Lecture Notes
in Business Information Processing 339

More information about this series at http://www.springer.com/series/7911

Witold Abramowicz · Adrian Paschke (Eds.)

Business Information Systems Workshops

BIS 2018 International Workshops
Berlin, Germany, July 18–20, 2018
Revised Papers

 Springer

Editors
Witold Abramowicz
Poznań University of Economics
and Business
Poznań, Poland

Adrian Paschke
Fraunhofer FOKUS
Berlin, Berlin, Germany

ISSN 1865-1348   ISSN 1865-1356 (electronic)
Lecture Notes in Business Information Processing
ISBN 978-3-030-04848-8   ISBN 978-3-030-04849-5 (eBook)
https://doi.org/10.1007/978-3-030-04849-5

Library of Congress Control Number: 2018962544

This Springer imprint is published by the registered company Springer Nature Switzerland AG
The registered company address is: Gewerbestrasse 11, 6330 Cham, Switzerland

Preface

In 2018 we had a great opportunity to organize the 21st edition of the International Conference on Business Information Systems, which has grown to be a well-renowned event for the scientific and business communities. This year the main topic of the conference was "Digital Transformation an Imperative in Today's Business Markets." The conference was jointly organized by the Fraunhofer Institute for Open Communication Systems, Germany, and Poznań University of Economics and Business, Poland, and was held in Berlin, Germany.

During each edition of the BIS Conference we make efforts to provide an opportunity for discussion about up-to-date topics from the area of information systems research. However, there are many topics that deserve particular attention. Thus, a number of workshops and accompanying events are co-located with the BIS Conference. Workshops give researchers the possibility to share preliminary ideas and initial experimental results and to discuss research hypotheses from a specific area of interest.

Seven workshops and one accompanying event took place during the 21st BIS Conference. We were proud to host well-known workshops such as AKTB (tenth edition), BITA (ninth edition), IDEA (fourth edition) and iDEATE (third edition) as well as new initiatives such as BSCT, SciBOWater, and QOD. Each workshop focused on a different topic: knowledge-based business information systems (AKTB), challenges and current state of business and IT alignment (BITA), digital enterprise engineering and architecture (IDEA), big data and business analytics ecosystems (iDEATE), Blockchain (BSCT), water management (SciBOWater), and data quality (QOD).

Additionally, BIS hosted a doctoral consortium. It was organized in a workshop formula, and thus the best papers from this event are included in the book. Moreover, all authors had the possibility to discuss their ideas on PhD theses and research work with a designed mentor.

The workshop authors had the chance to present their results and ideas in front of a well-focused audience; thus the discussion provided the authors with new perspectives and directions for further research. Based on the feedback received, authors had the opportunity to edit the workshop articles for the current publication. The volume contains 59 articles that are extended versions of papers accepted for BIS workshops. The volume opens with a paper presented by one of the keynote speakers: Prof. Francesco Archetti. In total, there were 122 submissions for all mentioned events. Based on the reviews, the respective workshop chairs accepted 58 in total, yielding an acceptance rate of 48%.

We would like to express our thanks to everyone who made the BIS 2018 workshops successful. First of all, our workshops chairs, members of the workshop Program

Committees, authors of submitted papers, and finally all workshops participants. We cordially invite you to visit the BIS website at http://bisconf.info and to join us at future BUS conferences.

July 2018

Witold Abramowicz
Adrian Paschke

Contents

Keynote Speech

Business Information Systems for the Cost/Energy Management
of Water Distribution Networks: A Critical Appraisal of Alternative
Optimization Strategies 3
    Antonio Candelieri, Bruno G. Galuzzi, Ilaria Giordani,
    Riccardo Perego, and Francesco Archetti

AKTB Workshop

Enhancing Clinical Decision Support Through Information Processing
Capabilities and Strategic IT Alignment 19
    Rogier van de Wetering

Ontology-Based Fragmented Company Knowledge Integration:
Possible Approaches 30
    Alexander Smirnov and Nikolay Shilov

Enhancing Teamwork Behavior of Services 38
    Paraskevi Tsoutsa, Panos Fitsilis, and Omiros Ragos

Business Rule Optimisation: Problem Definition, Proof-of-Concept
and Application Areas 51
    Alan Dormer

Profiling User Colour Preferences with BFI-44 Personality Traits 63
    Magdalena Wieloch, Katarzyna Kabzińska, Dominik Filipiak,
    and Agata Filipowska

The Benefits of Modeling Software-Related Exceptional Paths
of Business Processes 77
    Krzysztof Gruszczyński and Bartosz Perkowski

Process Mining of Periodic Rating Scale Survey Data Using
Analytic Hierarchy Process 86
    Dalia Kriksciuniene, Virgilijus Sakalauskas, and Roman Lewandowski

BITA Workshop

Determinants to Benefit from Enterprise Architecture Management –
A Research Model 101
    Ralf-Christian Härting, Christopher Reichstein, and Kurt Sandkuhl

Business and Information Technology Alignment Measurement - A Recent
Literature Review   112
   Leonardo Muñoz and Oscar Avila

Using Business Process Modelling to Improve Student Recruitment
in UK Higher Education   124
   Oluwatoyin Fakorede, Philip Davies, and David Newell

Stakeholder-Oriented and Enterprise Architecture Driven Cloud
Service Selection.   136
   Sabrina Kurjakovic and Knut Hinkelmann

Business-IT Alignment Improvement in Co-creation Value Networks:
Design of a Reference Model-Based Support   143
   Samaneh Bagheri, Rob Kusters, Jos Trienekens,
   and Paul W. P. J. Grefen

Ontology Development Strategies in Industrial Contexts   156
   Vladimir Tarasov, Ulf Seigerroth, and Kurt Sandkuhl

BSCT Workshop

Blockchain Backed DNSSEC   173
   Scarlett Gourley and Hitesh Tewari

The Proposal of a Blockchain-Based Architecture for Transparent
Certificate Handling   185
   Jerinas Gresch, Bruno Rodrigues, Eder Scheid, Salil S. Kanhere,
   and Burkhard Stiller

Blockchain-Based Distributed Marketplace   197
   Oliver R. Kabi and Virginia N. L. Franqueira

BlockChain Based Certificate Verification Platform.   211
   Axel Curmi and Frankie Inguanez

Blockchain-Based Management of Shared Energy Assets Using a Smart
Contract Ecosystem.   217
   Manuel Utz, Simon Albrecht, Thorsten Zoerner, and Jens Strüker

Research of Ethereum Mining Hash Rate Dependency on GPU
Hardware Settings   223
   Paulius Danielius, Tomas Savenas, and Saulius Masteika

Practical Deployability of Permissioned Blockchains   229
   Nitesh Emmadi, R. Vigneswaran, Srujana Kanchanapalli,
   Lakshmipadmaja Maddali, and Harika Narumanchi

Decentralized Energy Networks Based on Blockchain: Background,
Overview and Concept Discussion   244
  Mario Pichler, Marcus Meisel, Andrija Goranovic,
  Kurt Leonhartsberger, Georg Lettner, Georgios Chasparis,
  Heribert Vallant, Stefan Marksteiner, and Hemma Bieser

Enabling Data Markets Using Smart Contracts
and Multi-party Computation   258
  Dumitru Roman and Kien Vu

Opportunities, Challenges, and Future Extensions for Smart-Contract
Design Patterns.   264
  Carl R. Worley and Anthony Skjellum

A Multichain Architecture for Distributed Supply Chain Design
in Industry 4.0   277
  Kai Fabian Schulz and Daniel Freund

Invisible BlockChain and Plasticity of Money – Adam Smith Meets Darwin
to Buy Crypto Currency.   289
  Zeeshan-ul-hassan Usmani, Andre Waddell, and Rytis Bieliauskas

Blockchain-Based Internet Voting: Systems' Compliance
with International Standards   300
  Jordi Cucurull, Adrià Rodríguez-Pérez, Tamara Finogina,
  and Jordi Puiggalí

Chaining Property to Blocks – On the Economic Efficiency of Blockchain-
Based Property Enforcement.   313
  Janina da Costa Cruz, Aenne Sophie Schröder,
  and Georg von Wangenheim

On the Future of Markets Driven by Blockchain.   325
  Mario Cichonczyk

Smart Contract-Based Role Management on the Blockchain   335
  Cornelius Ihle and Omar Sanchez

Industrial Socio-Cyberphysical System's Consumables Tokenization
for Smart Contracts in Blockchain.   344
  Nikolay Teslya

SmartExchange: Decentralised Trustless Cryptocurrency Exchange   356
  Filip Adamik and Sokol Kosta

A Public, Blockchain-Based Distributed Smart-Contract Platform Enabling
Mobile Lite Wallets Using a Proof-of-Stake Consensus Algorithm   368
  Alex Norta, Patrick Dai, Neil Mahi, and Jordan Earls

Risk Engineering and Blockchain: Anticipating and Mitigating Risks   381
  Michael Huth, Claire Vishik, and Riccardo Masucci

IDEA Workshop

IT Infrastructure Capability and Health Information Exchange:
The Moderating Role of Electronic Medical Records' Reach   397
  Rogier van de Wetering

The IT Department as a Service Broker: A Qualitative Research   408
  Linda Rodriguez and Oscar Avila

Foster Strategic Orientation in the Digital Age: A Methodic Approach
for Guiding SME to a Digital Transformation   420
  Manuela Graf, Marco Peter, and Stella Gatziu-Grivas

TEA - A Technology Evaluation and Adoption Influence Framework
for Small and Medium Sized Enterprises   433
  Dominic Spalinger, Stella Gatziu Grivas, and Andre de la Harpe

iDEATE Workshop

Prescriptive Analytics: A Survey of Approaches and Methods   449
  *Katerina Lepenioti, Alexandros Bousdekis, Dimitris Apostolou,
  and Gregoris Mentzas*

Challenges from Data-Driven Predictive Maintenance in Brownfield
Industrial Settings   461
  Georgios Koutroulis and Stefan Thalmann

Big Data is Power: Business Value from a Process Oriented
Analytics Capability   468
  Rogier van de Wetering, Patrick Mikalef, and John Krogstie

SciBOWater Workshop

A Multiple-Layer Clustering Method for Real-Time Decision Support
in a Water Distribution System   485
  *Alexandru Predescu, Cătălin Negru, Mariana Mocanu, Ciprian Lupu,
  and Antonio Candelieri*

Automated Updating of Land Cover Maps Used
in Hydrological Modelling   498
  *Muhammad Haris Ali, Thaine H. Assumpção, Ioana Popescu,
  and Andreja Jonoski*

High-Performance Computing Applied in Project UBEST   507
  Ricardo Martins, João Rogeiro, Marta Rodrigues, André B. Fortunato,
  Anabela Oliveira, and Alberto Azevedo

A Comparative Study on Decision Support Approaches
Under Uncertainty.   517
  Panagiotis Christias

Plastic Grabber: Underwater Autonomous Vehicle Simulation
for Plastic Objects Retrieval Using Genetic Programming.   527
  Gabrielė Kasparavičiūtė, Stig Anton Nielsen, Dhruv Boruah,
  Peter Nordin, and Alexandru Dancu

Adaptation of Irrigation Systems to Current Climate Changes.   534
  George Suciu, Teodora Uşurelu, Cristina M. Bălăceanu,
  and Muneeb Anwar

QOD Workshop

ADEQUATe: A Community-Driven Approach to Improve
Open Data Quality   555
  Lőrinc Thurnay, Thomas J. Lampoltshammer, Sebastian Neumaier,
  and Tomáš Knap

Situation-Dependent Data Quality Analysis for Geospatial Data
Using Semantic Technologies.   566
  Timo Homburg and Frank Boochs

Indicating Studies' Quality Based on Open Data in Digital Libraries   579
  Yusra Shakeel, Jacob Krüger, Gunter Saake, and Thomas Leich

Syntactical Heuristics for the Open Data Quality Assessment
and Their Applications.   591
  Donato Pirozzi and Vittorio Scarano

Access Control and Quality Attributes of Open Data: Applications
and Techniques.   603
  Erisa Karafili, Konstantina Spanaki, and Emil C. Lupu

Doctoral Consortium

Measures for Quality Assessment of Articles and Infoboxes
in Multilingual Wikipedia   619
  Włodzimierz Lewoniewski

Supply Chain Modelling Using Data Science   634
  Szczepan Górtowski

Behavioral Biometrics in Mobile Banking and Payment Applications   646
    Piotr Kałużny

Modelling of Risk and Reliability of Maritime Transport Services.   659
    Milena Stróżyna

Mixed Methods Approach as Requirements Analysis of a Method
for Process Harmonization in Design Science Research   675
    Irene Schönreiter

Predicting Customer Churn in Electronic Banking.   687
    Marcin Szmydt

Assessing Process Suitability for AI-Based Automation.
Research Idea and Design   697
    Aleksandra Revina

Author Index   707

Keynote Speech

Business Information Systems for the Cost/Energy Management of Water Distribution Networks: A Critical Appraisal of Alternative Optimization Strategies

Antonio Candelieri[1]([✉]), Bruno G. Galuzzi[1], Ilaria Giordani[1],
Riccardo Perego[1], and Francesco Archetti[1,2]

[1] University of Milano-Bicocca, viale Sarca 336, 20126 Milan, Italy
{antonio.candelieri,bruno.galuzzi,ilaria.giordani,
francesco.archetti}@unimib.it,
riccardo.perego@disco.unimib.it
[2] Consorzio Milano Ricerche, via Roberto Cozzi 53, 20125 Milan, Italy

Abstract. The objective of this paper is to show how smart water networks enable new strategies for the energy cost management of the network, more precisely Pump Scheduling Optimization. This problem is traditionally solved using mathematical programming and, more recently, nature inspired meta-heuristics. The schedules obtained by these methods are typically not robust both respect to random variations in the water demand and the non-linear features of the model. The authors consider three alternative optimization strategies: *(i)* global optimization of black-box functions, based on a Gaussian model and the use of the hydraulic simulator (EPANET) to evaluate the objective function; *(ii)* Multi Stage Stochastic Programming, which models the stochastic evolution of the water demand through a scenario analysis to solve an equivalent large scale linear program; and finally *(iii)*, Approximate Dynamic Programming, also known as Reinforcement Learning. With reference to real life experimentation, the last two strategies offer more modeling flexibility, are demand responsive and typically result in more robust solutions (i.e. pump schedules) than mathematical programming. More specifically, Approximate Dynamic Programming works on minimal modelling assumption and can effectively leverage on line data availability into robust on-line Pump Scheduling Optimization.

Keywords: Pump Scheduling Optimization · Bayesian Optimization
Multi-stage stochastic programming · Reinforcement Learning

1 Introduction

The digital revolution in the water industry has just started, later than in other sectors notably energy, but will disrupt the sector in many, still unpredictable ways [1].

In this paper we consider the specific sector of the operations of an urban **Water Distribution Network** (WDN) as it is being impacted by the introduction of smart metering and the growing capability of sensing the network, specifically flow and

© Springer Nature Switzerland AG 2019
W. Abramowicz and A. Paschke (Eds.): BIS 2018 Workshops, LNBIP 339, pp. 3–13, 2019.
https://doi.org/10.1007/978-3-030-04849-5_1

pressures, and look to the new opportunities that this technological scenario is offering in the way of improving the networks operations. Indeed, the analysis of the new data streams has the potential of turning upside down all the aspects of network operations, for instance asset management, leak localization, network resilience evaluation, customer relationship management and energy cost optimization, water digital services.

Business information systems for the water sector will have to integrate these data streams and functionalities towards achieving technical and business objectives.

The authors have been active in several European and national projects, such as H2OLeak (national), ICeWater (European, FP7), DATA4WATER (European, H2020), PILGRIM (national) and PERFORM-WATER2020 (national), addressing the critical issues of leak management [2, 3], demand forecasting [4, 5] resilience evaluation [6] and, more recently energy cost optimization through innovative strategies for **Pump Scheduling Optimization** (PSO) [7].

Operating a WDN is a very energy intensive activity and a substantial part of this energy goes into operating pumps, either fixed or variable speed. A number of modelling and computational tools have been developed over the years [8] to optimize the energy consumption, meeting reliably customers' demand and respecting operational constraints, specifically pressure related.

PSO, described in Sect. 2, is a nonlinear problem due to the relation between flow and head pressure and its solution by mathematical programming requires some model simplification, e.g. linearization/convexification of objective functions and constraints set. Moreover, the water demand is to be assumed deterministic and known in advance. Under these conditions it's possible to apply highly efficient mixed integer linear programming (MINP) methods. Thus, the solution obtained, optimal for the model considered, might easily be unfeasible due to the simplification introduced and the assumptions on the demand. Therefore, its feasibility must be verified through a hydraulic simulation software, like EPANET [9]. Moreover, these methods require a complete and detailed knowledge of the WDN which is not always available, mostly in large scale systems built in different time stages.

Alternatively to MINP, several metaheuristics, such as Genetic Algorithms and Simulated Annealing among others, have been proposed to solve the PSO problem, such in [10], which proposes a two stage simulated annealing approach, or in [11], which uses Harmony Search to solve a multi-objective version of PSO.

The first strategy, analyzed in Sect. 3.1, is a black-box or simulation-based Global Optimization. This approach is based on **Bayesian Optimization** (BO) [12], does not require simplification/approximation, uses EPANET to evaluate the objective function, and to take care that the pressure constraints are satisfied.

The second strategy, reported in Sect. 3.2, is focused on the uncertainty on the water demand, whose probability distribution is assumed to be known a-priori. The aim is to approach PSO via **Multi Stage Stochastic Programming** (MSSP), by solving several water demand scenarios generated according to the distributions and represented through a scenario tree [13].

BO and MSSP are characterized by an off-line analysis, where the solution is the state of each pump for every time step (typically 1 h) of the optimization horizon (typically 24 h). However, the availability of on-line consumptions and operational data enables to formulate PSO as an on-line optimization/control problem. Indeed, the authors believe that the digitalization of WDN will offer opportunities for alternative optimization strategies free from the limitations of BO and MSSP and able to leverage the availability in smart grid of online data into strategies with the potential of simultaneously learning and optimizing. The third strategy, described in Sect. 3.3, is based on a Markov Decision Process (MDP), structured in term of states, transition dynamics and actions specified for each state and rewards. In this case the PSO problem is solved using the **Approximate Dynamic Programming** (ADP), a.k.a. **Reinforcement Learning** (RL) in the machine learning community, that does not require full knowledge of the system (i.e. transition dynamics and rewards), and tries actions, in different states, with the aim to learn something more about the system behavior (exploration) while exploiting current knowledge to infer a policy, even if not the best, with a good potential towards long term reward.

The three strategies can be tested both on benchmarks and real WDNs. However, since WDNs evolve along different trajectories both in terms of data model and availability as well as optimization goals, we do not provide a comparison between the numerical results obtained by using the three strategies on three different experimental settings. The main result of this paper is a set of new generation optimization strategies which, not necessarily as computationally efficient as deterministic mathematical programming, adapt to different operational and technological settings, and blend effectively learning from the environment (exploration) and optimization depending on the info gathered so far (exploitation).

Finally, in Sect. 4 we report the main conclusions and discussion about the benefits and limitations of the three strategies, depending on the different operational settings.

2 The Pump Scheduling Optimization Problem

A complex WDN can be represented by a set of **nodes** connected by **links**. The nodes consist of three subsets: **reservoirs**, **tanks** and **junctions**. Reservoirs are nodes that represent an infinite external source or sink of water to the network. Tanks are nodes with storage capacity, where the volume of water can vary with time during a simulation. Junctions are points in the network where links join and where water can leave the network to satisfy a certain quantity of water **demand**. We indicate with J, R, and K the set of junctions, reservoirs, and tanks, respectively.

The links consist of two subsets: **pipes**, that convey water from one point in the network to another, and **pumps**, that are used to increase the pressure within the network by generating enough water flow to satisfy the demand. We indicate with N, and N_p, the set of pipes and pumps, respectively.

Different decision variables can be defined related to the WDN analyzed over a planning horizon, generally divided into equally-sized time periods $t \in \{1, .., T\}$: the status $s_{i,t}$ of the pumps $i \in N_p$, the flow rate $q_{i,t}$ and the head-loss $h_{i,t}$ of the pipes $i \in N$, and the volume of water $v_{k,t}$ of the tanks $k \in K$. Typical parameters of the optimization problem are the set of the demands $D_{j,t} \geq 0$, for each junction node $j \in J$.

An example of benchmark WDN very used is the Anytown [11], reported in Fig. 1a. It consists of 37 pipes, 19 nodes, 1 tank and 1 reservoir, with 4 pumps installed at the source of supply water. The total water demand $D_t = \sum_{j \in J} D_{j,t}$ is reported in

Fig. 1b and ranges from a minimum of 161.51 *lps* to a maximum of 484.53 *lps*, with two peaks during a 24-h period, one around 10:00 and another around 20:00.

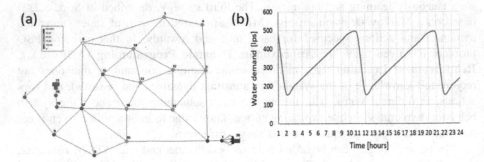

Fig. 1. (a) Topology of the water distribution system Anytown. (b) The hourly water demand of Anytown network over 24 h.

Generally, the PSO problem is formulated as the minimization of an objective function, representing the value of the energy consumption on the planning horizon [8, 14]:

$$\min E = \min\left(\sum_{i \in N_p} \sum_{t=1}^{T} \frac{C_t}{e_i} \cdot \lambda \cdot s_{i,t} \cdot h_{i,t} \cdot q_{i,t}\right), \tag{1}$$

where $e_i \in (0,1)$ represents the efficiency of the pump $i \in N_p$, C_t is the electricity cost, measured in \$ /kWh, and λ is an appropriate constant factor.

For feasibility reasons, the operational constraints [15] must be added to the formulation, such as the flow-rate or the water levels of tank(s) within a given range. An important set of constrains is related to **flow-continuity equations** for all the WDN's junctions:

$$\sum_{i \in N_j} q_{i,t} = D_{j,t} \, \forall j \in J, \, \forall t \in T \tag{2}$$

where N_j indicates the subset of links with a vertex in junction j and the flow $q_{i,t}$ is positive by convention. Another important set of constrains is related to the **flow-head-loss equations**:

$$h_{i,t} = \begin{cases} h_0 - r \cdot q_{i,t}^n, |\forall i \in N_p \\ r \cdot p_{i,t}^n + m \cdot q_{i,t}^2, |\forall i \in N \end{cases}, \forall t \in T \tag{3}$$

where r is the resistance coefficient, n is the flow exponent, m is the minor loss coefficient, and h_0 is the shutoff head for the pump. Finally, an important constrain is the **tank mass balance equation**, $\forall t \in T$:

$$v_{k,t} = v_{k,t-1} + \sum_{i \in N_k} q_{i,t}, \forall k \in K, \tag{4}$$

where N_k indicates the subset of links with a vertex in the tank node k.

This formulation of the PSO is a mixed integer non-linear problem that is computationally expensive to solve using a standard optimization software with no guarantee of global optimality.

The optimal pump schedule obtained by solving the PSO is limited to the decision variables $s_{i,t}$ which represent the status of each pump i at time step t. These variables are discrete (i.e., $\{0, 1\}$) in the case of on/off pumps, and continuous (e.g. in $[0, 1]$) in the case of variable speed pumps. However, a simple WDN such as Anytown have 4 ON/OFF pumps and, considering an hourly resolution and a 24-h horizon, this leads to an optimization problem with 96 discrete decision variables and, consequently, 4^{24} (i.e. $\approx 2.8 \cdot 10^{14}$) possible pump schedules.

3 Optimization Strategies

3.1 Global Optimization Through Bayesian Optimization

The first strategy presented in this work to solve the PSO problem uses a Global Optimization (GO) approach and, specifically, Bayesian Optimization (BO) [16, 17]. In this case the PSO problem is considered as a solution x^* of a global optimization problem of a black-box usually expensive-to-evaluate, objective function $f(x)$,

$$x^* = \mathrm{argmin}_x f(x) \tag{5}$$

where $x \in X \subset R^d$ is a point in a d-dimensional bounded-box space X. With respect to the PSO problem, $f(x)$ represents the energy cost E (Eq. 1), whereas the dimension d of the search space is given by $T \cdot N_p$ [7]. Each evaluation will require to run an EPANET simulation and, in case of possible warnings during the simulation run (i.e. some constraint is not satisfied) is possible to use a penalty on the objective function.

In BO the objective function f is modelled as a realization of a stochastic process, typically, a Gaussian Process (GP) on a probability space (Ω, Σ, P). A GP, which defines a prior distribution over the function f, is completely specified by its mean $\mu(x) : X \to R$ and a definite positive covariance function $k(x, x') : X^2 \to R$:

$$f(x) \approx GP(\mu(x); k(x, x')). \tag{6}$$

It can intuitively think of GP as analogous to a function, but instead of returning a single numeric value $f(x)$, it returns the mean and variance of a normal distribution over the possible values of $f(x)$.

The BO algorithm starts with an initial set of k points $\{x_i\}_{i=1}^k \in X$ and the associated observations $\{y_i\}_{i=1}^k$ with $y_i = f(x_i)$. At each iteration $\bar{k} \in \{k+1, \ldots, N\}$, the GP prior is updated using the Bayes rule, to obtain posterior distribution conditioned on the current training set $S_t = \{(x_i, y_i)\}_{i=1}^{\bar{k}}$ containing the past evaluated points and observations. For any point $x \in X$, the posterior mean $\bar{\mu}_t(x)$ and the posterior variance $\bar{\sigma}_t^2(x)$ of the GP, conditioned on S_t, are known in closed-form:

$$x_{\bar{k}+1} = \arg\max_{x \in X} U_{\bar{k}}(x; S_{\bar{k}}),$$ (7)

where $U_{\bar{k}}$ is a acquisition function to maximize. Solving this auxiliary problem does not involve the evaluation of the expensive objective function f, but only the posterior quantities of the GP and, thus, is considered cheap. Several acquisition functions have been proposed, such as the Probability of Improvement [18], the Expected Improvement [12], the Lower Confidence Bound (LCB) and Upper Confidence Bound (UCB) [19], and the Knowledge Gradient [20].

3.2 Multi-stage Stochastic Programming

The second strategy presented in this work to solve the PSO problem simplifies the original problem to a simple linear problem (LP), where the nonlinear relation coming from the objective function and/or some of the constrains above are circumvented.

A complex WDN can be simplified to only three nodes, one reservoir, one tank, and one junction, and two links, one pump from the reservoir to the junction node, and one pipe from the junction node to the tank. For each period t, a tank volume v_t and a pump flow rate q_t is defined, whereas the junction node has as demand $D_t = \sum_{j \in J} D_{j,t}$.

By this way, the original PSO problem is approximated by an LP problem [11, 21]:

$$\min_{q_1,\dots,q_T} \sum_{t=1}^{T} c_t \cdot q_t,$$ (8)

subjected to the following constrain:

$$v^{min} \leq v_1 + \sum_{l=1}^{t} (q_l - D_l) \leq v^{max}, \ \forall t \in T.$$ (9)

where c_t is an appropriate factor, representing the proportional factors between the energy and the pumped flow, and v^{min} and v^{max} represent the minimum and the maximum water level of the tank.

Such simple model can be used to describe a more complex model of water distribution in a synthesis stage [21], whereas an extended period simulation, using EPANET, can be used subsequently in order to verify the feasibility of the obtained pump schedule, in an analysis stage. If the demand pattern $\{D_t\}_{t=1}^{T}$ is known in advance, the optimal pumping policy is given by the optimal solution to the LP problem, solved by using any commercial code able to solve a MIL problem such as CPLEX.

The advantage of such formulation consists of the possibility to use the **Multi-stage stochastic programming** (MSSP) approach [22, 23], to manage a possible uncertain demand, in which, for example, the demand at each time follows a probability distribution. In this case the evolution pattern of the demand is treated as a stochastic process $D = (D_1, \dots, D_T)$ (sequence of random variables representing a random time series), and the flow rate q_t as a decision process $q = (q_1, \dots, q_T)$, that are interlinked into a sequence of alternating decisions and observations: $q_1, D_1, q_2, D_2 \ldots, q_T, D_T$. The decisions at each stage are made while considering that will be opportunities for modification and corrections at later stages (recourse decisions). The decision process is non-anticipative or implementable, i.e. the decision q_t at time t depends only on previous information $D_1, \ldots, D_{t-1}$. The MSSP formulation for the problem of Eq. (7) will be set as follow:

$$\min_{q_1, \ldots, q_T} \mathbb{E}\left[\sum_{t=1}^{T} c_t \cdot q_t(D_{[t]})\right], \tag{10}$$

subject to constraint (9) and where $q_t(D_{[t]})$ means that the solution q_t will be depends only on the demand until stage t and $\mathbb{E}$ represents the expected value as a function of the demand. The MSSP solves for an optimal policy which contains the first-stage decisions (values) and the recourse decisions (functions of revealed information).

Finding the functions $q_t(\cdot)$ which lead to optimal solution of the MSSP is done introducing a discrete approximation of space of the stochastic process by means of the **scenarios** [13], which are particular possibilities of how the process might be realized as the future unfolds. The stochastic process D is discretized into a finite set of scenarios $D^s = (D_1^s, \ldots, D_t^s) \in \Omega_T, \forall s = 1, \ldots S$, with a probability p_s where $\sum_{s=1}^{S} p_s = 1$. Each scenario, D^s, is defined as a possible realization of the stochastic process over the entire time horizon. The function $q_t(\cdot)$ is replaced by a corresponding finite number of vectors, equal to the different possibilities taken by the function $q_t(\cdot)$ as its input, and using a non-anticipativity requirement, that means that every pair of scenarios $D^k, D^l \in \Omega$, which are indistinguishable up to stage t (share the same history) have the same decision history up to stage t. A common way to represent such situation is through a **scenario tree** (Fig. 2) [13], consisting of nodes and arcs; each node represents a possible realization of the stochastic process, where the **root node** represents the first stage. In such a scenario tree, the path from the root node of the tree to each of its leaf nodes corresponds to a single scenario, and the event outcomes for scenarios that pass through the same intermediate node are identical for all stages up to that node.

3.3 Approximated Dynamic Programming

The third strategy, presented in this section, is based on Markov Decision Processes (MDP), a powerful framework to model a variety of sequential optimization problems and provide a robust mechanism to generate solutions online.

An MDP is based on a **state space** S, and an **action space** $\mathcal{A}$. A state consists of a set of possible decision variables $s_t = \{\xi_{1,t}, \ldots, \xi_{N,t}\}$ at a time step t. An action $a_t = a$ allows for moving from the current state $s_t = s$ to another state $s_{t+1} = \bar{s}$, according to the transition dynamics of the system. When transition dynamics is not known a-priori, as well as the immediate rewards associated to every state-action pair, Approximate Dynamic Programming (ADP) is used. Any ADP algorithm learns how to behave with the system to be optimized by directly interacting with it (aka "environment") while infers an optimal policy (i.e. a mapping from every state s to the action a associated to the highest long-term reward). More precisely, we consider **Q-Learning**, one of the

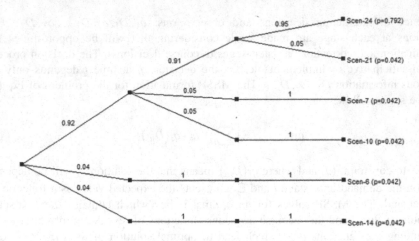

Fig. 2. Example of scenario tree.

most widely adopted ADP algorithm, well-known in the Reinforcement Learning community. It takes its name from the variable $Q(s, a)$ which represents the value of being in the state $s \in S$ and taking the action $a \in \mathcal{A}$ (i.e. state-action value function).

Q-Learning works "going forward in time", where the next action to perform is selected according to an ε-greedy policy, selecting a random action with probability ε (exploration) and the action with maximum value of $Q(s, a)$, (exploitation) with probability $1 - \varepsilon$.

After the selected action is performed, an immediate reward r value is observed along with the new state s', so the value of the state-action pair, $Q(s, a)$, is updated consequently:

$$Q(s, x) \leftarrow Q(s, x) + \alpha[\mathcal{R}(s, x) + \gamma \max_{x'} Q(s', x') - Q(s, x)] \qquad (11)$$

where α is the learning rate – which sets how much the old estimate of the Q-value has to change depending on the observed state and reward – and γ is the discount factor – which sets how much the future rewards impact on the update of the Q-value of the current state-action pair.

In case of the PSO problem, we have defined the state as a 2D vector consisting of the tank level and the average pressure (computed on all the WDN's junctions). The two vector components have been discretized on 5 levels each, leading to a discrete state space with size 25. An action is a vector with a number of components equal to the number of pumps, that is 4 in the Anytown case study. In our previous analysis we have considered on/off pumps, only [24]. Finally, the transition dynamics is not modelled – indeed, Q-Learning is "model-free" – and the reward is computed according to the energy costs associated to the actions performed.

Therefore Q-Learning does not provide, in one shot, an entire schedule for the 24 h horizon, but suggests the best action to perform (i.e. activation of each pump) at every decision step, working online with the WDN. Q-Learning proved to be an effective strategy even when the optimal policy is obtained on a deterministic case and then applied on the real-world system: it is robust with respect to demand variations/ uncertainty.

4 Conclusion and Discussion

In this paper, we have presented several approaches because PSO in WDN should be modelled and solved in different ways according to the objectives of the analysis, the data infrastructure and availability and in general the state of digitalization of the. network.

BO has the advantage that the problem formulation is not analytical but based on a hydraulic simulator that can take care, also in a detailed way, of operational objective and constraints. This simulation, based black-box optimization, is expensive because each evaluation of the model requires the run of simulation but has the advantage that the solutions proposed are hydraulically feasible. Moreover, BO alternates exploration stages, to acquire information on the model, and exploitation to improve the incumbent solution: this affects also early stage solutions proposed by the algorithm correspond to good quality schedules. This make possible to deal with WDN, as shown in [7], way larger than the theoretical scaling properties would suggest.

The MSSP solution we presented is analytically based and requires linearization of objective functions and constraints. This simplification makes it necessary to check the hydraulic feasibility of the proposed schedules. An advantage of the MSSP approach is that demand is no longer considered deterministic but can be uncertain, modeled through a probability distribution. The strategy is computationally demanding requiring the generation of a scenario tree and consequently a larger set of variables to simulate the possible evolution of the water demand.

The result of MSSP is not just a schedule but more generally a strategy mapping the water demand observed so far to the best flow provided by pumps for the current step (i.e. node of the scenarios tree).

The last strategy ADP/RL is completely data-driven which makes it, at least in principle, the natural choice where full digital infrastructure is already in place and can acquire and process online pressure, flows, water demand and energy consumption. There is no need to model or know a priori the water demand whose values are provided by sensor readings. Simulation is not needed because the sensory infrastructure is such that the state of the system is observable on line This strategy is also structure in phases of exploration (learning something more about the WDN behavior) and exploitation (using the current knowledge to improve on the best pump schedule obtained so far. Similarly, to MSSP, ADO/RL provides not only a solution but more generally a strategy mapping the water demand observed so far to the best flow provided by pumps for the current step (i.e. node of the scenarios tree). The difference is that in ADP/RL this strategy is inferred by interacting online with the WDN, instead of generating possible scenarios a-priori.

The focus of this paper is only energy operations management strategy which is enabled by smart water networks: besides the PSO problem it is important to remark that other operational functions are going to be disrupted by the online data availability as already demonstrated by the prototypes developed by the authors for leak management [25], demand forecasting [26, 27] and resilience evaluation [28, 29] in the previously cited European projects.

References

1. Stewart, R.A., et al.: Integrated intelligent water-energy metering systems and informatics: visioning a digital multi-utility service provider. Environ. Model Softw. **105**, 94–117 (2018)
2. Candelieri, A., Giordani, I., Archetti, F.: Automatic configuration of kernel-based clustering: an optimization approach. In: Battiti, R., Kvasov, D.E., Sergeyev, Y.D. (eds.) LION 2017. LNCS, vol. 10556, pp. 34–49. Springer, Cham (2017). https://doi.org/10.1007/978-3-319-69404-7_3
3. Candelieri, A., Soldi, D., Archetti, F.: Cost-effective sensors placement and leak localization - the Neptun pilot of the ICeWater project. J. Water Supply Res. Technol. AQUA **64**(5), 567–582 (2015)
4. Shabani, S., Candelieri, A., Archetti, F., Naser, G.: Gene expression programming coupled with unsupervised learning: a two-stage learning process in multi-scale, short-term water demand forecasts. Water **10**(2) (2018)
5. Candelieri, A., et al.: Tuning hyperparameters of a SVM-based water demand forecasting system through parallel global optimization. Comput. Oper. Res. (2018)
6. Candelieri, A., Giordani, I., Archetti, F.: Supporting resilience management of water distribution networks through network analysis and hydraulic simulation. In: 2017 Proceedings of the 21st International Conference on Control Systems and Computer, CSCS 2017, pp. 599–605 (2017)
7. Candelieri, A., Perego, R., Archetti, F.: Bayesian optimization of pump operations in water distribution systems. J. Glob. Optim. **71**(1), 213–235 (2018)
8. Mala-Jetmarova, H., Sultanova, N., Savic, D.: Lost in optimisation of water distribution systems? A literature review of system design. Water **10**(3) (2018). https://doi.org/10.3390/w10030307
9. Rossman, L.A.: EPANET 2: users manual, Washington, DC (2000)
10. McCormick, G., Powell, R.S.: Derivation of near-optimal pump schedules for water distribution by simulated annealing. J. Oper. Res. Soc. **55**(7), 728–736 (2004)
11. De Paola, F., Fontana, N., Giugni, M., Marini, G., Pugliese, F.: An application of the harmony-search multi-objective (HSMO) optimization algorithm for the solution of pump scheduling problem. Procedia Eng. **162**, 494–502 (2016)
12. Mockus, J.: Bayesian Approach to Global Optimization: Theory and Applications, vol. 37. Springer, Dordrecht (1989). https://doi.org/10.1007/978-94-009-0909-0
13. Dupacová, J., Consigli, G., Wallace, S.W.: Scenarios for multistage stochastic programs. Ann. Oper. Res. **100**(1), 25–53 (2000)
14. Ghaddar, B., Naoum-Sawaya, J., Kishimoto, A., Taheri, N., Eck, B.: A Lagrangian decomposition approach for the pump scheduling problem in water networks. Eur. J. Oper. Res. **241**(2), 490–501 (2015)
15. D'Ambrosio, C., Lodi, A., Wiese, S., Bragalli, C.: Mathematical programming techniques in water network optimization. Eur. J. Oper. Res. **243**(3), 774–788 (2015)
16. Močkus, J.: On Bayesian methods for seeking the extremum. In: Marchuk, G.I. (ed.) Optimization Techniques 1974. LNCS, vol. 27, pp. 400–404. Springer, Heidelberg (1975). https://doi.org/10.1007/3-540-07165-2_55
17. Archetti, F., Betrò, B.: A probabilistic algorithm for global optimization. Calcolo **16**(3), 335–343 (1979)

18. Kushner, H.J.: A new method of locating the maximum point of an arbitrary multi-peak curve in the presence of noise. J. Basic Eng. **86**(1), 97–106 (1964)
19. Auer, P.: Using confidence bounds for exploitation-exploration trade-offs. JMLR **3**, 397–422 (2002)
20. Frazier, P.I.: Knowledge-Gradient Methods for Statistical Learning. Princeton University, Princeton (2009)
21. Goryashko, A.P., Nemirovski, A.S.: Robust energy cost optimization of water distribution system with uncertain demand. Autom. Remote Control **75**(10), 1754–1769 (2014)
22. Puleo, V., Morley, M., Freni, G., Savić, D.: Multi-stage linear programming optimization for pump scheduling. Procedia Eng. **70**, 1378–1385 (2014)
23. Housh, M., Ostfeld, A., Shamir, U.: Limited multi-stage stochastic programming for managing water supply systems. Environ. Model Softw. **41**, 53–64 (2013)
24. Candelieri, A., Perego, R., Archetti, F.: Intelligent pump scheduling optimization in water distribution networks. In: 12th International Conference, LION 12, Kalamata, Greece (2018)
25. Candelieri, A., Archetti, F., Messina, E.: Analytics for supporting urban water management. Environ. Eng. Manag. J. **12**(5), 875–881 (2013)
26. Candelieri, A.: Clustering and support vector regression for water demand forecasting and anomaly detection. Water **9**(3) (2017)
27. Candelieri, A., Soldi, D., Archetti, F.: Short-term forecasting of hourly water consumption by using automatic metering readers data. Procedia Eng. **119**(1), 844–853 (2015)
28. Candelieri, A., Soldi, D., Archetti, F.: Network analysis for resilience evaluation in water distribution networks. Environ. Eng. Manag. J. **14**(6), 1261–1270 (2015)
29. Soldi, D., Candelieri, A., Archetti, F.: Resilience and vulnerability in urban water distribution networks through network theory and hydraulic simulation. Procedia Eng. **119** (1), 1259–1268 (2015)

AKTB Workshop

AKTB 2018 Workshop Chairs' Message

The 10th Workshop on Applications of Knowledge-Based Technologies in Business (AKTB2018) was organised in Berlin (Germany) in conjunction with 21th BIS2018 conference. The anniversary 10th workshop continues the successful series of AKTB workshops in Poznan, Berlin, Vilnius, Larnaca, Leipzig, etc. The workshop joined the researchers, practitioners and policy makers to gather for the discussion on the most urgent topics where the advanced IT may serve for their progress. The workshop called for sharing research knowledge of efficient computational intelligence methods for implementing business information systems in finance, healthcare, e-business and other application domains. We invited papers which provide advanced services for the information systems users, propose innovative solutions for smart business and process modelling, especially targeting digital transformation issues.

The AKTB2018 continue the tradition of delivering efficient computational solutions validated by the experimental research and based on the in-depth knowledge of business domains using smart data. Total number of 13 articles was submitted to the AKTB2018 workshop. Each paper was evaluated by two or three independent reviewers of the Program Committee. The highest ranked 6 articles were accepted for presentation during the conference and the second stage of reviewing before including them into the post-conference proceedings. The PC of AKTB2018 has invited one additional paper disclosing the Process Mining issues of Periodic Rating Scale Survey Data. The 20 outstanding researchers who represent prestigious scientific institutions from 9 countries joined the Program Committee as paper reviewers. They evaluated the quality of the articles by taking into account the criteria of its relevance to the workshop topics, originality, novelty, and quality of presentation.

We appreciate the level of work and expertise of the program committee members, whose reviews provided deep analysis of the submitted research works and highlighted valuable insights for the authors. High standards followed by reviewers enabled to ensure high quality of the workshop event, excellent presentations, intensive scientific discussions and added value to the post-conference workshop proceedings.

We would like to express our gratitude for the joint input to the success of AKTB 2018 to all authors of submitted papers, members of the program committee, Kaunas Faculty of Vilnius University, department of Information Systems of the Poznan University of Economics, Fraunhofer FOKUS, Freie Universität Berlin and to acknowledge the outstanding efforts of Organizing Committee of the 21th International conference BIS2018.

Virgilijus Sakalauskas
Dalia Kriksciuniene

Organization

Chairs

Dalia Kriksciuniene   Vilnius University, Lithuania
Virgilijus Sakalauskas   Vilnius University, Lithuania

Program Committee

Lia Bassa   Foundation for Information Society, Hungary
Tânia Bueno   Instituto de Governo Eletrônico, Brasil
Mario Hernandez   University of Las Palmas de Gran Canaria, Spain
Daning Hu   University of Zurich, Switzerland
Ferenc Kiss   Foundation for Information Society, Hungary
Irene Krebs   University of Technology Cottbus, Germany
Dalia Kriksciuniene   Vilnius University, Lithuania
Audrius Lopata   Vilnius University, Lithuania
Dhrupad Mathur   Director(IIP). SPJCM, United Arab Emirates
Elpiniki I. Papageorgiou   Technological Educational Institute of Central
                              Greece, Greece
Laima Papreckiene   Kaunas Technological University, Lithuania
Saulius Masteika   Vilnius University, Lithuania
Tomas Pitner   Masaryk University, Czech Republik
Jose Raul Romero   University of Córdoba, Spain
Vytautas Rudzionis   Vilnius University, Lithuania
Virgilijus Sakalauskas   Vilnius University, Lithuania
Leonard Walletzky   Masaryk University, Czech Republik
Darijus Strasunskas   NTNU, Norway
Margaret Tan   Nanyang Technological University, Singapore
Sebastiàn Ventura   Cordoba University, Spain
Danuta Zakrzewska   Technical University, Łódz, Poland
María Dolores Suárez   SIANI, Spain
Dumitru Dan Burdescu   Universitatea din Craiova, Romania
Enrique Herrera Viedma   Universidad de Granada, Spain

Enhancing Clinical Decision Support Through Information Processing Capabilities and Strategic IT Alignment

Rogier van de Wetering[✉]

Faculty of Management Science and Technology,
Open University of the Netherlands,
Valkenburgerweg 177, 6419 AT Heerlen, The Netherlands
rogier.vandewetering@ou.nl

Abstract. Hospitals heavily invest in Healthcare IT to improve the efficiency of hospital operations, improve practitioner performance and to enhance patient care. The literature suggests that decision support systems may contribute to these benefits in clinical practice. By building upon the resource-based view of the firm (RBV), we claim that hospitals that invest in a so-called information processing capacity (IPC)—the ability to gather complete patient data and information and enhance clinical processes—will substantially enhance their clinical decision support capability (CDSC). After controlling for common method bias, we use Partial Least Squares SEM to analyze our primary claim. Following the resource and capability-based view of the firm, we test our hypotheses on a cross-sectional data sample of 720 European hospitals. We find that there is a positive association between a hospital's IPC and clinical decision support capability (CDSC). IT alignment moderates this relationship. All included control variables showed nonsignificant results. Extant research has not been able to identify those IT-enabled capabilities that strengthen CDSC in hospital practice. This study contributes to this particular gap in the literature and advances our understanding of how to efficaciously deploy CDSC in clinical practice.

Keywords: Clinical decision support capability ·
Information processing capability · Health information exchange ·
Information capability · The resource-based view of the firm (RBV) ·
Strategic IT alignment · Hospitals

1 Introduction

Recent studies recognized that the adoption and effective use of information technology (IT) leads to productivity gains and benefits in a wide variety of markets and industries, including healthcare [1–3]. Modern hospitals use IT to transform healthcare delivery processes as a means to improve operational efficiencies, clinical quality, expand access and reduce costs, and increase patient satisfaction, among other benefits [3–9]. A particular IT-enabled innovation in the clinical practice is clinical decision support (CDS). CDS tries to improve the process of decision-making by providing doctors, nurses and

© Springer Nature Switzerland AG 2019
W. Abramowicz and A. Paschke (Eds.): BIS 2018 Workshops, LNBIP 339, pp. 19–29, 2019.
https://doi.org/10.1007/978-3-030-04849-5_2

clinicians with various modes of decision support (e.g., messages, alerts, reminders, consults) following strict clinical guidelines [10, 11]. Many past and recent studies attribute a broad range of benefits to the use of effectively deployed clinical decision support (CDSS) within the hospital enterprise [12, 13], although empirical evidence remains sparse.

Hence, various related factors motivate this work. First, from extant literature has emerged the widely accepted conclusion that IT can be beneficial for hospitals [14]. However, there have been limited studies on the antecedents and conditions underlying robust clinical decision support capability (CDSC) deployments in hospitals. Second, previous studies often have a narrow scope and focus on specific clinical outcomes of specific diseases [11]. Third, the targetted use of IT is becoming more important in hospitals, because it is not uncommon that IT can impede potential benefits [1, 15, 16]. Specifically, IT-productivity literature direct toward the use of IT plans in achieving alignment [17], synchronizing organizations' IT resources to gain benefits [18] and IT spending justifications as part of IT evaluations [18].

Motivated by these factors, this paper follows the premise of resource- and capability synchronization theories [19, 20] and focuses on the IT-driven aspects that enable CDSC in the hospital practice. This aspect is important because this will lead to a broader understanding of IT implementations in hospitals, CDSSs in particular [21]. Specifically, the literature suggested that a particular capability enables information flow and a hospital's information capability (IC) within (en beyond the boundaries of the hospital) and enhance the processes of health information exchange (HIE) [22–24]. This capability is called an information processing capability (IPC) [25]. Hospital's IPC represents their ability to gather complete patient data and information and to enhance clinical processes. Based on the above, we define the following research questions: *'To what extent does an IPC influence a hospital's CDSC?'* and *'What is the conditioning effect of IT alignment on this relationship?'*

This paper applies a positivistic approach whereby we focus on a strong theoretical grounding and research design, evidence, and a logical argument to find support for our central claim. Therefore, our work is structured as follows. We first review the relevant resource-based theory and subsequently propose our research model with the associated hypotheses. Then, we present the methods and results section then follows these sections. We end with our key findings, a discussion of the most important results, and we present some limitations of our current work and provide some direction for future research.

2 Theoretical Ground and Hypotheses Development

2.1 Resources and Capability-Based View

Building upon the resource-based view of the firm (RBV) recent literature contends that modern digital business strategies focus on strategic capability-building and the process of leveraging information systems and information technology (IS/IT) investments; even in healthcare [26–29]. The central premise of resource-synchronization theories within the context of IT is that strategic IT investments in the organization's IT platforms and IT resource portfolio are essential to develop and align firm-wide capabilities to gain benefits and performance enhancements [30–32]. In healthcare, we explicitly see a development the management and decision-makers want to make sure that their resources and investments in IS/IT are harnessed successfully [29]. Hence, hospitals are investing in information flow capabilities to enhance the processes of health information exchange (HIE) [22–24] and to capture a complete patient's picture and their behavior. IPC seems a substantial capability hospital should invest in.

We now follow this resource and capability based view and contend that a hospitals' IPC is deemed appropriate to enhance a hospital's clinical decision support capability (CDSC).

2.2 Information Processing Capability and Clinical Decision Support

IT plays a crucial role in hospitals to improve strategic and operational processes. Following established literature on IPC [33, 34], we know that organizations that have high levels of IPC are better equipped to collect and process internal and external data and information and provide a foundation for decision-making processes. Hence, in this research we regard IPC to represent to core IT-enabled capabilities, i.e., (1) health information exchange (HIE) capability and (2) information capability (IC). We will now elaborate on both of them.

An HIE capability enables hospitals to share and exchange health and patient data and information, e.g., medical reports, PACS images, clinical documentation, and medication lists across the organizations' boundaries [35]. Benefits of sharing information are well elaborated upon in literature, even in the public domain. This capability contributes to primary data and information needs in hospitals and is important for patient management, safety and in clinical decision making [36, 37]. Hence, HIE provides a foundation for hospital efficiency, reducing health care costs, and to enhance patient outcomes [24] by securely exchanging and the use real-time health data and information [22]. Developing an HIE capability allows hospitals to generate a complete patient image, which is essential in for clinical effectiveness, workflow efficiency, and patients' clinical journeys. However, the process of exchanging health information is not enough. It is conceivable that the obtained information needs to be exploited and leveraged even further by a complementary IT-enabled capability to create value in clinical practice. Another essential capability in the dynamic hospital environment is an IC. IC concerns a hospital's capability to acquire information effectively, subsequently view this information and use it in clinical practice. This capability is critical for a patient clinical journey as this is dependent on accurate information and its usage in practice. Such a capability is not restricted to any IT functions or departments [38]. Instead, in our view, IC represents a hospital-wide measure that generates IT/business value and enhanced clinical decision-support levels. Recent research showed that such an IT-enabled capability could only create value if appropriately leverage using a sophisticated IT infrastructure capability [29].

Moreover, various studies argue that hospital operations heavily depend on the process of acquisition, exchanging, analyzing, and use of health data within the organization and within the broader hospital ecosystem [39]. We, therefore, contend that hospitals that develop high levels of IC and HIE are better equipped to deploy and its CDSC in clinical practice. Hence, we contend that hospitals IPC will enhance the clinical decision support within the hospital enterprise and provides value-added services. Therefore, we define:

Hypothesis 1: *IPC is positively associated with a hospital's CDSC.*

2.3   IT Alignment

Investments in IS/IT, along with structured adoption and use, have been suggested to lead to multi-factorial advantages and competitive gains for organizations in various industries [40]. Despite massive investments in IT, organizations quite often fail to achieve improvements in their organizational performance due to their inability to align IT with organizational needs. Ever since the exposition of the 'productivity paradox' [41], organizations increasingly paid attention IS/IT investments, strategic IS/IT planning and its contributions to clinical operations. This development is even more so significant for hospitals, as clinical excellence and service to the community are critical factors for public hospitals [42].

Strategic IS/IT planning that was first addressed by King and Cleland [53] is a crucial activity within organizations and allows organizations to align both business and IT strategies. It is a process by which organizations effectively deploy sustainable business and IT strategies in which internal resources are integrated into external opportunities [43]. Therefore, it enables organizations to assess the existing and planned IS resources and can be regarded as a weapon to involve processes for the identification of opportunities for the use of the IT resources and capabilities [44]. The concept of strategic IT alignment is a central element of strategic IS/IT planning. Both in scientific literature and in practice, it is a well-known fact that achieving a state of IS/IT-alignment is a crucial step to leverage the maximum potential benefits [1, 45, 46], also in healthcare [47]. Literature addresses explicitly the importance of IT plans in achieving alignment [17] and in the process of managing organizations' IT resources [18] and subsequent IT spending justifications [18]. Hence, we define IT alignment as the extent to which hospitals have adequately synchronized their overall IT plan with the IT spending [17, 48]. Now, following both recognized work and more recent studies [46, 49, 50], we argue that the degree of IT alignment will positively influence the relationship between IPC and hospital's CDSC. Hence, we define:

Hypothesis 2: *The higher the degree of IT alignment, the stronger the positive relationship between IPC and CDSC.*

3   Methods

3.1   Data Collection and Sampling Procedure

To assess the proposed research model fit and examine the hypothesized relationships, we needed a high-quality, large-scale, and cross-sectional data. In our systematic search efforts, we found such a comprehensive cross-sectional dataset—the European Hospital

Survey: Benchmarking deployment of e-Health services (2012–2013). This particular dataset contains data from roughly 1,800 European hospitals and is distributed by the European Commission[1]. This survey aimed at benchmarking the level of eHealth adoption and use in acute hospitals across 30 European countries in Europe. In doing so, the research team focused on European acute hospitals and assessed a wide range of aspects from IT applications and the hospitals' IT infrastructure, health data and information exchange, as well as security and privacy issues. The final survey targeted the Chief Information Officers (CIOs) based on their knowledge of the various social, technical and organizational aspects.

Based on the concepts in our research model (see next section) and research scope, we in total conservatively removed 1033 cases with lots of missing data entries. This amount includes removed cases for data consistency and comparability, i.e., private and private not for profit hospitals ($N = 367$) and University hospitals ($N = 196$). These hospitals were removed from our sample as they typically are organized differently (than public hospitals) and have other financing mechanisms. Therefore, our final dataset includes 720 hospitals that represent most European countries. The 720 hospitals can be grouped as follows by firm size-class (based on the number of beds), 13% large (750+ beds), 27% medium (251–750 beds), 51% small (101–250 beds) and 9% micro (less than 100 beds).

To control for common method variance, *ex-post,* we performed Harman's single factor test using SPSS v24. In doing so, we included the relevant constructs in the analysis and found that one specific factor could not attribute to the majority of variance [51]. Hence, this data sample is not affected by CMB.

3.2 Items and Construct Definitions

Our research model's constructs are partly based on and inspired by past foundational, empirical and validated work [17, 29, 33, 35, 52, 53]. For this research, we incorporated a set of twelve survey items from the European Hospital Survey to operationalize HIE. This construct included questions on appointments, receiving laboratory reports, exchanging medical patient data, interaction with patients, transfer prescriptions, and exchange patient medication lists. We operationalized the IC construct by using 17 measurement items from the survey that focused on the use and input of specific clinical information. Hence, this construct includes questions on medication lists, lab, and radiology results, medical history, allergies, immunizations and ordered tests. Finally, we measured CDSC (our dependent construct), using six survey items as a representation of hospitals' capability to enhance the process of clinical decision making. This construct contained the measurements clinical guidelines, drug-drug interactions, drug-allergy alerts, drug-lab interactions, contraindications, alerts to a critical laboratory value. All the above items were measured on or rescaled to a Likert scale from 1 to 5.

---

[1] This dataset was distributed by the European Commission and is freely accessible through: https://ec.europa.eu/digital-single-market/en/news/european-hospital-survey-benchmarking-deployment-ehealth-services-2012-2013.

Following the core literature, we measured IT alignment as a product of the total hospital's IT budget (Likert scale from 1–5; Less than 1%–5%; More than 5%) and the presence of a formal IT Strategic plan (binary scale). We controlled our outcomes with the control variables 'fte in IT department', 'size' (based on beds), and 'type of hospital' (acute or general).

3.3 SEM Model Specification and Validation

For this research, we use Partial least squares (PLS)-SEM to assess our model's 'outer' and 'inner' model [54, 55]. PLS-SEM is a mature variance-based approach allow us to simultaneously test the measurement model (factor, block analyses) and structural model (to test our hypotheses). For parameter estimation, we use SmartPLS version 3.2.7. [56]. For our measurement model specification, we propose a reflective measurement model (Mode A) for both the first (HIE, CI, and CDSC) and second-order construct (IPC) through which the manifest variables are affected by the latent variables. We also use a bootstrapping procedure with 500 replications to obtain stable results to interpret the structural model. As for sample size requirements, the included data exceeds all minimum requirements.

3.4 Assessment of the Measurement Model

We assessed the psychometric properties of our model by subjecting the first-order constructs to internal consistency reliability, convergent validity, and discriminant validity tests [56]. First, we computed the composite reliability $(CR)^2$ values for each construct as this measure takes into account the different outer loadings of the manifest variables [54]. As can be seen from Table 1, all our CR values are above the threshold values (i.e., $CR \geq 0.7$). Next, we assessed all construct-to-item loadings (λ). We removed all manifest indicators with a loading of less than 0.6^3 from our model. In total, we removed seven indicators from the HIE construct, and eight from the IC construct. All indicators for CDSC were above ≥ 0.7.

In PLS model assessments, researchers must evaluate the measurement model by their convergent and discriminant validity [54, 57]. Hence, we examined the convergent validity by examining if the average variance extracted (AVE) is above the lower limit of 0.50 [57]. All values exceed the threshold value. We assessed discriminant validity through different, but related tests. First, we investigated, whether or not, particular cross-loadings load more strongly on other constructs than the outer loading on the associated construct. We also assessed the Fornell-Larcker criterion. In this process, we investigated if the square root of the AVEs of all constructs is larger than the cross-correlation (see entries in bold in Table 1 along the matrix diagonal). As can be seen from Table 1, all correlations among all constructs were below the threshold (0.70) [57]. As a final step in the measurement model assessment, we used a relatively

---

[2] Composite reliability is similar to Cronbach's alpha without the assumption of the equal weighting of variables.

[3] An even more liberal threshold is a loading value of 0.4 for exploratory studies, see [63].

new heterotrait-monotrait (HTMT) ratio measure of correlations approach by Henseler, Ringle, and Sarstedt [58]. This measure is calculated based on the mean of the correlations of indicators across constructs measuring different constructs, relative to the average correlations of indicators within the same construct. Our assessments show that all HTMT values are well below the 0.90 upper bound. Table 1 shows all relevant outcomes and suggests that our model's first-order reflective measures are now valid and reliable. The next step is to analyze the structural 'inner' model.

Table 1. Model assessment of reliability, convergent and discriminant validity.

	(1)	(2)	(3)	(4)
(1) IT alignment	**n/a**			
(2) Clinical decision support capability	0.101	**0.768**		
(3) Health information exchange	0.041	0.392	**0.751**	
(4) Information capability	0.040	0.412	0.368	**0.751**
AVE	n/a	0.589	0.565	0.564
CR	n/a	0.895	0.866	0.921

4 Analyses and Hypotheses Testing

We used a SmartPLS bootstrapping procedure to test the significance of the various path coefficients in our model. Hence, we found support for our first hypothesis; IPC, indeed, positively influences hospitals' CDSC ($\beta = .482$; $t = 14.649$; $p < .0001$). As for our second hypothesis (strategic alignment moderates the relationship between IPC and CDSC, H1), we also looked at the significance of the path coefficient ($\beta = 0.101$, $t = 2.910$, $p < .005$). Hence, we additionally found support for our second hypothesis, while all included control variables showed non-significant effects on CDSC: 'fte IT department' ($\beta = .023$, $t = 0.998$, $p = .226$), 'size' ($\beta = -.041$, $t = 1.214$, $p = .067$), and 'type' ($\beta = 0.050$, $t = 1.839$, $p = .319$). R^2 values, the coefficient of determination, of the endogenous constructs are commonly used to assess model fit [54]. The structural model explains 25.9% of the variance for digital capabilities ($R^2 = .259$), which is considered moderate to large. We also assessed the model's predictive power [54].

In doing so, we performed a blindfolding procedure (i.e., a sample re-use technique) in SmartPLS and calculated Stone-Geisser (Q^2) [59] values. $Q^2 > 0$ for the endogenous latent constructs indicate that models have predictive relevance. Results show that our Q^2 value (for CDSC) is well above 0 for both cross-validated redundancy ($Q^2 = 0.140$) and cross-validated communality ($Q^2 = 0.423$). These outcomes indicated the overall model's predictive relevance [54]. Figure 1 shows the main results of our structural analyses.

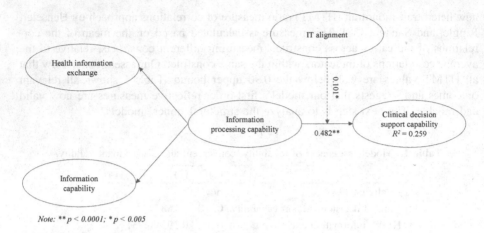

Note: ** p < 0.0001; * p < 0.005

Fig. 1. Structural model analysis.

5   Discussion, Conclusion, and Outlook

This study tried to investigate to what extent an IPC impacts the hospital's CDSC. This research is very relevant because hospitals are currently investing heavily in IT to improve strategic and operational processes. Following the RBV—through which relevant IT assets, resources and capabilities can be identified and assessed toward their importance [60]—we argued that hospitals that have high levels of IPC are better equipped to collect and process internal and external data and information and provide a foundation for decision-making processes. Our PLS results substantiate our claim, i.e., IPC significantly influences CDSC based on a sample of 720 European hospitals.

Moreover, we argued that IT alignment would moderate the relationship between IPC and CDSC based on synchronized IT resources, allocated IT budgets and assets. Next, to empirical evidence for our first hypothesis, we found support for the second claim. IT alignment indeed moderates this relationship and clarifies our model. Like [61], our findings help minimize confusions regarding the role of strategic IT alignment under the resource-based view. These findings are important, as IT not always yields significant productivity gains, also in healthcare [62].

Our outcomes demonstrate relevance for practice as well, as they suggest that greater efficiency gains and operational benefits can be gained through high levels of IPC within the hospital. Hence, IT-enabled processes that drive collaboration, coordination, and innovative diagnostic approaches have great potential to deliver higher quality for patients and physicians at a lower cost. Jones et al. [63] call this 'the definition of greater productivity.' Hospitals can, therefore, enhance CDSC by improving the capability to share and exchange health and patient, and invest in the capability to acquire, view and use information in clinical practice effectively.

Limitations constrain current results, so that future research could seek to address those. First, we focused on public hospitals. Future research might investigate whether or not our results also hold for other types of hospitals. Second, we did not uncover heterogeneity issues, as the scope of our work was limited. However, it is, worth investigating in detail potential differences among groups of hospitals taking into account, e.g., financial incentives for the adoption of IT, organization characteristics, and other potentially related digital capabilities.

To conclude, we believe hospitals can benefit from our results and that they could help decision-makers in the process of allocating their IT budget, resources and asset to facilitate decision-support in clinical practice.

References

1. Brynjolfsson, E., Hitt, L.M.: Beyond computation: information technology, organizational transformation and business performance. J. Econ. Perspect. **14**(4), 23–48 (2000)
2. Agha, L.: The effects of health information technology on the costs and quality of medical care. J. Health Econ. **34**, 19–30 (2014)
3. Lee, J., McCullough, J.S., Town, R.J.: The impact of health information technology on hospital productivity. RAND J. Econ. **44**(3), 545–568 (2013)
4. Haux, R.: Medical informatics: past, present, future. Int. J. Med. Inform. **79**(9), 599–610 (2010)
5. Ludwick, D., Doucette, J.: Adopting electronic medical records in primary care: lessons learned from health information systems implementation experience in seven countries. Int. J. Med. Inform. **78**(1), 22–31 (2009)
6. McGlynn, E., et al.: The quality of health care delivered to adults in the United States. New Engl. J. Med. **348**(26), 2635–2645 (2003)
7. Chiasson, M., et al.: Expanding multi-disciplinary approaches to healthcare information technologies: what does information systems offer medical informatics? Int. J. Med. Inform. **76**, S89–S97 (2007)
8. Curtright, J.W., Stolp-Smith, S.C., Edell, E.S.: Strategic performance management: development of a performance measurement system at the Mayo clinic. J. Healthc. Manag. **45**(1), 58–68 (2000)
9. Ahovuo, J., et al.: Process oriented organisation in the regional PACS environment. In: EuroPACS-MIR 2004 in the Enlarged Europe, pp. 481–484 (2004)
10. Garg, A.X., et al.: Effects of computerized clinical decision support systems on practitioner performance and patient outcomes: a systematic review. JAMA **293**(10), 1223–1238 (2005)
11. Romano, M.J., Stafford, R.S.: Electronic health records and clinical decision support systems: impact on national ambulatory care quality. Arch. Intern. Med. **171**(10), 897–903 (2011)
12. Elkin, P.L., et al.: The introduction of a diagnostic decision support system (DXplain™) into the workflow of a teaching hospital service can decrease the cost of service for diagnostically challenging Diagnostic Related Groups (DRGs). Int. J. Med. Inform. **79**(11), 772–777 (2010)
13. Kaushal, R., Shojania, K.G., Bates, D.W.: Effects of computerized physician order entry and clinical decision support systems on medication safety: a systematic review. Arch. Intern. Med. **163**(12), 1409–1416 (2003)
14. Buntin, M.B., et al.: The benefits of health information technology: a review of the recent literature shows predominantly positive results. Health Aff. **30**(3), 464–471 (2011)
15. Overby, E., Bharadwaj, A., Sambamurthy, V.: Enterprise agility and the enabling role of information technology. Eur. J. Inf. Syst. **15**(2), 120–131 (2006)

16. Weill, P., Subramani, M., Broadbent, M.: Building IT infrastructure for strategic agility. MIT Sloan Manag. Rev. **44**(1), 57 (2002)
17. Hirschheim, R., Sabherwal, R.: Detours in the path toward strategic information systems alignment. Calif. Manag. Rev. **44**(1), 87–108 (2001)
18. Chan, Y.E., Reich, B.H.: IT alignment: what have we learned? J. Inf. Technol. **22**(4), 297–315 (2007)
19. Wernerfelt, B.: A resource-based view of the firm. Strateg. Manag. J. **5**(2), 171–180 (1984)
20. Mithas, S., Tafti, A., Mitchell, W.: How a firm's competitive environment and digital strategic posture influence digital business strategy. MIS Q. **37**(2), 511–536 (2013)
21. Goh, J.M., Gao, G., Agarwal, R.: Evolving work routines: adaptive routinization of information technology in healthcare. Inf. Syst. Res. **22**(3), 565–585 (2011)
22. Van de Wetering, R., Versendaal, J.: How a flexible collaboration infrastructure impacts healthcare information exchange. In: Proceedings of the 31th Bled eConference Digital Transformation – Meeting the Challenges, Bled, Slovenia (2018)
23. Walker, J., et al.: The value of health care information exchange and interoperability. Health Aff. **24**, W5 (2005)
24. Hersh, W.R., et al.: Outcomes from health information exchange: systematic review and future research needs. JMIR Med. Informa. **3**(4), e39 (2015)
25. Galbraith, J.R.: Organization design: an information processing view. Interfaces **4**(3), 28–36 (1974)
26. Bharadwaj, A., et al.: Digital business strategy: toward a next generation of insights (2013)
27. Setia, P., Venkatesh, V., Joglekar, S.: Leveraging digital technologies: how information quality leads to localized capabilities and customer service performance. MIS Q. **37**(2), 565–590 (2013)
28. El Sawy, O.A., et al.: Research commentary-seeking the configurations of digital ecodynamics: it takes three to tango. Inf. Syst. Res. **21**(4), 835–848 (2010)
29. Van de Wetering, R., Versendaal, J., Walraven, P.: Examining the relationship between a hospital's IT infrastructure capability and digital capabilities: a resource-based perspective. In: Proceedings of the Twenty-Fourth Americas Conference on Information Systems (AMCIS). AIS, New Orleans (2018)
30. El Sawy, O.A., Pavlou, P.A.: IT-enabled business capabilities for turbulent environments. MIS Q. Exec. **7**(3), 139–150 (2008)
31. Mithas, S., et al.: Information technology and firm profitability: mechanisms and empirical evidence. MIS Q. **36**(1), 205–224 (2012)
32. Sheikh, A., Sood, H.S., Bates, D.W.: Leveraging health information technology to achieve the "triple aim" of healthcare reform. J. Am. Med. Inform. Assoc. **22**(4), 849–856 (2015)
33. Wang, E.T.: Effect of the fit between information processing requirements and capacity on organizational performance. Int. J. Inf. Manag. **23**(3), 239–247 (2003)
34. Tushman, M.L., Nadler, D.A.: Information processing as an integrating concept in organizational design. Acad. Manag. Rev. **3**(3), 613–624 (1978)
35. Vest, J.R., et al.: Challenges, alternatives, and paths to sustainability for health information exchange efforts. J. Med. Syst. **37**(6), 9987 (2013)
36. Kaelber, D.C., Bates, D.W.: Health information exchange and patient safety. J. Biomed. Inform. **40**(6), S40–S45 (2007)
37. Sutcliffe, K.M., Lewton, E., Rosenthal, M.M.: Communication failures: an insidious contributor to medical mishaps. Acad. Med. **79**(2), 186–194 (2004)
38. Marchand, D.A., Kettinger, W.J., Rollins, J.D.: Information orientation: people, technology and the bottom line. Sloan Manag. Rev. **41**(4), 69 (2000)
39. Jadad, A.R., et al.: The internet and evidence-based decision-making: a needed synergy for efficient knowledge management in health care. Can. Med. Assoc. J. **162**(3), 362–365 (2000)

40. Tallon, P.P., Pinsonneault, A.: Competing perspectives on the link between strategic information technology alignment and organizational agility: insights from a mediation model. MIS Q. **35**(2), 463–486 (2011)
41. Strassman, P.A.: Business Value of Computers. The Information Economic Press, New Canaan (1990)
42. Firth, L., Francis, P.: Understanding the lack of adoption of E-commerce in the health sector: the clinician's strategic perspective. In: IADIS Virtual Conference, Lisbon (2004)
43. Van de Wetering, R., Batenburg, R., Lederman, R.: Evolutionistic or revolutionary paths? A PACS maturity model for strategic situational planning. Int. J. Comput. Assist. Radiol. Surg. **5**(4), 401–409 (2010)
44. King, W.R.: Strategic planning for IS: the state of practice and research. MIS Q. **9**(2), 6–7 (1985). Editor's comment
45. Henderson, J.C., Venkatraman, N.: Strategic alignment: leveraging information technology for transforming organisations. IBM Syst. J. **32**(1), 4–16 (1993)
46. Gerow, J.E., et al.: Looking toward the future of IT-business strategic alignment through the past: a meta-analysis. MIS Q. **38**(4), 1059–1085 (2014)
47. Henderson, J.C., Thomas, J.B.: Aligning business and information technology domains: strategic planning in hospitals. J. Healthc. Manag. **37**(1), 71 (1992)
48. Luftman, J., Brier, T.: Achieving and sustaining business-IT alignment. Calif. Manag. Rev. **42**(1), 109–122 (1999)
49. Avison, D., et al.: Using and validating the strategic alignment model. J. Strateg. Inf. Syst. **13**(3), 223–246 (2004)
50. Van de Wetering, R., Batenburg, R.: Towards a theory of PACS deployment: an integrative PACS maturity framework. J. Digit. Imaging **27**(3), 337–350 (2014)
51. Podsakoff, P.M., et al.: Common method biases in behavioral research: a critical review of the literature and recommended remedies. J. Appl. Psychol. **88**(5), 879 (2003)
52. Wade, M., Hulland, J.: Review: the resource-based view and information systems research: review, extension, and suggestions for future research. MIS Q. **28**(1), 107–142 (2004)
53. Ravichandran, T., Lertwongsatien, C.: Effect of information systems resources and capabilities on firm performance: a resource-based perspective. J. Manag. Inf. Syst. **21**(4), 237–276 (2005)
54. Hair Jr., J.F., et al.: A Primer on Partial Least Squares Structural Equation Modeling (PLS-SEM). Sage Publications, Thousand Oaks (2016)
55. Henseler, J., et al.: Common beliefs and reality about PLS: comments on Rönkkö and Evermann (2013). Organ. Res. Methods **17**(2), 182–209 (2014)
56. Ringle, C.M., Wende, S., Becker, J.-M.: SmartPLS 3. Boenningstedt: SmartPLS GmbH (2015). http://www.smartpls.com
57. Fornell, C., Larcker, D.: Evaluating structural equation models with unobservable variables and measurement error. J. Mark. Res. **18**(1), 39–50 (1981)
58. Henseler, J., Ringle, C.M., Sarstedt, M.: A new criterion for assessing discriminant validity in variance-based structural equation modeling. J. Acad. Mark. Sci. **43**(1), 115–135 (2015)
59. Geisser, S.: A predictive approach to the random effect model. Biometrika **61**(1), 101–107 (1974)
60. Barney, J.: Firm resources and sustained competitive advantage. J. Manag. **17**(1), 99–120 (1991)
61. Akter, S., et al.: How to improve firm performance using big data analytics capability and business strategy alignment? Int. J. Prod. Econ. **182**, 113–131 (2016)
62. Lapointe, L., Mignerat, M., Vedel, I.: The IT productivity paradox in health: a stakeholder's perspective. Int. J. Med. Inform. **80**(2), 102–115 (2011)
63. Jones, S.S., et al.: Unraveling the IT productivity paradox—lessons for health care. New Engl. J. Med. **366**(24), 2243–2245 (2012)

Ontology-Based Fragmented Company Knowledge Integration: Possible Approaches

Alexander Smirnov[1] and Nikolay Shilov[2(✉)]

[1] ITMO University, St. Petersburg, Russia
smir@iias.spb.su
[2] SPIIRAS, St. Petersburg, Russia
nick@iias.spb.su

Abstract. Companies have multiple business process, some of which are supported by knowledge described via ontologies. However, due to their nature, the processes use different knowledge notation what causes a problem of integrating such fragmented heterogeneous knowledge. The paper investigates the problem of developing a single multi-domain ontology for integrating company knowledge taking into account differences between terminologies and formalisms used in various business processes. Different options of designing ontologies covering multiple domains are considered. Three of them: (i) ontology localization/ multilingual ontologies, (ii) granular ontologies, and (iii) ontologies with temporal logics are considered in details and analyzed.

Keywords: Knowledge management · Interoperability
Multi-domain ontology

1 Introduction

Development of knowledge management technologies enables companies to apply new technologies, workflows, and software tools. This, in turn, usually speeds up business processes and increases their flexibility and efficiency. However, different workflows often rely on different AI mechanisms caused by their nature. For example, product classification and feature definition can be done by using some general ontology model, and more specific domains, such as configuration models can be derived by inheriting or subclassing the ontologies within the general model. Rule-based language SWRL can be used for description of constraints. It is based on OWL and the resulting ontology can be an extension of OWL ontology. Configuration system in turn can be implemented using JESS what would require mapping of OWL-based configuration knowledge and SWRL-based constraints into Jess facts and Jess, respectively [1].

Thus, the variety of the elements of the resulting eco-system of information and knowledge representation can become really high. A possible scale of the problem was identified in [2] and presented in Fig. 1.

It is obvious that the problem of interoperability and integrity of fragmented company knowledge related to different workflows arises. The paper is aimed at investigating the possible problem of integrating fragmented company knowledge representing via ontologies. Various possibilities of developing ontologies to describe

© Springer Nature Switzerland AG 2019
W. Abramowicz and A. Paschke (Eds.): BIS 2018 Workshops, LNBIP 339, pp. 30–37, 2019.
https://doi.org/10.1007/978-3-030-04849-5_3

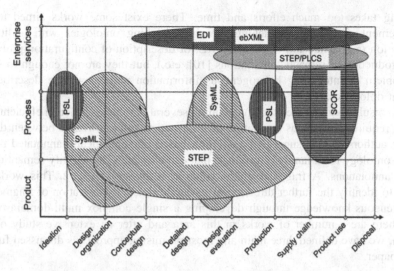

Fig. 1. Usage of different languages for information description [2].

several domains are considered. The most suitable ones are considered in detail and analysed. The research develops the earlier obtained results [3, 4] aimed at development of knowledge-based solutions for various company workflows. Though the carried out projects have led to substantial results in the areas complex product and system information management and configuration, it is still visible that the developed and existing knowledge management systems are separated. An important task would be to develop a way to integrate existing knowledge so that it could be freely used in different processes.

2 Ontologies for Multi-domain Knowledge Description

Ontologies are aimed at describing knowledge related to a certain domain in a machine-readable way. Ontologies make it possible to obtain, exchange and process information and knowledge taking into account their semantics and not just syntax. Ontology is a formal conceptualisation of a particular domain of interest shared among heterogeneous applications [5, 6]. An ontology usually includes concepts existing in the domain, relationships between them and axioms. Ontologies are thought to be a well-proven tool for solving the problem of interoperability. However, there still exist the problem of using different ontologies with different terminology and notation in applications addressing different tasks even within one company that has to be solved. E.g., the authors of [7] propose a model-driven interoperability framework for technical support of co-evolution strategy of products and manufacturing systems. They address connecting possible modules to all possible production capabilities managed on different software tools through establishing "connector framework" matching used ontologies.

Ontology matching [8] seems to be one of the solutions to this problem. But in reality, automatic ontology matching is still not reliable enough while manual ontology matching takes too much efforts and time. There exist some works aimed at the improvement of ontology matching through enriching ontologies with additional information (e.g., extension of DAML+OIL for description of configuration problems [9], introduction of semantic annotations [10], etc.), but they are not enough to solve the problem of integrating heterogeneous information and knowledge described in different ontologies.

As a result, it can be seen that maintaining several ontologies is not an efficient way since it requires continuous translation of information and knowledge between them.

The authors of [11] suggested a solution based on semantically annotated multi-faceted ontology for a family of products that can automatically identify semantically-related annotations. A fragment of the solution is shown in Fig. 2. This work has helped to identify the further direction of research aimed at integration of fragmented heterogeneous knowledge through developing a single complex multi-domain ontology. There are a number of works in this area and after an extensive study of the domain, we have defined three main and most promising approaches discussed further in the paper.

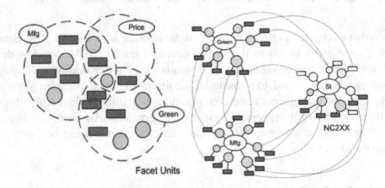

Fig. 2. A multi-faceted ontology for a family of products (adapted from [11]).

3   Approaches to Building a Multi-domain Ontology

3.1   Multilingual Ontology

The goal of multilingual ontologies is to resolve terminological issues that arise due to usage of different languages. Among the terminological issues the following can be selected [12]:

1. Existence of an exact equivalent. This is the easiest case when two terms have completely the same meaning. In real life (when talking of regular languages such as English or German) this is a rear situation, however in a company most of terminology would be the case. For example, "product" would mean the same both during the design stage and the production stage, or in the case reported earlier [3], "feature" during the design stage means the same as "characteristic" during the production stage.

2. Existence of several context-dependent equivalents. This case assumes that one can choose the right translation (the right equivalent) based on the situation. An example could be the term "modular product" that can stand for both product consisting of several modules or product with some variable characteristics. Treating such ambiguity for a person could be relatively simple but for a machine it can cause significant difficulties.
3. Existence of a conceptualization mismatch. This is an important issue for regular languages, standing for a lack of semantic equivalent for a given term. In case of ontologies used in business processes this is a much less common issue since the lack of a certain term in a business process usually would mean that it is just not used (not needed) in this process.

Such ontologies are built as an ontology with language-specific fragments with relationships between terms and it might be a straightforward enough solution for multi- domain ontology. This would really help to overcome the terminological issues, as well as to solve the problem of heterogeneity of information and knowledge between different business processes.

However, a multilingual ontology is formulated in a single formalism and collecting together, for example, procurement and configuration knowledge would not be possible without losing certain semantics. As a result, this approach can not solve the problem formulated. Multilingual support can be of high importance for global companies that have employees speaking in different languages but this is out of the scope of the presented here research.

3.2 Granular Ontology

Granular ontologies are based on the integration of ontology-based knowledge representation with the concept of granular computing. Granular computing is based around the notion of granule that links together similar regarding to a chosen criteria objects or entities ("drawn together by indistinguishability, similarity, proximity or functionality" [13]). The granules can also be linked together into bigger granules forming multiple levels of granularity.

From the knowledge representation point of view, a granule can be considered as a chunk of knowledge made about a certain object, set of objects or sub-domain [14]. A level is a collection of granules of similar nature. When speaking about corporate knowledge, lower-level granules can be related to particular business processes, and higher-level granules can combine knowledge related to macro-processes. The hierarchy of granules then would form a hierarchy of business processes of the company.

Granular ontologies seem to be a suitable solution to support multiple domains: they enable splitting the domain in smaller areas with consistent terminology and formalisms. The possibility to form a hierarchy (generalisation) is also beneficial due to the possibility to define generic concepts and relationships at higher levels.

However, business processes usually overlap in terms of used information and knowledge (Fig. 3). This means that there exist multiple processes that assume collaboration and usage of the same information and knowledge. Pure granular ontologies cannot solve the problem of terms having different meaning in different processes or different company departments. There are multiple efforts in the area of rough granular computing [15–17], however, they are not directly related to ontology design. As a result, additional research in this area is required. Another possibility is to extend a granular ontology with a concept that would enable certain "roughness" of it, and the following section proposes such a possibility.

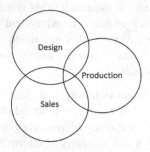

Fig. 3. Example of overlapping business processes.

3.3   Temporal Logics-Based Ontology

The authors of [18] propose to address the problem of terms having different meaning in different business processes or different company departments through usage of temporal logics.

The approach presented in [18] is based on the fuzzy extension of temporal logics to enable links and overlapping between different business processes. The metaphor used in the approach is based on the idea of different business processes as time intervals with fuzzy duration.

The ontology (ONT_{LC}) is described by the following formula:

$$ONT_{LC} = <C_{LC}, R_{LC}, O_{LC}, T_{LC}>, \text{ where}$$

C_{LC} is the set of concepts (all the concepts of the ontology used in all business processes),

R_{LC} is the set of relations between the concepts,

O_{LC} is the set of operations over concepts and/or relations,

T_{LC} is the set of temporal characteristics.

Since the ontology is aimed at separation of concepts between business processes, the systemic kernel is represented as the following triple:

$$ONT_S = <S, R_S, O_S>, \text{ where}$$

S is the set of business processes under consideration,

R_S is the set of relations between the processes,

O_S is the set of operations used on the processes.

As it was mentioned the different business processes are considered as time intervals $s = [t^-, t^+]$, with starting and ending time points t^- and t^+ respectively. However, in order to indicate the overlapping of processes, the intervals are considered to be fuzzy.

Though the usage of granular ontology with temporal logic as a notation for multi-domain knowledge representation looks complex, it can solve the heterogeneity problem arising from different mental models in different business processes. Besides, the "complexity" of this approach makes it possible to include different representations related to different processes preserving the expressiveness of the representations and languages used unlike multilingual ontologies. As a result, it was concluded that in the considered case the semantic interoperability support for fragmented company knowledge based on a multi-domain ontology should be implemented via the notation of granular ontology with temporal logic.

4 Conclusion and Future Work

The paper represents an analysis of the possible notations for building a multi-domain ontology supporting semantic interoperability.

Building a multi-domain segmented ontology basically consisting of a number of ontologies (sub-ontologies) can be based on using unchanged source ontologies and the overall structure of such an ontology would be simple and easy to process. However, this would lead to the necessity of continuous translation of information and knowledge between different representations and standards, which is not an easy task. The dynamic structure of the terminology would make this issue even more complex for solving. As a result, this solution was not accepted.

Multilingual ontologies can solve the problem of heterogeneity of information and knowledge but lack the possibility to support multiple problem-specific formalisms. This solution was not accepted wither but it was noted that multilingual support could be useful for global companies, which have employees speaking in different languages.

It was identified that the semantic interoperability for fragmented company knowledge should be based on granular multi-domain ontology extended with temporal logics elements. The pilot efforts related to building smaller ontologies with the purpose of validation of this approach proved its viability and potential efficiency. The future research is aimed at building a larger-scale ontology including real company data.

Acknowledgements. The paper is partially due to collaboration between SPIIRAS and Festo AG & Co KG, State Research # 0073-2018-0002, projects funded by grants ## 18-07-01201, 18-07-01272 of the Russian Foundation for Basic Research. The work has been also partially financially supported by the Government of Russian Federation, Grant 08-08.

References

1. Yang, D., Miao, R., Wu, H., Zhou, Y.: Product configuration knowledge modeling using ontology web language. Expert Syst. Appl. **36**, 4399–4411 (2009). https://doi.org/10.1016/j.eswa.2008.05.026
2. Rachuri, S., Subrahmanian, E., Bouras, A., et al.: Information sharing and exchange in the context of product lifecycle management: role of standards. Comput. Des. **40**, 789–800 (2008). https://doi.org/10.1016/j.cad.2007.06.012
3. Smirnov, A.V., Shilov, N., Oroszi, A., et al.: Changing information management for product-service system engineering: customer-oriented strategies and lessons learned. Int. J. Prod. Lifecycle Manag. **11**(1), 1–18 (2018). https://doi.org/10.1504/IJPLM.2018.091647
4. Oroszi, A., Jung, T., Smirnov, A., et al.: Ontology-driven codification for discrete and modular products. Int. J. Prod. Dev. **8**, 162–177 (2009). https://doi.org/10.1504/IJPD.2009.024186
5. Gruber, T.R.: A translation approach to portable ontology specifications. Knowl. Acquisition **5**, 199–220 (1993). https://doi.org/10.1006/knac.1993.1008
6. Staab, S., Studer, R.: Handbook on Ontologies. Springer, Heidelberg (2009). https://doi.org/10.1007/978-3-540-92673-3
7. Lafleur, M., Terkaj, W., Belkadi, F., Urgo, M., Bernard, A., Colledani, M.: An onto-based interoperability framework for the connection of PLM and production capability tools. In: Harik, R., Rivest, L., Bernard, A., Eynard, B., Bouras, A. (eds.) PLM 2016. IAICT, vol. 492, pp. 134–145. Springer, Cham (2016). https://doi.org/10.1007/978-3-319-54660-5_13
8. Smirnov, A., Shilov, N.: Ontology matching in collaborative recommendation system for PLM. Int. J. Prod. Lifecycle Manag. **6**, 322–338 (2013). https://doi.org/10.1504/IJPLM.2013.063210
9. Felfernig, A., Friedrich, G., Jannach, D., et al.: Configuration knowledge representations for semantic web applications. Artif. Intell. Eng. Des. Anal. Manuf. **17**, 31–50 (2003). https://doi.org/10.1017/S0890060403171041
10. Liao, Y., Lezoche, M., Panetto, H., Boudjlida, N.: Semantic annotations for semantic interoperability in a product lifecycle management context. Int. J. Prod. Res. **54**, 5534–5553 (2016). https://doi.org/10.1080/00207543.2016.1165875
11. Lim, S.C.J., Liu, Y., Lee, W.B.: A methodology for building a semantically annotated multi-faceted ontology for product family modelling. Adv. Eng. Inform. **25**, 147–161 (2011). https://doi.org/10.1016/j.aei.2010.07.005
12. Espinoza, M., Montiel-Ponsoda, E., Gómez-Pérez, A.: Ontology localization. In: Proceedings of the Fifth International Conference on Knowledge Capture - K-CAP 2009, New York, New York, USA, pp. 33–40. ACM Press (2009)
13. Zadeh, L.A.: Is there a need for fuzzy logic? Inf. Sci. (Ny) **178**, 2751–2779 (2008). https://doi.org/10.1016/j.ins.2008.02.012
14. Calegari, S., Ciucci, D.: Granular computing applied to ontologies. Int. J. Approximate Reasoning **51**, 391–409 (2010). https://doi.org/10.1016/j.ijar.2009.11.006
15. Jankowski, A., Skowron, A.: Toward rough-granular computing. In: An, A., Stefanowski, J., Ramanna, S., Butz, C.J., Pedrycz, W., Wang, G. (eds.) RSFDGrC 2007. LNCS (LNAI), vol. 4482, pp. 1–12. Springer, Heidelberg (2007). https://doi.org/10.1007/978-3-540-72530-5_1
16. Inuiguchi, M., Hirano, S., Tsumoto, S.: Rough Set Theory and Granular Computing. Springer, Heidelberg (2003). https://doi.org/10.1007/978-3-540-36473-3

17. Polkowski, L., Skowron, A.: Rough mereological calculi of granules: a rough set approach to computation. Comput. Intell. **17**, 472–492 (2001). https://doi.org/10.1111/0824-7935. 00159
18. Tarassov, V., Fedotova, A., Stark, R., Karabekov, B.: Granular meta-ontology and extended allen's logic: some theoretical background and application to intelligent product lifecycle management systems valery. In: Schwab, I., van Moergestel, L., Gonçalves, G. (eds) The Fourth International Conference on Intelligent Systems and Applications, INTELLI 2015, St. Julians, Malta, pp. 86–93 (2015)

Enhancing Teamwork Behavior of Services

Paraskevi Tsoutsa[1,2]([⊠]), Panos Fitsilis[3], and Omiros Ragos[1]

[1] Department of Mathematics, University of Patras, 26442 Patras, Greece
tsoutsa@teilar.gr, ragos@math.upatras.gr
[2] Department of Accounting and Finance,
University of Applied Sciences of Thessaly, 41110 Larisa, Greece
[3] Department of Business Administration,
University of Applied Sciences of Thessaly, 41110 Larisa, Greece
pfitsilis@gmail.com

Abstract. Nowadays, many large software systems that are developed for business are mainly built from services leveraging the benefits of interoperability. However, the development of new technologies such as Cloud Computing, Internet of Things and Cyber Physical Systems create additional concerns that claim to be integrated into the existing approaches of modeling services, their interaction and cooperation. In this research, we propose web services to automatically cooperate using the role modeling approach by enhancing service's interoperability through novel *service teamwork roles*. Teamwork contribution to the organizational performance has tracked attention of various research groups from several disciplines. In this direction, we contribute by determining the dominant teamwork roles that prevail during service group cooperation, link them with fifteen major teamwork factors that are recognized in agent-based teamwork, and indicate their primary teamwork behavior. A simulation using Monte Carlo presents results about how teamwork roles could affect and benefit the service cooperation.

Keywords: Services · Information systems · Composition · Role modeling Teamwork

1 Introduction

Web services play a central role in modern software development and business information systems. They are commonly considered for performing complex tasks, thus research has focused on the problem of the automatic cooperation and service composition. From a business perspective, service composition dramatically reduces the cost and risks of building new business applications in the sense that existing business logics are represented as services and could be reused [1]. However, realizing a fully automated service composition still presents several open issues [2, 3].

A basic limitation detected in most of existing research works on service composition is that, although web services work together as a group to achieve a common objective, they do not use any teamwork abilities which are commonly used in case of groups of human, agents or robots. The concept of developing *autonomously composite services capable of exhibiting teamwork behavior* is introduced as a challenge in this

© Springer Nature Switzerland AG 2019
W. Abramowicz and A. Paschke (Eds.): BIS 2018 Workshops, LNBIP 339, pp. 38–50, 2019.
https://doi.org/10.1007/978-3-030-04849-5_4

paper. A service capable of exhibiting teamwork behavior is one that effectively cooperate with multiple potential teammates on a set of collaborative tasks and is able to catch errors or prevent emergent behaviors that put in danger the overall team goal, i.e. the execution of the composite service. The study presented here therefore, aims to contribute to theory by adding a discussion of teamwork abilities to the service literature and introduces teamwork roles that could be adopted to service cooperation.

Teamwork has become an important research field contributing to organizational performance. In recent years, many scientists studied why humans succeed or fail in joint activities and a variety of models have been developed that follow social - psychological approaches for human team formation. Apart from human team working, another area where similar problems have been studied and such theories have been applied is the area of software agents and robots. As with humans, a group of software agents must accomplish given tasks by organizing themselves according to their individual characteristics and their role within the overall system. Furthermore, in the real world scenarios, complex teams are composed of both humans and software agents, where agents can play a variety of roles in their interactions with humans. They support humans in tasks that they jointly perform or independently work to carry out tasks for which they are responsible [4]. Moreover, as researchers in [5] observe, robots and agents could also be modeled as services, which is a central concept in this research.

According to the role modeling approach of service cooperation, services are modeled as a set of roles which belong to the role model of a domain [6]. Defining services as set of roles allows making an abstraction and helps to model also other entities that might exist and cooperate in the domain to form heterogeneous teams, e.g. teams of services, humans, agents and robots. By adopting this approach, services and other actors of the domain are treated as entities that are defined in terms of the roles they play. Roles are patterns of behavior; a similar approach is often used in human team modeling, where roles represent patterns of behavior and they are interrelated with the activities of other team members in pursuit of the overall team goal [7].

Towards this direction, in this research, we attempt to bring together role theories and models of both human and agent-based teamwork literature. The aim of the paper is to determine the *service teamwork roles* that prevail during service group interaction and provide their indicative behavior based on a core set of teamwork factors that are identified to agent-based teamwork. More analytically, we contribute by (i) presenting eight novel dominant *service teamwork roles*, (ii) habilitating these roles with indicative teamwork behavior that services need as participants of an optimal team in order to underlie the required teamwork abilities, (iii) creating an experiment using Monte Carlo simulation and present results about how a service role expressing a teamwork behavior largely affects and benefits the overall goal of a composed service.

The rest of this paper is organized as follows. Section 2 describes the background, in Sect. 3 we present a set of dominant service teamwork roles, in Sect. 4 an experiment is given to show how the approach can improve the performance of service execution, while the last section presents conclusion and ongoing work.

2 Background

2.1 Web Services and the Composition Problem

A *service* is essentially a semantically well-defined abstraction of a set of computational or physical activities involving a number of resources, with the aim to fulfill a customer need or a business requirement [1]. Services receive much attention due to their ability to facilitate seamless integration of information and they are the foundation of most of today's business information systems. Services can be hosted either locally or in web environments that are inherently dynamic, since web services appear and disappear during the time. The peculiarity of subjects and the plethora of available web services make their discovery and composition a complex process.

The problem of *service composition* is, in general, the problem of constructing a new composite service, by using available services that perform some desired functionality, when no single service satisfies it. To address this issue, many approaches have been proposed as a solution, with some of the initiatives to be CDL, WSCDL, OWL-S, WSMO, BPEL4WS, while some academic efforts are presented in [8–10]. While early studies in service composition problems have addressed almost exclusively the functional composition, recent studies have made efforts that aim to consider non-functional requirements as well. Using the role modeling approach, services can be modeled from a global perspective; such that their processes are mapped to the behavior is expressed by a role in the domain [6]. The semantics of the role model explicitly indicates how a service can be used. By using role modeling, a domain accomplishes a twofold abstraction between concrete services and their processes. Roles abstract over services while behaviors abstract over their processes.

Overall, several works exist on composition of web services, but despite this intense research activity there are still open issues concerning automation, decentralization, safety, reliability, scalability, adaptivity and many others [11, 12]. In addition, while there exist research efforts that go beyond functional composition, most of them consider service composition as a problem of defining a set of semantic annotations that indicate the sequence of processes to be executed for the composition and do not exploit other existing theories about teamwork and cooperation.

2.2 Teamwork Theory to Humans and Other Systems

Today's business environment is so complex that work is done in teams composed of members that are either humans, agents or robots where each of them is specialized in specific tasks. For example, teams of humans, robots, and virtual agents need to cooperate in production settings [13], while humans, together with various e-commerce cooperative agents offered by various providers having different standards, need to collaborate. The success of the production cooperative work depends on the team rather than the individual effort of each team member. As an example, in the context of Industry 4.0 (i4.0) [14], embedded systems are linked with business information systems and organizational processes are transformed to enable the real time collaboration among humans, machines and smart objects. In order for these entities to be effectively connected and collaborate as a team, models referring to team working literature is worth to be investigated.

Team working has been thoroughly studied by psychologists and human resource experts over the last decades. In early studies, some researchers have proposed models focused on specific characteristics that team members should have such as personality, functional expertise, competencies, goal orientations, teamwork orientations, etc. [15, 16]. As the team research matured, research moved firmly from dealing with single characteristics that teams and members should have to a variety of behaviors that team members should expose [17, 18]. Ultimately, existing research member's tasks and behaviors are often clustered into distinct roles within the system that are aligned with the expertise of each team member [19]. Increasingly, researchers propose that team-mates, along with the operational tasks that they perform in a team, they have also to play some other roles such that of coordinator, contributor, idea generator, etc. Indeed, as it is witnessed by empirical studies, these approaches are effective in a variety of contexts, tasks and domains [20].

The various models of team behavior proposed in the literature were investigated to identify and analyze the different teamwork factors among various types of teams in related areas and to indicate if and how they are inter-related. Generally, factors should address different collaboration attributes, such as (i) how the team is organizing itself, e.g. by creating rules for collaboration and communication, (ii) how the team is forming its strategy for future direction, e.g. by planning and decision making and (iii) how the team work together to achieve synergy, e.g. rules of trust and engagement. Fifteen primary factors revealed in the literature, which merit particular attention across different team tasks and group sizes [21]. In the following, we provide a brief description of the identified factors of teamwork associated with agent teamwork and the three dimensions in which they are clustered.

I. ORGANIZING FACTORS

- *Collaboration (COL):* The ability of team members to act collaboratively with mutual awareness when performing a task or carrying out the team activities needed to satisfy a shared goal.
- *Communication (COM):* Through communication, the members get the essential information to collaborate and achieve shared objectives.
- *Coordination (COO):* Members that jointly perform a task need to coordinate in order to avoid interdependence problems with other members of the team.

II. STRATEGY RELATED FACTORS

- *Planning (PLN):* The ability of members to plan, recognize and resolve conflicts in scheduled plans.
- *Learning (LRN):* The ability of members to "learn" as they identify new patterns in data that will enable participants to effectively discover opportunities and create strategies to improve teamwork experience.
- *Decision making (DM):* Decision making process and problem solving are essential for effective team performance, reasoning services usually exist in teams that are responsible for the system's decision-making process.

- *Evaluation (EVL):* The use of evaluation methodologies and metrics to determine the performance of the team members, the total team effectiveness and in what degree they achieve the intended effects.
- *Teamwork policies (POL):* Policies assuring the appropriate functionality of members according to domain and other safety rules.

III. SYNERGY RELATED FACTORS

- *Ad hoc team setting (ADH):* A team member's behavior that is able to cooperate with multiple potential unknown and heterogeneous members without pre-coordination in order to achieve a common goal.
- *Autonomy (AUT):* The ability of the member to assist the team by having a degree of reasoning and taking a decision.
- *Delegation (DLG):* The ability of a member to select tasks to delegate to other team members in order to increase flexibility and team performance when unavailability to perform a task occurs.
- *Joint-intention (INT):* The common intention, and the focus that team members demonstrate in order to handle unexpected failures and reach an optimal team behavior.
- *Knowledge of teammates' capabilities (KCT):* In order to improve collaboration, members learn about capabilities of their teammates and use that knowledge to improve team performance.
- *Knowledge sharing (KNL):* The shared understanding of the task to be performed, knowledge and beliefs, goals and intentions and plans of the team that members have which help them to reason and predict future system states.
- *Trust (TRS):* Team members take into account the issue of trust and the factors that help to build trusted relationships in order to adjust their behavior encompassing both social and ethical aspects.

Existing approaches in service modeling and teamwork provide the framework for the goal of this research paper. On the one hand, researchers investigate how complex objectives can be achieved by group of services, and on the other hand, *teamwork* models are formally defined in *agent teamwork*. Since these aims are far apart in the available service cooperation research, hence in the next section, we present eight service teamwork roles with the explicit purpose to combine the solutions of the above problems. According to our point of view, the primary objective for the composition is not only to develop a plan for the composition, but also to satisfy more composition requirements that are achieved by facilitating services with teamwork abilities.

3   Bringing Teamwork Abilities to Services

Motivated by the organizational behavior and the teamwork theory [21–23], in order to bring teamwork abilities to service cooperation, we argue that services, similarly to agents and robots except from functional behavior they have also to exhibit teamwork behavior when they cooperate. In case, that there do not exist member services that exhibit such behavior then other services should be included into the composition that will provide this behavior. To achieve this and based on the role modeling approach for service definition presented in [6], we introduce a role-model paradigm enhanced by service teamwork roles. We propose eight additional service teamwork roles to be involved during the composition process that aim to catch any emergent behavior that happens in a domain. The eight roles were derived by combining the teamwork theory focusing on the behavior of high performing human teams and the fifteen teamwork factors emerged from agent team working, which are actually the behavioral descriptors for these roles.

The enriched model can be proved beneficial to create more stable team of services, i.e. composite services such that their components-members promote better understanding and much more likely they are able to cooperate effectively and achieve their objectives.

3.1 Determining the Teamwork Roles for Services

In the following, we present the eight novel service teamwork roles could be exploited in modeling the service execution and cooperation process. The proposed roles are defined with the aim to meet the performance challenges that dynamic domains are facing, in terms of various non-functional objectives as they are also identified in [24, 25]. The main objective for all teamwork roles is to handle emergent behavior that occurs in the domain and arrest any misbehaving of other participants. We outline the behavior for each service teamwork role by coupling the desired behavior of service team members with the discoveries from agent-based teamwork.

1. The Developer role
Description: The main goal of the *developer* is to form new composite services. It is the "team builder" of the domain; it binds the appropriate services to the behaviors to be executed for the service composition. It generates a plan for the composition, then does an evaluation for candidates services enrolled to domain in order to select the most appropriate to play the role and finally makes the service allocation for the execution of behaviors. After the service allocation is completed, this role calls the *monitor* role to monitor how the team of the selected services is performing while executing the plan.
Primary behaviors: AUT, INT, KCT, KNL, COO, COL, COM, DM, POL, EVL, PLN

2. The Organiser role
Description: The *Organiser* monitors the global schedule and implements ways of making things work. It keeps track of accomplishments and how teams are progressing relative to goals and timelines ensuring that standards and processes are upheld. It keeps track of queues, average time responses and urgent. It receives maintenance queries and schedules them. In case a service is unavailable, it delegates the execution of the behavior to another available and appropriate service. When a gap between services that run for an existing plan occurs, it re-assigns the service execution to another service and substitutes the missing services in order to fill the gap.
Primary behaviors: ADH, DLG, INT, KCT, KNL, TRS, COO, COL, COM, DM, POL, EVL, PLN

3. The Promoter role

Description: The *promoter* helps bridge and connect members of the team with services outside of the team. It works in a twofold aspect by searching for new opportunities and exploring possibilities inside and outside of the domain. It takes feedback from organiser and producer roles and, if the system has unused available services, searches for new opportunities to promote their usage. If the system is overloaded, it looks for solutions, e.g. other resources inside or outside of the domain that could help. After analysis, it recommends products of the domain to new markets. It has the ability to present the availability of the overall system to other roles.

Primary behaviors: ADH, INT, KCT, TRS, COO, COL, COM, DM, POL

4. The Monitor role

Description: The monitor role monitors the whole process of composition and the team functionality in the domain. It receives the plan for the execution and informs the involved services to participate, e.g. informs a drilling machine that has a work to do. If a service is unavailable, it proceeds with the next candidate service. This role is enabled to achieve cooperation between peer roles by catching errors that might occur during communication. For example, there are web services which might be inherently unreliable e.g., due to the failure of the hosting. Role implementations that rely on such resources need to be able to adapt to such situations. Its main purpose is to help roles to execute a behavior with success by providing the necessary information. If emergent behavior occurs, that could be adapted it will contact the *adviser* role. When a manufacturing service is out of order, the monitor role will inform the maintainer role in order to take care of it while, in case a service suffers from overload, informs the organiser role to re-plan the production process.

Primary behaviors: ADH, AUT, INT, KCT, KNL, TRS, COO, COL, COM, DM, POL, EVL, PLN

5. The Producer role

Description: The *Producer* role works on a systematic way to produce work outputs. It is the doer of the domain; this role characterizes, for example, all manufacturing services. They individually keep track of queues, balances, etc. If smart machines play this role, they have a list of tasks to do in order to know their schedule. According to these lists, they inform about under using or if they exceed workload capacity.

Primary behaviors: ADH, AUT, DLG, KCT, KNL, COO, COL, COM, DM, POL

6. The Adviser role

Description: Upon to a user request for a service, the *adviser* of the domain takes the request and searches if it matches according to its semantic similarity with existing goals of the domain repository. If it is so, it retrieves a plan and provides it to the *developer* role in order to proceed with the service allocation. Otherwise, it informs the *developer* role to search for a new plan. It gathers information and advices other roles. It concerns about data accuracy and checks the data integrity while helps on making data decisions. For some services, e.g. the IoT services that are enrolled to the domain and bring data from the physical world (e.g., via sensors), a degree of unreliability and uncertainty is introduced. The adviser role needs to analyze and check the data integrity to assure accuracy and consistency, if decisions based on those data are to be taken. It

accesses and tests the applicability of new approaches proposed by the *innovator* role. It assists the team by analyzing previous plan executions taking into consideration previous errors and recommends solutions, e.g. bad communication.
Primary behaviors: KCT, KNL, COO, COL, COM, DM, POL, LRN

7. The Innovator role

Description: The *Innovator* checks new updates for services to substitute outdated ones, tests new plan workflows that are send by developer and keeps the identity if there exists a change either for a new plan or for a new service. It searches for new opportunities for services that have similar goals and consider them as new resources, explores possibilities and searches for new solutions from services deployed in the web, accessing and testing the applicability of new approaches to form novel services.
Primary behaviors: KCT, KNL, TRS, COO, COL, COM, DM, POL

8. The Maintainer role

Description: The *Maintainer* role maintains the team functionality. It receives queries for maintenance of services, e.g. manufacturing services that have maintenance errors. If resources inside the domain cannot overcome a problem, it informs the promoter role to search for providers outside of the domain. It keeps the configuration of the system. It ensures that standards and processes are upheld and maintains team functionality.
Primary behaviors: ADH, KCT, KNL, COO, COL, COM, DM, POL, PLN

4   An Experiment to Prove the Benefit of Using Teamwork Roles

In this stage of research, gathering real data would be impractical. The simulation in this situation is the first step towards the real application that will use real data from an enterprise. We use Monte Carlo simulation [26] to demonstrate some benefits of adopting our approach during service execution. Monte Carlo simulation is a probabilistic analysis technique that artificially simulates a dynamic process by running it several times and directly observing the results. Using Monte Carlo simulation, which is based on statistical measures of the problem variables, we address the stochastic uncertainty issue of order receipt.

Let us consider a simple production system, which consists of two smart production machines $\{m_1, m_2\}$ which use one-phase production and they are situated at the same manufacturing level (the transfer cost from one machine to the other is considered zero). The machines have different capacity $\{c_1 = 5, c_2 = 10\}$, their processing times are equal $\{pt_1 = pt_2 = 10\ min\}$ and they produce products of the same type. The objective is to check availability of the system in serving the incoming orders. We perform simulation to produce the quantity in demand of the incoming orders and see what happens in a long run when they should produce hundreds of orders.

For the execution of the system, initially, we make the following assumptions:

(a) For representing the customer order quantity (q_t), a random number generator is used, producing 1.000 random numbers in the interval [1, 15].
(b) Customer orders arrive according to random numbers produced in the interval [1, 25] for representing the minutes that a new customer order arrives. Furthermore, we assume that customer orders are served in a FIFO order.
(c) The scheduling production algorithm is quite straightforward since we assume that "small" customer orders are handled by machine m_1, while "large" customer orders are handled by machine m_2. This is an assumption that usually fits well into production environments. In our case, we consider as a "small" customer order an order that contains less than ten order items $(q_t < 10)$, while a "large" customer order is any customer order with ten or more than ten order items $(q_t \geq 10)$.
(d) Further, let us name *"successful order"* the order that it's demanded quantity start to be produced straight from the minute the order is received. In case the production machines are busy producing products for previous orders, then the order is characterized as *"unsuccessful"*.

Table 1. Part of the data matrix during Run 1.

t_i (min)		1	14	21	36	57	73	76
q_t (items)		10	3	14	6	14	13	5
m_1 work time (min)		1	14	24	36	57	73	76
m_1 order phase1	phase2		3		5 | 1			5
Preparation time (OPT_i)			10		20			10
Order wait time (WOT_i)								
Machine idle time (IT_{mi})		13		12	1	16	3	6
m_2 work time (min)		1	14	21	41	57	77	97
m_2 order phase1		10		10		10	10	
m_2 order phase2				4		4	3	
Preparation time (OPT_i)		10		20		20	24	
Order wait time (WOT_i)							4	
Machine idle time (IT_{mi})		3	7		16			

We run the simulation twice. In the first run, the simulation do not take into account our collaboration framework, while in the second run, it exploits our proposed framework that demonstrates teamwork behavior for the production of items requested.

For doing so, both smart machines, except playing the *DOER* role they are also running equipped with *Delegation* (DLG primary behavior). Generally, this primary behavior belongs to *ORGANISER* and to *PRODUCER* roles, since an *ORGANISER* should be able to delegate work to other system's components at a higher level by

Table 2. Part of the data matrix during Run 2 with delegation.

t_i (min)	1	8	24	39	42	65	82
q_t (items)	6	15	7	9	3	13	3
m_1 work time (min)	1	21	24	44	44	65	82
m_1 order phase1	5		5		3		
m_1 order phase2 / phase3	1		2				3
Preparation time (OPT_i)	20		20		10		10
Order wait time (WOT_i)					2		
Machine idle time (IT_{mi})		3			13	17	
m_2 work time (min)	1	8	28	39	49	65	85
m_2 order phase1		10		9		10	
m_2 order phase2		5				3	
Preparation time (OPT_i)		20		10		20	
Order wait time (WOT_i)							
Machine idle time (IT_{mi})	7		11		16		

considering the whole production plan. Similarly, a smart machine that plays the *PRODUCER* role should be able to delegate work to other similar machines, which are idle during the production. In case that the machines could not have this behavior, then the team of machines could be equipped by a service that will play the *ORGANISER* role and will take care of the delegation. Part of the data matrix without the use of delegation is shown in Table 1, the table continues to the right for more produced orders, while in Table 2 the results after delegation are presented.

The simulation data are used to estimate the performance of the production plan in employing these two machines. For this purpose, we use the following indicators that present the objective of the scenario.

(a) The probability of a customer order to successfully start to be produced on time is equal to:

$$PO_i = \frac{number\ of\ sucessfull\ orders}{number\ of\ total\ orders}$$

(b) The Waiting Order Time (WOT_i) for a customer order that is waiting to be served from the production machines is calculated as equal to:

$$WOT_i = Time_{start\_produce} - Time_{arrived}$$

(c) The Order Preparation Time (OPT_i) for an order is the time between customer order arrival time and the finishing time of all production order items. This is calculated as equal to:

$$OPT_i = Time_{finish\_produced} - Time_{arrived}$$

(d) The Idle Time of m_i (IT_{mi}) is the idle time for each machine, the time each machine is waiting without serving customer orders. We calculate the idle time for a machine by subtracting the time that the production for an order is finished from the time a new order starts to be produced in the same machine:

$$IT_{mi} = \sum_{i=1}^{1000} \left(t_{start_{i+1}} - t_{finish_i} \right)$$

(e) Idle Time % ($IT\%_{mi}$) is the percentage of idle time over the total duration of the simulation. More specifically it is calculated as equal to:

$$IT\%_{mi} = \frac{IT_{mi}}{Total\ Simulation\ Time}$$

The results in Table 3 indicate that there is a significant improvement with the introduction of delegation primitive behavior in our production measurements, which is expected since the utilization of machines is done intelligently. Further, customer orders are executed faster leading to improved customer satisfaction. More specifically:

Table 3. Comparison of Run1 and Run2.

	PO_i	WOT_i	OP_i	IT_{mi}	IT_{mi}
Run 1 (without delegation)	48%				
Machine1 (m_1)		10.3 min	24.8 min	3.813 min	42%
Machine2 (m_2)		7.8 min	26.4 min	5.586 min	58%
Run 2 (including delegation)	74%				
Machine1 (m_1)		4.3 min	19.2 min	5.405 min	48%
Machine2 (m_2)		1.5 min	16.5 min	5.895 min	52%

- the probability (PO_i) of executing a customer order immediately, without delay, is increased from 48% to 74%,
- the average Waiting Order Time (WOT_i) for customer orders, time orders are waiting to be served from production machines is lowered for 10.3 min to 4.3 min for m_1, and from 7.8 min to 1.5 min for m_2,
- the average Order Preparation Time (OPT_i) for an order, the time between customer order arrival time and the finishing of all production order items is decreased from 24.8 min to 19.2 min for m_1, and from 26.4 min to 16.5 min for m_2 and
- the idle time is better balanced since these smart machines are in collaboration. This implies that more orders could be planned during next production periods.

5   Conclusion and Future Research

Collaborative work performed by teams require teamwork abilities. In this paper, we study a broadened view of service cooperation, one grounded in teamwork abilities of services. We outline the principles for eight service teamwork roles which is a fundamental building block for an architecture where business information systems use services to work together not always in a predefined manner. The main goal was to exploit teamwork roles and factors were identified within the research literature on both human and agent based teamwork and use them in the role modeling approach of service composition by employing teamwork roles in the process.

In this stage of research, gathering real data would be impractical. In order to test the necessity of the proposed approach, we run an inaugural simulation, about a simple scenario, where using Monte Carlo simulation we assess the production potential of a business. The inferences we draw from the simulation indicate that there is a significant improvement in the production measurements with the introduction of the delegation primitive behavior. This is the first step towards creating a more complicated scenario where all defined roles will contribute, using real data from business environment, in order to exploit the benefits of the framework. Our ongoing research agenda includes (i) formalizing the teamwork roles and defining their analytical primitive behaviors that should be extracted from each team role according to the proposed role descriptions, (ii) statistically validate the model by using a simulation framework to evaluate the impact of real teamwork services in business environments.

References

1. Sheng, Q.Z., Qiao, X., Vasilakos, A.V., Szabo, C., Bourne, S., Xu, X.: Web services composition: a decade's overview. Inf. Sci. **280**, 218–238 (2014)
2. Jula, A., Sundararajan, E., Othman, Z.: Cloud computing service composition: a systematic literature review. Expert Syst. Appl. **41**(8), 3809–3824 (2014)
3. Tosi, D., Morasca, S.: Supporting the semi-automatic semantic annotation of web services: a systematic literature review. Inf. Softw. Technol. **61**, 16–32 (2015)
4. Van Wissen, A., Gal, Y., Kamphorst, B.A., Dignum, M.V.: Human-agent teamwork in dynamic environments. Comput. Hum. Behav. **28**(1), 23–33 (2012)
5. Liemhetcharat, S., Veloso, M.: Synergy graphs for configuring robot team members. In: International Conference on Autonomous Agents and Multi-agent Systems, pp. 111–118 (2013)
6. Tsoutsa, P., Fitsilis, P., Ragos, O.: Role modeling of IoT services in industry domains. In: Proceedings of the 2017 International Conference on Management Engineering, Software Engineering and Service Sciences, pp. 290–295 (2017)
7. Driskell, T., Driskell, J.E., Burke, C.S., Salas, E.: Team roles: a review and integration. Small Group Res. **48**, 482–511 (2017). https://doi.org/10.1177/1046496417711529
8. Rao, J., Kungas, P., Matskin, M.: Logic-based web services composition: from service description to process model. In: ICWS, pp. 446–453. IEEE Computer Society (2004)
9. Giacomo, G.D., Patrizi, F., Sardina, S.: Automatic behavior composition synthesis. Artif. Intell. **196**, 106–142 (2013)

10. Berardi, D., Calvanese, D., Giacomo, G.D., Lenzerini, M., Mecella, M.: Automatic service composition based on behavioral descriptions. Int. J. Coop. Inf. Syst. **14**(4), 333–376 (2005)
11. Rodríguez, G., Soria, Á., Campo, M.: AI-based web service composition: a review. IETE Tech. Rev. **33**(4), 378–385 (2016)
12. Zeshan, F., Mohamad, R.: Semantic web service composition approaches: overview and limitations. Int. J. New Comput. Archit. Appl. (IJNCAA) **1**(3), 640–651 (2011)
13. Schwartz, T., et al.: Hybrid teams of humans, robots, and virtual agents in a production setting. In: Proceedings - 12th International Conference on Intelligent Environments, IE 2016, pp. 234–237 (2016)
14. Rojko, A.: Industry 4.0 concept: background and overview. Int. J. Interact. Mobile Technol. (iJIM) **11**(5), 77–90 (2017)
15. Delarue, A., Van Hootegem, G., Procter, S., Burridge, M.: Teamworking and organizational performance: a review of survey-based research. Int. J. Manag. Rev. **10**(2), 127–148 (2008). https://doi.org/10.1111/j.1468-2370.2007.00227.x
16. Mathieu, J.E., Tannenbaum, S.I., Kukenberger, M.R., Donsbach, J.S., Alliger, G.M.: Team role experience and orientation: a measure and tests of construct validity. Group Organ. Manag. **40**, 6–34 (2015). https://doi.org/10.1177/1059601114562000
17. Rousseau, V., Aube, C., Savoie, A.: Teamwork behaviors: a review and an integration of frameworks. Small Group Res. **37**(5), 540–570 (2006)
18. Salas, E., Cooke, J., Rosen, M.A.: On teams, teamwork, and team performance: discoveries and developments. Hum. Factors **50**(3), 540–547 (2008)
19. Kozlowski, S.W.J., Grand, J.A., Baard, S.K., Pearce, M., Durso, F.: Teams, teamwork, and team effectiveness: implications for human systems integration. In: Handbook of Human Systems Integration (CDM), pp. 1–30 (2015)
20. Berlin, J.M., Carlstrom, E.D., Sandberg, H.S.: Models of teamwork: ideal or not? A critical study of theoretical team models. Team Perform. Manag. Int. J. **18**(5–6), 328–340 (2012). https://doi.org/10.1108/13527591211251096
21. Tsoutsa, P., Fitsilis, P., Ragos, O.: Teamwork behavior: a review to interconnect Industry 4.0 entities. In: Ferreira, L., Lopes, N., Silva, J., Putnik, G., Cruz-Cunha, M., Ávila, P. (eds.) Technological Developments in Industry 4.0 for Business Applications, pp. 1–25. IGI Global, Hershey (2019). in press. https://doi.org/10.4018/978-1-5225-4936-9
22. Margerison, C.J., McCann, D.: Team Management: Practical New Approaches. Mercury Books, San Francisco (1990)
23. Belbin, R.M.: Team roles at work: a strategy for human resource management. zitiert in: Teamarbeit und Teamentwicklung 321 (1993)
24. Zeshan, F., Mohamad, R.: Semantic web service composition approaches: overview and limitations. Int. J. New Comput. Archit. Appl. (IJNCAA) **1**(3), 640–651 (2011)
25. Nacer, H., Aissani, D.: Semantic web services: standards, applications, challenges and solutions. J. Netw. Comput. Appl. **44**, 134–151 (2014)
26. Rubinstein, R.Y., Kroese, D.P.: Simulation and the Monte Carlo method, vol. 10. Wiley, Hoboken (2016)

Business Rule Optimisation: Problem Definition, Proof-of-Concept and Application Areas

Alan Dormer[✉]

Department of Information Technology, Monash University, Clayton, Australia
Alan.dormer@monash.edu

Abstract. Business rules have been applied to a wide range of manufacturing and services organisations. Decisions around quality control, customer acceptance, and warranty claims are typical applications in day-to-day operation. They all have two things in common; there are multiple assessment criteria such as profit, revenue, and customer satisfaction, and the quality of the decisions made have an impact on the performance and sustainability of the organisation. This paper presents a solution to the novel problem of optimising the structure and parameters of automated business rules where there is the possibility to refer some decisions to a human expert. The difference here is that although the business rules are deterministic and repeatable, human decisions are generally neither. This research problem is multi-disciplinary, and the solution comprises elements of business process management, mathematical optimisation, simulation, machine learning, probability, and psychology. The paper describes a potential solution, some initial results when applied to a problem in the financial services sector and identifies further areas of application.

Keywords: Business process management · Business Intelligence
Mathematical optimisation · Machine learning · Decision support

1 Introduction

A business rule is a rule that defines or constrains some aspect of a business. Business rules are intended to assert business structure or to control or influence the behaviour of the business [1]; rules exist within a business process and become an integral part of it, for example by controlling the processing, flow or direction of products through a factory or the delivery of services to customers. Business process management (BPM) is a discipline in operations management that uses various methods to discover, model, analyse, measure, improve, optimize, and automate business processes [2]. As such seeking to understand and optimise the impact of rules on business processes falls within the remit of BPM. Rules are also related to Business Intelligence (BI) as the knowledge and insights obtained can be codified into rules and then used by many less expert and less experienced staff.

Business rules are very common within industry, particularly the service sector. They enable consistent decision making by individuals and a degree of automation using business rules engines. Generally, rules add value to an organisation by reducing

W. Abramowicz and A. Paschke (Eds.): BIS 2018 Workshops, LNBIP 339, pp. 51–62, 2019.
https://doi.org/10.1007/978-3-030-04849-5_5

cost (either replacing human decision makers completely or by less experienced staff) and providing greater transparency and consistency.

However, there is another important aspect to business rules: the nature of the rules can determine the quality of the outcome for the organisation as defined by profit, revenue, and/or customer satisfaction. In a simple case of customer acceptance, if we set the acceptance criteria too high we risk rejecting too many good customers; if we set it to low, we accept too many bad customers. Similar considerations apply in quality control in manufacturing, investment decisions, or processing insurance claims, for example.

The challenge for the rule designer is how to construct a set of rules that, when applied, maximises revenue, minimises cost, limits resource requirements, and maintains customer satisfaction, or a combination thereof over the range of customers that we expect to serve or products that we expect to make.

For example, insurance claims depend on information, some of which is easy to obtain and some not so, such as:

- Type of claim
- Size of claim
- Cause of claim
- Circumstances
- Number of previous claims
- Length of time policy has been in force

No two claims will be the same, so we are aiming to find that set of rules that maximises the expected value of the outcome for the organisation based on the existing and anticipated customer profile. The most common outcome measures include profit, revenue and customer satisfaction, so in many cases we have a multi-criteria optimisation problem.

2 Research Contribution

Business rules do have an impact on an organisation and they can be optimised to achieve certain outcomes or key performance indicators (KPI's), such as the percentage of customers accepted [3] and [4]. Business rules also have an impact on organisational performance in retail [5] and inventory management [6]. Rules can also be optimised to allocate work to a range of human decision makers based on their skill levels and availabilities [7]. We can go further and seek to optimise business rules to maximise the expected profit of an organisation [8, 9]. Rules can also be combined with optimisation techniques on a case by case basis [10]. Here, we are looking at the ability to optimise the rules in advance so that the overall expected profit is maximised, with the potential for rules to operate alongside human decision makers.

There is a large body of work in machine learning where costs and consequences can be incorporated into a decision tree. For example, [11] considers the cost of obtaining information and [12] considers the cost of classification errors. Generally, this research is an extension of a methodology rather than solving a specific business problem.

Business Process Optimisation (BPO) is an area of research that considers a business problem that focusses predominately on the processes required to produce an outcome at minimum time and/or cost, and the way that tasks and activities are created, ordered and interlinked, [13]. Rules, where cases or components are directed one way or the other, are not considered and the cost model is *deterministic* [14]. It is also worth noting that the general direction of machine learning and business rules research is to make the best decision possible; in effect supplanting a human decision maker. In this paper we are admitting the possibility that some cases would be better directed to a human, should it be *cost effective* to do so.

The research contribution of this paper is the formulation and proof-of-concept solution of the business rule optimisation problem where:

- The objective function is the *expected* benefit to the enterprise
- Business rules are automated with the potential for certain decisions to be referred to a human expert
- The human expert is imperfect and subject to error
- We consider human decisions and outcomes

3 Theory

3.1 Problem

There are many examples of business rules in the services sector, ranging from commercial (for which we gave several examples in the introduction), to social such as medical diagnosis and assessing issues around child protection where a decision must be made on a course of action.

Normally business rules resolve to one of TRUE (such as ACCEPT or PROCEED) or FALSE (REJECT or STOP) [1] but in this paper we have allowed the possibility for the rules to reach a third state, namely REFER to a human expert.

The human expert is not perfect, and the problem is to create a set of rules, that, when combined with the potential to refer cases to the (imperfect) human expert, will result in the best economic outcome for the organisation.

3.2 Definition

For simplicity and clarity, the definition below applies to the process of loan or credit application, but the basic structure applies to similar problems.

Let $\{x_i\} 1 \leq i \leq n$ be the set of cases (applicants) that are presented to the business rules. Each case x_i is characterised by a set of m attribute values $A_i = \{a_{i1}, , \ldots, a_{im}\}$ with a_{ij} real, integer or categorical and a quality $c_i \in \{GOOD, BAD\}$.

We also have two types of determination for x_i. The determination made by the rules:

$$rd_i \in RD = \{ACCEPT, REJECT, REFER\}.$$

and the determination made by the human:

$$hd_i \in HD = \{NONE, ACCEPT, REJECT\}$$

We represent the business rule by a function $rd : A \rightarrow RD$ with $rd_i = rd(A_i)$ and similarly we represent the human decision making by a function $hd : A \rightarrow HD$ with $hd_i = hd(A_i)$.

We also have:

p_i = the potential profit from a good case (full repayment), and
l_i = the potential loss from a bad case (default)
e_i = the expense of the human processing the case

We can this determine the expected economic value of a case and its determination denoted by $g_i = g(c_i, rd_i, hd_i, p_i, l_i, e_i)$.

In conclusion, we are seeking to find that set of rules that maximises the objective, G, across all the cases:

$$G_{max} = \max_{rd} \sum_{i=1}^{n} g_i$$

4 Solving the Problem

To formulate this as an optimization problem, we need to determine the degrees of freedom, objective function and constraints.

4.1 Degrees of Freedom

In the context of the problem defined above, we have two essential choices:

1. What attributes do we require (the elements of A in Sect. 3.2)?
2. What business rules do we apply (the function rd in Sect. 3.2)?

There are normally well-known attributes that make a difference to the outcome and thus, enable us to make a determination, and the question is generally which ones do we include from such a list?

We could choose any function for the rules, rd, but in normal business practice business rules are expressed as chain of IF-THEN-ELSE logic (or decision tree) with logical tests based on the numerical value or category of the attributes [1].

In some cases, there is value in including functions of attributes or derived attributes as additional inputs to the rules. Examples include the ratio of loan: income in the case of mortgage applications, or number of standard deviation from the mean, in case of quality control.

4.2 Objective Function

Earlier, we identified that the objective could be multicriteria with profit and customer satisfaction as typical quantities of interest. Such multicriteria problems can be addressed by a weighted sum to create one overall objective function.

If we take this approach we are looking to maximise the expected value of the objective function which can be expressed as the expected values of:

- Gains from good cases accepted $\sum_{c_i=GOOD\ and\ (rd_i\ OR\ hd_i)=ACCEPT}\ p_i$
- losses from bad case accepted $\sum_{c_i=BAD\ and\ rd_i\ OR\ hd_i=ACCEPT}\ l_i$
- cost of processing information $\sum_{hd_i=ACCEPT\ OR\ REJECT}\ e_i$
- abandoned transactions $at(m)\sum_{c_i=GOOD}\ g_i$

Where $at(m)$ is a function that estimates the probability that a customer will abandon the transaction as we ask for more information [15]. This can only be an approximation because we cannot identify the customers or whether we would have accepted them or not, but for economic and customer satisfaction reasons, we need to be mindful of the number of attributes we request.

4.3 Basic Data

To create optimal business rules, we need a data set of cases (with all the relevant attributes), determinations and outcomes. It is important to note that we are not just interested in determinations as these will not necessarily be accurate, as humans make mistakes. We also need data on outcomes. For example, borrowers may default later; diseases may be misdiagnosed and eventuate later, children can be returned to their parents and subsequently abused. Also, if we are considering the place of human experts in any optimised system, we need to know how well they perform.

4.4 Choice of Attributes

The classical feature selection problem considers the performance of the rules with different attributes [16]. However, in our case, we are not incurring costs for every attribute we might have at our disposal, we are incurring costs for the attributes that we ask for and use. Unless we are using a paper application form, the questions we ask can follow the path through the rules. The path followed through the rules will depend on the responses (attributes) made by the applicant (case). At some point, the expected benefit of asking another question will be exceeded by the costs of information processing and the probability that the transaction will be abandoned.

So, if we ask for attributes as the rules need them, there is no feature selection problem in the classical sense; we simply stop asking for more information when its value is outweighed by the associated costs.

4.5   Incorporating Human Experts

One of the potential decisions of the business rules is to refer the case to a human expert. In this case we need to know whether it is worth incurring the additional cost of the human expert. The LENS model [17] provides a framework to model and understand the accuracy of the rules and the accuracy of the human expert (true positives, false positives, etc.). Essentially, we need to know the probability that a case is good and the probability that a case is good if it is deemed to be by human expert, and the expected benefits and costs for each. Based on the definition in Sect. 3.2 we have:

$$IF(P(c_i = GOOD|rd_i = ACCEPT))p_i$$
$$> P(c_i = GOOD|hd_i = ACCEPT)(p_i - e_i)THEN\ rd_i = ACCEPT$$
$$ELSE\ rd_i = REFER$$
$$IF(P(c_i = GOOD|rd_i = REJECT))p_i$$
$$> P(c_i = GOOD|hd_i = ACCEPT)(p_i - e_i)THEN\ rd_i = REJECT$$
$$ELSE\ rd_i = REFER$$

Note that it is important to compare the cases where the rules ACCEPT and REJECT as in either case a human decision may be cost-effective, for example, if the rules cannot effectively split a leaf.

4.6   Solution Methods

There are many methods for solving optimisation problems. Evolutionary computing has been extensively used in BPO to solve problems around the selection and sequencing of business processes to deliver a desired outcome [13]. Mixed integer (often linear) programming is used in similar problems in supply chain [18].

Given that business rules (as we have delimited them above) are equivalent to a decision tree [19] we have used a decision tree approach. We allow for fact that the problem is asymmetrical (potential profits don't always equal potential losses) and that the stopping criteria is based on the net benefit (expected additional gain less the cost of asking for and processing the additional attribute). The probability that the rules make a correct determination is calculated from the validation set (correct classifications compared to incorrect) and we have modelled the decisions of the human expert using logistical regression. For each leaf of the tree we use these probabilities combined with the potential profits and losses for each case to determine:

- The expected value of acting upon the determination of the rules
- The expected (net) value of referring to the human expert

We then select the highest value, provided at least one of them is positive. If both are negative, all the cases within the leaf are rejected.

If we set:

$$Rg_i = P(c_i = GOOD|rd_i = ACCEPT)\ \text{and}$$
$$Hg_i = P(c_i = GOOD|hd_i = ACCEPT)\ \text{then}$$

Expected net benefits are equal to:

$Rg_ip_i - (1 - Rg_i)l_i$ from the rules decision
and $Hg_ip_i - (1 - Hg_i)l_i - e_i$ from the human decision

4.7 Testing the Algorithms

The rules are created using the training set (two thirds of the cases selected at random) and then the rules and algorithms are used on the validation set (the other third) assess the acceptance and rejection on cases where we know the human decisions and outcomes and can calculate the profits and losses. This enables us to calculate the difference in net profit between using the human only and the human and the rules.

5 Results

The credit application problem has been analysed using data from Lending Club [20]. Lending Club is a peer-to-peer lender that makes data available on applications, acceptances and outcomes. The process consists of an initial screen, on limited data, and certain selected applicants are invited to provide more detailed information for further analysis and verification, with remainder being rejected.

5.1 Initial Screening Process

The first part of the process has been modelled and optimised using the decision tree approach with the simplifying assumption that the human expert is always correct [9]. This was necessary as the initial screening process only had data on acceptance and rejection, but not outcomes. An allowance was made for the cost of the human expert, but there was no data on customers who decided not to proceed and abandoned the process. But it is known [15] that the more data you ask for, the more likely it is that customers do abandon transactions.

With these assumptions it can be shown that the optimal solution is to process about 80% of customers with the rules alone with the remainder referred to the human expert. This gives a net revenue (income less expenses) of about 2% greater than if the cases were processed by the human alone.

If we look at the GOOD and BAD cases in any leaf, we have:

$$\text{Net gain from the rule decision} = \sum_{c_i=GOOD} p_i - \sum_{c_i=BAD} l_i$$

And the net gain from the (assumed perfect) human expert

$$= \sum_{c_i=GOOD} p_i - \sum_{c_i=GOOD\,OR\,BAD} e_i$$

5.2 Detailed Assessment

In this case we had data on acceptance, rejection, and outcomes. The rules were created from a decision tree and the accuracy of the rules was determined from the validation set and the accuracy of the human expert was modelled using logistical regression. The latter was chosen so that, at any leaf, by using the mid-point, the accuracy of the human could be determined.

There was a problem with determining the accuracy of the rules as the data on outcomes was only available for the cases judged to be good by the human expert. Thus, whilst it was possible to determine the probability that a case x_i that had been accepted ($hd_i = ACCEPT$) was good ($c_i = GOOD$) it was not possible to do the same for those cases that had been rejected. In execution, the rules could very well accept a case that the human had rejected ($hd_i = REJECT$), and for which the outcome c_i was unknown.

To calculate the optimum allocation of cases between the rules and the human expert we took a conservative approach and assumed that the unknown cases that the rules accepted were bad ($c_i = BAD$), and in that case the optimum allocation was 70% to the rules and the gain over the human alone was about 4% in additional net revenue. If we assume that those cases were good the net benefit is nearly 7%. In this problem, the false positives (as determined by the human) were 15%. In the absence of any other information we could reasonably assume some symmetry, in which case 15% of the unknown cases were good. In that case the benefit would be about 4.5%.

6 Other Examples

There are many examples of business rules that fit the generalisation above. Table 1, below, gives examples of such business rules.

Table 1. Examples

Application	Loan approval	Child protection	Medical diagnosis
Case	Loan applicant	Child of interest	Patient
Class	Good Bad	Abused At risk Not at risk	Healthy Diseased
Determination	Accept Reject	Do nothing Monitor Act	Do nothing Tests Treat
Attributes	Credit score Income Security	Parents History Observations	Symptoms Test results
Business rules	Credit policy	Statute	Medical procedure
Automated rules	Application website	Triage	Screening test
Output from rules	Accept, reject or refer	No case, low priority, high priority	Negative, positive (refer)
Human expert	Underwriter	Social worker	Doctor

The examples above are straightforward classification problems. There are many other examples, such as paying insurance claims, recruitment decisions, procurement decisions, investment decisions, product quality assessment, and so on. There are other problems - that are not classification problems – that are typically rule driven. These include transport, logistics and manufacturing. Below are some examples.

6.1   Freight Transport

The allocation of routes and loads to trucks for pick-up and delivery [21] is often rule driven to cater for day to day changes. For example:

- Deliveries and pick-ups are clustered using rules around the location
- Minimum loading rules are used to drive efficiency
- Empty running is avoided as far as possible

Here, we could use optimisation to determine the best set of rules using anticipated or historical orders. Effectively we are finding the rules that would result in the most cost-effective operation over the period in equation. Each day may not be optimal, but the cumulative result would be better than it would have been had the rules not been optimised.

6.2   Public Transport

Another example is disruption management in public transport [22]. When a train is potentially going to be late certain decisions must be made, such as:

- Cancel the service or turn back early
- Hold back connecting services
- Delay it further to save delaying others

There are rules that can be used such as:

- Less than 5 min late, hold connections
- More than 5 min late don't hold
- More than 15 min turn back early and don't delay others
- More than 30 min cancel

The impact of these rules can be determined by simulation and subsequently the rules can be optimised using historical data using criteria such as minimise overall passenger delay minutes or minimise the worst delay.

6.3   Manufacturing

Scheduling plays an important part in efficient manufacturing [23] where the time to change from one product to another may be a significant part of the overall production time. Rules can be employed to reduce this, for example in painting we can have rules around going from light colours to dark, or in plastic bag manufacture we start with large bags first to avoid burning out the heating elements that seal the bags. But it is never that simple as there are urgent jobs that need to be fitted in. Again, looking at the rules in the wider context and building rules that are more sophisticated and creating good and bad sequences is another potential example of rule optimisation.

6.4 Mobile Workforce Management

Rules may be used to allocate mobile workforce - such as maintenance technicians or roadside assist - to a queue of jobs and jobs as they are called in [24]. Rules include:

- Suitability (skills and experience)
- Location of job within a service area
- Allocation of next job

On the last point, the rules are typically applied to distance to be travelled, time to serve (travel time + time to complete current job), maximum waiting time, etc. These can be optimised by analysing their impact on previous and anticipated demand patterns and optimising the rules around:

- Geographical service areas
- Allocation of workers to areas
- Allocation of the next job to the next available worker

7   Conclusion

We have explored the idea of business rule optimisation for the classification (accept or reject) problem that occurs in the services and manufacturing sector and developed a problem statement and formal description of the problem. This problem exists in credit applications, insurances claims, investment decisions and quality control, to name a few.

The concept has been developed to include both automated rules and human judgement, considering the costs of obtaining and processing information, and a solution method using an extension of decision trees has been developed. This method has been applied to real data for credit approval, for both the initial screening and detailed evaluation. The results are encouraging, suggesting that rules could deal with 70–80% of all cases leading to an increase in net revenue between about 2% and 7%.

The method developed can be applied to the examples in Table 1. The problems in Sect. 6 are different, but there is a basic similarity; it is that of optimising a set of fixed business rules, in advance, across a range of anticipated scenarios. In effect, we are keeping the inherent simplicity of a fixed set of rules whilst maximising the expected benefit of their application over time.

Given the wide range of business processes using business rules, there is considerable scope for further research in this area.

References

1. Business Rules Group: Final Report, Revision 1.3, July 2000
2. Jeston, J., Nelis, J.: Business Process Management. Routledge, Abingdon (2014). ISBN 9781136172984
3. Wang, O., Liberti, L.: Controlling some statistical properties of business rules programs. In: Battiti, R., Kvasov, D.E., Sergeyev, Y.D. (eds.) LION 2017. LNCS, vol. 10556, pp. 263–276. Springer, Cham (2017). https://doi.org/10.1007/978-3-319-69404-7_19
4. Wang, O., Liberti, L., D'Ambrosio, C., de Sainte Marie, C., Ke, C.: Controlling the average behavior of business rules programs. In: Alferes, J.J.J., Bertossi, L., Governatori, G., Fodor, P., Roman, D. (eds.) RuleML 2016. LNCS, vol. 9718, pp. 83–96. Springer, Cham (2016). https://doi.org/10.1007/978-3-319-42019-6_6
5. Kunz, T.P., Crone, S.F.: The impact of practitioner business rules on the optimality of a static retail revenue management system. J. Revenue Pricing Manag. 14(3), 198–210 (2015)
6. Quinzaños, J.M., Cartas, A., Vidales, P., Maldonado, A.: iDispatcher: using business rules to allocate and balance workloads. In: DSS, pp. 110–119, May 2014
7. Hegazi, M.O.: Measuring and predicting the impacts of business rules using fuzzy logic. Int. J. Comput. Sci. Inf. Secur. 13(12), 59 (2015)
8. Dormer, A.: Optimising business rules in the services sector. Int. J. Soc. Behav. Educ. Econ. Bus. Ind. Eng. 6(10), 2580–2584 (2012)
9. Dormer, A.: A framework for optimising business rules. In: Abramowicz, W. (ed.) BIS 2017. LNBIP, vol. 303, pp. 5–17. Springer, Cham (2017). https://doi.org/10.1007/978-3-319-69023-0_1
10. Taylor, J.: Decision Management Systems: A Practical Guide to Using Business Rules and Predictive Analytics. IBM Press, Indianapolis (2011). ISBN 0-13-288438-0
11. Turney, P.D.: Cost-sensitive classification: empirical evaluation of a hybrid genetic decision tree induction algorithm. J. Artif. Intell. Res. 2, 369–409 (1995)
12. Zadrozny, B., Langford, J., Abe, N.: Cost-sensitive learning by cost-proportionate example weighting. In: Third IEEE International Conference on Data Mining, ICDM 2003, pp. 435–442. IEEE, November 2003
13. Vergidis, K., Tiwari, A., Majeed, B.: Business process analysis and optimization: beyond reengineering. IEEE Trans. Syst. Man Cybern. Part C (Appl. Rev.) 38(1), 69–82 (2008)
14. Laguna, M., Marklund, J.: Business Process Modeling, Simulation and Design. CRC Press, Boca Raton (2013)
15. Rajamma, R.K., Paswan, A.K., Hossain, M.M.: Why do shoppers abandon shopping cart? Perceived waiting time, risk, and transaction inconvenience. J. Prod. Brand Manag. 18(3), 188–197 (2009)
16. Chandrashekar, G., Sahin, F.: A survey on feature selection methods. Comput. Electr. Eng. 40(1), 16–28 (2014)
17. Brunswik, E.: The essential Brunswik: beginnings, explications, applications, new directions in research on decision making. In: Research Conference on Subjective Probability, Utility and Decision Making, Helsinki, Finland (1985)
18. Jonsson, P., Kjellsdotter, L., Rudberg, M.: Applying advanced planning systems for supply chain planning: three case studies. Int. J. Phys. Distrib. Logist. Manag. 37(10), 816–834 (2007)
19. Quinlan, J.R.: Generating production rules from decision trees. In: IJCAI, vol. 87 (1987)
20. Lending Club. https://www.lendingclub.com/info/download-data.action. Accessed 9 Feb 2017

21. Berbeglia, G., Cordeau, J.F., Gribkovskaia, I., Laporte, G.: Static pickup and delivery problems: a classification scheme and survey. Top **15**(1), 1–31 (2007)
22. Jespersen-Groth, J., et al.: Disruption management in passenger railway transportation. In: Ahuja, R.K., Möhring, R.H., Zaroliagis, C.D. (eds.) Robust and Online Large-Scale Optimization. LNCS, vol. 5868, pp. 399–421. Springer, Heidelberg (2009). https://doi.org/10.1007/978-3-642-05465-5_18
23. Graves, S.C.: A review of production scheduling. Oper. Res. **29**(4), 646–675 (1981)
24. Naveh, Y., Richter, Y., Altshuler, Y., Gresh, D.L., Connors, D.P.: Workforce optimization: identification and assignment of professional workers using constraint programming. IBM J. Res. Dev. **51**(3.4), 263–279 (2007)

Profiling User Colour Preferences
with BFI-44 Personality Traits

Magdalena Wieloch, Katarzyna Kabzińska, Dominik Filipiak,
and Agata Filipowska[✉]

Department of Information Systems, Faculty of Informatics and Electronic Economy,
Poznań University of Economics and Business, Poznań, Poland
agata.filipowska@ue.poznan.pl
http://www.kie.ue.poznan.pl

Abstract. Nowadays, a lot of attention is paid to personalisation of services and content presented to a user. Personalisation is based on profiles of a users built on top of diverse data: logs, texts, pictures, etc. The goal of the paper is to analyse a connection between a type of user's personality and his colour preferences, to enable for personalisation. To reach this goal, correlations between outcomes of BFI-44 Personality Traits and colour preferences inspired by Plutchik's Wheel of Emotions for individual users were analysed. 144 respondents had been surveyed with a questionnaire to enable the analysis. The results were analysed using linear models for different personality traits. Outcomes, together with their quality assessment, are presented in the paper.

Keywords: User profiling · Online social networks · User profile
Activity recognition and understanding

1 Introduction

Knowing preferences of a customer or user is a key to achieve success. These preferences may relate to e.g. their interests, locations visited or people followed on social media. On the other hand, these preferences may also relate to colours of products recommended or displayed to a user. We would like to check whether one's colour preferences depend on their personality – previous research suggests that there's a connection. For instance, politicians and TV presenters usually dress in blue, as this is a colour most of people like, for instance.

A number of researchers proposed theories to explain the notion of personality. For example, BFI-44 is the best known and the most frequently used personality test. The Wheel of Emotions, which is another approach, is a psychological model which presents 24 emotions in groups of 3 – each group of emotions is shown on one of 8 main colours. The colours themselves used on the Wheel of Emotions doesn't carry any special meaning, though – it is just Plutchik's loose interpretation. These colours are just one of countless approaches to the problem of colour categorisation. In his wheel, each colour has 4 hues of intensity

© Springer Nature Switzerland AG 2019
W. Abramowicz and A. Paschke (Eds.): BIS 2018 Workshops, LNBIP 339, pp. 63–76, 2019.
https://doi.org/10.1007/978-3-030-04849-5_6

and every hue complies with different intensity levels of a given emotion. Colour palette, which in the case of the Wheel of Emotions was just a tool for presenting emotions, was an inspiration for this research.

The main motivation behind this work is connecting results of the BFI-44 personality test and the 8 basic colours, in order to explore relationships between personality of respondents and colours that they fancy. Researchers have already recognised the importance of this subject. Zuckerman-Kuhlman Personality Questionnaire [32] or Eysenks [8] personality tests have been previously used to measure personality traits – participants had to grade pictures with specific plain colours. These techniques have been rarely used in research, though – only several publications that use these questionnaires. Ferwerda et al. [6] grappled with the issue of predicting personality from colours of posted pictures. In this case, the Big Five model was applied in order to have a full view of personality traits.

The aim of our research is to analyse users' personalities and their colour preferences with the Big Five Inventory, also known as BFI-44 [17], and the 8 basic colours. The analysis is based on pictures published on Flickr, as images are ubiquitous on Online Social Media and they can facilitate expansion of the existing body of knowledge about users and their colour preferences.

The paper is structured as follows. A short review of the existing body of knowledge is presented in the next section. Section 3 presents details of the data preparation process. In our approach, images with dominant colours inspired by Plutchik's Wheel of Emotions have been randomly chosen from the Flickr database using the snowball sampling method. They were attached to the questionnaire with the original BFI-44 test. The following section presents findings of the questionnaire. Section 5 delivers models, explaining relation between colour preferences and the personality traits. Connections between traits and colours have been examined using linear models. Finally, conclusions are presented in the last section.

2   Related Work

2.1   Analysis of Pictures

The two most popular approaches used to analyse images on the open social media (OSM) encompass: clustering [13] and determining sentiment of an image [22]. Following Souza et al. [31], one can enlist the following topics connected to OSM pictures' analysis: engagement connected with them [3,35], self-presentation in social media [7,30], prediction of age and gender from the visual content [16], recognising the basic personality types from photos basing on the Big Five Inventory questionnaire [6].

Images themselves can be divided into 8 groups, based on their content: activities, captured photos, fashion, friends, food, gadgets, pets and selfies. Friends and selfies are the most popular categories on Instagram, forming almost 50% of the all photos. Publishing a selfie online is a way of attracting the attention. Such photos collect more likes and comments [7].

Users adapt their behaviour differently on each social platform, depending on the type of that platform, user's age and gender. By combining comments, hashtags and content of photos and using appropriate algorithms, it is possible to identify these details. Thanks to BFI-44, past studies have yielded some important insights into personality, emotions, and reactions of users. Researchers focused on user profiling, photos and texts such as questionnaires [14], comments [20], hashtags [9], and captions [25].

2.2 Big Five Personality Traits

The Big Five Inventory (BFI-44) is a personality test (based on the Big Five Model) and consists of 44 questions that measure the Big Five traits [17] such as Extraversion/Introversion, Agreeableness/Antagonism, Conscientiousness/Lack of Direction, Neuroticism/Emotional Stability, and Openness/Closeness to Experience. Following Ahrndt et al. [1], these five personality features can be defined as follows:

- *Extraversion* is related to interactions with other people and gaining the energy from them, contrary to being more independent (e.g. action-oriented, outgoing and energetic behaviour vs. inward, solitary and reserved behaviour).
- *Agreeableness* stems from being trustful, helpful and optimistic, contrary to being antagonistic and sceptical (e.g. cooperative, friendly and compassionate behaviour vs. detached, analytical and antagonistic behaviour).
- *Conscientiousness* is connected to the level of self-discipline and acting dutifully, contrary to spontaneity (e.g. efficient, organised and planned behaviour vs. careless, easy-going and spontaneous behaviour),
- *Neuroticism* reflects the inability in dealing with stress, contrary to emotional stability and confidence, addressed the level of emotional reaction to events (e.g. nervous, sensitive and pessimistic behaviour vs. emotionally stable, secure and confident behaviour).
- *Openness* relies on creativity (e.g. curious, inventive and emotional behaviour vs. consistent, cautious and conservative behaviour).

Some researchers sought to understand other phenomena, such as loneliness or sadness. Pittman [26] established a link between social media use and offline loneliness. Students who are active online usually feel less lonely in real life. By the examination of norms of expressing emotions in OSM, Lup et al. [21] claim that there is a relation between Instagram usage and depression symptoms. Waterloo et al. [34] have carried an extensive study on sadness, anger, disappointment, worry, joy, and pride. These studies proved that positive expressions are perceived better than negative by users across all OSM platforms. Some scholars claim that there are differences in a way of expressing emotions between men and women. In other papers, colours of photos taken in two cities in a certain period of time were compared [11]. Other researchers tried to tackle the problem of sentiment analysis from visual content [4]. The standard positive/negative/neutral classification can be extended by combining visual content, comments and colours of the photo.

2.3   Colours

A universal approach for dividing colours has not been found yet. Some methods are focused on solely blue, green, and red [19]. On the other hand, Ferwerda et al. attached orange, violet and yellow to the aforementioned set [6]. Some scholars investigate so called low-level features, such as chrominance [24]. Plutchik's Wheel of Emotions [27] includes 24 emotions (8 basic emotions with 4 intensity levels) presented on 8 colours (each of them has 4 hues and the least intense one does not carry a meaning). Despite the representation of emotions as colours, there are no connections between them, since it was not the purpose of wheel's author. Among many approaches for choosing basic colours palettes, this work is inspired by those from the common illustrations of Plutchik's Wheel of Emotions which are pink, green, blue, dark blue, red, dark green, orange, and yellow.

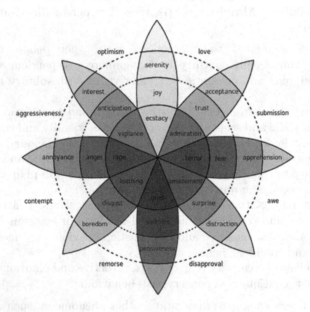

Fig. 1. Plutchik's Wheel of Emotions. Source: Borth et al. [4] (Color figure online)

When it comes to recognising leading colours of the pictures, it is necessary to define the dominant colour of every pixel [23,28]. A colour can be found in the colour palette or a lookup table. Determining which colour is dominant is tightly coupled with the number of pixels having the same colour in an image. The colour with the biggest number of pixels is therefore defined as a dominant colour of an image. The dominant colour can be found in the palette of colours. The most popular colour representation scheme is the RGB (Red-Green-Blue) palette [2], but it is complicated to define hues ranges within one colour using this palette. Therefore, HSV scale [5], which is an abbreviation from Hue-Saturation-Value, can be used for this task. After defining the range of hue within one colour, the saturation and values have to be stated. On contrary, defining colour ranges for the RGB colour palette is much more complex. Therefore, using the HSV palette and converting it to the RGB colour palette gained popularity in related research (see Table 1 for a comparison).

Table 1. RGB and HSV colour spaces.

Channel	Range	Unit	Description
R	0–255	8 bits	Intensity of red (black to white)
G	0–255	8 bits	Intensity of green (black to white)
B	0–255	8 bits	Intensity of blue (black to white)
H	0–360	degree	Hue
S	0–100	percent	Saturation (bright to dark)
V	0–100	percent	Value (black to white)

Source: Ha et al. [10]

3   Data Collection

Our experiment is based on a questionnaire, which is a combination of the standard BFI-44 test and assessment of Flickr images. The latter are used to examine links between the user's personality and their colour preferences. This section describes the process of preparation to our experiment. It entails Flickr data collection and processing, questionnaire preparation, and the description of the scoring formula used.

3.1   Questionnaire

Flickr[1] is one of the most popular OSM platforms. It is image oriented, which makes it particularly useful in our experiment. Flickr has a convenient API, which facilitates preparing a sample. Therefore, we decided to collect the pictures from this service by:

1. Following an approach similar to the ones presented by Machajdik and Hanbury [22] and Jamil et al. [15], a random photographer was chosen using the *#photography* hashtag.
2. Using snowball sampling [3,12,20], users followed by that photographer were selected (329 users plus the photographer).
3. Following Min and Cheng [23], for each selected Flickr profile, the most recent 100 pictures (or less if they had fewer photos) have been chosen using Flickr API. This resulted in acquiring 32,056 photos in total.
4. For every photo, a number of pixels for every colour has been encoded using the RGB palette.

---

[1] http://flickr.com.

5. Values in the RGB scale were converted to the HSV model, as an extension of previous ranges in order to enhance their perception by human eyes and therefore simplify the detection of more hues of colours.

6. The downloaded images were divided into 9 categories (8 categories according to chosen basic colours and a category for these colours that are not included in any of the remaining categories).

7. Ranges for specific colours were created using a table of colours[2] and Rapid Tables[3] in order to adjust them to the 8 selected colours.

8. Having assigned the categories of colours, a number of pixels corresponding to the one of 9 categories was assigned to each image.

9. Following Min and Cheng [23] and Potluri and Nitta [28], an assumption that the colour that has the largest number of pixels is the dominant colour of the photo determines the category of it was made.

10. Pictures where one of the colours from colour palette was dominant create 20.79% of the primary sample (the rest fell to the category not represented in any of colours' categories).

As the dominant colour in a picture may be not obvious for a human eye, the acceptance threshold was set for the percentage of pixels of dominant colour in the pictures. 70% of pixels in the photo have to constitute the dominant colour [33]. The resulting set was then manually checked to delete pictures with inscriptions, faces and vibrant symbols that can create biases in further research. From each of the 8 categories of photos, 4 randomly chosen pictures were selected. It resulted in a sample of 32 photos. The scale for grading pictures was the same as in the questions from BFI-44:

- 1 – disagree strongly,
- 2 – disagree a little,
- 3 – neither agree nor disagree,
- 4 – agree a little,
- 5 – agree strongly.

Pictures were divided into 8 categories according to the chosen colour palette. After that, user preferences for colours were calculated. Questions from BFI-44 were divided into groups that correspond to personality traits (each one has two opposite features, such as extraversion/introversion) from the Big Five model. The questionnaire also contains questions about gender and age. Combined with the original 44 questions from BFI-44, a questionnaire was created and posted on the Internet. The number of points for the opposite features was reversed on the scale to enable summing up the points for each trait.

3.2   Scoring Formula

A mathematical formula (Eq. 1) used in the scoring process was developed for the purposes of this research. The scoring process was carried out as follows:

---

[2] https://mehrarodgers.wordpress.com/2013/05/05/final-project/.
[3] http://www.rapidtables.com/web/color/RGB_Color.htm.

1. At first, a number of questions for each of the five features was determined.
2. The number of points (P) for every trait was summed up.
3. For every question, the minimal number of points was one. Therefore, the minimal number of points for each trait equals the number of the questions about it (min).
4. The middle of the scale is the number of the questions about the trait multiplied by three as it was the middle of the scale (M).
5. Maximum (max) is the minimum multiplied by five which is the largest number of points that could be marked by a participant of the survey.

The result of the calculations is the percentage of a given trait (F). If it is smaller than 50%, then it is treated as a value of the opposite trait by subtracting 100% minus the given value. The same process was performed in the case of scoring photos in order to determine how often a photo was liked.

$$F = \left(50 + \frac{100}{\max - \min} \left(\sum P - M\right)\right) [\%] \tag{1}$$

4 Questionnaire Findings

144 responses to the questionnaire (of which there were 92 coming from women and 52 from men) were collected. The scoring process was performed according to the BFI scoring (for the questions concerning personality and pictures as well) applying the Eq. 1. The results of scoring are presented in Fig. 2. The vast majority of surveyed liked blue photos. They graded it 66% on average and the median was close to 69%. Dark green, the second most liked colour, had the mean score equal to 56% and the median about 59%. Drawing conclusions, dark green also has a positive impact on the most of the people. On contrary, respondents did not like yellow photos, as they scored 42% on average and the median at the level of 44%. The rest of the colours was rated around 50%. The mean and median values are presented in Fig. 3.

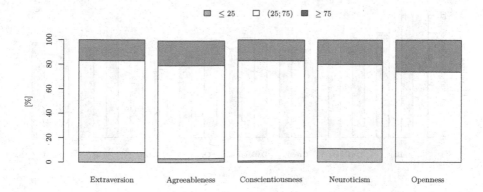

Fig. 2. Percentage of participants by trait. Source: own elaboration

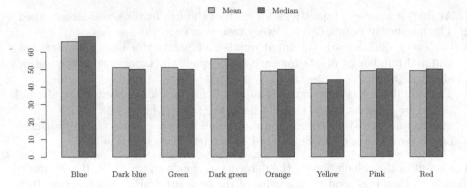

Fig. 3. Colour preferences. Source: own elaboration

In the case of personality traits, respondents were divided into 3 groups, for each trait separately (18 in total). For Extraversion, respondents were classified as follows:

– extreme extroverts (Extraversion trait equal to 75% or more),
– extreme introverts (Extraversion trait equal to 25% or less),
– people who were between those two ends (more than 25% and less than 75%).

The rest of traits was treated in the same manner. For each trait, the moderate (between) group was the largest and there are not many people who present extreme types. There was also no person who was classified into the group of Closeness to experience (Openness is the opposite trait) and there was only one person classified in the Lack of direction group (Conscientiousness is the opposite trait). Figures 4, 5, 6, 7 and 8 depict mean colour preferences. On each plot, there are two or three series of data - one or two for the first and last quartile and the one for moderate values.

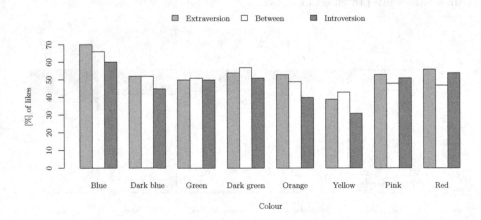

Fig. 4. Mean colour preferences among extrovert/introvert people. Source: own elaboration

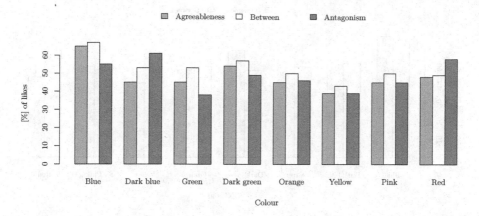

Fig. 5. Mean colour preferences among agreeable/antagonistic people. Source: own elaboration

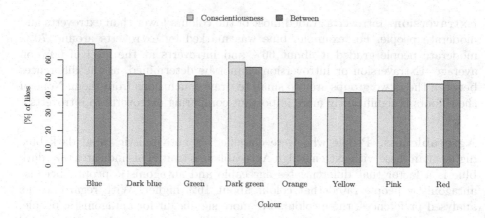

Fig. 6. Mean colour preferences among conscientious people. Source: own elaboration

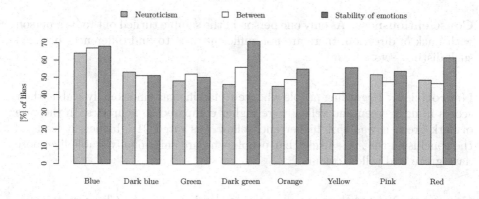

Fig. 7. Mean colour preferences among neurotic/stable people. Source: own elaboration

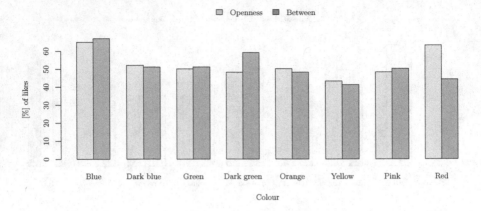

Fig. 8. Mean colour preferences among open/closed to experience people. Source: own elaboration

Extraversion. Introverts graded most of the colours lower than extroverts and moderate people. For example, blue was marked by extroverts around 70%, moderate people graded it about 66% and introverts at the level of 60% on average. Extraversion or Introversion cannot be determined, as the differences between these two groups are too small to draw conclusions from them. None of the colours is significantly more important comparing extroverts to introverts.

Agreeableness. People who were classified as antagonistic rated dark blue higher than these with extreme high Agreeableness trait. This indicates that dark blue is a factor that differentiates agreeable and antagonistic people, because antagonistic people rated that colour about 16% higher. With regard to the analysed preferences, these colours are more significant for antagonistic people, so perhaps they are more likely to fancy them. The rest of the colours was graded lower or the same as in the Agreeableness group, except for dark blue and red.

Conscientiousness. As only one person in the sample turned out to be a person with Lack of direction, there are not sufficient data to find differences between such distinct sets.

Neuroticism. Regarding people who were classified as emotionally stable, their scores in dark green and yellow were higher compared to neurotics. In the case of dark green it was 25% higher and yellow was rated 21% higher. It leads to the conclusion that it is likely that people who are emotionally stable like more dark green and yellow colours.

Openness. None of the respondents were classified into the Closeness to experience group, therefore a comparison of these groups can not be conducted.

5 Establishing Links Between BFI-44 and Colours

This study used a linear regression model in order to analyse the relationship between the Big Five personality traits and user's colour preferences. The least-squares method was applied for obtaining the model. As a result, 5 different models (for each trait separately) were obtained. We used Gretl and standard linear regression. Statistical significance was accepted at the $\alpha = 0.05$ level [18,29]. To choose models which fit the data best, R^2 values and cross-validation have been used. After rejecting insignificant variables and choosing the right models, the final regression formulas are as follows:

$$\text{Extraversion} = 0.527720 \cdot blue + 0.336480 \cdot orange$$
$$\text{Agreeableness} = 0.526617 \cdot blue + 0.172206 \cdot darkgreen + 0.239923 \cdot orange$$
$$\text{Conscientiousness} = 0.532727 \cdot blue + 0.215184 \cdot darkgreen + 0.192177 \cdot red$$
$$\text{Neuroticism} = 0.424213 \cdot blue + 0.262295 \cdot green + 0.185821 \cdot red$$
$$\text{Openness} = 0.510553 \cdot blue + 0.225479 \cdot orange + 0.337031 \cdot red$$

The statistical features (quality assessment) of the obtained models are presented in Table 2. All of the variables in each model are statistically significant. Uncentered R^2 values (notice the lack of intercepts) for every model are close to 0.9 and indicate a good explanation of the dependent variables by independent variables. Observations emerging from these models are summarised in Table 3.

Table 2. Evaluation of models created (statistical features of models).

	Average	Standard deviation	R-squared	Adjusted R-squared	F-statistics	P-value (F)
Extraversion	53.51563	17.53756	0.884671	−0.196736	544.6285	2.50e-67
Agreeableness	59.22068	16.79134	0.885038	−0.554949	361.8292	5.27e-66
Conscientiousness	59.51003	15.38935	0.909029	−0.460811	469.6478	3.64e-73
Neuroticism	53.84115	19.90443	0.822532	−0.485069	217.8366	1.00e-52
Openness	64.70486	13.6531	0.915415	−0.997652	508.6554	2.16e-75

Source: own elaboration

Table 3. Significant colours for each trait from linear regression models. Source: own elaboration

Extraversion	Agreeableness	Conscientiousness	Neuroticism	Openness
Blue	Blue	Blue	Blue	Blue
Orange	Dark green	Dark green	Green	Orange
	Orange	Red	Red	Red

Source: own elaboration

Blue is significant for all of personality traits, which means that this colour has a low discriminatory value. Blue and dark green are significant for Agreeableness and Conscientiousness. In the case of Openness, red and orange were important. Some colours are not strongly linked with any of the personality traits, such as yellow and pink. All the results are summarised in Table 3.

6 Summary and Conclusions

This paper presents how colours can be connected with personality traits. A questionnaire based on Big Five Inventory (BFI-44) and a sample of photos (in colours from the chosen colours' palette inspired by Plutchik's Wheel of Emotions) was created. The developed models show the relation between colours and the strength of the trait, comparing results of scoring the pictures by opposite traits provides information about criterion of differentiating people with opposite traits. Regarding extroverts and introverts, their marks are quite comparable, thus the conclusions about the preferences can not be done. Dark blue is a colour that distinguishes agreeable people and antagonists as the latter gave this colour much higher rank. Regarding differences between neurotics and those who are emotionally stable, the latter group preferred dark green and yellow.

Colours and emotions related to specific personality traits can lay the foundations for creating the profile of user's preferences in OSM. In our case, the data was collected from Flickr, but it could be taken from any social network that relies on images. A larger data sample might be considered in future work. One may also test different machine learning approaches in the process of profiling. A sample from a different part of the world might be considered in order to spot cultural differences. Results from this study can be helpful for marketing, due to revealed ties between colours and personality traits.

References

1. Ahrndt, S., Aria, A., Fähndrich, J., Albayrak, S.: Ants in the OCEAN: modulating agents with personality for planning with humans. In: Bulling, N. (ed.) EUMAS 2014. LNCS (LNAI), vol. 8953, pp. 3–18. Springer, Cham (2015). https://doi.org/10.1007/978-3-319-17130-2_1
2. Azmi, M.A.S.B., Mazli, N.B., Yusof, Y., Hassan, M.F.H.A.: Study of RGB color classification using fuzzy logic. In: ETERD 2010 Proceedings. ACM (2010)
3. Bakhshi, S., Shamma, D.A., Gilbert, E.: Faces engage us: photos with faces attract more likes and comments on Instagram. In: Proceedings of the 32nd Annual ACM Conference on Human Factors in Computing Systems, pp. 965–974. ACM (2014)
4. Borth, D., Ji, R., Chen, T., Breuel, T., Chang, S.F.: Large-scale visual sentiment ontology and detectors using adjective noun pairs. In: Proceedings of the 21st ACM International Conference on Multimedia, pp. 223–232. ACM (2013)
5. Chaudhari, R., Patil, A.: Content based image retrieval using color and shape features. Int. J. Adv. Res. Electr. Electron. Instrum. Eng. 1(5), 67–72 (2012)
6. Ferwerda, B., Schedl, M., Tkalcic, M.: Predicting personality traits with Instagram pictures. In: Proceedings of the 3rd Workshop on Emotions and Personality in Personalized Systems 2015, pp. 7–10. ACM (2015)
7. Geurin-Eagleman, A.N., Burch, L.M.: Communicating via photographs: a gendered analysis of olympic athletes' visual self-presentation on Instagram. Sport Manag. Rev. 19(2), 133–145 (2016)

8. Ghorawat, D., Madan, R.: Correlation between personality types and color shade preference. Int. J. Indian Psychol. **1**(04), 70–79 (2014)
9. Giannoulakis, S., Tsapatsoulis, N.: Evaluating the descriptive power of Instagram hashtags. J. Innov. Digit. Ecosyst. **3**(2), 114–129 (2016)
10. Ha, S.V.U., Pham, N.T., Pham, L.H., Tran, H.M.: Robust reflection detection and removal in rainy conditions using LAB and HSV color spaces. REV J. Electron. Commun. **6**(1–2), 13–19 (2016)
11. Hochman, N., Schwartz, R.: Visualizing Instagram: tracing cultural visual rhythms. In: Proceedings of the Workshop on Social Media Visualization (SocMedVis) in Conjunction with the Sixth International AAAI Conference on Weblogs and Social Media (ICWSM-12), pp. 6–9 (2012)
12. Hosseinmardi, H., Mattson, S.A., Rafiq, R.I., Han, R., Lv, Q., Mishra, S.: Detection of cyberbullying incidents on the Instagram social network. arXiv preprint arXiv:1503.03909 (2015)
13. Hu, Y., Manikonda, L., Kambhampati, S., et al.: What we Instagram: a first analysis of Instagram photo content and user types. In: ICWSM (2014)
14. Jackson, C.A., Luchner, A.F.: Self-presentation mediates the relationship between self-criticism and emotional response to Instagram feedback. Pers. Individ. Differ. **133**, 1–6 (2018). https://doi.org/10.1016/j.paid.2017.04.052. ISSN: 0191-8869
15. Jamil, N., Sa'adan, S.A.: Automatic image annotation using color K-means clustering. In: Badioze Zaman, H., Robinson, P., Petrou, M., Olivier, P., Schröder, H., Shih, T.K. (eds.) IVIC 2009. LNCS, vol. 5857, pp. 645–652. Springer, Heidelberg (2009). https://doi.org/10.1007/978-3-642-05036-7_61
16. Jang, J.Y., Han, K., Shih, P.C., Lee, D.: Generation like: comparative characteristics in Instagram. In: Proceedings of the 33rd Annual ACM Conference on Human Factors in Computing Systems, pp. 4039–4042. ACM (2015)
17. John, O.P., Srivastava, S.: The big five trait taxonomy: history, measurement, and theoretical perspectives. Handb. Pers.: Theory Res. **2**(1999), 102–138 (1999)
18. Labovitz, S.: Criteria for selecting a significance level: a note on the sacredness of 0.05. Am. Sociol. **3**, 200–222 (1968)
19. Liu, L., Preotiuc-Pietro, D., Samani, Z.R., Moghaddam, M.E., Ungar, L.H.: Analyzing personality through social media profile picture choice. In: ICWSM, pp. 211–220 (2016)
20. Liu, T.Y., Scollon, C.N., Zhu, W.: Social Informatics: 7th International Conference, SocInfo 2015, Beijing, China, December 9–12, 2015, Proceedings, vol. 9471. Springer, Heidelberg (2015)
21. Lup, K., Trub, L., Rosenthal, L.: Instagram# instasad?: exploring associations among Instagram use, depressive symptoms, negative social comparison, and strangers followed. Cyberpsychology Behav. Soc. Netw. **18**(5), 247–252 (2015)
22. Machajdik, J., Hanbury, A.: Affective image classification using features inspired by psychology and art theory. In: Proceedings of the 18th ACM International Conference on Multimedia, pp. 83–92. ACM (2010)
23. Min, R., Cheng, H.: Effective image retrieval using dominant color descriptor and fuzzy support vector machine. Pattern Recogn. **42**(1), 147–157 (2009)
24. Pazda, A.D.: Colorful personalities: investigating the relationship between chroma, person perception, and personality traits. Ph.D. thesis, University of Rochester (2015)
25. Perkins, J., Dutson, S., Quinn, R., Greene, Y., Nautu, T., Davis, E.J.: Is every picture worth 1,000 likes?: a content analysis of the images and messages on popular Instagram accounts (2017)

26. Pittman, M.: Creating, consuming, and connecting: examining the relationship between social media engagement and loneliness. J. Soc. Media Soc. **4**(1), 66–98 (2015)
27. Plutchik, R.: Emotion: A Psychoevolutionary Synthesis. Harpercollins College Division, New York (1980)
28. Potluri, T., Nitta, G.: Content based video retrieval using dominant color of the truncated blocks of frame. J. Theor. Appl. Inf. Technol. **85**(2), 165 (2016)
29. Simes, R.J.: An improved bonferroni procedure for multiple tests of significance. Biometrika **73**(3), 751–754 (1986)
30. Smith, L.R., Sanderson, J.: I'm going to Instagram it! An analysis of athlete self-presentation on Instagram. J. Broadcast. Electron. Media **59**(2), 342–358 (2015)
31. Souza, F., et al.: Dawn of the selfie era: the whos, wheres, and hows of selfies on Instagram. In: Proceedings of the 2015 ACM on Conference on Online Social Networks, pp. 221–231. ACM (2015)
32. Tao, B., Xu, S., Pan, X., Gao, Q., Wang, W.: Personality trait correlates of color preference in schizophrenia. Transl. Neurosci. **6**(1), 174–178 (2015)
33. Wang, P., Zhang, D., Zeng, G., Wang, J.: Contextual dominant color name extraction for web image search. In: 2012 IEEE International Conference on Multimedia and Expo Workshops (ICMEW), pp. 319–324. IEEE (2012)
34. Waterloo, S.F., Baumgartner, S.E., Peter, J., Valkenburg, P.M.: Norms of online expressions of emotion: comparing Facebook, Twitter, Instagram, and Whatsapp. New Media Soc. (2017). https://doi.org/10.1177/1461444817707349
35. Zhong, C., Chan, H.W., Karamshu, D., Lee, D., Sastry, N.: Wearing many (social) hats: how different are your different social network personae? arXiv preprint arXiv:1703.04791 (2017)

The Benefits of Modeling Software-Related Exceptional Paths of Business Processes

Krzysztof Gruszczyński[✉] and Bartosz Perkowski

Department of Information Systems, Poznań University of Economics
and Business, al. Niepodległości 10, 61-875 Poznań, Poland
k.gruszczynski@live.com

Abstract. A business process is a collection of activities leading to increase customer's satisfaction. With organizations depending on the software's reliability, this satisfaction might be dramatically reduced with the growing number of failures that might harm the business process related to the client. In this paper, we identify the reasons for organizations to model their business processes including exceptional paths. We begin with the summary of existing research on benefits of business process modeling. Then we analyze current status in the subject of techniques and tools for mapping exceptional paths in process. By carrying out a case study, we verify what conditions should be met for the organization to gain benefit from visualizing the process paths taken as a result of software failure occurrence.

Keywords: Business process modelling · Exceptional process paths
Software reliability

1 Background

A software without defects, supporting execution of business processes, would be a priceless asset for every organization operating on many different applications every day. Every software failure generates a cost for the organization, therefore defects in the source code of application should be prevented. But in the real life, it is almost impossible to create a fully reliable software. Failures introduce chaos to the world of business processes, where the standard paths of process are visualized. Is devoting time on mapping other – exceptional paths, profitable?

Analyzing existing approaches to identify and classify benefits of applying business process modeling was the first stage of this research. During this phase, based on the literature analysis performed, we discovered three categories of benefits. The most common is the possibility to analyze, measure and optimize existing processes. Secondly, creating shared knowledge of how the organization works is also a valuable advantage of applying business process modeling tools and techniques. Additionally, organizations begin to perceive the role of business process models in developing software solutions by providing more reliable requirements.

Business process modeling is the activity of creating representations of organization's current and future business processes [3], thus being an effective technique for analyzing and improving them [1]. Creating business process models is the essential

© Springer Nature Switzerland AG 2019
W. Abramowicz and A. Paschke (Eds.): BIS 2018 Workshops, LNBIP 339, pp. 77–85, 2019.
https://doi.org/10.1007/978-3-030-04849-5_7

step for the organizations, having an aim of applying business process management methods [4]. The elementary information, that a business process model consists of, is the flow of activities in the process. More information (like performance metrics) can be added to the model to allow for a more thorough analysis [4]. By using visualizations of business processes, it is possible to discover bottlenecks and implement simplifications to overwhelmed business processes. Those activities lead to achieve higher customer satisfaction and responsiveness to customer demands [5].

Optimizing business processes is a significant benefit, but applying business process modeling also affects current processes being performed at the moment [1]. One of the main goals of implementing business process modeling is performing conformance checking to verify, if the process is executed as desired. Also, it emphasizes understanding of the performance metrics and the flow of activities more clearly than standard text, data tables or charts, thus allowing for a more complex quality description [5].

Another advantage of modeling business processes is the creation and promotion of an organization's shared meaning between internal and external stakeholders involved in the business process, by using process models [1, 14]. According to [5], business process modeling allows formalizing existing knowledge, increasing its reusability and reducing the cost of knowledge transfer. With business process models being more available to all participants in the process, it is easier for them to solve problems of how activities should be performed and why [9].

Through business processes being often the core of software systems, business process models are widely used as a guide for developing new features or creating applications supporting organization's activities. Business process models are usually a valuable source for requirements analysis, thus providing reliable specifications for developing software [11, 13]. They also allow the identification of processes with the need for automation [8].

A complex research in identifying benefits of implementing business process modeling was conducted by [4]. As a result, they discovered 10 most compelling benefits and ordered them by relevance for 3 groups of stakeholders – academic, practitioners and vendors. The highest ranks are achieved by the following benefits: process improvement possibilities, a better understanding of business processes and enhanced communication between business process stakeholders. It is worth noting, that for different groups of stakeholders, ranking lists of benefits also differentiate.

[9] in their paper explored the reasons for organizations to use process mapping software. They collected data by telephone interview with project managers responsible for process mapping solutions in their organizations. They resulted in a complex classification scheme of benefits with descriptions and 21 reported factors. Results were also analyzed by the sector of the industry of each respondent, thus allowing for identification of the most desirable benefits or business process modeling for each group. Some of the identified benefits are reduced auditing costs, creating a framework for major facility development and sharing knowledge base.

The main goal of this stage of our research was to explore existing literature, that reveals advantages of modeling business processes. It is common for most papers treating business process modeling to present at least fundamental benefits perceived by most stakeholders, who analyze or execute business processes. Additionally, there is literature regarding thoroughly this matter, depicting more complex classifications of profits for different groups of interests. The outcome of this stage will be used while carrying out a case study in this research.

2 Modeling Business Process Exceptional Paths

The essence of every business process model is the flow of activities adding value to the organization. Therefore, the "happy path" of the process describes how should the process be executed as desired. But in the real life, the situation is often much more complicated. An exception caused by internal or external factor might be the trigger for the process to run its unwanted path. Those undesired situations are usually not considered in the business process models [12]. In most cases, they require human control to be completed [10].

One of the most important reasons to include undesired scenarios in the process model is the possibility to monitor all varieties of a process with performance indicators set up [12]. Modeling exceptional circumstances allows analyzing the process fully and verifying if exceptions are handled correctly and efficiently [6]. That leads to the process optimization and increasing its reliability by uncovering the main vulnerabilities and the ways they are being dealt with. But including too many exceptional paths in the model with low occurrence rates might cause the overflow of information and decrease the usability of a model, especially if the business logic is mixed with exception handling procedures [2]. That significantly reduces the possibility for stakeholders to understand and analyze the modeled process.

[12] in their paper introduce the concept of mal-process – a collection of activities executed intentionally, potentially harmful to the organization. Modeling those undesired branches of the normal process increases the organization's understanding of what really happens, when problems arise and allows measuring those cases. Handling unexpected exceptions in processes is thoroughly described in [7]. They propose a framework for workflow systems supporting unstructured actions executed beyond the model. Exception handling functions, diagnosis, and strategies can also be found there.

To avoid manual operations in handling exceptional flows of business processes, [2] presents a dynamic and flexible model based on worklet – "a small, discrete workflow process that acts as a late-bound sub-net for an enabled workitem" [2]. Using a service-oriented architecture of YAWL, their solution consists of sub-services dynamically selecting a proper process path and handling exceptions at runtime. That allows maintaining clarity in process models with business logic in the middle and a separated set of exceptional flows automatically included in the model when an exception occurs.

[6] introduces common patterns for modeling exceptional paths in business processes for 3 modeling notations. Each pattern features a description and illustrations in UML, BPMN, and Little-JIL. Patterns rely on 3 exception handling behaviors – selecting an alternative path, inserting an additional task and canceling the process. They increase consistency of modeled processes and provide common solutions for modeling exceptional scenarios.

The purpose of this section was to investigate motivation for including unwanted paths in business process models. Modeling undesired process flows is a complex activity that might create additional value allowing an organization to work better.

But organizations must be cautious, as it is also possible to cause damage by lowering readability of existing process models. Different techniques and patterns supporting modeling exceptional scenarios were also analyzed, we will use them further in our research.

There is a lack of existing research regarding strategies for handling exceptions that occur while executing a given process step. Thus our approach cannot be com-pared with other results. We plan to expand our research on other use cases in future to verify the business value of our study more thoroughly.

3   Case Study

3.1   Collecting Data

To verify the need for modeling exceptional paths in a process model, we carried out a case study on a real data collected from KRUK group – one of the leading enterprises on the European debt collection market. For our analysis, we selected a process of verifying clients email address. The data for our case study comes from three different sources: software failure tracking system (BugTracker), the main system used in KRUK Group (Delfin) and the source code of applications stored in subversion system (SVN). We also asked domain experts (both software developers and system owners) for their help in modeling the process correctly.

The main work during this stage was to collect proper data from failure collection system. BugTracker stores over 2 million records of failures from all applications used in KRUK Group. Our need was to extract the failure data that comes from two applications – Delfin, which is used by the contact center employee to start a process and EmailVerifier, which is used by the client and is accessible over the Internet. We followed these steps:

1. Extraction of data regarding Delfin and EmailVerifier from the whole failure data set.
   With this achieved, we had the proper data from the system used exclusively in email verification process (EmailVerifier) and a large volume of data recorded from other operational processes using Delfin system.
2. Selection of the main data attributes needed for further analysis.
   Within the primary extraction, we ended up with data described by 38 attributes. We chose the minimum set of attributes valuable for the process analysis (Table 1).
3. Filtering records from Delfin failures data set not connected with the email verification process.
   We eliminated from our set all elements that were generated during execution of other processes. We left failure records generated from the software module used in email verification process and additionally filtered them by text using keyword "verif".

Table 1. Sample data from the failure tracking system.

Failure id	System id	Error date	User comment	Message	Type name
2777556	Delfin	2017-09-21 12:08	During sending verification email	Sending email failed	Kruk.Delfin.Email. EmailNotAddedToEmail QueueException
2639528	Delfin	2017-07-17 14:19	Unable to send verification link to the client	Status HTTP 400: Bad Request	Kruk.Delfin.Email.Bad RequestException
2584108	EVerifier	2017-06-02 17:39	NULL	Procedure or function 'DEL_EContactIn CaseLog_Add' expects parameter '@EContactIn CaseId', which was not supplied	System.Data.SqlClient. SqlException
2553908	EVerifier	2017-05-14 22:03	NULL	A network-related or instance-specific error occurred while establishing a connection to SQL server	System.Data.SqlClient. SqlException

After we had prepared proper data from failure tracking tool, we were able to continue our research on the process model analysis. Our list of failure data consisted of 396 records from 3 different methods in the source code of applications, meaning that 99.75% of email verifications process instances executed as desired, without failure occurrence. But the remaining 0.25% was the target of further analysis.

3.2   Business Process Model Analysis

The aim of the investigated business process is to confirm the correctness of client's email address stored in KRUK's database. If the email address becomes verified, the company will use it to contact the client. The email verification process begins after contact center employee receives an email address from the client with a data processing agreement. After the employee submits the received data to the system, a unique link to the verification website is generated. The employee prepares an email content that will be sent to the client with a generated unique link. When the client receives an email from KRUK, he opens the embedded link in the web browser. The verification system opens and the client is asked to select the type of data that will be used for validation (for example date of birth). The verification system compares data submitted by the client with data stored in the database. If they match, client's email

address will become verified and will be used as a way of communication with the
client. For the needs of our study, we modeled business process using BPMN (Fig. 1).

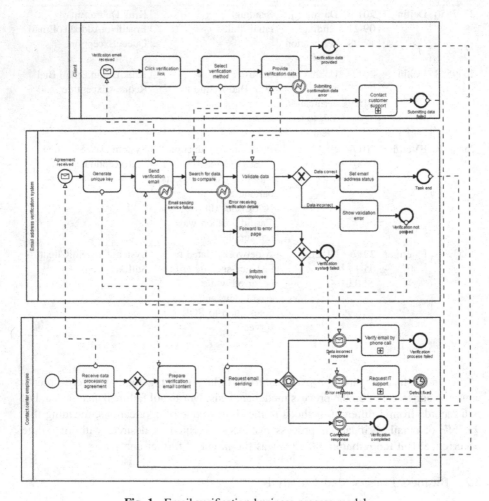

Fig. 1. Email verification business process model.

With the data from the failure tracking system, we were able to identify 3 activities
of the process that were the most error-prone (Table 2). With the help of domain
experts, we modeled exceptional paths to identify steps taken to remove defects
causing failures. All failures occurring during the execution of the email verification
process involve IT staff as the only servicemen capable of removing the defect. When a
failure occurs, the process starts from the beginning and requires participation of a
contact center employee.

In Sect. 2 we discussed benefits of modeling business processes. In our case study,
we focused on the exceptional paths in the process to verify the need for modeling

Table 2. Activities with failure occurrences.

Activity	Number of failures	Solution	Caller	Impact on the process
Provide verification data	37	Request IT support	Client	Repeating the process
Send verification email	114	Request IT support	Employee	Repeating the process
Search for data to compare	245	Request IT support	Client	Repeating the process

them. We identified 396 failure records regarding the analyzed process, meaning that 396 process instances were repeated. Given this, in addition to the process model extended with exceptional paths, KRUK stakeholders benefited with:

1. The common understanding of how the process is executed in the real life.
   Software developers involved in developing the email verification product and process experts realized the scale of the problem with failures and the lack of automation in removing them. The model also helped to visualize that too many failures occur when the company's client uses the product.
2. Identification of bottlenecks and a good starting point to provide root cause analysis optimizing the process.

Including exceptional paths in the process model allows not only to improve the process but also to make it more secure and reliable. When software defects are eventually fixed, the process model can be simplified to increase its readability.

4 Conclusions and Future Work

One of the key aspects of business process management is the business process modeling. It is vital to visualize activities performed during the process execution to achieve benefits mentioned in [1, 3–5, 11]. Those are above all efficient knowledge management, process improvement directions and clearer definitions of software requirements.

In our research, we aimed at mapping the aforementioned benefits on the reasons of modeling exceptional paths in business process models which are taken as a result of software failure. We carried out a case study based on the real data provided by a debt collecting company and analyzed one of the core processes regarding managing client's personal information. We extracted data from the failure tracking system, we modeled business process and connected failure occurrence records with proper steps in the process. A report with conclusions presenting paths of investigated process and measures was provided to process expert and software developers in KRUK. As a result, proper steps were taken to enhance system's reliability.

It is worth mentioning that though gaining benefits from mapping exceptional paths in business processes caused by failures is possible, estimating this activity's cost is fundamental. It requires knowledge of domain experts and software developers to create a process model and visualize how the process behaves when problems occur. This kind of knowledge doesn't usually exist at the primary stage of designing process – it is acquired by executing more process instances and requires monitoring. Also, when the failure occurrence rate is extremally rare or defects are entirely removed from source code after their first occurrence, visualizing additional steps in the process model might decrease its readability.

In our future research, we will try to measure and compare the cost of standard process path with the cost of the exceptional path. This information will provide the basis for stakeholders of the business process to decide if removing defects in software is profitable according to the incurred cost of failures. This will allow for the more balanced direction of developing the organization's internal software.

References

1. Abu Rub, F.A., Issa, A.A.: A business process modeling-based approach to investigate complex processes: software development case study. Bus. Process. Manag. J. **18**(1), 122–137 (2012)
2. Adams, M., Ter Hofstede, A.H.M., Edmond, D., van der Aalst, W.M.P.: Worklets: a service-oriented implementation of dynamic flexibility in workflows. In: Meersman, R., Tari, Z. (eds.) OTM 2006. LNCS, vol. 4275, pp. 291–308. Springer, Heidelberg (2006). https://doi.org/10.1007/11914853_18
3. Eikebrokk, T.R., Iden, J., Olsen, D.H., Opdahl, A.L.: Understanding the determinants of business process modelling in organisations. Bus. Process. Manag. J. **17**(4), 639–662 (2011)
4. Indulska, M., Green, P., Recker, J., Rosemann, M.: Business process modeling: perceived benefits. In: Laender, A.H.F., Castano, S., Dayal, U., Casati, F., de Oliveira, J.P.M. (eds.) ER 2009. LNCS, vol. 5829, pp. 458–471. Springer, Heidelberg (2009). https://doi.org/10.1007/978-3-642-04840-1_34
5. Kalpic, B., Bernus, P., Muhlberger, R.: Business process modelling and its applications in the business environment. In: Leondes, C.T. (ed.) Intelligent Knowledge-Based Systems, pp. 288–345. Springer, Boston (2005). https://doi.org/10.1007/978-1-4020-7829-3_10
6. Lerner, B.S., Christov, S., Osterweil, L.J., Bendraou, R., Kannengiesser, U., Wise, A.: Exception handling patterns for process modeling. IEEE Trans. Softw. Eng. **36**(2), 162–183 (2010)
7. Mourão, H., Antunes, A.J.: Supporting effective unexpected exception handling in workflow management systems within organizational contexts (1998)
8. Pietroń, R.: Best practices in business process modelling. Inf. Syst. Manag. **5**(4), 551–562 (2016)
9. Rowell, J.: Do organisations have a mission for mapping processes? Bus. Process. Manag. J. **24**(1), 2–22 (2018)
10. Simões, D., Thuan, N.H., Jonnavithula, L., Antunes, P.: Modelling sensible business processes. In: Dang, T.K., Wagner, R., Küng, J., Thoai, N., Takizawa, M., Neuhold, E. (eds.) FDSE 2015. LNCS, vol. 9446, pp. 165–182. Springer, Cham (2015). https://doi.org/10.1007/978-3-319-26135-5_13
11. Snoeck, M.: Bridging business process modelling and domain modelling. In: Enterprise Information Systems Engineering. The Enterprise Engineering Series. Springer, Cham (2014). https://doi.org/10.1007/978-3-319-10145-3_10

12. Sundaram, D., Erik Rohde, M.: Mal-processes: explicitly modelling the deviant. In: Barjis, J. (ed.) EOMAS 2010. LNBIP, vol. 63, pp. 164–178. Springer, Heidelberg (2010). https:// doi.org/10.1007/978-3-642-15723-3_11

13. van der Aalst, W.M.P.: Challenges in business process analysis. In: Filipe, J., Cordeiro, J., Cardoso, J. (eds.) ICEIS 2007. LNBIP, vol. 12, pp. 27–42. Springer, Heidelberg (2008). https://doi.org/10.1007/978-3-540-88710-2_3

14. vom Brocke, J., Schmiedel, T., Recker, J., Trkman, P., Mertens, W., Viaene, S.: Ten principles of good business process management. Bus. Process. Manag. J. **20**(4), 530–548 (2014)

Process Mining of Periodic Rating Scale Survey Data Using Analytic Hierarchy Process

Dalia Kriksciuniene[1], Virgilijus Sakalauskas[1(✉)],
and Roman Lewandowski[2]

[1] Institute of Applied Informatics, Vilnius University,
Universiteto str.3, Vilnius, Lithuania
{dalia.kriksciuniene,
virgilijus.sakalauskas}@khf.vu.lt
[2] Management Faculty, University of Social Sciences, Lodz, Poland
r.lewandowski@ameryka.com.pl

Abstract. The main purpose of our research is to propose original algorithm to evaluate the dynamic behavior of processes from the survey data collected with the help of periodically repeated surveys based on Likert scale questions. This approach supposes the usage of AHP (Analytic Hierarchy Process) for assessment the factors influencing the process behavior. Our idea is to use the aggregated periodic rating scale data as alternatives inputs for AHP evaluation. The practical usefulness of proposed process quality evaluation technique was proved by examining particular Polish rehabilitation hospital service quality changes over time frame from 2008 to 2017.

Keywords: Process mining · Healthcare system
AHP (Analytic Hierarchy Process) · Likert scale

1 Introduction

To explore the run of some processes that usually are dependent from behavior, sentiments and satisfaction of participating members, we apply the questionnaires, surveys to learn the participants' opinion about the process they are involved. More often this situation appears when evaluating the quality of service provided by social infrastructure, healthcare level secured by some hospital, knowledge level achieved by educational institution, satisfaction from used service or purchased goods. To examine such process behavior usually is used rating scale data obtained from public opinion poll or survey with Likert scale questions. A Likert scale let us to measure attitudes or opinion of respondents and rate the answers on a level of agreement from 'strongly agree' to strongly disagree [Joshi et al. 2015; Murray 2013].

There are a lot of methods to analyze the rating scale data. Recommendations for analysis, interpretation, literature review and reporting of scores derived from Likert-type scales are presented in recent work of [Robert Warmbrod 2014]. The [Jamieson 2004] outlines some common pitfalls seen in practice when using Likert scales. The article of [Harpe and Pharm 2015] explains the situations, when parametric and non-parametric analytical techniques is more appropriate for rating scale data.

© Springer Nature Switzerland AG 2019
W. Abramowicz and A. Paschke (Eds.): BIS 2018 Workshops, LNBIP 339, pp. 86–95, 2019.
https://doi.org/10.1007/978-3-030-04849-5_8

The Likert scale data is easy to summarize but, hard to interpret. You can compare the responses with results from previous similar survey or find some in advance known process behavior description. Usually such comparison is hard realized. So the task of constructive interpreting the Likert scale responses leaves to researcher. Usually they use simple statistical location and variation characteristics like mean, median, mode, standard deviation, percentile, its confidence intervals and so on.

In this paper we analyze more complicated situation. We study the process changes over time by the help of repeated surveys. We want to find the way for analyzing and comparing the data retrieved from multiply Likert scale based surveys. The proposed research method is described in Sect. 2. The practical implementation of introduced testing idea on the data of rehabilitation hospital service quality changes over time is done in Sect. 3. The paper is finished with main findings and final conclusions of research done.

2 Research Method

The main task of the research is to propose the algorithm for process mining of periodically collected numeric rating scale data by using AHP (Analytic Hierarchy Process).

Let us assume we investigate behaviour of some process. It may be quality of healthcare in some hospital, educational achievement for given school or university, service level of some society and so on. The general approach of exploring patterns of process changes is based on selecting some factors influencing this process by different weights (see general framework in Fig. 1).

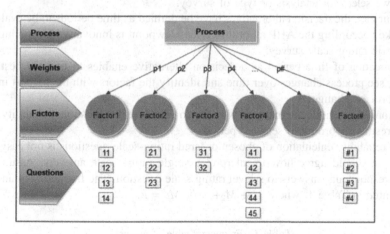

Fig. 1. Framework for process investigation

To investigate the factors, we can employ the survey with rating-scale (Likert scale) questions.

The main problem is how to interpret the answers and get the meaningful assessment of factor importance. Other challenge arises in case we collect survey answers periodically and look for process changes along the specific time frame. These problems make the core of our research in this article.

Let the $\{F_i\}_{i=1}^n$ denotes the set of factors. The survey rating-scale questions we assigned to most appropriate factors. The set of $Q_1^i, Q_2^i, \ldots, Q_{ki}^i$ denotes questions assigned to F_i, having any quantity of ordered response levels. For the research of the process evaluation task we employ AHP method (Saaty 1980; Ishizaka and Labib 2011; Kriksciuniene and Sakalauskas 2017). Application of AHP means that we exercise four major steps:

1. Problem modeling in the hierarchical form;
2. Valuation of factor weights by pairwise comparisons;
3. Weight aggregation into the priority vector by using the eigenvalue method;
4. Ranking the decision alternatives.

The factors of quality evaluation of the hospital were arranged into two level hierarchical tree (Fig. 1). The experts have been employed for the group decision of the consistent factors weights. During AHP evaluation procedure they use the pairwise comparison of factor importance and merge joint decision as a priority vector (Saaty 1980). The $W = \{p_i\}_{i=1}^n$ denotes the generalised and consistent vector of weights of the factors forming first level of the decision tree.

The last step of the AHP method consists of selecting and ranking the decision alternatives which, in general, are defined as entities or objects characterized by the weighted hierarchical tree of factors. For this stage different types of decision alternatives can be discussed. It highly depends on the process we try to investigate; the factors we select for analysis or type of survey.

In our case the decision alternatives have be defined as time periods to be evaluated and ranked according the AHP algorithm. This viewpoint is innovative for mining data of numeric rating scale survey.

Application of time period as a decision alternative enables to find the best time periods, see process changes over time and identify the factors with the highest impact on the process changes.

To rank the periods alternatives, we need to calculate the questions reliability from survey results according to selected period.

The reliability calculation of chosen ordered rating-scale questions is not easy task. Firstly, we should agree how to interpret a single rating-scale answers. Assume we have R respondents answers to s-level rating scale question. The frequency of answers is presented in Table 1, where $M_1 + M_2 + \ldots + Ms = R$.

Table 1. Frequency table of answers

1-strongly disagree	2-moderate disagree	..	..	..	s-strongly agree
M_1	M_2	.	.	.	M_s

The aggregation the answers to single indicator can be done by many different ways. We can use top-box or top two box scoring, net top box, customer experience index, Z-score to percentile rank and other raw responses aggregation to single indicator [Measuring U 2018; Joshi 2015; Murray 2013; Subedi 2016].

For answers aggregation to single indicator we introduce new method, which takes count not only on content of answers, but also consider the response rate of respondents. This let us get more reliable rating-scale questions evaluation.

As we have ordered categories, accepting its degree of arbitrariness, we might give scores to the categories from **1**-'strongly disagree' to **s**-'strongly agree', and then produce an aggregated reliability index using formula:

$$ARI_s = \frac{M_1 \cdot 1 + M_2 \cdot 2 + \ldots + M_s \cdot s}{(M_1 + M_2 + \ldots + M_s) \cdot s} \tag{1}$$

ARI_s is positive and equals to 1 only in case all respondents choose 'strongly agree' answer. So the bigger is ARI_s the more respondents agree with our statement.

In other hand, we need to assure sufficiently active participation in survey. The number of respondents directly affect the significance of the research. Consequently, we advise to supplement the aggregated reliability index with the response rate of respondents. Let U-stands for the number not-responded participants to given question. Then for selected alternative we can define generalized respondents aggregated reliability index (RARI), which takes account on the response rate of respondents:

$$RARI_s = ARI_s \cdot \frac{R}{R + U} \tag{2}$$

This index takes a value equal to 1 only in case we have the answers from all respondents, and they all choose 'strongly agree' answer.

These calculations can be done for every alternative-periods of time. So, using this procedure we can rank all the time periods from best to worst and try to identify the sources allowing to reach the best results.

3   Experimental Research of the Method

The data for our experimental research was given by one rehabilitation hospital in Poland. The administration of this hospital from 2008 to 2017 have distributed to patients the survey about the quality of treatment, personnel helpfulness, infrastructure and admission conditions. The main purpose of such questioning was the intention to find the positive and negative factors of rehabilitation process, assess the influence of specific actions and find the quality improvement patterns over the time. The survey answers were collected as the numeric rating scale data, so direct comparison the quality and efficiency of rehabilitation in specific time frame was not easy task. The following research will show possible solution of this problem.

We'll try to get not only the estimation of the rehabilitation hospital service quality changes over time frame from 2008 to 2017. The survey consists of 20 Likert-scale questions (Table 2) with different number of rating-scale levels –from 2 to 5.

Table 2. The questions of survey

1.	Were there any difficulties with getting a referral to the hospital?
2.	Is it easy to contact the hospital?
3.	Was the date of admission to hospital in line with your expectations?
4.	How do you assess the organization of admitting to the hospital?
5.	How do you assess the staff in the department?
6.	Did the staff help acclimatize to hospital environment?
7.	Has the staff facilitated contact with relatives?
8.	Was the staff responding promptly to the patient's needs?
9.	How do you assess the treatment procedures?
10.	Did the staff inform in a clear and exhaustive way about the performed procedures?
11.	Did the staff perform all the treatments with due diligence?
12.	Did the staff provide comprehensive information about the disease and treatment?
13.	Did recommended treatment program meet your expectations?
14.	Are the treatment effective?
15.	Were the tips for further treatment comprehensive?
16.	Was the quality of the equipment appropriate to your requirements?
17.	Were the meals delicious?
18.	Were the meals aesthetically served?
19.	How do you assess the therapists - educator?
20.	Were leisure activities organized by the hospital?

The answers of all possible respondents to specific question were collected and presented as a frequency table. An example of such frequency table (answers to question no. 11) is presented in Table 3.

As we see from Table 3, the data was collected every quarter of the year and distributed according the patient's department: A1, REH, AR, GOŚ, DZIENNY. This let us make the quality investigation not only by time periods but also evaluate the efficiency of rehabilitation by departments.

According the research framework described in previous section we need to select the set of factors mostly influencing the rehabilitation quality and distribute the questions to groups related to these factors. For this task we have involved seven hospital specialists. They have selected 4 factors: Process of admission to hospital; Personnel helpfulness; Quality of treatment; Infrastructure and food. The questions related to these factors we can see in Table 4.

The next step is to evaluate the factors weights. We have asked the hospital specialists to assess the consistent factors weights using the pairwise comparison of factors importance. The results of factors evaluation by 7 experts are shown in Table 5.

Table 3. A part of frequency table (answers to question no. 11)

11. Did the staff perform all the treatments with due diligence?

Quarter year	Department	Yes	Rather yes	Rather no	No	No answer
I 2008	REH	25	7	1	0	0
I 2008	AR	84	16	0	0	5
I 2008	GOŚ	2	0	0	0	0
I 2008	DZIENNY	26	18	0	0	2
II 2008	REH	16	8	0	0	0
II 2008	AR	56	14	0	0	1
II 2008	GOŚ	6	2	0	0	0
II 2008	DZIENNY	9	6	0	0	1
III 2008	REH	25	9	2	1	0
III 2008	AR	90	23	2	1	2
III 2008	GOŚ	5	8	0	0	0
III 2008	DZIENNY	35	15	0	0	2
III 2008	A1	8	2	0	0	1
IV 2008	REH	13	5	0	0	0
IV 2008	AR	64	9	1	0	2
IV 2008	GOŚ	15	5	0	1	1
IV 2008	DZIENNY	34	10	1	1	0
I 2009	REH	46	6	1	0	2
I 2009	AR	63	9	1	0	1
I 2009	GOŚ	18	13	1	0	0
I 2009	DZIENNY	39	11	2	0	0
I 2009	A1	5	0	0	0	0
...	...	...	...	...	...	...
IV 2017	DZIENNY	14	4	4	0	0

Table 4. Questions related to specific factor

Factors	Questions no.
Process of admission to hospital	1–4
Personnel helpfulness	5–11
Quality of treatment	12–15
Infrastructure and food	16–20

From the last column of the table, we see calculated consistency ratio (CR) of weight distribution. From practice of AHP application, we know that CR couldn't exceed 10%. Our experts' decision follows this rule.

Now we can choose the alternatives and calculate its priority vectors for every factor. As alternatives we selected the annual time period from 2008 to 2017 and estimate its value for specific questions. Using formulas 1–2 for calculation alternatives

Table 5. Factors weights along the group of expert decision

Specialists, experts	Process of admission to hospital	Personnel helpfulness	Quality of treatment	Infrastructure and food	CRmax
A	10.80%	14.70%	66.60%	8.00%	5.00%
B	6.30%	15.50%	71.90%	6.30%	3.30%
C	5.20%	12.50%	66.90%	15.40%	8.50%
D	9.80%	22.80%	52.90%	14.50%	8.00%
E	6.40%	17.70%	57.90%	18.00%	4.60%
F	8.00%	14.90%	59.10%	18.00%	7.70%
G	7.60%	31.20%	47.90%	13.30%	7.50%
Group result	**7.80%**	**17.70%**	**61.90%**	**12.50%**	**3.20%**

priority vector and taking into account determined factor weights we got following result about the rehabilitation hospital service quality changes over 2008–2017 (Fig. 2):

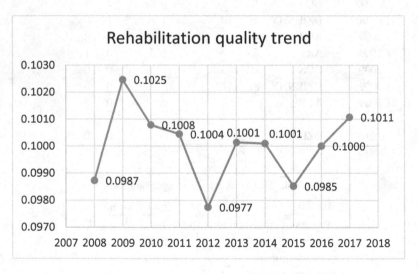

Fig. 2. Annual rehabilitation quality changes

General trend (Fig. 2) shows some points of rapid change and we have asked the hospital authorities to justify trend variation. The sharp increase of satisfaction between years 2008–2009 correlates with the significant rise of the level of payment for healthcare services by Polish national payer. The 2012 drop was related to the personnel crisis. In the region a new rehabilitation centre was established and some staff was proposed there a leading position and leave the hospital. The rise in 2016 and 2017 may be due to the government law about incremental long-term pay rise for all healthcare employees.

On the next figure (Fig. 3) we presented the annual service quality changes over all departments.

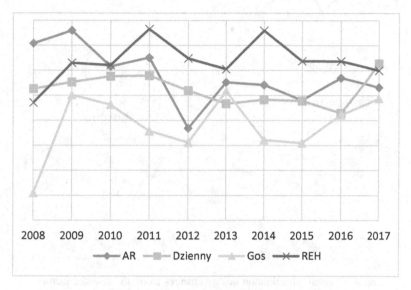

2008   2009   2010   2011   2012   2013   2014   2015   2016   2017

—◆— AR   —■— Dzienny   —▲— Gos   —✕— REH

Fig. 3. Annual rehabilitation quality changes over apartments

According the hospital authorities the 2008 was the year where the "Gos" department was under construction and temporarily was located in less comfortable facility. This also explains the 2009 upswing when the department return to the renewed facility. The 2013 peak may collocate with giving the "Gos" department additional new rooms. The somehow continuous decline of satisfaction in "AR" department is due to increasing number of patients without sufficient employment growth and facility expansion. Both "Dzienny" and "REH" departments are operating in stable environment, thus the fluctuation of patients' satisfaction is not high.

The last figure (Fig. 4) shows the annual pattern of selected factors influencing the patients' satisfaction in rehabilitation process.

Going further into details concerning particular fields of quality it is worthy to notice that the improvement of healthcare financing and employment of more staff in 2009 is significantly reflected in three dimensions where the personnel is the critical factor, i.e. personnel helpfulness, quality of treatment and process of admission to hospital. Similarly echoed is the staff crisis in 2012. Persistent progress of satisfaction of the process of admission to hospital from 2012 may be related to greater involvement of ICT solutions allowing better interaction between hospital and patients'

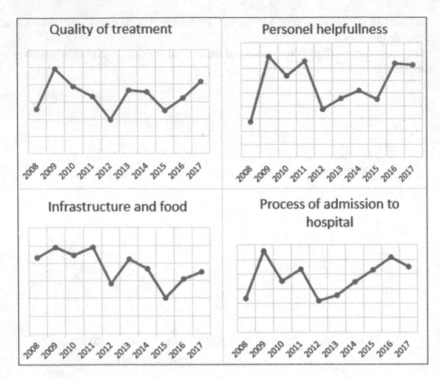

Fig. 4. Annual rehabilitation quality changes along the selected factors

parents. The results about the patients' satisfaction in rehabilitation process highly correlates with the sources of changes disclosed by hospital authorities. So, the method of analysis the periodic rating scale data using AHP give us meaningful results and can be used in practice.

4   Conclusions and Main Results

The investigation of applying AHP for tracking temporal change of compound quality indicator enabled to draw the following conclusions:

1. Widespread application of Likert scale for customer surveying provides data which could be used for enhanced interpretation of its results in time range. However existing methods for processing results, measured by Likert scale do not enable continuous comparative evaluation among different surveying events.
2. The article proposes original approach for processing Likert scale–based survey data for estimating compound characteristics of time periods and further performing time series analysis by applying concept of evaluation of alternatives by AHP framework.
3. The proposed approach is employed for design of compound indicator for quality evaluation in the application domain of person centered healthcare.

4. Experimental evaluation was performed by processing longitudinal survey data, collected at one rehabilitation Hospital in Poland. Application of quality change by proposed AHP-based approach is correlated to implementation of strategic management decisions and programs.

Acknowledgement. This work was performed within the framework of the COST action "European Network for cost containment and improved quality of health care" http://www.cost. eu/COST_Actions/ca/CA15222, and was also supported by funding from National Science Centre, Poland (grant number: 2015/17/B/HS4/02747).

References

Joshi, A., Kale, S., Chandel, S., Pal, D.K., Scale, L.: Explored and explained. Br. J. Appl. Sci. Technol. **7**(4), 396–403 (2015)

Subedi, B.P.: Using Likert type data in social science research: confusion, issues and challenges. Int. J. Contemp. Appl. Sci. **3**(2), 36–49 (2016)

Ishizaka, A., Labib, A.: Review of the main developments in the analytic hierarchy process. Expert Syst. Appl. **38**(11), 14336–14345 (2011)

Warmbrod, R.J.: Reporting and interpreting scores derived from Likert-type scales. J. Agric. Educ. **55**(5), 30–47 (2014)

Murray, J.: Likert data: what to use, parametric or non-parametric? Int. J. Bus. Soc. Sci. **4**(11), 258–264 (2013)

Jamieson, S.: Likert scales: how to (ab)use them. Med. Educ. **38**, 1217–1218 (2004)

Kriksciuniene, D., Sakalauskas, V.: AHP Model for Quality Evaluation of Healthcare System. In: Damaševičius, R., Mikašytė, V. (eds.) ICIST 2017. CCIS, vol. 756, pp. 129–141. Springer, Cham (2017). https://doi.org/10.1007/978-3-319-67642-5_11

Measuring U. https://measuringu.com/interpret-responses/ (2018)

Saaty, T.L.: The Analytical Hierarchy Process. McGraw Hill, New York (1980)

Harpe, S.E., Pharm, D.: How to analyze Likert and other rating scale data. Curr. Pharm. Teach. Learn. **7**(6), 836–850 (2015)

BITA Workshop

BITA 2018 Workshop Chairs' Message

A contemporary challenge for enterprises is to keep up with the pace of changing business demands imposed on them in different ways. There is today an obvious demand for continuous improvement and alignment in enterprises but unfortunately many organizations don't have proper instruments (methods, tools, patterns, best practices etc.) to achieve this. Enterprise modeling, enterprise architecture, and business process management are three areas belonging to traditions where the mission is to improve business practice and business and IT alignment (BITA). BITA is many times manifested through the transition of taking an enterprise from one state (AS-IS) into another improved state (TO-BE), i.e. a transformation of the enterprise and it's supporting IT into something that is regarded as better. A challenge with BITA is to move beyond a narrow focus on one tradition or technology. There is a need to be aware of and able to deal with a number of dimensions of the enterprise architecture and their relations in order to create alignment. Examples of such dimensions are: organizational structures, strategies, business models, work practices, processes, and IS/IT structures. Among the concepts that deserve special attention in this context is enterprise architecture management (EAM). An effective EAM aligns IT investments with overall business priorities, determines who makes the IT decisions and assigns accountability for the outcomes. IT governance is also a dimension that traditionally have had a strong impact on BITA. There are ordinarily three governance mechanisms that an enterprise needs to have in place, (1) decision-making structures, (2) alignment process, and (3) formal communications. This workshop aimed to bring together people who have an interest in BITA. We have invited researchers and practitioners from both industry and academia to submit original results of their completed or ongoing projects. We have encouraged broad understanding of possible approaches and solutions for BITA, including EAM and IT governance subjects. Specific focus was on practices of business and IT alignment, i.e. we have encouraged submission of case study and experiences papers. The workshop received 11 submissions. The program committee selected 6 submissions for presentation at the workshop. We thank all members of the program committee, authors and local organizers for their efforts and support.

Ulf Seigerroth
Kurt Sandkuhl
Julia Kaidalova

Organization

Chairs

Ulf Seigerroth (Chair)   Jönköping University
Kurt Sandkuhl (Co-chair)   Rostock University
Julia Kaidalova (Co-chair)   Jönköping University

Program Committee

Marite Kirikova   Riga Technical University Latvia
Vladimir Tarasov   Jönköping University, Sweden
Milena Stróżyna   Poznan University of Economics and Business,
                                 Poland
Nikolay Shilov   SPIIRAS, Russia
Björn Johansson   Department of Informatics, School of Economics
                                 and Management, Lund University, Sweden
Michael Fellmann   University of Rostock, Institute for Computer
                                 Science, Germany
Jānis Grabis   Riga Technical University, Latvia
Julia Kaidalova   Jönköping University, Sweden
Stijn Hoppenbrouwers   HAN University of Applied Sciences,
                                 The Netherlands
Andreas L Opdahl   University of Bergen, Norway
Janis Stirna   Stockholm University, Sweden
Birger Lantow   University of Rostock, Germany
Alexander Smirnov   SPIIRAS, Russia

Determinants to Benefit from Enterprise Architecture Management – A Research Model

Ralf-Christian Härting[1](✉), Christopher Reichstein[1](✉),
and Kurt Sandkuhl[2](✉)

[1] Aalen University of Applied Sciences, Business Administration,
Aalen, Germany
{ralf.haerting, christopher.reichstein}@hs-aalen.de
[2] Institute of Computer Science, Rostock University, Rostock, Germany
kurt.sandkuhl@uni-rostock.de

Abstract. A successful digital transformation in enterprises requires surpassing infrastructural flexibility within firms and high IT competency to accomplish changing business requirements. Digital Enterprises are challenged to combine business and IT to gain from existing technological achievements. Previous studies showed that there are certain factors influencing the benefit of Enterprise Architecture Management. However, there are some more influencing factors due to the digital transformation that were not taken into consideration yet. An alternative research approach investigates more factors and helps to get a deeper insight of impact factors. This paper draws on a first approach to investigate additional factors and their impact on EAM. The approach is based on a profound literature research in order to build a new empirical research model. In addition, the indicators were examined in a case of industrial digital transformation. It is shown that factors aggregated to the determinants IT Landscapes, internal as well as external Business Environments and the level of EAM Establishment have substantially impact on the benefit of EAM in enterprises.

Keywords: EAM · Enterprise Architecture · Impact factors · Benefit of EAM
Use of EAM · Qualitative study · IT Business Alignment

1 Introduction

Enterprise Architecture Management (EAM) is a crucial task for enterprises and their IT infrastructure [1, 13]. Therefore, it is an often discussed topic for management and research [2]. It also plays an important role in implementing new digital strategies [3]. The different developments of digitization embrace new technologies (Hadoop, RFID et al.), services (cloud services et al.) and applications with new business models [4]. To include such challenges specific frameworks like SEAM [4], ESARC [3] or "Internet of Things reference architecture" have been developed.

Previous studies have explored the effects of various important impact factors regarding the perceived benefit of EAM in enterprises [1, 5–8, 12], but did not focus on the tremendous impact of the digital transformation. Digitization is a driver for the development of new business models with innovative products. Approaches to digital

© Springer Nature Switzerland AG 2019
W. Abramowicz and A. Paschke (Eds.): BIS 2018 Workshops, LNBIP 339, pp. 101–111, 2019.
https://doi.org/10.1007/978-3-030-04849-5_9

transformation can be found across sectors, including traditional sectors such as services and manufacturing [36]. This results in additional impact factors which were not taken into account within existing quantitative approaches. An additional (e.g. qualitative) research approach might be useful to investigate more factors in relation to the digital transformation to get a deeper insight, which finally can help to classify these factors into relevant determinants. Therefore, this paper will explore determinants of the perceived benefit of EAM and impact factors behind based on a structured literature research. The paper proceeds as follows. In the following Sect. 2, the research methods are described. Then, in Sect. 3, the research model and the determinants to benefit from EAM are defined. Section 4 investigates the use of the impact factors in an industrial digital transformation case. Finally, this paper presents impact factors obtained from the literature research as well as an outlook for future work.

2   Research Methods

To prove whether there are some more important impact factors as found in the first research experience about benefits of EAM [12], the examination were enhanced with current literature starting from the year 2009. By searching for additional factors influencing the benefit of EAM, a common approach based on an extensive and structured literature research and intensive reading has been followed [9, 10, 30].

The authors searched for the keywords "Enterprise Architecture Management", "Enterprise Architecture" and "EAM" within the databases SpringerLink, AISel, Web of Knowledge, EbscoHost, IEEexplore and Science Direct. To limit the results, often used search items "Business Environment", "IT Landscape", "Internal Business", "EAM Establishment", "Benefit" and "Impact Factor" were added to the above-mentioned keywords. 20 articles from different well-known journals were selected and checked according to quality by using the internationally accepted journal ranking relevant to business research [10], the SCImago Journal & Country Rank as well as Core Conference Rank [11]. Table 1 shows the used articles, a short summary, the ranking of the journals in which they are published (if existing), and the impact factor.

Table 1. Summary of literature review

Author	Summary	Ranking	Competitive environment	IT landscape	Internal business	EAM establishment	Firm size	Industry complexity
Wegmann [4]	Definition of systemic paradigm to provide a theoretical foundation for alleviating practical problems.	C			X			
Schmidt et al. [2]	Exploration of the impact of the perceived benefit of EAM in enterprises with a literature-based research model.		X	X	X	X		
Sandkuhl et al. [14]	Basic concepts and purposes as well as quality and possibilities for the analysis of company models are shown.		X		X			

(continued)

Table 1. (*continued*)

Author	Summary	Ranking	Competitive environment	IT landscape	Internal business	EAM establishment	Firm size	Industry complexity
Hanschke [15]	The relevant core tasks are the management of the Enterprise Architecture (EA), the IT development management, the technology management as well as EAM governance.		X	X	X	X		
BITKOM [16]	EA describes the interplay between business processes and IT in the company and thus provides a strategic, conceptual and organizational framework for the design of IT landscape.		X			X		
Aier et al. [17]	Literature overview of the current state of EA comparing a number of publications from recent years.	B		X		X		
Wigand et al. [18]	Competitive strategies must re-evaluate the business-management goals of flexibility, time, quality and cost to ensure business success in the global marketplace.				X			
Pereira and Sousa [19]	The alignment between Business and IT can be aggregated into four different dimensions. The paper presents some heuristics to ensure such alignment.				X			
Luftmann [20]	Approach for assessing the maturity of the business-IT alignment.				X			
Luftmann and Brier [21]	This article develops a methodology that leverages the most important enablers and inhibitors to business-IT alignment.	C			X			
Hanschke [22]	Overview of the objectives and benefits of EAM. Practical examples show how to implement EAM successfully.					X		
Timm et al. [23]	This work reveals a need for a reference EA that tailors utility enterprises demands towards EAM and derives implications for the development of such a reference EA.	C					X	X
Hanschke et al. [24]	Based on expert interviews an integration of the TOGAF ADM and Scrum has been developed and evaluated following the Design Science research process.	C						X
Lakhrouit and Ba [25]	A method to evaluate the EA complexity and facilitating decisions between different architecture scenarios.	C		X				
Plataniotis et al. [26]	This paper extends the approach with concepts from the problem space domain of the EA, such as goals, principles, and requirements.		X					

(*continued*)

Table 1. (*continued*)

Author	Summary	Ranking	Competitive environment	IT landscape	Internal business	EAM establishment	Firm size	Industry complexity
Banaeianjahromi and Smolander [27]	Analysis of the available literature on determining the role of EA to identify gaps and state-of-the-art in research.	C		X	X			
Hinkelmann et al. [28]	The paper deals with Next Generation Enterprise Information Systems in the context of Enterprise Engineering.	D			X			
Geerts and O'Leary [29]	Architecture for integrating cloud computing and enterprise systems based on the Resource-Event-Agent (REA) model.	C		X				X
Azevedo et al. [31]	Ontological analysis of concepts focusing in particular on the resource, capability and competence.	C		X				
Alwadain et al. [32]	Empirically and theoretically grounded insights into EA evolution, in particular in relation to the introduction of SOA.	C		X				

3   Determinants to Benefit from EAM: A Research Model

To prove how to benefit from EAM, the authors build a research model based on literature review guidelines by Cooper et al. [9]. The model (see Fig. 1) consists of six determinants including 22 indicators and two moderating effects (firm size and industry).

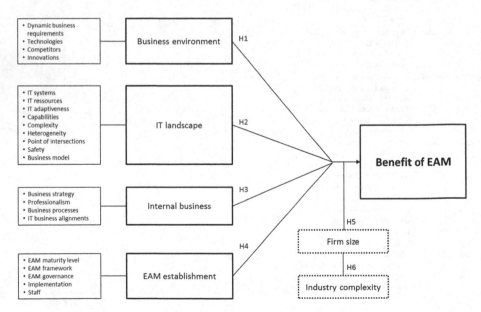

Fig. 1. Research model

Recent research studies have shown that there are potential drivers to benefit from EAM [1, 12]. In the following, the impact factors showing how to benefit from EAM are represented and hypotheses are constructed.

The frequent change of business requirements has a positive impact on the perceived benefits of EAM [12]. Beneath adapting the corporate strategy, continuous process improvement, new laws and regulations and technical innovations a competitive Business Environment is one of the major challenges for enterprises, as well in the industrial as in the service sector. EAM is an approved tool to overcome the challenges of a competitive business environment [16, 26]. Requirements for a useful EAM are a customized, efficient and flexible IT solution and an effective information supply. All can contribute significantly to differentiation. Information supply consists of knowledge about customer needs, competitors, competitive products and the costs and benefits of the products [15]. The improvement of transparency and control capability of the organization results in a value contribution of EAM [16, 26].

Hypothesis 1: A competitive Business Environment positively influences the benefits of EAM.

The use of EAM is recommended for enterprises with a high complex IT Landscape because of the positive link between the IT Landscape complexity and the perceived benefit of EAM [12]. For a better handling of IT Landscapes they should be well-structured, that means the reduction of the complexity [32]. This means making the IT Landscape comprehensible and manageable by simplification on all levels with standardization and homogenization, elimination of redundancies and dependencies, as well as organizational measures [15, 25]. Therefore, several analyses are needed: The cover analyses over several levels leads to the detection of gaps and redundancies in the IT support of business processes. Interface, complexity and heterogeneity analyses lead to the improvement of the level of integration [27, 29]. The resulting transparency leads to a more efficient way to improve the planning of the IT strategy, the IT/Business Alignment and the optimization of business processes [17, 31].

Hypothesis 2: A well-organized IT Landscape positively influences the benefits of EAM.

In this context Internal Business consists of enterprise strategy, specific corporate functions, business processes and IT-Business-Alignment. The enterprise strategy is needed for the definition of the IT strategy and essential for long-term success [14]. Information systems, which are aligned with the enterprise strategy, are able to raise business processes to a higher level of efficiency and create economies of scale [18]. Business processes and specific functions are both part of the business architecture, which is crucial for the business of the enterprise [15]. IT Business Alignment is the application of Information Technology in an appropriate and timely way [19, 20] and a crucial topic for IT Management [4, 27]. The benefit of EAM can be very extensive by implementing a high level of IT Business Alignment [12, 28]. A distinctive degree of IT Business Alignment is recommended and is very important for the majority of enterprises [12, 21].

Hypothesis 3: A well-structured Internal Business positively influences the benefits of EAM.

An established and sustainable EAM requires the arrangement of a EAM governance [16]. The EAM governance has to be adjusted to the EAM maturity level, the enterprise and its general architecture, as well as its processes and guidelines of modelling to ensure the quality of the EAM database [22]. The assessment of the EAM maturity level is important to get implementable expectations [15]. The EAM framework should be developed in participation with affected stakeholders. Results of the EAM framework are the general aim and the first implementation level of EAM [15]. An adjusted EAM governance is needed for all levels of implementation [17]. EAM benefits also from EA knowledge by training IT staff with EAM basics as well as fundamental skills [12].

Hypothesis 4: A high level of EAM establishment positively influences the benefits of EAM.

In addition to these four determinants, there are firm and industry specific control variables to consider. Established frameworks like TOGAF and COBIT or actual approaches regarding IoT aspects like ESARC are often too complex and expensive for small and medium sized enterprises (SMEs) [23]. For them, EAM is not able to reduce complexity of IT infrastructure, although there are many frameworks of EAM available. As a result, firm size might positively affect the influences regarding the benefit of EAM [23]. It can be assumed that the bigger the firm, the more it might benefit from these factors. Sectors with complex technologies or processes like the electronic, utility or plant engineering industries are expected to benefit from EAM [23] as they do have more complex requirements towards their information systems. In some sectors like utility or telecommunication industry, trade liberalization also leads to more competitiveness [24, 29]. Thus, an effective and efficient management of EA helps to create competitive advantages. The more complex the product or service of a firm, the higher the benefit of EAM [29]. As a result, the control variable "Industry Complexity" positively affects the influences regarding the benefit of EAM.

4   Industrial Case of Digital Transformation

Although the determinants and indicators presented in the previous section are anchored in literature and grounded in a thorough conceptual analysis, we consider a validation of the research model as important before conducting further qualitative studies. As a first validation step, we decided to apply the research model in an industrial case. The primary aims of this validation step are to validate first the feasibility of operationalizing the indicators, second the feasibility of capturing indicator values in practice, and third fitness of the indicators for the determinants.

4.1   Case Study Company

The industrial case is a producer of outdoor power products including, e.g., chainsaws, trimmers, robotic lawn mowers and garden tractors. The company offers products and services for both the private and industrial market. The company is in a transformation process where many of the products are enhanced and redefined by equipping them with sensors and actuators and by defining and transforming the accompanying services. Many of the products for professional customers do not only have built-in embedded systems but also networking abilities. The built-in embedded systems are used for controlling the different mechatronic sub-systems of the product and for collecting information when the product is in use. Example: for a fleet of trimmers and garden tractors used by a housing company, sensors can collect vibration information of the individual devices to predict maintenance needs; for the overall fleet, statistics of the device use and runtimes can be applied for economic calculations and to detect the need for additional devices.

Since many of the products offer similar functionality regarding networking and built-in sub-systems, the case study company designed and implemented reusable services and components for either products or back-office infrastructure. From an enterprise architecture management perspective, the challenge is to integrate these product-related components and services into the general enterprise architecture of the company, which so far was focused on administrative and resource planning issues. Without integration, there would be a danger of developing services for the products again which already exist for the enterprise (e.g., license management, customer identification, security services). On the other hand, the lifecycle of product-related components is much shorter than the lifecycle of enterprise applications, which leads to conflicts in architecture management [35].

The case study company has a defined enterprise architecture and the management of the architecture (roles, processes, policies) is implemented. The company currently undergoes a digital transformation process, which is also visible in company strategies and resource allocations. This makes the case a good basis for the intended validation of the research model.

4.2   Validation of Indicators

In a first validation step, we checked if the proposed indicators (shown in Fig. 1 on the left) could be operationalized and captured in the case study company:

- Future business requirements are frequently analyzed in the case study company, including competing enterprises, new technologies or related innovations. The results of this analysis are captured in internal documents or in reports provided by consultancies. The indicators for the business environment can be captured by analyzing the reports and documents and possibly be rated according to their level of detail or up-to-date-ness.
- The IT landscape is captured within the enterprise architecture model and the related information systems, like the configuration management database (CMDB). Most of the indicators listed in the research model are readily available and are already evaluated by the case study company for roadmap planning. However, the

indicator "business model" is not visible and from the perspective of the research model, it should be considered to move this indicator to another determinant or to split it into several indicators.

- The internal business is in the case study company divided into production, development, operation and administration. Business processes are defined; business strategy is broken down to business line level and documented. The level of professionalism and business/IT alignment can be interpreted in different ways and would – from the perspective of the case study company – call for further refinement.
- The indicators related to "EAM establishment" can be directly linked to the extent and way roles, structures, processes, landscape and implementation are established, defined, documented and in operation. In the case study company, a collection of general policy documents, process and mandate descriptions and the system support for "IT landscape" management exist.

The above analysis of the indicators also gives some hints regarding the fitness of the indicators for the determinants. The business model might have to be moved to another determinant. Professionalism and business/IT alignment probably need a refinement. Furthermore, it was observed that staff-related issue could be a candidate for another determinant. This, however, is not grounded by the available literature. Table 2 summarizes the validation results.

Table 2. Summary of indicator validation

	Feasible to operationalize the indicators?	Feasible to capture values in use case?	Fitness of indicators to determinants?
Business environment	Yes – by rating explicit documentation and level of detail	Yes – from frequent reports on market and technology developments	Yes
IT landscape	Yes – by using the operationalization implement in EAM systems, like planning IT	Yes – EAM system is available	Yes – with exception of "business model"
Internal business	Yes – with focus on refinement levels of processes and details of strategies and with exception of "professionalism" and "IT business alignments"	Yes – business processes and business strategy are defined and documented	Yes
EAM establishment	Yes – with focus on documentation and implementation of EAM structures and processes	Yes – partly using the same sources as for "IT landscape"	Yes

5 Conclusion and Outlook

Enterprise Architecture reflects the IT infrastructure and business processes. It shows how to align business and IT components in conjunction with the objectives and strategies of enterprises [1]. Aligning business processes and IT is an important task of general management. In addition, EAM plays a crucial role in implementing the vision of digital enterprises [33]. Based on the determinants *Business Environment* (external), *IT Landscape*, *Internal Business* as well as *EAM Establishment*, the authors found four main factors with 22 indicators positively influencing the benefit of EAM. Moreover, there are two moderating effects found, Firm Size and Industry Complexity, which positively affect the influences with respect to the benefit of EAM.

This paper is based on a first approach to investigate additional factors and neglected impact factors with respect to the benefit of EAM in relation to digital transformation. An extensive and structured literature research shows a new conceptual research model with clear influencing factors and related indicators. Applied to an industrial digital transformation case study most of the proposed indicators could be operationalized and values could be captured. Also the indicators have been proved suitable for the determinants with exception of "business model". In this context, the authors claim that some influencing factors and indicators were incorrectly represented or even missing within past researches.

Still, there are some limitations within this research. First, a further qualitative research approach might investigate more detailed factors or indicators. Second, the empirical research model should be proved by a quantitative approach. In addition, there are general limitations regarding our qualitative research design as there might be even more databases and valuable work (e.g. paper in supposedly poorer journals) to consider when reviewing literature. Additionally, it was not possible for us to find relevant papers from A-Journals within literature research. Furthermore, it was not our intention to test the hypotheses in the industrial case, as this would require the possibility of comparison or benchmarking with other companies. The validation of the indicators was purely textual/argumentative, which is why future investigations can start here by operationalizing the presented constructs in the presented study model.

Academics can learn from a new classification of influencing factors and related indicators regarding the benefit of EAM and can improve previous study designs. The theoretical research model with testable hypotheses can be optimized and more domain-specific correlations can be explored. The paper makes a valuable contribution to practice as they can use the proposed factors of each hypothesis to initiate own EAM endeavours. Thus, practitioners can use the classification to evaluate and improve current EAM implementations. Future research might be able to develop new models on the benefit of EAM in relation to digital transformation whereupon industry sector specific adoptions of the classification can be considered [34].

References

1. Lange, M., Mendling, J., Recker, J.: An empirical analysis of the factors and measures of enterprise architecture management success. Eur. J. Inf. Syst. **25**, 411–431 (2016)
2. Möhring, M., Schmidt, R., Härting, R.-C., Bär, F., Zimmermann, A.: Classification framework for context data from business processes. In: Fournier, F., Mendling, J. (eds.) BPM 2014. LNBIP, vol. 202, pp. 440–445. Springer, Cham (2015). https://doi.org/10.1007/978-3-319-15895-2_37
3. Zimmermann, A., et al.: Decision case management for digital enterprise architectures with the Internet of Things. In: Neves-Silva, R., Jain, L., Howlett, R.: Proceedings of the 8th KES International Conference on Intelligent Decision Technologies Smart Innovation, Systems and Technologies (KES-IDT 2016), pp. 27–37. Springer, Heidelberg (2016). https://doi.org/10.1007/978-3-319-39627-9_3
4. Wegmann, A.: The systemic enterprise architecture methodology (SEAM) - business and IT alignment for competitiveness. In: International Conference on Enterprise Information Systems 2003 (ICEIS 2003), pp. 483–490 (2003)
5. Tamm, T., Seddon, P.B., Shanks, G., Reynolds, P.: How does enterprise architecture add value to organizations? Commun. Assoc. Inf. Syst. **28**(10), 141–168 (2011)
6. Niemi, E.: Perceptions from literature and practice, evaluation of enterprise and software architectures: critical issues, metrics and practices: AISA Project 8. University of Jyväskylä, Information Technology Research Institute (2008)
7. Schmidt, C., Buxmann, P.: Outcomes and success factors of enterprise IT architecture management: empirical insight from the international financial services industry. Eur. J. Inf. Syst. **20**(2), 168–185 (2011)
8. Cooper, D.R., Schindler, P.S., Sun, J.: Business research methods (2013). http://sutlib2.sut.ac.th/sut_contents/H139963.pdf. Accessed 19 Feb 2015
9. Cooper, H.M.: Synthesizing Research – A Guide for Literature Reviews, vol. 3. Sage, Thousand Oaks (1998)
10. Hennig-Thurau, T., Walsh, G., Schrader, U.: VHB-JOURQUAL: Ein Ranking von betriebswirtschaftlich-relevanten Zeitschriften auf der Grundlage von Expertenurteilen. Z. betriebswirtsch. Forsch. **56**(9), 520–545 (2004)
11. Computing Research & Education: Conference rankings. http://www.core.edu.au/index.php/conference-rankings. Accessed 20 July 2016
12. Schmidt, R., Möhring, M., Härting, R.-C., Reichstein, C., Zimmermann, A., Luceri, S.: Benefits of enterprise architecture management – insights from European experts. IFIP Working Conference on The Practice of Enterprise Modeling, pp. 223–236. Springer, Heidelberg (2015). https://doi.org/10.1007/978-3-319-25897-3_15
13. Ross, J.W., Weill, P., Robertson, D.C.: Enterprise Architecture As Strategy, vol. 1. Harvard Business School Press, Brighton (2006)
14. Sandkuhl, K., Wißotzki, M., Stirna, J.: Unternehmensmodellierung: Grundlagen, Methode und Praktiken. Berlin, Wiesbaden: Springer (2013). https://doi.org/10.1007/978-3-642-31093-5
15. Hanschke, I.: Strategisches Management der IT-Landschaft: Ein praktischer Leitfaden für das Enterprise Architecture Management, vol. 2. Carl Hanser, Munich (2010)
16. BITKOM: Enterprise Architecture Management – neue Disziplin für die ganzheitliche Unternehmensentwicklung (2011). https://www.bitkom.org/Bitkom/Publikationen/Leitfaden-EAM-Enterprise-Architecture-Management.html. Accessed 10 July 2016
17. Aier, S., Riege, C., Winter, R.: Unternehmensarchitektur – Literaturüberblick und Stand der Praxis. Wirtschaftsinformatik **50**(4), 292–304 (2008)

18. Wigand, R.T., Picot, A., Reichwald, R.: Information, Organization and Management: Expanding Markets and Corporate Boundaries. Wiley, Hoboken (1997)
19. Pereira, C.M., Sousa, P.: Enterprise architecture: business and IT alignment. In: Proceedings of the ACM Symposium on Applied Computing, pp. 1344–1345 (2005)
20. Luftman, J.: Assessing business-IT alignment maturity. In: Strategies for Information Technology Governance, vol. 4, p. 99 (2004)
21. Luftman, J., Brier, T.: Achieving and sustaining business-IT alignment. Calif. Manag. Rev. **42**, 109–122 (1999)
22. Hanschke, I.: Enterprise Architecture Management – einfach und effektiv: Ein praktischer Leitfaden für die Einführung von EAM. vol. 2, Munich (2011)
23. Timm, F., Wißotzki, M., Köpp, Ch., Sandkuhl, K.: Current state of enterprise architecture management in SME. In: INFORMATIK 2015 - 45. Jahrestagung der Gesellschaft für Informatik, Workshop Digital Enterprise Architecture, DEA 2015, Cottbus, Germany (2015)
24. Hanschke, S., Ernsting, J., Kuchen, H.: Integrating agile software development and enterprise architecture management. In: 48th Hawaii International Conference on System Sciences (HICSS), pp. 4099–4108 (2015)
25. Lakhrouit, J., Ba, K.: Evaluating complexity of enterprise architecture components landscapes. In: 10th International Conference on Intelligent Systems: Theories and Applications, pp. 1–5 (2015)
26. Plataniotis, G., De Kinderen, S., Ma, Q., Proper, E.: A conceptual model for compliance checking support of enterprise architecture decisions. In: 17th Conference on Business Informatics, vol. 1, pp. 191–198 (2015)
27. Banaeianjahromi, N., Smolander, K.: What do we know about the role of enterprise architecture in enterprise integration? a systematic mapping study. J. Enterp. Inf. Manag. **29** (1), 140–164 (2016)
28. Hinkelmann, K., Gerber, A., Karagiannis, D., Thoenssen, B., van der Merwe, A., Woitsch, R.: A new paradigm for the continuous alignment of business and IT: combining enterprise architecture modelling and enterprise ontology. Comput. Ind. **79**, 77–86 (2016)
29. Geerts, G.L., O'Leary, D.E.: A Note on an Architecture for Integrating Cloud Computing and Enterprise Systems using REA. Int. J. Acc. Inf. Syst. **19**, 59–67 (2015)
30. Rouhani, B.D., Mahrin, M.N.R., Nikpay, F., Ahmad, R.B., Nikfard, P.: A Systematic Literature Review on Enterprise Architecture Implementation Methodologies. Inf. Softw. Technol. **62**, 1–20 (2015)
31. Azevedo, C.L., Iacob, M.E., Almeida, J.P.A., van Sinderen, M., Pires, L.F., Guizzardi, G.: Modeling resources and capabilities in enterprise architecture: a well-founded ontology-based proposal for archimate. Inf. Syst. **54**, 235–262 (2015)
32. Alwadain, A., Fielt, E., Korthaus, A., Rosemann, M.: empirical insights into the development of a service-oriented enterprise architecture. Data Knowl. Eng. **105**, 39–52 (2015)
33. Lapalme, J., Gerber, A., Van der Merwe, A., Zachman, J., De Vries, M., Hinkelmann, K.: Exploring the future of enterprise architecture: a zachman Perspective. Comput. Ind. **79**, 103–113 (2016)
34. Romero, D., Vernadat, F.: Enterprise information systems state of the art: past, present and future trends. Comput. Ind. **79**, 3–13 (2015)
35. Sandkuhl, K., Seigerroth, U., Kaidalova, J.: Towards Integration Methods of Product-IT into Enterprise Architectures. In: EDOC Workshops, pp. 23–28. IEEE (2017)
36. Härting, R.C., Reichstein, C., Jozinovic, P.: The Potential value of digitization for business – insights from German-speaking experts. In: Eibl, M., Gaedke, M. (eds.) Informatik 2017, Jahrestagung der Gesellschaft für Informatik. Lecture Notes in Informatics (LNI), vol. 1647, Gesellschaft für Informatik, Bonn (2017)

Business and Information Technology Alignment Measurement - A Recent Literature Review

Leonardo Muñoz[(✉)] and Oscar Avila[(✉)]

Department of Systems and Computing Engineering, School of Engineering,
Universidad de los Andes, Bogotá, Colombia
{l.munozm,oj.avila}@uniandes.edu.co

Abstract. Since technology has been involved in the business context, Business and Information Technology Alignment (BITA) has been one of the main concerns of IT and Business executives and directors due to its importance to overall company performance, especially today in the age of digital transformation. Several models and frameworks have been developed for BITA implementation and for measuring their level of success, each one with a different approach to this desired state. The BITA measurement is one of the main decision-making tools in the strategic domain of companies. In general, the classical-internal alignment is the most measured domain and the external environment evolution alignment is the least measured. This literature review aims to characterize and analyze current research on BITA measurement with a comprehensive view of the works published over the last 15 years to identify potential gaps and future areas of research in the field.

Keywords: Fit · Coherence · Relationship · Measurement · Measuring
Assessing · Evaluating · Qualitative · Quantitative · Model

1 Introduction

Currently all organizations are leveraged by technology at different levels, from the operational to the strategical. Due to this growing relationship, several frameworks and approaches have been developed to model and achieve alignment between traditional business structures and the technology domain. The main objective of these Business and Information Technology Alignment (BITA) models and methods is to transform the way business and Information Technology (IT) domains understand each other in terms of objectives and requirements in business execution.

In this line of ideas, one of the biggest problems in organizations is the misalignment between business and IT objectives and needs. Because each of these domains works independently for their improvement through individual frameworks, the result is failed projects and delays in overall company performance. For this reason, BITA has been one of the main concerns of business and IT directors in the last decade [1–3], due to the fact that BITA helps to close the gaps in communication and

© Springer Nature Switzerland AG 2019
W. Abramowicz and A. Paschke (Eds.): BIS 2018 Workshops, LNBIP 339, pp. 112–123, 2019.
https://doi.org/10.1007/978-3-030-04849-5_10

interaction between Business and IT domains in organizations. This implies that also measuring and evaluating such alignment is an important concern.

The importance of BITA measurement in the organizations is that it constitutes one of the main sources of information for the decision-making process. Commonly, BITA measurement have been focused on the "classical" internal alignment, which is related to the measurement of the alignment between the business strategy and processes and the IT resources. But, the modern organizations must have to evaluate two other alignment levels that are, the alignment with the external environment and the alignment with uncertain future evolutions [4]. These alignments with the environment and future evolutions àre not currently the focus on the BITA measurement area, what means that the organizations are not prepared to the modern enterprise environment which is in continuous and fast changing. This lack of focus on the alignment with future evolutions and external environment could be one of the main problems of organizations because they depend on the changing external market. The BITA measurement at these levels could improve the sustainability and growth of the companies.

Considering this concern, the main objective of this article is to evaluate the most recent works in the literature of BITA measurement to identify their contributions to the three alignment levels above mentioned: classical strategic alignment, alignment with the external environment and alignment with the external evolutions. Based on the evaluation results, our purpose is to present the potential gaps and propose future areas of research. This article is organised as follows: the second section describes the study methodology and evaluation framework to review existing literature, which includes evaluation categories, criteria and questions. The third section describes how the research literature was evaluated. The fourth section describes the application of the framework and the synthesis and analysis of corresponding results. Finally, in the fifth section, the findings and conclusions are presented to lay foundations for future research.

2 Study Methodology and Evaluation Framework

The literature review process includes:

(i)   *Planning.* It consists in the selection of the categories and criteria which will be used to design the evaluation framework for the selected articles.
(ii) *Realization.* This step consists in the definition of the research terms to make the search and selection of the articles to be evaluated.
(iii) *Synthesis and analysis.* This step presents the evaluation framework application to the selected articles and the analysis of the results for each research question.

2.1 Planning

This work aims to evaluate the last 15 years of research literature on BITA measurement methods and approaches. For the evaluation of this set of articles, the proposed framework in [5] was adopted as a basis to develop a personalized evaluation framework. To classify the BITA approaches, the Strategic Alignment Model (SAM) [6] proposed by Henderson and Venkatraman was also adopted as one of the base criteria to evaluate the scope of the works being reviewed. Based on this, a characterization framework was defined to review current research on BITA measurement methods and approaches. This framework has three main categories, each with specific criteria for proposing research questions (See Table 1).

Table 1. Proposed evaluation framework.

Category	Criteria	Questions
Context	Objective	What is the main objective of the article?
Alignment	Strategic alignment	Which organizational domains of the business context can be aligned?
		According to the SAM alignment model, which is the alignment sequence of the applied model?
	Environment alignment	Which external environment elements of the business and IT are aligned?
	Future alignment	Which temporal dimensions are approached by the alignment model used?
	Alignment level	Which alignment levels are addressed?
Measurement	Method type	Which is the type of measurement method approached?
	Measurement nature	Which is the nature of the measurement method approached?
	Metrics	Which are the measurement criteria and metrics of the method?
	Methodology	Which are the steps included in methodology applied?

Context. This category looks for identifying the objective of the reviewed works and identifying common characteristics in such objetives.

Alignment. This category aims to understand the alignment scope of BITA measurement models in terms of the three alignment levels mentioned above (see introduction section). This analysis is intended to know at which alignment levels measurement is made at each approach. According to [4], in BITA we can classify the alignment in: First, the classical-internal alignment that aims to align all the organization areas with IT. Second, the alignment with the environment, referring to the external actors and events which could affect the organization. Finally, the alignment with uncertain evolutions related to future changes in the internal domains of the organization and the external environment.

Measurement. This category examines the nature, the type and other details of the measurement method. This is the focus of our work and for this reason it is the main section of the proposed framework in this article (see Table 1).

3   Realization

For conducting the identification of the related articles, SCOPUS was adopted as search tool, keeping in mind it is the largest and one of the main scientific abstract and citation databases [7].

To find the set of academic articles for the evaluation, the search query showed below was used on the SCOPUS platform:

TITLE-ABS("Alignment" OR "Match" OR "Fit" OR "Fitness" OR "Strategic alignment" OR "Coordination" OR "Link") AND TITLE-ABS("Business and IT" OR "Business/IT" OR "Business-IT" OR "Business/IS" OR "Business and IS" OR "Business-IS" OR "Business and Information Systems" OR "Business and Information technology" OR "Business and Information technologies") AND TITLE-ABS ("Measurement" OR "Assessment" OR "Measure" OR "Assess" OR "Evaluation" OR "Evaluate" OR "measuring" OR "evaluating" OR "assessing")

The search yielded 386 results. A second filter was made by scanning the titles and abstracts to obtain a set of articles that were closely related to the measurement topic. Following, through the reading and detailed review, the final set was defined, consisting of 22 articles which present different methods and approaches for BITA measurement [8–29]. The proposed evaluation framework was applied to this set of articles, answering each of the research questions in each category and criteria. For the analysis of this set, reference works such as Henderson and Venkatraman and Luftman were used. These are fundamental for the BITA research and its measurement.

4   Synthesis and Analysis

For the synthesis and analysis, we review the selected works with respect to each research question in the framework. In general, we found that the approaches in current literature are not homogenous. The synthesis of the review is presented below.

4.1   Context

Which is the Main Objective of the Research Work?
Across the 22 articles reviewed, we found that the focus in the last years of research was to present new methods and approaches for measuring alignment without a case study application (46% of the articles); articles that apply alignment methods to different specific cases of study (36% of the articles) and articles that present both, new approaches and its application (18% of the article). Many of the new proposed approaches have one or more previous frameworks as the base of development, producing thus enhanced methods through the adoption of one of the existing approaches or a mix of them.

4.2   Alignment

What Organizational Domains of the Business Context Can be Aligned?
Despite the variety of terminology, most of the reviewed works rely on to two main Business and IT modelling approaches:

First, the *EA metamodels* in [10–16], where layers, domains or other elements involved in alignment measuring are: Business architecture, data architecture, application architecture, and technology architecture.

Second, the *SAM* in [8, 9, 12, 14, 16–22, 25–29] in which the aligned domains are: Business Strategy, IT strategy, Business Infrastructure, IT infrastructure.

To standardize and simplify the evaluation of the literature, we adopted the SAM, which is described in Fig. 1a, as the base of characterization.

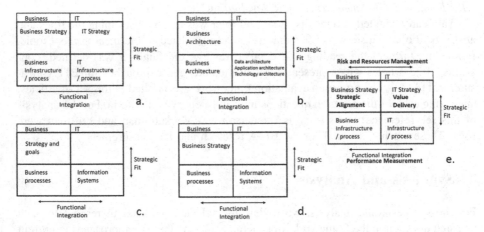

Fig. 1. a. SAM domains [6]; b. EA domains mapped into SAM domains; c. L.-H. Thevenet proposed alignment mapped into SAM; d. Doumi et al. Proposed alignment model mapped into SAM; e. SAM and COBIT (Bold) domains combined

According to our decision of relying on the SAM as reference framework, we map in the Fig. 1b the common EA domains used by the reviewed works, such as the domains of the EA Planning (EAP) [30], the layers of TOGAF [31] and the Zachman's levels [32]. Those are the most widespread EA models according to [33].

Differing from these common models, we have found some variants in terminology in the reviewed articles that we have mapped into the SAM domains. Thus, the Fig. 1c shows the mapping of the Thevenet's approach [23] and the Fig. 1d the mapping of the Doumi's approach [24]. In other custom cases we found that the SAM is combined with other frameworks. For instance, [18] presents a mix of the SAM and COBIT which we have mapped in the Fig. 1e.

In this way we found that in BITA measurement, Business Infrastructure and IT infrastructure has been the focus in the 86% of the articles. The IT and Business strategies are only considered as main evaluated domains in 50% and 68% of the reviewed articles, respectively. This last finding reveals a lack of focus in the strategic layer.

Table 2. Alignment sequence classification

Alignment perspective	Figure 2	Figure 3	Figure 4	Figure 5	Figure 6
Quantity of articles	13	2	1	1	3
Articles where sequence is addressed	[8, 11, 12, 14-20, 22, 23,24]	[11, 12]	[10]	[21]	[9, 13, 25]

According to the SAM, Which is the Alignment Sequence of the Applied Model?
In order to describe the relationship or alignment between domains in which measurement is addressed in the reviewed works, we use alignment sequences of the SAM [6]. To this end, we use the domain roles used in [5] and the alignment perspectives proposed in [34] (See Table 2). The following domain roles are thus considered:

Anchor: the starting domain of the alignment sequence, represented by a square.
Pivot: the intermediate domain involved in the alignment sequence, represented by a circle.
Impacted: the final point of the alignment sequence, represented by an arrow head

The following alignment perspectives are considered:

Strategy Execution Perspective. It refers to a top-down sequence where the IT enables the business infrastructure and processes to execute the business strategies (see Fig. 2 in Table 2).

Technology Potential. In this perspective the focus is on the fit between business and IT strategies to enable new business strategy based on the technology application (see Fig. 3 in Table 2).

Competitive Potential. This perspective the focus is on the fit between business and IT strategies to do more competitive the business processes (see Fig. 4 in Table 2).

Service Level. This perspective focuses on deliver IT services and resources to enable business processes (see Fig. 5 in Table 2).

Functional Integration. This sequence focuses on the integrations of the business processes with the IT services and resources without an IT strategy (see Fig. 6 in Table 2).

Considering the elements defined above for the evaluation of alignment sequences, the Table 2 show the quantity of research works that correspond better to each alignment perspective as well as the reference to those works. The results shows that the sequence in which alignment measurement is most carried out is Strategy Execution. This reflects that the traditional alignment sequence is the most addressed in the reviewed measurement approaches. The remaining sequences have a low development in the reviewed works.

Last, two of the reviewed articles [26, 27] are not included in the alignment sequence evaluation, because these are focused on developing frameworks to classify the current evaluation methods. Also, the works [28, 29] have not been included because they address alignment measurement in all the sequences, due to they are a SAMM [28] application cases.

Which External Environment Elements of the Business and IT are Aligned?
In this question, we use three external elements as possible responses [35]:

Actors: It refers to the external networks of actors present in the environment where organizations are involved.

Uses: It refers to the demands of the external environment of the organization, specifically referring to IT uses.

Issues: It groups all the external problematic situations where the organization could be involved and the barriers for the achievement of the objectives.

In the review, all the measurement methods and approaches focus only on the classical-internal level and, due to this, there are no external elements considered in the assessments. There is therefore a lack of external environment alignment measurement methods. This constitutes one of the main gaps that must be approached in future BITA measurement research.

Which Temporal Dimensions are Approached by the Alignment Model Used?
To answer this question, we have adopted two temporal states for the organizations [35]:

As-Is: referring to the current state.
To-Be: referring to the expected future state.

In this order, in all the reviewed work, the current state of the organization or *As-Is* is assessed. This show that measuring alignment of the current organizational and IT elements is the main objective of the BITA measurement processes. Even though the explicit assessment of the future state or *To-Be* is presented as the base for performance improvement, only three works [8, 20, 21] address alignment at this time-pitch. For instance, a fuzzy logic method is used in [8] to predict the future state based on the *As-Is* and the alignment sequence. The contributions of these three works are important because one of the main BITA measurement objectives is to establish a path for future action, but in general most of the methods only gives a diagnosis at the As-Is state.

Which Alignment Levels are Addressed by the Work?
In this review we found that in the 100% of the BITA measurement approaches, the classical-internal alignment level is the focus, only one approach of BITA measurement

in [8] is related with the future state through a fuzzy logic expert system and there is no explicit focus on the external environment alignment. The articles [20, 21] mention the To-Be as desired state based on predictions but it is not really addressed and not is the main topic of the papers.

4.3 Measurement

Which is the Type of Measurement Method Approached?

According to [36] we adopted two options as possible response for the measurement type:

The *model-based* type which is focused on assessing the strength or quality of the link or relationship between the modelled elements in business and IT domains. Generally, the information used to carry out such measurement is obtained from documented models in the organization.

The *perception-based* type in which the evaluation is made from the perception of the actors (users, managers, etc.) in the different domains and levels of the organization. Generally, the information to undertake this type of measurement is obtained from surveys and interviews.

In our review we have found that approximately half of the reviewed works have each of these types of measurement, for model-based [8–10, 12, 13, 21, 23, 24, 26, 27] and for perception-based [11, 14–20, 22, 25, 28, 29]. It is logical, keeping in mind that the Luftman's method [28] (perception-based oriented) and the EA frameworks (model-based oriented) are the most widely adopted in the business environment.

Some of the last works like in [12], have begun to combine both perception and model-based measurement methods. This seems to be a more complex but also a more complete measurement approach.

Which is the Nature of the Measurement Method Approached?

To evaluate the nature of the measurement method, we define two classification categories, which are linked to the type criterion in last question, as possible response:

Qualitative nature: in this category the methods that yield a result are based on the quality of the alignment. These are not based on exact quantifiable scores that measure the alignment level. Conversely, they are mostly based on the perceptions of the quality of the fit between business and IT elements.

Quantitative nature: in this category the methods yield quantifiable scores based on the relationship between the modelled elements in the business and IT domains.

When reviewing the works, we found that the nature of the measurement methods used and developed are more oriented toward qualitative approaches. The results show that 50% of the articles have a qualitative nature and are based on evaluation scales that define a quality level of the alignment in the organizations [10, 11, 16, 17, 19, 20, 22, 25, 26, 28, 29], but with a wide range of error. It could be due to the high ambiguity of the comprehensive vision of the alignment in an enterprise scenario. The remaining reviewed articles are distributed in quantitative approaches in [9, 13, 15, 21, 23, 24, 27] (32%) and a mix of quantitative/qualitative approaches in [8, 12, 14, 18] (18%). The mixed nature could address a diagnosis with a more exact classification of the alignment levels, including a wide range of aspects that are defined as not only technically oriented.

Which are the Measurement Criteria and Metrics of the Method?
In the measurement process a variety of measurement criteria and metrics are defined, which are necessary to quantify or qualify the level of BITA. These criteria and metrics are closely related to the nature of the measurement method as the metrics define such nature. In the reviewed literature, the most adopted criteria by the reviewed articles (55%) correspond the SAMM six criteria, proposed by Luftman [28], which are used to measure the maturity of the BITA. The SAMM criteria are:

1. Communication
2. Competency/Value Measurements
3. Governance
4. Partnership
5. Technology Scope
6. Skills

Each one of these criteria are evaluated by using a five-level scale, in which each level possesses a list of defined best practices to be assessed in the organization. In some cases, the SAMM is completely adopted [28, 29], but, in general, the developed methods customize the five evaluation levels and the formulation of best practices as in [22] by using the Likert scale. Such changes are made in order to find a better match with the specific organizational departments and their culture. In this way, they obtain more accurate results in the assessment application.

In the remaining articles, in second position, some libraries of EA misalignment symptoms are included as the criteria and metrics base. These libraries are the comparative base to obtain quantifiable rates with the EA modelled elements in the organization. Finally, in our review we found that, in a lower proportion, some methods have custom metrics based on the experts' definitions and perceptions and in other modelling elements, like the ontologies, where the metrics are the rate of mapped ontologies from each domain in the organization. In these remaining metrics we also found: Key Performance Indicators (KPIs), COBIT control objectives and Crucial success factors (CSF).

Which are the Steps Included in Methodology Applied?
In this compilation of BITA measurement literature it is difficult to find a common structure of application methodology. This difficulty is due to the wide variety and heterogeneity of the current methods. Nevertheless, we found three general steps that are fundamental in any BITA measurement method. These steps are:

1. Describe the organization context by using modelling tools to have a parametrized scenario to work with.
2. Customize the BITA measurement tools to the context, organization departments and culture.
3. Assess all the organization departments.

5 Conclusions

The first conclusion of this literature review is that, in general, the measurement of the classical-internal BITA has been widely developed, supported in the need of performance improvement in the functioning of the organizations, at the level of internal processes and IT resources use. However, there is a lack of focus in BITA on the external environment of the companies. This is an important finding due to the current fast changing markets where traditional and modern companies are converging and competing. In addition, the new managing models such as outsourcing, offshoring and join-ventures in which alignment with external actors is indispensable has also increased the need for BITA measurement with the external extended organization.

The external BITA measurement could be addressed by including in the models and methodologies some frameworks such as Porter's five forces, presented in [37], which can help to complement the scope of the current methods and models.

Despite the fact that the SAM and the EA Frameworks are widely adopted, the selection of adequate tools and guidelines for BITA and its measurement continues to be complex due to the high ambiguity that BITA involves. The current advances are the basis for possible first steps toward a common standard for BITA, producing mixes of the methods, and producing more complete frameworks that are also contextualized with the organizations. The potential gap here is to find a common BITA standard which could be dynamic and flexible enough for the variety of organization contexts and approaches.

References

1. Luftman, J., Derksen, B.: Key issues for IT executives 2012: doing more with less. MIS Q. Exec. **11**, 207–218 (2012)
2. Luftman, J., Lyytinen, K., ben Zvi, T.: Enhancing the measurement of information technology (IT) business alignment and its influence on company performance. J. Inf. Technol. **32**(1), 26–46 (2017)
3. Luftman, J., Derksen, B., Dwivedi, R., Santana, M., Zadeh, H.S., Rigoni, E.: Influential IT management trends: an international study. J. Inf. Technol. **30**, 293–305 (2015)
4. Avila, O., Goepp, V., Kiefer, F.: ATIS: a method for the complete alignment of technical information systems. Int. J. Comput. Integr. Manuf. **24**(11), 993–1009 (2011)
5. Avila, O., Goepp, V., Kiefer, F.: Understanding and classifying information system alignment approaches. J. Comput. Inf. Syst. **50**(1), 2–14 (2009)
6. Henderson, J.C., Venkatraman, N.: Strategic alignment: leveraging information technology for transforming organizations. IBM Syst. J. **32**(1), 4–16 (1993)
7. Mongeon, P., Paul-Hus, A.: The journal coverage of web of science and scopus: a comparative analysis. Scientometrics **106**(1), 213–228 (2016)
8. Nadali, A., Pourdarab, S., Mazloumi, A., Nosratabadi, H.E.: Maturity assessment of business/IT alignment using fuzzy expert system. In: Communications in Computer and Information Science, CCIS, vol. 194, pp. 724–738 (2011)
9. Etien, A., Rolland, C.: Measuring the fitness relationship. Requir. Eng. **10**, 184–197 (2005)

10. Ori, D.: Misalignment symptom analysis based on enterprise architecture model assessment. In: Proceedings of the International Conferences on ICT, Society and Human Beings 2014, Web Based Communities and Social Media 2014, e-Commerce 2014, Information Systems Post-Implementation and Change Management 2014 and e-Health 2014 - Part of the Multi Conference, pp. 191–198 (2014)

11. Wagter, R., Proper, H.A., Witte, D.: Enterprise coherence assessment version. In: Harmsen, F., Grahlmann, K., Proper, E. (eds.) PRET 2011. LNBIP, vol. 89, pp. 28–52. Springer, Heidelberg (2011). https://doi.org/10.1007/978-3-642-23388-3_2

12. Őri, D.: An artifact-based framework for business-IT misalignment symptom detection. In: Horkoff, J., Jeusfeld, M.A., Persson, A. (eds.) PoEM 2016. LNBIP, vol. 267, pp. 148–163. Springer, Cham (2016). https://doi.org/10.1007/978-3-319-48393-1_11

13. Őri, D.: Misalignment symptom detection with XML-based enterprise architecture model analysis. In: CEUR Workshop Proceedings, vol. 1859, pp. 153–157 (2017)

14. Plazaola, L., Flores, J., Vargas, N., Ekstedt, M.: Strategic business and IT alignment assessment: a case study applying an enterprise architecture-based metamodel. In: Proceedings of the Annual Hawaii International Conference on System Sciences, no. 4439103 (2008)

15. van der Raadt, B., Hoorn, J.F., van Vliet, H.: Alignment and maturity are siblings in architecture assessment. In: Pastor, O., Falcão e Cunha, J. (eds.) CAiSE 2005. LNCS, vol. 3520, pp. 357–371. Springer, Heidelberg (2005). https://doi.org/10.1007/11431855_25

16. Rakgoale, M.A., Mentz, J.C.: Proposing a measurement model to determine enterprise architecture success as a feasible mechanism to align business and IT. In: Proceedings - 2015 3rd International Conference on Enterprise Systems, ES 2015, pp. 214–224 (2016)

17. Cuenca, L., de Dios Milla, J., Boza, A.: Business and IT alignment in companies of Valencian community in Spain. Direccion y Organizacion 55, 38–43 (2016)

18. Hosseinbeig, S., Moghadam, D.K., Vahdat, D., Moghadam, R.A.: Combination of IT strategic alignment and IT governance to evaluate strategic alignment maturity. In: 2011 5th International Conference on Application of Information and Communication Technologies, AICT 2011, no. 6110901 (2011)

19. Khanfar, M., Zualkernan, I.A.: Assessing the IT-business alignment maturity in a hospitality and exhibition company. In: 2010 2nd International Conference on Engineering System Management and Applications, ICESMA 2010, no. 5542653 (2010)

20. Silvius, A., Waal, B.D.: Assessing business and IT alignment in educational organizations. In: 2010 International Conference on Computational Intelligence and Software Engineering, CISE 2010, no. 5677247 (2010)

21. Sarandis, M.: A simulation-based approach for IT and business strategy alignment and evaluation. Int. J. Bus. Inf. Syst. 10(4), 369–396 (2012)

22. Khaiata, M., Zualkernan, I.A.: A simple instrument to measure IT-business alignment maturity. Inf. Syst. Manag. 26(2), 138–152 (2009)

23. Thevenet, L.-H.: Modeling strategic alignment using INSTAL. In: Song, I.-Y., et al. (eds.) ER 2008. LNCS, vol. 5232, pp. 261–271. Springer, Heidelberg (2008). https://doi.org/10.1007/978-3-540-87991-6_32

24. Doumi, K., Baïna, S., Baïna, K.: Strategic business and IT alignment: representation and evaluation. J. Theor. Appl. Inf. Technol. 47(1), 41–52 (2013)

25. Umoh, E., Sampaio, P.R.F., Theodoulidis, B.: Measuring and evaluating business-IT alignment for RAD projects using the REFINTO framework and tool. In: Proper, E., Gaaloul, K., Harmsen, F., Wrycza, S. (eds.) PRET 2012. LNBIP, vol. 120, pp. 96–119. Springer, Heidelberg (2012). https://doi.org/10.1007/978-3-642-31134-5_5

26. El-Mekawy, M., Rusu, L., Perjons, E.: An evaluation framework for comparing business-IT alignment models: a tool for supporting collaborative learning in organizations. Comput. Hum. Behav. **51**, 1229–1247 (2015)
27. Goepp, V., Petit, M.: Towards an enterprise architecture based strategic alignment model an evaluation of SAM based on ISO 15704. In: ICEIS 2013 - Proceedings of the 15th International Conference on Enterprise Information Systems, vol. 3, pp. 370–375 (2013)
28. Luftman, J.: Assessing IT/business alignment. Inf. Syst. Manag. **20**(4), 9–15 (2003)
29. Sledgianowski, D., Luftman, J.: IT-business strategic alignment maturity: a case study. J. Cases Inf. Technol. **7**, 102–120 (2005)
30. Spewak, S., Hill, S.C.: Enterprise Architecture Planning: Developing a Blueprint for Data, Applications, and Technology. Wiley, Hoboken (1992)
31. The Open Group: The Open Group Architecture Framework TOGAF™ Version 9, Basharat Hussain (2009)
32. Zachman, J.A.: A framework for information systems architecture. IBM Syst. J. **26**(3), 276–292 (1987)
33. Minoli, D.: Enterprise Architecture A to Z: Frameworks, Business Process Modeling, SOA, and Infrastructure Technology. CRC Press, Boca Raton (2008)
34. Luftman, J.N., Lewis, P.R., Oldach, S.H.: Transforming the enterprise: the alignment of business and information technology strategies. IBM Syst. J. **32**(1), 198–221 (1993)
35. Avila, O., Garces, K.: Change management support to preserve business - information technology alignment. J. Comput. Inf. Syst. **57**(3), 218–228 (2017)
36. Avila, O.: Contribution à l'alignement complet des systèmes d'information techniques. Thèses de doctorat, Université de Strasbourg, Strasbourg (2009)
37. Porter, M.E.: How competitive forces shape strategy. Harv. Bus. Rev. (1979)
38. Calder, A., Moir, S.: The Calder-Moir framework. In: IT Governance: Implementing Frameworks and Standards for the Corporate Governance of IT, Ely, Cambridgeshire, pp. 97–106. IT Governance Publishing (2009)

Using Business Process Modelling to Improve Student Recruitment in UK Higher Education

Oluwatoyin Fakorede$^{(\boxtimes)}$, Philip Davies, and David Newell

Department of Computing and Informatics, Faculty of Science and Technology,
Bournemouth University, Poole, UK
{Ofakorede, Daviesp, Dnewell}@bournemouth.ac.uk

Abstract. We consider how the student recruitment process might be improved to optimize performance with particular reference to the clearing process. A Design Science Research (DSR) methodology was used which entails learning through artefact production and data was collected from interviews, observation and document analysis. The logic of the clearing process was modelled using a process-oriented modelling technique. An 'As Is' clearing process model was created to analyze the process, and a 'To Be' clearing process model developed. The improved model has been verified by domain experts and promises to enhance the clearing process in terms of cost saving and resource utilization.

Keywords: UK higher education · Process modeling · Recruitment process
Business process improvement · BPMN · Clearing

1 Introduction

Around 700,000 prospective students seek admission through the Universities and Colleges Admissions Service (UCAS) to over 380 higher education institutions (HEI) in the UK each year [1]. There is fierce competition amongst universities to recruit and retain students with almost 50% of universities' income being sourced from tuition fees [2]. Clearing is an extension of the higher education (HE) application process run by UCAS which can be used by applicants who do not have a place at a university or a higher education institution [3]. Clearing allows applicants to find courses that still have places available. According to UCAS, around one in eight people accepted onto a full-time university course arrived through clearing [4].

The clearing process is divided into early clearing, which runs from the beginning of July to mid-August, and main clearing which starts from mid-August when the A-levels results are released. This work focusses on main clearing from the university perspective [5]. From an economic view point, the idea of 'student as customer' has developed since the increase in tuition fees which has meant it is harder to fill places from clearing and consequently important to optimize and effectively manage the application experience. In this paper we use business process modelling to identify non-value-adding activities in the clearing process. The clearing process improvement is iteratively achieved through the analysis of the process models. The use of a structured technique to support the improvement of a process from the 'As Is' to the

© Springer Nature Switzerland AG 2019
W. Abramowicz and A. Paschke (Eds.): BIS 2018 Workshops, LNBIP 339, pp. 124–135, 2019.
https://doi.org/10.1007/978-3-030-04849-5_11

'To Be' state is a complex and difficult one which requires significant consideration of process improvement methodologies [6, 7] and lies outside the scope of the present work. This paper's originality lies in the application of process modelling to identify issues in the recruitment process in the UK HEI which so far no one has investigated. The paper is structured as follows: Sect. 2 describes choosing a business process modelling technique. Section 3 explains the use of BPMN-based process improvement models. Section 4 describes the methodology while data gathering sources are revealed in Sect. 5. Section 6 presents the implementation of the DSR methodology using BPMN and Sect. 7 presents conclusions and future work.

2 Choosing a Business Process Modelling Technique

Aguilar-Saven [8] has classified business process modelling techniques in two dimensions. The first dimension is based on four levels of functionality; level 1 - Descriptive for learning, level 2 - Decision support for process development/design, level 3 - Decision support for process execution and level 4 - IT enactment. The second dimension is based on whether the model is active (allows interaction between the model and the user) or passive (does not allow interaction).

Another author, Vergidis et al. [9] proposed three classifications of business process modelling techniques as follows (Fig. 1):

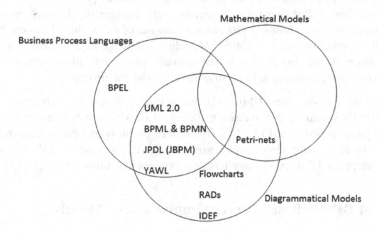

Fig. 1. Classification of business process modelling techniques according to Vergidis et al. [9].

1. Diagrammatic models: This entails the use of diagrams to represent a business process model e.g. Flowcharts, Role Activity Diagrams, IDEF. These techniques can be used to give fast and informal representation of a business process, but they lack the semantic capacity to depict a more complex construct [9].
2. Formal or Mathematical Models: These models have been accurately defined and analyzed to glean quantitative information from them. Petri-nets (see Fig. 1) are business modelling techniques that can be visually represented using standard

notations but with formal or mathematical underpinning [10]. The disadvantage of mathematical models is that they can be tedious to create and maintain [11].

3. Business Process Languages: These bridge the gap between the diagrammatical models and formal models. Where diagrammatical models lack semantics to capture complex constructs and formal models are too complex, business process languages based on XML reduce the complexity of formal models without losing consistency and capacity for analysis e.g. BPEL. Figure 1 shows business process languages that can be expressed diagrammatically e.g. YAWL, JBPM etc.

Several business process graphical notations can be used to model different aspects of processes in the business process lifecycle depending on the objective of the phase such as requirements analysis, mapping business requirements to IT Services, data flow between processes, modelling interaction between the model and the user, business process improvement, process simulation etc. These graphical notations can be grouped into three categories [12]:

1. Data-oriented Notations: The objective is to capture the flow of data e.g. Data Flow Diagrams. As this study is not about how data is stored or transformed in a process, DFDs will not be suitable to model the clearing process.
2. Role-oriented Notations: The objective is to capture the specific roles in an organization and their interaction with others. Role Activity Diagrams (RADs) capture humanistic processes and their interactions. As this study is not about human factors, it will not be suitable to model the clearing process [13].
3. Process-oriented Notations: The objective is to capture the flow of operational activities in or across business processes. Examples of this include Business Process Modeling Notation (BPMN), Unified Modeling Language Activity Diagrams (UML AD). Since the clearing process is best viewed from an operational perspective the process-oriented notation is most suitable to model the process.

BPMN is chosen over UML AD because the Object Management Group (OMG) BPMN version 2.0 includes a mapping of BPMN to a business process execution language called WSBPEL [14]. This makes business process models created in BPMN to be executable. On the other hand, UML AD does not include any specification of mapping UML AD to any business process execution language [15].

3   Use of BPMN-Based Process Improvement Models

As discussed above, a single process can be captured using multiple process models, from different perspectives, at different levels of abstraction using different modelling languages [16]. However, BPMN-based process improvement has not received much attention. Business process improvement approaches in HEIs are scarce as indicated by Daurte and Martins [17]. Their work focused on the gathering of practices and knowledge and the communication between stakeholders to improve business processes. They presented an extension to the Business Process Maturity Model (BPMM) for HEI which includes five maturity levels that capture the degrees of organization transformations. Their improvement was aimed at the transition of institutions from maturity level 2 to 3 and validated by experiment at the University of Algarve [17].

Process improvement in HEI was carried out by Gamil [13] who focused on process improvements from a human resource perspective; showing roles, activities and interactions within an organization. This informed the use of Role Activity Diagrams (RAD) to model the student journey processes using RADs-RichPicture model to identify improvements in role-oriented services and therefore adopted a Role-oriented notation to capture the processes.

Another related work by Al-Medlej [18] investigated the factors that influence the decision-making process in Saudi Arabia HEI and explored ways to manage these factors in order to exert a positive influence on the process and proposed a new approach towards a more efficient decision-making process.

There are other non-HEI related BPMN-based process improvement models. For example, Khabbazi et al. [19] in their work engaged the use of BPMN 2.0 to capture and analyze the "As Is" complex inbound logistics of an industrial system. The logistic process entails all activities with respect to the inbound movement of the resources and information including the ordering, procurement, auction and purchasing processes. A "To Be" inbound logistics business process model was proposed to specify the structure and the behavior of the system.

Silvia et al. [20] presented the improvement of a government public service via the analysis of the Key Performance Indicator (KPI) and Critical Success Factor (CSF), while the process model was designed using BPMN. The Service Engineering Framework (SEF) research methodology was used which entails three phases: (1) Identification Phase (the performance of the existing business process using CSF and KPI analysis) (2) Design Phase (the current and proposed processes modelled using BPMN with Bizagi modeler software) and (3) Design Validation was performed using the time analysis level of Bizagi modeler software [21]. The result of the business process improvement showed that the speed of various services provided had increased by a minimum of 58.1%.

Mpardis and Kotsilieris [22] created a process model that captures the procedures involved in approving a loan request using BPMN with Intalio|Designer. The process model was mapped to a BPEL 2.0 process server for execution. BPEL outputs were analyzed by Matlab based on some specific KPIs. The benefits of their approach could lead to reduction in cycle time and in-crease in output per employee.

There is lack of research work that analyses the admission process of UK HEI using the BPMN technique.

4 Methodology

The Design Science Research (DSR) methodology is used here in preference to the SEF methodology because the CSF and KPI analysis is not required. Design Science provides a set of synthetic and analytical techniques for carrying out research in Information Systems [23, 24]. This set of techniques formulates new knowledge or theory through the design of novel or innovative artefacts, followed by an analysis (which includes reflection and abstraction) of the performance of the artefacts to understand and improve the behavior of the information system.

DSR has four main process stages, where each stage has a specific output. The stages we apply here are:

1. **Awareness of Problem:** The problem needs to be identified, for example from an area of challenge in an organization. The problem is made manifest by creating the 'As Is' clearing process model using BPMN 2.0. In this case the problem was identified through involvement in the clearing process in the chosen university which led to the identification of clearing recruitment challenges. One problem identified was that applicants may select university "A" on UCAS Track without a prior offer from university A. On the other hand, upload of offer (made by universities) confirmations to UCAS happen only when the university is selected by the applicant. An applicant who already has an offer from university "A" may instead select University "B". Since staff are required to follow up on the applicants with offers, this activity could be a waste of time and resources. The output of this phase is a proposal for improved design.
2. **Suggestion:** The proposal from stage 1 is transformed into a tentative design. In this case the tentative design is the same as the proposal. The suggestion stage is part of the solution design. The cognitive process involved is **Abduction** because the suggestion offered to solve the identified problems are abducted from the existing process of knowledge base in the problem area [23, 25].
3. **Development:** This is the concluding part of the solution design. The artefacts can be constructs (vocabulary and symbols), models (abstractions and representations), methods (algorithms and practices) and instantiations (implemented and prototypes systems) [23, 24]. In this case, the tentative design was developed into the 'To Be' clearing process model. Five progressive versions of the model were developed through an iterative process until a final validated version (see Fig. 2) which is an accurate representation of the UK HE clearing process. The cognitive process involved is **Deduction** because it involves a move from the general to the specific.
4. **Evaluation:** This phase entails the evaluation of the artefact based on performance measurements such as time saving and resource utilization. This was achieved through simulations used to compare various scenarios and domain experts. The cognitive process involved at this stage is called Deduction because knowledge deduced from the analysis of contradictions or deviations from expectations.

5   Data Gathering and Verification

The clearing process is regulated by UCAS and is the same for all UK HEs. The choice of HE was determined by access to data sources. The quality of data gathered was verified using verification strategies [26]. Verification of data is the process of establishing the validity and reliability of data. The relevant verification strategies used were appropriate sampling and concurrent data analysis. We gathered data from three independent sources; Interviews, Document Study and Observation.

1. **Interviews:** Interview was chosen to ensure that relevant questions are answered, and responses can be more in-depth. Both structured and semi-structured approaches were adopted to allow flexibility and adaptation and to elicit more in-depth and personalized responses. To guarantee the reliability of the interview data, we selected an appropriate sample [26] consisting of participants who have significant roles and adequate knowledge of the clearing process. Nine interviews were conducted involving seven members of staff involving; a senior management team member, academic staff, admissions staff, administrative staff, a business intelligence team member, IT services and one member of staff from UCAS. The interviews varied between 20 to 120 min duration and were recorded and transcribed for analysis. Both personal data and materials gathered were treated as confidential. The interviews covered areas such as; the student recruitment process; the clearing process from a UCAS perspective, HE perspective and student perspective; admission target setting; how admission estimates are generated, benefits of improving the process and verification of process models. The interview transcripts were coded into broad themes according to the research objectives.

2. **Document study:** Document study was chosen to gain background and context information, help generate interview questions, develop understanding, and discover insights relevant to UK HEI admissions. The Schwartz principles [27] of fair admissions and several reports on HE admissions relevant to the research objectives were downloaded from Ucas.com [3] and studied. Minutes of meetings and administrative reports for the same UK university were also examined using thematic analysis [28]. The codes used in the interview transcripts were applied to the content of the documents generating an integrated data gathered by different methods. The data obtained from document study was iteratively analyzed concurrently [26] with the data obtained from interviews to ensure uniformity.

3. **Observation:** Participant observation [29] was engaged to understand how the clearing process works. This was achieved through personal involvement [30]. As data verification process entails checking, confirming and being certain [26], the data obtained from observation was cross-checked with the data obtained from the above two sources to establish the quality of the data [31].

6 Implementing the DSR Methodology Using BPMN

DSR Stage 1 Awareness of Problem

The information obtained from the interviews, document study and observation were translated into 'As Is' process models. The clearing process was modelled using BPMN (Fig. 2) which represents the 'As Is' collaborative clearing process between UCAS, Applicant and University. An initial validation process was conducted to seek expert opinion on the process model to verify that it is an accurate, and acceptable description of the current clearing process. All the activities, interactions and explicitness of the elements were checked and validated through discussion with staff members whose roles and activities are represented in the model. Feedback and comments were received which informed the iterative creation of the 'As Is' clearing process.

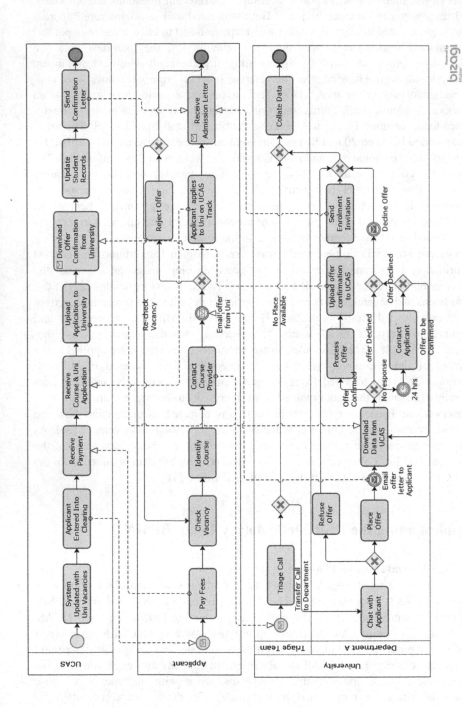

Fig. 2. 'As Is' Collaborative Clearing Process between UCAS, Applicant and University

The process begins when the UCAS system is updated with university vacancies available for applicants to view. The details of the applicants who do not hold any offers are entered into clearing on the UCAS TRACK system. The applicant is notified to pay clearing fees. Once the fees are paid, they can check vacancies available in various universities, identify the course they would like to study and contact the course provider by making a phone call. The triage team at the university receives the call, discusses entry requirements with the applicant and confirms whether spaces are available on the desired course. If places remain the call is transferred to the relevant department. Each department would have three to four academics available to talk to the applicant. If the applicant is given an offer at this stage, an admission letter is then emailed to the applicant. The applicant then has 24 h to apply to the university via UCAS TRACK.

All applications made on UCAS TRACK are uploaded to the university every two hours during clearing. The university downloads data from UCAS and processes the offers. Once the offer is processed, the confirmation is uploaded to UCAS. UCAS updates the student records and sends a confirmation letter to the applicant. The university then sends an enrolment invitation to the applicant. If the university discovers the applicant has not applied through UCAS TRACK, the applicant will be contacted, reminded, and given a further 24 h to apply. All phone calls, enquiries, offers, declines and refusals are collated and stored in a student records management system.

DSR Stage 2 Suggestion

Examining the current clearing process reveals the following issues:

(1) Offers are made by the university before applicants can apply to the university on UCAS TRACK. These offers are verbal confirmations and may come from many universities at the same time. There is no way for UCAS to monitor these offers because they are not registered with UCAS until the applicant goes to TRACK, selects the university. The university only receives the application when UCAS uploads the data to the university. The university will then confirm with UCAS that an offer has been made to the applicant. As a result, time and resources utilized to speak to the applicant could end up being wasted as the applicant may choose to accept an offer from another University.

(2) If the student does not apply within 24 h, the clearing staff have to chase up the applicant expending more time and resources on an applicant that may have accepted an offer from another University.

(3) UCAS TRACK is rendered ineffective in allowing UCAS to ensure that applicants do not have more than one offer.

The above-mentioned issues were confirmed as suggested in [25] by admissions domain experts with several years of experience in student's admissions.

DSR Stage 3 Development

To address these issues, a 'To Be' clearing process model was created to improve the process as shown in Fig. 3. Starting from when the applicant is given an offer, an admission letter is emailed to the student by the university. The university also uploads all offers to UCAS. When the student gets the admission letter, they can go to UCAS to confirm or reject the offer and formally apply to the University. Meanwhile, UCAS

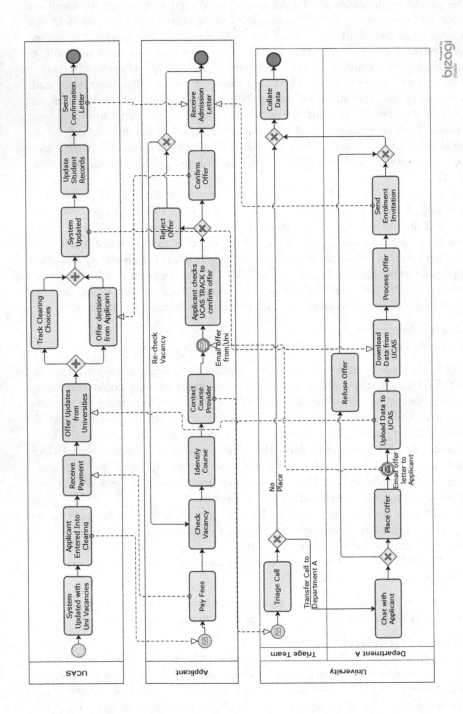

Fig. 3. 'To be' Clearing Process between UCAS, Applicant and University

would have a tracking activity which runs parallel to the offer decision notification from the applicant. The confirmations and rejections are available to the university for download. Once downloaded by the University, the offer confirmations can be processed and the invitation for enrolment is sent to the applicant.

DSR Stage 4 Evaluation
The first step in the evaluation phase is to validate the improved process model that it is an accurate, and acceptable description of the clearing process. All the activities, interactions and explicitness of the elements were checked and validated through discussion with staff members whose roles and activities are represented in the model.

Feedback and comments were received which informed the iterative creation of the 'To Be' clearing process. The benefit of this improved process is that it is simple, more efficient and less time wasting. Business process (BP) simulation [30] was employed to confirm that the model is error-free and to evaluate the performance of the clearing process models (both As-Is and To-Be) using Bizagi process modeler's [21] time analysis and resource analysis levels. The benefit for applicants is that they will finish with all the offers they have received in their TRACK account and they select the university of their choice, and the university receives the information. The benefit for the university is that it would save time, cost and resources expended in chasing applicants. The model only represents one department, it is expected that the proposed model would yield even cumulative benefits when applied to all faculties within the University.

7 Conclusion and Future Work

We have demonstrated that process modelling can be useful in identifying unnecessary or non-value activities in the clearing process model of a UK HEI facilitating the creation of an improved process model to allow for goal optimization such as time saving, resource utilization etc. The choice of a suitable modelling technique enabled the process model to accurately capture the business logic in the clearing process, thereby enabling the analysis of the process operations. After running simulations on both current and the proposed models using BP simulation with Bizagi tool, the outcome was that the proposed clearing process model was more efficient and saved time. Other benefits are allowing UCAS to effectively manage and track offers made by universities, students would be able to see all verbal offers made by Universities in their TRACK account, and universities would not need to waste time and resources to chase up applicants who have decided to accept an offer from another university. Further work is needed to understand how the process models (current and proposed) will behave under certain resource constraints when simulated. As the modelling technique (BPMN) supports simulation, a what-if-analysis will be performed on the improved process to determine how the process model would behave under various scenarios [32]. Furthermore, future work will investigate the development of business process heuristics that would support the actual act of process improvement.

References

1. Attenda: Delivering a highly successful confirmation and clearing process (2013). http://www.attenda.com/wp-content/uploads/2014/01/UCAS-Case-Study.pdf. Accessed 16 May 2016
2. Universities UK: Patterns and trends in UK higher education (2017). http://www.universitiesuk.ac.uk/facts-and-stats/data-and-analysis/Documents/patterns-and-trends-2017.pdf. Accessed 24 Jan 2018
3. UCAS.com (2017). https://www.ucas.com/corporate/about-us/our-services. Accessed 19 Nov 2017
4. UCAS: Top ten reasons why clearing is an important route into higher education (2016). https://www.ucas.com/corporate/news-and-key-documents/news/top-ten-reasons-why-clearing-important-route-higher-education. Accessed 11 Apr 2018
5. UCAS: Admissions Guide and Decision Processing Manual (2015)
6. Zellner, G.: A structured evaluation of business process improvement approaches. Bus. Process Manag. J. **17**(2), 203–237 (2011). https://doi.org/10.1108/14637151111122329
7. Rashid, O.A., Ahmad, M.N.: Business process improvement methodologies: an overview. J. Inf. Syst. Res. Innov. **5**, 45–53 (2014)
8. Aguilar-Saven, R.S.: Business process modelling: review and framework. Int. J. Prod. Econ. **90**, 129–149 (2004). https://doi.org/10.1016/S0925-5273(03)00102-6
9. Vergidis, K., Tiwari, A., Majeed, B.: Business process analysis and optimization: beyond engineering. IEEE Trans. Syst. Man Cybern. Part C (Appl. Rev.) **38**, 69–82 (2007). https://doi.org/10.1109/TSMCC.2007.905812
10. Van der Aalst, W.M.P., Ter Hofstede, A.H.M., Weske, M.: Business process management: a survey. In: Conference on Business Process Management (2003)
11. Koubarakis, M., Plexousakis, D.: A formal framework for business process modelling and design. Inf. Syst. **27**(5), 299–319 (2002)
12. Tay, M.: Notations for Business Process (Part 1) – RAD, EPC and BPMN. http://blog.maxconsilium.com/2013/09/process-notation-p1.html. Accessed 22 Nov 2017
13. Gamil, N.: Process improvement in higher education institutions, Faculty of Science and Technology, Bournemouth University (2015)
14. OMG: Business process model and notation specification version 2.0. (2011). http://www.omg.org/spec/BPMN/2.0/About-BPMN/. Accessed 18 Oct 2017
15. OMG: The unified modeling language specification version 2.5. (2015). http://www.omg.org/spec/UML/About-UML/. Accessed 18 Oct 2017
16. Weidlich, M., Mendling, J.: Perceived consistency between process models. Inf. Syst. **37**(2), 80–98 (2012)
17. Daurte, D., Martins, P.V.: Higher education business process improvement achieving BPMM level 3. In: 2014 9th International Conference on the Quality of Information and Communications Technology, Portugal, p. 319. http://ieeexplore.ieee.org/stamp/stamp.jsp?tp=&arnumber=6984089&tag=1. Accessed 22 Jan 2018
18. Al-Medlej, H.I.: Decision Making Process in Higher Education Institutions – The Case of Saudi Arabia, Middlesex University (1997)
19. Khabbazi, M.R., Hasan, M.K., Sulaiman, R., Shapi'I, A.: Business process modeling for domain inbound logistics system: analytic perspective with BPMN 2.0. J. Basic Appl. Sci. Res. **3**(9), 569–578 (2013). http://www.diva-portal.org/smash/get/diva2:828124/FULLTEXT01.pdf. Accessed 20 Jan 2018

20. Silvia, S., Yustianto, P.: Business process improvement of district government innovation service. Case study Cimahi Tengah District of Cimahi. In: 2016 International Conference on Information Technology Systems and Innovation (ICITSI), Bandung, Bali (2016)
21. Bizagi. https://www.bizagi.com/en/products/bpm-suite/modeler
22. Mpardis, G., Kotsilieris, T.: Bank loan process modelling using BPMN. In: Developments in E-Systems Engineering (2010). https://doi.org/10.1109/DESE.2010.45
23. Vaishnavi, V., Kuechler, B.: Design science research in information systems (2004). http://www.desrist.org/design-research-in-information-systems/. Accessed 1 May 2017
24. Hevner, A.R., March, S.T., Park, J., Ram, S.: Design science in information systems research. MIS Q. **28**(1), 75–105 (2004)
25. Offermann, P., Levina, O., Schonherr, M., Bub, U.: Outline of a design science research process. https://wise.vub.ac.be/sites/default/files/thesis_info/outline_of_design_science_research_process.pdf. Accessed 12 Apr 2018
26. Morse, J.M., Barret, M., Mayan, M., Olson, K., Spiers, J.: Verification strategies for establishing reliability and validity in qualitative research. Int. J. Qual. Methods **1**(2), 13–22 (2002). https://doi.org/10.1177/160940690200100202
27. Higher Education Steering Group. Fair Admissions to Higher Education: Recommendations for Good Practice. https://www.spa.ac.uk/sites/default/files/Admissions-review-Schwartz-2004.pdf. Accessed 20 Sept 2017
28. Bowen, G.A.: Document analysis as a qualitative research method. Qual. Res. J. **9**(2), 27–40 (2009)
29. Mill, C.: Comparison of research methods (2015). https://themille17.org/wp-content/uploads/2015/07/Comparison-of-Research-Methods.pdf. Accessed 13 June 2017
30. Personal attendance at clearing event at a UK University, 14 August 2017
31. Lambert, M.: A Beginners Guide to Doing Your Education Research Project. SAGE Publications, London (2012)
32. Aguilar, M., Rautert, T., Pater, A.: Business process simulation: a fundamental step supporting process centered management. In: Winter Simulation, pp. 1383–1392. ACM, Phoenix (1999)

Stakeholder-Oriented and Enterprise Architecture Driven Cloud Service Selection

Sabrina Kurjakovic[1]([✉]) and Knut Hinkelmann[2]

[1] University of Camerino, Camerino, Italy
sabrina.kurjakovic@unicam.it
[2] FHNW University of Applied Sciences and Arts Northwestern Switzerland,
Olten, Switzerland
knut.hinkelmann@fhnw.ch

Abstract. In the last decade the number of cloud services has grown significantly. However, it is still a challenge for enterprises to describe functional requirements in a user-friendly way in order to select cloud services. This study introduces an approach to increase the practical relevance of business IT alignment research. We integrate insights from organizational buying behaviour into enterprise architecture modeling. The result consists of a concept and web-based platform. It enables business users without expert knowledge in modeling to exploit the potential of enterprise architecture for cloud service selection.

Keywords: Business IT alignment · Enterprise architecture
Cloud service selection · Reference models

1 Introduction

An essential prerequisite for successful strategy implementation is a proper alignment of business and information technology [1]. It is of major importance to thoughtfully select appropriate software services which support the business processes of an enterprise. Nowadays there is a manifold software landscape. In the last decade the number of cloud services has grown significantly. However, it is still a challenge for enterprises to describe their requirements in a user-friendly way to find appropriate cloud services. A majority of the current cloud research focuses on non-functional aspects, such as security and performance, targeting technically experienced cloud users. Only a minority of the studies address functional aspects and considers various kinds of business stakeholders with different knowledge levels [2]. This is also reflected in practice. Getapp.com, for example, is one of the most popular cloud app platforms for cloud service discovery and evaluation [3]. However, most of the selection criteria address non-functional requirements. Moreover, the distributed nature of cloud services challenges traditional requirements elicitation concepts. In comparison to on-premise software suppliers, cloud service providers often operate remotely and have less opportunities to meet customers face to face. This calls for an approach where the cloud service evaluation can be conducted remotely assisted by an automated system. The largest group of cloud services are Software as a Service (SaaS) applications. Horizontal SaaS, such as e-mail or collaboration tools, can cover various industries. Vertical

© Springer Nature Switzerland AG 2019
W. Abramowicz and A. Paschke (Eds.): BIS 2018 Workshops, LNBIP 339, pp. 136–142, 2019.
https://doi.org/10.1007/978-3-030-04849-5_12

SaaS are targeted to specific industry sectors. We suggest an approach, which draws upon enterprise architecture and enterprise ontologies for cloud service selection to describe the functional requirements for vertical SaaS. The result consists of a concept and web-based platform that (1) guides enterprises in describing their requirements (2) enables cloud service provider to describe their cloud offers (3) establishes a matching between user requirements and cloud offers to retrieve cloud service proposals that meet the business needs.

This paper is organized as follows. Section two demonstrates the body of knowledge. Section three depicts the research methodology which is based on design science research. In section four the overall approach is described. Section five introduces the prototype of the web platform from business perspective drawing upon mock-ups. Section six includes the conclusion and outlook.

2 Literature Review

At first glance cloud services are closely related to web services. Latter are loosely-coupled, modular software applications used across the internet. Web services draw upon a set of standards and are made available through interfaces. Most of the current techniques for service specification address web services, for example the Web Service Description Language (WSDL) [4]. The growth of cloud services in the past decade calls for a unified specification which addresses the nature of cloud services. Studies have been conducted in this area, but so far, a widely accepted standard doesn't exist. A majority of the conducted cloud service selection studies focus on cloud services in general investigating on non-functional requirements [5–11]. However, in comparison to web services, SaaS services address enterprises and individuals and hence require a greater involvement by users. There is a lack of contributions addressing cloud service selection from functional perspective supporting non-technical users in decision making. Currently semantic approaches and ontologies are considered as the most promising approach for classification and normalization of domain knowledge [2, 12].

The discipline of enterprise architecture management (EAM) supports business IT alignment and provides a holistic view on the enterprise. Enterprise architecture (EA) models represent all relevant business structures, IT structures and their relationships of an enterprise. They can be used as a means for analysing the business situation and for communication between stakeholders and are also exploited for strategic alignment [13]. There are a number or contributions addressing the problem of adjusting enterprise architecture models and methods for better support of specific business scenarios. However, there is room for further scientific contribution and future research should address (1) the stakeholder categories who use a model, (2) the stakeholder concerns that are supported with specific models and (3) the representation of the model, which has to be understandable for the target group [14].

3   Research Methodology and Application Scenario

This study is based on the design science research approach [15] which includes five steps: (1) awareness of the problem, (2) suggesting a draft for the solution, (3) developing the solution, (4) evaluating the solution and (5) drawing conclusions. The application domain is provided by an established Swiss vendor for enterprise resource planning software for garages and body shops. A qualitative research method was applied. We conducted 12 semi structured interviews with customers and developed use case scenarios. We evaluated various modeling languages and developed an approach for business and cloud perspective modeling and matching. We suggested a draft for the solution and work currently on the development of the solution (web-based platform). The evaluation of the final solution draws upon usability testing and qualitative and quantitative research methods. We will provide test users (decision makers from garages and body shops) with a personal computer and internet access. Each participant will perform a specific scenario on the web platform. The participants describe their business requirements in order to retrieve corresponding cloud service proposals. Subsequently a quantitative survey will be conducted. The survey will be complemented with semi-structured face to face interviews. The goal is to gain insights about the effectiveness and usability of the web platform.

4   The Approach

Figure 1 shows an overview of the approach which serves as a basic framework for the development of a browser-based application. The approach includes a modeling method supported by reference models and an enterprise ontology in the backend. A modeling method consists of a modeling language (syntax, semantics and notation) and a modeling procedure [16]. Figure 1 depicts the concept that is described in four layers. The first layer shows the modeling procedure: (1) Configure, (2) define, (3) refine and (4) evaluate represent the steps of the requirements elicitation process from business user perspective. The steps (1) add and (2) describe are performed by the cloud service provider to describe the cloud service offers.

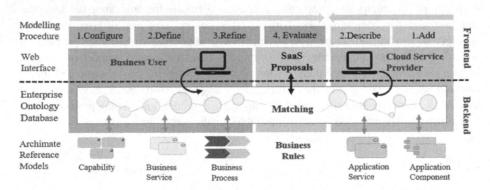

Fig. 1. Overview of the approach

The second layer represents the interface consisting of a web platform which queries an ontological database in the backend. We provide both the business user as well as the cloud service provider with a specific website. The website guides the user through the modeling procedure. Layer three shows the enterprise ontology which includes all basic concepts required to model the knowledge and reason about it. We suggest using Archimate [17] as underlying framework for the enterprise ontology. Archimate allows modeling the business, application and technical architectures and provides an appropriate level of abstraction. To describe the business architecture, we draw upon the Archimate concepts capabilities, business services and business processes. The cloud services are described with application components and application services. The semantics of the modeling concepts are formalized in the enterprise ontology called Archimeo [18].

Cloud service proposals are identified through a matching between the Archimate strategy/business and application layer. The ontology includes a set of mapping rules (business rules) which have been derived from the use case scenarios. Layer four shows the reference models for the different architectures. Reference models [19] are generic, conceptual models for a specific domain, which formalize recommended practices. Based on the insights from 12 interviews with practitioners, for each step of the modeling procedure we developed reference models. Reference models make the solution more accessible to non-expert users. Instead of modeling from scratch users can only select the relevant part of the model at run time. The goal is to enhance user-friendliness by reducing and simplifying the modeling effort.

5   The Business Perspective

This section introduces the prototype of the browser-based web application by focusing on the requirements description from the business perspective. We identified two stakeholder perspectives in small and medium enterprises which are important with respect to functional requirements: the management-oriented and the task-oriented perspective. The smaller the enterprise, the more important it is to successfully consider both perspectives when selecting a cloud service. In small enterprises the owner is often involved in both management tasks (e.g. developing the strategy) and daily tasks (e.g. performing a service). The bigger the enterprise, the more a division of tasks can be observed and the more people are involved in the cloud service selection process. Our approach enables decision makers in both small and large enterprises to describe their requirements according to their role and knowledge level. We suggest using the Archimate concepts of capabilities and business services to address the management-oriented perspective. Business processes represent the task-oriented perspective and are used to further refine the requirements. Figure 2 shows the starting point of the requirements elicitation process. The development of the interfaces aimed at increasing user-friendliness and accessibility. We suggest the artifacts based on the type of information that has to be represented. In a first step the user is asked to define the industry in which the enterprise is active in. In a second step, which is not shown in the figure, the subsector of the industry can be selected. For example, a user selects 'Automotive' as industry and 'Garage' as subsector. The industry is used as a categorization system since each subsector has its own specific set of capabilities. Since Archimate doesn't include the concept of industry, we added some concepts to the Archimate metamodel. The next step is the selection of the capabilities of the enterprise. Figure 2 depicts on the right side a snippet of an industry specific capability map for a garage. Capabilities [20] answer simply 'what' a solution should be able to do on a high level (management-oriented perspective).

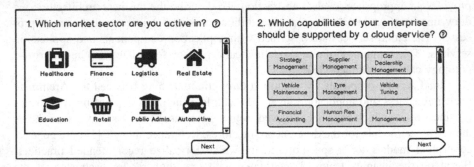

Fig. 2. Selecting the industry and capabilities

Possessing a capability doesn't necessarily mean that this capability generates value and subsequently profit for the enterprise. Therefore, after defining the capabilities, the user is asked to define for each capability corresponding business services as depicted in Fig. 3 on the left side. Business services can be internal or offered to external customers. For example, the top bar in Fig. 3 shows the capability Financial Accounting. It includes three business service proposals: General Accounting, Payroll Accounting and Financial Reporting. In the example below only the business service Payroll Accounting should be supported by a cloud solution.

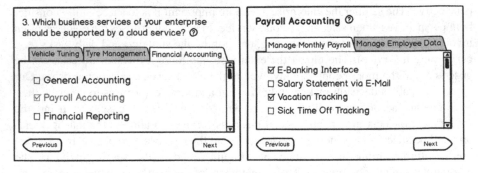

Fig. 3. Selecting the business services and refining the business processes

Figure 3 depicts on the right side the final step of the cloud service selection process. The concept of business processes is used to refine the requirements on a solution in more detail (task-oriented perspective). Employees who perform daily tasks, such as a bookkeeper, know the processes of an enterprise. They can provide more detailed information about the requirements since it has a direct impact on their daily work. We analysed various ERP cloud solutions and identified features that are normally not necessarily expected as 'must be' standard functionality. We extracted these features and provide the user with the opportunity to add these features as additional information to the business process. In the example in Fig. 3 E-Banking Interface and Vacation Tracking have been selected as relevant application features. In a final step the business user can retrieve cloud service proposals. The concept of the matching has been validated with use cases. We described business requirements, as they occur in garages and body shops, with the concepts of business capabilities, business services and business processes. We modeled vertical SaaS service bundles with the concepts of application components and application services. The business requirements and cloud service perspective have been matched in two steps. First there is a check whether there are cloud services which correspond with the capabilities and business services of a specific use case. If the answer is yes, then we check in a second step if there are cloud services which satisfy the requirements on business process level. The result consists of cloud service proposals.

6   Conclusion and Outlook

This study shows how the potential of enterprise architecture and tool automation (web-based platform) can be exploited for cloud service selection. The approach increases the practical relevance of business IT alignment. In this article, we focused on the conceptual solution, for which a prototype was realized to show its feasibility. It will now be integrated into a web platform. Currently only functional requirements are addressed. However, non-functional requirements, such as security, play an important role. In the next step, the approach will be extended by integrating non-functional requirements too.

References

1. Henderson, J.C., Venkatraman, H.: Strategic alignment: leveraging information technology for transforming organizations. IBM Syst. J. **32**(1), 472–484 (1993)
2. Sun, L., Dong, H., Hussain, F.K., Hussain, O.K., Chang, E.: Cloud service selection: state-of-the-art and future research directions. J. Netw. Comput. Appl. **45**, 134–150 (2014)
3. GetApp: Discover, Compare, and Choose the Best Business Apps (2018). getapp.com. Accessed 20 May 2018
4. Christensen, E., Curbera, F., Greg, M., Weerawarana, S.: Web Services Description Language (WSDL) 1.1. https://www.w3.org/TR/2001/NOTE-wsdl-20010315. Accessed 03 June 2018
5. Godse, M., Mulik, S.: An approach for selecting Software-as-a-Service (SaaS) product. In: CLOUD 2009 – 2009 IEEE International Conference on Cloud Computer, pp. 155–158 (2009)
6. Boussoualim, N., Aklouf, Y.: Evaluation and selection of SaaS product based on user preferences, pp. 299–308. IEEE, May 2015

7. Limam, N., Boutaba, R.: Assessing software service quality and trustworthiness at selection time. IEEE Trans. Softw. Eng. **36**(4), 559–574 (2010)
8. Afify, Y.M., Moawad, I.F., Badr, N.L., Tolba, M.F.: A semantic-based Software-as-a-Service (SaaS) discovery and selection system. In: 8th International Conference on Computer Engineering and Systems, pp. 57–63, November 2013
9. Chen, Y., Zhu, Y.: SaaS vendor selection basing on analytic hierarchy process. In: Proceedings - 4th International Joint Conference on Computational Sciences and Optimization, CSO 2011, pp. 511–515 (2011)
10. Karim, R., Ding, C., Miri, A.: An end-to-end QoS mapping approach for cloud service selection. In: 2013 IEEE Ninth World Congress on Services, pp. 341–348 (2013)
11. Wen, P.X., Dong, L.: Quality model for evaluating SaaS service. In: Proceedings - 4th International Conference on Emerging Intelligent Data and Web Technologies, EIDWT 2013, pp. 83–87 (2013)
12. Rehman, Z.U., Hussain, O.K., Hussain, F.K.: User-side cloud service management: State-of-the-art and future directions. J. Netw. Comput. Appl. **55**, 108–122 (2015)
13. Ahlemann, F., Stettiner, E., Messerschmidt, M., Legner, C., Hobbs, G.: EAM governance and organisation. In: Ahlemann, F., Stettiner, E., Messerschmidt, M., Legner, C. (eds.) Strategic Enterprise Architecture Management. Management for Professionals, pp. 81–110. Springer, Heidelberg (2012). https://doi.org/10.1007/978-3-642-24223-6_4
14. Sandkuhl, K., et al.: From expert discipline to common practice: a vision and research agenda for extending the reach of enterprise modeling. Bus. Inf. Syst. Eng. **60**(1), 69–80 (2018)
15. Peffers, K., Tuunanen, T., Rothenberger, M.A., Chatterjee, S.: A design science research methodology for information systems research. J. Manag. Inf. Syst. **24**(3), 45–77 (2007)
16. Karagiannis, D., Kühn, H.: Metamodelling platforms. In: Proceedings of the Third International Conference EC-Web, no. 2455 (2002)
17. The Open Group: ArchiMate 3.0.1 Specification (2018). http://pubs.opengroup.org/architecture/archimate3-doc/. Accessed 07 May 2018
18. Hinkelmann, K., Laurenzi, E., Lammel, B., Kurjakovic, S., Woitsch, R.: A semantically-enhanced modelling environment for business process as a service. In: 2016 4th International Conference on Enterprise Systems (ES), pp. 143–152 (2016)
19. Rosemann, M.: Application reference models and building blocks for management and control. In: Bernus, P., Nemes, L., Schmidt, G. (eds.) Handbook on Enterprise Architecture. International Handbooks on Information Systems, pp. 595–615. Springer, Heidelberg (2003). https://doi.org/10.1007/978-3-540-24744-9_17
20. Freitag, A.: Towards a theoretical foundation for business capabilities. In: Freitag, A. (ed.) Applying Business Capabilities in a Corporate Buyer M&A Process, pp. 64–104. Springer, Heidelberg (2015)

Business-IT Alignment Improvement in Co-creation Value Networks: Design of a Reference Model-Based Support

Samaneh Bagheri$^{(\boxtimes)}$, Rob Kusters, Jos Trienekens,
and Paul W. P. J. Grefen

Industrial Engineering Department, Eindhoven University of Technology,
5600 MB Eindhoven, The Netherlands
{s.bagheri,r.j.kusters,j.j.m.trienekens,
p.w.p.j.grefen}@tue.nl

Abstract. Prior research has not adequately addressed business-IT alignment (BITA) improvement, especially in a business network situation of a co-creation value network (VN). In a VN setting, IT is regarded as a major facilitator of actors' collaboration to realize their joint objectives, i.e. to deliver seamless customer experience through providing mass-customized integrated solutions. To effectively use IT, a sufficient degree of BITA for key capabilities of a VN is required. Furthermore, BITA as a moving target should be improved continuously over time.

In this paper, BITA improvement in a VN setting is studied. We focus on BITA improvement for the key capabilities of a VN and design support for it. To this end, we adopt a dynamic capability perspective due to its ability to explain how organizations can improve their operational capabilities and processes to adjust to a changing environment. We design a reference model-based approach that enhances the 'business process management' dynamic capability of a VN by enabling co-development of business processes with their supporting IT-based systems. This co-development facilitates BITA improvement. This paper presents the research process of the design of our support. As a proof of concept, the results for one of the key capabilities of a VN (i.e., customer understanding) is presented and discussed.

Keywords: Business-IT alignment improvement · Reference model
Key capabilities · Co-evolution · Dynamic capability
Co-creation value network

1 Introduction

Alignment of business and information technology (BITA) continues to be an important challenge for firms [1, 2]. Furthermore, BITA is a moving target due to changes in the organization's external and internal environments. It means that BITA should be continuously improved over time [2–5]. Achieving better BITA may be even more challenging in a co-creation value network (VN) setting where a set of autonomous actors collaborate to accomplish their joint goal (i.e., co-creating mass-

© Springer Nature Switzerland AG 2019
W. Abramowicz and A. Paschke (Eds.): BIS 2018 Workshops, LNBIP 339, pp. 143–155, 2019.
https://doi.org/10.1007/978-3-030-04849-5_13

customized integrated solutions). BITA improvement in a VN setting is difficult due to the complexity of this context, such as lack of central decision maker, complex inter-organizational business processes, and diversity of working environments of the actors [6–8]. Co-creation value implies delivering a seamless customer experience by providing integrated solutions in which value is defined by or with the customers [9, 10]. As the provision of integrated solutions is often beyond the resources of an individual firm, multiple firms together with their mutual customers collaborate in the context of VN to access to complementary resources [11]. In a VN setting, IT is regarded as a major facilitator of collaboration [12]. To achieve business values of IT, a sufficient degree of alignment (fit) between the business side and IT side of a VN is required [1, 3, 4]. BITA improvement entails a more efficient use of IT among actors of a VN, contributes to sustaining a profitable collaboration, and facilitates joint value creation [6, 7].

While the earlier literature on BITA typically concentrated on alignment at one point in time, addressing a continuous process of BITA improvement has received much more attention in recent studies [7, 13, 14]. BITA improvement can occur when the business side and the IT side co-evolve [2, 5]. By taking into account this co-development, BITA improvement has been investigated from a theoretical perspective of dynamic capabilities [7, 13]. However, this literature does not explain how a dynamic capability with the aim of BITA improvement can be systematically developed. Additionally, in this literature, there is a lack of explanation on how to co-develop business with IT.

In this paper, we look at BITA improvement in a VN setting and aim to design support for it. We focus on BITA improvement for the strategic areas of key capabilities of a VN. If the degree of BITA for key capabilities is low, a VN will struggle to achieve its shared goals [15]. Key capabilities are used for implementation of key business processes. IT-based systems can facilitate this implementation. To continuously improve key business processes with their supporting systems, a business process management (BPM) dynamic capability is necessary [16]. Furthermore, the development of both capabilities (i.e., operational capabilities for process execution) and dynamic capabilities (i.e. abilities to improve operational capabilities) can be facilitated by organizational learning [17–19]. In this regard, Zollo and Winter [17] introduce a capability development model in which the role of the learning is highlighted.

We use this model as a basis to design our support for BITA improvement. According to Zollo and Winter [17], organizational learning starts with the accumulation of experiences. However, it is a time-consuming process. With the aim of BITA improvement, we provide a specific addition to this model. To accelerate learning, we propose a reference model-based approach which is to the best of our knowledge is new. We suggest identifying, classifying, and using, systematically, relevant external knowledge from literature which can accelerate/kick-start the learning process. In doing so, we will design and use reference models. In general, a reference model refers to a generic abstract conceptual model that describes essential elements of a particular domain. It helps to establish a common understanding about that domain [20, 21].

Following design science as a research approach, we design and evaluate a reference model-based approach to support the enhancement of the 'business process management' (BPM) dynamic capability. We argue that reference model-based learning process can enhance the BPM dynamic capability. This dynamic capability can support the co-development of key business processes with supporting IT-based system. It can thus facilitate BITA improvement. As a proof of concept, the results for the key capability of customer understanding is presented and discussed.

The outline of the paper is as follows. Section 2 describes related work. Sections 3 and 4, respectively, explains research setting and the research design. Research results are described in Sect. 5. Discussion and conclusion are presented in Sect. 6.

2 Related Works

While prior research has typically focused on BITA as an event at one point in time, addressing a continuous process of BITA improvement has received much more attention in recent studies [7, 13, 14]. In this regard, BITA improvement has been investigated through a theoretical perspective of dynamic capability with an emphasis on co-evolution of business with IT [7, 13, 22].

The dynamic capabilities theory is mainly concerned with the intentional change in a firm's capabilities and business processes [17, 19, 23]. The term dynamic capability refers to learned and stable pattern of activities for systematically improving business processes [17]. Three examples of works from a review of recent literature on BITA improvement from the dynamic capabilities perspective are given here. By conducting a longitudinal case study, Chen et al. [5] provide snapshots of alignment across time and link this to the dynamic capabilities of IT acquisition, integration, and reconfiguration. Schwarz et al. [24] by focusing on dynamic capability, investigate the effect of BITA on firm performance. Baker et al. [13] emphasize the dynamic nature of BITA improvement and propose an approach to measure a dynamic capability that aims at BITA improvement. From this review, we have identified three points:

1. The main focus is on strategic BITA, e.g., alignment between strategic goals of the business and IT. However, these studies do not explain how strategic objectives can be realized.
2. There is a lack of detailed explanation of how a dynamic capability which aims at BITA improvement can be developed. The current literature only highlights the importance of a dynamic capability for BITA improvement, in general. But research lacks an understanding of a specific dynamic capability and the mechanisms which underpin its enhancement.
3. Although the co-development of business and IT has been emphasized in this literature, there is a lack of research that explains how to do this systematically.

In summary, the prior studies on BITA improvement from a dynamic capability perspective have provided useful insights into the general role of a dynamic capability. However, very little is known about how a dynamic capability with the aim of BITA improvement can be enhanced. It is also unclear how the co-development of processes with their supporting IT-based systems can be carried out.

3 Research Setting

A research setting of this study is specified by making four choices: one on context, two on theoretical perspective, and one on scope selection within the second theoretical perspective.

Firstly, as our focus is on BITA improvement over time, we are looking at a specific type of a VN which can be characterized as a longer-term (opposed to temporary) and reasonably stable collaborative environment [25]. The reason for this is to provide time to learn and improve. In that setting, actors closely work together based on longer-term shared goals and a shared understanding of the way to achieve their joint goals.

Secondly, we look at BITA from a capability-based theoretical perspective with a focus on key capabilities [26]. The reason for this focus is that the central premise of the BITA literature is to prioritize IT efforts for key capabilities effectively [15]. Firms that target IT initiatives in their key capabilities are likely to realize higher value from their IT than those that are less focused on their IT deployment [4, 15, 27]. The strategic significance of key capabilities, which are fundamental to a firm in realizing its business objectives, has been discussed in a capability-based theory [28, 29]. The term "capabilities" refers to the firm's abilities to perform business processes, i.e., day-to-day operational activities, to turn a current profit [23].

Thirdly, BITA improvement has been studied from a theoretical perspective of dynamic capabilities. By taking into account co-development of business and IT, the dynamic capability theory has been considered a suitable perspective from which to study BITA improvement [2, 5, 13, 22].

Fourthly, there are some concrete dynamic capabilities, such as product development [30], process re-engineering [17], and BPM [31]. For the purpose of this study, we focus on the BPM dynamic capability, which is dedicated to business process improvement [31, 32] and which supports both incremental and radical improvement [31].

In summary, with a longer-term view of collaboration in a VN setting, we look at a BITA improvement in the key capabilities of a VN. Key capabilities are used to execute key inter-organizational business processes that can be supported by IT-based systems. Value networks need to improve and update their BPM dynamic capability which will allow them to continually improve their key business processes and their supporting IT-based systems [16]. We design support to enhance this dynamic capability.

To provide a clear structure for our discussion on BPM dynamic capability, the well-known model of Zollo and Winter [17] is used (Fig. 1). This model describes the systematic enhancement of dynamic capabilities by learning mechanisms. It should be noted that this model was developed from a perspective of a single organization. However, given that learning is a generic process, the logic of capability development by learning is transferable and applicable to the network settings such as VN [33].

Regarding the first learning mechanism; i.e., experience accumulation, organizations can learn from their own experience as well as from the experience of their network partners by accumulating experience over time [34]. Learning from experience

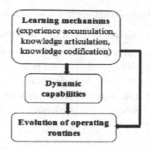

Fig. 1. Capability development model [17]

accumulation thus could be a time-consuming process. To accelerate learning, we propose a reference model-based approach which is to the best of our knowledge is new. We argue that reference model-based learning process can enhance the BPM dynamic capability. This dynamic capability can support the co-development of key business processes with supporting IT-based system. It can thus facilitate BITA improvement.

4 Research Design

The objective of this paper is to design a reference model-based approach to support BITA improvement for the key capabilities of a VN. A designed support will enhance the BPM dynamic capability by enabling the co-development of key business processes and their supporting IT systems. We step from BITA improvement to co-development. This choice is supported by literature. It has been acknowledged that co-development of business and IT can lead to BITA improvement [2].

Our reference model-based approach is designed by following a design science. Design science research is an iterative approach for the design and evaluation of an artifact, where steps in the iteration take both relevance (i.e., importance for the application field) and rigor (i.e., alignment with the academic state of the art) into account [35, 36]. As illustrated in Table 1, our reference model-based approach consists of step 4 supported by steps 1 to 3. From step 1 to 3, we design and evaluate a reference model for a particular key capability. In step 4, we design and evaluate a process that uses a reference model with the aim of BITA improvement. It should be stated that step 4 and the other steps are independent.

Step 1: Identifying Key Capabilities of a VN. As specified in the research setting, we focus on BITA improvement for the key capabilities of a VN. The key capabilities are identified in a structured way from literature. This is done by following a systematic literature review (SLR) approach as suggested by [37]. The identified key capabilities are then classified and described in a structured way by using a structured classification approach in Metaplan sessions [38]. (Full information of this step is presented in one of our previous papers [39]).

Table 1. A reference model-based approach to support BITA improvement

Steps for the design of a reference model	Design of a process to use a reference model
Step 1: Identifying key capabilities of a VN Step 2: Selecting a specific key capability and identifying its key business processes Step 3: Designing and evaluating reference models in relation to the key business processes of the selected key capability	Step 4: Designing and evaluating a reference model-based user requirements elicitation process for co-development of key business processes with their supporting IT-based systems

Step 2: Selecting a Specific Key Capability and Identifying Its Key Business Processes. To be able to design a concrete reference model, we should specify it for a specific key capability. Considering a generic reference model would be unlikely to be adequately precise and meaningful to be used to design support for BITA improvement, and as a consequence, no concrete proof of concept could be expected.

Given that capabilities are embedded in business processes [17, 23], and in order to provide a base for developing reference models, key business processes of the selected key capability are identified. To achieve this, an SLR is conducted.

Step 3: Designing and Validating Reference Models for the Key Business Processes of the Selected Key Capability. To develop the reference models, we do not follow an experience accumulation approach as suggested by Zollo and Winter [17]. Instead, we develop them by introducing outside knowledge, i.e. from literature. We develop and validate our reference models by following this methodology:

– Design phase:
  • Conducting an SLR: By doing this, sufficient relevant knowledge of prior studies is identified systematically.
  • Structured classification: By conducting structured classification in Metaplan sessions, the identified information from literature is classified in a reference model.
– Evaluation phase:
  • Evaluation of the validity of the designed reference model by conducting multiple case studies.

Step 4: Designing and Applying a Reference Model–Based User Requirements Elicitation Process. We design a process to use the reference model with the aim of co-development of key business processes with their supporting IT-based systems. To do this, we focus on the user requirements elicitation process of IT-based systems. The development of IT-based systems should be derived from the requirements of business processes. The success of those systems depends on how well they meet user requirements. If systems functionalities properly meet user requirements, the business and IT will be aligned better [6, 40, 41].

Until now, the majority of user requirements elicitation studies with the aim of addressing BITA were based on a pure asking strategy [42, 43]. According to Davis [44], the asking strategy is aimed at relatively simple situations that provide users with a well-defined structure to support requirement identification. A co-creation value network setting is usually more complex [8, 45]. To compensate for the limitation of the asking strategy in a more complex situation a VN setting, using it in conjunction with other elicitation strategies, e.g., a reference model strategy, is required [44]. A reference model strategy, by providing additional structure and by supporting for asking focused and more-detailed questions, can help in to deal with the added complexity caused by the VN setting.

Accordingly, we design a reference model–based user requirements elicitation process of the IT-based system which aims to improve BITA by addressing a set of recognized elicitation problems (e.g., weak knowledge of application domain, communication flaws) [46]. To do so, two-phase research according to the design science approach is followed. In the design phase, a reference model-based user requirements elicitation process is designed [47]. The combinations of asking strategy with a reference model strategy are used to design our artifact. The reference model strategy is realized by means of a particular reference model and the asking strategy is realized by means of a particular elicitation technique. In the evaluation phase, the applicability and usefulness of the designed artifact for the co-development is evaluated in case studies.

5 Research Results

The results of our designed reference model-based approach (Table 1) are presented here. To demonstrate the feasibility of the approach and as a proof of concept, the results of one of the key capabilities, i.e., customer understanding is also explained.

Step 1: In our previous work, the key business capabilities of a VN were identified from literature and classified in a structured way. They are customer understanding, partnership, trust-based interaction, engagement, design, and delivery of integrated solutions, knowledge management, and process orchestration and coordination [39].

Step 2: As mentioned above, in this paper, we focus only on the key capability of customer understanding. The importance of this key capability is emphasized in literature. As, an in-depth understanding of customer needs is regarded as a first step towards delivering seamless customer experience [48, 49]. To identify key business processes of customer understanding, we realize that this capability is an abstract construct and needs further conceptualization. Therefore, we used the concept of customer knowledge management in a VN setting (VN-CKM), because customer knowledge is essential for understanding and expression of customer needs [48, 50]. In order to get the right customer knowledge to the right people at the right time and to handle it systematically, firms in general and VN specifically should have the capability to manage their customer knowledge. We thus focused on this VN-CKM capability. In our prior work, the VN-CKM key processes were identified from literature. They are customer knowledge creation, storage/retrieval, transfer, and application processes [51].

Step 3: Two concrete reference models, respectively, the VN-CKM process and the VN-CKM challenge reference models, were designed and validated. The reason for creating these two types of reference models was that when talking to people about their tasks and roles, talking about abstract objectives and goals would have been too difficult. But talking about the things people do and the problems and barriers that affect their work would be much easier. Consequently, developing a reference model which describes the business processes or challenges will be aligned with topics that people can easily talk about. Thus, we expected that the VN-CKM process and the VN-CKM challenge reference models can be understood by people and are likely to be used by them. In our prior works, these reference models were designed and validated [52, 53]. In the VN-CKM process reference model, the four key processes of customer knowledge management in a VN are characterized regarding their sub-processes activities, control, and outcome (Table 2).

Table 2. Example part of VN-CKM process reference model [52]

Process	Sub process	Activity	Control		Outcome
			Formal	Informal	
Knowledge creation	Tacit-tacit (Socialization)	Contextual understanding of customer experience and problems, socializing in relaxed environments	-	Briefing sessions; reciprocal interactions; dialogues	Mutual understanding of customer problems in the context of usage, Increasing social cohesion in a network

In the VN-CKM challenge reference model (Table 3), challenges in relation to knowledge exchange in a VN setting are classified into five challenge areas and 28 challenge types.

Table 3. Example part of VN-CKM challenge reference model [53]

Challenge area	Challenge types
Network Structure Challenges	Transactive memory
	Relationship
	Complex network
	General distance
	Cultural distance

Step 4: A reference model–based user requirement elicitation process by using a Delphi technique was designed (Fig. 2). A theoretical justification of the selection of a Delphi technique is presented in one of our previous papers [47].

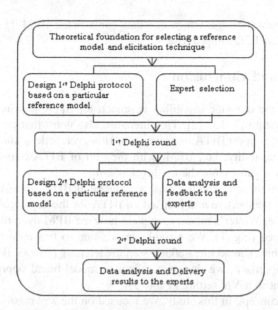

Fig. 2. A reference model–based user requirements elicitation process

According to the structure of a Delphi technique, eligible participants should be selected based on specific criteria. A two-round Delphi session are guided by Delphi protocols which are based on a reference model. While the first round is for individual brainstorming, the second round is for verification of the results of the first round, and for justification of the expert's opinion based on a controlled feedback (Further information is presented in one of our previous papers [55]). Based on the advantages of using a reference model (e.g., a template for communication, creating a shared understanding) and the benefits of a Delphi technique (e.g., eliminates undesirable group effects, and support asynchronous communication) our artifact was designed to address one class of elicitation problems in a VN setting. These problems as suggested by [46] are: weak knowledge of application domain, communication flaws between the project team and users, terminological problems, users with difficulties in separating requirements from previously known solutions, missing traceability, incomplete requirements, and inconsistent requirements.

We also designed two instances of this artifact, respectively, based on the VN-CKM process reference model and the VN-CKM challenge reference model. Their applicability and usefulness in dealing with the elicitation problems were evaluated in two separate studies. The two elicitation problems of 'communication flow' and 'weak domain knowledge,' which addresses well by the empirical data, are also acknowledged as the two main barriers in achieving better BIA [1, 54, 55]. We can thus conclude that our designed artifact contributes to dealing with these BIA problems and thus contributes to the BITA improvement. We thereby contribute to enhancing the BPM dynamic capability of a VN. Furthermore, during evaluation phase, participants came up with suggestions for improvements of VN-CKM processes and their supporting IT-based systems. Those suggestions indicated the viability of our designed artifact for the co-development, which can thus enhance the BPM dynamic capability of a VN and support BITA improvement.

6 Discussion and Conclusion

The usefulness of the dynamic capability approach for BITA improvement has been highlighted in literature [7, 13, 22]. This literature also notes that co-development of business and IT can support BITA improvement. However, little is known about how a specific dynamic capability, i.e., BPM, with the aim of BITA improvement can be enhanced and how it can enable the co-development.

To contribute to these research gapes, we looked at BITA improvement from the dynamic capability perspective and focused on BITA for the key capabilities of a VN. We used the Zollo & Winter's model to explain how the BPM dynamic capability of a VN can be enhanced (Fig. 1). We provide an addition to this model by including a reference model which can accelerate/kick-start the learning process. Based on a design science research approach, we design a reference model-based approach to support BITA improvement in a VN setting (Table 1).

As a proof of concept, in this study, we focused on the key capability of customer understanding and developed and used two relevant reference models for that, i.e., the VN-CKM process and the VN-CKM challenge reference models. To provide comprehensive support for BITA improvement for all strategic areas of key capabilities of a VN, we suggest that future research will develop reference models for the other key capabilities of a VN. Furthermore, alignment initiatives in a VN setting involve considerable complexity and can take substantial time to improve. Thus as BITA improvement is a long-lasting effort, due to time restrictions of this research, we could not evaluate the actual improvement of BITA in practice. The results of evaluation of the proposed approach provide a good indication of the overall validity, applicability, and usefulness of this artifact. However, more empirical investigation, especially through conducting longitudinal case studies, can enhance the confidence in the findings.

Our reference model approach presents a novel perspective and contributes to the ongoing discussion of BITA improvement in a VN setting. However, we do not claim that the process-based and challenge-based reference models and the Delphi elicitation technique are the only options available. Other types of reference models (e.g., goal-based reference model) and other types of user requirements elicitation techniques might be useful as well, and should be investigated in future studies.

References

1. Luftman, J., Lyytinen, K., Ben Zvi, T.: Enhancing the measurement of information technology (IT) business alignment and its influence on company performance. J. Inf. Technol. **32**(1), 26–46 (2017)
2. Gerow, J.E., Thatcher, J.B., Grover, V.: Six types of IT-business strategic alignment: an investigation of the constructs and their measurement. Eur. J. Inf. Syst. **24**(5), 465–491 (2015)

3. Henderson, J.C., Venkatraman, H.: Strategic alignment: Leveraging information technology for transforming organizations. IBM Syst. J. **32**(1), 472–484 (1993)
4. Tallon, P.P.: A process-oriented perspective on the alignment of information technology and business strategy. J. Manag. Inf. Syst. **24**(3), 227–268 (2007)
5. Chen, R.-S., et al.: Aligning information technology and business strategy with a dynamic capabilities perspective: a longitudinal study of a Taiwanese Semiconductor Company. Int. J. Inf. Manag. **28**(5), 366–378 (2008)
6. Pijpers, V., et al.: Using conceptual models to explore business-ICT alignment in networked value constellations. Requir. Eng. **17**(3), 203–226 (2012)
7. Coltman, T., et al.: Strategic IT alignment: twenty-five years on. J. Inf. Technol. **30**(2), 91–100 (2015)
8. Grefen, P., Turetken, O.: Advanced business process management in networked E-business scenarios. Int. J. E-Bus. Res. (IJEBR) **13**(4), 70–104 (2017)
9. Vargo, S.L., Lusch, R.F.: Evolving to a new dominant logic for marketing. J. Mark. **68**(1), 1–17 (2004)
10. Aarikka-Stenroos, L., Jaakkola, E.: Value co-creation in knowledge intensive business services: a dyadic perspective on the joint problem solving process. Ind. Mark. Manag. **41**(1), 15–26 (2012)
11. Gebauer, H., Paiola, M., Saccani, N.: Characterizing service networks for moving from products to solutions. Ind. Mark. Manag. **42**(1), 31–46 (2013)
12. Camarinha-Matos, L.M.: Collaborative networked organizations: Status and trends in manufacturing. Annu. Rev. Control **33**(2), 199–208 (2009)
13. Baker, J., et al.: Conceptualizing the dynamic strategic alignment competency. J. Assoc. Inf. Syst. **12**(4), 299 (2011)
14. Zhang, M., et al.: Evolvement of business-it alignment: a conceptual model and intervening changes from resource allocation. IEEE Access **6**, 9160–9172 (2018)
15. Ravichandran, T., Lertwongsatien, C., Lertwongsatien, C.: Effect of information systems resources and capabilities on firm performance: a resource-based perspective. J. Manag. Inf. Syst. **21**(4), 237–276 (2005)
16. Trkman, P.: The critical success factors of business process management. Int. J. Inf. Manag. **30**(2), 125–134 (2010)
17. Zollo, M., Winter, S.G.: Deliberate learning and the evolution of dynamic capabilities. Organ. Sci. **13**(3), 339–351 (2002)
18. Zahra, S.A., Sapienza, H.J., Davidsson, P.: Entrepreneurship and dynamic capabilities: a review, model and research agenda. J. Manag. Stud. **43**(4), 917–955 (2006)
19. Vera, D., et al.: Knowledge-based and contextual factors associated with R&D teams' improvisation capability. J. Manag. **42**(7), 1874–1903 (2016)
20. Thomas, O.: Understanding the term reference model in information systems research: history, literature analysis and explanation. In: Bussler, C.J., Haller, A. (eds.) BPM 2005. LNCS, vol. 3812, pp. 484–496. Springer, Heidelberg (2006). https://doi.org/10.1007/11678564_45
21. Frank, U.: Evaluation of reference models. Reference modeling for business systems analysis, pp. 118–140 (2007)
22. Yeow, A., Soh, C., Hansen, R.: Aligning with new digital strategy: a dynamic capabilities approach. J. Strat. Inf. Syst. **27**(1), 43–58 (2018)
23. Teece, D.J.: Explicating dynamic capabilities: the nature and microfoundations of (sustainable) enterprise performance. Strat. Manag. J. **28**(13), 1319–1350 (2007)
24. Schwarz, A., et al.: A dynamic capabilities approach to understanding the impact of IT-enabled businesses processes and IT-business alignment on the strategic and operational performance of the firm. Commun. Assoc. Inf. Syst. **26**(1), 4 (2010)

25. Camarinha-Matos, L.M.: Collaborative networks: a mechanism for enterprise agility and resilience. In: Mertins, K., Bénaben, F., Poler, R., Bourrières, J.-P. (eds.) Enterprise Interoperability VI. PIC, vol. 7, pp. 3–11. Springer, Cham (2014). https://doi.org/10.1007/978-3-319-04948-9_1

26. Schryen, G.: Revisiting IS business value research: what we already know, what we still need to know, and how we can get there. Eur. J. Inf. Syst. **22**(2), 139–169 (2013)

27. Wang, Y., et al.: IT capabilities and innovation performance: the mediating role of market orientation. CAIS **33**, 9 (2013)

28. Grant, R.M.: The resource-based theory of competitive advantage: implications for strategy formulation. Calif. Manag. Rev. **33**, 114–135 (1991)

29. Teece, D.J.: A capability theory of the firm: an economics and (strategic) management perspective. N. Z. Econ. Pap. (2017). https://doi.org/10.1080/00779954.2017.1371208

30. Eisenhardt, K.M., Martin, J.A.: Dynamic capabilities: what are they? Strat. Manag. J. **21**, 1105–1121 (2000)

31. Ortbach, K., et al.: A dynamic capability-based framework for business process management: theorizing and empirical application. In: 2012 45th Hawaii International Conference on System Science (HICSS). IEEE (2012)

32. Lehnert, M., Linhart, A., Roeglinger, M.: Exploring the intersection of business process improvement and BPM capability development: a research agenda. Bus. Process Manag. J. **23**(2), 275–292 (2017)

33. Lichtenthaler, U., Lichtenthaler, E.: A capability-based framework for open innovation: complementing absorptive capacity. J. Manag. Stud. **46**(8), 1315–1338 (2009)

34. Schwens, C., Kabst, R.: How early opposed to late internationalizers learn: experience of others and paradigms of interpretation. Int. Bus. Rev. **18**(5), 509–522 (2009)

35. Peffers, K., et al.: A design science research methodology for information systems research. J. Manag. Inf. Syst. **24**(3), 45–77 (2007)

36. Hevner, A., et al.: Design science in information systems research. MIS Q. **28**(1), 75–105 (2004)

37. Kitchenham, B.: Procedures for performing systematic reviews. Keele, UK, Keele University **33**(2004), 1–26 (2004)

38. Habershon, N.: Metaplan (R): achieving two-way communications. J. Eur. Ind. Train. **17**(7), 8–13 (1993)

39. Bagheri, S., Kusters, R.J., Trienekens, J.: Business-IT alignment in PSS value networks: a capability-based framework. In: Camarinha-Matos, L.M., Afsarmanesh, H. (eds.) PRO-VE 2014. IAICT, vol. 434, pp. 273–284. Springer, Heidelberg (2014). https://doi.org/10.1007/978-3-662-44745-1_27

40. Ullah, A., Lai, R.: A systematic review of business and information technology alignment. ACM Trans. Manag. Inf. Syst. (TMIS) **4**(1), 4 (2013)

41. Aversano, L., Grasso, C., Tortorella, M.: Managing the alignment between business processes and software systems. Inf. Softw. Technol. **72**, 171–188 (2016)

42. Ullah, A., Lai, R.: Modeling business goal for business/it alignment using requirements engineering. J. Comput. Inf. Syst. **51**(3), 21–28 (2011)

43. Bleistein, S.J., et al.: B-SCP: a requirements analysis framework for validating strategic alignment of organizational IT based on strategy, context, and process. Inf. Softw. Technol. **48**(9), 846–868 (2006)

44. Davis, G.B.: Strategies for information requirements determination. IBM Syst. J. **21**(1), 4–30 (1982)

45. Camarinha-Matos, L.M., et al.: Collaborative networked organizations–Concepts and practice in manufacturing enterprises. Comput. Ind. Eng. **57**(1), 46–60 (2009)

46. Fernandez, D.M., et al.: Naming the pain in requirements engineering. Empir. Softw. Eng. **22**(5), 2298–2338 (2017)
47. Bagheri, S., Kusters, R.J., Trienekens, J.J.: Eliciting end users requirements of a supportive system for tacit knowledge management processes in value networks: a Delphi study. In: 2017 International Conference on Engineering, Technology and Innovation (ICE/ITMC). IEEE (2017)
48. Payne, A.F., Storbacka, K., Frow, P.: Managing the co-creation of value. J. Acad. Mark. Sci. **36**(1), 83–96 (2008)
49. Zomerdijk, L.G., Voss, C.A.: NSD processes and practices in experiential services. J. Prod. Innov. Manag. **28**(1), 63–80 (2011)
50. Jaakkola, E., Hakanen, T.: Value co-creation in solution networks. Ind. Mark. Manag. **42**(1), 47–58 (2013)
51. Bagheri, S., Kusters, R., Trienekens, J.: Business-IT alignment in PSS value networks linking customer knowledge management to social customer relationship management. In: ICEIS 2015, pp. 249–257. SciTePress (2015)
52. Bagheri, S., Kusters, R., Trienekens, J.: The customer knowledge management lifecycle in PSS value networks: towards process characterization. In: Academic Conferences and Publishing International Limited Reading, UK (2015)
53. Bagheri, S., et al.: Classification framework of knowledge transfer issues across value networks. Procedia CIRP **47**, 382–387 (2016)
54. Preston, D.S., Karahanna, E.: Antecedents of IS strategic alignment: a nomological network. Inf. Syst. Res. **20**(2), 159–179 (2009)
55. Alaceva, C., Rusu, L.: Barriers in achieving business/IT alignment in a large Swedish company: what we have learned? Comput. Hum. Behav. **51**, 715–728 (2015)

Ontology Development Strategies in Industrial Contexts

Vladimir Tarasov[1]([✉]), Ulf Seigerroth[1], and Kurt Sandkuhl[1,2]

[1] School of Engineering, Jönköping University, Jönköping, Sweden
{Vladimir.Tarasov,Ulf.Seigerroth,Kurt.Sandkuhl}@ju.se
[2] Institute of Computer Science, Rostock University, Rostock, Germany
Kurt.Sandkuhl@uni-rostock.de

Abstract. Knowledge-based systems are used extensively to support functioning of enterprises. Such systems need to reflect the aligned business-IT view and create shared understanding of the domain. Ontologies are used as part of many knowledge-bases systems. The industrial context affects the process of ontology engineering in terms of business requirements and technical constraints. This paper presents a study of four industrial cases that included ontology development. The study resulted in identification of seven factors that were used to compare the industrial cases. The most influential factors were found to be reuse of ontologies/models, stakeholder groups involved, and level of applicability of ontology. Finally, four recommendation were formulated for projects intended to create shared understanding in an enterprise.

Keywords: Business and it alignment · Knowledge management
Ontology engineering · Industrial development context

1 Introduction

Knowledge management is an established practice in many industrial areas and public authorities with the general objective to contribute to a systematic identification, capturing, integration and maintenance of knowledge important for the organization [1]. The IT support for knowledge management typically consists of different systems tailored to the organizational needs, such as knowledge management systems, decision support systems or knowledge portals. A typical feature common for these systems is that they incorporate or built upon a clearly defined terminology, often formalized as taxonomy, dictionary, semantic net or ontology, which forms the basis for knowledge representation and definition of rules in the systems. From an organizational perspective, it is important that this terminology is shared by both business and IT stakeholders, because sharing knowledge essentially depends on a common understanding of the terminology used. From an organizational perspective, knowledge management and sharing a terminology contributes to business and IT alignment (BITA). BITA is a concept that cuts through a number of dimensions of enterprises and BITA can

W. Abramowicz and A. Paschke (Eds.): BIS 2018 Workshops, LNBIP 339, pp. 156–167, 2019.
https://doi.org/10.1007/978-3-030-04849-5_14

be addressed from different perspectives. In general, strategic, structural, social and cultural dimensions of BITA can be identified [2]. Another way to address BITA is to say that we need to create both horizontal- and vertical alignment between business and IT. Horizontal BITA means to apply a product lifecycle perspective which would include activities such as: product development, manufacturing, production design, production planning, production, logistics, time to, and launch on market, sales, predictive maintenance, customer involvement etc. Vertical BITA, on the other hand, will include aspects such as: strategy, vision, organization, business models, processes, infrastructures, technologies and all the way down to components, people, algorithms, micro services etc. Regardless of which dimensions are in focus for the current BITA effort, there is an apparent need for a shared and clear common terminology.

In this paper we therefore focus on a specific aspect of knowledge management and BITA: the development of ontologies representing the shared terminology in an enterprise or in a selected application domain within an enterprise. The paper investigates how industrial context affects development strategy in an industrial ontology engineering projects.

2   Background

2.1   Ontology Engineering

There are a number of methodologies for ontology development. Ontology 101 proposes a seven-step method to create an ontology using an ontology editing environment, such as Protégé [3]. The method introduces competency questions and ontology reuse as well as practical advice on ontology design. Another well-known ontology development methodology is METHONTOLOGY [4]. It contributes with a general framework for ontology development, which describes series of activities for development, management and support sub-processes. In addition, METHONTOLOGY proposes ontology life cycle as a series of evolving prototypes. The On-To-Knowledge methodology is focused on application-driven ontology development [5]. According to this method, engineering and industrial experts should actively be involved in the development of an ontology, in particular during the early stages of ontology engineering. Agile approach to ontology development is reflected in the eXtreme Design (XD) methodology that emphasises the use of ontology design patterns, customer involvement, task-oriented design, and collaborative and incremental development [6]. These methods focus on a collaborative, incremental, and iterative process of ontology development.

2.2   Business and IT Alignment

As been mentioned in the introduction, BITA is a concept that cuts through a number of dimensions of enterprises and BITA can be addressed from different perspectives. An important dimension of BITA is to bridge the gap between organizational context and technology. Several scholars have emphasized the need to capture both organization (business) and technology during design and implementation of Information System (IS) (e.g. cf. [7]). One way to approach this is to create a common vocabulary that will serve as abstraction of complex enterprises and support communication, dissemination and reuse of knowledge [8]. Formalized common vocabularies are able to capture different aspects of enterprise practices in terms of procedures, operations, and management and thus bridge the gap between organizational context and technology to facilitate BITA [9].

A promising way to link organizational context and technology is to view enterprises from an action perspective where actions are performed by humans and artefacts. Socio-instrumental pragmatism [10] incorporates human, organizational, and IS/IT-enabled actions within a single, coherent taxonomy or ontology. This concern of theorizing actions has also been acknowledged by actor-network theory (ANT) [11], where technology and people are both regarded as social actors. As identified by Goldkuhl and Ågerfalk [12] it is necessary, therefore, to acknowledge both the social in the technical and the technical in the social—a duality that is a main concern within BITA. Research has shown that alignment of business with IT is often addressed as a top concern of IT and business practitioners [2]. De Haes and Van Grembergen [13] discuss various practice-oriented frameworks such as Enterprise Governance of IT (EGIT), and COBIT and Val IT. They argue, in particular, that implementation of EGIT impacts the achievement of specific IT goals, which in turn impacts the achievement of business goals.

2.3   Related Work

Previous work of relevance for our research originates from two areas of computer science: experience reports on ontology development and case descriptions reporting on industrial ontology engineering. In the scientific literature, there are only a few publications which systematically investigate experiences and reflect on practices from ontology engineering. Almeida Falbo [14] discusses strong points and weaknesses of the SABiO (Systematic Approach for Building Ontologies) ontology development approach and derives improvement opportunities. Park et al. [15] report on the development of an ontology based on the guidelines provided by METHONTOLOGY, examines the utility of the method and discusses the drawbacks and disadvantages. Mizoguchi [16] presents focuses on the practice of ontological engineering and presents results and experiences without addressing any specific method. Brusa et al. [17] reflect experiences from merging different ontology development methods in software engineering and outlines best practices. Finally, Hristozova et al. [18] report on lessons learnt during the development of an ontology using the EXPLODE method for value-added publishing. Furthermore, our previous work in [19,20] report on experiences from ontology construction in practice, which is substantially extended in this paper by including additional cases and another methodical approach for comparing cases and strategies.

3   Research Approach

Our research was driven by the following research question which originated from the observation that in particular industrial development projects ontologies were quite different from their construction process:

What are the factors in industrial ontology engineering projects that affect ontology construction?

The research method used for working on this research question is a combination of literature study and multiple case study. Based on the research question defined, we started identifying research areas with relevant work for this question and analyzed the literature in these areas. The purpose of the analysis was to find existing studies which systematically analyze experiences of ontology engineering and present theories about factors and their origin. Due to the focus on engineering processes, an additional area to investigate are methodologies for ontology construction with their built-in possibilities to adapt to industrial requirements. The summary of the results are presented in Sect. 2.3.

Since the literature study returned only "candidates" for factors to be investigated rather than proven theories, we decided to perform a multiple case study in order to gather information pertinent for the subject area. Qualitative case study is an approach to research that facilitates exploration of a phenomenon within its context using a variety of data sources. This ensures that the subject under consideration is not explored from only one perspective, but rather from a variety of perspectives which allows for multiple facets of the phenomenon to be revealed and understood. Yin differentiates various kinds of case studies: explanatory, exploratory and descriptive [21]. The case studies presented in Sect. 4 have to be considered as descriptive, as they are used to describe the phenomenon of ontology engineering in the real-life context in which it occurs. Based on the case study results, we conclude that there are certain factors to consider. This argumentative-deductive part of our work is discussed in Sect. 5.

As we aim at investigating factors for industrial ontology engineering, our focus has to be on data sources containing very detailed reports and rich case descriptions. This type of report is quite sparse in scientific literature on ontology engineering (see Sect. 2.3). Thus, we decided to use case studies of ontology development projects performed in our own research groups. We selected four projects (see next section) where not only the original project documentation was available to us but also the personnel involved in the project could be contacted and interviewed. The projects analysed originated from School of Engineering at Jönköping University (Sweden), research group computer science and informatics, and Rostock University (Germany), research group business information systems who in some projects jointly worked on the tasks. The analysis of the projects was done in distributed teams using a joint list of aspects to be investigated.

4   Industrial Cases

4.1   OSTAG

The project Ontology-based Software Test Case Generation (OSTAG) was supported by the Knowledge Foundation and aimed at improving the automation of testing activities related to software systems. The technical purpose was to create a method for deriving test case data from an ontology representing the requirement specification and domain for a software system. One of the industrial cases was provided by the participating company, Saab Avionics and originated from the avionics domain. A software requirements ontology was developed representing the requirements of a software component pertaining to an embedded system located in an airplane [22]. The developed ontology includes three specific pieces of knowledge: (1) a meta model of the software requirements, (2) the domain knowledge of the application, e.g. general knowledge of the hardware and software, electronic communication standards, etc., (3) all the requirement specifications defined in the SRS documents provided by Saab. The ontology was created with Protégé and was written in OWL (Web Ontology Language). The final version of the ontology contained 43 concepts, 37 object properties, 12 datatype properties, and 206 instances in total. The ontology was utilised to create software test cases by using inference rules, coded in Prolog, that represented the expertise of an expert software tester [23].

During the development, the team of two ontology engineers worked as a pair and followed an iterative and incremental process. There were five iterations, which resulted in four major versions of the requirements ontology. The followed methodology was the combination of the steps in Ontology 101 [3], and the activities in the supporting process in METHONTOLOGY [4]. Lightweight competence questions (CQs) were also used to guide the creation of the ontology. A project workshop with the participating companies was conducted in the beginning of each iteration, which included presentation of the current results and feedback from the industry experts. Moreover, four meetings with the developers and testers from Saab were arranged to discuss the issues encountered during the acquisition and specification steps. The evaluation of the requirements ontology consisted of its use in the test case generation in every iteration and a evaluation session with the developers and testers from Saab. The feedback was used by the knowledge engineering team to modify the ontology. The HermiT reasoner was used to check the consistency of the ontology.

4.2   CLICK

The second case was the CLICK project financed by the Vinnvård Programme[1]. The focus of CLICK was on supporting networking among researchers in a number of Vinnvård-financed projects spread throughout Sweden. The technical objective of this project was to create an on-line service to facilitate the

---

[1] http://www.vinnvard.se/.

task of seeking collaborators for joint work on producing scientific artefacts [24]. Each researcher was modelled by a profile that represented competences of the researcher and was comprised of major research areas, published papers, engagement in projects, and known co-workers. The search of potential collaborators was based on matching the researcher's profile against others' profiles. The resulting competence profiles were represented as sets of linked instances in the competence profile ontology saved in OWL. The ontology was created with TopBraid Composer and contained 52321 concepts, 11 object properties, 14 datatype properties, and 22790 instances in total. The most part of data needed for the creation of competence profiles was pulled from two publicly available data sources: PubMed (the database of citations for biomedical literature) and DiVA (Academic Archive On-line) through schema transformations. The rest of the data was imported from proprietary files.

The ontology development was carried out as an inherent part of the software development process, which followed agile approach. Consequently, the ontology development process was a combination of Ontology 101 [3] with elements of XD [6]: an iterative process with close involvement of the main stakeholder. The profile ontology creation started with the reuse of the thesaurus of MeSH (Medical Subject Headings)[2]. During the eight project iterations, five prototypes of the on-line service was developed, including five versions of the profile ontology. An ontology engineer and two domain experts were working on the ontology continuously. The representatives of the main stakeholder (the Vinnvård Programme) were part of several workshops, which focused on detailed project updates and in-depth discussions of the prototypes. These workshops contributed to gathering requirements to the ontology and elaboration of the ontology design. Moreover, two rounds of interviews with end users were carried out during the user study. The user interviews resulted in creation of several user stories that contained requirements to the content of the ontology profiles. Between the interview rounds a workshop with a bigger group of end users was arranged. This user workshop resulted in identification of important expertise to model in a profile as well as in prioritization of the tasks in the ontology development plan.

4.3   SEMCO

The third industrial case originates from automotive industries and the SEMCO project (Semantic modeling of Components in automotive industries) [25]. Automotive manufacturers and suppliers have to manage a large number of product variations and their integration into a specific car model. Many products are designed as product families consisting of configurable components prepared for reuse across different product instantiations. In order to manage and control variety, manufacturers and suppliers increasingly recognize the need to manage project entities like models, documents, metadata, and classification taxonomies in such a manner that the integrative usage of these entities is supported. In SEMCO, the application scenario guiding the development of an ontology was

---

[2] http://www.ncbi.nlm.nih.gov/mesh.

the integration of different kinds of structures reflecting the artefacts and their interrelations. On the one hand, model hierarchies had to be captured, structured and implemented on different modelling levels (system, software, hardware, etc.), which also included model instances (artefacts) to be managed. On the other hand, networks of terms and taxonomies had to be considered as equally important. These networks represented organizational structures, product structures or taxonomies originating from customers closely related to artefacts. Explicit denotation of these relationships proved beneficial for identification of reuse potential of components or artefacts. The ontology construction was performed in a Swedish automotive supplier of safety components implemented as software-intensive systems. The development process applied is an enhanced version of the METHONTOLOGY process [4]. Most important knowledge sources were (1) a description of the suppliers internal software development process with defined procedures for all major aspects of software development and software project management and (2) documentation of two example cases for requirement handling, including original customer requirements, system and functional requirements, and (3) interviews and working sessions with members of the software development department were conducted including project manager, software developers and engineers. The resulting ontology consisted of 379 concepts and with an average depth of inheritance of 3.5 [25].

4.4 SEMA

Object recognition in videos is the topic of a research project funded by the State Ministry for Economics of Mecklenburg-Western Pomerania. Partners in this project are Future TV, an innovative company from Rostock (Germany) in the field of media and entertainment, Fraunhofer-Institute IGD-Rostock and the chair Business Information Systems. The core intention of the project is to develop a fully automatic tagging of arbitrary video films which provides information about the objects visible in the video in different scenes and at different points in time. This information about the video content could be used to select the most relevant video for the interests of a consumer or what commercials would fit best to the video content and the user watching the video-to give just two examples. From a technical perspective, the project aims at combining different techniques from artificial intelligence to improve precision of the object recognition and at the same time reduce the computational workload. The sub-project of Rostock University is called "Semantic Assistance for Object Recognition in Videos (SEMA)" and has a planned runtime of 24 months starting in April 2018.

The requirements to the ontology in SEMA are that two quite diverse areas have to be covered and integrated. One area is the content of the videos, i.e. the application domains from which the video content is taken has to be reflected. For the initial phase of the project this includes economics, home décor, selected parts of men's fashion, sports and cars. Later on, the content might be extended which requires a design of the ontology prepared for change and extension. The other area is the recognition of situations in videos in the context of demand profiles of individual users or of companies targeting customers in this context. Although this area is to some extent dependent on the content of the videos (first area) it also includes own structures and knowledge, for example needed for structuring demands, targets and situations.

Development of the ontology is done in a mixed group of knowledge engineers from research, marketing people and domains experts from the company, and software engineers from the company aiming at integrating the ontology into the existing content management system. The development approach used is to first build an application ontology overarching both areas mentioned above and afterwards identify existing ontologies or conceptual models for the content areas under consideration, re-engineer and integrate them. To some extent, this approach is inspired by the methodology proposed in [3] and the ontology pattern based work by [26].

5   Comparison of the Cases

The comparison of the cases discussed in the previous section aims at tackling the research question formulated in Sect. 3. Some input to answering this question is already available from previous research on ontology development methodologies (Sect. 2.1) which identifies factors such as:

- The possibility to reuse existing ontologies and how this changes the construction process,
- The representation selected for the ontology and how thus might change the way of coding it, or
- The required level of formality which affects the time required for the development and potential application level of an ontology.

For the above aspects, our work aims at evaluating whether they can be confirmed in our industrial cases. What from our observation is not sufficiently addressed in existing research (see Sect. 2.3) are the effects of stakeholder involvement, ontology update cycles and technical constraints on the ontology development process. Ontology update cycle in this context refers to the expected need for changing or adapting the ontology to new usage scenarios or to changing domain knowledge. Furthermore, we designed our study based on the assumption that the effects on ontology engineering projects not only manifest in the development process but also in other aspects of the project organisation. More concrete, we consider:

- The roles established in the engineering team (e.g. knowledge engineer, tool expert, knowledge analyst),
- The stakeholders involved from the organisation under consideration (e.g. domain experts, project manager or process owner),
- The steps and activities of the development process,
- The artefacts created during the development process.

Table 1. Comparison of the cases with respect to the factors

Aspect to Compare	OSTAG	CLICK	SEMCO	SEMA
Reuse of ontologies or models	No	Moderate (taxonomy, bibliographic information)	No	Extensive (taxonomies, standards)
Representation of ontology	OWL	OWL	Frames (OKBC-based)	OWL
Level of applicability	Problem solving	Shared conceptual model	Process reuse	Process reuse
Roles in engineering team	Project manager, Tool specialist, Knowledge Engineer	Project manager, Tool specialist, Knowledge Engineer, Reuse Engineer	Project manager, Tool specialist, Knowledge Engineer	Project manager, Tool specialist, Knowledge Engineer, Reuse Engineer
Stakeholder groups involved	Domain experts (Engineers)	Domain experts, Business Area Experts, End Users	Domain experts (Engineers)	Domain experts, Business Area Experts
Activities/Process	"Ontology 101" enriched by METHONTOLOGY	"Ontology 101" with elements of XD	"Ontology 101" enriched by METHONTOLOGY	"Ontology 101" plus reuse sub-process
Artefacts to be produced	CQ, Ontology	Ontology, Competence Profiles	CQ, Ontology	CQ, Ontology, Ontology Patterns

With the three factors mentioned in the literature and the four organizational aspects identified above, we all in all have seven aspects to consider for each case. We produced Table 1 comparing the cases regarding the seven aspects.

The observations made in our industrial cases confirmed that the possibility to reuse either ontologies or related conceptual models changes the construction process massively. In SEMA, the project with most intense reuse, a specific sub-procedure was designed and performed for managing reuse. This sub-procedure consisted of the essential activities of identification of potentially reusable models, in-depth check of suitability (from content and technical perspective), selection of what exactly to integrate, integration into ontology and quality check. This kind of sub-process was not required in the other projects. In CLICK, the reuse was determined by the domain and required only integration activity.

The level of formality is mentioned in the literature as a factor influencing the construction process. Formality level also affects potential applications of an ontology. However, it is not clearly defined in literature how to "measure" or determine the level of applicability in a "standardized" way. Alan Newell's idea of knowledge levels was applied in our case comparison [27]. Newell's view is that data structures (symbols) can be used to represent knowledge in a knowledge base, but those symbols cannot generate intelligent behaviour—unless some process is applied to those symbols. This means we have to distinguish the symbols in a knowledge base (knowledge representation) from the knowledge (capacity for rational behaviour) that the symbols can be used to generate. We cannot share knowledge bases if we do not also share the inference engines (or mental processes) that bring our knowledge bases to life. The level of applicability of ontologies could be differentiated according to the knowledge levels reflected in the knowledge bases. The most simple levels are only a known representation format (level 1) and additionally a shared vocabulary (level 2). In an ontology, we usually reach the next formality level (3), a shared conceptual model. If inference rules are properly and completely defined, the "process reuse" level (4) is given i.e. the process to be performed by interpreter when using the shared conceptual model is defined. The most complex level (5) is the problem solving level which requires completeness of knowledge base and inference rules with the problem and solution space. The highest applicability level is observed in the OSTAG case due to the complexity of the task to be solved—test case generation.

Roles in the engineering team, stakeholder groups involved in the construction process and tasks/activities to perform seem to be mutually reflective. Whenever domain experts without engineering background or end users have to be involved, there seems to be the need for business analyst in the engineering team in addition to knowledge engineers. If there is a high formality requirement, senior experts in the representation used are required. In reuse situations, the role of reuse engineer should be established. Moreover, in the CLICK project the intensive involvement of end users was necessary because the ontology requirements were not specified by the customer. Instead, the requirements were gradually refined through participative design during several iterations in line with the XD methodology, which differs from the other projects.

Regarding the representation of ontology, there was little variation. Nevertheless, the choice of tools to use in the project needs to be taken into account by the project management. Finally, the artefacts to be delivered affected the ontology development in one case. The creation of competence profiles in CLICK required extensive population of the ontology, which was carried out through data integration from the publicly available sources.

6   Conclusions

This paper presented the results of the literature study and multiple case study aimed at determining the factors that affect ontology development strategy in the context of industrial projects. The seven factors were identified and subsequently used to compare the four industrial cases. The most influential factors are reuse of ontologies/models, stakeholder groups involved, and level of applicability of ontology. The results can be utilised to develop formalized common vocabularies capturing both organization (business) and technology to facilitate BITA. Our recommendations derived from the analysis of the case comparison are as follows.

Recommendation 1: In projects with substantial reuse of existing conceptual models or ontologies, establish the role of a reuse engineer and explicitly define a reuse sub-procedure to be followed.

Recommendation 2: In projects with many non-expert modellers as domain experts or end users, integrate a person/role with experience in explicating implicit knowledge or in participatory work. This is essential when ontology requirements are to be gathered in a series of project iterations.

Recommendation 3: Use Alan Newell's proposal of knowledge levels to define the
level of applicability of the required result. If the applicability level exceeds
the shared conceptual model level, integrate a knowledge engineer specialising
in rule engines and inference mechanisms into the team.

Recommendation 4: Whenever creation of artefacts implies extensive population
of an ontology, investigate early in the project what data source are available
and how they can be integrated in an automated manner.

References

1. Hislop, D.: Knowledge Management in Organizations: A Critical Introduction. Oxford University Press, Oxford (2013)
2. Chan, Y.E., Reich, B.H.: IT alignment: what have we learned? J. Inf. Technol. **22**(4), 297–315 (2007)
3. Noy, N.F., McGuinness, D.L.: Ontology development 101: A guide to creating your first ontology. Technical report, Stanford Knowledge Systems Laboratory (2001). KSL-01-05
4. Fernández-López, M., Gómez-Pérez, A., Juristo, N.: METHONTOLOGY: from ontological art towards ontological engineering. In: Proceedings of the Ontological Engineering AAAI 1997 Spring Symposium Series, American Association for Artificial Intelligence, March 1997
5. Sure, Y., Staab, S., Studer, R.: On-to-knowledge methodology (OTKM). In: Staab, S., Studer, R. (eds.) Handbook on Ontologies, pp. 117–132. Springer, Heidelberg (2004). https://doi.org/10.1007/978-3-540-24750-0_6
6. Presutti, V., Daga, E., Gangemi, A., Blomqvist, E.: eXtreme design with content ontology design patterns. In: Blomqvist, E., Sandkuhl, K., Scharffe, F., Svatek, V. (eds.) Proceedings of the Workshop on Ontology Patterns (WOP 2009), Collocated with the 8th International Semantic Web Conference (ISWC-2009), pp. 83–97 (2009)
7. Gibson, C.F.: IT-enabled business change: an approach to understanding and managing risk. MIS Q. Exec. **2**(2), 104–115 (2003)
8. Frank, U.: Multi-perspective enterprise modeling: foundational concepts, prospects and future research challenges. Softw. Syst. Model. **13**(3), 941–962 (2014)
9. Seigerroth, U.: Enterprise modeling and enterprise architecture: the constituents of transformation and alignment of business and IT. Int. J. IT/Bus. Alignment Gov. **2**(1), 16–34 (2011)
10. Goldkuhl, G., Röstlinger, A.: Towards an integral understanding of organisations and information systems: Convergence of three theories. In: The 5th International Workshop on Organisational Semiotics, Delft (2002)
11. Latour, B.: Technology is society made durable. A Sociology of Monsters: Essays on Power, Technology, and Domination, pp. 103–131. Routledge, London (1991)
12. Goldkuhl, G., Ågerfalk, P.J.: IT artifacts as socio-pragmatic instruments: reconciling the pragmatic, semiotic, and technical. Int. J. Technol. Hum. Interact. **1**(3), 29–43 (2005)
13. Haes, S.D., Grembergen, W.V.: Analysing the impact of enterprise governance of IT practices on business performance. Int. J. IT/Bus. Alignment Gov. **1**(1), 14–38 (2010)

14. de Almeida Falbo, R.: Experiences in using a method for building domain ontologies. In: Proceedings of the 16th International Conference on Software Engineering and Knowledge Engineering, SEKE 2004. International Workshop on Ontology in Action, OIA 2004, pp. 474–477 (2004)
15. Park, J., Sung, K., Moon, S.: Developing graduation screen ontology based on the methontology approach. In: Fourth International Conference on Networked Computing and Advanced Information Management, NCM 2008, vol. 2, pp. 375–380 (2008)
16. Mizoguchi, R.: Ontological engineering: foundation of the next generation knowledge processing. In: Zhong, N., Yao, Y., Liu, J., Ohsuga, S. (eds.) WI 2001. LNCS (LNAI), vol. 2198, pp. 44–57. Springer, Heidelberg (2001). https://doi.org/10.1007/3-540-45490-X_5
17. Brusa, G., Caliusco, M.L., Chiotti, O.: Building ontology in public administration: a case study. In: Simperl, E.P.B., Hepp, M., Tempich, C. (eds.) Proceedings of the First International Workshop on Applications and Business Aspects of the Semantic Web (SEBIZ 2006). Collocated with the 5th International Semantic Web Conference (ISWC-2006) (2007)
18. Hristozova, M., Sterling, L.: Experiences with ontology development for value-added publishing. In Cranefield, S., Finin, T.W., Tamma, V.A.M., Willmott, S. (eds.) Proceedings of the Workshop on Ontologies in Agent Systems (OAS 2003) at the 2nd International Joint Conference on Autonomous Agents and Multi-Agent Systems, pp. 17–24 (2003)
19. Sandkuhl, K., Öhgren, A., Smirnov, A.V., Shilov, N., Kashevnik, A.: Ontology construction in practice - experiences and recommendations from industrial cases. In: Cardoso, J.S., Cordeiro, J., Filipe, J. (eds.) ICEIS 2007 - Proceedings of the Ninth International Conference on Enterprise Information Systems, pp. 250–256 (2007)
20. Sandkuhl, K., Smirnov, A., Shilov, N., Koç, H.: Ontology-driven enterprise modelling in practice: experiences from industrial cases. In: Persson, A., Stirna, J. (eds.) CAiSE 2015. LNBIP, vol. 215, pp. 209–220. Springer, Cham (2015). https://doi.org/10.1007/978-3-319-19243-7_21
21. Yin, R.K.: Case Study Research and Applications: Design and Methods. Sage Publications, Thousand Oaks (2017)
22. Tan, H., Ismail, M., Tarasov, V., Adlemo, A., Johansson, M.: Development and evaluation of a software requirements ontology. In: Exman, I., Llorens, J., Fraga, A. (eds.) Proceedings of the 7th International Workshop on Software Knowledge, SKY, (IC3K 2016), INSTICC, vol. 1, pp. 11–18. SciTePress (2016)
23. Tarasov, V., Tan, H., Ismail, M., Adlemo, A., Johansson, M.: Application of inference rules to a software requirements ontology to generate software test cases. In: Dragoni, M., Poveda-Villalón, M., Jimenez-Ruiz, E. (eds.) OWLED/ORE -2016. LNCS, vol. 10161, pp. 82–94. Springer, Cham (2017). https://doi.org/10.1007/978-3-319-54627-8_7
24. Tarasov, V., Höglund, P., de Roos, P.: Ontology-based eService enabling collaboration of researchers in healthcare. In: eChallenges e-2012 Conference Proceedings, IIMC International Information Management Corporation Ltd. (2012)
25. Sandkuhl, K., Billig, A.: Ontology-based artefact management in automotive electronics. Int. J. Comput. Integr. Manuf. 20(7), 627–638 (2007)
26. Blomqvist, E.: Semi-automatic Ontology Construction based on Patterns. Ph.D. thesis, Linköping University (2009)
27. Newell, A.: The knowledge level. Artif. Intell. 18(1), 87–127 (1982)

BSCT Workshop

BSCT 2018 Workshop Chairs' Message

We have a great pleasure to hand over to the readers the volume that contains papers selected for presentation at BSCT 2018: 1st Workshop on Blockchain and Smart Contract Technologies held on July 19–20, 2018 in Berlin, Germany. The event was co-organized with the 21st International Conference on Business Information Systems. It was a debut of the workshop and judging by the numbers - a very successful one.

In fact, the mentioned success of the event exceeded wildest expectations of the organizers. When we planned the organization of this new workshop we knew that there is an urgent and growing need from the researchers as well as business perspective to meet on the common ground in order to facilitate and accelerate the exchange of ideas and knowledge in the area of the workshop. In our conservative estimates we presumed the number of submissions to be around 15. But the submission system pointed this number in a week before the deadline. Two days before the deadline the number doubled. Ultimately the process ended with 46 submissions, tripling the initial anticipations. On the one hand we were really excited with the achieved level but on the other hand we were full of doubts whether we will be able to stand up to the high quality organizational characteristics that we are all accustomed to. As one may expect such abundance raise numerous organizational issues.

After all, the whole set of mentioned 46 papers were thoroughly reviewed. We managed to administer around 130 reviews in a short period of time. As a result of the review process 21 works were accepted for presentation and publication after additional editorial review. This way we reached the very decent level of acceptance rate at around 45%. The workshop covered a wide area of topics. There are also many challenges appearing on the horizon as the blockchain technologies are in a phase of swift advancement. Despite some turbulences on the cryptocurrencies markets we are certain that the blockchain and smart contract will thrive, develop and continue to emerge in many new usages. That is why we are strongly convinced that the workshop as a platform for discussion and sharing thoughts will be even more important in the years to come.

As a final point, the chairs would like to express their heartfelt gratitude to all the participants and especially authors whose attendance and contribution allowed to organize this very successful event. We believe that the workshop is all about community. Therefore the voice of the participants is of utmost importance to us. Programme Committee members are those people whose role is always undervalued. That is why we would like to state the words of our deepest thankfulness towards them. It is only thanks to their knowledge, sound judgment and kind support that the workshop took place in its final shape. Without this hard work of the PC the organizers would not be able to make the selection of the best works.

Finally, as usual we would like to direct our sincere appreciation to the organizers of the hosting conference (BIS2018). Without doubts their organizational know-how and assistance was one of key factors of success. The next BIS Conference will take place in Seville, Spain which for sure will be the venue of the 2nd Workshop on Blockchain and Smart Contract Technologies as well. Thus we would like to invite all this year participants, submitters and newcomers to the planned event in 2019.

Saulius Masteika

Erich Schweighofer

Piotr Stolarski

Organization

Chairs

Saulius Masteika	Laboratory of Decision Support and Dispute Management, College of Business, Victoria University, Australia
Erich Schweighofer	Centre for Computers and Law, University of Vienna, Austria
Piotr Stolarski	Poznań University of Economics and Business, Department of Information Systems, Poland

Program Committee

Rainer Alt	Leipzig University, Germany
Emmanuelle Anceaume	IRISA, France
Adrian Florea	'Lucian Blaga' University of Sibiu, Romania
François Charoy	Université de Lorraine – LORIA – Inria, France
Nicolas T. Courtois	University College London, UK
Sergi Delgado-Segura	Universitat Autònoma de Barcelona, Spain
Ernestas Filatovas	Vilnius University, Lithuania
Vladislav V. Fomin	Vilnius University, Lithuania
Jaap Gordijn	Vrije Universiteit Amsterdam, The Netherlands
Aquinas Hobor	National University of Singapore, Singapore
Constantin Houy	Institute for Information Systems at DFKI (IWi), Germany
Raja Jurdak	Commonwealth Scientific Industrial and Research Organization, Australia
Monika Kaczmarek	University Duisburg Essen, Germany
Kalinka Kaloyanova	University of Sofia, Bulgaria
Salil S. Kanhere	The University of New South Wales, Australia
Gary Klein	University of Colorado Boulder, USA
Eva Kühn	Vienna University of Technology, Austria
Romaric Ludinard	IMT Atlantique, France
Raimundas Matulevicius	University of Tartu, Estonia
Bill Maurer	University of California, USA
Massimo Mecella	Sapienza University of Rome
Remigijus Paulavičius	Vilnius University, Lithuania
Cristina Pérez-Solà	Universitat Autònoma de Barcelona, Spain
Sushmita Ruj	Indian Statistical Institute, India
Sherif Sakr	The University of New South Wales
Kouichi Sakurai	Kyushu University, Japan
Davor Svetinovic	Masdar Institute of Science and Technology, United Arab Emirates
Herve Verjus	Université de Savoie – LISTIC – Polytech'Savoie, France
Hans Weigand	Tilburg University, The Netherlands
Anna Wingkvist	Linnaeus University, Lithuania

Blockchain Backed DNSSEC

Scarlett Gourley$^{(\boxtimes)}$ and Hitesh Tewari

Trinity College Dublin, Dublin, Ireland
gourleys@tcd.ie, htewari@cs.tcd.ie

Abstract. The traditional Domain Name System (DNS) does not include any security details, making it vulnerable to a variety of attacks which were discovered in 1990. The Domain Name System Security Extensions (DNSSEC) attempted to address these concerns and extended the DNS protocol to add origin authentication and message integrity whilst remaining backwards compatible. Yet despite the fact that issues with DNS have been well known since the late 90s, there has been very little adoption of DNSSEC. This paper proposes a new system using blockchain technology. Our system aims to provide the same security benefits as DNSSEC whilst addressing the concerns that led to its slow adoption.

Keywords: Blockchain · DNS · DNSSEC · Fragmentation
Amplification attack · X509

1 Introduction

The DNS is a hierarchical and decentralised naming service, which translates human readable, more readily memorable names into IP addresses. In its original form is insecure and suffers from a number of protocol attacks. These include DNS spoofing/cache poisoning [14], DNS hijacking [4], and DNS rebinding [10].

A solution to this was the introduction of DNSSEC. However, DNSSEC also suffers from various problems, namely IP fragmentation [17], potential denial of service attacks [12], and complicated key management. This has caused a slow adoption of DNSSEC, with only 4% of second level domains signed [5].

In this paper we propose an alternative security extension set for DNS. This system aims to provide a client all the security benefits that DNSSEC grants, i.e. origin authentication and message integrity. We also wish to reduce responses to fit into a 512-byte UDP packet as per the original DNS standard [11], and to simplify the key management. This is in order to mitigate possible availability issues associated with DNSSEC. Finally, we intend to produce a protocol which minimises the number of requests necessary for signature validation.

This work was supported, in part, by Science Foundation Ireland grant 13/RC/2094 and co-funded under the European Regional Development Fund through the Southern & Eastern Regional Operational Programme to Lero - the Irish Software Research Centre (www.lero.ie).

© Springer Nature Switzerland AG 2019
W. Abramowicz and A. Paschke (Eds.): BIS 2018 Workshops, LNBIP 339, pp. 173–184, 2019.
https://doi.org/10.1007/978-3-030-04849-5_15

2   Background

In this section, we present the current DNSSEC system and how it operates. We also provide a brief introduction to the X.509 Public Key Infrastructure (PKI) and blockchain technology.

2.1   DNSSEC

DNSSEC is a set of security extensions which provides origin authentication and message integrity to DNS. It does this by using public key based digital signatures. To facilitate this, some new resource records (RRs) were added [2]:

- **RRSIG** records contain a digital signature
- **DNSKEY** records contain a signing key
- **DS** records contain the hash of a DNSKEY
- **NSEC** and **NSEC3** records map a denial of existence to a domain range.

RRs are grouped together to form RRsets. The RRset is digitally signed to form an RRSIG record [2].

Each zone has a Zone Signing Key (ZSK) pair. The private key portion is used to digitally sign the RRsets. The public portion is stored as a DNSKEY record in the name server. This DNSKEY also needs signing in order to prove its integrity. Each zone also has a Key Signing Key (KSK), which is used to sign the RRset of DNSKEY records. The public portion of the KSK is also stored as a DNSKEY record [2].

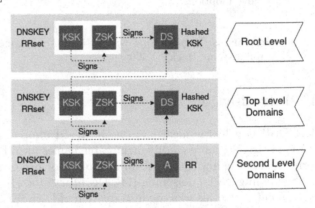

Fig. 1. Chain of trust

A DS RR is created by generating the hash of the public portion of the KSK. This hash is added to the parent zone (e.g. google.com would place their DS RR in the com zone). The parent would sign these DS RRs with their ZSK [2]. This carries up to the root server, where the root KSK is stored on the client's machine. Figure 1 contains a visualisation of this trust chain.

2.2   PKI

A PKI is a system for managing, distributing and revoking digital certificates [18]. A digital certificate is a digitally signed electronic document that contains information on the owner, intended to bind their identity and public key. These are created and issued by trusted third parties, known as Certificate Authorities (CAs) [18].

X.509 is a digital certificate standard that is used in many internet protocols, such as HTTPS [7]. In order for an entity to receive an X.509 certificate, they must create a Certificate Signing Request (CSR) which includes their identity and their public key. This CSR gets sent to a Registration Authority [9]. A Registration Authority is approved by a CA to accept, reject and revoke certificates [8,9]. If the CSR is accepted, an X.509 certificate signed by the CA is returned to the entity [9].

Once a certificate is returned to the owner, it can be used to establish a secure connection using their public key. In order to verify the certificate's public key, the CAs public key that signed the certificate must also be validated. This verification process is continued up until a trusted certificate, which is stored on the client's machine. Once a trusted signature is identified, it can be believed that the public key contained in the original certificate belongs to the certificate owner [9,18].

3 Related Work

The issue with DNSSEC lies with the need to have a chain of trust up to the root server. This leads to an excessive number of requests, and hence signed responses. If a domain name was bound to a public key in a trusted manner, we could remove this chain of trust.

Blockchain based PKIs have been proposed numerous times. Blockstack operates a complete naming system where namespaces can be registered [1]. However, any user can buy any name as there is no dispute authority. This means organisations will have difficulty registering their trademarked and copyrighted names.

X509Cloud is a framework which allows X.509 certificates to be added to a public blockchain network [16]. When a CSR is accepted the certificate is not only sent back to the individual, but it is also broadcasted on the X509Cloud blockchain network [16]. Each CA participating in the system will verify the certificate is valid. Once the transaction is validated it is grouped with other transactions into a block which is also be broadcasted. If the block is accepted, the next bundle of transactions is validated.

This framework offers a very simple solution which solves several issues. It allows organisations to distribute certificates to those within it in a convenient and secure way. It also solves the issues associated with CRLs, where it can take time for the changes to propagate through the network. Lastly, it creates an always up to date data store of the current X509 certificates that are in use by those participating in the system.

4 Protocol Design

The aim of this section is to create a DNS security extension, which does not suffer from common issues which arise in DNSSEC deployment. If the keys in

the DNS hierarchy are replaced with some other PKI, we can link an identity
with these keys [18]. We can therefore remove DNSKEY and DS RRs from the
DNS hierarchy and simply check the repository of whatever PKI we are using.

4.1   CSK

A Combined Signing Key (CSK) is what will be used to refer to a DNSSEC
configuration which uses a single key. This CSK is simply a KSK which also
operates as a ZSK, i.e. the DNSKEY RRset is signed by the same key which
signs all other RRsets in that zone. DNS software for authoritative servers can
enable this configuration. A flag is simply used to indicate the KSK signs all
RRsets [6].

4.2   PKI

The X509Cloud blockchain network will be used as the store for X.509 certificates. A single certificate which associated a domain name with a CSK is created.
An X.509 certificate is often created for a domain so that other internet protocols
can be used, and this same certificate could simply be used to sign DNS RRs.

4.3   Protocol

It is important to note that at any given stage in the resolution, the X509Cloud
blockchain network acts as a secure and trusted store. The root KSK is no longer
used as a trust anchor, so if the A RR for a name server was cached the resolution
could securely start from there.

A look-up where we would like the IPv4 address of google.com and know the
IP address of the name server which contains this would operate as follows:

1. A client initiates a normal lookup for the domain google.com, which gets
   forwarded to a recursive resolver
2. The recursive resolver will query the google.com name server for the
   google.com A RR
3. The google.com name server will respond with the A RR for google.com and
   a signature
4. The recursive resolver will search for the most recent entry of the google.com
   certificate in the X509Cloud blockchain network, check the validity of the
   certificate, and validate the signature
5. The verified A RR will be forwarded back to the client.

Once again, this could simply begin at the com name server if the IP address
for the google.com name server was not known. The ability to begin a resolution
from anywhere speeds up the verification process considerably as each level does
not need to be validated (Fig. 2).

The following is an example verification on the example.scarlett domain
which has a single certificate containing its CSK:

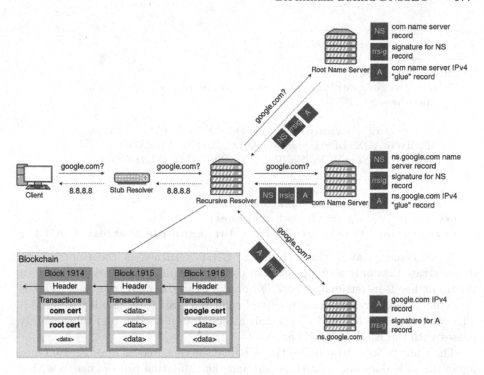

Fig. 2. Proposed protocol

```
1  $ ./bin/main @localhost -v 2 -t NS -val-RR -t A
       example.scarlett.
2
3  Querying for: example.scarlett.
4
5  _____
6  Verifying Resource Record
7  _____
8  RRSIGs of type NS to validate: 1
9  Failed to get certificate example.scarlett. ZSK from the
       database: 11
10
11 DNSKEY string: example.scarlett. IN DNSKEY 257 3 13
       tP2dIWHtAQXTDDSrUNM8EjBQDzLC3DJkKBqWAtd34+
       WpgxtN7KKSFimHCYsdHaNPuLjWEGR0pgWhG9yFL8unCQ==
12
13
14 Trying to verify with zsk...no zsk
15 Trying to verify with ksk...success
16 Verification result of RRSIG 0 for example.scarlett.: All OK
17
18
```

```
19  ─────────────────────────────────────────
20  Verifying  Resource  Record
21  ─────────────────────────────────────────
22  RRSIGs of type A to validate: 1
23  Failed to get certificate example.scarlett. ZSK from the
       database: 11
24
25  DNSKEY string: example.scarlett. IN DNSKEY 257 3 13
       tP2dIWHtAQXTDDSrUNM8EjBQDzLC3DJkKBqWAtd34+
       WpgxtN7KKSFimHCYsdHaNPuLjWEGR0pgWhG9yFL8unCQ==
26
27
28  Trying to verify with zsk...no zsk
29  Trying to verify with ksk...success
30  Verification result of RRSIG 0 for example.scarlett.: All OK
```

A NS (Line 8) and "glue" (Line 22) RR is returned in the response. To demonstrate that only a single key is in use, the output for the resolver shows a failure at line 9 in retrieving the ZSK for the `example.scarlett` zone. This is expected. A single certificate is used and creates a KSK (or CSK) key at line 11. The validation fails at line 14 for a ZSK as one does not exist, and subsequently passes with the KSK (or CSK) at line 15.

The same process to validate the A RRSIG is repeated at lines 22–29. Once again the ZSK does not exist (Line 25) and the validation process passes with a single key (Line 28–30).

This protocol provides us with origin authentication and message integrity. The number of requests are also reduced. We reduce key management to a single certificate rather than multiple keys, making it simpler. However, the question on if RRSIGs suffer from IP fragmentation still exists.

5   DNSSEC Response Sizes

Statistics on DNSSEC were gathered by studying the zonefile of the **net** zone, which consists of approximately 35 million entries and 15 million different second level domains. Responses from these second level domains that were DNSSEC enabled were inspected.

Around 1.63% of second level domains in the **net** zone are signed. Figure 3 shows the distribution of DNSSEC algorithms that are used by these.

5.1   DNSKEY

DNSKEY requests were expected to yield the largest response. Figure 4 shows a histogram of a variety of RSA algorithms.

Algorithm 7 yielded the smallest response size. This explains its prevalent use shown in Fig. 3, as many zones will attempt to reduce the size of their DNSSEC responses in order to avoid accessibility issues. Algorithm 7 returns the smallest response as the signature uses a SHA-1 hash function which produces

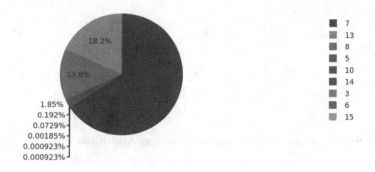

Fig. 3. Distribution of DNSSEC algorithms

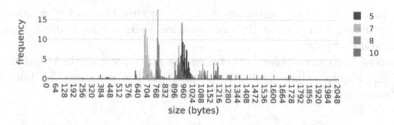

Fig. 4. DNSKEY RR response sizes from RSA algorithms

the smallest message digest. However, SHA-1 has been proven to cause colliding message digests, which can limit the security of a signature using this hash function [15].

Algorithm 8 produces the next smallest response size. This algorithm uses a SHA-256 hash, which is a trade-off between the resulting size of the message digest (and hence signature), and the security of the hash function.

Algorithm 10 uses a SHA-512 hash function which produces the largest signature. This would explain why many of the responses using this algorithm are very large.

It can be observed that a significant majority of these responses from all algorithms are above 512 bytes, which would not fit inside of a traditional DNS packet [11].

Figure 5 compares the most common RSA algorithm against the most common ECDSA algorithm, as determined from Fig. 3. Each of these peaks show the various forms of DNSKEY configurations.

The majority of responses using Algorithm 13 fit in a 512 byte packet. The only exception to this is key rollovers or excessively complicated DNSSEC set ups. On the contrary, a minimal amount of Algorithm 7 responses fit inside a packet of this size.

Our proposed protocol would not suffer from these large DNSKEY responses as these RRs are extracted from the DNS and instead placed in the blockchain.

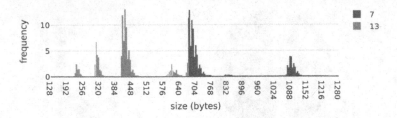

Fig. 5. DNSKEY RR response sizes from Algorithms 7 and 13

5.2   A and AAAA

If IPv4 and IPv6 address responses do not fit within the packet restriction of
512 bytes in order to prevent IP fragmentation then neither will NS responses
which contain a "glue".

Response sizes were observed between the most popular RSA and ECDSA
algorithms. Figure 6 shows 99.9% of DNSSEC A RR responses for both algorithms comes within the 512 byte packet limit.

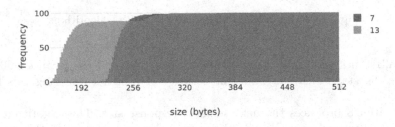

Fig. 6. A RR response sizes from Algorithms 7 and 13

Figure 7 also demonstrates that 99.9% of DNSSEC AAAA RR responses
using either algorithm fits in a 512 byte UDP packet.

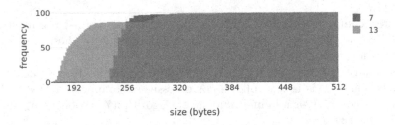

Fig. 7. AAAA RR response sizes from Algorithms 7 and 13

5.3 NS

It is important that a NS and "glue" RR is not subject to IP fragmentation, as this accounts for a significant portion of DNS traffic.

First, the response sizes for the most popular RSA and ECDSA algorithms were analysed. Figure 8 shows that 99.9% of responses using both algorithms fit inside a 512 byte UDP packet. This is an exceptionally important observation, as this could mean that key algorithms do not need to be restricted to ECDSA algorithms.

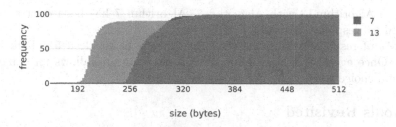

Fig. 8. NS RR response sizes from Algorithms 7 and 13

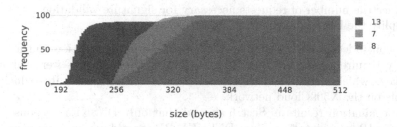

Fig. 9. NS RR response sizes from Algorithms 7, 8 and 13

However, Algorithm 7 produces the smallest responses, as shown in Fig. 4. Algorithm 8 is the next most commonly used algorithm, which also results in larger responses due to the use of a SHA-256 hash function. Figure 9 shows that 99.5% of these responses also fit inside a 512 byte packet.

This means that there is a significant amount of freedom in what choice of algorithm can be used when DNSKEY RRs have been extracted from the hierarchy, as most responses will not suffer from IP fragmentation.

5.4 NSEC

DNS traffic can potentially consist of a lot of NSEC responses, and so it is important to consider the implication it would have on IP fragmentation. Figure 10

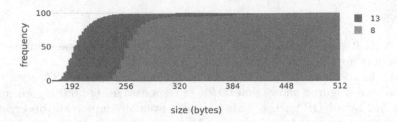

Fig. 10. NSEC RR response sizes from Algorithms 8 and 13

compares Algorithm 13 with Algorithm 8. Algorithm 7 has been omitted as it uses NSEC3 responses instead.

99.9% of responses using these two algorithms fit inside a 512 byte UDP packet. Once again, this is an important observation and allows for a flexible algorithm choice when using the proposed protocol.

6   Goals Revisited

The goals that were listed in Sect. 1 were:

- Provide the client with origin authentication
- Provide the client with message integrity
- Reduce the size of DNSSEC responses to the traditional DNS packet size
- Reduce the number of requests necessary for signature validation
- Simplify the key management

We concluded in Sect. 4 that both client origin authentication and message integrity requirements were met. This is evident as signatures were validated using keys which were linked to a zone's identity using certificates which are available on the X509Cloud network.

The evaluation results in Sect. 5 showed that only DNSKEY responses suffered from IP fragmentation. Since DNSKEY RRs would not exist anymore, and public keys are instead stored in the blockchain, this does not impact the system described in Sect. 4. It appears the system would be capable of returning over 99% of responses in a single UDP packet, regardless of the choice of algorithm.

We describe in Sect. 4 that a convoluted validation process is no longer necessary, as the blockchain allows us to trust the certificate at any level in the DNS lookup process. This produces far less requests than traditional DNSSEC. We can conclude the number of requests necessary are reduced.

As for key management, all that needs to be done is to sign each RRset which is already performed in traditional DNSSEC. Only a single key is necessary for the proposed protocol. The need to place DS RRs in the zone above is also eliminated. It can be concluded that our proposed system's key management is simpler.

Not only is the key management simpler, but it is also extraordinarily flexible. If a more fitting PKI were discovered tomorrow, this could easily be integrated with the system with no impact on the DNSSEC response sizes from Sect. 5.

7   Future Work

Due to the fact that not all zones are DNSSEC enabled, a resolver is unsure if it should expect a signature in the response. In traditional DNSSEC, the DS record in the parent zone tells a resolver that the child is DNSSEC enabled. However, the protocol described in Sect. 4 does not use DS records.

This leaves a resolver open to a man in the middle attack, where an attacker can pretend a zone is not DNSSEC enabled by omitting signatures. The following are several potential solutions that could be implemented to mitigate this:

- If a certificate for a particular zone exists on the blockchain, then the resolver will expect a signature to be returned.
- A flag is passed to a name server in the OPT pseudo RR could be returned from the name server to the resolver specifying if the child domain is DNSSEC enabled.
- A flag could be added to the NS RR that that indicates if that name server is DNSSEC enabled.

One of our aims was to try and keep the protocol flexible, allowing the PKI to be agnostic to the overall protocol, and keeping the choice of algorithm for signatures open. An ECDSA key is much smaller than an equivalently secure RSA key [3], but validation is slower than RSA validation [13]. The affects of this on a resolver is undetermined. More research could be performed into this, especially relating NSEC3 records.

References

1. Ali, M., Nelson, J.C., Shea, R., Freedman, M.J.: Blockstack: a global naming and storage system secured by blockchains. In: USENIX Annual Technical Conference, pp. 181–194 (2016)
2. Arends, R., Austein, R., Larson, M., Massey, D., Rose, S.: Resource records for the DNS security extensions. Technical report (2005)
3. Barker, E., Barker, W., Burr, W., Polk, W., Smid, M.: Recommendation for key management part 1: general (revision 3). NIST Spec. Publ. 800(57), 1–147 (2012)
4. CactusVPN: All you need to know about DNS hijacking (2017). https://www.cactusvpn.com/beginners-guide-online-security/dns-hijacking/
5. Communications, D.: DNSSEC deployment report (2018). http://rick.eng.br/dnssecstat/
6. Internet System Consortium: Linux man page (2018). https://linux.die.net/man/8/dnssec-signzone
7. Cooper, M., Dzambasow, Y., Hesse, P., Joseph, S., Nicholas, R.: Internet x. 509 public key infrastructure: certification path building. Technical report (2005)
8. Ford, W., Baum, M.S.: Secure Electronic Commerce: Building the Infrastructure for Digital Signatures and Encryption. Prentice Hall PTR (2000)
9. Housley, R., Ford, W., Polk, W., Solo, D.: Internet x. 509 public key infrastructure certificate and CRL profile. Technical report (1998)
10. Jackson, C., Barth, A., Bortz, A., Shao, W., Boneh, D.: Protecting browsers from DNS rebinding attacks. ACM Trans. Web (TWEB) 3(1), 2 (2009)

11. Mockapetris, P.: RFC 1035-domain names-implementation and specification, November 1987 (2004). http://www.ietf.org/rfc/rfc1035.txt
12. van Rijswijk-Deij, R., Sperotto, A., Pras, A.: DNSSEC and its potential for DDoS attacks: a comprehensive measurement study. In: Proceedings of the 2014 Conference on Internet Measurement Conference, pp. 449–460. ACM (2014)
13. van Rijswijk-Deij, R., Sperotto, A., Pras, A.: Making the case for elliptic curves in DNSSEC. ACM SIGCOMM Comput. Commun. Rev. 45(5), 13–19 (2015)
14. Son, S., Shmatikov, V.: The Hitchhiker's guide to DNS cache poisoning. In: Jajodia, S., Zhou, J. (eds.) SecureComm 2010. LNICST, vol. 50, pp. 466–483. Springer, Heidelberg (2010). https://doi.org/10.1007/978-3-642-16161-2_27
15. Stevens, M., Bursztein, E., Karpman, P., Albertini, A., Markov, Y.: The first collision for full SHA-1. In: Katz, J., Shacham, H. (eds.) CRYPTO 2017. LNCS, vol. 10401, pp. 570–596. Springer, Cham (2017). https://doi.org/10.1007/978-3-319-63688-7_19
16. Tewari, H., Hughes, A., Weber, S., Barry, T.: X509cloud-framework for a ubiquitous PKI. In: Military Communications Conference (MILCOM), MILCOM 2017. IEEE, pp. 225–230. IEEE (2017)
17. Van Den Broek, G., van Rijswijk-Deij, R., Sperotto, A., Pras, A.: DNSSEC meets real world: dealing with unreachability caused by fragmentation. IEEE Commun. Mag. 52(4), 154–160 (2014)
18. Younglove, R.W.: Public key infrastructure. How it works. Comput. Control Eng. J. 12(2), 99–102 (2001)

The Proposal of a Blockchain-Based Architecture for Transparent Certificate Handling

Jerinas Gresch[1]([✉]), Bruno Rodrigues[1], Eder Scheid[1], Salil S. Kanhere[2], and Burkhard Stiller[1]

[1] Communication Systems Group (CSG), Department of Informatics (IfI), University of Zurich (UZH), Zürich, Switzerland
jerinas.gresch@gmail.com, {rodrigues,scheid,stiller}@ifi.uzh.ch
[2] Networked Systems and Security Group (NetSyS), UNSW Sydney, Sydney, Australia
salil.kanhere@unsw.edu.au

Abstract. Diplomas have high importance in society since they serve as official proofs for education. Therefore, it is not surprising that forgeries of such documents have become commonplace. Thus, employers ordinarily have the diplomas manually verified by the issuer. Blockchain creates opportunities to overcome these obstacles, as it has revolutionized the way in which people interact with each other. Based on this, a holistic solution that includes issuance and verification of diplomas can be realized. This paper presents a proposal of a blockchain based system for managing diplomas called UZHBC (University of ZuricH BlockChain).

Keywords: Blockchain · Education · Diploma · Verification Digitalization

1 Introduction

In an increasingly competitive market, a diploma from a higher education institution has a major relevance in the labor market. Diplomas are seen as a sign of capability, certifying the level of education and skills of individuals. Globally, enterprises are having difficulties in finding skilled professionals to fill up vacancies [17]. Unfortunately, this has led to an increase in *diploma fraud* which ranges from inflating academic grades to outright fake diplomas. There now exist several 'diploma mills', *i.e.*, unscrupulous organizations with the sole purpose of providing illegitimate academic degrees and diplomas. The number of individuals "owning" fake credentials globally is hard to estimate. In 2015 the Association of Certified Fraud Examiners [13] estimated that only in US (United States) about 41% of job applicants presented falsified information about their education. In 2017, it is estimated that about 500 fake doctoral diplomas are sold monthly in the US [14].

© Springer Nature Switzerland AG 2019
W. Abramowicz and A. Paschke (Eds.): BIS 2018 Workshops, LNBIP 339, pp. 185–196, 2019.
https://doi.org/10.1007/978-3-030-04849-5_16

Recognition and accreditation systems are commonly used to verify which institutions are recognized (*i.e.*, trusted or reputable) and authorized to award academic or professional qualifications. However, this system is not always effective in countries where the recognized higher education institutions cannot meet the demand of certified professionals required by the labor market. This creates a fertile ground for these 'diploma mills' to sell fake credentials to unqualified individuals attempting to take advantage of this shortfall. In this regard, the digitalization of the processes of issuing and verifying diplomas including cryptography primitives to ensure the identity of the diplomas becomes increasingly important to ensure that enterprises are recruiting truly qualified individuals.

Currently, the majority of diplomas is granted in a paper-based format, which can easily be faked and scanned into a digital representation. As a countermeasure, many universities implement mechanisms [20] or use services [6] to issue and verify a digital representation of the paper-based diploma. The verification can be automated by including the identity of the diploma into a central database, which can be accessed by a company wishing to verify the credentials. However, this process is rather ad-hoc and there are no unified mechanisms or standards in place such as a public registry, that is maintained by multiple institutions and accessible for everyone.

As mentioned in [8,21], there is not a perfect type of diploma certification. While paper-based diplomas are still seen as the cheaper and safest form of accreditation, it has some drawbacks in contrast to digital-based diplomas. For example, paper-based diplomas require more manual tasks for issuing and verifying diplomas than a digital one, and the security of these diplomas are as high as the level and expertise that one has to include security features such as watermarks or invisible fibers. In contrast, digital diplomas are more simple to be issued and verified against a central database maintaining these diplomas, and their security relies on available security cryptographic protocols.

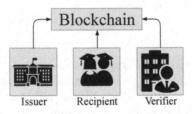

Fig. 1. Stakeholders

Digital diplomas using a centralized database, however, have some drawbacks that blockchain-based approach can overcome. For example, centralized databases are a single point of failure and using a blockchain (*c.f.*, Fig. 1), issued diplomas cannot be tampered with as data stored in a block is replicated across the blockchain network. Once blocks are distributed, any party connected to the blockchain can access the stored diplomas, meaning that any verifier in possession of a diploma can easily verify the authenticity of the diploma.

Furthermore, hashes can create a link between the original paper-based diploma which is held by the recipient to a verifier, which can then check whether the hash stored by the issuer represents the original diploma.

Recently, there have been works [2,4,5] on the use of blockchain technology for creating a standardized platform for issuing and verifying diplomas. Thus, the infrastructure maintaining the information related to the diplomas is transparently replicated by the chain of nodes, so that it is not possible to change diplomas issued by previously authorized institutions. This way, only diplomas created by valid issuers are published and the falsification of diplomas can be omitted. Based on these works, a blockchain based end to end system is presented in this paper, implementing an approach to issue and verify diplomas at the University of Zurich (UZH).

This paper is structured as follows: In the next section, known projects related to this approach will be discussed. Thereupon the identified requirements as well as the structure of the prototype are presented. In Sect. 4, a preliminary evaluation that illustrates how the proposed framework meets the requirements is shown. The paper ends with a final consideration.

2   Related Work

When blockchain is used for the issuance of diplomas, there is an opportunity not just to verify a degree certificate, but to enrich and add value to the verification ecosystem. In its purest form, a blockchain acts like a shared, replicated, append-only database where participants can depending share, write, access and participate in the validation process [3,16]. By providing a trustworthy, decentralized, and publicly available data storage, blockchain has become a disruptive technology that has seen interest from many application domains beyond FinTech (Financial Technology) area. Although the application of blockchains in education is in its infancy, there are many interesting projects (blockchain-based or not) that have explored the possibility of digital diplomas as a countermeasure to fake diplomas.

BADGR [1] and Mozilla Open Badges [12], both present unified solutions for managing the entire educational history of students by collating all digital certifications acquired by them at different academic institutes and associating it with a single identity. Although these solutions do not use blockchain, they demonstrate how to integrate multiple certifications into a student identity.

The goal of blockchain in the educational area is to create a digital certificate into an automatically verifiable piece of information that can be consulted by third parties through an immutable proof system. According to [8], blockchain can be implemented in two distinct ways in the area of education. While the first requires that diplomas be stored in plain text to create a publicly available database, the second requires that only the hash of a diploma be stored to secure the digital certificate awarded to the student. Therefore, published student data can be seen by anyone, as they are not containing any confidential information. As the diplomas are required to be tamper-proof, using a blockchain as a decentralized storage is appropriate.

The first notable use case storing a hash of diplomas is Blockcerts [11], an initiative by the MIT (Massachusetts Institute of Technology) to create an open standard for issuing and verifying credentials on the Bitcoin blockchain. The stored diplomas are accessible via an App termed Blockerts wallet, which enables students to get a verifiable, tamper-proof version of their diploma which they can share with employers, schools, family, and friends. Blockcert is seen as an enabler towards digital certificates in the blockchain.

Similar to the approach of Blockcerts, the National Research and Education Network of Greece (GRNET) [4] are also storing the hashes of diplomas in a blockchain in order to protect the confidential student data. The goal is to create a system that can verify student diplomas on the Cardano blockchain reducing the manual verification process and cases of fake diplomas. However, the GRNET project [4] differs from Blockcerts [11] in the sense that it can store not only hashes of diplomas, but also the entire verification process. Verification requests, successful or unsuccessful proof and the forwarding of the result to its requester are steps that will be stored.

BCDiploma [2], EduCTX [18] and UNIC (University of Nicosia) [19] have started their blockchain-based projects to issue and verify diplomas. BCDiploma and EduCTX share the same goal towards a global certification network of higher academic institutions. However, UNIC aims to digitize and decentralize their internal processes having issued their first academic certificates as a proof of concept. Although these approaches are already mature, they either are not meeting the requirements of the UZH or are not easy to integrate into the structure of a university. Therefore, this work shows a prototype that, besides considering these works as starting points, taking into account specific requirements raised from the UZH. For instance, the ease of deployment into their existing IT infrastructure, extending the existing functionality to create diplomas.

To guarantee the authenticity of a document, digital signatures can also be used. However, the UZH stated not to apply this solution, mainly because of cost reasons. Also, software exists that can bypass those protections and manipulate the content of a document [22].

3   System Overview

This Section discusses key requirements for such a system (*c.f.*, Sect. 3.1). Further, it is presented the development of the prototype based on the architecture design and the performed implementation are detailed (*c.f.*, respectively, Sects. 3.2 and 3.3).

3.1   UZH Requirements

Table 1 presents the requirements derived from interviews with stakeholders. This includes the student administration office, that is responsible for the verification. Also, the faculty of economic science, which issues the diplomas for all economic students, was questioned. To not violate any legal aspects, the data privacy protection department of the UZH was interviewed. For all IT relevant topics, the UZH employs the *Zentrale Informatik*[1] (ZI), who provides IT infrastructure, software and services for students and employees of the UZH (herein termed legacy system). While, RQ (Requirements) 1–4 are related to the issuer, *i.e.,* conditions that UZH demands from the system, RQ5–6 are related with the requirements for a company that wants to verify diplomas. The most named requesters of verifications by the student administration office were background check companies. Finally, RQ7 is related to the delivery of the diploma in a digital form to the student.

Table 1. Requirements elicited during Interviews with Stakeholders

Issuer	
RQ1	Only authorized UZH departments are allowed to issue diplomas
RQ2	Diploma data should be confidential to its recipients
RQ3	Process of issuing and verifying diplomas should abstract technical complexities
RQ4	Multiple diplomas should be processable in batch
Verifier	
RQ5	Verification capabilities should be accessible to any company
RQ6	Diplomas should be verified autonomously
Recipient	
RQ7	Graduates should receive their diplomas in a digital format

- **RQ1:** related to the guarantee that diplomas can only be issued by authorized issuing instances, for example, UZH faculties. Thus, diploma mills are not able to fabricate any certificates. For the verifiers, it is important to be ensured that the diplomas can only be issued by the university.
- **RQ2:** addresses the confidentiality of student data, which should only be accessible by the student and potential verifiers. Also, the 'right to be forgotten' defined in the new GDPR (General Data Protection Regulation) declares that data of consumer (*i.e.,* students) cannot be permanently stored [15]. Hence, the diploma itself cannot be stored in the blockchain. The blockchain should therefore store a hash of the document in order to prove the authenticity of the digital diploma sent to the student.
- **RQ3:** defines that technical details involved in the process of issuing diplomas must remain transparent to involved users (issuers, verifiers and recipients). In this sense, the use of blockchain (or any other infrastructure) for issuing or verifying diplomas should not require technical know-how from the users (*e.g.,* extracting the hash of a diploma at the verification process).
- **RQ4:** relates to the system scalability concerning the ease to create and verify multiple diplomas at once, as in a bash service. The goal is to avoid manual exchange of information between companies wishing to verify diplomas and the university as an issuer instance.

[1] Zentrale Informatik: http://www.id.uzh.ch/de.html.

- **RQ5:** allows anyone in possession of a diploma hash to verify its authenticity. As any company that receives a diploma from a graduate might want to verify its authenticity, this functionality has to be publicly accessible.
- **RQ6:** describes an always available service with an automated response of the verification. If the diploma is authentic, the system has to recognize it, whereas tampered documents need to be rejected.
- **RQ7:** graduates shall receive their diplomas in a digital format. Physical diplomas can get lost or damaged, whereas digital diplomas are not affected by these problems. In addition, forgery of physical documents is generally easier.

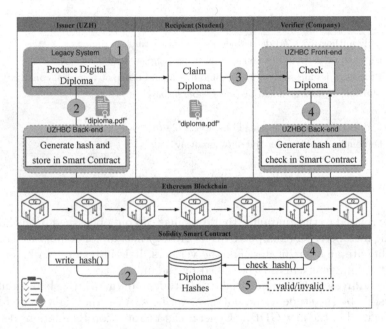

Fig. 2. UZHBC system architecture.

3.2   Design

Overall, the system (*c.f.,* Fig. 2) is divided in three different parts. The first covers issuer requirements and the second covers recipient (graduate student) requirements. The third is related to companies wishing to verify a diploma sent by recipients. At the UZH side, the issuing instance, the system is embedded into the legacy system, taking as input diplomas in a digital form (.PDF files). Currently, these digital diplomas are not sent to students but used to print paper-based diplomas which are then granted to graduate students.

In the first step, the issuing institution has to create the digital diploma, which is part of UZH legacy system workflow. Currently, the generated digital diploma (PDF document) is used only for printing the paper-based diploma and it is not made available to the recipient. In a second step, the UZHBC back-end requires this PDF document as input to generate an one-way hash function corresponding to the paper-based diploma. This hash will be stored in a smart contract, that is deployed on the Ethereum blockchain. A verifier company that receives the diploma from a student could then verify the authenticity of the document without contacting the university. Therefore, the verifier can use the UZHBC front-end, that takes the digital diploma as an input to check the authenticity of the hash. This hash will be compared with all hashes that are contained in the smart contract. If it exists, the verification will return successfully and informs the company that the diploma is authentic. If no match occurs, the system also gives a feedback.

3.3   Implementation Details

3.3.1   Front-End

The user can interact with the system through an HTML5 and JavaScript-based web page. To cover the two functionalities, issuing and verifying, two input fields are provided. These inputs expect documents from the type PDF and are meant to insert the diplomas. The calculated hash of the documents will also be displayed. Also, a password field is provided, which is needed to regulate the writing access into the blockchain. The screens to issue and verify are depicted in Figs. 3 and 4.

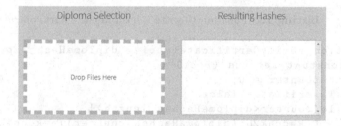

Fig. 3. Front-end interface to issue diplomas

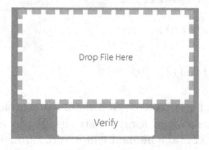

Fig. 4. Front-end interface to verify diplomas

3.3.2 Back-End

The back-end has the functions to take the documents from the input fields, convert them to hashes and send them to the smart contract. The hashes are calculated with the SHA-3 checksum, which takes any kind of data as input and returns a hash with the size of 256 bits [10]. To interact with the Smart Contract deployed on the Ethereum blockchain, the web3.js-Library is used [7]. Also, the associated owner of the smart contract is used as a standard account to send transactions and requires a password. Also, Web3 handles the connection between client and *Geth*. *Geth* is the official Ethereum client and is responsible for creating the local copy of the Ethereum's network state. *Geth* must be syncing in the background to run this application and needs to be attached to *localhost:8545* in order to communicate with web3 client.

3.3.3 Smart Contract

The smart contract contains only two functions. The write function issueCertificate is responsible to store the hashes into the smart contract. Also, it is only possible to call this function as an owner of the contract, which is the university. The dedicated code is depicted in Listing 1.1.

```
1    function issueCertificate(string _diplomaHash) public {
2        if (msg.sender != owner)
3            revert();
4        diplomaHashes.push(_diplomaHash);
5    }
```

Listing 1.1. Function to write a hash in the smart contract

```
1    function verifyCertificate(string diplomaHash_) public
         constant returns (bool) {
2    uint counter = 0;
3    bool verified = false;
4    while(counter<diplomaHashes.length){
5        if(keccak256(diplomaHashes[counter])==keccak256(
             diplomaHash_)){
6            verified = true;
7            return verified;
8        }else{
9            counter++;
10           }
11   }
12   return verified;
13   }
```

Listing 1.2. Function to check if the smart contract contains a hash

The hashes are stored in an array of strings. When a verification request occurs, the verifyCertificate method will iterate through the array of hashes. If any hash in the array matches with the given hash from the parameter, the method returns true as an indicator of a verified diploma. At the moment, Solidity, the underlying programing language of smart contracts, does not provide functionalities to compare strings. Therefore, the function `keccak256()` is used to hash the strings which allows to make them comparable again. The dedicated code is depicted in Listing 1.2. Since this is a prototype, the Smart Contract is deployed on the Rinkeby testnet of the Ethereum blockchain.

4 Preliminary Evaluation

This Section discusses the preliminary evaluation of the UZHBC prototype. An analysis is conducted to verify whether the prototype can satisfy the requirements identified in Sect. 2. Likewise, the fulfillment of the requirements by the related work was analyzed and compared against the prototype. This comparison is presented in Table 2.

Table 2. Related Work on Requirements

	Blockcerts	GRNET	EduCTX	UNIC	BCDiploma	BADGR	UZHBC
RQ1	✗	✓*	✓*	✓	✗	✗	✓
RQ2	✓	✓	✗	✓	✓*	✗	✓
RQ3	✗	✗	✗	✗	✗	✗	✓
RQ4	✓	✓	✗	✓	✓	✗	✓
RQ5	✓*	✓*	✓*	✓	✓	✓	✓
RQ6	✓	✓	✓	✓	✓	✓	✓
RQ7	✓	✓	✓	✓	✓	✓	✓

Note: * indicates that the requirements has been partially met.

The UZH consists of seven faculties whereas each faculty includes many departments. In UZHBC, each of these faculties would represent an issuing instance able to record diploma hashes into the blockchain. Other blockchain-based approaches such as Blockcerts [11] and BCDiploma [2] extended the number of issuers in their works. For example, new issuing institutions can register itself on the platform which could work as a universal diploma verifier. However, at some point, new issuers would have to prove their ability to certify diplomas to the developers of the platform. This dependency between developers and issuers cannot be neglected, and a fully automated process cannot be achieved. The most critical issue is that this prototype is intended to solve the falsification of diplomas through individuals or diploma mills. Therefore, granting issuing rights needs to be strictly regulated and the ability to add issuers is not desired. However, it is important to note that the different UZH faculties are acting independently. The requirements to graduate, deadlines to be met, and the entire process of graduating are different at each faculty. Thus, a faculty has to be considered as an autonomous entity with respect to the issuance of diplomas.

The provided UZHBC functionalities achieve the requirement (RQ1) as presented in Listing 1.2, which shows that writing access is only granted to the actual owner of the smart contract, the UZH. Similar to Blockcerts and BCdiploma, GRNET [4] and EduCTX [] allow multiple issuers. Nevertheless, write permissions are not readily granted. While GRNET consists of a group of predefined universities as issuers, new universities at UniCTX should be selected by the existing participants.

Regarding the RQ2, a hash generated through a one-way function is used to represent the diploma. By only recording the hash, one is not possible to identify confidential data about the actual content of the diploma. To verify the authenticity of a diploma, a verifier needs an actual diploma document sent by a student (e.g., in a job application). The provided functionality for verification generates a hash again, and if this hash is already contained in the smart contract, it can be considered as authentic. Issued hashes are publicly available without compromising the confidentiality of its owner.

As depicted in Table 2, many approaches also use cryptographic hashes. BCDiploma [2] store encrypted diploma data and claims to solve the problem of the new GDPR "right to be forgotten" [15]. Diplomas can be decrypted through a persistence key, which is unique and kept by the owner of the diploma. However, losing this key implies that the diploma cannot be retrieved anymore and encrypted data would remain on the blockchain.

Intensive acceptance and usability test scores with the university and verifiers are required to gain more insights concerning system practicability. However, the amount of interaction with the system, which can be seen as the actual additional effort, require fewer interactions in contrast to other approaches. This includes sending invitations or transaction addresses, registration, maintaining a hash list, etc. Therefore, it must be stated that comparing different approaches is not straightforward since these are slightly different concerning their functionalities. As UZHBC currently offers two interaction possibilities (recording and verifying), complexity is reduced to a minimum (RQ3). For example, these functionalities are translated into a simple action at the front-end, such as dragging a file into a field.

The UZHBC can verify the authenticity of diplomas without relying on manual intervention by the university. However, it requires some additional steps to achieve this. At the point where the paper-based diplomas are delivered to graduates, the digital equivalents have to be processed into the system. The extra effort can be limited since the prototype allows to prepare as many documents as desired. As the UZH handle diplomas in batches (for printing), it is also feasible to use the prototype and RQ4 can be met.

As confidential data is not disclosed in the verification process, the front-end interface can be publicly accessible (RQ5). Other approaches (e.g., Blockcerts [11] and EduCTX [18]) uses invitation mechanisms, where the graduates sends a link to his academic credentials. With UZHBC (and UNIC [19]), this invitation is handled by sending the digital diploma in a job application. The interface of verification is accessible to everyone, but without a diploma, it is useless. It is important that awareness of such a system needs to be spread, so employers know where to verify the received diplomas.

Background-check companies, headhunters and also regular companies are the typical entities that need to verify student diplomas. This task is currently seen as rather time-consuming as there is no automated verification system for diplomas currently in Switzerland. Thus, the process relies on the manual interaction between the employer, university, and graduate. Nonetheless, universities in Switzerland are not allowed to send any information without the consent of the graduate. Thus, verification requests are rather time-consuming. Based on UZHBC, verifiers are only required to send the received digital diploma to the front-end verification provided UZH. Therefore, the hash will be generated again and checked at the blockchain whether it is authentic or not, fulfilling the initial requirement from the employers (RQ6).

From the perspective of the recipients, *i.e.,* graduate students, digital diplomas would be granted in addition to the conventional paper-based diplomas [9]. At the moment, these are obtained by scanning the paper-based document to have a digital equivalent. To fulfill RQ7, the UZH will deliver, through the UZHBC system, these documents added to the paper-based diplomas. However, this requirement relies on the cooperation of the university concerning its internal regimentations. This is also a prerequisite for the other related work, as all the academic credentials are handled digitally.

5   Final Considerations

The digitalization of the processes within the UZH for issuing and verifying diplomas including cryptography primitives to ensure the identity of the diplomas becomes an increasing necessity. In this paper, it was presented a prototype tailored to the UZH needs to record and verify diplomas issued by its faculties. The first step was to determine the requirements of the university's stakeholders to create an initial prototype which demonstrates the functionalities and highlight advantages. Subsequently, other improvements are foreseen as future work. For instance, as the project started as a research initiative by the authors in contact with the technical UZH department, the UZH board of directors also need to approve the project. Then, the system should include adaptations fully comply with the university's internal regulations. Also, further universities or colleges should be included as issuers in Switzerland. As the UZH is not the only institution that has to deal with diploma fraud, verification is a general concern.

References

1. Badgr.io: Make your badges meaningful with Badgr, May 2018. https://info.badgr.io
2. BCDiploma: Degrees Certified on the Blockchain, August 2017. https://bit.ly/2rp95qC
3. Bocek, T., Stiller, B.: Smart contracts – blockchains in the wings. In: Linnhoff-Popien, C., Schneider, R., Zaddach, M. (eds.) Digital Marketplaces Unleashed, pp. 169–184. Springer, Heidelberg (2018). https://doi.org/10.1007/978-3-662-49275-8_19

4. Castor, A.: Cardano blockchain's first use case: proof of university diplomas in Greece, January 2018. https://bit.ly/2DVsrYt
5. Durant, E., Trachy, A.: Digital Diploma debuts at MIT, October 2017. https://bit.ly/2xPRWXC
6. My eQuals: The Official Platform of Australian and New Zealand Universities, January 2017. https://bit.ly/2qjHtE9
7. Ethereum: Ethereum JavaScript API, February 2015. https://github.com/ethereum/web3.js
8. Grech, A., Camilleri, A.F.: Blockchain in education. Technical report (2017)
9. Jerinas, G.: Survey about digital academic certificates, May 2018. https://bit.ly/2wLFXyP
10. Andrée, M.: SHA-3 and Keccak checksum utility, November 2017. https://github.com/maandree/sha3sum
11. MIT Registrar's Office: Digital diploma pilot program faqs, September 2017. https://bit.ly/2JYw4zT
12. Mozilla: Open Badges, May 2018. https://openbadges.org/
13. Musee, N.M.: An academic certification verification system based on cloud computing environment. Ph.D. dissertation, University of Nairobi (2015)
14. Park, H., Craddock, A.: Diploma mills: 9 strategies for tackling one of higher education's most wicked problems, December 2017. https://bit.ly/2DoEeyu
15. General Data Protection Regulation (GDPR): Right to erasure ('right to be forgotten'), May 2018. https://bit.ly/2zMT9Vl
16. Rodrigues, B., Bocek, T., Stiller, B.: The use of blockchains: application-driven analysis of applicability. In: Pethuru Raj, G.D. (ed.) Blockchain Technology: Platforms, Tools and Use Cases, Advances in Computers, vol. 111, pp. 163–198. Elsevier (2018). https://doi.org/10.1016/bs.adcom.2018.03.011, https://www.sciencedirect.com/science/article/pii/S006524581830024X
17. Rutkowski, J.: From the shortage of jobs to the shortage of skilled workers: labor markets in the EU new member states (2007)
18. Turkanović, M., Hölbl, M., Košič, K., Heričko, M., Kamišalić, A.: EduCTX: a blockchain-based higher education credit platform. IEEE Access (2018)
19. University of Nicosia: Academic certificates on the blockchain, March 2018. https://bit.ly/2I5G3mj
20. USD: University of South Denmark. The Digital Diploma, January 2018. https://bit.ly/2I3Bid5
21. Warasart, M., Kuacharoen, P.: Paper-based document authentication using digital signature and QR code. In: International Conference on Computer Engineering and Technology (ICCET 2012), April 2012
22. Zeichick, A.: Can blockchain solve your document and digital signature headaches? April 2018. https://bit.ly/2tstjkx

Blockchain-Based Distributed Marketplace

Oliver R. Kabi and Virginia N. L. Franqueira(✉)

Cyber Security Research Group, College of Engineering and Technology,
University of Derby, Derby DE22 1GB, UK
o.kabi1@unimail.derby.ac.uk, v.franqueira@derby.ac.uk

Abstract. Developments in Blockchain technology have enabled the creation of smart contracts; i.e., self-executing code that is stored and executed on the Blockchain. This has led to the creation of distributed, decentralised applications, along with frameworks for developing and deploying them easily. This paper describes a proof-of-concept system that implements a distributed online marketplace using the Ethereum framework, where buyers and sellers can engage in e-commerce transactions without the need of a large central entity coordinating the process. The performance of the system was measured in terms of cost of use through the concept of 'gas usage'. It was determined that such costs are significantly less than that of Amazon and eBay for high volume users. The findings generally support the ability to use Ethereum to create a distributed on-chain market, however, there are still areas that require further research and development.

Keywords: Blockchain · Smart contract · Ethereum · E-commerce
Distributed systems

1 Introduction

In order to exchange physical goods online, internet users utilise third party marketplaces to mitigate some of the associated risks of trading with unknown Internet users and to also facilitate the processing of the financial transaction. Buyers and sellers expect that the third party marketplace will act as a trusted intermediary and provide the service of connecting and protecting peers wishing to exchange goods, in exchange for a fee that is likely a percentage cut of the transaction. Despite these protections, reported instances of non-payment and non-delivery crimes amounted to over $138 million in losses for victims in the USA in 2016 [14].

The use of extremely large and reputable marketplaces, such as eBay and Amazon, offer better protection to users from retail fraud than small, unknown alternative marketplaces, however this in turn creates powerful centralised corporations with vast quantities of personal information about users, which can be processed and sold [19]. Recent events have brought to light the issue of data

© Springer Nature Switzerland AG 2019
W. Abramowicz and A. Paschke (Eds.): BIS 2018 Workshops, LNBIP 339, pp. 197–210, 2019.
https://doi.org/10.1007/978-3-030-04849-5_17

privacy, creating wide spread concern regarding the collection and use of user data by large corporations [11]. Alongside this are concerns regarding the security of our sensitive financial information online. Again, recent events such as the Equifax data breach have highlighted the risks of sharing financial information, even with large, previously trusted financial corporations [7]. In order to exchange currency online users must provide sensitive personal and banking information, exposing their data to the risk of a data breach and thus exposing the user to the risk of identity theft. Large marketplaces pose a double threat of information security to users, as users must expose both their personal information, that is valuable for the study and manipulation of populations through big data analysis, as well as their banking information which could be used for identity theft, should it be compromised.

Recent developments in Blockchain technology have enabled the creation of Smart Contracts, self-executing contracts that are stored and executed on the Blockchain nodes, allowing secure decentralised applications to be developed. Buterin et al. [8] suggest many applications for smart contracts, including on-chain decentralised marketplaces, however they provides no details on such an application. By using Smart Contracts to create an on-chain decentralised marketplace, the requirement of a large central entity to co-ordinate the marketplace functions are removed, which in turn provides a method to remove data aggregation and user exposure to the threats posed.

The contribution of the paper is threefold. First, it reports on the design and implementation of blockchain technology for a distributed physical goods marketplace application, in order to enable trading of goods without the requirement of a trusted third party market operator using the Ethereum framework. Second, it evaluates the developed proof-of-concept marketplace system in terms of performance, based on *gas* used for computation by the smart contracts on the blockchain, and scalability. Third, it discusses issues and insights gained which give directions to future research & development.

The reminder of the paper is organised as follows. Section 2 provides background on traditional online marketplaces, related work and the Ethereum framework. Section 3 enumerates requirements for online marketplaces and presents the architecture of the proof-of-concept system. Section 4 elaborates on the aspects of the developed system and the testing performed. Section 5 evaluates the system in terms of performance and scalability, while Sect. 6 provides discussion based on the work done, issues faced and suggestions for future work. Finally, Sect. 7 draws conclusions.

2   Background

This section reviews (in Sect. 2.1) current online commerce and the technologies employed by existing centralised marketplaces to facilitate the online exchange of goods and services, despite the prevalence of fraud and other risks faced by online peers. Following this related work is discussed to provide a basis for our design. It also reviews the Ethereum framework (in Sect. 2.3), which is used to implement the decentralised marketplace proof-of-concept system.

2.1   Online Commerce

While online commerce provides convenience to consumers, online retail fraud is one of the top three crime types reported in the United States of America with losses of $138 million for victims in the US in 2016 [14]. These losses are for non-payment or non-delivery of goods exchanged between online peers, which highlights the risks faced by both buyer and sellers in online marketplaces.

To combat the increased opportunity for fraud that exists on the trustless web, a number of legal and technological solutions are employed. A number of these solutions will now be detailed.

Centralised Marketplaces. Centralised marketplaces act as an intermediary between buyers and sellers, helping to facilitate the exchange of goods for currency. A peer is able to list an item for sale, which another peer is then able to purchase in exchange for currency via a payment provider like PayPal or a credit card provider like VISA. Consumers may mitigate the risk of fraud by using large trusted online retailers or marketplaces such as Amazon or eBay. Even when making purchases from third parties via these large marketplaces, the marketplace acts as an intermediary between the consumer and seller, mediating any disputes that may arise from the transaction.

Escrow Services. A more traditional form of intermediary that can be utilised are escrow services. In this process, the buyer and seller agree upon a mutually trusted third party, that will be responsible for the funds until the conditions of the transaction, as agreed upon by all parties, have been met. Should any dispute arise the third party will provide arbitration and attempt to resolve the dispute. However as shown by Grazioli and Jarvenpaa [16], most users are unable to distinguish fraudulent websites, leaving consumers open to fraudulent online escrow services.

Reputation Systems. Many online marketplaces, including Amazon and eBay, provide reputation systems which provide a metric for users to judge one another and determine the risk of partaking in an exchange with another particular user. These trust and reputation systems are being used successfully by online commercial applications to promote good behaviour by users [18]. Resnick and Zeckhauser [25] report that reputation profiles used on eBay were predictive of future performance and they found that users participate in reputation systems the majority of the time, despite the incentives to free ride.

2.2   Related Work

Subramanian [27] provides an analysis of decentralised marketplaces on the blockchain based on the current theory and literature. He identifies advantages of using blockchain-based marketplaces to include, faster transaction times, reduced costs and increased privacy and security for users. He also provides an analysis of the decentralisation possibility for various product and service categories, including physical products which he states may only achieve partial decentralisation due to the complexities of providing decentralised B2B support, accounting, payment and reputation systems.

Notheisen, Cholewa, and Shanmugam [23] implemented a real-world asset marketplace with a private blockchain, using the ethereum framework to create a digital motor vehicle asset register. The system provides automated transfer of ownership along with immutable records of vehicle history. The study also introduced methods to reduce the risk arising from the immutability of blockchain transactions. By providing abort mechanisms, both buyer and seller may disengage from the transaction before final confirmation and exchange of funds and property. The application shifts the centralisation onto a single government authority to provide verification of vehicle information and condition, however it's benefits provide a system that requires less work to participate in and maintain compared to existing vehicle registration methods.

Mobius [20] provides protocols for smart markets however the aim is more specifically for providing a marketplace for autonomous agents to trade data and micro services, specifically with the world of IoT in mind.

Nasonov et al. [21] propose a big data platform that companies can use to sell, exchange and process Big Data sets. Such an application would provide a valuable mechanism for companies to improve their business organisation through the application of knowledge extracted from such data sets.

Eskandari et al. [13] studied the possibility of using smart contracts to implement a derivatives market that would remove the need for an intermediary broker. They highlight gaps in the current infrastructure, stopping the development of secure and autonomous derivatives markets, particularly the lack of decentralised data feeds, as this may lead to potential vulnerabilities should centralised feeds become compromised. They also highlight issues raised by new development concepts such as gas usage, and limiting the gas usage during computation.

2.3   Ethereum

Ethereum extends the application of the blockchain technology used by Bitcoin to provide a Turing complete scripting language. Scripts can be committed to the blockchain via transactions, indefinitely making them publicly accessible. This enables the ability to encode arbitrary state transition functions, and as such the ability to create decentralised blockchain-based applications, otherwise known as Dapps.

Smart Contracts. The Turing-complete scripting language incorporated into Ethereum allows for the creation of smart contracts as envisioned by Szabo [29]. Scripts can be included within transactions as in Bitcoin, however contracts also have their own addresses that can send and receive transactions, allowing parts of the contract to be executed upon receiving a transaction. Smart contracts are able to communicate with one another through messages allowing for complex interactions to be developed such as Decentralised Autonomous Organisations [9].

Ether and Gas. Gas, which is directly exchangeable for Ether (ETH) at a consistent real price, is the unit used to fuel the computations of byte-code within the EVM and storage of data on the blockchain. The use of a resource to fuel contracts protects from malicious and infinitely looping code from being executed on the chain without the cost of computation being paid for.

Contracts and transactions have a fixed start price to pay the miner for his computational power. Each specific computation also has predefined gas costs, such as additions, subtractions, memory stores and retrievals, as such the total cost of computation can be estimated on compilation of the code. However as ethereum is still being developed, changes could cause the gas cost of a contract function to change.

3   System Design

To effectively investigate the research question, an adaptation of the Design Science Research (DSR) methodology set out by Vaishnavi and Kuechler [30] will be used. This process involves investigating a known problem through the design and creation of an artefact, which can then be evaluated through discussion and reflection as a potential solution to the original problem.

The intent is to provide a system for the trading of physical goods similar to eBay, meaning that both the physical characteristics and the value of the goods will be extremely varied. As such the automatic verification of physical exchange of goods is a problem beyond the scope of what is currently achievable by this paper. In order to resolve disputes during exchange, such as non-delivery, misrepresented goods or fraudulent claims, some form of centralisation will be required, such as an escrow and arbitration process.

We used abstract story-like descriptions using non-technical language to define the required behaviour of the system, inspired by Agile software development [24]. Table 1 contains a list of user stories from the perspective of the various user types of the application. The users are subdivided into "Buyers", those wishing to purchase items, and "Sellers", those wishing to list and sell items. These requirements are identified using a sequential numbering Rn to provide easy referencing.

The application is designed to have a back-end consisting of two Solidity smart contracts hosted on the Ethereum public blockchain, along with a HTML/CSS/JS front end UI application. The web application will use the web3 API to interact with the smart contracts. Figure 1 provides a diagram of the systems architecture.

3.1   Back-End

The back-end will consist of two smart contracts written in Solidity, the Marketplace Agent contract and the Escrow Agent contract. Each will act as a sort of repository for the business data they are required to administer and store, with

Table 1. User stories encompassing the requirements of the blockchain-based distributed marketplace system.

ID	User story
R1	As a seller I am able to list items for sale with a listing name and price in Ether
R2	As the seller of a purchased listing, I am able to approve the linked escrow for the aforementioned listing
R3	As the seller of a purchased listing, my ethereum account is funded with the proceeds of a sale once the buyer has approved/finalised the linked escrow, once the listed goods have exchanged possession
R4	As a buyer I am able to browse existing listing for sale
R5	As a buyer I am able to purchase an available listing
R6	As a buyer I am able to fund an escrow for the purchase of a listing
R7	As the buyer of a listing, I am able to approve the linked escrow for the aforementioned listing
R8	As the buyer or seller of a listing, I am able to request and receive impartial mediation of an escrow in the event of a issue with the exchange of goods

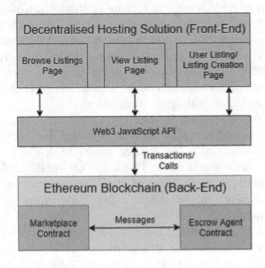

Fig. 1. System architecture

their implementation based on the pattern described by Hitchins [17]. These contracts will now be further described.

Marketplace Contract. The marketplace contract will provide the business logic which orchestrates the process of listing, browsing and purchasing of items. It will also handle the logistical information exchange between a buyer and a seller required to enable the logistics of a physical exchange.

Escrow Agent Contract. The escrow contract will provide the business logic to reduce and mitigate risk for both buyers and sellers in the exchange of physical goods over the internet. This logic will form an escrow contract between the buyer and seller that is paid out automatically in the event that both the buyer and seller approve the escrow. Logic for disputing the escrow will also be provided, in which case the escrow can be paid out by an arbitrator to either the buyer or the seller.

3.2 Front-End

While the smart contracts provide all the business logic of a marketplace, using them via an API would not be user friendly and as such a JavaScript web application will be implemented to provide a front-end that can be accessed via a web browser.

The front-end of the marketplace will consist of a typical web application. This will be comprised of a JavaScript application that utilises the Web3 API to interact with both the marketplace and escrow contracts along with HTML pages to provide a graphical user interface.

4 System Implementation

The requirements R1-R8 (Table 1) were processed into a Kanban style to-do list, allowing the development of the application in a Behaviour-Driven Development (BDD) fashion [26] This allowed the developer to better react to an evolving understanding of the development processes and methods within the Ethereum framework. The development environment consisted of the components and tools enumerated in Table 2.

The architecture of the smart contract implementation is described by the UML diagram of Fig. 2. The source code for the components which compose the architecture of the system shown in Fig. 1, i.e. the Marketplace and Escrow Agent contracts, the "browser listing page", "view listing page", "user listing/listing creation page", and "user orders page" can be found on GitHub: https://github.com/Howserr/onchain-market.

5 System Evaluation

The proof-of-concept system has been tested and evaluated in terms of white-box testing, black-box testing [22] and cost of use for users. Test scripts and full results are also available on GitHub.

White-Box Testing. A suite of 74 unit tests were created during development to provide white box test coverage of both smart contracts, MarketplaceAgent and EscrowAgent. These tests were organised as BDD structures using the Mocha architecture. Naming of the groups and individual tests followed the behavioural language style of "given, when, then". These tests were created to

Table 2. Tools used for the implementation of the proof-of-concept system

Software	Version	Purpose
Web3	1.0	Provides a JavaScript API for Ethereum blockchains by implementing the Ethereum JSON RPC API; it allows front-end web applications to interact with blockchains
Ganache	1.1.0	Ethereum blockchain JavaScript implementation which runs in-memory; it removes the need for a local blockchain client for local testing and provides additional tools to aid in development of smart contracts
Truffle	4.1.7	Part of Ethereum development framework which provides a compilation, testing and deployment pipeline for Dapp developers
Mocha	5..0	Included as part of Truffle in order to provide a unit testing framework for Solidity contract code/
MetaMask	4.5.5	Extension for the Chrome web browser that enables interaction with the Ethereum blockchain, as required for the use of Dapps
NodeJS	8.11.1	Provides a development framework for Truffle and enables use of NPM, the NodeJS package manager, for the installation of JavaScript dependencies

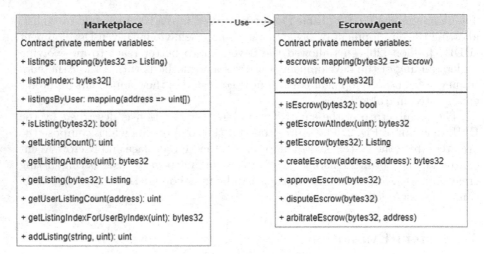

Fig. 2. Smart contracts UML diagram

run using the Truffle testing framework which runs against a local in-memory blockchain, i.e., Ganache.

Black-Box Testing. A set of 8 test cases were created to meet the requirements R1-R8; all of the test cases were successful except the script for R8, the ability for an arbitrator to provide arbitration of a disputed listing/escrow. This test failed because the front-end functionality for arbitrators was not implemented due to security issues created by the single arbitrator solution of our artefact. This problem, along with potential solutions, is discussed further in Sect. 6.

Performance Testing. This section presents the results of performance testing the implemented artefact in terms of the costs of use. The quantity of gas used by each action that requires sending a transaction to the blockchain was recorded using Ganache. In order to calculate a cost based on the gas used, the exchange price of gas was determined to be 1 gwei per unit. This exchange price is based on the current *Gas Price Standard* at ETH Gas Station [1]. The costs of use for the artefact are displayed in Table 3.

It should be noted that the execution of Solidity code is deterministic and the gas used is calculated as the sum of the gas used by the EVM opcodes executed. As such measurements of gas usage were not repeated.

The costs for selling on Amazon and eBay were calculated based on the pricing models detailed on their seller information pages [2,3]. The calculations were based on an item in the Consumer Electronics category, the second most preferable category of goods to buy online [4]. In both cases we used the cheapest fee structure available, those targeted at sellers running online stores, however the subscription cost is not included in the calculation. For Amazon the *consumer electronics* referral fee percentage of 8% (minimum $1.00) was used and consequently it would be a non-media item so no closing fee is charged. As such, the cost to sell an item on Amazon given the stated assumptions, is *8% of the listing price*. The cost to sell an item on eBay given the same assumptions is 10% of the total value of sale. The results of these calculations are displayed in Table 4.

Table 3. Combined buyer and seller use costs of listing and selling an item in Gas, ETH and USD (rounded up to 2 decimal places).

Behaviour	Gas cost	ETH cost	USD cost
Add listing	163192	0.0001632	$0.07
Purchase listing	237384	0.0002374	$0.10
First approval (seller)	45524	0.0000455	$0.02
Second approval (buyer)	37050	0.0000370	$0.02
Total cost	483150	0.004831	$0.21

Comparison. By comparing Tables 3 and 4 it can be seen that the combined cost of both a buyer and seller for selling an item using the artefact will be significantly lower than the costs of selling even a $10 item on either Amazon or eBay. As the costs of usage for the artefact are based on the gas used rather than a marketplace commission, the costs would not scale based on the price of the item being exchanged as it would on Amazon or eBay.

Table 4. The costs of selling items of specific prices on popular online marketplaces in USD.

Item price	Amazon cost	eBay cost
$10	$1.00	$1.00
$50	$4.00	$5.00
$100	$8.00	$10.00
$1000	$80.00	$100.00

6   Discussion

This section discusses issues faced during implementation of the artefact, and suggests future work.

6.1   Escrow Arbitration

Our initial design intent was to use a similar system to that employed by existing marketplaces, in which administrative members of the marketplace community would take turns to fulfil the role of arbitrator when required. During the development phase it became obvious that the planned method of arbitration was fundamentally flawed when used within a decentralised system as it creates centralisation and a requirement of trust in a closed group of administrators. As such this requirement was not fulfilled and instead we suggest it as a subject for further study. Insights into the problem based on the current literature will now be provided.

Group Escrow. The use of group escrow protocols in order to facilitate the exchange of physical goods using cryptocurrencies has been studied previously [15]. A protocol using group escrow techniques could be developed in order to solve the requirement of trust in a single arbitrator. A number of arbitrators would be selected from a pool of registered arbitrators who would then individually review the available information pertaining to the exchange of goods and vote on the party to which the balance of the escrow should be awarded to. This then presents the problem of finding consensus between the arbitrators, a problem which the literature provides many potential avenues for solution.

Proof-of-Stake Consensus. The Casper Proof-of-Stake protocol being developed as a replacement for Proof-of-Work by the Ethereum Foundation [10] provides potential solutions for encouraging good peer behaviour within a consensus system. Aspects of this protocol could be applied to group arbitration such as by requiring would-be arbitrators to stake Ether. By doing this, the stake of malicious actors can be slashed, in order to create a disincentive to such behaviour, while arbitrators that form the majority could be rewarded with a share of a fee charged as part of the arbitration process, when it is requested. The shared fee would be collected from the balance of the escrow.

Such an arbitration protocol would reduce the potential impact of malicious actors within the centralised process. It could be utilised as a separate arbitration service for many forms of transaction within applications on the decentralised web.

6.2   Logistics Integration

During an online exchange of physical goods the logistics of the physical exchange are likely to involve a logistics carrier due to the potential distances. Currently the system has no functionality to help peers organise this crucial part of the exchange of goods, or to help arbitrators understand the current state of the logistic process of the exchange. By introducing the ability for courier logs to be recorded against an escrow, the state of the exchange could be better tracked providing arbitrators with rich information to better perform their role, reducing the risk of participation for good peers. Logistical updates could be made via an interaction with the smart contract from the logistics provider, which would of course require their co-operation. However, such functionality would require authorised access such that logistic logs on the escrow could not be fraudulently created by anyone but the logistics provider; else the logs would no longer be dependable for arbitration. In order to provide authorisation to update logistics logs, logistic providers would need to have an Ethereum account verified and approved for access to the specific escrow. This creates the requirements for a process to verify that a given Ethereum account belongs to a specific and legitimate logistics provider. The integration of logistical elements into a distributed on-chain marketplace provides an opportunity for further work.

6.3   Reputation System

The introduction of an eBay style reputation system would help sellers and buyers to better identify safe, low risk peers to exchange goods with [18]. An average of a users feedback scores could be displayed as part of their profile to help peers better judge the risk of potential exchanges.

An alternative option would be to use a reputation system protocol designed for peer-to-peer networks. Swamynathan et al. [28] suggest such a system to address user collusion and short-lived online identities, the main causes of erroneous and misleading values in reputation systems. A similar reputation system that is blockchain based was introduced by Dennis and Owen [12], however no implementation currently exists for practical use.

6.4   Decentralised Front-End Hosting

The developed implementation is a locally deployed proof of concept artefact, however any real marketplace would be required to be publicly accessible. The back-end of the application, the smart contracts, would be hosted on the blockchain, however the front-end is a standard web application and so requires a web hosting solution. The simplest solution would be to use a standard web hosting service, however this would centralise the front-end and drastically reduce the points of failure required to make the application inaccessible. Decentralised web hosting options are under development, such as the IPFS peer-to-peer hypermedia protocol [6] or the ethereum foundation developed Swarm [5], a peer-to-peer storage and content distribution platform. However at the current time, while both are available to use, development of the systems is still ongoing and as such neither would be suitable for production environment use. Works to study the deployment of a Dapp front-end to a decentralised hosting platform should be undertaken.

7 Conclusion

To evaluate the applicability of an on-chain marketplace for physical goods, first the current blockchain literature was reviewed and then an proof-of-concept artefact was designed. The artefact was implemented to meet the basic requirements of a physical goods marketplace, captured in 8 requirements (R1–R8). It was then successfully tested against the requirements using white box and black box testing to verify the software. Performance measurements were taken regarding the gas usage of various behaviours of the marketplace, which were analysed against figures from existing centralised marketplaces. Our successful acceptance testing and performance testing of the artefact provides a demonstration of the Ethereum framework's testing and quality assurance capabilities – a key requirement for production applications. Discussion of the shortcomings of the generated artefact were presented, such as the vulnerabilities of a single escrow arbitrator and the difficulties regarding integrating logistics information and logs. Ultimately, it was concluded that an on-chain marketplace is indeed feasible, however, further study and development of the technology is required before a production implementation becomes practical.

References

1. ETH Gas Station. https://ethgasstation.info/. Accessed 01 May 2018
2. How much does it cost to sell on eBay? https://sellercentre.ebay.co.uk/private/what-fees-youll-pay. Accessed 01 May 2018
3. Sell on Amazon - Pricing and Fees. https://services.amazon.co.uk/services/sell-online/pricing.html. Accessed 01 May 2018
4. Total Retail 2017. https://www.pwc.com/gx/en/industries/assets/total-retail-2017.pdf. Accessed 01 May 2018
5. Ethersphere/swarm, December 2017. https://github.com/ethersphere/swarm
6. Benet, J.: IPFS-content addressed, versioned, P2P file system. arXiv preprint arXiv:1407.3561 (2014)
7. Berghel, H.: Equifax and the latest round of identity theft roulette. Computer 50(12), 72–76 (2017)
8. Buterin, V.: A next-generation smart contract and decentralized application platform (2013). https://github.com/ethereum/wiki/wiki/White-Paper. Accessed 02 May 2018. Document constantly updated by different people

9. Buterin, V.: Bootstrapping a decentralized autonomous corporation: part I. Bitcoin Mag. (2013). https://bitcoinmagazine.com/articles/bootstrapping-a-decentralized-autonomous-corporation-part-i-1379644274/

10. Buterin, V., Griffith, V.: Casper the friendly finality gadget. arXiv preprint arXiv:1710.09437 (2017)

11. Colangelo, G., Maggiolino, M.: Data Accumulation and the Privacy-Antitrust Interface: Insights from the Facebook Case for the EU and the US (2018), Working Paper No. 31/2018. https://ssrn.com/abstract=3125490

12. Dennis, R., Owen, G.: Rep on the block: a next generation reputation system based on the blockchain. In: Proceedings of the 10th International Conference for Internet Technology and Secured Transactions (ICITST), pp. 131–138. IEEE (2015)

13. Eskandari, S., Clark, J., Sundaresan, V., Adham, M.: On the feasibility of decentralized derivatives markets. In: Brenner, M., et al. (eds.) FC 2017. LNCS, vol. 10323, pp. 553–567. Springer, Cham (2017). https://doi.org/10.1007/978-3-319-70278-0_35

14. FBI: 2016 internet crime report (2016). https://pdf.ic3.gov/2016_IC3Report.pdf. Accessed 02 May 2018

15. Goldfeder, S., Bonneau, J., Gennaro, R., Narayanan, A.: Escrow protocols for cryptocurrencies: how to buy physical goods using bitcoin. In: Kiayias, A. (ed.) FC 2017. LNCS, vol. 10322, pp. 321–339. Springer, Cham (2017). https://doi.org/10.1007/978-3-319-70972-7_18

16. Grazioli, S., Jarvenpaa, S.L.: Perils of internet fraud: an empirical investigation of deception and trust with experienced Internet consumers. IEEE Trans. Syst. Man Cybern. - Part A: Syst. Hum. 30(4), 395–410 (2000)

17. Hitchens, R.: Solidity CRUD - Part 1 (2017). https://medium.com/@robhitchens/solidity-crud-part-1-824ffa69509a. Accessed 01 May 2018

18. Jøsang, A., Ismail, R., Boyd, C.: A survey of trust and reputation systems for online service provision. Decis. Support Syst. 43(2), 618–644 (2007)

19. Leber, J.: Going head to head with Google and Facebook, Amazons next big business could be advertising. MIT Technology Review (2014)

20. Mochi Inc.: Mobius: a universal protocol suite for the blockchain ecosystem and real world data, November 2017. https://mobius.network/mobius_white_paper.pdf. Accessed 02 May 2018

21. Nasonov, D., Visheratin, A.A., Boukhanovsky, A.: Blockchain-based transaction integrity in distributed big data marketplace. In: Shi, Y., et al. (eds.) ICCS 2018. LNCS, vol. 10860, pp. 569–577. Springer, Cham (2018). https://doi.org/10.1007/978-3-319-93698-7_43

22. Nidhra, S., Dondeti, J.: Black box and white box testing techniques-a literature review. Int. J. Embed. Syst. Appl. (IJESA) 2(2), 29–50 (2012)

23. Notheisen, B., Cholewa, J.B., Shanmugam, A.P.: Trading real-world assets on blockchain. Bus. Inf. Syst. Eng. 59(6), 425–440 (2017). https://doi.org/10.1007/s12599-017-0499-8

24. Ramesh, B., Cao, L., Baskerville, R.: Agile requirements engineering practices and challenges: an empirical study. Inf. Syst. J. 20(5), 449–480 (2010). https://doi.org/10.1111/j.1365-2575.2007.00259.x

25. Resnick, P., Zeckhauser, R.: Trust among strangers in Internet transactions: empirical analysis of eBay's reputation system. In: The Economics of the Internet and E-Commerce, pp. 127–157. Emerald Group Publishing Limited (2002)

26. Smart, J.F.: BDD in Action: Behavior-Driven Development for the Whole Software Lifecycle. Manning Publications, Shelter Island (2014)

27. Subramanian, H.: Decentralized blockchain-based electronic marketplaces. Commun. ACM **61**(1), 78–84 (2017)
28. Swamynathan, G., Almeroth, K.C., Zhao, B.Y.: The design of a reliable reputation system. Electron. Commer. Res. **10**(3–4), 239–270 (2010)
29. Szabo, N.: Formalizing and securing relationships on public networks. First Monday **2**(9) (1997). https://doi.org/10.5210/fm.v2i9.548
30. Vaishnavi, V., Kuechler, W.: Design science research in information systems (2004). http://desrist.org/desrist/content/design-science-research-in-information-systems.pdf

BlockChain Based Certificate Verification Platform

Axel Curmi and Frankie Inguanez

Malta College of Arts, Science and Technology, Paola PLA9032, Malta
{axel.curmi.a100445,frankie.inguanez}@mcast.edu.mt
http://ict.mcast.edu.mt

Abstract. This research is still in progress and focuses on using the blockchain for the verification of the authenticity of issued certificates. In this first stage of the research we are presenting a prototype that allows the registration of academic institutions and its respective institutes/faculties, registration of student cohorts and issuing of certificate awards. The issued certificates are registered on the blockchain so that any third party who would need to verify the authenticity of a certificate can do so, independently of the academic institution, even in the event that such institution has closed. The next phase of this research aims to extend the prototype to the registration of medical records on the blockchain with a focus on the privacy of sensitive data and allowing the owner of the information to control user access to the documents. The final phase of the research will involve gathering user and corporate feedback on the proposed prototypes.

Keywords: Blockchain · Smart contracts · Certificates
User-access control

1 Introduction

Satoshi Nakamoto, out of a need to secure transactions for cryptocurrencies, introduced a new concept of how we could store transaction data without the need for a centralised point of authority. Nakamoto described this system as "an ongoing chain of hash-based proof-of-work" [8], nowadays known as the blockchain. The blockchain is considered to be the next revolutionary technology ever since the internet was first introduced, as it is constantly challenging us to change the way we use technology in our daily lives [10]. In this research we set out the hypothesis: the integrity of certificates, be it academic or medical, should ideally be in a decentralised system, that will be able to survive beyond the lifetime of the issuing institution/entity. We have opted to split this research into three stages:

1. **Stage 1: Technology Familiarisation:** where a prototype is created using the blockchain for the verification of academic certificates;

W. Abramowicz and A. Paschke (Eds.): BIS 2018 Workshops, LNBIP 339, pp. 211–216, 2019.
https://doi.org/10.1007/978-3-030-04849-5_18

2. **Stage 2: Privacy Enhancement:** a second prototype is created which will hold important medical health records of patients, with a main focus on the privacy concerns/issues;
3. **Stage 3: Market Acceptance:** a study is performed to gather user and corporate acceptance as well as the possibility of having inter blockchain network communication.

The motivation behind this research is that systems developed for the blockchain have an absence of a central point of authority which controls, filters and manipulates content, as well as the fact that recently, countries around the globe are working towards finding various ways to use the blockchain for their own purposes, including Malta which is aiming to be the "The blockchain island" and has already attracted companies such as Neufund [9] and Binance [11]. Thus in this paper, we document the first stage of this research as a second year undergraduate research project, leading to the final year in which the subsequent two stages of the research will be performed.

2   Literature Review

In order to solve issues related to centralised forms of systems a decentralised system can be created using a blockchain network [10]. By using this network, the data is not stored in a centralised location, instead, it is distributed between all participants, also known as a distributed ledger. With this design, the users do not have to trust each other nor a central point of authority. Instead, every participant in the blockchain holds every record of data stored in the network throughout its lifetime, and is able to contribute to the creation of new blocks. However if the newly added blocks are verified by means of the consensus algorithm, and added to the blockchain, it can never be deleted nor updated, not even by the creator. Furthermore in [10], the researchers also describe how the blockchain works and states that rather than relying on the intermediary, the participants of the network agree on a verification protocol called the consensus algorithm (examples of these are: Proof of work and Proof of Stake), which allows the participants to reach an agreement and mutual trust. Currently Bitcoin and Ethereum use a proof of work based consensus algorithm, however, other algorithms are currently being researched as a replacement, due to the cost inefficiency and potential damage to our environment. Any certificate should be immutable and unable to be corrupted, as that would invalidate the certificate, thus making the blockchain structure ideal. The lack of central authoritative power is also very ideal in this scenario, because if one is looking to retrieve or validate a specific certificate, they can do so without the need for permission or control from the intermediary. The number of research publications is increasing exponentially and spreading around the globe [13], next a few notable research will be reviewed.

In [14] the researchers address the lack of privacy users deal with when using third-party applications, more specifically mobile applications which are constantly collecting personal data without the knowledge or control of the user.

The researchers implemented a protocol which turns the blockchain structure into a trust-less automated access-control manager, which is done by combining the blockchain and off-chain storage. To accomplish this the user has to install an application which uses this privacy platform, as the user signs up for the first time an identity is generated and sent along with the permission settings to the blockchain. The data collected on the device is encrypted with the identity and sent to the blockchain along with appropriate encryption details from the off-chain storage. The user can access and opt-out of the data collection at any given time, and the service can freely access data it was given permission to.

The EduCTX blockchain platform is focused for higher education credits and grading, where higher education institutions form part of a peer-to-peer network and students have a wallet within the network. This would allow the students and organisations to verify the credits that a student has [12]. Other proposals have also been researched such as using the MultiChain Platform [7]. The exchange of healthcare information across institutions has been proven to be very beneficial [4] and a number of solutions have been researched to do just that using the blockchain network such as in BlocHIE [6].

3   Research Methodology

The main aim of this research is to demonstrate that having certificates published on the blockchain would improve the authenticity of the certificate while also improving the quality of life for certificate holders, certificate issuers, and employers. As physical certificates could be falsified, lost or damaged, and if the issuing entity is from a different country or no longer exists, the verification of the certificate could be cumbersome and lengthy. With the proposed platform, certificates can no longer be falsified due to the high level of cryptography in the blockchain, known as proof-of-work, and if the certificates get lost or damaged, one can simply access their storage with their credentials and download to print a copy of the certificate. Students will also be allowed to access and freely share their awards with anyone by just sharing their public key and certificate ID. Employers will then easily verify the authenticity of the specified certificate as there would no longer be the need for a central point of authority to verify for them, this is especially the case when the issuing entity no longer exists. To confirm this concept, a prototype of the proposed platform was developed to allow issuers to register with the application, and later on be able to issue their certificates on the blockchain network. In order to implement this prototype we split it into three phases (see Fig. 1).

1. **Phase 1: Institution, cohort, and student registration:** This phase consisted of designing and developing an off-chain storage system along with the interfaces required with which institutions could interact with so that they would be able to register themselves for approval. Once the institutions register they would have the status of pending, and the owner of the platform is required to approve or reject such registrations. Once an institution is

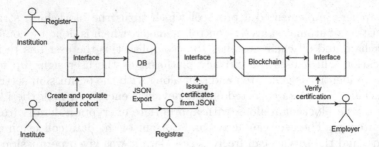

Fig. 1. The three phases of the prototype

approved, it will have the ability of issuing certificates on the blockchain with our smart contract. Another tool is also implemented to allow the administration to create student cohorts and add students to their respective cohort, after this is done the administration is able to finalise the changes and download a JSON file containing the cohort and respective students, this JSON file is then passed-on to the registrar or the person in charge of the institution's public key and private key credentials.

2. **Phase 2: Issuing of certificates:** In this phase an interface was developed to allow communication between the registrar, their Ethereum wallet and the smart contract. When the registrar has successfully received the JSON file, they can now start the issuing process - assuming the registrar is already logged into the institution's Ethereum wallet (in this case Metamask was used). The registrar inputs the requested JSON file and the platform will make sure it is valid by performing client-side validation. When the data has been loaded successfully the registrar is able to issue the certificates by approving the transaction between the institution's account and the smart contract.

3. **Phase 3: Certificate viewing and validation:** An interface was developed to allow students to access and view their certificates while also allowing potential employers to check and validate the integrity of the students certification without having the need to check with the institution. This is done by entering the certificate holder's ID and certificate ID, and automatically the platform calls the smart contract in order to retrieve the certificate with the given details, if an empty response is returned, that would mean that the certification does not exist and is invalid, otherwise if a detailed certificate is returned, that would mean that the certification exists and it's details are shown on screen.

4   Evaluation

Since we used the Ethereum network to build a public blockchain application, we could not store the certifications privately. Instead certificates are publicly visible and everyone is able to make a function call to check any given certification, having said this we made sure that no private information is being stored on the blockchain and instead only store the holder address and certificate details. Following this, we can explore another framework for building distributed applications such as Hyperledger fabric, which is mainly used to build permissioned applications and thus providing the ability to store private information on the blockchain without being exposed to everyone [3].

Scalability and size are two major limitations with this platform, as well as blockchain itself. This is because every certificate which is issued with this platform is recorded and stored within the blockchain, in this case the minimum size taken for one certificate is 40 bytes, the exact amount of bytes can not be calculated as strings are dynamically allocated and could vary in size depending on the length of the strings used. According to [5] the number of students attending higher educational institutions is roughly 207 million, which means that if every student has had only a single certification issued with this platform, the minimum amount of storage required is roughly 10.8 gigabytes. Another important fact one should consider is that certain certificates could no longer be relevant, this is especially the case when certificates expire or higher level certificates are awarded, in this case a network such as [1] would be very ideal as it supports cross blockchain atomic swaps, this means that old and non-relevant certificates could be archived in an archive blockchain, while the higher level and relevant certificates would still be accessible on the main blockchain.

Certificate count per block is another limiting factor in this platform, this is because if we try to issue too many certificates at once, it would result in an error message from the Ethereum virtual machine (EVM) and no certificates would be issued. This is because the blocks in the blockchain must not exceed a specific size. To solve this we could split certification transactions into smaller transactions, making each transaction much smaller. Another limitation of this platform would be that due to the nature of smart contracts and blockchain applications, whenever the data in the smart contract has to be modified in one way or another, a payment fee has to be paid in order to compensate for the computational power used by the Ethereum virtual machine (EVM).

One major limitation with the current version of Ethereum is it's transactions complete per second, this is because Ethereum can handle much less transactions per second compared to companies like VISA and PayPal. However [1] and [2] provide a solution for this limitation and make transactions near-instant by providing an off-chain scaling solution. Due to the fact that certifications do not need to be issued as fast as monetary transactions, this limitation does not affect this platform on the same level that it affects the Ethereum blockchain.

5   Conclusion

This research confirms that anything which is considered valuable, such as certificates, can be stored on the blockchain, and thus being immutable and incorruptible. Thus it is being proposed that in the next stage of this research, focus is given to securing the data and controlling user access. It is being also recommended to investigate the combination of blockchain and off-chain storage structure, similar to what was implemented in [14], in order to implement an advanced medical health recording system which would also allow end users to opt-in and opt-out from having their medical data used by medical researchers. This research has not investigated on how the validity of documents on the blockchain is verified, yet this needs to be addressed in the subsequent phases. The blockchain technology is a very recent and emerging technology which is met with mixed feelings and understanding by the general public.

References

1. Lightning Network scalable, instant bitcoin/blockchain transactions. https://lightning.network/. Accessed 27 June 2018
2. The Raiden Network fast, cheap, scalable token transfers for ethereum. https://raiden.network/. Accessed 28 June 2018
3. Androulaki, E., et al.: Hyperledger fabric: a distributed operating system for permissioned blockchains. In: Proceedings of the Thirteenth EuroSys Conference, p. 30. ACM (2018)
4. Dixon, B.E., Cusack, C.M.: Measuring the value of health information exchange. In: Health Information Exchange, pp. 231–248. Elsevier (2016)
5. U.G.E.M.R.U.I.I. for Education Planning (IIEP): Six ways to ensure higher education leaves no one behind (2017)
6. Jiang, S., Cao, J., Wu, H., Yang, Y., Ma, M., He, J.: Blochie: a blockchain-based platform for healthcare information exchange (2018)
7. Kaltyshev, M., et al.: Proof of university certificate using blockchain technology (2018)
8. Nakamoto, S.: Bitcoin: a peer-to-peer electronic cash system (2008). https://www.bitcoin.com/bitcoin.pdf
9. O'Brien, C.: Berlinís neufund wants to help turn malta into blockchain island (2018). https://venturebeat.com/2018/04/17/berlins-neufund-wants-to-help-turn-malta-into-blockchain-island/
10. Puthal, D., Malik, N., Mohanty, S.P., Kougianos, E., Yang, C.: The blockchain as a decentralized security framework (future directions). IEEE Consum. Electron. Mag. **7**(2), 18–21 (2018). https://doi.org/10.1109/MCE.2017.2776459
11. Sanchez, H.: Malta determined to become the ëblockchain islandí: regulations, adoption, binance headquarters (2018). https://cointelegraph.com/news/malta-determined-to-become-the-blockchain-island-regulations-adoption-binance-headquarters
12. Turkanović, M., Hölbl, M., Košič, K., Heričko, M., Kamišalič, A.: EduCTX: a blockchain-based higher education credit platform. IEEE Access **6**, 5112–5127 (2018). https://doi.org/10.1109/ACCESS.2018.2789929
13. Yli-Huumo, J., Ko, D., Choi, S., Park, S., Smolander, K.: Where is current research on blockchain technology?–A systematic review. PloS one **11**(10), e0163477 (2016)
14. Zyskind, G., Nathan, O., et al.: Decentralizing privacy: using blockchain to protect personal data. In: 2015 IEEE Security and Privacy Workshops (SPW), pp. 180–184. IEEE (2015)

Blockchain-Based Management of Shared Energy Assets Using a Smart Contract Ecosystem

Manuel Utz[1(✉)], Simon Albrecht[1,2], Thorsten Zoerner[3], and Jens Strüker[1]

[1] Fresenius University of Applied Sciences, Frankfurt, Germany
manuel.utz@hs-fresenius.de
[2] University of Freiburg – Information Systems Research, Freiburg, Germany
simon.albrecht@is.uni-freiburg.de
[3] StromDAO UG, Mauer, Germany

Abstract. Energy markets are facing challenges regarding a changing energy generation and consumption structure, as well as the coordination of an increasing number of assets, devices and stakeholders. We address these challenges by introducing a blockchain-based smart contract ecosystem as our contribution to extant research. Apart from blockchain-specific benefits (e.g. data integrity and smart contract execution), the ecosystem fosters energy-blockchain research through the creation of digital assets. Doing so, we address research gaps identified by previous authors. From our work, we can derive economic implications regarding the foundation of local energy markets, the incentivization of grid-stabilizing behavior and the settlement of collective action problems.

Keywords: Blockchain · Energy · Smart contract · Asset management
Proof-of-Authority · Ethereum · Microgrid

1 Introduction

The energy transition from centralized power plants to distributed energy assets challenges existing utility business models due to a higher market participation of customers and coordination of an increasing number of Internet of Things (IoT) devices. Simultaneously, innovations of blockchain technologies, such as the inclusion of an application layer in Ethereum have been portrayed as a potential building block to address these challenges. Despite being discussed extensively in the press, the academic community has identified substantial research gaps regarding the technology. For instance, (a) the relevance of scientific work to focus on smart contracts in IoT environments, such as the sharing of virtual property [1]; (b) further investigation of group decision making in cases of lacking consensus and implications for value creation [2]; and (c) a necessity to elaborate on research gaps regarding new intermediaries in value chains and the implementing of business logic in smart contracts [3].

W. Abramowicz and A. Paschke (Eds.): BIS 2018 Workshops, LNBIP 339, pp. 217–222, 2019.
https://doi.org/10.1007/978-3-030-04849-5_19

We address the identified research gaps by introducing a blockchain-based ecosystem of smart contracts, executing business logics for the management of energy assets in a shared environment (a). This ecosystem utilizes a complexity-reducing consensus mechanism to solve collective action problems (b) and constitutes a major element for alternative value streams and business roles (c), that can be filled by stakeholders of the energy sector. The introduced ecosystem was developed based on a design science approach [4].

Our approach has several implications for research and practice. First, we present the system framework for a novel smart contract ecosystem based on the Proof-of-Authority (PoA) consensus mechanism. Second, we describe the business logic of interdependent smart contracts, operating on the application layer for several energy-related use cases in which the system can be deployed. Third, we present the potential and economic implications of such a deployment.

The remainder of the paper is structured as follows: First, we describe the fundamental background of our energy-focused use case, as well as related literature and previous approaches. Subsequently, we present the components, interdependencies and functions of the smart contract ecosystem. Next, we critically discuss the economic implications of our work and finally we lay out future research steps.

2   Background

The energy market is currently being transformed by two mutually dependent dynamics: The decentralization of energy generation and the digitalization of grid and market communication. The increasing number of residential microgrids is an indicator for this development. Energy assets such as photovoltaic (PV) panels pose major challenges to the traditional energy system, which is designed for uni-directional flows of energy and information [5]. From an economic perspective, a higher level of self-consumption leads to a reduction in electricity costs for residents [6]. At the same time, system costs for the macrogrid rise due to fixed costs for grid infrastructure. Therefore, one of the key challenges is to efficiently integrate energy market players into a decentralized system. Existing market mechanisms and processes are neither designed to integrate numerous small generation plants into the energy market, nor to manage them within microgrids. From an economic perspective it is not only necessary to transform business models, e.g. from electric utilities into energy service providers [7], but also to find ways of implementing those models into the real world. In recent years blockchain technology has been used to address the mentioned challenges. Prototype attempts of creating a consensus system for peer-to-peer energy trade and microgrid market places have been made [8]. In those projects, it has been shown that consensus of the amount and price of electricity between peers can be achieved by using blockchains.

When managing microgrids various implications with regard to technical feasibility, overall social sustainability, economic compatibility and regulatory frameworks have to be taken into consideration [8]. On-site power generation units such as PV-panels and electrical storage options such as batteries are shared energy assets as their electricity output is consumed by residents or fed into the public grid. For each actor, different levels of uncertainty apply to those assets. For investors the return on investment of installed energy assets is a key figure, whereas for residents the prices and origin of consumed electricity might be paramount. From a governments perspective the integration of fluctuating energy of microgrids into the public macrogrid might be a technical and regulatory concern.

Due to an increased complexity of small-scale and volatile power generation and the emergence of residential microgrids traditional business models and underlying processes of energy utilities need to be modified to be part of the energy transition [7]. Value chains of energy retailers and grid operators will change. Therefore, it is fundamental to find economically feasible ways to integrate microgrids in public grid infrastructure. For that purpose, electricity tariffs that fit the needs of residential microgrids e.g. by encouraging consumption behavior favorable for grid stabilization have been designed. Future residential microgrid tariffs should not only be based on volumetric billing but also include some charge for the usage of installed energy assets [6]. However not only will the role perception of energy utilities be changed but consumers might also become prosumers that sell electricity to their peers or into the grid made possible by process innovation based on blockchain technology [8].

As wholesale markets have been designed for predictable and non-fluctuating power-plants new frameworks for small-scale energy trading and incentives for integrating fluctuating on-site power generation are being investigated. When blockchain-technology is applied to manage processes within decentralized market networks small-scale and economically efficient transactions of renewable energy are made possible. The real-live applicability of such market places based on blockchain has been reviewed in a case study of the Brooklyn Microgrid [9]. A previously made top-level analysis on different system design features and implications for respective use cases within the energy sector has pointed out the applicability of complexity-reducing consensus mechanisms, such as PoA for energy-related use cases [10].

As the reviewed literature shows, the management of energy assets in microgrids proves to be difficult, new business roles and models are demanded. Simultaneously new ways for residents of microgrids to become active energy market actors open up by the emergence of the blockchain technology. However, the process innovation possibilities that blockchains entails for energy markets are currently focused on peer-to-peer trading scenarios and the integration in energy markets. This paper provides a major contribution in form of blockchain-based process management of transactions between microgrid energy assets. The approach goes beyond previous ones, as tokenization enables a multitude of use case applications such as grid management, energy product certification or the integration of electric vehicles. Using blockchain platform design ontologies [11], we will outline the components of our smart contract ecosystem for the digital energy asset management in the subsequent section.

3 Smart Contract Ecosystem Design

The system framework is a coinless PoA implementation of the Ethereum blockchain protocol [12]. It has been established to maintain irrevocable consensus on complex flows of energy and therefore acts as a single, decentralized market communication bus for settling and clearing transactions between energy market participants. Since the network is unrestricted, anyone can deploy their own node. However the PoA consensus mechanism allows transactions to only be verified by authorities. This form of internal governance does not only significantly reduce the energy consumption per transaction verification but also increases internal security. To become an authority node, one has to be voted in by another authority node. The energy sector market logic is encapsulated in smart contracts as entities on the blockchain. Smart contracts are based on the ERC-20 Ethereum token standard [13] and the programming language Solidity. For the management of energy assets such as battery storages, solar panels and electric cars, smart contracts are logically combined within business logics. By using these logics entire business processes. Further software components such as Python or JavaScript e.g. for smart home control build the interface between the digital infrastructure and energy assets. Indices representing the share of green electricity in an area and also devices like smart meters act like applications on the blockchain ecosystem. As both their data input is transferred to designated smart contracts by using software components (e.g. command-line tools) electricity consumers are enabled to put their consumption in perspective to local energy generation. In the following paragraph, six smart contracts and their interaction will be explained.

StromDAO Node: The purpose of this smart contract is the authorization of a blockchain node after a meter point reading has been stored the first time. A public and private key set will be generated as soon as a first meter point reading is created.

Meter Point Reading (MPR): The purpose of the MPR smart contract is to deploy meter readings to the blockchain. Every meter point holds a private key and is able to sign its own transactions. The private key is only known to the meter point operator.

> **Input:** Meter point reading of smart meter.
> **Output:** Storage of reading and time on blockchain.

Settlement. In the settlement smart contract, a consensus of transactions between different meter points is created. As each meter point is linked to a balancing group the delivery and consumption of energy can be settled.

> **Input:** Meter point reading of A, B and C.
> **Output:** Consensus for energy delivery from balancing group of meter point A (energy production meter) to meter points B and C (consumption meters).

Single Clearing. The clearing process is the next logical step after settlement. In this smart contract, the stored settlements of different meter points are connected to prices of the individual electricity tariffs. The tariff information has been stored during the creation of the StromDAO Node.

> **Input:** Settlement transactions of meter points A, B and C.
> **Output:** Liability stored within the blockchain.

Electricity Account: This ledger shows the current credits and liabilities regarding consumption and generation of a meter point. It can be linked to a crypto wallet or a standard bank account.

Input: Liabilities of meter point B and C to meter point A.
   Output: Debit credit account.

MP Token. By using this smart contract, the meter point readings are tokenized as digital assets on the blockchain. A power and a time token are created for every watt hour since the last meter point storing. The tokens do not have an intrinsic value, they proof the origin and time of generation or consumption. Much like traditional green energy certificates their value is determined by the demand for renewable energy.

Input: Meterpoint reading.
   Output: Power and time tokens.

4   Discussion of Economic Implications

The outlined smart contracts are the foundation for various energy asset use cases. A first one is the design of electricity tariffs that encourage consumption behavior favorable for grid stabilization within residential and industrial microgrids. Due to tokenized meter point readings and smart meters as nodes on the blockchain, the origin of each kilowatt hour can be tracked. Based on their behavior, residents within the microgrid, consuming at peak times, might get a financial bonus built into the electricity tariff. Moreover, simplified billing and invoicing models for the pro-rata utilization of energy assets such as PV-panels and battery storage can be designed. The flexible energy balancing and settlement capabilities of the ecosystem support vehicle charging use cases such as dynamic electricity pricing. A fourth use-case is the pooling of distributed production and consumption in co-productive micro community markets enabling cost-efficient and transparent peer-to-peer energy trade. Finally, the smart contract ecosystem offers capabilities for autonomous swarm orchestration, connecting micro markets to operate seamlessly on the public grid.

5   Conclusion and Outlook

In this paper, we introduced an operational smart contract ecosystem on top of a PoA blockchain network, as well as designated use cases for deployment and underlying economic implications. The described system constitutes a building block to address concurrent challenges of the energy sector. Doing so, we further address previously identified research gaps [1–3] in form of a blockchain-based process management.

Apart from the contribution of the smart contract ecosystem, we can derive the following real-world implications from our use case formalization: (1) The system enables the incentivization of grid-stabilizing energy consumption behavior as the electricity consumers are enabled to put their consumption in perspective to local energy production. (2) The settlement of collective action problems through precise tracking and consensus finding of assets' properties is reached by energy assets acting as blockchain agents and settling electricity transactions e.g. via dynamic price ranges within the SingleClearing smart contract. (3) The foundation of dynamic energy markets, as the described blockchain ecosystem is used to establish an energy market communication to connect assets regardless of their size. In contrast to centralized management systems our distributed system creates an information synchrony and provides trust-supplement among network participants. Previous projects are mainly focused on designing peer-to-peer trading platforms. These transactions do not represent digital assets as described in this paper. Through tokenizing, digital assets are created enabling a multitude of use case applications.

For future work we will perform a scalability test and then deploy the smart contracts in a real-world environment, using the infrastructure of a demonstration project we are currently working on.

References

1. Yli-Huumo, J., Ko, D., Choi, S., Park, S., Smolander, K.: Where is current research on blockchain technology?—a systematic review. PLoS ONE **11**, e0163477 (2016)
2. Risius, M., Spohrer, K.: A blockchain research framework - what we (don't) know, where we go from here, and how we will get there. Bus. Inf. Syst. Eng. **59**, 385–409 (2017)
3. Beck, R., Avital, M., Rossi, M., Thatcher, J.B.: Blockchain technology in business and information systems research. Bus. Inf. Syst. Eng. **59**, 381–384 (2017)
4. Crnkovic, G.D.: Constructive research and info-computational knowledge generation. In: Magnani, L., Carnielli, W., Pizzi, C. (eds.) Studies in Computational Intelligence, vol. 314, pp. 359–380. Springer, Berlin Heidelberg (2010). https://doi.org/10.1007/978-3-642-15223-8_20
5. Green, J., Newman, P.: Citizen utilities: the emerging power paradigm. Energy Policy **105**, 283–293 (2017)
6. Fridgen, G., Kahlen, M., Ketter, W., Rieger, A., Thimmel, M.: One rate does not fit all: an empirical analysis of electricity tariffs for residential microgrids. Appl. Energy **210**, 800–814 (2018)
7. Helms, T.: Asset transformation and the challenges to servitize a utility business model. Energy Policy. **91**, 98–112 (2016)
8. Mengelkamp, E., Gärttner, J., Rock, K., Kessler, S., Orsini, L., Weinhardt, C.: Designing microgrid energy markets. Appl. Energy **210**, 870–880 (2017)
9. Mengelkamp, E., Notheisen, B., Beer, C., Dauer, D., Weinhardt, C.: A blockchain-based smart grid: towards sustainable local energy markets. Comput. Sci. Res. Dev. **33**, 207–214 (2018)
10. Albrecht, S., Reichert, S., Schmid, J., Strüker, J., Neumann, D., Fridgen, G.: Dynamics of blockchain implementation - a case study from the energy sector. In: Proceedings of the 51st Hawaii International Conference on System Sciences, pp. 3527–3536 (2018)
11. Glaser, F.: Pervasive decentralisation of digital infrastructures: a framework for blockchain enabled system and use case analysis. In: Proceedings of the 50th Hawaii International Conference on System Sciences (2017)
12. Zoerner, T.: Fury network energychain. https://github.com/energychain
13. Vogelsteller, F., Buterin, V.: ERC-20 Token Standard, September 2017. https//github.com/ethereum/EIPs/blob/master/EIPS/eip-20-tokenstandard

Research of Ethereum Mining Hash Rate Dependency on GPU Hardware Settings

Paulius Danielius[✉], Tomas Savenas, and Saulius Masteika

Vilnius University Kaunas Faculty, Muitines St. 8, 44280 Kaunas, Lithuania
paulius.danielius@mif.vu.lt,
{tomas.savenas, saulius.masteika}@knf.vu.lt

Abstract. Cryptocurrency mining with GPUs for profit has a fine edge of finding the best rate for mining power versus energy consumption. In this research we explore different GPU settings, namely memory clock and core voltage influence on mining performance measured as hash rate. Additionally, we look for opportunities to lower power consumption. Experiment using combined power of five commonly available graphics cards showed improvement of hash rate with increased memory clock frequencies, and lower power consumption with decreased core voltages. However, these dependencies are not linear, and some other factors, like different memory chips on otherwise similar graphics card models may give contradicting results.

Keywords: Ethereum · Ethash · Mining efficiency · Hash rate
GPU voltage · GPU memory clock

1 Introduction

The driving force of all cryptocurrencies is the *blockchain* technology. Each transaction within the specific *blockchain* is confirmed by the consensus of a majority of the members [6, 10].

There are several different types of consensus algorithms. The most widely used is *proof of work.* In *proof of work* the computational power of processing unit is employed to solve extremely difficult cryptographic puzzle. However, the drawbacks of this method are enormous power consumption, long transaction confirmation times, and accumulating mining activity in areas with cheap power supply [2].

The second most popular cryptocurrency, Ethereum [4, 5] had seen many improvements over Bitcoin and addressed several of its limitations [13]. Ethereum uses different *proof of work* algorithm, called *Ethash*. Still, the drawback of being computationally intensive remains, and there are considerations of changing this algorithm in favor of *proof of stake* [7], which is the most common alternative to *proof of work*.

In case of *proof of stake*, there is no mining (coin creation). All coins exist from the very beginning, and stakeholders are paid solely in transaction fees. The next block creator is picked depending on the amount of coins he owns, and block commitment to *blockchain* can vary in different *proof of stake* systems. This type of consensus algorithms is not without its own problems, which several other, less common, consensus algorithms are trying to address [2].

© Springer Nature Switzerland AG 2019
W. Abramowicz and A. Paschke (Eds.): BIS 2018 Workshops, LNBIP 339, pp. 223–228, 2019.
https://doi.org/10.1007/978-3-030-04849-5_20

Given sheer rise of popularity of cryptocurrency mining, the demand for capable hardware skyrocketed and induced fierce competition among hardware manufacturers. The shift from CPU to GPU based mining was followed by more specialized hardware pieces such as FPGA and ASIC. The history of this hardware evolution is explored in excellent review of Taylor [12].

Although presently Bitcoin is mostly mined by using ASIC, Ethereum is still mined with GPUs. The problem there is a shortage of scientifically tested experiments looking for best settings of different GPU parameters. Because of this energy usage and mining process efficiency usually is not optimal. The mining difficulty of cryptocurrencies using *proof of work* consensus is constantly increasing, so every finding which allows to maximize hashing efficiency per consumed power unit is a must, if miners want to maintain a positive economic balance for longer time.

The aim of this research is to analyze which settings influence Ethereum GPU mining efficiency and power consumption the most and find the optimal combination of settings for higher profit.

The paper is organized as follows. Section 2 introduces mining of *Ethash* based cryptocurrencies. Section 3 describes hardware setup used for experiment and tested GPU parameters. Section 4 presents experiment results. Section 5 concludes.

2 Mining of Ethash Based Cryptocurrencies

There are several cryptocurrencies, powered by *Ethash proof of work* hashing algorithm, most popular of them are Ethereum (ETH), Ethereum Classic (ETC), Metaverse ETP (ETP), Expanse (EXP) and some others. Mining *Ethash* based coins is the most profitable choice for AMD RX series GPU card owners, because they perform better at *Ethash* than any other algorithm [3]. In general, AMD cards were considered better choice for mining than Nvidia cards, because of better performance/cost ratio and GCN microarchitecture and instruction set, which allow for better *integer* computation speed, hence – faster cryptographic puzzle-solving. Nvidia cards were better optimized for gaming than any other purpose. However, this may look different with newer Nvidia cards, especially of *Titan* series.

Ethash has one significant difference as compared to Bitcoin hashing algorithm – it is memory hard (a. k. a. memory bound). The characteristic feature of such design is limited efficiency gain with emerging ASIC hardware [11], which is specialized solely for cryptocurrency mining.

Properly setting up a card for mining means finding best performance/energy consumption rate. For this purpose, several parameters may be adjusted: *core voltage, power limit, temperature limit, core clock, memory clock* and *fan speed*. The most important of them for increasing mining performance (especially for memory intensive *Ethash*), is *memory clock*, while lowering the voltage allow to use less power [9].

The research of Balanyuk, Silnov, Goncharov [1] proposed an alternative to increasing memory clock frequency – the results show that lowering memory clock together with memory latency may yield a significant gain of GPU productivity. However, as this method involves changing video card BIOS settings and causes the strong heat up of the card, we have not used it in our experiment. We do not propose this method either, because changing BIOS voids warranty of the card in most of the cases.

The second component needed for mining is mining software. There are several software packages to choose from. The most popular is *Claymore*, which is free, frequently updated and may have an edge over other programs, for example it is about 8% faster than *EthMiner* [8].

3   Experimental Setup

GPU machine with following setup was used for our experiment:

Motherboard: Gigabyte X99-UD4-CF; CPU: 12 × Intel(R) Core(TM) i7-5820K, 3.30 GHz; RAM: 8 GB; drive: KINGSTON SV300S37A240G, 250 GB; GPUs:

1. ASUS Ellesmere RX 580 115-D000PIL-100 SK Hynix
2. ASUS Ellesmere RX 580 115-D000PIL-100 SK Hynix
3. ASUS Ellesmere RX 480 115-D000PIL-100 Samsung
4. AMD Ellesmere RX 480 113-D0090101-100 Samsung
5. AMD Ellesmere RX 480 113-D0090101-100 Samsung

Operating system: EthOS 1.3.1; mining software: Claymore v11.6.

During the experiment hash rates of each separate GPU together with combined hash rate and power consumption of each GPU were measured for different core voltage and memory clock frequency combinations.

Four different GPU core voltage settings were used: default (lowered by 5% as default by EthOS and Claymore settings), then lowered by 10%, 15% and 20%.

Within each voltage setting, 14 different memory clock frequencies by 50 MHz increments were tested in range from 1600 MHz to 2250 MHz, as a result, under-clocked (lower than default 2000 MHz) and overclocked (higher than 2000 MHz) frequencies were covered.

We did not test higher than default core voltage settings, because increasing the voltage increases power consumption and heating up of the cards, which may lead them to clocking down to stay within their set power and heat limits, which defeat the purpose of the experiment.

4   Experimental Results

During all four test sets with different voltage settings we found that GPU-1 and GPU-2 performed considerably worse, than the rest, especially with higher than default 2000 MHz memory clock frequency settings (Fig. 1, default voltages). This could be explained due to different memory chip manufacturer.

Figure 2 displays combined hash rates of all five GPUs across tested range of memory clock frequencies with all four voltage settings. The results show, that 10% lower voltage setting (2nd column in each group) did not have considerable impact on hash rate, and on highest memory clock frequency the difference from default voltage setting was only 0.19 Mh/s. With 15% lower voltage setting (3rd column in each group)

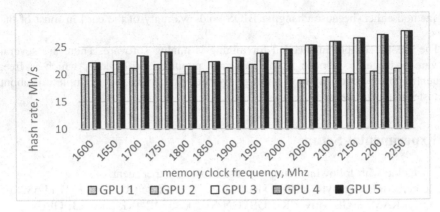

Fig. 1. Hash rate dependency on GPU memory type

the differences were slightly higher and for highest point reached 0.65 Mh/s. The biggest differences showed up with 20% lower voltage setting (4th column in each group) which for three highest memory clock frequencies reached 1.21, 1.87 and 3.47 Mh/s respectively.

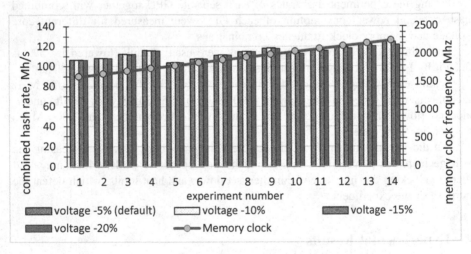

Fig. 2. Hash rate dependency on GPU memory clock frequency and core voltage

In addition, Fig. 2 shows that decreasing memory clock frequency from default 2000 MHz (9th group of columns) causes drop of hashing power, which continues down till 1800 MHz, and then the next setting of 1750 MHz (4th group) suddenly increases it by more than 11 Mh/s. Further lowering memory clock frequency starts to decrease the hashing power again.

Increasing memory clock frequency over default setting causes to drop hashing rate slightly, and this is due significant performance decrease of first two GPUs.

Performance of the other three actually increased as seen in Fig. 1, and at the end only the contribution of these resulted in higher combined hashing power as compared with default memory clock frequency.

Lowering core voltages resulted in decrease of power consumed by GPUs (Fig. 3). The differences were consistent within entire memory clock frequency range. Average power savings were 37, 110 and 154 W for 10%, 15% and 20% lower voltage settings respectively as compared to default voltage setting. The total power savings using highest tested memory clock settings could be measured up to 359, 1007 and 1445 kW/h annually for given hardware setup.

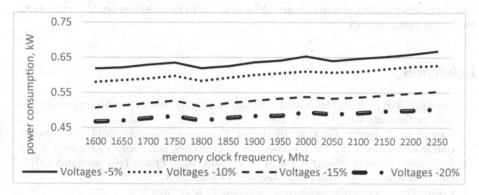

Fig. 3. Power consumption dependency on GPU core voltage and memory clock frequency

However, considering significant drop in hash rate with 20% lower voltages, the decrease by 15% proved to be better choice.

Our findings suggest that for best hash rate of RX 480 video cards it is recommended to increase memory clock frequency (e.g., 2250 MHz). For tested RX 580 cards the default memory clock frequency proved to be the best setting.

For minimizing power consumption, it is recommended to lower core voltage (e.g., 15%). In addition, if the priority is to minimize power consumption, lower memory clock frequency may be chosen (e.g., 1750 MHz), which provided very similar hashing results to default setting. As RX 580 Radeon cards with Hynix memory chips showed considerably worse performance (this may be attributed to specifics in chip architecture), we recommend using cards with Samsung memory chips.

For more broader hashing efficiency comparison, experiment including video cards with GeForce GPUs could be made. Also, it may be worthwhile to look for further multiobjective optimization using Pareto analysis.

5   Conclusions

Tweaking GPU settings like memory clock frequency and core voltage may significantly impact its hash rate and power consumption. However, the hash rate dependence on these settings is not linear. Different vendors hardware components on the same video card model may also provide greatly different results, therefore it is highly recommended to check card components manufacturer before going to invest in a greater amount of GPU cards.

In our experiment we found out that increasing memory clock frequency in general should improve hash rate (although different memory chips may give contradicting results), the sweet spot however should be found by experimenting. Lowering memory clock frequency also may be an option to consider, because at some point very similar results as with default setting could be reached, and, in addition, power consumption could be cut back.

Decreasing core voltage gives good results in lowering power consumption without affecting hash rate, but at certain point (20% lower than default) this could start to make too big negative impact.

References

1. Balanyuk, Y.B., Silnov, D.S., Goncharov, D.E.: Applying memshift technology to increase GPU performance (2018)
2. Castor, A.: A (Short) Guide to Blockchain Consensus Protocols (2017). https://www.coindesk.com/short-guide-blockchain-consensus-protocols/. Accessed 17 May 2018
3. Coinguides: What is Ethash? A List of all Ethash coins – Ethash PoW algorithm (2018). https://coinguides.org/ethash-coins/. Accessed 17 May 2018
4. Coinranking. https://coinranking.com/. Accessed 20 May 2018
5. Collin: Cryptocurrency List – Which Are the Top-Rated Altcoins? (2018). https://cybermentors.org.uk/cryptocurrency-list/. Accessed 17 May 2018
6. Efanov, D., Roschin, P.: The All-pervasiveness of the blockchain technology. Procedia Comput. Sci. **123**, 116–121 (2018)
7. Lielacher, A.: What Has Been Happening with Ethereum in 2018? (2018). https://cryptonews.com/exclusives/what-has-been-happening-with-ethereum-in-2018-1628.htm. Accessed 20 May 2018
8. Murray, M.: How to Mine Ethereum (2017). https://www.thegeekpub.com/11292/how-to-mine-ethereum/. Accessed 15 May 2018
9. Murray, M.: Overclocking a Mining GPU (2017). https://www.thegeekpub.com/11350/overclocking-a-mining-gpu/. Accessed 15 May 2018
10. Nakamoto, S.: Bitcoin: a peer-to-peer electronic cash system (2008). https://bitcoin.org/bitcoin.pdf
11. Pradeep, V.: Ethereum's Memory Hardness Explained, and the Road to Mining It with Custom Hardware (2017). https://www.vijaypradeep.com/blog/2017-04-28-ethereums-memory-hardness-explained/. Accessed 20 May 2018
12. Taylor, M.B.: The evolution of bitcoin hardware. Computer **50**(9), 58–66 (2017). https://doi.org/10.1109/MC.2017.3571056
13. Vujičić, D., Jagodić, D., Ranđić, S.: Blockchain technology, bitcoin, and ethereum: a brief overview. In: 17th International Symposium INFOTEH-JAHORINA, 21–23 March 2018 (2018)

Practical Deployability of Permissioned Blockchains

Nitesh Emmadi$^{(\boxtimes)}$, R. Vigneswaran, Srujana Kanchanapalli,
Lakshmipadmaja Maddali, and Harika Narumanchi

TCS Innovation Labs, Hyderabad, India
{nitesh.emmadi1,vigneswaran.r,srujana.k,lakshmipadmaja.maddali,
h.narumanchi}@tcs.com

Abstract. Ever since the evolution of cryptocurrencies, there has been profound interest in employing the underlying Blockchain technology for enterprise applications. Enterprises are keen on embracing the advantages of Blockchain in applications ranging from FinTech, Supply chain, IoT, Identity Management, Notary, Insurance and to many other domains. Blockchain is often spoken of as the third disruption after computers and the internet, and is being studied for application in several domains. A blockchain, as used in most cryptocurrencies, does not require any authorization for participants to join or leave the system, and hence is referred to as a *permission-less* blockchain. However, enterprise applications cannot operate in such models. Enterprise applications operate in a regulated, *permissioned* blockchain setting. This paper provides an industry focused insight into the practicality and feasibility of permissioned blockchains in real-world applications. In particular, we consolidate some non-trivial challenges that should be addressed in making the *permissioned* blockchain practically deployable in enterprises.

Keywords: Permissioned blockchain · Challenges · Smart contracts
Enterprises

1 Introduction

It is always desirable to have a system which is not controlled by a single entity. A system that is governed by multiple entities is inherently more trusted in the sense that a single malicious entity in charge cannot manipulate the system. For instance, the cryptocurrency Bitcoin [1] is one such system that functions without a central controlling authority. Rather, it is controlled collectively (in agreement) by the parties involved in the system, thereby distributing the trust. Bitcoin enables monetary transactions without the need for a central authority like a bank. Such systems are referred to as having decentralized trust i.e., systems where trust does not depend on any one specific entity. It is this feature that drew the attention of academia and industry.

The core primitive that enables decentralization in Bitcoin is blockchain. Blockchain can simply be viewed as a shared append-only database with entries

W. Abramowicz and A. Paschke (Eds.): BIS 2018 Workshops, LNBIP 339, pp. 229–243, 2019.
https://doi.org/10.1007/978-3-030-04849-5_21

(transactions) agreed upon by all the involved parties. The entries are grouped into a *block* and appended to the ledger. A typical blockchain as in Bitcoin is referred to as *permission-less* blockchain. It means that entities can join/leave the blockchain network without any restrictions. The identities of these entities are not verified i.e., the entities are anonymous. However, enterprise applications cannot do the same. Enterprises need the entities to have verified identities in order to enable accountability and traceability. Hence, they need a permissioned model of blockchain or *permissioned* blockchain.

Another important difference between *permission-less* and *permissioned* blockchain is the consensus (agreement) mechanism. *Permission-less* blockchains are suitable for trust-less environments without accountability due to anonymity. They often employ a computationally intensive mechanism, usually *proof of work* [5] for consensus. Proof of work is a self-rewarding computational challenge for block formation, to be solved by any of the entities in the network. The entity that solves the puzzle propagates the solution along with the block to other parties in the network. Acceptance of the propagated block by other peers establishes correctness of the solution and block formation. Moreover, computational complexity of the proof of work guarantees that it is in-feasible to tamper with the ledger without significant computational effort. In case of *permissioned* blockchains, the entities in the system have verified identities. Hence, consensus can be reached simply through non-repudiating interactions. This study focuses only on *permissioned* blockchains due to their applicability in enterprise environments.

The paper is organized as follows: In Sect. 2 we give a brief overview of blockchain. Section 3 outlines the blockchain in a permissioned environment. In Sect. 4 we demonstrate the applicability of blockchain in different usecases. Section 5 we describe how blockchain adds value to commonly occurring usecases and in Sect. 6 we emphasize on the challenges in making the blockchain practically deployable.

2   Brief Overview of Blockchain

Blockchain is a shared ledger that enables mutually distrusting parties to transact with each other without any central authority. The participants together form a peer-to-peer network of nodes with a common ledger (Fig. 1). Blockchain, as its name implies, is a *chain of blocks*. Each block consists of a set of entries (transactions in case of cryptocurrencies) to be included in the blockchain and each new block is chained to the preceding block. All entries are appended to the ledger based on the consensus (agreement) of the involved parties. This ensures that the ledger is always consistent among all the parties.

2.1   Chaining the Blocks: Hashchain

The chaining in blockchain is done by a special cryptographic primitive called *hash function*. A hash function is a one-way function that takes any arbitrary

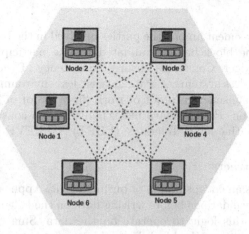

Fig. 1. Blockchain network

string as input and easily computes another string of pre-determined length. Important properties of a hash function are:

- Given the output, it should be computationally in-feasible to find input
- Highly sensitive to changes in input, that is, a single bit change in input should affect several bits of the output
- Computationally in-feasible to change the message without changing the hash
- Computationally in-feasible to find two messages with the same hash.

In blockchain, the blocks are chained together by including the hash of a block in the next block (Fig. 2). This method is called *hash-chaining*. This way of chaining in blockchain makes it immutable, that is, for a continuous chain of blocks, if modification is done on a block "n" and a new hash is produced, then all the blocks after "n" will produce hashes that are different from the previously known hashes. The hash function ensures integrity and provides tamper evidence of the blockchain. Also, the fact that the ledger is shared among the parties ensures that one malicious party cannot alter the ledger without the knowledge of others.

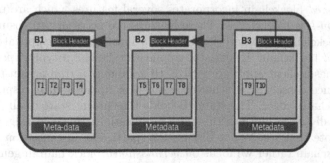

Fig. 2. Blockchain

2.2 Consensus

Consensus is an agreement among the parties involved in the blockchain network. All the data in the blockchain is validated by the participants before being written into the ledger. Consensus ensures consistency of the ledger across all parties. Permission-less systems operate in trust-less environments and thus rely on consensus mechanisms like proof of work [5] or proof of stake [2] or proof of space [3] and so on. *Permissioned* blockchains rely on consensus mechanisms like Practical Byzantine Fault Tolerance (PBFT) [7], SIEVE [8] and so on.

2.3 Smart Contracts

A smart contract is an encapsulation of business logic. Applications have several computations and validations before writing data on the ledger. Smart contracts enable embedding this logic to operate on the data. Smart contracts handle reading or writing data on the blockchain. Smart contracts are executed by one or more parties independently to ensure the correctness of data processing, and to impart trust to the system. The results of the smart contract execution from various parties is used for consensus purposes.

2.4 Properties of a Blockchain

The following are some interesting properties of blockchain that are applicable to both permission-less and permissioned environments:

- **Decentralization:** Blockchain enables mutually distrusting parties to engage with each other without a central authority.
- **Transparency:** Shared ledger ensures all the transactions are visible to all involved parties.
- **Integrity:** Immutable ledger preserves the integrity of the data. Shared ledger obtained through consensus ensures tamper detection.
- **Availability:** Shared ledger ensures there is no single point of failure.

Blockchain is being studied for application in enterprise use-cases for one or more of the above advantages.

3 Blockchain for Enterprises

A *permissioned* blockchain incorporates several features which are not present in *permission-less* blockchains. These features are necessary to ensure applicability of blockchains to enterprises. Figure 3 illustrates the application flow of *permissioned* blockchain. Briefly, the application flow of a typical *permissioned* blockchain has a client application SDK that submits a transaction proposal to the peer. Once consensus is achieved, each peer updates their respective copy of the blockchain ledger. The stateDB holds the current state of all the entities (users). Finally Peers notifies the client applications that the ledger has been updated. Note that we do not discuss any particular instantiation of *permissioned* blockchain rather we focus on *permissioned* blockchain in general. Some of these features include:

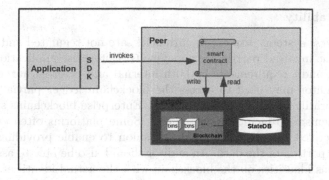

Fig. 3. Application flow of *Permissioned* blockchain

3.1 Privacy and Security

Blockchain is a shared ledger visible to all the involved parties. However, enterprise applications are concerned about security and privacy of the customers' data. For example, two contending businesses availing services on the same blockchain do not wish their data to be available to each other.

The privacy and security requirements in *permissioned* blockchain can be listed as follows:

- **Confidentiality:** A transaction on blockchain should not be accessed by an unauthorized party.
- **Unlinkability:** Different transactions of the same user should not be linked to each other by an unauthorized party.
- **Anonymity:** Any transaction recorded on the blockchain should not be associated with the user by an unauthorized party.

Cryptographic primitives ensure confidentiality, unlinkability and anonymity in blockchain.

3.2 Attribute Based Access Controls

Attribute based access controls is a security mechanism that provides access based on the attributes of the requester. Most enterprise applications are modeled with attribute based access controls for flexibility and granularity. This is necessary in order to define access privileges based on attributes of the individuals accessing an application, rather than on the individuals themselves. *Permissioned* blockchain platforms should provide attribute based access controls in order to enable enterprises to realize the applications with granular access controls. In the *permissioned* blockchains, these access control mechanisms are embedded into smart contracts Sect. 2.3.

3.3 Auditability

Permission-less systems, like cryptocurrencies, are not regulated and cannot be audited as the involved parties are anonymous. Enterprise applications have to comply with audit requirements by both internal and external authorized parties. The auditor may need to access the blockchain ledger partially or fully, either temporarily or on a continuous basis. Enterprise blockchains should provide a mechanism to facilitate such audits. Some platforms often encrypt the data with derived keys in a hierarchical fashion to enable providing access to only specific portion of the data. An auditor should also be able to associate the pseudonymous identities on the blockchain with the actual identities.

4 Do You Need a Blockchain?

The advantages of blockchain are being studied for several applications ranging from IoT to international monetary transfers and more. Blockchain has the potential to provide significant value addition to some but not all applications. It is easy to get carried away by the hype around blockchain. Hence, a critical evaluation of the applicability of blockchain in use-cases is needed.

Figure 4[1] provides guidelines for evaluating applicability of blockchain for use cases. The original flowchart from [4], assumes the existence of an always-online trusted third party (TTP) for certain use-cases. However, there is no such thing in the real world. Another important modification is at the "multiple writers" flow. Blockchain is also being considered for applications involving a

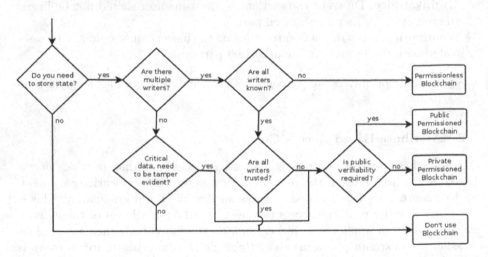

Fig. 4. Do you need a blockchain? (This is a modified version of flowchart from [4])

---

[1] The modifications are based on independent comments from Prof. Bart Preneel, University of Leuven, Belgium at BLOCKCHAIN 2017 Workshop and Sitaram Chamarty, TCS Innovation Labs, Hyderabad.

single writer, for example Land Records Registry or Motor Vehicles Registry or Logging (System Logs/Event Logs). These category of use-cases depend on blockchain for long-term integrity purposes. This kind of use-cases are valid only if the data entry to the blockchain is trusted.

Note that Fig. 4 classifies *permissioned* blockchains into *Public Permissioned* blockchain and *Private Permissioned* blockchain. The distinction arises from the public verifiability of blockchain data. Public Permissioned blockchain can be publicly verified by anyone whereas in a *Private Permissioned*, it is not allowed.

5   Use-Cases

In this section, we present several enterprise use-cases and explain how blockchain adds value in each case. We only consider how blockchain improves the operational efficiency of the usecases rather than focusing on design choices.

5.1   Global Payments

International transfers in banking is often a tiring process. Consider an international transfer request submitted to a local bank. The local bank could not process the payment directly as it does not deal with foreign exchange. The local bank requests foreign exchange from a Forex bank that deals with foreign exchange. This foreign exchange then has to be routed to the receiver through another routing bank. In the current banking system, this settlement is done with several requests among the banks and can take significant effort.

Blockchain can be used to speed up the process of payments across multiple banks. Blockchain can bring all the banks into a single network and transactions can be made easily. All the requests for money transfer done between banks are recorded in the blockchain. So, it reaches all the parties involved in the blockchain system. This makes the reconciliation process instantaneous and improves the speed of the payments.

5.2   Delivery Versus Payment (DVP)

Delivery versus payment, or DVP, is a common form of settlement for securities. The process may involve transfers of two securities in such a way as to ensure that delivery of one security occurs if and only if the corresponding delivery of the other security occurs. This is done to avoid settlement risk where one party fails to deliver the security when the other party has already delivered the payment. The parties in DVP use-case are buyer, seller, clearing house, bank and securities issuer. In the usual scenario, the process of settlement is done by the parties after ensuring that securities are transferred. This induces delay in the settlement process.

With blockchain, the settlement can be reached atomically on the shared ledger. For a securities exchange, both buyer and seller submit transactions to the blockchain. The transaction submitted by the seller contains a message to the corresponding asset issuer to transfer a particular asset to the buyer, and a message to the DVP provider to receive corresponding payment in return. Similarly, the transaction submitted by the buyer includes a message to the bank to transfer payment to the seller, and a message to the DVP provider to receive the asset in return. The DVP provider makes sure that both occurs in an atomic way. The buyer's and seller's transaction also includes post trade settlement instructions to the Clearing house. This triggers the Clearing house to submit transactions to both the bank and the security issuer to get the settlement done. Blockchain improves the operational efficiency by providing atomic on-chain settlements.

5.3   Digital Identity (eKYC)

Enterprises need to validate identity of their customers before providing services. This is essential for regulatory and compliance purposes. The process of identifying and verifying identity of clients is generally referred to as "Know Your Customer (KYC)". It is redundant and often expensive for all the organizations to verify their customers independently. It is also an inconvenience for customers to provide the same information to different organizations at different times.

It can be seen that a blockchain can enable data sharing between multiple organizations and eliminate redundant verification. If one organization verifies KYC of a user and records it in a blockchain, the other organizations can access the information from the blockchain without independently repeating the KYC process time and again. This eliminates unnecessary expenses for the organizations and improves the user experience while also recording the details of the KYC in a tamper-evident database. Blockchain, in this case, improves operational efficiency through data sharing.

5.4   Receivables Registry

Receivables registry is a peripheral process for Trade Receivables Discounting System (TReDS). Receivable registry maintains financing invoices in TReDS. The invoices are registered into the system by TReDS operators or banks. The invoices can be queried by other financiers in the system. It is possible for parties to register the same invoice fraudulently for multiple financing.

Duplication of invoices can be solved by leveraging blockchain among the parties. With blockchain, a duplicate entry can easily be detected by validating against the shared ledger. Different parties can have the full copy of the same receivables registry and process the invoice independently without worrying about duplicate entries being registered. Blockchain enables different parties to register, update, search and query invoices on the receivables registry, serving to prevent fraud by efficiently detecting duplicates.

5.5   Supplychain

Supplychain tracks the life cycle of a product from manufacturing to purchase by the end user. Blockchain is believed to add immense value to the supply chain ecosystem. A typical supplychain management system requires maintaining records for products, tracking shipments and notifying related parties about the status. Transparency in such workflows enhances the operational efficiency as the updates are visible to all the involved parties. Blockchain enables transparency in the flow. In turn, this helps identify counterfeit products entering into the supply chain midway (not introduced at the origin itself). Also, the effectiveness greatly depends on the type of product. For example, one way of eliminating chip counterfeits is to capture the location where the microchips were created and process the specific port of entry [20]. If there is a mismatch in the port of entry, the microchips would be held by customs and a notification is sent to the appropriate parties detailing the counterfeits. Blockchain also improves inventory management by providing real-time visibility.

Moreover, blockchain can also be leveraged for recording the provenance of high value assets like diamonds [16]. Blockchain can help track diamonds by creating a permanent record of the asset's history and ownership. Blockchain ledger provides proof of authenticity for the asset.

5.6 Internet of Things

Internet of Things (IoT) is a network of physical devices that exchange data streams. IoT usually consists of low-powered and low-storage devices like sensors. These suffer from resource constraints and can only perform limited tasks. Blockchain, on the other hand, deals with huge amount of storage(and possibly computations). When blockchain and IoT are imagined together it is usually the IoT infrastructure outside the sensors that is imagined in the blockchain scenario.

Blockchain is being studied in IoT use-cases to deal with access controls, data storage, auditability, decentralized (autonomous) networks, and so on [11]. However, the problems outside the blockchain system in IoT still exists and can devalue the blockchain advantages. Extensive study and further research into the practical aspects is needed.

5.7 Travel Ecosystem

Airlines travel ecosystem consists of travel providers, Global Distribution System (GDS), and travel buyers. Travel providers are service providers such as airlines, hotels, and so on and the travel buyers include consumers such as travel agencies or individual travelers. GDS is a network of travel providers and travel buyers. Air ticket or hotel booking can be done directly through the airline/hotel's website. However, that direct mode of booking is a very small proportion. More than 60% of bookings are indirect, through travel agencies or third parties. GDS plays a predominant role in aggregating the seat availability related information from various airlines. A recent study has shown that three GDSs dominates the market with 99% of market share [10]. Though GDS is trusted, there is a possibility of monopoly given that the GDS has significant negotiating power. Moreover, due to the complex pricing rules, it is hard to verify that the offers provided by travel providers are genuine.

There is a need for a trusted intermediary to enable airline search, multiple airline combinations search, visibility for providers to enable them to provide better services. A blockchain can be leveraged as an intermediary (with or without replacing GDS) to enable data sharing and transparency. Blockchain can provide a transparent trustworthy network and prevent disputes in the system.

6   Challenges

Blockchain in the current state is not practically deployable for almost all usecases. In this section, we highlight several challenges in *permissioned* blockchains. These challenges are generic and prevail in all the usecases.

6.1   Throughput

All the current enterprise applications rely on centralized databases to store data. Centralized databases are very efficient and are capable of handling a high number of read/write operations without much latency. However, blockchains are decentralized and hence inherently slower due to consensus. The throughput issue has two aspects.

- implementation related: choice of various options (for example, "execute-order-validate" vs "order-execute" paradigms) and tunables such as payload size, batch size, block latency and so on [19].
- intrinsic: because by definition, what was previously the equivalent of one simple database *insert* or *update* is now a much more complex process that involves several messages going back and forth between several nodes, and so on.

This makes application of blockchain more ideal for low throughput use cases dealing with high value (or at least notional value) transactions. There is a need to improve throughput of blockchain to accommodate it in wider applications.

6.2   Consensus

Consensus mechanisms are complex and inefficient due to several factors like message complexity, communication rounds between nodes, etc. This severely impacts the throughput. Significant industry and academic research is concentrated on improving efficiency. Alternate solutions, such as trusted computing, are being evaluated as replacement in this regard. Also, a single consensus algorithm that suits all types of blockchain use cases is almost impossible to achieve. Thus there is a need for pluggable consensus framework with parameter tuning such as message/computational latency. Designing such a framework with automatic consensus algorithm suggestions is a challenge.

6.3   Query Efficiency

As per the confidentiality requirement, data in the blockchain is encrypted, thus making it harder to query efficiently. There is a need to investigate cryptographic primitives like searchable encryption in order to solve this problem. The usual searchable encryption schemes allow queries on data encrypted under single key. However, the data on blockchain is encrypted under several different one-time keys. Searchable encryption schemes that can handle such requirement are necessary to improve query efficiency.

6.4   Privacy and Confidentiality

Achieving privacy and confidentiality in a shared ledger is a challenge. The current solutions depend on standard cryptographic primitives to achieve privacy and security. However, these solutions are either inefficient or do not quite solve the problem. Though new paradigms like Zero Knowledge Proofs (ZKPs) for developing anonymous credentials (Identity Mixer [9]) or privacy-preserving smart contracts [12] are being explored in this regard, there are still open issues. For instance, cryptographic algorithms and their implementations demand more scrutiny before actually being deployable in the real world. Dependence on such novel and not yet widely deployed cryptographic primitives induce risk in dealing with customers' privacy and confidentiality.

6.5   Key Management

Usability in security has been a challenge for ages. Most current systems depend on passwords for protection. Though the password is the most well-known security mechanism, it still suffers from lack of "non-repudiation". Blockchain systems, therefore, require users to use asymmetric cryptographic keys. Storing the privatekeys is an unmanageable risk with current levels of user education. Though several secure wallets for key storage are developed, they are often exploited. The immutable nature of data on the ledger adds several more challenges in key rotation and key loss.

6.6   Inter-blockchain Communication

Enterprise applications often involve multiple systems communicating with each other. To cater to this kind of application, use-cases are now envisioned in a multi-blockchain model, which is basically a collection of blockchains. Establishing cross blockchain communication without compromising integrity guarantees, privacy and confidentiality is a big challenge. There is a need to develop proper cryptographic mechanisms to ensure privacy in this setup.

Moreover, applications developed on different *permissioned* blockchain platforms should be able to communicate with each other. Standard communication protocols and mechanisms must be supported uniformly by all the blockchain platforms.

6.7 Auditability

Auditability allows authorized entities (internal/external) to audit transaction records. To perform an audit, auditors should be given a means to investigate the activity of users or their transactions. The current *permissioned* blockchains envision pseudonymous identities and encrypted transactions for privacy and confidentiality. Auditability requires a provision to de-anonymize the users and link their pseudonymous identity to the original identity at the time of enrollment and also de-classify encrypted transaction data. This can be done by providing necessary secret keys to the auditors. However, the accessibility of blockchain endangers the privacy and confidentiality of users if the secret keys are shared to other parties. Alternatively, access control mechanisms can be leveraged to avoid sharing the keys but this introduces the additional requirement of proving the correctness of the data accessed. Auditability still remains one of the important requirement to be fulfilled. Hence, there is a need to develop comprehensive mechanism for dealing with the audit management. Zero-Knowledge Proofs can be potential solution to present proofs of correctness to the auditors.

6.8 Compliance with the Privacy Regulations

Compliance with privacy regulations can be more challenging in the blockchain world. For instance, General Data Protection Regulation (GDPR) mandates a "Right to Forget" feature for customers. The immutable nature of blockchain is contrary to this requirement. There are mutable blockchain [18] solutions which can cater to these needs, however they call into question the very basis of what makes a blockchain attractive for given use. Thus, more research is needed to make blockchains compliant with regulations.

6.9 Migration

Migration of data from existing applications to new blockchain systems can be a problem. The data models for blockchain application can differ from the existing systems. The data migration has to be seamless and ensure services without disruption.

6.10 Interoperability with Existing Systems

One of the crucial challenges in developing blockchain systems for existing applications is interoperability of blockchain with existing components in the applications. Rather than creating entirely new applications, it is better to remodel existing applications at certain levels to embed the blockchain. The blockchain system should be able to integrate itself with the other existing components in the application like query engines, front-end systems, UI systems and etc. This makes it necessary to structure new data models so as to retain sufficient query capability to support existing front-end systems and UIs.

6.11   Smart Contract Security

In recent times, several vulnerabilities in various smart contracts have been exploited in the blockchain platforms like Ethereum [6]. The immutability of blockchain makes dealing with the after-math very challenging. Security bugs in applications are inevitable. Therefore some notions of resilience need to be explored in order to avoid irreversible damages.

6.12   Standardization

Standardization ensures systems or services to better realize their objectives in secure and robust manner. Standardization of blockchain is important in realizing real-word applications. Blockchain standardization enables interoperability, compatibility, security, regulatory compliance. Standards also encourage innovation and embed more confidence in building applications.

6.13   Oracles

Often the smart contracts in a blockchain are required to validate transactions based on information from external systems. Some smart contracts may have to be triggered based on information from the physical world. To a blockchain, such information is delivered by external entities referred to as oracles. An oracle acts as an interface between the blockchain and external systems. Relying on oracles for such information is a necessary risk. There is a need to mitigate the risk by ensuring the authenticity of information transmitted to the blockchain. Another important challenge is confidentiality and privacy of oracle queries. Some solutions like Town Crier [14], Oraclize [15] explore oracles in context of decentralized applications.

6.14   Certificate Authority and Revocation Lists

The current *permissioned* blockchains rely on traditional Public key infrastructure (PKI) to manage identities of the entities. Even though the blockchain is decentralized, this certificate issuing system for issuing the certificates is based on a central authority. This could lead to issuance of spurious certificates to unauthorized parties. Therefore, the PKI infrastructure used in blockchain must be made decentralized. Even if a malicious entity obtains a certificate from the CA it can be easily detected by other nodes. There are solutions such as [13, 17] that provide transparency and prevent misbehavior however further study is necessary to incorporate such solutions into *permissioned* blockchains. Similarly, it is also necessary to have a decentralized solution for certificate revocation (CRL or OCSP).

7 Conclusion

A comprehensive elucidation of current industrial experience with blockchains have been provided in this paper. It is necessary for market players to understand and evaluate the practical aspects of blockchain applications before deploying blockchain based applications. Our study enumerates several challenges and limitations in current blockchain models that need to improved before the full potential of blockchain can be realized. Blockchain is believed to be the third disruption, however, our understanding suggests that it is **"not yet"**.

Acknowledgements. We thank Dr. Sumanta Sarkar and Dr. Sachin Lodha from Tata Consultancy Services for their insightful feedback. We also thank anonymous reviewers for their valuable comments in improvising the paper.

References

1. Nakamoto, S.: Bitcoin: a peer-to-peer electronic cash system (2009). https://bitcoin.org/bitcoin.pdf
2. King, S., Nadal, S.: Ppcoin: peer-to-peer crypto-currency with proof-of-stake. Self-published paper, 19 August 2012. https://peercoin.net/assets/paper/peercoin-paper.pdf
3. Dziembowski, S., Faust, S., Kolmogorov, V., Pietrzak, K.: Proofs of Space. In: Gennaro, R., Robshaw, M. (eds.) CRYPTO 2015. LNCS, vol. 9216, pp. 585–605. Springer, Heidelberg (2015). https://doi.org/10.1007/978-3-662-48000-7_29
4. Wüst, K., Gervais, A.: Do you need a Blockchain?. IACR Cryptology ePrint Archive 2017/375. https://eprint.iacr.org/2017/375.pdf
5. Back, A.: Hashcash: a denial-of-service countermeasure (2002). http://www.hashcash.org/papers/hashcash.pdf
6. Ethereum. https://www.ethereum.org/
7. Castro, M., Liskov, B.: Practical byzantine fault tolerance. In: Third Symposium on Operating Systems Design and Implementation, OSDI, USENIX (1999)
8. Cachin, C., Schubert, S., Vukolic, M.: Non-determinism in byzantine fault-tolerant replication. In: International Conference on Principles of Distributed Systems, OPODIS (2016)
9. Identity Mixer. https://www.zurich.ibm.com/identity_mixer/
10. Blockchain in Air ticketing. https://medium.com/@PasschainBlog/is-blockchain-necessary-in-airline-ticketing-d4e089910bd3
11. Shafagh, H., Burkhalter, L., Hithnawi, A., Duquennoy, S.: Towards Blockchain-based auditable storage and sharing of IoT data. In: ACM CCSW (2017)
12. Kosba, A., Miller, A., Shi, E., Wen, Z., Papamanthou, C.: Hawk: The blockchain model of cryptography and privacy-preserving smart contracts. In: IEEE Symposium on Security and Privacy, SP (2016)
13. Fromknecht, C., Velicanu, D., Yakoubov, S.: A Decentralized Public Key Infrastructure with Identity Retention. https://eprint.iacr.org/2014/803.pdf
14. Zhang, F., Cecchetti, E., Croman, K., Juels, A., Shi, E.: Town Crier: an authenticated data feed for smart contracts. In: ACM SIGSAC Conference on Computer and Communications Security, CCS (2016)
15. Oraclize. http://www.oraclize.it/#projects

16. Everledger. https://www.everledger.io/
17. Certificate Transparency. https://www.certificate-transparency.org/
18. Ateniese, G., Magri, B., Venturi, D., Andrade, E.: Redactable blockchain -or-rewriting history in bitcoin and friends. In: IEEE European Symposium on Security and Privacy (Euro SP) (2017)
19. Androulaki, E., et al.: Hyperledger fabric: a distributed operating system for permissioned blockchains. In: EuroSys (2018)
20. Supplychain Traceability: Anti-counterfeiting. https://wiki.hyperledger.org/_media/groups/requirements/hyperledger-_supply_chain_traceability-_anti_counterfeiting.pdf

Decentralized Energy Networks Based on Blockchain: Background, Overview and Concept Discussion

Mario Pichler[1]([⊠]), Marcus Meisel[2], Andrija Goranovic[2],
Kurt Leonhartsberger[3], Georg Lettner[4], Georgios Chasparis[1],
Heribert Vallant[5], Stefan Marksteiner[5], and Hemma Bieser[6]

[1] Software Competence Center Hagenberg GmbH (SCCH), Hagenberg, Austria
mario.pichler@scch.at
[2] Institute of Computer Technology (ICT), TU Wien, Vienna, Austria
[3] Department of Renewable Energy, University of Applied Sciences Technikum
Wien, Vienna, Austria
[4] Energy Economics Group (EEG), TU Wien, Vienna, Austria
[5] DIGITAL – Institute of Information and Communication Technologies,
Joanneum Research, Graz, Austria
[6] Avantsmart, Oberwaltersdorf, Austria

Abstract. This paper provides a snapshot of the globally ongoing decentralization of (business) relations in the energy sector. This tendency can be observed in other domains as well and is accompanied by new digital technological developments. Blockchain technology is assigned disruptive potential when it comes to realize those decentralization ideas. This hype about Blockchain is mainly company-driven without a solid academic basis yet. The authors are currently involved in several research efforts for utilizing distributed energy resources like photovoltaic systems, batteries and electric cars for the setup of energy communities and marketplaces. The paper, therefore, presents detailed investigations of background and motivations for decentralization and the building of (local) energy communities and (peer-to-peer) marketplaces for sustainable utilization of renewable energies. An overview of recent related Blockchain-based works is presented, and the current state and feasibility for the realization of the envisioned decentralized solutions are discussed. In this way, the work aimed at contributing to a research-based decision foundation for upcoming Blockchain-based decentralization efforts.

Keywords: Energy decentralization · (Local) renewable energy communities
Blockchain-based energy networks

1 Introduction

In 2008, Bitcoin was invented with the aim of creating a peer-to-peer (P2P) currency that removes the need for trusted third parties like banks [1]. Especially Bitcoin's underlying technology – Blockchain – caught the attention of several domains. Even in the energy sector, where disruption is currently underway, in which (private) owners of

W. Abramowicz and A. Paschke (Eds.): BIS 2018 Workshops, LNBIP 339, pp. 244–257, 2019.
https://doi.org/10.1007/978-3-030-04849-5_22

renewable energy sources, e.g., photovoltaic (PV) systems, could directly sell their surplus energy to others. Traditional energy consumers are becoming producers, which are referred to as prosumers, and represent equal peers in the energy system.

As a consequence of these disruptions, todays energy systems, in particular, regional and local distribution networks are facing increasingly complex challenges. A main driver are high numbers of private, decentralized, fluctuating generators, combined with electricity storages, a rising share of e-mobility, and the increasing electrification of building heating systems, as well as the selfish use of private flexibilities opposed to grid and system-friendly behaviors. From today's perspective, these developments will escalate driven by flexible tariffs, the increasingly active and unregulated market participation of prosumers, and new business models this paper tries to investigate.

The following structure explains the logical flow of arguments throughout the paper: Sect. 2 introduces the background of the ongoing energy decentralization efforts heading towards enabling (local) renewable energy communities. The subsections highlight concrete opportunities and challenges of these decentralization tendencies, by already having in mind Blockchain as supportive technology. Section 3 presents an overview of identified active, recent Blockchain initiatives for decentralized energy solutions. Preparatory for this overview, the first subsection refers to and shortly presents a scheme for distinguishing different types of hitherto Blockchain applications in the energy sector. Subsequent to the overview of Blockchain-based energy networks, a mapping of the investigated systems to these application types is done in the last subsection. Section 4 discusses gained experiences concerning Blockchain potential to support aforementioned opportunities and challenges, together with limitations and open issues. Section 5 concludes the paper and presents a short outlook on further activities.

2 Decentralization in the Energy Sector

Decentralization in the energy sector is currently a highly relevant topic, also in Europe. A lot of initiatives, new laws and directives on European and national levels have been recently elaborated. The Strategic Energy Technology (SET) Plan [2] is putting energy research & innovation at the heart of the Energy Union in Europe, aligned with the Energy Union research and innovation priorities.

2.1 (Local) Renewable Energy Communities

The "Winter Package" [3] introduces the concept of energy cooperatives or "Energy Communities", as they are called in Annex1 [4] and Annex2 [5]. They empower active consumers of the Energy Union to participate (generate, consume, store, share, trade, and sell back renewably generated energy) in energy markets. This includes incentives for self-consumption of locally and regionally produced energy as well as for activation of flexibility to help stabilize the overall energy system.

At the moment, the primary drivers for such communities are a potential increase of self-consumption and energy self-sufficiency for prosumers as well as the enhanced use of local energy generation, reinforced by new opportunities brought by digitalization and new smart technologies. For example, the Energy Package provides the appropriate collaborative environment for the implementation of Smart Grids and roll-out of smart metering systems across Europe. In the proposal for the internal electricity market, a specific role is given to "Energy Communities". Hence, it is crucial to think beyond the currently existing regulatory framework and to create a new regulatory space regarding local energy communities.

Several EU member states have prepared legislative changes to allow for more onsite self-consumption of electricity coming from PV. Belgium, for example, recently announced to allow direct lines between companies that consume renewable electricity in the area of another company. Greece, as one of the first EU countries in this regard, has adopted a new energy law in 2017, allowing energy communities to lease corresponding parts of the grid from the distribution system operator (DSO). In Germany, the so-called "Mieterstrom" – where tenants are buying electricity produced on site – is regulated within the Renewable Energy Sources Act (EEG), and since 2017 projects implementing such solutions are being subsided.

The legislative change of the energy law in Switzerland (Energiegesetz EnG, 30.09.2016) allowed for so-called "Eigenverbrauchsgemeinschaften" (EVG), i.e., self-consumption communities, in which pro-/consumers in spatial proximity are allowed to form a decentralized electricity production facility for self-consumption.

2.2   User Centered Business Models

While the centralized energy market structure has a limited number of decision makers, decentralized structures may involve a large number of actors, among which specific market and business models need to be coordinated, requiring specialized methods. Within the given regulatory framework, mainly two general types of energy communities have been established. In company organized energy communities, such as sonnenCommunity [6] or EnBWsolar+ [7], energy providers manage the community of prosumers as their customers and offer tariffs and trading options. Their customers remain in contractual relationship with the energy provider or utility. On the other hand, there are bottom-up, community-organized projects, legal forms of associations that allow prosumers to be co-owners or investors. In Germany, for example, an energy trading community in Bammental [8] sets precedence on how a community with about 80% of prosumers owns and organizes the local energy system. In energy systems of the future, new players and stakeholders are gaining in importance: households, municipalities, business holders producing and consuming energy at the same time will become prosumers. Full-service providers will be offering the whole service beginning with planning, installation and ending up with operations and maintenance. New business models can be based on cooperative models, where users and stakeholders are deeply involved or "carefree" solutions, where customers just click a join button and the service behind takes care of all organizational and legal processes. The challenge for new market participants, established utilities, and grid operators is to find their place in the competitive value chain. Following questions are still unsolved:

1. Identification of stakeholders, assignment of roles (e.g., customers, stakeholders)
2. Deep understanding of stakeholders and customers motivations
3. Designing attractive value propositions for all involved stakeholders
4. Conceptual work on new revenue streams, applying successful business model patterns on current topics based on new technologies (e.g., platforms, Blockchain)
5. Search for profitable and scalable business models where all stakeholders benefit.

The integration of users and stakeholders into research and development processes, and users' active participation in early stages of projects is crucial for understanding the customer perspective. The implementation and market acceptance depends on the approval of solutions being supportive to underlying values and needs, and the general willingness of users to integrate solutions into their practices and everyday life.

The Austrian Living Lab Act4Energy [9], founded in 2018, is currently forming a user community in the energy region of southern Burgenland which supports R&D projects to develop and test new decentralized energy networks, including PV, storage, e-mobility, and Blockchain applications. An analysis of three case studies in Austrian Climate and Energy Model (CEM) regions conducted by IIASA [10] on participatory governance and existing possibilities for inhabitants to engage into decision-making processes regarding energy transition in their communities shows that decision-making within projects is usually assigned to informed and organized public. However, inhabitants are mostly excluded from decisions on the project definitions, needs of the project or the implementation process.

2.3 (Decentralized) Control Strategies for Energy Optimization

With the continuously growing renewable energy generation, users need to be flexible in adjusting their energy consumption, giving rise to demand-response mechanisms.

Demand response refers to the ability of each user to respond to specific requests reported by the network operator by changing its load [11, 12]. This response may be performed either in the form of a commitment of the consumer to reduce electricity during peak hours [13], or by introducing financial incentives that affect prices during peak hours [14, 15]. Some examples of currently implemented demand-response programs are the "Scheduled Load Reduction Program (SLRP)" and "PJM Demand-Response" programs in the USA. In these programs, a demand-response aggregator announces an electricity deficit to customers and schedules a demand-response plan in the day ahead. Customers join the demand-response plan voluntarily for monetary credits (rewards).

The problem of optimally defining the amount of flexibility requested by each user (in a commitment-based approach) or the amount of financial incentives provided to each user (in an incentive-based approach) is currently drawn significant attention due to its computational complexity. Examples of commitment-based approaches have been presented in [16, 17], while examples of incentive-based approaches include [15, 18]. Incentives or own interests are also present under such frameworks, given the ability of the end-users to vary their electricity use patterns given the current conditions (e.g., the price of electricity, PV generation, state of the storage equipment).

Several challenges naturally emerge, including (a) accurately predicting the flexibility of the end-users, (b) optimally and equitably utilizing the provided flexibility subject to user-defined constraints, and (c) exploiting local coordination mechanisms to guarantee efficiency for the global (operator's) objectives.

2.4   Trust, Privacy, Security and Interoperability

Through the excessive use of intelligent distribution algorithms in smart grids, the proliferation of the Internet Protocol (IP) is expected to rise in the power grid significantly. This factor has a severe impact from a security perspective, for it both makes control devices susceptible to the broad range of security vulnerabilities of IP networks and also potentially makes these devices (through misconfigurations) accessible to threats from the Internet [19]. Ukraine, for example, was struck by large-scale cyber-attacks on their power distribution network, causing complete blackout events [20]. Typically, attacks within the distribution grid aim at the Advanced Metering Infrastructure (AMI), the Distributions Automation (DA), and monitoring feeders. These attacks can cause malfunctions, trip distribution network feeders, distort power grid data, or violate user privacy by extraction of sensitive information [21].

Necessary protection actions are, therefore, essential to be in place to reduce the attack surface of the overall system against cyber threats. These include measures for device security, identity management, communication line and data storage security.

A further important issue is a compliance with the General Data Protection Regulation [22], which has to be addressed by carefully selecting which data will be collected or processed and which data will be transmitted. Data and all communication channels need to be protected from unauthorized access and also its integrity and authenticity need to be ensured. Therefore, technologies which exploit or combine different key-exchange methods, consisting of signature, encryption algorithm and key length, cipher mode, as well as hash-algorithm, which are considered secure for the foreseeable future [23] need to be found.

In general terms, trust, privacy, security and interoperability issues are currently huge challenges, even though, if traditionally centralized business models will be increasingly decentralized. To ensure that data remains in the exclusive possession of the respective user, a secure architecture by introducing Blockchain building blocks seems to be a viable solution to guarantee cybersecurity, interoperability, provenance, privacy and, therefore, ensuring also GDPR compliance [24, 25].

3   The Case of Blockchain for Decentralized Energy Solutions

Blockchain and decentralized business models and applications built on top of it are recognized as some of the most significant disruptions since the invention of the Internet. However, a thorough overview of available Blockchain implementation flavors that provides a research-based decision foundation for other interested parties to follow is still missing. A systematic review on Blockchain technology research until 2016 showed that most work ($\sim 80\%$) is related to Bitcoin systems, while other relevant topics suffer from detailed investigations [26].

In the following paragraphs, we will explore the continuously evolving Blockchain-based business models and proposed solutions in the energy domain. As this is currently a very active field, for identifying and selecting, we will concentrate on finding active, recent initiatives for developing new decentrally organized energy business models. An overview of Blockchain applications in microgrids until mid of 2017 is given in [27].

The current state of knowledge regarding development and exploitation of Blockchain technology and applications in the energy sector is heavily driven by start-ups and initiatives at municipal, local, and regional levels.

3.1 Types of Blockchain Applications in the Energy Sector

Energy Cities, a European association of local authorities in energy transition for over 30 years with over 1,000 member cities through 30 countries, in [28] distinguished the following types of Blockchain applications, covering current use, needs, and near-future trends of the energy sector: transaction processing, document asset ownership and management, energy certification and verification, real-time monitoring and analysis of energy use, invoicing and allocation processes, remuneration in a real or virtual currency, creation of an online marketplace for (local/regional) energy, peer-to-peer renewable energy transactions in a decentralized system, offsetting CO_2 emissions and rewarding the implementation of sustainable measures, facilitating the development of e-Mobility as a service.

While this list of different application types helps in classifying existing Blockchain energy applications, in most cases, the started initiatives are aiming at the creation of an online marketplace for (local/regional/global) energy and/or peer-to-peer renewable energy transactions in a decentralized system. This means, the other listed types are more or less partly included in those kinds of projects as well.

3.2 Overview of Blockchain-Based Energy Networks

According to a news-message at bitcoinist.com [29], the UK based company _Verv_ has facilitated the first Blockchain energy trade transaction in the U.K. with its P2P energy trade pilot project in the Banister House Estate. The developed technology consists of two parts: (1) the Verv Home energy assistant that identifies the power usage of individual appliances in a household using artificial intelligence. And (2) the Blockchain-based P2P energy trading solution that allows households to trade generated excess electricity with a neighbor who has a higher demand. With this technology, one kWh of solar power generated from an array of solar panels on one of the roofs of an apartment block was sent to another residential building on April 11, 2018.

WePower [30] aims at changing how energy is developed and distributed, and provides a Blockchain-based green energy trading platform. When a renewable energy producer requires capital to finance the initial cost of a renewable energy project, he may sell a portion of the energy to be produced in the future, on the WePower platform. The buyer/investor acquires this energy in the form of internal energy tokens. One internal energy token represents 1 kWh to be produced at a particular future time. Each energy token acts as smart contract indicating: (1) type of energy, (2) time of energy production and delivery, and (3) price tag. This smart contract represents a standard power purchase agreement between the renewable energy producer and energy buyer. As a result, energy producers can trade directly with the green energy buyers (consumers and investors). The platform is connected to the energy grid, the local energy exchange market and energy end users. It receives data about the produced and consumed energy and about the energy price from the energy grid, and energy exchange markets.

Hive Power [31] aims at developing a solution for the creation and management of local energy communities on the Ethereum blockchain. All participants are guaranteed to benefit from their participation, and at the same time achieve a technical and financial optimum for the entire community. This optimum shall be reached through a market mechanism that incentivizes the participants to collaborate with each other by coordinating their energy production and consumption.

Thereby, the Hive Power platform also takes into account technical aspects, such as cables, power rating, and voltage limits to provide an optimal solution for multiple objectives. It also provides an energy trading mechanism for energy communities. The so-called HONEY algorithm exploits customers' flexibility to match production and consumption optimally, such that the community's welfare is maximized and grid technical constraints are satisfied. This selling of flexibility as a service helps system operators balancing the grid.

In collaboration with meter producers, Hive Power is building a Blockchain-ready energy meter, which allows tokenizing energy safely. The developed and used Hive Token (HVT) is a standard Ethereum ERC20 token managed by a smart contract which gives access to the Hive Power platform and its management.

For the realization of its P2P distributed green energy market, the *Pylon Network* [32] created its Ethereum-based blockchain that solves specific challenges of the energy sector, like the need for high rate transaction speed and storage and processing of vast amounts of data as well as scalability and versatility requirements. The Pylon Network targets renewable energy cooperatives (RECs) and aims at helping energy sellers having better knowledge of energy flows. Similar to Hive Power, it combines a smart meter (Metron) and Blockchain technology to certify energy flows and enable virtual transactions using tokens (green kW production units/coins). This technology allows the renewable energy community to manage demand and optimize the energy flows in real-time. For certification and payments, the Pylon coin is used which enables micro-payments in real-time and traces by whom, when, and where each kWh of energy in the community was produced and consumed. A full-scale pilot for the Spanish market is expected in 2018 and shall later be expanded to other countries like the United Kingdom and Germany.

Tal.Markt [33] is a digital marketplace for local renewable energy trading, which is based on a private blockchain. It was developed for the Wuppertal area by Wuppertal Stadtwerke Energie & Wasser AG (WSW) in cooperation with Elbox. On one hand, energy producers can sell their surplus energy from renewable energy sources and thereby earn an additional income. On the other hand, energy consumers can create a personal electricity mix by choosing energy producers and energy sources, e.g., solar system, biogas plant or wind turbine. Thereby, the consumer gets a guarantee of the origin of the consumed energy. If no energy from these sources is available, e.g., no solar energy when the sun is not shining, WSW supplies the energy consumer with energy from a combined heat and power plant. Tal.Markt especially targets energy producers, which will lose support by the Erneuerbare Energien Gesetz (EEG), which expires in 2020. Currently, a requirement for participation is that the energy producer's installation is above 30 kW.

The *Inuk* [34] application, developed by the French start-up Inuk, focuses on carbon emission offsetting. Users can calculate their carbon footprint based on their daily activities, like getting food delivered or traveling. Inuk offers the user to offset their carbon emissions by investing in solar energy production. The Inuk model enables small solar energy producers to obtain higher prices for generated energy, thus contributing to the development of local clean energy. Inuk cooperates with solar energy producers, mainly in France, whose plants must comply with specific quality criteria and be equipped with sensors for real-time monitoring of energy production. Based on the UN Framework Convention on Climate Change (UNFCCC), the equivalent of the carbon emissions in green electricity is calculated. Thereby, the public Ethereum blockchain is used to guarantee transparent emission offsetting.

The pilot project *Power-ID* [28], led by the Swiss Federal Institute of Technology ETH in Zurich, aims to create a local peer-to-peer energy marketplace in Walenstadt (canton St. Gallen). Thereby, the marketplace focuses on solar energy and energy storage systems, like batteries. For energy payments, matchmaking and allocation of network costs, the Ethereum blockchain is utilized. The network costs are calculated according to the actual degree of self-sufficiency, which means that if external energy sources, like other networks, are used, the network costs include costs for their usage.

The TECSOL spin-off *Sunchain* [35] wants to realize self-consumption of solar energy independent of the production point. Therefore, a virtual network of solar energy producers and consumers using the Blockchain is created. It utilizes its private blockchain, based on Hyperledger Fabric, to store encrypted and signed energy production and consumption data. The distribution system operator is involved in this process and receives allocation coefficients for energy distribution between the self-consuming network participants. Possible applications based on the network are, besides off-site self-consumption, collective-self consumption, e.g., in multi-apartment buildings, and power exchange between buildings.

A further notable international initiative is *Restart Energy* [36], which is developing a decentralized energy trading platform based on Blockchain that will enable anyone to trade energy in any deregulated energy market in the world. *Enosi* [37], *SunContract* [38], and *Green Power Exchange* [39] are developing platforms to support self-sufficient energy communities and P2P energy trading between their members. *EnergiMine* [42] aims at building a decentralized global energy market by rewarding energy efficient behavior. The Energy Web Foundation is developing a Blockchain-based transactive energy implementation framework that includes *EW Origin* [40], a customizable, open-source decentralized application for renewable energy and carbon markets, and a decentralized autonomous area agent *(D3A) market model* [41].

In Austria, just a few projects are focusing on Blockchain applications for the energy sector so far. The *Urban Pioneers Community* project [43], carried out by Wien Energie and Riddle & Code, is a pilot project on cross-property electricity trading infrastructures based on Blockchain technology in Vienna. The project explores how new energy pricing models based on Blockchain and smart meters could work. In that way, energy transactions can be carried out autonomously by the system.

A similar approach has been developed in a project (*Salzburg Blockchain Pilot*) by the Austrian consortium consisting – amongst others – of the Center for Safe Energy Informatics (ZSE), University of Applied Sciences Salzburg, Salzburg AG and Verbund AG. In their project, the Blockchain technology is used to enable residents of a multi-party residential building to transfer their shares of PV electricity to their neighbors within the same building – thus, allowing for higher energy self-consumption rates and increasing the overall efficiency of the building's electricity consumption [44].

3.3 Summary: Mapping of Investigated Systems and Application Types

Table 1 summarizes the investigated systems and assigns them to the Blockchain application types introduced in Sect. 3.1. It reveals that lots of recent effort is spent for online energy marketplaces and P2P energy transactions, which are both supportive for (local) renewable energy communities as motivated in Sect. 2.

4 Discussion

In the following, the gained experiences concerning Blockchain potential to support the opportunities and challenges of the ongoing decentralization tendencies in the energy sector introduced in Sect. 2, together with limitations and open issues, are discussed.

4.1 Blockchain Support for (Local) Renewable Energy Communities and User Centered Business Models

The presented overview in Sect. 3 revealed that a bigger part of ongoing Blockchain initiatives in the energy domain is aiming at realizing (local) renewable energy communities.

Further research efforts are needed to investigate new value chains, including new actors relevant in energy communities such as municipalities, energy cooperatives, aggregators, and citizens. The concepts of local energy and grid communities, based on the ongoing decentralization movement in the energy domain, create opportunities for new market players to enter the energy market and to build up new value chains. New entrants like startups or IT-companies will take over the role of full-service providers. Everyone in the new value chain has to define their new business model.

However, besides offering new possibilities, the complexity of Blockchain might even expose "small" consumers participating in a local energy marketplaces to unacceptable price risks, as argued in [28].

Table 1. Mapping of investigated Blockchain-based energy systems and Blockchain application types in the energy sector

Systems	Application types									
	Transaction processing	Document asset ownership and management	Energy certification and verification	Real-time monitoring and analysis of energy use	Invoicing and allocation processes	Remuneration in a real or virtual currency	Online marketplace	Peer-to-peer renewable energy transactions	Offsetting CO2 emissions & rewarding sustainable measures	e-Mobility as a service
Verv	X			X				X		
WePower	X	X	X	X		X	X	X		
Hive Power						X	X			
Pylon Network			X	X			X	X		
Tal.Markt	X	X	X				X			
Inuk							X		X	
Power-ID	X	X	X		X		X	X		
Sunchain	X	X	X					X		X
Restart Energy							X	X		
Enosi	X	X	X		X	X	X	X		
SunContract		X				X	X	X		
Green Power Exchange						X	X	X		
EnergiMine			X				X		X	
EW Origin	X		X							
D3A	X	X		X	X		X	X		
Urban Pioneers Community	X				X		X			
Salzburg Blockchain Pilot	X			X				X		

4.2   Blockchain Support for Decentralized Control Strategies for Energy Optimization

The realization of advanced decentralized control strategies utilizing Blockchain technology is partly addressed by some of the investigated works. An important related issue concerns the exploitation of energy transaction histories captured on a blockchain for the prediction of future energy transactions.

In [45, 46], the authors reported about the conceptualization of a decentralized battery energy storage network to compensate for schedule deviations. Thereby, Blockchain was already identified as potential enabling technology. In an ongoing and proposed follow-up effort [47, 48], this concept will be extended to (1) include further kinds of flexibilities like heat pumps, boilers, and electric vehicles, and (2) develop user-centered, grid- and system-friendly integrated, local and regional energy systems including local and regional markets based on Blockchain technology. Parts of the introduced Hive Power system [31] are closely related to these conceptualizations and will, therefore, be further investigated and observed.

4.3   Blockchain Support for Trust, Privacy, Security and Interoperability

Blockchain technology claims to solve fundamental trust problems in decentralized applications. A considerable challenge for the future, however, is to provide trust-worthiness among different blockchains and establish secure and transparent mechanisms to settle apart drifted statements, which do not match to the interrelated ecosystem but were supplied by these blockchains. For example who has the authority and what happens when the reported CO_2 certificates do not fit energy transfer reported by the sensor values at different grid monitoring points?

4.4   Limitations and Open Issues

Alongside the development of Blockchain-based solutions for energy markets and economics, which represent the primary objectives with the works presented in the overview of Blockchain-based energy networks (cf. Sects. 3.2 and 3.3), further potential applications of Blockchain technology need to be investigated. There are many attempts for promising applications, but implementations often lack a holistic, customer-centered, cyber-physical system considering point of view. According to [28], some of these initiatives exclusively focus on the technological aspects, leaving aside further essential elements, in the light of the envisioned disruptions in the energy sector.

While the presented international initiatives are quite ambitious in their goals, it is not yet clear, except Verv, how far the developments of these experimental and pilot activities, as sketched in the development timelines of the corresponding white papers, have gone already. The amount of different white papers and the lack of feasible applications is a success story for openly shared research. The Austrian projects are quite focused but of comparably limited scope.

To reach a readiness technology level, Blockchain needs to be thoroughly under-stood by a broad array of stakeholders, involving everyone from customers to producers, from technologists to economists etc. Blockchain, as of today, is not a ready to use off the shelf technology but needs to be made measurable by technology experts on each application scenario. A thorough overview of available Blockchain implementations providing a research-based decision foundation is currently missing. The work at hand represents one step for improving this situation.

5 Conclusion and Outlook

Blockchain technology bears the potential to disrupt whole economic sectors by decentralizing traditional business relations. The energy sector is one of the early adopters, but as the presented mapping of investigated applications and types shows, in early stages as well. These disruptions are just starting with potentially far-reaching social and socio-economic consequences [49]. It is therefore necessary – also for Austria – to keep up with, and even shape these developments, especially from a scientific point of view as this (technology) domain is currently heavily driven by technology start-ups. Therefore, the authors are currently participating in and initiating activities for building an Austrian Energy Blockchain Experts Group/Cluster to tackle open issues, limitations, and also strengthening Austria's international position. An essential building block in doing so is "Smart Grid Control", a flagship project recently proposed with the Austrian Green Energy Lab – a global testbed for the integrated energy system [48, 50].

Acknowledgments. The research reported in this paper has been supported by the Austrian Ministry for Transport, Innovation and Technology, the Federal Ministry for Digital and Economic Affairs, and the Province of Upper Austria in the frame of the COMET center SCCH.

References

1. Nakamoto, S.: Bitcoin: A Peer-to-peer Electronic Cash System (2008)
2. European Commission - The Strategic Energy Technology (SET) Plan: https://publications.europa.eu/en/publication-detail/-/publication/771918e8-d3ee-11e7-a5b9-01aa75ed71a1/language-en/format-PDF/source-51344538
3. EC - Clean Energy For All Europeans (2016). https://ec.europa.eu/transparency/regdoc/rep/1/2016/EN/COM-2016-860-F1-EN-MAIN.PDF
4. EC - Clean Energy For All Europeans – ANNEX 1. (2016). https://ec.europa.eu/energy/sites/ener/files/documents/1_en_annexe_autre_acte_part1_v9.pdf
5. EC - Clean Energy For All Europeans – ANNEX 2 (2016). https://ec.europa.eu/transparency/regdoc/rep/1/2016/EN/COM-2016-860-F1-EN-ANNEX-2-PART-1.PDF
6. Sonnenbatterie. https://sonnenbatterie.de/de-at/sonnencommunity
7. ZuHausestrom. https://zuhause.enbw.com/solarenergie
8. Bündnis Bürgerenergie BBEn e.V. https://www.buendnis-buergerenergie.de/fileadmin/user_upload/downloads/Bericht_2017/Broschuere_Buergerenergie17_96dpi.pdf
9. Innovation lab act4energy. https://nachhaltigwirtschaften.at/en/sdz/projects/enics.php

10. Komendantova, N.: Energy transition in the Austrian climate and energy model regions: a multi-risk participatory governance perspective on regional resilience. Procedia Eng. **212**, 15–21 (2018). https://doi.org/10.1016/j.proeng.2018.01.003
11. Albadi, M.H., El-Saadany, E.F.: A summary of demand response in electricity markets. Electric Power Syst. Res. **78**(11), 1989–1996 (2008). https://doi.org/10.1016/j.epsr.2008.04.002
12. Conejo, A.J., Morales, J.M., Baringo, L.: Real-time demand response model. IEEE Trans. Smart Grid **1**(3), 236–242 (2010)
13. Ruiz, N., Cobelo, I., Oyarzabal, J.: A direct load control model for virtual power plant management. IEEE Trans. Power Syst. **24**(2), 959–966 (2009)
14. Triki, C., Violi, A.: Dynamic pricing of electricity in retail markets. 4OR **7**(1), 21–36 (2009)
15. Xu, Y., Li, N., Low, S.H.: Demand response with capacity constrained supply function bidding. IEEE Trans. Power Syst. **31**(2), 1377–1394 (2016)
16. Chen, C., Wang, J., Kishore, S.: A distributed direct load control approach for large-scale residential demand response. IEEE Trans. Power Syst. **29**(5), 2219–2228 (2014)
17. Nguyen, H.K., Song, J.B., Han, Z.: Distributed demand side management with energy storage in smart grid. IEEE Trans. Parallel Distr. Syst. **26**(12), 3346–3357 (2015)
18. Li, N., Chen, L., Dahleh, M.A.: Demand response using linear supply function bidding. IEEE Trans. Smart Grid **6**(4), 1827–1838 (2015)
19. Wagner, M., Kuba, M., Oeder, A.: Smart grid cyber security: a german perspective. In: 2012 International Conference on Smart Grid Technology, Economics and Policies (SG-TEP), pp. 1–4, Nuremberg (2012)
20. Liang, G., Weller, S.R., Zhao, J., Luo, F., Dong, Z.Y.: The 2015 Ukraine Blackout: Implications for False Data Injection Attacks. IEEE Trans. Power Syst. **32**(4), 3317–3318 (2017)
21. Tang, Y., Chen, Q., Li, M., Wang, Q., Ni, M., Fu, X.Y.: Challenge and evolution of cyber attacks in cyber physical power system. In: 2016 IEEE PES Asia-Pacific Power and Energy Engineering Conference (APPEEC), pp. 857–862, Xi'an (2016)
22. European Parliament and Council: Regulation on the protection of natural persons with regard to the processing of personal data and on the free movement of such data, and repealing Directive 95/46/EC (Data Protection Directive), L119, 4/5/2016, pp. 1–88 (2016)
23. Sheffer, Y., et al.: Recommendations for Secure Use of Transport Layer Security (TLS) and Datagram Transport Layer Security (DTLS) (No. RFC 7525). Internet Engineering Task Force. Internet Requests for Comments (2015)
24. Schwerin, S.: Blockchain and privacy protection in the case of the european general data protection regulation (GDPR): a delphi study. JBBA **1**(1), 1–75 (2018)
25. Dorri, A., Kanhere, S.S., Jurdak, R., Gauravaram, P.: Blockchain for IoT security and privacy: the case study of a smart home. In: 2017 IEEE International Conference on Pervasive Computing and Communications Workshops (PerCom Workshops), pp. 618–623, Kona, HI (2017)
26. Yli-Huumo, J., Ko, D., Choi, S., Park, S., Smolander, K.: Where is current research on blockchain technology? a systematic review. PLoS ONE **11**(10), e0163477 (2016). https://doi.org/10.1371/journal.pone.0163477
27. Goranović, A., Meisel, M., Fotiadis, L., Wilker, S., Treytl, A., Sauter, T.: Blockchain applications in microgrids: an overview of current projects and concepts. 43rd Annual Conference of the IEEE IES, IECON 2017, pp. 6153–6158, Beijing (2017)
28. Donnerer, D., Lacassagne, S.: Blockchain and Energy Transition: What challenges for cities? Energy Cities, Licence Creative Commons Attribution (2018). http://www.energy-cities.eu/IMG/pdf/energy-cities-blockchain-study_2018_en.pdf
29. First Ever Blockchain Energy Trade Completed in the UK. http://bitcoinist.com/first-ever-blockchain-energy-trade-completed-uk/

30. WePower WP. https://drive.google.com/file/d/0B_OW_EddXO5RWWFVQjJGZXpQT3c
31. Hive Power WP. https://c.fastcdn.co/u/a25ac79a/29853262-0-Hive-Power-WP-1.3.pdf
32. Pylon Network Whitepaper. https://pylon-network.org/wp-content/uploads/2017/07/170730_WP-PYLON_EN.pdf
33. Tal.Markt. https://wsw-talmarkt.de/#/frequently-asked-questions
34. Inuk. https://www.inuk.co/howdoesitwork
35. Sunchain. http://www.sunchain.fr/english-1
36. Restart Energy Whitepaper. https://restartenergy.io/Restart_Energy_Whitepaper.pdf
37. Enosi Whitepaper. https://enosi.io/images/file/whitepaper_24_04_18.pdf
38. SunContract Whitepaper. https://suncontract.org/tokensale/res/whitepaper.pdf
39. Green Power Exchange Whitepaper. https://drive.google.com/file/d/1Qvn7e9Q_NhURYM2-wkru6zP10P6L-w3x/view
40. Energy Web Foundation – EW Origin. https://energyweb.org/origin/
41. D3A Market Model. https://energyweb.org/wp-content/uploads/2018/04/EWF-D3A-ConceptBrief-FINAL201804.pdf
42. EnergiMine Whitepaper. https://energitoken.com/whitepaper/WPEnglish.pdf
43. Blockchain im Block: Strom-Sharing im Wiener Viertel Zwei. https://derstandard.at/2000073939772/Blockchain-im-BlockStrom-Sharing-im-Viertel-Zwei
44. Blockchain-Pilotprojekt gestartet. https://www.fh-salzburg.ac.at/en/about-us/news/news/details/article/blockchain-pilotprojekt-gestartet-1
45. Moisl, F., Pichler, M., Chasparis, G., Leonhartsberger, K., Lettner, G.: Development of a decentralized small battery energy storage network to compensate for schedule deviations. In: D. Schulze (ed.), NEIS 2017: Conference on Sustainable Energy Supply and Energy Storage Systems, pp. 169–174, VDE Verlag, September (2017)
46. Leonhartsberger, K., et al.: System relevant applications for battery storage systems. In Proceedings of the 33rd PLEA International Conference (PLEA 2017), vol. III, pp. 4595–4602, July (2017)
47. Flex+ project. https://projekte.ffg.at/projekt/2926622
48. Green Energy Lab. http://www.greenenergylab.at/
49. Markey-Towler, B.: Anarchy, blockchain and utopia: a theory of political- socioeconomic systems organised using blockchain. The JBBA 1(1), 1–14 (2018)
50. Supper, S., Keding, M., Lettner, G., Schwab, T., Stricker, K.: Green Energy Lab: Accelerating User-centric Integrated Solutions for the Renewable Energy System of Tomorrow (2017). http://www.greenenergylab.at/wp-content/uploads/2017/09/Green-Energy-Lab-Presentation-September-2017.pdf

Enabling Data Markets Using Smart Contracts and Multi-party Computation

Dumitru Roman$^{(\boxtimes)}$ and Kien Vu

SINTEF AS, Oslo, Norway
dumitru.roman@sintef.no, kienv91@gmail.com

Abstract. With the emergence of data markets, data have become an asset that is used as part of transactions. Current data markets rely on trusted third parties to manage the data, creating single points of failure with possibly disastrous consequences on data privacy and security. The lack of technical solutions to enforce strong privacy and security guarantees leaves the data markets' stakeholders (e.g., buyers and sellers of data) vulnerable when they transact data. Smart Contracts and Multi-Party Computation represent examples of emerging technologies that have the potential to guarantee the desired levels of data privacy and security. In this paper, we propose an architecture for data markets based on Smart Contracts and Multi-Party Computation and present a proof of concept prototype developed to demonstrate the feasibility of the proposed architecture.

Keywords: Multi-party computation · Smart contracts · Data markets

1 Introduction

The online behavior of users (e.g., online shopping, interacting on social media) leaves a trail of digital footprints. Nowadays, these digital footprints are in most cases accumulated and traded by various online organizations, offering "free" services to the users. Companies, such as Facebook and Google, are using individuals' personal data to profile users and provide them so called "targeted ads". As a result, they are basically feeding on the users' data to gain tremendous profits, leaving the user without any possibilities to actually monetize their own digital footprints in a transparent data market.

Besides the delicate legal and ethical aspects of exploiting user data (see for example the recent Cambridge Analytica scandal), a major reason for the difficulty of users to monetize their data in a data market is the lack of technical solutions to enforce the desired levels of privacy. When it comes to selling individuals' personal data, one of the main issues is trustworthiness. Generally, individuals do not want to sell their data to a counter-party and have the risk that that party will sell the data further to others for a higher price, or misuse the data for another purpose than the individual initially agreed to.

© Springer Nature Switzerland AG 2019
W. Abramowicz and A. Paschke (Eds.): BIS 2018 Workshops, LNBIP 339, pp. 258–263, 2019.
https://doi.org/10.1007/978-3-030-04849-5_23

Two key technologies are emerging as essential to allow such a data market to be established. The first one is *secure multi-party computation* (hereby referred to as MPC)[1]. MPC is a technology that allows data to be shared in a secret form (i.e., encrypted), while at the same time allowing meaningful computations to be performed on the data, the results of which could be shared with a third-party willing to pay for them. At no point in this process are data exposed in clear form, meaning that no parties involved in sharing the data and computing on the data can have access to the data, other than the owner of the data. By enabling calculation without removing encryption, MPC is the first cryptography-based technology that permits multi-owner data sharing and processing, ensuring that only data owners are allowed to access their data.

The second technology is *smart contracts* (hereby referred to as SC)[2]. A smart contract is a software program that typically runs in a decentralized infrastructure and once started it cannot be changed. A SC can facilitate, verify, and automatically enforce transactions giving it the potential to preserve data provenance in a data market context, where data ownership is essential. By design, a SC is being executed on a Blockchain which is an open distributed ledger that can record transactions between parties efficiently and in a verifiable and permanent way.

This paper explores the combination of MPC and SC technologies in the context of data markets. It proposes an architecture for combining MPC and SC as baseline technologies for data markets, and reports on a successful proof of concept prototype developed to demonstrate the feasibility of the proposed architecture.

The remainder of the paper is organized as follows. Section 2 provides an overview of the proposed data markets architecture combining MPC and SC. Section 3 describes the implemented proof of concept prototype. Finally, Sect. 4 discusses relevant related works, summarizes the paper, and outlines potential future work.

2   Architecture for Data Markets Using Smart Contracts and Multi-party Computation

Figure 1 shows the proposed architecture for data markets based on combining MPC and SC technologies. The key stakeholders in the market would be companies or individuals that subscribe either as a *buyer* or *seller* depending on the terms of the smart contract.

As depicted in Fig. 1, the architecture is divided by design time and run time. The design time infrastructure includes the design of the smart contract and algorithm and their deployment in the run time infrastructure:

- *Smart contract*: A program containing information about the business logic and transactional events of the contract (e.g., how and when data will be exchanged, when and how much the sellers will be paid, etc.), payment information (buyers'/ sellers' wallet addresses), the reference to the algorithm that will run on the data, and the address of the MPC Engine that will execute the algorithm.

---

[1] https://en.wikipedia.org/wiki/Secure_multi-party_computation.
[2] https://en.wikipedia.org/wiki/Smart_contract.

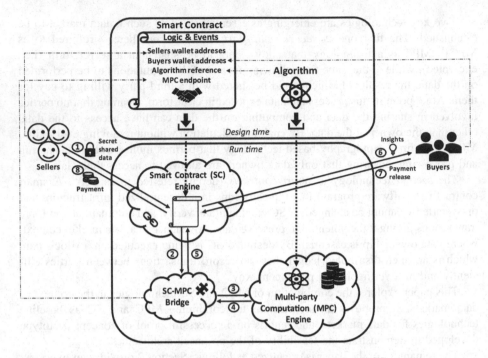

Fig. 1. Architecture for data markets using MPC and SC

- *Algorithm:* The MPC algorithm that will run on the (secret shared) data.

The run time infrastructure consists of three components:

- *SC Engine*: The engine where the smart contract will be deployed.
- *SC-MPC Bridge*: A component for ensuring communication between the SC Engine and the MPC Engine. This component is needed since MPC engines are currently not designed to communicate with SC engines.
- *MPC Engine*: The engine where the desired algorithm will be executed on (secret shared) data.

A typical process this architecture would support at runtime is as follows: the data sellers secret share their data as part of the SC execution (1); the SC execution passes the data to the SC-MPC bridge (2) which in turn supplies it to the MPC engine (3), returning the result of the computation to the SC-MPC bridge (4), which is then passed to the SC executing engine (5) triggering the message with the result in form of insights to the buyers (6). Upon receiving of the result, the buyers release the payment (7) and the SC execution enters the final state of executing the payment to the sellers (8).

3 Proof of Concept Prototype

The above architecture was implemented in a proof of concept prototype to test its feasibility. A set of concrete technologies have been selected for the implementation of the architecture as follows.

For the SC engine, Ethereum[3] [1] was chosen. The SC is written in *Solidity*[4] – a high-level, statically typed, and Turing complete programming language. Ethereum, compared to other SC frameworks such as NEM[5] and EOS[6], appears to be the most mature development framework for smart contracts to date.

By design, the SC executed on the Ethereum blockchain is isolated from the outside world. The reason is that Ethereum uses a peer-to-peer network protocol and it uses miners as peers to validate each block on the chain. Hence, each miner must get the same result to reach consensus. In other words, if the SC allows communication with external sources it would lead to the risk of never getting the same result and never achieving consensus. Based on this, a mechanism to allow the communication with the outside world and send/receive events outside of the Solidity SC is needed, in our particular case to receive secret shared data and pass it to the SC-MPC bridge. For this, we chose the Oraclize[7] library. Oraclize is an open-source library that works as a data carrier between the SC and the outside world. Oraclize ensures that data fetched from the data source is genuine and untampered. To guarantee this, Oraclize combines the returned data with a document called authenticity proof. In our case, this proof ensures that the secret shared data has been successfully sent and received by the SC-MPC bridge.

For the MPC engine, the Sharemind MPC[8] framework [2] was chosen. Sharemind, compared to all the other existing MPC frameworks, provides high-level libraries and tools to enable application development by non-cryptographers on a business-process implementation level, making it easier to write MPC algorithms. It provides a programming language called *SecreC* [3] that allows the users to write algorithms to be computed on the secret shared data. All the intermediate and final results are encrypted and only the allowed user making the query can decrypt the result. Sharemind consists of different nodes that act as independent hosts processing the specified algorithm. The algorithm is created outside the framework, however when it is deployed to the MPC engine, it is the Sharemind hosts that will evaluate and authorize the execution of the algorithm.

The SC-MPC bridge is a component that was needed to connect the Ethereum environment with Sharemind. This component was implemented from scratch since no implementations for this previously existed (Sharemind does not provide REST APIs necessary for Oraclize to communicate with). The component was implemented as a

---

[3] https://ethereum.org.

[4] https://github.com/ethereum/solidity.

[5] https://nem.io.

[6] https://eos.io.

[7] http://www.oraclize.it.

[8] https://sharemind.cyber.ee.

Web service allowing the SC deployed on Ethereum to invoke Sharemind functions. For this particular architecture, Node.js was used to implement the SC-MPC bridge.

Regarding the components for the particular choice of technologies selected for the prototype, what needs to be deployed would be one SC for every algorithm. These SCs need to be deployed onto the main Ethereum blockchain network. The SC-MPC needs to be hosted as a Web service by a third party. The algorithms used to do computation on the secret shared data need to be written in SecreC and deployed to the Sharemind hosts.

4   Relevant Related Works, Discussions, and Outlook

The approach proposed in this paper differentiates from other emerging initiatives such as Datum[9] [4], Enigma[10] [5], and Insights Network[11] [6] in the choice and particular combination of existing technologies that enable secret sharing of data, computation on secret shared data, and a transparent transactional system that allows transactions to be realized within the same framework.

- The Enigma project aims to provide a privacy protocol that enables the creation of decentralized applications that guarantee privacy. The protocol Enigma is building also advertises the use of MPC. By building the protocol directly on top of the blockchain, it removes the need of a bridge as proposed in our architecture. However, it is a project under development and no public releases exist to date.
- Datum is a project for creating a decentralized marketplace for social and IoT data. Datum provides a working product in the form of an application that allows users to submit their personal data and get paid in the Datum currency. Datum encompasses a decentralized data storage running on a smart contract blockchain. However, they do not allow any form of external computation on personal data.
- Insights Network is a data exchange based on combining blockchain technology, smart contracts, and secure multi-party computation. It is based on the EOS blockchain and a custom MPC system. Like Enigma, it is a project under development, with little technical details about the emerging implementation available to date.

The design of the architecture and its implementation in a prototype has come with different challenges. For example, one of the challenges is the process of writing smart contracts and deploying them onto the Ethereum ecosystem. The language and framework itself is easy to setup and use, but the "gas", a resource that is accumulated during deployment to the blockchain, is dependent on the amount of gas provided with the SC. The error handling mechanism for debugging smart contracts does not provide intuitive error messages, so one cannot be sure if too little or too much gas has been

---

[9] https://datum.org.

[10] https://enigma.co.

[11] https://insights.network.

sent. That makes it important for users to be careful about everything they write in the SC.

In terms of the proposed architecture, the SC-MPC bridge component was needed, mainly due to the lack of mechanisms for communication between existing SC engines and MPC engines. For example, if future implementations of Etherum and Sharemind provide REST APIs, the need for such a bridge would potentially be eliminated, simplifying the architecture.

In this paper, we proposed an architecture for combining MPC and SC for the purpose of implementing data markets. Our proof of concept prototype demonstrates that combining MPC and SC is practically feasible with existing technologies. As part of future work, we plan to evaluate the prototype by testing its scalability. We want to check to what degree it can handle, for example, thousands of transactions at the same time. The challenges that may arise are related to cost efficiency and latency. Also, blockchain technology is undergoing rapid changes and new frameworks and technologies often emerge. It means that we have to be on the lookout for emerging technologies that may be suitable as mechanisms to be used in the development of future data markets. Finally, it is worth mentioning that the architecture and proof of concept reported in this paper represent a first concrete realization of the reference architecture for trusted data marketplaces introduced in [7].

Acknowledgements. This work is partly funded by the EC H2020 projects euBusinessGraph (Grant number: 732003), EW-Shopp (Grant number: 732590), and TheyBuyForYou (Grant number: 780247). We thank the Sharemind team for promptly answering questions regarding Sharemind.

References

1. Ethereum White Paper (2013). https://github.com/ethereum/wiki/wiki/White-Paper
2. Bogdanov, D.: Sharemind: programmable secure computations with practical applications, Doctoral dissertation (2013)
3. Jagomägis, R.: Secrec: a privacy-aware programming language with applications in data mining. Master's thesis, University of Tartu (2010)
4. Datum White Paper v15 (2017). https://datum.org/assets/Datum-WhitePaper.pdf
5. Zyskind, G., Nathan, O., Pentland, A.: Enigma: decentralized computation platform with guaranteed privacy. arXiv preprint arXiv:1506.03471 (2015)
6. Insights Network - A Blockchain Data Exchange White Paper (2017). https://s3.amazonaws.com/insightsnetwork/InsightsNetworkWhitepaperV0.5.pdf
7. Roman, D., Stefano, G.: Towards a reference architecture for trusted data marketplaces: the credit scoring perspective. In: International Conference on Open and Big Data (OBD). IEEE (2016)

Opportunities, Challenges, and Future Extensions for Smart-Contract Design Patterns

Carl R. Worley[1]([✉]) and Anthony Skjellum[2]

[1] Clemson University, Clemson, SC 29634, USA
cworley@g.clemson.edu
[2] University of Tennessee at Chattanooga,
701 E. ML King Jr. Blvd, Chattanooga, TN 37403, USA
tony-skjellum@utc.edu

Abstract. Blockchains enable the trustless establishment of long-term consensus. The primary paradigm for extending this capability to generalized use cases is *smart contracts*. Smart contracts have the advantages of trustlessness, immutability, transparency, censorship-resistance, and DDoS resistance, but suffer from immutability, chain-boundedness, high cost of storage and execution, and poor parallelizability. While the advantages of smart contracts create many opportunities, their unique properties impose important constraints. A suite of design patterns are therefore proposed as one methodology for addressing these constraints while taking full advantage of the opportunities that smart contracts provide.

Keywords: Blockchain · Design pattern · Smart contract
Pattern language · Ethereum

1 Introduction

In this section, we cover blockchain background, then introduce smart contracts and design patterns. We leverage these discussions to put the remainder of this paper in context.

1.1 Bitcoin and Blockchain

Nakamoto (a pseudonym) announced Bitcoin in 2008 as a practical solution to the problem of safely storing and transferring digital currency [1]. The Bitcoin network is composed of nodes, each of which stores a ledger representing the current state of each user's balance. When one user transfers a bitcoin to another, the transferring user broadcasts a signed message announcing the transaction. Other nodes in the network recognize the transaction, verify its soundness, and add it to their copy of the public ledger.

© Springer Nature Switzerland AG 2019
W. Abramowicz and A. Paschke (Eds.): BIS 2018 Workshops, LNBIP 339, pp. 264–276, 2019.
https://doi.org/10.1007/978-3-030-04849-5_24

The aforementioned description suffers from a fatal flaw: a user can broadcast two valid transactions that spend the same bitcoin. This overlap creates a race condition in which the long-term consensus is determined by the exact order of transactions that is established as canonical. If there is no such long-term consensus, a user can spend the same coin multiple times, rendering the currency useless. To solve the problem of this "double-spending" attack, the transactions that are broadcast to the Bitcoin network are collated into a data structure called a "block". Each block contains the hash of the previous block, creating a sequence of blocks in which each builds on the security of the previous. Changing one block would change its hash, requiring the arduous recomputation of the hashes of all subsequent blocks.

Blocks are created by network nodes called miners. Each miner proposes a block and then must perform a process called proof-of-work (PoW) that establishes that block's validity. All network nodes accept as valid the blockchain with the longest visible proof-of-work. Modifying a block, recalculating its hash, and performing proof-of-work on all subsequent blocks at a rate faster than the entire rest of the network is impractical, rendering the longest chain a stable consensus.

1.2   Smart Contracts

While their inception was solely as digital currency, blockchains are suitable for *any* application where a distributed system must converge on a long-term consensus on the ordering of events. Alternative blockchains, like Namecoin [2], achieve distributed consensus on non-currency applications. Because of the competition between miners, it is more efficient to generalize a blockchain's functionality as much as possible [3]. This need for multiple applications has led to the emergence of blockchains that support *smart contracts*.

First proposed by Nick Szabo in 1994, a smart contract is any transactional protocol that enforces the terms of a contract [4]. While Szabo noted that many existing technologies, such as point-of-sale (PoS) terminals, formed a crude approximation of smart contracts, the idea never came into the fore because there was rarely a way to ensure proper execution. Ethereum has emerged as the first true smart-contract platform [5]. Ethereum allows users to perform transactions that execute smart contracts using a blockchain to ensure the smart contracts are applied to a global state in an order that converges on consensus. This provides the secure, decentralized platform that smart contracts require in order to be both robust and practical.

Since Ethereum is currently the most popular smart contract platform, this paper focuses primarily on examining smart contracts with the assumption that they are executed on the Ethereum blockchain. Many of the principles discussed here can generalize to alternative smart contract systems, but the variety of conceivable platforms is too large to be covered here.

1.3 Design Patterns

Design patterns were first conceived of in the field of architecture, where they were used to describe general principles of structural design [6]. The term has since generalized to refer to methods of conceptual organization in any field. Design patterns became especially influential in software engineering upon the publication of the book *Design Patterns: Elements of Reusable Object-Oriented Software* [7]. Software is inherently complex, and design patterns describe solutions that arise time and again to manage this complexity. Instead of reinventing the wheel, it is useful to recognize common software patterns, abstract them away from any specific context(s), and provide a general description of the pattern to guide future software development.

There are several concepts used to describe design patterns (or pattern languages, when discussed in a more semantic context) [6]. The design pattern is identified by its **Name**. To show the concept's validity, several **Examples** are usually given. Next, the **Problem** the design pattern is meant to solve must be examined. The balance of **Forces**, or various conflicts of interest that give rise to the problem, are examined. This balance gives rise to the **Solution**.

High-quality, relevant design patterns are important for smart contracts because of a property discussed throughout this paper: immutability. This key concern means that smart contracts are unchangeable once deployed; their core code cannot be modified after deployment. If a system is designed poorly, there is often nothing a developer can do to remedy the situation after the fact. Immutability makes good software engineering practice more important than in almost any field; the standard of care has to be much more like a CMM-5 "Efficient" gestalt (e.g., medical devices and human flight) because of the criticality of any residual faults [8]. Much web technology and many modern online programs use just-in-time and agile approaches to software upgrades and deployment; bug fixes and rollbacks are routine strategies of such systems. When mixed with smart contracts, agile systems require much greater bug-prevention approaches in the software-development lifecycles. Design patterns comprise part of such a CMM-based approach to quality software.

The remainder of this paper discusses the unique properties of smart contracts, as well as the design patterns that emerge by analysis and abstraction of these properties. It must be noted that traditional design patterns for object-oriented software are also often useful for smart contracts. A decentralized application can use the Adapter or Flyweight patterns [7] just as well as any other object-oriented system. Instead of discussing typical design patterns and how they're useful for smart contracts (which is interesting in itself to improve quality), this paper focuses on identifying design patterns that are unique to or see exceptional use in smart contracts. Our chief goal is advancing a discussion of design patterns specifically in the context of smart contracts.

2 Strengths and Weaknesses of Smart Contracts

As a prerequisite for exploring options to improve smart contract practices through design patterns, while considering potential future improvements to them, it is germane to review their key strengths and weaknesses.

2.1 Strengths

Trustlessness. Smart contracts are executed when the validity of an Ethereum block is determined [5]. This validation occurs in every full node in the network, with a valid block defined as one that emerges from the proper application to the global state of the smart contracts that are executed in the block's transactions. Because the execution of a smart contract is verified by every node in the network, there are no trusted authorities responsible for ensuring proper execution. Validation exists "in the ether."

Immutability. Because the Ethereum blockchain, like Bitcoin, converges on a long-term consensus, smart contract execution can be said to be immutable. Here, "immuability" is used to imply not that the contract never changes state but that the contract does not change state by any mechanism other than the internal logic of that contract.

If a transaction is broadcast, included in a block, and then incorporated into the longest blockchain, the probability of a successful attack that undoes the transaction becomes negligible within minutes [1]. Since transactions can only transfer Ether (the ethereum currency), pass messages to contracts, and/or create contracts, there is no mechanism for an outside entity to modify the contract. If a contract is programmed to behave in a certain way, then it will always behave that way.

Transparency. The Ethereum blockchain is public by design. Any user who wishes can run a full node, which necessitates downloading the blockchain. This data, once stored on a local machine, can be examined at leisure. It contains a history of all miners, transactions, contract creations, and contract calls that have been performed since the genesis block. There are several blockchain explorer tools that make this process easier (e.g., [9]).

Censorship-Resistance. The distributed, pseudonymous nature of Ethereum makes it inherently censorship-resistant. Censoring individual users is challenging because someone can always create an account that hasn't been linked to themselves in some easy-to-detect way. Censoring access to specific contracts or specific types of transactions would require a static analysis of each transaction that would likely introduce sufficient overhead to significantly decrease a miner's chance of creating a valid block before another does. Moreover, if only a few miners try to censor, the censored transaction will still be accepted when a non-malicious miner includes it in a block.

DDoS-Resistance. The distributed nature of Ethereum implies a high degree of DDoS-resistance. Even if a single miner were overwhelmed by broadcast transactions, the vast majority of the network would still remain active. If an attacker were to try to deny service by using the majority of the blockchain resources, the cost would be prohibitive. Ethereum's gas system means that smart contract execution and storage space are expensive.

2.2 Weaknesses of Smart Contracts

Immutability. One of the biggest strengths of smart contracts, immutability, is also one of their biggest drawbacks. Since they are immutable, flawed smart contracts cannot be repaired and can be exploited indefinitely. A famous example is "the DAO attack," where an attacker managed to withdraw 3.6 million Ether because of bugs in the smart contract code [10]. Because the blockchain is immutable, there was no on-chain mechanism for recovering such lost funds.

Chain-Boundedness. Smart contracts execute in an environment that is totally determined by the world-state of the blockchain and the messages passed to the contract by its caller [11]. The contract is totally isolated from the outside world; a smart contract cannot directly affect anything beyond the blockchain environment. It is impossible to write a smart contract that submits a web request, for example. Off-chain sources can examine the blockchain state for the occurrence of particular events, butf smart contracts cannot initiate external activity themselves. This property protects all nodes that execute the contracts but severely limits a given contract's utility.

Cost of Use. Scalability is one of the chief concerns of blockchain technology [12]. At present, all resources associated with the network are extremely scarce. Ethereum uses gas, a unit of accounting of computation, to manage this scarcity. Each step in a smart contract's execution costs an amount of gas [5], and the gas price in Ether of a transaction affects the likelihood of inclusion in new blocks. At the time of writing, the average gas price was 10 gwei [13], or 10^{-8} Ether, creating an average transaction fee of 50 cents (USD) [14].

3   Design Patterns

Design Patterns provide reusable abstractions with known cohesion, coupling, and semantic properties, without the burden of specific code implementations. Here, we apply them to smart contracts, the main contribution of this paper. First, we consider low-level patterns, then oracles, and finally high -level patterns. A summary of all such patterns is given in Table 1.

3.1   Low-Level Patterns

This subsection discusses various low-level patterns. A pattern is placed in this category if it occurs in most non-trivial smart contracts.

Table 1. Design patterns by category

Category	Pattern
Low-Level	Key-value Store
	Address Mapping
	Authorization
Oracle	Judge
	Ticker Tape
	Vote
	Anti-Oracle
	Blocklist
	Announcement
	Bulletin Board
High-Level	Token
	Migration

Key-value Store

- **Problem:** Many smart contracts store nontrivial amounts of data. A common use case is a contract that serves a registry, storing data in a manner that takes advantage of the blockchain's censorship-resistant and DDoS-resistant nature. How can this data be stored and retrieved effectively?
- **Forces:** The contract must be capable of dynamically allocating space to store new data. It must be capable of providing the data and differentiating it from other possible return values.
- **Solution:** A key-value store is well-suited to blockchain data management, where the store is dynamically resizable and provides a value given a specific key.
- **Examples:** Ethereum Name Service (ENS) is a key-value store that maps .eth domains to machine-readable data, such as Ethereum addresses [15].

Address Mapping

- **Problem:** Smart contracts often interact with various users, all of whom must be tracked independently. How can relationships between the smart contract and user accounts be managed correctly?
- **Forces:** Since any user account can send a message to the contract, the solution must be capable of dealing with *any* account, even ones it has never interacted with before. It must be capable of relating these accounts to contract-relevant data.
- **Solution:** Establish a mapping from addresses to contract-relevant data, defined for all possible Ethereum addresses. In the case of accounts that the contract has never interacted with, the mapping is from the address to a default value of the codomain (the set being mapped to). This mapping may be changed by the contract to other values of the type.

- **Examples:** The Solidity programming language [16] contains native support for mappings that are defined for all elements of the domain. Mappings from the native address type are used for managing users in many contracts, such as the OpenZeppelin implementation of ERC20 tokens [17].

Authorization [18]

- **Problem:** A smart contract may need to transition to a new state that isn't defined by its internal logic because of some external event or internal flaw. Since smart contracts are immutable, how can this transition be performed?
- **Forces:** The contract's immutability means that the potential for unspecified state changes needs to be present in the contract at its creation. The contract should not transition to these novel states unless required to do so.
- **Solution:** Establish a permissioning system where the contract is hard-coded to perform special actions in response to specific users. This permission may come from a single user or a vote of many, and privileges may range from setting state variables to completely destroying the contract. The exact details of the permissions and privileges must be specified at creation.
- **Examples:** The OpenZeppelin Ownable contract [19] allows a contract to have a specific "owner." The contract may be transferred between owners and may allow executing of some functions only by said owner.

3.2   Oracles

Due to the chain-boundedness of smart contracts, a variety of patterns have emerged for the supply of data to on-chain contracts. Contracts that serve as interfaces between the outside world and the blockchain are called oracles [18].

Judge

- **Problem:** Multiple parties are participating in a contract that is dependent on real-world data.
- **Forces:** The contract must determine the proper state of the real world in a manner that satisfies all participating parties.
- **Solution:** All parties identify a third-party actor that they all trust. This entity is given Authorization to update the contract with real-world state.
- **Examples:** An escrow contract where the release of funds is determined by a third-party.

Ticker Tape

- **Problem:** A contract must constantly supply up-to-date information about some real-world data.
- **Forces:** The contract must be able to update its internal state regularly to reflect changes in the world.

- **Solution:** Create a contract whose only purpose is to store regularly updated data about the external world. Use the Authorization pattern to allow a trusted source to update the state periodically/regularly. This contract is a service to other contracts that use the data.
- **Examples:** A contract that contains the recorded temperature each day in a given city.

Vote

- **Problem:** A contract must supply data that cannot rely on a single source. A large number of data sources are present and must be decided between.
- **Forces:** The contract must accept data from multiple sources and resolve any disputes among them.
- **Solution:** Allow the input sources to vote on the correct answer. And, provide disincentives for voting incorrectly, as determined by the eventual consensus.
- **Examples:** A group of users of some decentralized application vote on an upgrade to that application. Since there is no trusted authority guiding the application, a vote of users is necessary.

Anti-Oracle

- **Problem:** Information from different sources on the blockchain must be accessed off-chain.
- **Forces:** The data must be easily accessed at once in a non-contract context. The data from the blockchain cannot necessarily be parsed from this context.
- **Solution:** Create an off-chain daemon that periodically examines the blockchain for specific events and collates the records of those events into a single off-chain source. Off-chain entities can then read a well-formatted digest of the relevant information.
- **Examples:** A client that tracks the interactions of all the contracts in its decentralized application.

Blocklist

- **Problem:** A contract needs to record a set of entities that will be disallowed access to some asset off-chain.
- **Forces:** The contract must be easily readable, with fast lookup times and no false negatives.
- **Solution:** Define a contract that stores a Bloom filter coefficient set. Off-chain clients may download the coefficients to calculate with the Bloom filter.
- **Examples:** A contract could be used to track certificate revocations or the Ethereum addresses of stolen cryptocurrency.

Announcement

- **Problem:** Information from different sources on the blockchain must be accessed by entities on-chain.

- **Forces:** The data must be easily accessed by smart contracts.
- **Solution:** Create a contract that serves as a space where Authorized contracts can post announcements. These announcements can then be viewed by any other contract.
- **Examples:** An application that serves as an exchange for different cryptocurrencies might have interest in tracking the average price of exchange on-chain.

Bulletin Board

- **Problem:** A contract must supply irregular updates on real-world data, from multiple sources.
- **Forces:** The contract must be able to be prompted when an update is needed, and it must be able to accept results from any source. The contract must also contain a decision process to recognize the validity of update data.
- **Solution:** Create a Bulletin Board contract, where requests for data can be posted and answered by users. Define a decision process for acceptance of the answers, perhaps using the Vote or Judge patterns, and expose the answer data.
- **Examples:** A mathematician requires an answer to a difficult problem. The mathematician posts a contract that, when provided with a provably-correct solution, offers a reward to the solver.

3.3   High-Level Patterns

This section describes patterns that are neither oracles nor low-level enough to be ubiquitous. They are high-level organizing schema for entire smart contract applications.

Token [18]

- **Problem:** A contract needs a flexible unit of accounting for access to a certain resource.
- **Forces:** The unit of accounting must be fungible, collectible, and countable.
- **Solution:** Define a token, or contract-based cryptocurrency. Use the Address Mapping pattern to associate each Ethereum address with a balance and provide functions for transfer of balance between users.
- **Examples:** The ERC20 standard defines the interface for tokens [20].
- **Variants:** While the traditional token represents a fungible asset of fixed supply, there are variants such as non-fungible tokens [21] or tokens that can be regularly minted [22].

Migration

- **Problem:** A contract has a defined lifespan, passing through multiple stages related to its development or obsolescence.

- **Forces:** Since a contract is immutable, the lifespan must be taken into consideration in the contract's original code. The current state of the development must be tracked, even if the original contract has ceased to exist.
- **Solution:** Create a special Migration contract that serves as a pointer to the current version of the contract. When the contract is upgraded, the Migration contract is updated with a pointer to the latest version.
- **Examples:** The smart contract development suite Truffle has built-in functionality for Migration contracts with every project [23].

4   Related Work

In [18], the authors introduce design patterns for smart contracts in a more abbreviated form of this paper. To the best of our knowledge, this is only other paper published to-date that considers design patterns for smart contracts. The authors cover a broad range of aspects of smart contracts, platforms, and other salient matters while relegating design patterns to a small section. There, they present nine patterns overall (of which four are integrated into our taxonomy above and cited).

The other five patterns not mentioned here were excluded because they appear too straightforward to constitute a significant design abstraction in practical software (e.g., they offer a "math" pattern that guards execution of specific logic, a simple abstraction of an `if` statement).

Another useful contribution of [18] that is different from this current paper is the previous paper's empirical quantification of design patterns according to their proposed usage taxonomy. That presentation is at a level much higher than design patterns alone. The authors consider which of their nine patterns are used in each of their contract kinds and how frequently in practice. For instance, they considers "financial contracts," "notary contracts," "games contracts," and "library contracts".

5   Future Directions

As one can infer from the previous discussion, many design patterns exist concerning the retrieval of data from off-chain sources. Even more design patterns will likely emerge for this aspect because of the chain-boundedness of smart contracts. Another area ripe for further development is in the idea of Migrations. The immutability of smart contracts makes planning their lifecycles extremely important. The Migrations pattern is mostly just a pointer to the current location of the contract. It would be useful to determine design patterns for initiating contract state changes, deleting contracts, or any other step in a contract's lifecycle.

Identifying more design patterns in smart contracts will likely require several considerations:

1. What goal is the contract intended to serve?

2. What is the long-term lifecycle of the contract?
3. What situations involve interactions with the contract?
4. What inputs is the contract given? What outputs does it produce? What is the functional relationship between these inputs and outputs?
5. How does the contract interact with other contracts, if at all?

If these considerations provide the same answer in several different contracts, they may constitute a pattern. Since blockchains are transparent, these questions are more easily answered than they would be in other software. Static analysis of EVM bytecode stored in the blockchain state could answer many of the above questions for an unknown smart contract. Such work is underway in our research group, for instance.

One could envisage opt-in rules to utilize certain minimal design patterns with robust, 3rd-party implementation libraries to ensure contract safety. Implementation could also be required to include Migration and/or to subject smart contracts to third-party scrutiny prior to launch in order to be rated, such as a "UL listing" or other certification. While such auditing is not guaranteed to remove all residual faults, it could improve quality, which is of immediate concern. The best smart contracts would utilize as much highly tested, quality-controlled software as possible, with design patterns presenting abstractions and specific libraries providing merited solutions. These could be coupled with full UML models for such patterns [24,25] for enhancing the software development lifecycle. This would allow further elaboration of the patterns' limitations and applicability. Such rigor would be supportive toward achieving CMM-4 or CMM-5-type quality (which is strictly adherence to specifications) [8] in such critical software.

6   Conclusion

We posited that posing recurring aspects of smart contracts as software design patterns would have utility. Then, we proposed a suite of low-level, oracle-type, and high-level design patterns as one methodology for addressing the constraints of smart contracts while producing "best practices" that ideally will lead to more robust, well-developed smart contracts while reducing financial losses from buggy implementations. Because of the immutability property, high reliability software development and reuse of carefully vetted components is essential to robust contracts. Recognizing design patterns is a key step to generating designs based wherever possible on recognized patterns with reliable, well-tested implementation options. Potential future directions are sketched as well. Our set of patterns is not exhaustive but exemplary. Many more can be defined as we build up a pattern catalog for smart contracts.

Acknowledgment. This material is based upon work supported by the National Science Foundation under Grants Nos. 1547164, 1547245, and 1821926. Any opinions, findings, and conclusions or recommendations expressed in this material are those of the authors and do not necessarily reflect the views of the National Science Foundation.

References

1. Nakamoto, S.: Bitcoin: a peer-to-peer electronic cash system (2008). https://bitcoin.org/bitcoin.pdf
2. Namecoin. https://namecoin.org/
3. Worley, C., Skjellum, A.: Blockchain tradeoffs and challenges for current and emerging applications: generalization, fragmentation, sidechains, and scalability. In: Slated for Inclusion at IEEE Blockchain 2018, Halifax (2018)
4. Smart contracts. http://www.fon.hum.uva.nl/rob/Courses/InformationInSpeech/CDROM/Literature/LOTwinterschool2006/szabo.best.vwh.net/smart.contracts.html
5. Ethereum white paper. https://github.com/ethereum/wiki/wiki/White-Paper
6. Alexander, C., Ishikawa, S., Silverstein, M.: A Pattern Language: Towns, Buildings, Construction. Oxford University Press, Oxford (1977)
7. Gamma, E., Helm, R., Johnson, R., Vlissides, J.: Design Patterns: Elements of Reusable Object-Oriented Software. Addison-Wesley, Boston (1994)
8. Anonymous. The capability maturity model. https://en.wikipedia.org/wiki/Capability_Maturity_Model. Accessed 27 May 2018
9. Etherscan. https://etherscan.io/
10. Vessenes, P.: Deconstructing the DAO attack: a brief code tour. https://etherscan.io/
11. Ethereum yellow paper. https://github.com/ethereum/yellowpaper
12. Croman, K., et al.: On scaling decentralized blockchains. In: Clark, J., Meiklejohn, S., Ryan, P.Y.A., Wallach, D., Brenner, M., Rohloff, K. (eds.) FC 2016. LNCS, vol. 9604, pp. 106–125. Springer, Heidelberg (2016). https://doi.org/10.1007/978-3-662-53357-4_8
13. Eth gas station. https://ethgasstation.info/
14. Average transaction fee historical chart. https://bitinfocharts.com/comparison/ethereum-transactionfees.html
15. Ethereum name service. https://ens.domains/
16. Solidity. http://solidity.readthedocs.io/en/v0.4.21/
17. OpenZeppelin standard token implementation. https://github.com/OpenZeppelin/openzeppelin-solidity/blob/master/contracts/token/ERC20/StandardToken.sol
18. Bartoletti, M., Pompianu, L.: An empirical analysis of smart contracts: platforms, applications, and design patterns. In: Brenner, M., et al. (eds.) FC 2017. LNCS, vol. 10323, pp. 494–509. Springer, Cham (2017). https://doi.org/10.1007/978-3-319-70278-0_31
19. OpenZeppelin ownable implementation. https://github.com/OpenZeppelin/openzeppelin-solidity/blob/master/contracts/ownership/Ownable.sol
20. ERC-20 token standard. https://github.com/ethereum/EIPs/blob/master/EIPS/eip-20.md
21. ERC-721. http://erc721.org/
22. OpenZeppelin mintable token implementation. https://github.com/OpenZeppelin/openzeppelin-solidity/blob/master/contracts/token/ERC20/MintableToken.sol
23. Running migrations. http://truffleframework.com/docs/getting_started/migrations
24. Anonymous. Unified modelling language. https://en.wikipedia.org/wiki/Unified_Modeling_Language. Accessed 27 May 2018

25. Object Management Group/ISO. ISO/IEC 19505–1:2012 - information technology - Object Management Group Unified Modeling Language (OMG UML) - part 1: Infrastructure, 20 April 2012. ISO.org. Accessed 10 Apr 2014
26. Worley, C., et al.: Scrybe: a 2nd-generation blockchain technology with lightweight mining for secure provenance and related applications (2018). Unpublished paper, under revision

A Multichain Architecture for Distributed Supply Chain Design in Industry 4.0

Kai Fabian Schulz[1]([⊠]) and Daniel Freund[2]

[1] Technische Universität Berlin, Straße des 17. Juni 135, 10623 Berlin, Germany
kai.f.schulz@campus.tu-berlin.de
[2] DAI-Labor, Technische Universität Berlin,
Ernst-Reuter-Platz 7, 10587 Berlin, Germany
daniel.freund@dai-labor.de

Abstract. The Fourth Industrial Revolution is centered around a self-organized production. Cyber-physical systems can be used to collect and share data for tracking, automation and control as well as evaluation and documentation. This has a wide-reaching impact on business models. Instead of a linear approach, concentrating on a single company, the focus needs to be on the complete production ecosystem represented by a dynamic and self-organized network, including the supply chain. The interconnectedness of the cyber-physical systems in these networks is rooted in the Internet of Things, but also shared business processes. Performance, stability, security as well as data integrity and access control hereby represent a major contributing factor, calling for a new concept of information processing systems.

The blockchain is a distributed ledger combining cryptographic and game-theoretic concepts, which enable immutable transactions and automatic consensus of the parties involved about its state. Blockchains have evolved as a fast-developing technology, promising increased efficiency and security in many scenarios, especially use cases that primarily rely on all kinds of transactions.

The paper follows a design science approach, examining the implications of blockchain and the industrial Internet of Things in Industry 4.0 (I40) on supply chain management. I40's implications on supply chains are discussed and connected with favorable characteristics of blockchain technology. Based on this analysis, requirements for a decentralized enterprise information processing system are derived, resulting in a reference model for distributed supply chains of I40.

Keywords: Blockchain · Supply chain · Industry 4.0 · Distributed supply chain · Multichain

1 Introduction

I40 represents a paradigm shift in traditional manufacturing and production techniques towards a self-organized production, meaning that products can control their own manufacturing process, which has the potential to transform the complete value chain [1, 10, 12]. "In the world of Industrie 4.0, people, machines, equipment, logistics systems and products communicate and cooperate with each other directly. Production

W. Abramowicz and A. Paschke (Eds.): BIS 2018 Workshops, LNBIP 339, pp. 277–288, 2019.
https://doi.org/10.1007/978-3-030-04849-5_25

and logistics processes are integrated intelligently across company boundaries to make manufacturing more efficient and flexible. This facilitates smart value-creation chains which include all of the lifecycle phases of the product" [11]. The inclusion of all lifecycles in the planning and engineering process is called a through-engineering across the entire value chain [13]. The evolution of I40 emanates from a technology push caused by the second machine age [2, 10]. At the same time, an application-pull enforces the systematic implementation of the above technologies. This application-pull is triggered by sustainability requirements, shorter development periods whilst the demand for flexibility has increased, emanating from a shift from a seller's to a buyer's market and resulting in 'batch size one'. Furthermore, the aforementioned conditions call for faster decision-making processes that will require a higher degree of decentralization [10]. Current business processes as well as management and organizational structures are seen as the potentially biggest hurdle to access the potential advantages of I40 [9].

The paper at hand motivates the innovation of existing information processing systems in the context of I40 and examines possibilities to meet the specific requirements in this context through the application of blockchain technology.

Other than taking a technical perspective on blockchain implementation in I40, a multichain-architecture involving various technologies under development is proposed that facilitates distributed supply chains in future industry ecosystems and lays a foundation for future development towards fully automated multi-stakeholder I40 applications. The research methodology is based on a literature research, a technology monitoring and design science approach, based on the information systems research framework of Hevner et al. [8] as a problem-solving paradigm has been used for the elaboration of the multichain architecture. More specifically, this paper utilizes the three-cycle view of design science research [7]. The initiation of the relevance cycle was achieved by a technology monitoring that has been conducted to identify the current status quo of blockchain application in supply chains. A technology monitoring is part of a set of methodologies for technology forecasts [4].

2   Implications of Industry 4.0 on Supply Chains, Company Structure and Information Processing Systems

Schrauf, Berttram [14] see the digital supply chain at the center of the digital enterprise. When projecting the self-organization approach of I40 onto supply chains, the IoT most certainly provides the most valuable technology for the supply chain, providing optimal visibility of and information on materials and products that are the basis for automation processes. In a supply chain, equipment and upstream products can be equipped with IoT devices so that the materials or upstream products become objects in the IoT. This can be utilized to achieve a decentralized and self-coordinated material flow [1].

Additionally, the mass production of individual products affects supply chain strategy and design, since individualized products are necessarily demand-driven. This resembles a traditional make-to-order process, in respect of the individuality of products and should result in an agile strategy. I40, however, allows for new concepts for the management of global production and supply systems. With its self-organization approach and real-time communication, I40 promotes efficiency in supply chains, which, as a result, can still be pull-based because they do not need to rely on stock in later production stages. Distributed sub-systems can become interconnected and communicate directly and in real-time. Demand-forecasting causing the bullwhip effect can be substantially reduced thanks to real-time information, also enabling the automatic redirection of material flows to another production site in case of an outage [1]. Thus, supply chains will become hyper-reactive in a way that is almost proactive. Machines equipped with sensors, actuators and visual systems can fulfill orders they have received from other machines, which these in return have commissioned based on e.g. sensor input from the physical environment.

Industry 4.0 requires information processing systems to promote integrability and interoperability that enable versatile and flexible production processes. "The most successful companies will use better communications to integrate suppliers and customers' needs into all value-creation activities" [13]. This will have implications on overall supply chain design, implying a paradigm shift from a linear supply chain design to a network-centric one. "The vertical networking of Industry 4.0 requires new IT solutions. In many cases, existing IT infrastructures are very fragmented and result in poor networking" [13].

The through-engineering over all lifecycle phases means that data must be securely available across the entire value chain. The demand to share data in many interrelated networks requires information access to be restrictable with an efficient users' rights management and to protect all data against cybersecurity risks. The vision of 'Ubiquitous Computing' that connects devices and opens up information processing and management information systems to other systems calls for a new holistic security concept. "With the increased connectivity and use of standard communications protocols that come with Industry 4.0, the need to protect critical industrial systems and manufacturing lines from cybersecurity threats increases dramatically" [12]. Connected machinery and asset information in the cloud pose a possible threat, since they will arouse the interest of hackers. "The extensive networking (...) and the high levels of data sharing involved in I40 will greatly increase the demands made on data security" [13].

Security concerns can represent a bottleneck in I40, which can be addressed by blockchain technology. Blockchain technology represents a tamper-proof way to record transactions in a distributed digital ledger and is supposed to have a great impact on the design and the implementation of digital business processes, bringing along the potential to streamline and accelerate them [15]. It promises to enable an infinitely scalable ledger that can be shared between all participants in a supply chain and that can be utilized to securely store all asset tracking data in real-time. While some solutions for blockchain-enhanced, distributed supply chains are already under development, the technology monitoring has shown that no market player has pulled clear with a mature and broadly applicable product that supports open standards. In general, standardization in the blockchain space seems a long way off.

3   Blockchain Technology

Blockchain technology embeds trust in a network through immutable data records and distributed network consensus, exchanging the need for intermediaries with crypto-graphic trust, thereby accelerating processes [15]. Similar to the provisioning models of cloud computing blockchains can be permissioned networks or unpermissioned networks depending on their purpose of application. Public blockchains provide better censorship resistance and, through their openness, can be used by many entities, nurturing network effects [3]. Certain aspects of private or consortium blockchains can be valuable for enterprise applications. In private chains or consortium chains, functionalities such as improved data privacy, configuring blockchain rules, reverting and modifying transactions can be of advantage. The implementation of consensus mechanisms such as PoA provides much faster transaction finality and leads to increased transaction speed and decreased transaction cost, promoting scalability. Even if the decentralization aspect is diluted, private blockchains still provide cryptographic authentication, audibility and features such as zero-knowledge proofs. Smart Contracts extend the capabilities of the blockchain as a secure distributed ledger to also enable automated and secure modifications of information on the blockchain [15]. They can be used to create arbitrary rules on a blockchain and can encapsulate complicated business logic that automates transactions based on supply chain events.

Utilizing smart contracts, tamper-proof tracking and trustless transactions, the blockchain in connection with the IoT enables automated operations within an SCM system [15]. Regarding IT security, blockchain technology offers the appropriate measures through public key cryptography and cryptographic hash functions. Security is furthermore embedded by a decentralized network consensus amongst several parties with disparate interests. This is especially useful, when parties don't want to exchange information directly, but need to verify the integrity of this information. Because every participant in the blockchain network has a copy of the ledger and the blocks form a chronological sequence of records, data manipulations are transparent and easy to reconstruct.

Furthermore, supply chains can become more trustable through the irreversibility of transactions. The embedded trust of the blockchain requires less clearances and reviews and can give unique identities to machines in the IoT so that machines can autonomously decide, which machine to trust and which services to offer to which machine. This automation potential is especially important for the reactiveness and agility of I40 supply chains; e.g. in case of a blocked transport route in an adaptive multimodal transport chain, goods can be automatically redirected, utilizing IoT information. Thanks to blockchains, the rapid change of plan is accountably trackable and payment streams regarding compensation for transport can be redirected in a trusted manner. In both cases, a blockchain is a suitable infrastructure. In all cases, an SCM tracks and monitors relevant production and product information. This information can refer to the parties involved in a certain transaction, the state of a product, e.g. its price or quality, a transaction or manufacturing date and location. The concatenation of blocks in the blockchain ensures that all data can be traced back to its very origin, which would be the raw materials in most cases. This can have a great impact an ecological responsibility of manufacturing and can be utilized to satisfy environmentally and socially conscious customers, since they can be confident in the data's integrity.

Taken together, the blockchain could improve efficiency and transparency in supply chain, but also increase the visibility of goods within them. Building confidence in supply chain networks has, until now, been costly because it is effortful and exhaustive, requiring a lot of intermediaries or trusted relationships between company employees [5].

4   Integrating Blockchains into Supply Chain Management Systems

Future enterprise information processing systems will be built on a network-centric design and support decentralized decision making. Ecosystems thrive on compatibility and openness for innovations. Enterprise application of blockchains is inherently more valuable when it incorporates an interoperable, versatile concept instead of only focusing on an isolated use case. This way, a complete ecosystem of intertwining systems can be created. In [5, 21–25] blockchain is presented as a freight logistics solution, a solution for improved pharmaceutical security, an integrated food supply chain and real-time logistics respectively. Also, blockchains is presented as a way to reduce fraud, increase supply chain visibility and to provide better means for supply chain optimization as well as demand forecasting.

Ideally, an ecosystem of autonomously communicating applications is able to provide sufficient automation capabilities for I40. Systems big enough to cope with a large amount of data, fast enough to cope with a high frequency of transactions, specialized to be extremely secure for certain purposes or to be easily accessible for customers have to be split up in subsystems that need one hub, bringing them all together. A beneficial ecosystem would be able to incorporate more specialized solutions for certain business cases, solutions specialized on IoT communication and enterprise systems focused on e.g. security and auditability. To guarantee future-proofness through openness and versatility, the bedrock of this ecosystem is therefore a hub that is optimally not provided by a proprietary solution and sufficiently decentralized. To construct such a system, three essential pillars are identified.

4.1   Core Functionality

Given the scenario of a consortium of supply chain network, participants that do not necessarily trust each other but mutually benefit from cooperation, a blockchain can provide trusted interactions without a central authority or intermediaries.

The toolkit for such a blockchain can be the Parity Ethereum Client. Each Parity Ethereum Client runs a full or light node in the P2P network and can be paired with a user interface, which can be customized to support file management, business processes, smart contracts configuration as well as account and rights management. On top, the client features permissions. Permissions span the configuration of an individual node's role as well as the definition of which nodes can connect to the network and connect to each other. On an account level, the type of transactions individual nodes can perform can be constricted. Furthermore, it is possible to regulate gas price within the blockchain and to introduce new validators to the blockchain in a distributed manner through any arbitrary rule, that can be implemented in a smart contract, e.g. a majority vote.

This offers a possibility to set up a configurable Ethereum-based blockchain for the decentralized and tamperproof exchange of supply chain and other relevant documents, whilst maintaining enough flexibility to implement the design requirements of an individual consortium network. Through a 'pluggable consensus', namely the possibility to choose a consensus algorithm – PoW (Ethash), PoA (Aura, Tendermint) and potentially PoS (Aura, Tendermint), but theoretically any functioning implementation of Byzantine Fault Tolerance.

4.2   File Storage

In the attempt to offer a distributed storage capability that is consistent with the decentralization paradigm, certain aspects of the traditional blockchain concept aren't useful for data storing purposes. Confirmation time of blocks is not acceptable for common data queries and not all data needs to be stored forever and immutable, either because it is to be actually replaced, has expired, or for simple reasons of costs for capacity. However, this only holds true if data is stored on the blockchain itself. P2P file systems such as IPFS (ipfs.io), decentralized cloud file storages such as Storj (storj. io) or Ethereum Swarm (github.com/ethersphere/swarm), but also decentralized database systems such as OrbitDB (https://github.com/orbitdb) or Bluzelle (bluzelle.com) can provide a far higher performance and provide means to be in consistence with the overall decentralization concept of a distributed supply chain.

IPFS is already integrated into the Parity technology stack. Built on a set of proven core technologies with the vision of a permanent World Wide Web, one of IPFS's purposes is that of an encrypted file or data sharing system. The link to (a large) amount of data can be stored in an IPFS link that is included in a blockchain transaction. This way the data becomes timestamped and is secured on the blockchain. At the same time, this provides a way to make the content addressable. The hyperlinks stored in the blocks form a Merkle directed acyclic graph (DAG) that supports the building of a versioned distributed file system. The implemented BitSwap protocol for block exchange ensures that also rare files are sufficiently distributed in the system.

The functionalities descried as hitherto have already been bundled by Parity Technologies in a product called SEDACS [19], which is licensed under a commercial license, but since most of its components are open sourced, it can be recreated with reasonable effort. When building on top of Parity Ethereum, Secret Store or other open source technologies of Parity Technologies and IPFS, customers can choose to connect these parts on their own or to resort to SEDACS. All technologies except SEDACS are licensed under a GNU GPLv3 free copyleft license, meaning that these technologies can be implemented for commercial use, unless they are redistributed within a commercially licensed software package. In comparison to e.g. Chronicled's offering SEDACS does not rely on central vendor servers or similar centralized services, but instead is based on federated servers, owned by each participant in the supply chain consortium or potentially by certain third parties that do not trust the consortium with verifying the data.

4.3   Interoperability

The need for interoperability on a distributed supply chain accrues from individualized product and service development, resulting in connected processes handled by different channels [10]. Because I40 spans the complete product lifecycle, interoperability of IT systems is indispensable. Cyber-physical Systems (CPS) along the value chain have to be interconnected in an overarching network and integrated in a distributed IT infrastructure [6]. Traditionally, interoperability can be achieved in a lot of ways and mainly concerns compatible data formats or APIs. The problem with these is, though, that they are not immutable and can be copied without notice. Blockchains can provide these security, but up to now always a closed system. I40 enterprises will presumably deploy private and consortium chains for their purposes, but the need for flexibility and the integration and cooperation of changing partners in a supply chain network requires these chains to be possibly open to others.

Polkadot is a 'heterogeneous multi-chain' concept. "The heterogeneous nature of this architecture enables many highly divergent types of consensus systems interoperating in a trustless, fully decentralised 'federation', allowing open and closed networks to have trust-free access to each other" [18]. Among multichain protocols, Polkadot has been identified as most suitable as it allows for the interaction of smart contracts located in disparate blockchains. It aims at providing a central relay chain, which decouples the consensus mechanism from the state-transition mechanism so that blockchains running on different logics can be linked. Another multi-chain approach is Cosmos an "inter-blockchain commu-nication protocol" [20]. The "Cosmos Hub" represents the equivalent of a relay chain, but since Cosmos is focused on the secure interchange of tokens whilst Polkadot focuses on the secure exchange of data in general, the latter has been identified to be more suited for a supply chain network application as it allows for the in-teraction of smart contracts located in disparate blockchains. The relay chain functions as a bedrock for numerous parallel chains, called parachains. Data from parachains is forwarded through the relay chain. This forwarding takes place in a validated parachain block via a Remote Procedure Calls (RPC).

Polkadot is designed for both public and private/consortium chains, opening up the possibility to integrate the two. Polkadot is also expected to be interoperable with the public Ethereum blockchain [18]. This opens up possibilities for the inclusion of data hosted on the public Ethereum chain, which could be an elegant way to integrate customers in an otherwise private/consortium enterprise blockchain setting.

5   Distributed Multichain Supply Chain Design

Based on the previous analysis, we suggest the following architecture for distributed supply chains of I40, in which

- **Parity SEDACS** provides blockchain-federated handling of asset tracking-data and documents, e.g. shipping documents or certificates.
- **Polkadot** is used as a connector from SEDACS to IoT blockchains that are suited to handle the amount of IoT data and provide M2M communication, but also to any

other possible chain such as financial institutions and insurances or the public blockchain network.

- **IoT** blockchains can be individually maintained by network participants and relevant asset-tracking data is forwarded to SEDACS (Fig. 1).

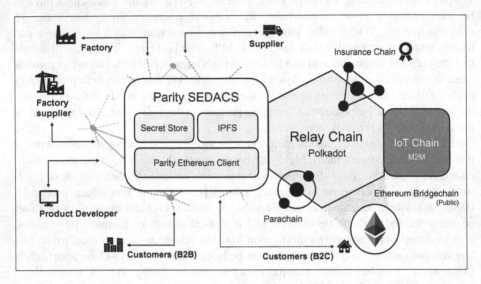

Fig. 1. Distributed supply chain design, partially based on [6, 18].

This answers the need for secure authentication, non-repudiation and integrity of data in a decentralized network and aims at combining several best-of-breed systems. Each of the chains focuses on further attributes – authorization, auditability and governance, availability and scalability – while always serving the purpose of security and are described in further detail in the following subchapters.

5.1   Corporate Network – Authorization, Audibility and Governance

Corporate network participants are directly connected in their own Ethereum-based chain. The overall functionality is based on Parity SEDACS, which bundles several core technologies. SEDACS allows for decentralized exchange of documents and will further promote decentralized decision making, the governance of network features and participants and the management of authorizations. It will as well provide a tamper-proof audit trail for internal and external review for e.g. auditors. PoA offers instant transaction confirmation by the trusted nodes, which implies freely configurable block times suited to individual needs, and high security, since the nodes within the corporate SEDACS network are, in a real-world scenario, more trustable than random nodes in a public network, since their identity is known and at stake. Moreover, malicious actions, e.g. in case a node is taken over, are countered thanks to the decentralization of validation rights.

Thus, a closely knit corporate network can be established, in which new actors can be introduced upon encoded rules. The consortium type of blockchain with PoA supports privacy and security as well as reactivity and configurability, so that individual corporation requirements can be mapped, while still maintaining the major advantages of blockchain technology. The exclusivity of the corporate blockchain enables a close cooperation of companies, but isolates this chain from wider networks, such as a network with customer identities and the IoT. Therefore, Polkadot is used to connect the more exclusive corporate network – offering higher performance and privacy – to the outer world, providing availability for customers. Customers thus are included into certain activities within the corporate network's I40 value chain. Since I40 heavily relies on IoT data, this data is also selectively included from external blockchain sources. Furthermore, Polkadot offers the opportunity to include other corporate networks to connect e.g. financial institutions and insurances that provide services to the corporate network.

5.2 Customer Integration – Availability

Geisberger, Broy [6] foresee the direct integration of customers into a decentral CPS. The relay chain enables a solution, which differentiates between B2B and B2C customers. While B2B customers are highly engaged and have their own security arrangements, B2C customers are naturally less involved in the value chain of a product of their choice. Thus, B2B customers are still directly integrated in the information processing system represented by SEDACS. B2C customers, on the contrary, are not required to have a permanent account for SEDACS that they have to maintain and that open possible security risks. However, customers as private persons will most likely keep their online identify on a secure blockchain solution for Identity Verification (IDV) and Know-Your-Customer (KYC) purposes. Civic (civic.com) and Blockstack (blockstack.org) propose current solution not based on Ethereum, while others such as SelfKey (selfkey.org) plan to provide a KYC solution for Ethereum. Either way, publicly accessible IDV and KYC systems can be integrated via the Ethereum bridgechain or a parachain. If they are Ethereum-based, they can also be built on top of the same Ethereum chain that runs SEDACS.

5.3 IoT Connection – Performance

The amount of data in the IoT requires different blockchain specifications other than needed for document sharing capabilities as in SEDACS. For simple value transfer infrastructures based on Unspent Transaction Outputs (UTXO), a DAG can be deployed as well to make single transactions interdependent [18]. A DAG-based ledger is being developed e.g. by IOTA with Tangle (iota.org). This approach is (at least momentarily) impractical regarding state changes: the ability to communicate a system state is a prerequisite for systems interaction [18]. Other blockchain solutions that could enable M2M communication in the IoT are developed by Filament (filament.com), ubirch (ubirch.de), Engima (enigma.co) and Moeco (moeco.io). Most importantly, IoT blockchain parameters can be aligned to promote transaction throughput, while neglecting transaction ordering.

Even if no prevailing solution can be identified yet, the interoperability approach of Polkadot makes it possible to realize the interconnection of any IoT focused blockchain with a document- and access rights-focused blockchain. With Polkadot, a system providing fast and efficient M2M communication is most favorable blockchain-based for maximum compatibility but could possibly also be DAG-based or simply incorporate IoT data via a blockchain oracle.

In an application scenario, certain IoT tracking data is forwarded to a SEDACS Ethereum-based private chain, where the involved parties manage this data and use it for further processing and administration. Conversely, IoT objects can be required to wait for permissions that are granted in SEDACS and then forwarded to the IoT chain.

6 Conclusion

In a first step, changing demands for information processing system due to the current developments around I40, especially in respect of SCM, have been outlined. The research design was based on the design science approach of Hevner et al. [8], while limiting the scope to the first half of the design cycle. Following, the high-level features of a blockchain were introduced and beneficial factors that can address the needs of I40 SCM systems were touched. Subsequently we proposed a design for distributed I40 supply chains, based on the design science approach.

The outlined design of distributed I40 supply chains incorporates technologies that are as well still under development. Their successful finalization is a prerequisite for the functioning of the solution as presented. Furthermore, the initial solutions will most likely fall short of the centralized systems. Still, the suggested advantages exist on a theoretical level and the utilized decentral systems are under heavy development, fueled by public interest in and experimentation with cryptocurrencies and tokens. The limitations described above can best be characterized by Foster's S-Curve for assessing technological threats, in which the current state of new technology is less capable than existing technology, but the new technology incorporates higher potential.

The paper has cycled through the first of three cycles of the design science approach. Future research should close the first cycle with concrete field tests. The results can then be used to cycle through phases 2 and 3. These would include evaluating the technology design as well as the induction of new theoretical concepts based on the results of the evaluation.

The concepts of blockchains that act as a hub and connector for disparate blockchains inherits a much broader vision and potential than presented in this paper and can have far-reaching consequences in many areas. The more there are application scenarios, the faster and more diligent the development of such technologies will be, facilitating the development of a distributed I40 supply chain design. Furthermore, the design with Polkadot will also enable Ethereum-based chains to interact with other blockchain technologies likely to be used in a corporate context such as Hyperledger Fabric (hyperledger.org/projects/fabric) or Quorum (jpmorgan.com/global/quorum), but also enable customers to pay with a cryptocurrency non-native to the corporate network within the latter.

References

1. Bauer, W., Schlund, S., Marrenbach, D., Ganschar, O.: Industrie 4.0. Volkswirtschaftliches Potenzial für Deutschland. Edited by Fraunhofer IAO BITKOM (2014)
2. Brynjolfsson, E., McAfee, A.: The Second Machine Age. Work, Progress, and Prosperity in a Time of Brilliant Technologies. Norton, New York (2014)
3. Buterin, V.: On Public and Private Blockchains. Ethereum Blog (2015). https://blog.ethereum.org/2015/08/07/on-public-and-private-blockchains/. Accessed 08 Feb 2018
4. Cuhls, K.: Methoden der Technikvorausschau - eine internationale Übersicht. Edited by Fraunhofer Institut für System- und Innovationsforschung (ISI). Fraunhofer IRB Verlag. Stuttgart (2008)
5. Field, A.M.: Blockchain for freight? (1542–3867). J. Commer. **18**(5), 88–92 (2017)
6. Geisberger, E., Broy, M.: agendaCPS Integrierte Forschungsagenda Cyber-Physical Systems (acatech STUDIE). Springer, Heidelberg (2012). https://doi.org/10.1007/978-3-642-29099-2
7. Hevner, A.: A three cycle view of design science research. Scand. J. Inf. Syst. **19**(2), 4 (2007)
8. Hevner, A., March, S.T., Park, J., Ram, S.: Design science in information systems research. MIS Q. **28**(1), 75–105 (2004)
9. Huber, W.: Industrie 4.0 in der Automobilproduktion. Ein Praxisbuch. Springer, Wiesbaden (2016). https://doi.org/10.1007/978-3-658-12732-9
10. Lasi, H., Fettke, P., Feld, T., Hoffmann, M.: Industry 4.0. Bus. Inf. Syst. Eng. **6**(4), 239–242 (2014)
11. Plattform Industrie 4.0: What is Industrie 4.0. Federal Ministry for Economic Affairs and Energy, Federal Ministry of Education and Research (2017). http://www.plattform-i40.de/I40/Navigation/EN/Industrie40/WhatIsIndustrie40/what-is-industrie40.html. Accessed 28 Dec 2017
12. Rüßmann, M., et al.: Industry 4.0. The Future of Productivity and Growth in Manufacturing Indudtries. The Boston Consulting Group (BCG) (2015). https://www.bcg.com/publications/2015/engineered_products_project_business_industry_4_future_productivity_growth_manufacturing_industries.aspx. Accessed 15 Dec 2017
13. Schlaepfer, R.C., Koch, M.: Industry 4.0. Challenges and solutions for the digital transformation and use of exponential technologies. Deloitte (2015). https://www2.deloitte.com/content/dam/Deloitte/ch/Documents/manufacturing/ch-en-manufacturing-industry-4-0-24102014.pdf. Accessed 15 Dec 2017
14. Schrauf, S., Berttram, P.: Industry 4.0. How digitization makes the supply chain more efficient, agile, and customer-focused. Strategy& (2016). https://www.strategyand.pwc.com/reports/industry4.0. Accessed 15 Dec 2017
15. Schütte, J., et al.: Blockchain und Smart Contracts. Technologien, Forschungsfragen und Anwendungen. In: Prinz, W., Schulte, A.T. (eds.) Fraunhofer-Gesellschaft (2017)
16. Szozda, N.: Industry 4.0 and its impact on the functioning of supply chains. Logforum **13**(4), 401–414 (2015)
17. Wahlster, W.: Semantic technologies for mass customization. In: Wahlster, W., Grallert, H.-J., Wess, S., Friedrich, H., Widenka, T. (eds.) Towards the Internet of Services: The THESEUS Research Program. CT, pp. 3–13. Springer, Cham (2014). https://doi.org/10.1007/978-3-319-06755-1_1
18. Wood, G.: Polkadot. Vision for a heterogeneous multi-chain framework (2016). https://polkadot.io/. Accessed 12 Dec 2017
19. Parity (2018): Secure Data Access Control System. Wiki. Parity Technologies Ltd. Available online at https://paritytech.github.io/wiki. Accessed 3 Feb 2018

20. Kwon, J., Buchman, E.: Cosmos. A Network of Distributed Ledgers. White-paper. Cosmos (2018). https://cosmos.network/about/whitepaper. Accessed 16 Jan 2018
21. Garrett, R.: How blockchain is transforming the supply chain. Supply Demand Chain. Exec. **18**(2), 10–14 (2017). http://search.ebsco-host.com/login.aspx?direct=true&db=bth&AN= 123453671&site=ehost-live
22. Haughwout, J.: Blockchain. A single, immutable, serialized source of truth: blockchain technology could help introduce higher levels of security to and confidence in supply chain transactions. Mater. Handl. Logist. **72**(8), 27–29 (2017)
23. Morley, H.R.: Weighing in on Blockchain. Blockchain technology touted as means to share container weights to meet global regulations. J. Commer. (1542-3867) **18**(19), 10A–13A. http://search.ebsco-host.com/login.aspx?direct=true&db=bth&AN=125674290&site=ehost-live
24. Shanley, A.: Could Blockchain Improve Pharmaceutical Supply Chain Security? Pharm. Technol., 34–39 (2017a). http://search.ebsco-host.com/login.aspx?direct=true&db=bth&AN= 124570785&site=ehost-live
25. Shanley, A.: Real-time logistics. Internet of things, advanced analytics, and blockchain solutions such as smart contracts promise to give manufacturers more control over products and supply chains. Pharm. Technol. Eur. **29**(10), 46–48 (2017b). http://search.ebscohost.com/login.aspx?di-rect=true&db=bth&AN=125734814&site=ehost-live

Invisible BlockChain and Plasticity of Money – Adam Smith Meets Darwin to Buy Crypto Currency

Zeeshan-ul-hassan Usmani[1(✉)], Andre Waddell[2], and Rytis Bieliauskas[3]

[1] Misk Innovation, Riyadh, Saudi Arabia
zusmani78@gmail.com
[2] University of Nicosia, Nicosia, Cyprus
[3] Coingate, Vilnius, Lithuania

Abstract. This paper will attempt to compare evolution in nature (based on Darwin's theory of evolution by natural selection), with similar processes happening in money, especially in the current iteration of money (cryptocurrencies), and the underlying blockchain technology. This paper will review the history and evolution of money up to this point, shortly explain Darwin's theory of evolution by natural selection, compare the similarities between evolution by natural selection in nature with evolution in blockchain technology and cryptocurrencies, and will examine the potential paths for the blockchain technology and cryptocurrencies to evolve in the future.

Keywords: Evolution of money · Crypto currencies · BlockChain
Darwinian evolution for crypto currencies

1 Introduction

Women, wealth, worldly possessions - these are the themes that have fueled stories from time immemorial. However, little did we know that the concept of money would one day be turned upside down? A lot has been changed in last the 2,000 years including the concept of money itself. It is worth mentioning that contrary of gradual decent of biological evolution, money always evolves in big jumps, from barter to writing on clay sheets, from commodity based money to precious coins, from gold-backed paper currency to sovereignty-backed fiat and from digital credit-debt registers to state-issued bonds. The world is standing at the right moment – an ever-connected environment is calling for the next jump – a money that is able to evolve new traits, programmable, best suited for machine-to-machine and machine-to-human interfaces for the globalized world and where people can conduct trust-worthy transactions without intermediaries. In a world where close to 100% of the population has access to cell phones, while only half has the access to toilets or tooth brushes, it would be disappointing to see if money does not evolve. The base DNA of world economics has changed through technology in the last two decades. The same environment that was once suitable for the fiat money is harming us now in more ways than we can imagine.

© Springer Nature Switzerland AG 2019
W. Abramowicz and A. Paschke (Eds.): BIS 2018 Workshops, LNBIP 339, pp. 289–299, 2019.
https://doi.org/10.1007/978-3-030-04849-5_26

The rest of the paper aims to decipher the ideology of blockchain and how similar it is with natural evolution. From Aristotle's Scala Naturae – the chain of being to Adam Smith's invisible hand, the dynamics and evolution of money is always been the invisible chain of transactions and transfers among human populace. Let's dive deeper to find out how natural the ideological revolution and prophecy of blockchain is to human life.

2   A Brief History of Money

Like biology, money is a historical science, where one constructs a historical narrative of a chain of events with tentative information and recorded details about the environment in which it takes place to explain the role, place and importance of money.

Some thirty thousand years ago, humans lived an itinerant life, rallying sustenance from the land from wherever it could be found. Drifting from place to place was the norm for man, some in search of commodities or animals and some to escape harsh weather. After all, what needs did they have to sustain a nomadic life - a pair of clothes or two, some tools, perhaps some pottery. When they crossed paths with a neighboring tribe or clan, they would exchange one of their own goods for something of theirs - wheat in exchange for fish, a utensil or two in exchange for a blanket. There existed no concept of currency, notes or legal tender - wealth was not owned in this form. Limited ownership, limited desires, communal living; life was carefree.

Competitiveness, however, is in the essence of man, and alas crept into how man began to value himself. What one owned, and how much of it, began to acquire the tinge of swagger and vanity. Wealth in the form of notes and cash was still non-existent, but the ownership of commodities and livestock was inequitably distributed. Also, people had distinct skills. This disparate ownership of commodities and skills gave rise to an arrangement of mutual transactions, which we know today as the barter system. Man spent some twenty thousand years, including the Ice Ages, bartering.

In some form or another, the barter system abides in the world even today. People exchange gifts with each other, for example, or share harvests. Even today, on account of international sanctions, Iran trades various commodities from other countries in exchange for oil. In his book 'Debt: the first 5000 years', David Graber argues that the barter system is used when transactions are made between strangers, such as between people of different tribes or clans. Among the people of a certain tribe or clan, on the other hand, the sentiments of offering favors, or offering commodities on loan, prevails. Barter, and eventually currency, was used when there was a scarcity of trust; within the community, the tradition of favors or trust kept the society together. With blockchain's decentralized trust and community consensus, the life of money is coming full circle to where it has begun.

Money is one of the oldest technologies in existence – it is older than the wheel. Throughout history, many different things were used as money, and they all had five distinct characteristics – they had to be relatively scarce, portable, fungible, divisible and easily recognizable.

Money eliminated the drawbacks of the barter system. It solved the double coincidence of wants. As a medium of exchange, you get money when you sell goods/services to whosoever and use that money to buy goods/services from whoso-ever have them for sale. Money solved the problem of absence of common. It acted as a unit of value; a yardstick to measure the worth of all goods and services. It resolved the problem of difficulty of storing wealth (purchasing power). It allowed a standard of deferred payment, a system which allowed you to plan future expenditures. Money facilitated the exchange of goods and services and enabled the sophistication of trade. It increased productivity and efficiency, production planning and consumption. It was utilized to revive the economy from depression and promoted economic welfare.

The first specie of money was commodity money – shells, beads, rare stones, metals, even cow dung and salt – were once used as money. Next came the specie of fiat money – where the underlying value came not from any material good used to create the money, or at least redeemable for the money, but from the faith in the government minting the money (centralized sovereignty). Now, we see the new species of money based on cryptographic algorithms – math-based money – where the value comes from voluntary use, and public mathematical algorithms and consensus (algo-rithmic governance), enabling various functions unavailable in other monies.

The value of fiat money is an act of faith, they worth what claimed, only because people believed in it.

The Yapese in Polynesia used enormous stones as currency. The stones themselves were useless as physical objects. They were only used to note value. Transactions were made not by physically moving the stone, but by publicly announcing that this par-ticular stone belongs not to you anymore, but to someone else. A 'public ledger' going from person to person, made everybody aware of who owned how many rai stones at a particular time. Thus the people of the island, via oral tradition, kept a record of who was the owner of how much wealth. A hole resembling that of a donut was traditionally kept in the middle of this stone so that it could be carried from one place to another with the help of rods. But for all practical purposes, no physical movement of the stone was ever required. This is illustrated by an event when one of the stones as it was being transported; fell from a canoe into the ocean. The Yapese agreed that the lost stone still represented value and still belonged to the same person as before. Future transactions were settled based on the stone, even though no one ever saw it again [1]. This is very similar to how cryptocurrencies work, as the units of account in cryptocurrencies are valueless as digital objects themselves, they are only used to note value. The trans-actions in cryptocurrencies are also usually made by publicly announcing that from now on those particular cryptocurrency units belong to someone else. This message is sent to other users of that cryptocurrency and signed using a digital signature, which ensures that everyone can check the validity of the message, but no one can change or forge it [2]. Consider the properties of the rai: it was scarce, it was durable and it was not possible to make a copy of it. There is much for us to learn from this story of the rai stone money. This will also help us in making sense of bitcoin and blockchain.

3   Darwin's Theory of Evolution by Natural Selection

Darwinian evolution comprises of three steps: Variation – the variants in a new generation doesn't need to be directed, it can be as blind and random as they can. Selection – a criterion to judge the best fit for the environment (this providing direction), and Inheritance – the retention of key traits of the previous generation for a stable cumulative capability of the species.

Natural selection in biology is the different rates of survival and reproduction, due to differences of traits, properties, behavior and products of behavior of individual organisms. When individuals of a species reproduce, regardless if it happens by splitting (for example in microbes) or by combining DNA of two individuals (sexual reproduction, like in most mammals, birds, etc.), there is always a slight chance of a random mutation happening and therefore the resulting individual(s) having new or changed traits, which their "parents" did not have. In some cases, these traits (or changes to them) happen to improve the chances of those individuals who have them to survive and/or reproduce in their current environment, which increases the chance of these traits to be passed on to the offspring. Over time, the traits which enable higher rates of survival/reproduction become prevalent, while "competing" traits subside. As the ability of a trait to enable higher survival/reproduction rate depends on the environment (for example, thick fur might be beneficial in a cold climate, but would be a disadvantage in a hot climate), when individuals of the same species migrate to different environments, they develop different traits over generations. There is no particular moment when a new species is "born" – every offspring belongs to the same species as their parents, yet over a sufficiently long timeframe, the difference in various traits between individuals living in different environments becomes so big, that they cannot be considered the same species anymore [3].

4   History of Blockchain Technology

Blockchain technology was invented in 2008, by a person or group of people under the pseudonym Satoshi Nakamoto, as part of the stateless cryptocurrency called Bitcoin. While cryptocurrencies might be possible without a blockchain, a blockchain cannot exist without a cryptocurrency providing the incentives model and anti-spam measures. There have been recent attempts to redefine the definition of the word "Blockchain" (e.g. so-called "private blockchains") to use it to describe any several-decades-old distributed-ledger technology (DLT) [4].

Bitcoin was released as a white-paper in 2008, and as a working programming code in 2009. As both the code and the white-paper are open-source, this enabled other people to copy Bitcoin while making slight modifications to its code. These modified copies (called "altcoins") are then usually released as open source software as well. While the modifications themselves are artificial, people still naturally select which cryptocurrency they wish to use, as all cryptocurrencies are (at least at the current moment) completely voluntary. This is similar to how traits are selected in nature. There were at least 10,000 paper currencies in circulation in late eighteenth century issued by various banks and corporates.

There have been several notable tries to improve Bitcoin, but most attempts have so far failed to create something better. Here are the few most noteworthy attempts:

Ethereum - a Blockchain based system which enables creation of complex smart contracts and is, by design, Turing-complete. The Turing-completeness, and the fact that all the functionality is implemented on the same layer, is the main flaw of Ethereum, as Turing-completeness hugely increases the attack surface, and everything happening on the same layer ensures that any fault in any single contract affects the whole system. The best example of this was the DAO contract, where a flaw in the contract ultimately resulted in the whole system splitting in two (Ethereum and Ethereum Classic) [5]. A better and long-term viable approach is the one of Bitcoin – keep layer-1 focused only on security, while implementing additional functionality and scalability using layer-2, layer-3, etc. protocols. The functionality of Ethereum has already been implemented in Bitcoin a few months ago, by using a layer-2 protocol called Rootstock [6]. However, just as in the biological world, sometimes a first-mover advantage is sufficient to become the dominant species. If some species already occupy an environment, another species, even if they are more suited to survive in that environment per se, might fail to become dominant, as the species already living in that environment would prevent that. The same could be applied to blockchain, and other technological innovations – quite often the technologically-better solution did not become the dominant one, simply because another technologically-inferior (but "good enough") solution came first.

Peercoin - this is the first cryptocurrency which implemented proof-of-stake consensus mechanism instead of the usually used proof-of-work (on a side note, all fiat currencies can be considered as Proof-of-Labor as well, as the currency in hands prove the amount of labor went into earning that money). Proof-of-stake is based on the users getting more voting power over the current state of the ledger based on the amount of cryptocurrency units that they own, as opposed to proof-of-work, where the voting power is earned by performing complex mathematical calculations. So far, proof-of-stake has proven to be highly unpopular, with Peercoin's capitalization being about 1900 times lower than the capitalization of Bitcoin at the moment of writing [7].

Freicoin - a cryptocurrency which implemented demurrage (a penalty for holding/saving the cryptocurrency units instead of spending them). This has been done to address the claim made by some traditional economists that a deflationary system (like Bitcoin is) would result in "deflationary spiral", as people would not be willing to spend their coins in hopes of the value of those coins rising in the future (in reality however, price increases in Bitcoin correlate with increased, not reduced, number of transactions). In Freicoin, the demurrage fee is about 5% annually, i.e. if a user owns 100 Freicoins, and does not move them for a year, after the year passes they would have 95 Freicoins left. Total capitalization of Freicoin is currently about 545,000 times lower than capitalization of Bitcoin [8].

Monero and Zcash: two cryptocurrencies trying to implement anonymity/privacy improvements, as these features are currently lacking in Bitcoin. These improvements seem to be much more valued by the community than those offered by Peercoin and Freicoin, with the market cap of Monero being about 37 times lower [9] and Zcash being about 115 times lower [10] than that of Bitcoin. The reason why these improvements might not be enough for another cryptocurrency to overtake Bitcoin is that unlike in the animal world, where traits cannot move horizontally between species, in cryptocurrencies any useful feature can be copied and implemented to any other compatible cryptocurrency.

Bitcoin Cash - while not having any technological improvements at all (actually, the opposite is true, as several technological improvements like Segregated Witness and Replace-by-Fee flagging functionality which are present in Bitcoin were removed from Bitcoin Cash), Bitcoin Cash deserves a mention as it was the first cryptocurrency to try a new approach to gain popularity – instead of spending time working on technological improvements (there are currently 3 people working on Bitcoin Cash code [11] as compared to 469 people working on Bitcoin code) [12], the vast majority of time and resources are spent on marketing, spreading misinformation about Bitcoin, and deliberately trying to confuse non-technologically-savvy users into thinking that Bitcoin Cash is the "real" Bitcoin. This approach has worked quite well, as the current capitalization of Bitcoin Cash is only about 7 times lower than that of Bitcoin. This approach has inspired many other new cryptocurrencies to do the same, and currencies such as Bitcoin Gold and Bitcoin Diamond were created. There is also a cryptocurrency called Litecoin Cash, a fork of Litecoin that has been release recently and is current at 219 position based on market capitalization. Such behavior is similar to behaviors of parasites in the biological world, as well as those animals employing camouflage and mimicry to appear to be other species than they actually are, for example insects looking like a branch of a tree, or a non-venomous snake looking like a venomous one.

5 Cryptocurrencies and Natural Selection

There is a Darwinian struggle for survival, between the current cryptocurrency heavyweights. This is a new paradigm that requires money to be decentralized or smart (programmable). Cryptocurrencies possess these traits, gold and fiat currencies do not. Cryptocurrencies have added heightened competition. All currencies are in a state of hyper-evolution. Growing distrust in centralized entities has encouraged many to consider alternatives stores of value. Sovereignty, once a trait necessary for the survival of a currency, has fallen out of favor. Centralized failures have created growing awareness that a decentralized world is possible. Historically, the existence and survival of any entity, be it plant, animal, corporation, or currency is subject to the laws of natural selection. However, there have been several mass-extinction events during the history of life. Such an event happens when the environment changes so drastically and/or so rapidly, that most of the species existing at that time fail to adapt quickly enough and are annihilated. An example of such an event is an asteroid hitting Earth, which made the dinosaurs go extinct. Fiat financial system's mass-extinction event has already occurred. It began with the birth of the Internet, peer to peer technological revolution and the 2008 Financial Crisis. Fiat is sliding into irrelevancy. The internet of money (cryptocurrencies led by Bitcoin) and the Internet-of-Things (IoT) era has already begun. During this period, fiat may very well become extinct and be replaced by cryptocurrencies. The average life of a fiat currency is 27 years. The main reasons for fiat currencies failing are monetary reforms, hyperinflation, wars, and changing geopolitical climates (for example, countries declaring independence). Even without failure, all fiat currencies continually lose value, which was not the case with most commodity-based currencies.

As easy accessibility is needed for currencies to gain widespread acceptance, currently cryptocurrencies still use the on-ramps interacting with the legacy currency systems. While everyone can acquire cryptocurrencies simply by accepting them as payment for their work, goods, or services, a lot of people still choose to use exchanges for purchasing (and selling) cryptocurrencies. These third-party institutions safeguard the private keys and facilitate trades. In a way, they benefited from centralization – governments' acceptance enabled entrepreneurship and investor confidence. Long term, exchanges, especially centralized ones, are not needed at all. Fully decentralized exchanges already exist (not only crypto-to-crypto, but fiat-to-crypto as well), for example Bisq [13].

Markets are not constant – the only constant is fluctuation and change. Market participants must therefore also adapt. While several years ago, the most popular cryptocurrency to be used in Darknet markets has been Bitcoin, recently Monero has become the currency of choice on the Darknet, as it has much better anonymity/privacy features than Bitcoin [14].

The ability to adapt should not be equated to being easily changeable. Sometimes, individuals or species ability to remain unchanged and uninfluenced by outside factors are actually the best adapted to the environment, especially if the environment, and the influencing factors, are harmful. Recently there has been an attack planned to be performed against Bitcoin, named SegWit2x (not to be confused with SegWit). Several largest companies using Bitcoin, and the majority of the miners, have tried to hijack the development of Bitcoin, to give it to their own corporate-backed developers [15]. The whole Bitcoin community fought together to prevent this from happening, and in the end, they were victorious – the attack has been canceled a few weeks before its supposed date [16]. This is similar to what happens in nature, when the whole biotope reacts to and defends from a foreign invader, especially if it threatens to destroy the whole habitat, or a human organism reacting to and defending from a virus.

There are several scenarios of how cryptocurrencies might evolve in the future. One possible way is for one or several largest cryptocurrencies to survive, while all others become obsolete. This is akin to situations in nature, where one or several species become dominant and extinguish other competing species. This can happen even without specifically trying to eradicate another species, an example of which is how Homo Sapiens wiped out Neanderthals by spreading diseases which infected the Neanderthals and sped up their annihilation [17].

Blockchain technology is at an evolutionary juncture. Will the future be dominated by permissioned or permission-less blockchain technology, or could the two coexist? Darwinian history has shown that, competing and analogous species tend to coexist for extended periods of time, until there is a divergence, creating separate species, sometimes ones that are vastly different or sometimes one obliterating the other [21].

The future of blockchain may be a social experiment for betterment of humanity [22]. These solutions could be either benevolent, or malevolent, or both. As the world becomes more polarized and populism ascends [23], nation states and countries might choose individual interests and self-preservation.

Private and consensus blockchains [24], might be given exclusive legitimacy. These blockchains' efficiency benefits could be exploited but their permissioned qualities, that are inherently centralized and hierarchical, where monopolistic and oligopolistic tendencies thrive, will be promoted. Russia might issue its own state cryptocurrency [25]. China, in theory, has heavily regulated its domestic cryptocurrency space, but in practice, it still wants to utilize the benefits of the technology, albeit within the sphere of China's control and centralized infrastructure.

Nation states and countries if they provide the infrastructure that solves the "last mile issue", could permit blockchain technology to evolve, but it would be in a permissioned ecosystem, that will be highly censored and nationalistic.

Another possibility is for thousands of cryptocurrencies to continue to exist, in an interconnected and inter-operable way (cryptocurrencies are already very easily inter-operable), for example using some sort of meta-protocol to easily move between cryptocurrencies. Such technology already exists and is called Atomic Swaps (although for it to be able to be used, both cryptocurrencies must support the Lightning Network, so as a prerequisite for that they both need SegWit or another type of transaction malleability fix integrated). This is similar to how in nature different species develop equilibrium and symbiotic inter-species relationships, helping each other to find food, shelter, or otherwise improving each other's odds of survival [18].

What is clear, regardless of how the cryptocurrency and blockchain landscape evolves, blockchain technology will be used more and more widely in the future, as it offers huge benefits for companies, such as cost reduction, increased traceability, disintermediation, censorship resistance, data immutability, and other [19].

6 Future Evolution of Crypto and Blockchain

New cryptocurrencies will continue being created and will keep trying to improve on various aspects of cryptocurrencies and Blockchain technology. However, there might soon come a time where new methods of such software evolving will be possible. One of the most likely cases of where/how it might happen is ransomware. Ransomware is a computer software which locks (encrypts) files on a user's computer without their consent, and then requests a ransom to be paid in cryptocurrency to unlock the files. Such software also tries to spread itself to other computers using various methods, such as emailing itself to all contacts in the original user's contact book, trying to look for network vulnerabilities to be able to spread to other computers connected to the same network etc. [20]. While at the moment such software is created by some particular developer or group of developers, and spreads without making any random changes in itself, it might be possible to develop ransomware which would make random changes in its code before spreading, therefore emulating biological evolution.

Another method would be to create modular ransomware software which would function completely autonomously, and which would use the money collected from ransoms to hire programmers to improve it, as well as purchase hosting, VPN access, or any other services which might improve its chance to collect more ransoms. If it was modular, any improvement made by a particular programmer could be made in such a way that the programmer who codes the particular change would receive some part of the ransom money as well, thus incentivizing programmers to work on such software. While this method would be a little bit different from the biological evolution than the aforementioned method of random changes, it would still be closer to biological evolution than the current traditional methods of software development.

If we ignore the current limitations of blockchain technology, the future might look even more promising than described above. Security of the Internet-of-Things is an issue. In the world of the smart city, with many IoT devices transmitting information, security will be of utmost importance. Technology has been evolving rapidly, but security has lagged [26]. If IoT devices malfunction or are sabotaged – the results can be fatal. Self-flying airplanes crashing, mistakes during automated surgery, lift bridges opening at the wrong time, etc. It is predicted that the blockchain can resolve IoT's security issues. As one potential solution, IoT devices could be embedded with Plantoids – a Blockchain-Based Artificial Life. Plantoids are autonomous entities which are completely independent and self-sufficient. An ecosystem designed for spontaneous Darwinian-like evolution. The non-visible part of a Plantoid is a DAO – a Distributed Autonomous Organization with a set of smart contracts that manage the Plantoid's life cycle and reproduction [27].

Environment has a huge impact in Darwinian-like evolution. Some male insects elicit dominance in their environment and assure the propagation of their genes. For example, bees and fruit flies, influence the behavior and physiology of their female mates, when they inject semen into them [28]. In the case of the female fruit fly, after she is impregnated, her rate of egg laying increases, her receptivity to mating with other fruit fly's decreases, and her life span shortens. She also stores the male fruit fly's sperm, thus guaranteeing future continuance of his genes. Darwin natural selection-survival of the fittest is at play in these insects' mating ritual, ultimately controlling the fertility of unwanted insects [29].

Plantoid entities in IoT devices are in many ways like insects; the dominant and most effective and efficient iterations will be the preferred choices to be embedded (impregnated) into IoT devices. Thus, these Plantoids, like those lucky bees and fruit flies, will propagate. Lesser Plantoids will be discarded, become extinct. IoT devices will need to navigate very hostile and fluid environments. Plantoid type smart contracts embedded in these devices would need to recalibrate and recreate themselves on the fly. A smart city of the future will not be smart, if its IoT devices continuously collide with each other, or even worse, crash into you. It remains to be seen which cryptocurrencies will fuel these smart contracts. But in Darwinian-like evolution, the one that facilitates the adaption of this technology wins. A cryptocurrency that is used in billions of IoT devices wields enormous influence.

7   Conclusion

Evolution of cryptocurrencies and Blockchain technology has a lot of parallels with the natural world, and in many situations behaves and responds in patterns reminiscent to those seen in nature. As Blockchain technology is based on programming code and can therefore incorporate other innovations made in information technologies, such as artificial intelligence, in the future blockchain technology will most likely follow the laws of natural selection even more closely when it does now and can perhaps even be a part of what we would call a "self-aware" or at least "fully-autonomous" artificial intelligence. We see the digital currencies will be only form where a computer can charge humans for their work. We like to extend this work further to develop a holistic theory of evolution for crypto currencies keeping in mind Adam Smith's invisible hand and building a framework for blockchain to analyze, monitor and enhance the future evolutionary changes in this space.

References

1. Goldstein, J., Kestenbaum, D.: The Island of stone money. National Public Radio. http://www.npr.org/blogs/money/2011/02/15/131934618/the-island-of-stone-money. Accessed 17 Feb 2018
2. Nakamoto, S.: Bitcoin: a peer-to-peer electronic cash system (2008). https://bitcoin.org/bitcoin.pdf. Author, F.: Article title. Journal 2(5), 99–110 (2016)
3. Darwin, C.: On the Origin of Species by Means of Natural Selection, or the Preservation of Favoured Races in the Struggle for Life. John Murray, London (2003). Modern reprint Darwin, C., Huxley, J.: On The Origin of Species. Signet Classics. ISBN 0-451-52906-5
4. Sheth, A.P., Larson, J.A.: Federated database systems for managing distributed, heterogeneous, and autonomous databases. ACM 22(3), 183–236 (1990). https://doi.org/10.1145/96602.96604
5. Wirdum, A.V.: Ethereum's DAO forking crisis: the Bitcoin perspective. Bitcoin Mag. https://bitcoinmagazine.com/articles/ethereum-s-dao-forking-crisis-the-bitcoin-perspective-1467404395/. Accessed 17 Feb 2018
6. Nova Mining: Rootstock (RSK): Smart contracts on Bitcoin. Medium. https://medium.com/novamining/rootstock-rsk-smart-contracts-on-bitcoin-9ef28e135193. Accessed 14 Dec 2018
7. Peercoin (PPC): CoinMarketCap. https://coinmarketcap.com/currencies/peercoin/. Accessed 17 Feb 2018
8. Freicoin (FRC): CoinMarketCap. https://coinmarketcap.com/currencies/freicoin/. Accessed 17 Feb 2018
9. Monero (XMR): CoinMarketCap. https://coinmarketcap.com/currencies/monero/. Accessed 19 Feb 2018
10. Zcash (ZEC): CoinMarketCap. https://coinmarketcap.com/currencies/zcash/. Accessed 17 Feb 2018
11. Bitcoin Cash Developer Chart: CoinGecko. https://www.coingecko.com/en/coins/bitcoin-cash/developer. Accessed 17 Feb 2018
12. Bitcoin Developer Chart: CoinGecko. https://www.coingecko.com/en/coins/bitcoin/developer. Accessed 17 Feb 2018
13. Bisq – The P2P Exchange Network. https://bisq.network/. Accessed 17 Feb 2018
14. DHS says darknet criminals are switching from Bitcoin to Monero. Deep Dot Web. https://www.deepdotweb.com/2017/09/20/dhs-says-darknet-criminals-switching-bitcoin-monero/. Accessed 15 Feb 2018
15. Yago, E.: Bitcoin's bogeyman cometh: why SegWit2x is a 51% attack. CoinDesk. https://www.coindesk.com/bitcoins-bogeyman-cometh-segwit2x-51-attack/. Accessed 17 Feb 2018
16. Suberg, W.: SegWit2x is dead, long live Bitcoin! price hits all-time high as hard fork canceled. Cointelegraph. https://cointelegraph.com/news/segwit2x-is-dead-long-live-bitcoin-price-hits-all-time-high-as-hard-fork-canceled. Accessed 17 Feb 2018

17. Perry, P.: What killed off the Neanderthals? You might not like the answer. Big Think. http://bigthink.com/philip-perry/guess-what-killed-off-the-neanderthals-you-might-not-like-the-answer. Accessed 17 Feb 2018
18. McElroy, K.: Symbiosis: when living together is win-win. Cosmos. https://cosmosmagazine.com/social-sciences/symbiosis-when-living-together-win-win. Accessed 17 Feb 2018
19. Marr, B.: 5 Blockchain opportunities no company can afford to miss. Forbes. https://www.forbes.com/sites/bernardmarr/2018/02/07/5-blockchain-opportunities-no-company-can-afford-to-miss. Accessed 17 Feb 2018
20. Bull, G.: Blockchain: a solution in search of a problem? Retrieved from consultative group to assist the poor. http://www.cgap.org/blog/blockchain-solution-search-problem. Accessed 29 May 2018
21. Darwin, C.: The Origin of Species by Means of Natural Selection (1917)
22. Kakushadze, Z., Liew, J.K.-S.: CryptoRuble: from Russia with love. Retrieved from CryptoRuble: From Russia with Love Risk, January 2018, Zura Kakushadze Quantigic Solutions LLC; Free University of Tbilisi Jim Kyung-Soo Liew Johns Hopkins University - Carey Business Scho, pp. 53–54, 20 Pages Posted: 26 Oct 2017 (2018). Accessed 17 Jan 2018
23. Lu, D.L.: Bitcoin: speculative bubble, financial risk and regulatory response. Butterworths J. Int. Bank. Finan. Law, March 2018. https://www.researchgate.net/profile/Lerong_Lu/publication/323874289_Bitcoin_Speculative_Bubble_Financial_Risk_and_Regulatory_Response/links/5ab0fb0aa6fdcc1bc0bee3b6/Bitcoin-Speculative-Bubble-Financial-Risk-and-Regulatory-Response.pdf
24. Proteous, D.: Banking and the last mile: technology and the distribution of financial services in developing countries. World Bank (2006)
25. Sawson, T.: Consensus-as-a-service: a brief report on the emergence of permissioned, distributed ledger systems (2015)
26. What is ransomware? Trend Micro USA. https://www.trendmicro.com/vinfo/us/security/definition/ransomware. Accessed 17 Feb 2018
27. Prisco, G.: Plantoids: the first blockchain-based artificial life forms. Bitcoin Mag. https://bitcoinmagazine.com/articles/plantoids-the-first-blockchain-based-artificial-life-forms-1482768916/. Accessed 17 Feb 2018
28. Colonello, N.A., Hartfelder, K.: She's my girl - male accessory gland products and their function in the reproductive biology of social bees. Apidologie 36, 231–244 (2005)
29. Wolfner, M.F.: Tokens of love: functions and regulation of drosophila male accessory gland products. 27(3), 179–192 (1997). Elsevier. https://doi.org/10.1016/S0965-1748(96)00084-7

Blockchain-Based Internet Voting: Systems' Compliance with International Standards

Jordi Cucurull$^{(\boxtimes)}$, Adrià Rodríguez-Pérez, Tamara Finogina, and Jordi Puiggalí

Scytl Secure Electronic Voting S.A., C. Enric Granados 84,
08008 Barcelona, Spain
{jordi.cucurull,adria.rodriguez,tamara.finogina,jordi.puiggali}@scytl.com

Abstract. Blockchain has emerged as the technology claiming to change the way services are delivered nowadays, from banking to public administrations. The field of elections, and specifically internet voting, is not an exception. As a distributed audit layer, it is expected that blockchain technology will provide more transparency to such services, while preventing that a simple agent can tamper with electoral electronic data. Elections require a challenging combination of privacy and integrity. However, a system that would store ballots in clear on a public blockchain, while transparent, would not comply with secret suffrage, one key principle for democratic elections. For this reason, the motivation of this paper is to assess the potential of blockchain technology in internet voting. To this end we analyse several blockchain-based internet voting systems and their degree of compliance against a set of commonly accepted properties of internet voting, namely those of the Council of Europe. This has allowed us to identify a set of common features and challenges on how blockchain can contribute to the conduct of e-enabled elections.

Keywords: Blockchain · Privacy · Verifiability · e-Voting
Council of Europe · Survey

1 Introduction

In the last years, blockchain has emerged as the technology claiming to change the way services are provided. From banking [27] to public administrations [8], several applications are emerging whose underlying technology is blockchain. The field of elections, and specifically internet voting, is another example. As a distributed audit layer, it is argued that blockchain technology will improve the transparency of such services, while preventing that a simple agent can tamper with electoral electronic data. On the other hand, however, elections require a challenging combination of privacy and integrity [10]. Thus, systems that would store ballots in clear on a public blockchain, while transparent, would not comply with secret suffrage, one of the key principles for democratic elections. In this

© Springer Nature Switzerland AG 2019
W. Abramowicz and A. Paschke (Eds.): BIS 2018 Workshops, LNBIP 339, pp. 300–312, 2019.
https://doi.org/10.1007/978-3-030-04849-5_27

context, the paper enquires whether blockchain-based internet voting meets the requirements for democratic elections.

Thus, in Sect. 2 we will first identify which criteria should be used as the properties that an internet voting system is expected to comply with. To do so, we will analyse the standards of the Council of Europe, and especially the recently updated Recommendation Rec(2017)5 on standards for e-voting. Following, Sect. 3 of the paper analyses in detail different proposals for blockchain-based voting. Finally, in Sect. 4 we compare these systems against the properties identified, and identify common trends and challenges on how blockchain can contribute to the conduct of e-enabled elections and referendums. Therefore, our main contribution is an analysis on whether several blockchain-based internet voting systems comply with a set of accepted properties.

2   International Standards on i-Voting

The principles for democratic elections are well established in international human rights instruments [17]. Its first expression in contemporary international law can be found in the Universal Declaration of Human Rights [29], enshrined in its article 21. However, and due to the lack of juridical value of the Declaration, this right will not be considered as such until its later inclusion in article 25 of the International Covenant on Civil and Political Rights (ICCPR) [30]. Several regional human rights instruments have also embraced such right. It is the case, for instance, of the European Convention on Human Rights (ECHR), which in its Protocol I, article 3, requires "[t]he High Contracting Parties [...] to hold free elections at reasonable intervals by secret ballot, under conditions which will ensure the free expression of the opinion of the people in the choice of the legislature" [11]. Yet, such rights tend to be described in general terms, requiring for elections to be held "by secret ballot" and "to ensure the free expression" (ECHR), or "by universal and equal suffrage", "held by secret ballot" and "guaranteeing the free expression of the will of the people" (ICCPR). Thus, they do not allow us to evaluate whether an internet voting system is compliant with their provisions or not.

2.1   The Council of Europe's Recommendation Rec(2017)5 on e-Voting

Electronic voting in general and internet voting in particular are neither generally permitted by human rights nor ruled out a priori. Instead, its acceptability depends on the standards implemented in the process [16]. At the same time, the Council of Europe claims to be the only organisation that has set intergovernmental standards in the field of e-voting[1]. The Council adopted a first

---

[1] See for instance: https://www.coe.int/en/web/electoral-assistance/e-voting. On their side, other authors are more cautious and argue that "Rec(2004)11 [was] the only international document regulating e-voting from a legal perspective" [28] or that "[t]he Council of Europe is the only international organisation to have issued recommendations on the regulation of the use of e-voting" [14].

recommendation already in 2004, setting clear requirements for those elections that involved "the use of electronic means in at least the casting of the vote" [23]. Years later, however, it was acknowledged that there was a need to update the Recommendation Rec(2004)11 of the Committee of Ministers to member states on legal, operational and technical standards for e-voting [18]. As a result, and after two years of update works, the Council of Europe adopted a new recommendation. The Rec(2017)5 of the Committee of Ministers to member States on standards for e-voting [22]. The new Recommendation contains legal standards on e-voting which set objectives that e-voting systems shall fulfil to conform to the principles of democratic elections [14]. Thus, the Recommendations sets standards on what an e-voting system is required to do [19], while leaving how each standard is achieved to be defined in national regulations. Such standards are grouped under each of the five principles for democratic elections, as identified by the Venice Commission in its Code of Good Practice in Electoral Matters [15], namely: universal, equal, free, and secret suffrage[2]. Since the goal of this paper is to evaluate whether blockchain-based internet voting proposals can meet the requirements of democratic elections, the standards of the new Recommendation seem like a good place to start our analysis. At the same time, however, it is necessary to take into account that national regulations may require additional principles to those identified in the Recommendation [12], and that these national regulations may set clear technical requirements on how each standard is to be achieved [9]. Following, we list the main standards that have been identified as applicable to blockchain-based internet voting from the Rec(2017)5[3]:

- **Safe aggregation:** Where electronic and non-electronic voting channels are used in the same election or referendum, there shall be a secure and reliable method to aggregate all votes and to calculate the result.
- **Authentication:** Unique identification of voters in a way that they can unmistakably be distinguished from other persons shall be ensured. The e-voting system shall only grant access after authenticating a person with the right to vote.
- **Equal voting rights:** The e-voting system shall ensure that only the appropriate number of votes per voter is cast and stored in the electronic ballot box and included in the election result.

---

[2] No specific standards are considered for the fifth principle (direct suffrage), nor for the fre-quency of elections. On the other side, the Recommendation does identify a set of standards that could be linked to the procedural guarantees that the Code considers as part of the European Electoral Heritage, i.e. respect for fundamental rights, regulatory levels and stability of electoral law and other procedural safeguards.

[3] We may have excluded some standards, mainly because they refer to the user interface of an e-voting system (which is client-side, and thus has little to do with the use of blockchain technology). This is the case of standards 1, 2 and 4, for example. We have also excluded the standards related to Regulatory and organisational requirements, Transparency and observation, Accountability nor Reliability and security of the system, since they do not refer to what an e-voting system is supposed to do, but rather to how national legislation should include when it comes to regulate e-voting and/or to procedural guarantees on how the standards can be audited and certified.

- **Integrity:** The voter's intention shall not be affected by the voting system, or by any undue influence.
- **Vote correctness:** The e-voting system shall advise the voter when casting an invalid e-vote.
- **Cast-as-Intended verifiability:** The voter shall be enabled to verify that his or her intention is accurately represented in the vote. Any undue influence that has modified the vote can be detected.
- **Recorded-as-Cast verifiability:** The voter shall be enabled to verify that the sealed vote has entered the electronic ballot box without being altered. Any undue influence that has modified the vote can be detected.
- **Counted-as-Recorded verifiability:** The e-voting system shall provide sound evidence that each authentic vote is accurately included in the respective election results. The evidence should be verifiable by means independent from the system.
- **Eligibility:** The system shall provide sound evidence that only eligible voters' votes have been included in the respective final result. The evidence should be verifiable by means that are independent from the e-voting system.
- **Confidentiality:** E-Voting shall be organized in such a way as to ensure at any stage of the voting procedure that the secrecy of the vote is respected.
- **Receipt-freeness:** An e-voting system shall not provide the voter with a proof of the content of the vote cast for use by third parties.
- **Election fairness:** The e-voting system shall not allow the disclosure to anyone of the number of votes cast for any voting option until after the closure of the electronic ballot box. This information shall not be disclosed to the public until after the end of the voting period.
- **Anonymity:** The e-voting process, in particular the counting stage, shall be organised in such a way that it is not possible to reconstruct a link between the unsealed vote and the voter. Votes are and remain anonymous.

2.2 Beyond the Council of Europe Standards: A Critical Account of Rec(2017)5

At this point it is also worth mentioning some limitations that we have identified when it comes to the new Recommendation by the Council of Europe. Specifically, there are two properties that should be additionally required to any internet voting system, namely: long-term privacy and scalability.

- **Long-term privacy:** Standards related to secret suffrage in the new Recommendation require that confidentiality is preserved at any stage during the voting procedure, while anonymity focuses on the counting stage. Yet, it is worth considering whether privacy and anonymity should be required even when an election has concluded. If we take into account the rationale behind secret suffrage, i.e. to ensure that voters are able to express their opinion freely [24], one could argue that such properties should be also preserved after election time. As a matter of fact, and with a view to preserve this, paper-based voting regulations usually require for paper ballots to be destroyed after the counting has concluded. The threat of a future breach of voter anonymity is especially accurate in internet voting, where votes are digitally signed while encrypted to provide the properties of integrity and eligibility as described above. In current internet voting systems, key-sharing schemes are combined with encryption to prevent that votes can be decrypted before they are anonymized, since such a process would require several agents to collude and reconstruct the election private key [25]. Yet, the complexity of current encryption schemes relay on the insufficient computation power of conventional computers to break them. This would not preclude, however, that a quantum computer, whose computing power is expected to be much greater, would be able to easily break such encryption schemes based on a brute force attack and compromise the anonymity as preserved in current internet voting. Since the information stored in a blockchain can never be deleted or modified, the risk of breaking voters' anonymity in the long-term is specially accrued to these systems.

- **Scalability:** One of the key principles for democratic elections is universality, meaning the right of all adult citizens to vote in a given election. At the same time, blockchains are well know for its limited scalability. To put an example, Bitcoin's blockchain takes around 10 mins to confirm a transaction and has a global throughput of 7 transactions per second [13]. If we take into account the number of voters that may have the right to cast a vote during an election, and a system only allows one voter to cast their vote at a time, while requiring a n-minutes delay for a voter to cast their vote after another, one could well consider that such system is actually preventing voters from expressing their free will. Thus, we consider scalability as a key standard for democratic elections.

3   Blockchain-Based Internet Voting Systems

In what follows we describe a set of blockchain-based internet voting proposals in order to assess whether they are compliant with the properties identified above[4].

3.1   FollowMyVote

FollowMyVote [1] is an electronic voting system implemented on top of the financial platform BitShares, which is based on a blockchain implemented with the Graphene software[5]. Each vote is represented as a transaction in the blockchain which is associated to a digital asset for the election and that consumes a certain amount of fees.

Voters' anonymity and authenticity is based on the use of two pairs of keys for signing the votes using Elliptic Curve Cryptography. No vote encryption is provided. One of the pairs is related to the voter identity while the other is

---

[4] While we have aimed at being exhaustive, we have selected those systems for which information was available at the time of writing this paper.

[5] http://docs.bitshares.eu/.

not. Both pairs are known to be linked, but the exact mapping of pairs remains unknown. As they describe in their website, FollowMyVote uses a blind signature approach, where the Identity Verifier signs a blind token and, later, a Registrar signs the unblinded token. However, it is unclear how the Registrar can be sure that this last token is related to the first one. One would expect some type of Zero Knowledge Proof, however no details are provided. Then the token is included in the vote cast.

Verifiability and auditability are provided off-the-shelf, because votes are published in the blockchain without encryption. Thus, voters can check whether their individual vote is correctly recorded and counted. However, this approach enables the computation of partial results before the end of the election and enables vote selling and coercion.

3.2   XO.1 SecureVote

The XO.1 Secure Vote [5] is a fully decentralised electronic voting system[6], that is currently based on Ethereum's blockchain and InterPlanetary File System (IPFS) for the storage of the votes. Its authors claim to have a solution for guaranteeing voters' anonymity based on an engine called Copperfield[7]. The voting is conducted via a smartphone application. Once the votes are received by the voting system servers, they are stored in ballot boxes that are aggregated into data structures called pallets, which are published to the IPFS distributed filesystem and anchored to the blockchain. The system is verifiable and its source code is available on GitLab[8].

The voter authentication and authenticity of the votes is guaranteed because each voter has two pairs of keys, one related to the voter's identity, which is the one whitelisted in the electoral roll, and another one that is ephemeral. The votes cast are signed with a voter's ephemeral key. Two processes of shuffle are performed: the first is to break the relation between the voter identity keys and the voter ephemeral keys; and the second is to break the relation between the votes and their signatures. The CoinShuffle algorithm [26] or a Mixnet can be used for this purpose.

The speed and scalability are ensured by encapsulating ballot boxes in pallets during the voting phase. These pallets, which may account for 10-100 MBs, are stored in IPFS, which provides off-the-shelf immutability when combined with blockchain. Each pallet includes a header that is used to link pallets among them and to anchor them in the blockchain. Since the immutabilisation in the blockchain is done at the granularity level of a pallet, the number of blockchain transactions used is much smaller than in systems where each vote is stored within a transaction. This allows the system to be highly scalable. As a matter

---

[6] https://gitlab.com/exo-one/svst-docker/blob/master/svst-docs/secure.vote.white. napkin.md.

[7] The process for a patent application was initially launched, although it was discontinued later on. See Australian Patent 2017900257.

[8] https://github.com/swarmfund/sv-voting-mvp.

of fact, their authors claim that the system can hold up to 10 million votes per minute, as demonstrated in a stress test run in March 2017[9].

The data of the system is public, thus it can be easily audited. For each vote cast, a receipt is returned. The receipt is composed of a nonce and the location of the vote. The authors claim the receipt is not cryptographic to prevent breaking voter secrecy. In addition, a mechanism called Duress mode is included to prevent coercion. The mechanism allows voters to obtain a receipt of a different vote. So they can show the contents of another vote to the coercer. This is based on giving the voter a real and a non-real PIN. The non-real PIN presents a vote that is not the one actually counted.

3.3 Votem CastIron

Votem has an electronic voting system called CastIron [4], which is built on top of a custom blockchain based on a Proof-of-Authority consensus algorithm[10]. The votes are registered in individual transactions of a private blockchain run by several trusted voting authority partners. Mobile apps and a desktop website are the voting channels provided for voters to cast their vote.

Voter authenticity is provided by means of third party authenticators that sign the voters' pseudonym if they have correctly authenticated. When the votes are cast they are also signed by the voter, although no information is provided about the key used to sign them. Voters' anonymity and confidentiality, as well as election fairness, are provided through the use of ElGamal vote encryption and later by mixing the ballots during the counting process.

The system is end-to-end verifiable. It provides Cast-as-Intended verifiability through two mechanisms based on the Cast-or-Challenge validation mechanisms (one directly executed by the voter and another one distributed and executed by several servers), i.e. the voter is offered the possibility to decrypt the vote and verify the selections encrypted were correct or cast the vote. This process can be repeated a number of times until the voter is convinced that the system is honest and then they cast a real vote. It can provide Recorded-as-Cast verifiability through a Public Verifier, which is a node with read-only access to the transactions of the blockchain. Finally, it offers Counted-as-Recorded verifiability by means of Zero Knowledge Proofs that ensure the correctness of the mixing and decryption processes during the counting stage.

Anti-coercion measures consist of (1) allowing multiple voting and counting only the last vote cast, to prevent the over-the-shoulder coercion, and (2) separate multiple contest ballots in multiple independent ballots, to prevent the Italian attack.

3.4 Polys

Polys [2] is an electronic voting system based on ElGamal encryption and the Ethereum blockchain technology. When a voter wants to cast a vote, the vote

---

[9] https://bit.ly/2J6EqIK.
[10] https://en.wikipedia.org/wiki/Proof-of-authority.

is signed with a key that is an alias of the voter. The aliases are present in the electoral roll of the system, thus ensuring that only one vote per voter is finally counted and keeping (or preserving) voters' anonymity. The votes are encrypted with an Election Key, of which the private part is divided in multiple shares given to the electoral board members. Then the vote is cast as an Ethereum transaction that is immutabilised in the blockchain. When the election finishes, an homomorphic tallying is performed, i.e. the encrypted votes are multiplied, the result decrypted and then the Shanks' algorithm (used to perform the logarithm of the decrypted data) applied to obtain the final results. The system is based on the use of a private Ethereum blockchain (at least in its Pro version according to their website). This ensures escalability, since it is not subject to the performance constrains of a public blockchain. However, at the same time this reduces the security strength offered by its immutabilisation.

3.5 Voatz

Voatz [3] is an electronic voting system based on blockchain about whose authors have not published any technical information. In commercial videos, they claim it is secure, tamperproof and that it provides voter anonymity and vote verifiability (without stating which type). The system includes facilities for voter registration direclty from the smartphone, by providing biometric features such as the voter fingerprint and picture. No information is provided regarding the type of blockchain used.

3.6 Agora

Agora is a blockchain-based electronic voting system that provides end-to-end encryption and verifiability. A high level description of the system [7] and code are available[11]. The system is based on a permissioned blockchain, which includes a set of write permissioned nodes called Cothority and a Byzantine consensus mechanism called SkipChain [21]. All the information produced in the voting system, including ballots, configuration and consensus proofs, are immutabilised in this blockchain. In addition, this blockchain is immutabilised in a tamper-resistant append-only log called Catena [31] which is built on top of the Bitcoin blockchain.

The system guarantees the anonymity of voters, the authenticity and secrecy of the votes and it is designed to prevent coercion and vote buying. The anonymity of the votes is based on the use of the Neff-shuffle-based [20] mix-net.

The electronic voting system also provides all the verifiability properties desirable in an electronic voting system, i.e. Cast-as-Intended, Recorded-as-Cast and Counted-as-Recorded verifiability. The Cast-as-Intended property is achieved by a Cast-or-Challenge validation mechanism. This process can be repeated a number of times until the voter is convinced that the system is honest and then they cast a real vote. The Recorded-as-Cast verifiability is achieved

---

[11] https://github.com/agoravoting/agoravoting-project/wiki.

by the voters verifying that the encrypted vote is correctly published in the blockchain. The Counted-as-Recorded verifiability is ensured by accessing to the data used during the counting period and because of the availability of the Zero-Knowledge Proofs produced by the mixing and the decryption processes.

Agora introduces a token called VOTE that is given as a reward to auditors and observers for validating election data and for checking election transactions respectively. At the beginning of each election, a new bonus pool for the mentioned incentives is created and funded by the customers of the system.

3.7   Horizon State

Horizon State is a platform for community engagement and it supports voting. The authors claim that the system is secure and auditable, since all the ballots are published in the blockchain and cannot be manipulated. The whitepaper [6] that describes the platform does not mention whether ballots are encrypted, which raises doubts about the robustness of the voter anonymity and confidentiality offered by the system and the fact that it may be possible to get results before the election has finished. The authors claim that their solution has been already used in commercially available systems, specifically in the voting application MiVote[12] of Australia. It is worth mentioning that in the website of this system the use of encryption is mentioned. Further, it is unclear what verifiability properties are provided.

The platform is built on top of Ethereum and makes use of a custom ERC20 token[13] called Decision Token (HST). Each vote cast is stored as an Ethereum transaction, which makes the system not scalable to nation-wide elections. However, their authors mention several proposals, such as the Raiden Network off-chain scaling solution[14], in which Ethereum developers are working that may increase the performance.

4   Discussion

Table 1 summarises which of the identified properties in Sect. 2 are claimed to be implemented by the blockchain-based internet voting systems of Sect. 3.

Most of the systems do not provide the safe-aggregation property, thus they cannot be integrated into a transitioning context where multiple election channels are deployed (e.g. a paper-ballot election). In most cases, safe-aggregation is impossible to achieve due to the way in which voters' anonymity is provided. If the vote is cast with an anonymised identifier, it is impossible to identify which votes have to be discarded because we cannot relate them with the voters that have already cast a vote through a different channel.

As expected, all the systems claim to offer voter authentication and voter anonymity. These are two very basic requirements of electoral systems. The

---

[12] https://www.mivote.org.au/.

[13] https://github.com/ethereum/EIPs/blob/master/EIPS/eip-20.md.

[14] https://raiden.network/.

Table 1. Properties of the blockchain voting systems analyzed

	Safe-aggregation	Authentication	Authentication type	Equal voting rights	Integrity	Vote correctness	Cast-as-Intended	Recorded-as-Cast	Counted-as-Recorded	Eligibility	Confidentiality	Receipt freeness	Election fairness	Anonymity	Long-term Privacy	Scalability
FollowMyVote	○	●	A	●	●	○	●	●	●	●	○	○[a]	○	●	●	○
XO.1 SecureVote	○	●	B	●	●	○	●	●	○	●	●	●	●	●	○	●[b]
Votem	●	●	C	●	●	(2)	●	●	●	●	●	○[c]	●	●	○[d]	●
Polys	○	●	D	●	●	●	○	?	?	●	●	●	●	●	○	●
Voatz	?	●	E	(1)	●	?	?	?	?	●	?	?	?	●	○	?
Agora	(1)	●	C	(1)	●	○	●	●	●	●	●	●	●	●	○	●
Horizon State	?	●	?	?	●	?	?	?	?	?	○	?	○	●	○	○

Legend: ● Implemented ○ Not implemented ? No information. *Types of authentication*: A) Blockchain identity with a pair of keys, B) Pair of keys, C) 3rd party authentication, D) Token + Ethereum pair of keys, E) Several authentication attributes. *Notes*: (1) Not explicitly mentioned, but the architecture allows it. (2) Only when the distributed Cast-as-Intended mechanism is used

[a] However, the vote can be revoked
[b] 10 million votes/min
[c] But multiple voting is possible
[d] But votes are in a private blockchain

former prevents multiple voting by the same voter and unauthorized voters from participation in the election, while the latter ensures that a ballot cannot be linked to a particular voter. Furthermore, there is no single type of authentication mechanism used. However, in most of the cases the voter always has or obtains a pair of keys to sign the vote.

Integrity is provided by all the systems as it is an off-the-shelf property of any blockchain. However, almost no system provides vote correctness. The only one that directly offers this property is Polys, since it implements homomorphic tally and it is customary from this type of system. Votem can also verify correctness, but only if the distributed Cast-as-Intended protocol is used (and for votes that will not be counted).

All the systems provide auditability, but not all of them provide specific verifiability mechanisms. For example, Polys does not provide Cast-as-Intended verifiability and it does not seem to provide Counted-as-Recorded verifiability (considering the documentation available). Others provide specific mechanisms, such as Votem or Agora.Vote. And one of the systems, FollowMyVote, provides full verifiability, but at the expense of storing all the votes in plaintext, which breaks the election fairness property.

In general, most of the systems encrypt the votes before they are cast in order to guarantee the properties of confidentiality and election fairness. However, there are exceptions (e.g. FollowMyVote or HorizonState). In some cases, no information is provided on whether encryption is used (i.e. Voatz).

While all the systems make use of blockchains, their scalability varies and depends on system's design. For example, FollowMyVote is not scalable because it stores each vote in a different transaction and makes use of a public blockchain, which usually has constrains on the number of transaction per second that can be accepted for all its users. Other systems, such as Votem, Polys and Agora.Vote, despite storing each vote in a different transaction, are considered to be scalable because they use a private or permissioned blockchain that is dedicated to the election system, thus not subject to strong performance constraints. And other systems, such as XO.1 Secure Vote, store the votes off-chain and generates a proof of integrity that is the data actually stored in the blockchain. Proofs of integrity, e.g. a hash, are much smaller than a vote and can be issued less frequently. Therefore, the requirements for the use of blockchain are much smaller than its constraints.

Assuming that the anonymisation mechanism is strong, only one of the blockchain voting systems can be considered to support Long-term Privacy: FollowMyVote, because it is the only system that uses a voter anonymity mechanism that is not based on encryption. The rest of them use encryption algorithms to protect the votes that are not quantum-resistant. As a consequence, the systems that make the actual votes public and immutable are subject to a potential future privacy breach, i.e. if the votes are public and immutable, there may also be available in the future when the quantum computers are ready to break their encryption algorithms. If the votes are not public or at least available only to authorized auditors, such as in Votem, the effects of a possible future encryption breach can be reduced.

5 Conclusions

In this paper, we have identified the set of core principles for democratic elections and also analyzed the main properties of seven blockchain-based electronic voting systems. This has showed us to obtain several insights.

First, almost half of the analyzed systems do not seem to be compatible with other traditional voting channels, i.e. no safe-aggregation, such as on-site paper or postal voting. Also, vote correctness is not covered by almost any system since in most cases an incorrect ballot can be detected only during a vote-counting procedure. Another controversial aspect is scalability, which can hinder their adoption for large elections. Systems that map one vote to one transaction are not scalable in public blockchains due to their low performance. One possible solution is to aggregate several votes into an off-chain database or to use private blockchains and, later, publish integrity proofs or commitments to a public blockchain. However, it is worth mentioning that the security of these solutions might be affected due to the data unavailability to all stakeholders and periodically scheduled immutabilization. Nevertheless, the most relevant conclusion is that the majority of the systems do not provide Long Term Privacy, while keeping the encrypted votes public in blockchains. The combination of non-quantum-resistant cryptography and the immutable publication of the encrypted votes carries significant risks in the long-term. When quantum computers get mature enough, the encryption of those votes could be easily broken and their content revealed. Thus, breaking voters' anonymity in the future. The effects of quantum computer attacks can be mitigated at the expense of reduced verifiability by publishing just the votes' hashes or using a private or permissioned blockchain and restricting the access to auditors and observers only.

Overall, we consider that the blockchain technology can be used to develop electronic voting systems that fulfill almost all the principles for democratic elections. However, we warn researchers against storing votes on public blockchains due to long-term privacy concerns.

References

1. FollowMyVote. https://followmyvote.com/
2. Polys whitepaper. https://polys.me/assets/docs/Polys_whitepaper.pdf
3. Voatz. https://voatz.com/
4. Votem CastIron Whitepaper. https://www.votem.io/#whitePaper
5. XO.1 Secure Vote. https://secure.vote
6. Horizon State (2017). https://horizonstate.com/horizon_state_white_paper.pdf
7. Agora. Agora - bringing our voting systems into the 21st century v0.2. https://agora.vote/Agora_Whitepaper_v0.2.pdf
8. Anand, A., McKibbin, M., Pichel, F.: Colored coins: bitcoin, blockchain, and land administration. Poverty the World Bank - Washington DC, 20–24 March 2017. http://cadasta.org/resources/white-papers/bitcoin-blockchain-land/
9. Barrat, J., Goldsmith, B.: Compliance with international standards: Norwegian e-vote project. Technical report, International Foundation for Electoral Systems, Norwegian E-Vote Project (2012)
10. Bernhard, M., et al.: Public evidence from secret ballots. In: Krimmer, R., Volkamer, M., Braun Binder, N., Kersting, N., Pereira, O., Schürmann, C. (eds.) e-Vote-ID 2017. LNCS, vol. 10615, pp. 84–109. Springer, Cham (2017). https://doi.org/10.1007/978-3-319-68687-5_6
11. Council of Europe. Protocol I to the European Convention on Human Rights and Fundamental Freedoms (1952)
12. Bundesverfassungsgericht (German Constitutional Court). Decision 2 BvC 3/07, 2 BvC 4/07, March 2009
13. Croman, K., et al.: On scaling decentralized blockchains. In: Proceedings of 3rd Workshop on Bitcoin and Blockchain Research (2016)
14. Driza Maurer, A.: Updated European standards for e-voting. In: Krimmer, R., Volkamer, M., Braun Binder, N., Kersting, N., Pereira, O., Schürmann, C. (eds.) E-Vote-ID 2017. LNCS, vol. 10615, pp. 146–162. Springer, Cham (2017). https://doi.org/10.1007/978-3-319-68687-5_9
15. European Commission for Democracy through Law (Venice Commission). Code of good practice on electoral matters - guidelines and explanatory report (2003)
16. Grabenwarter, C.: Report on the compatibility of remote voting and electronic voting with the standards of the council of Europe. Technical report, European Commission for Democracy through Law (Venice Commission) (2004)

17. Lécuyer, Y.: Le droit à des élections libres. Editions du Conseil de l'Europe - Council of Europe Publishing (2014)
18. Driza Maurer, A.: Ten years council of Europe Rec(2004) 11: lessons learned and outlook. In: Krimmer, R., Volkamer, M. (eds.) 6th International Conference on Electronic Voting, Proceedings Electronic Voting 2014 (EVOTE 2014), pp. 111–117. e-Voting. CC GmbH, October 2014
19. Driza Maurer, A.: Report on the scope and format of the update of Rec(2004)11. Technical report, Council of Europe (2015)
20. Neff, C.A.: A verifiable secret shuffle and its application to e-voting. In: Proceedings of the 8th ACM Conference on Computer and Communications Security, CCS 2001, pp. 116–125. ACM, New York (2001)
21. Nikitin, K., et al.: CHAINIAC: proactive software-update transparency via collectively signed skip chains and verified builds. In 26th USENIX Security Symposium (USENIX Security 2017), pp. 1271–1287. USENIX Association, Vancouver (2017)
22. Council of Europe. Recommendation CM/Rec (2017) 5 of the Committee of Ministers to member States on standards for e-voting (2017)
23. Council of Europe. Recommendation Rec (2004) 11 of the Committee of Ministers to member states on legal, operational and technical standards for e-voting (2004)
24. Parliamentary Assembly of the Council of Europe. Resolution 1590 (2007) - Secret ballot - European code of conduct on secret balloting, including guidelines for politicians, observers and voters (2007)
25. Puiggalí, J., Chóliz, J., Guasch, S.: Best practices in internet voting. In: NIST: Workshop on UOCAVA Remote Voting Systems, Washington DC, August 2010
26. Ruffing, T., Moreno-Sanchez, P., Kate, A.: CoinShuffle: practical decentralized coin mixing for bitcoin. In: Kutyłowski, M., Vaidya, J. (eds.) ESORICS 2014. LNCS, vol. 8713, pp. 345–364. Springer, Cham (2014). https://doi.org/10.1007/978-3-319-11212-1_20
27. Scott, B.: How can crypto currency and blockchain technology play a role in building social and solidarity finance? In: UNRISD Working Paper, Geneva (2016)
28. Stein, R., Wenda, G.: The council of Europe and e-voting: history and impact of Rec (2004) 11. In: Krimmer, R., Volkamer, M. (eds.) 6th International Conference on Electronic Voting: Verifying the Vote, EVOTE 2014, Lochau/Bregenz, Austria, 29–31 October 2014, pp. 1–6. IEEE (2014)
29. The United Nations. Universal Declaration of Human Rights, December 1948
30. The United Nations General Assembly: International covenant on civil and political rights. Treaty Ser. **999**, 171 (1966)
31. Tomescu, A., Devadas, S.: Catena: efficient non-equivocation via bitcoin. In: 2017 IEEE Symposium on Security and Privacy (SP), pp. 393–409, May 2017

Chaining Property to Blocks – On the Economic Efficiency of Blockchain-Based Property Enforcement

Janina da Costa Cruz⊙, Aenne Sophie Schröder⁽⊠⁾⊙,
and Georg von Wangenheim⊙

University of Kassel, Blockchain-Center.eu,
Möncheberstr. 1, 34117 Kassel, Germany
aschroeder@uni-kassel.de

Abstract. Within the last two years, much has been written about the blockchain and distributed ledger technologies. However, few actual use cases related to real world phenomena have been proffered in that literature. Most applications remain entirely in the virtual world or their descriptions remain on a very abstract and speculative level. In this paper we study one possible application on the powers of blockchain technology to real-world problems. In particular, we study the economic feasibility, effectiveness and efficiency of blockchain-based registries for property of chattel and the technical enforcement of the rights listed in such registries. For the example of smartphones, we show that their, and their owners' registration in a blockchain may achieve a most desirable results from registration, theft becomes less attractive. An additional advantage, which we also briefly touch on, is that the use of smartphones as collateral without possession may become possible. We study under what conditions the benefits from registration is feasible in a blockchain-based distributed ledger and why they are not implemented under less complex technologies such as registries owned and administered by producers of smartphones.

Keywords: Asset tokenization · Incentive analysis · Blockchain application

1 Introduction

Nearly ten years ago, Satoshi Nakamoto (2008) published his brilliant white paper on the Bitcoin blockchain in which he combined the concepts of blockchains and distributed ledgers with an incentive structure that induces people to run full nodes in a number making it extremely difficult to change the information stored in the blockchain on distributed ledgers and that make it more attractive to strengthen the system than to invade it (Kroll et al. 2013; Chiu 2017). Blockchains have evolved in large numbers and some of them are constructed in a way that induces their users to heavily trust in the immutability of information stored on them. Capabilities of blockchains have grown beyond the mere storage of information up to Turing complete frameworks like Ethereum which allow, inter alia, to design so-called 'smart contracts'.

© Springer Nature Switzerland AG 2019
W. Abramowicz and A. Paschke (Eds.): BIS 2018 Workshops, LNBIP 339, pp. 313–324, 2019.
https://doi.org/10.1007/978-3-030-04849-5_28

The combination of safe storage of information and the possibility to design 'smart contracts' has induced many writers to suggest to establish registers of rights in assets (Swan 2015; Government Office for Science 2016). As the very concept of rights registration of the land register type also rests on the idea of bits of information that are never altered but only amended, it is hardly surprising that several countries, as Sweden (Arruñada 2018; Kairos Future 2017), Georgia (Shin 2016) and Honduras (Collindres et al. 2016; Tapscott and Tapscott 2016) have taken up the idea for the registration of rights in real estate or at least contracts on such rights. However, the proposal to register rights in chattel, receivables and intangible assets has remained on the level of mere suggestions with little details. Proffered in academic journals, popular books and internet forum entries and blogs (Swan 2015; IBM 2016) these proposals lack empirical application and a discussion of their effects on incentive structures as well as costs and benefits of such registration. We strive to contribute to filling this gap from a law-and-economics perspective. Therefore, we study the possibilities of registering ownership of, and other rights in, smartphones in a blockchain. Smartphones are particularly suitable for this discussion as theft does play a major role in their use: The number of stolen smartphones has more than doubled from 2009 (102 023 cases) to 2013 (236 550 cases) (Deutscher Bundestag 2014). They are also specific in that registration of property may technically be intertwined with their functioning, a characteristic which they share with all other technical items that are attached to the internet (for details in the internet of things see Wortmann and Flüchter 2015).

We are aware of the fact that both advantages could also be realized by other modes of registration and therefore start our paper Sect. 2 with a description of such non-blockchain registration possibilities. This allows us to examine the differences between blockchain registration and e.g. proprietary registers of producers of smartphones in the rest of the paper. We continue with a description of some technical details that connect smartphones and their functioning to information in a blockchain. We then Sect. 3 turn to the economics of theft of blockchain-secured smartphones. In our conclusions Sect. 4 we will consider the extension of the concept of blockchain registration of chattel to other movables.

2   Technical Background of Smartphone Registration

Registration of smartphones and incapacitation of stolen phones has been provided by their producers, but the ensuing protection from theft is widely ineffective and technical protection of liens has never been attempted to the best of our knowledge. In this section, we describe the most important efforts in this direction and provide first economic explanations for their failure. We do not discuss purely software-based security applications as it is easy to make them ineffective, sometimes even by simply uninstalling them (Nield 2017). We then suggest a blockchain-based registration mechanism that overcomes most of the reasons for the failure of other registration tools.

2.1 Existing Technical Protection

Based on the International Mobile Equipment Identity (IMEI), a 15-digit number allegedly uniquely identifying smartphones, several firms and non-profit organizations in most countries provide Equipment Identity Registers (EIR) to protect smartphones from theft by interrupting their connectivity to communication networks. The basic principle according to which all existing systems of this kind work is the following. EIR providers produce black, grey and white lists of smartphones' IMEIs (Ministry of Communications of Telecommunications 2017). In the first place, the IMEI is registered in a white list. When an owner reports theft of his or her phone, the IMEI gets grey-listed and after some checks blacklisted. Operators of communication networks are supposed to check the lists whenever a mobile device tries to connect to the network and deny access if the IMEI is black listed (GSMA 2016).

However, the system does not work as imagined for a number of reasons. First of all, the IMEI attached to a smartphone during the production process is unique but it is not impossible to change it (GSMA 2016). Although changing the IMEI is illegal in many countries,[1] a simple google search yields at least five tools and tutorials how to change the IMEI. But even if the IMEI actually were unique and impossible to change, the complex structure of the system would still imply that in the interaction of operators, EIR providers and owners of smartphones a stable equilibrium of non-participation exists, and the system seems to be unable to leave this equilibrium, whether or not another equilibrium exists. Stability of this equilibrium is rooted in several problems of the incentive structures. As the number of EIR providers is large on a world-wide level and the market for stolen smartphones is world-wide operators would have to check a large number of EIRs to safely exclude stolen items from their communication network. As they can only loose from blocking smartphones from traffic, their incentives to participate are minute. In effect, most access providers fail to participate for example in Germany, where only Vodafone checks a small number of EIRs (Bitkom 2014).

2.2 The Blockchain Solution

To solve the problem of lacking operators' incentives to enforce blacklists blocking, we suggest replacing these traditional forms of registration by tokenization in a blockchain and thus provide a workable example for using blockchains as a register for movables with technical enforcement supporting legal rights in assets.

We propose the IMEI to represent the smartphone on the blockchain as a "colored coin" (Swanson 2014). A pair of an IMEI and a public key would be stored on the smartphone as well as on a blockchain. The verification of the identity of owner and possessor could be performed on demand and automatically about every ten minutes by a hardwired component that verifies the identity of the IMEI-public-key-pair on the smartphone with that on the blockchain. If the pairs do not coincide, the smartphone stops working. Of course, this would only work as long as the smartphone and thus the

---

[1] If manipulations of the IMEI serve for being able to use or sell stolen items, e.g. German law even treats this as a criminal offense according to Section 269 of the Criminal Code.

component is connected to the internet. But as smartphones are almost useless in dead spots or in flight mode, the goal of destroying the usability of a smartphone for periods, in which the pairs of IMEI and public key on the blockchain and the component do not match, is still reached if a control can only take place with a working internet connection. If there was a possibility to create a software that fools the hardwired component pretending the smartphone was offline while it was not, the blockchain-mechanism would no longer work while the smartphone would still be fully usable and the whole concept could collapse. That possibility would have to be technically explored and excluded in order to guarantee the effectiveness of the blockchain register.

If the blockchain used for tokenization is safe from invasion and capture either by a proof-of-work mechanism and sufficient size as e.g. the Bitcoin and the Ethereum blockchain or by other mechanisms like permission or proof of stake, the only remaining threat to property proof by blockchain registration are man-in-the-middle attacks, where the attacker fools the smartphone by pretending a fake blockchain with false property information is the real one. If the device requesting authentication from the blockchain is implemented close enough to the hardware, such attack would be difficult as well.

In case of theft, the owner may transfer the IMEI-coin to a different public key of his. Consequently, the pairs of the IMEI and the public key on the blockchain and on the smartphone would not match anymore and the smartphone would stop working. It is unlikely that the thief would keep the smartphone offline in order to avoid the blocking mechanism of the blockchain-connected component due to the negligible usability of smartphones without internet. The thief hence could not use the stolen smartphone, and neither could he sell his loot because a potential buyer would see that the smartphone is stolen and would also be unable to use it, and neither could he sell his loot because a potential buyer would see that the smartphone is stolen and would also be unable to use it.

When selling the smartphone, the owner now would be obliged to transfer the IMEI-coin on the blockchain to a public key named by the buyer using his private key. The buyer may then change the public key stored on the smartphone to his one. Hence, the new owner may command the blockchain mechanism that causes the smartphone to stop working by transferring the IMEI-coin to a different public key.

From the technical side, tokenization has some similarities to producer-run registers, but avoids some of the problems obstructing the latter's dissemination into markets and adds an additional feature: easing the use of smartphones as collateral.

Producer-run registers add more problems: Buyers of smartphones lose privacy by registration and legally re-selling a mobile-phone becomes more cumbersome and has to be announced to the register for otherwise the buyer of a used smartphone could never be safe from extortion by the seller who would still have the power to blacklist and thus block the phone.

Tokenization of property in smartphones facilitates their use as collateral for credits in the following way. Traditionally, pledges require possession (Livingston 2007; Wigmore 1897). That makes it unattractive to use objects of value which are used every day as pledges for securing loans. In jurisdictions in which pledges without possession are legal or replaced by sophisticated legal constructions like the German "Sicherungsübereignung", a conditional transfer of property by way of security, the French "gage sans dépossession" or the Italian "pegno non possessorio", chattel as collateral suffers from the obvious risk of accidental destruction or bona fide transfer of property to a third party. The United States already introduced registers for security rights with Art. 9 UCC. Although the goal was to reduce insolvency risks by publicity in an economical way (Sigman 2008) the UCC provision comes with substantial transaction costs for providing comprehensive information (Livingston 2007) and registration fees (Sigman 2008).

Here, the blockchain can score as only the public key is essential. A further advantage is the potential internationality which comes with the decentralized structure of distributed ledger technology, hence a blockchain solution would address the call for a "European Security Right (ESR)" (Flessner 2008). With tokenization of property, pledging of movables does not necessarily become legal but it becomes possible by technical enforcement. Transferring the token to the creditor hinders the owner of the item from further transfers of property and thus secures the credit. At the same time, the creditor can easily block the smartphone by transferring the property token to an address unknown to the phone so that its functioning is effectively blocked, which gives the borrower a strong incentive to pay his rates. The creditor has no incentive to abuse the token except for its opportunistic retention after the credit has been paid back. However, backing the credit contract by a smart contract may exclude this risk too. If the credit has to be paid back on the same blockchain as property in the item is tokenized on (or on a connected blockchain), a smart contract may automatically trigger the return of the token to the borrower as soon as the loan has been paid back in full. Additionally, the smart contract may exclude any transfer of property by the lender for the time during which the borrower fulfils his duties from the credit contract.

Nevertheless, the advantage of securing credits via blockchain pledges is more relevant for specific default and not so much for general default (insolvency) due to Armour's (2008) argument that in case of insolvency debtors will lose everything anyways while securitization only causes a redistribution amongst creditors.

3   Modeling the Economics of Blockchain-Secured Smartphones

To better understand the interaction of producers, owners and thieves of smartphones with respect to theft protection, we suggest a simple model based on a standard inspection game. This model will also allow us to predict, evaluate and compare the effects of registering ownership of smartphones on or off the blockchain.

3.1   Owners and Thieves

We start from the interaction between owners E and (potential) thieves T of smartphones.

Assumption 1: Owners E of smartphones enjoy utility V from owning and possessing a smartphone:

$V = v$ if they own and possess it and do not choose a particular behavior in order to exclude theft;

$V = v - a$ if they own and possess it and do actively choose a particular behavior with the cost of a in order to exclude theft;

$V = s$ (with $s \ll v$) if they do not possess their smartphone anymore because it has been stolen, where v is the net utility from owning and possessing a smartphone, α is the individual's cost of individually protecting the phone against theft and s is the individual's expected value of the phone after theft and its possible return.

Assumption 2: Thieves T may prepare theft (action t) or not. They earn utility N:

$N = \lambda$ if they successfully steal a smartphone, which they do if they meet an inactive owner of a smartphone;

$N = -\sigma$ if they prepare theft but meet an owner of a smartphone who actively protects his property;

$N = 0$ if they do not prepare theft.

If only two individuals, one from each population, interact or if all individuals within a population are identical, the following matrix describes payoffs for the four possible action combinations (Fig. 1):

Table 1. Payoffs in simple enforcement game

E		t	not t
	not a	s, λ	$v, 0$
	a	$v - a, -\sigma$	$v - a, 0$

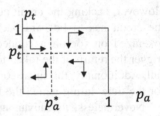

Fig. 1. Dynamic adaption with homogeneous agents

The figure to the right describes the dynamics of mutual adaptation of the probabilities p_a that the owner is active against theft and p_t that the thief prepares theft with the unique Nash equilibrium being given by $(p_a^*, p_t^*) = \left(\frac{\lambda}{\lambda+\sigma}, \frac{a}{v-s}\right)$. The expected utilities in the Nash equilibrium are $E(V) = v - a$ and $E(N) = 0$.

This simple model allows a first glance on the effects of producers' actions to help owners to protect against theft. We have to distinguish between three technology types of such actions.

(a) Technologies decreasing the costs a of the behavior that owners can employ to protect their smartphone against theft, (or increase the value v of smartphones that are not stolen).
(b) Technologies increasing the value s of stolen smartphones
(c) Technologies that reduce the value λ of stolen smartphones or increase the costs σ of preparing theft without success.

We note that technologies of type a increase the expected utility of owners. If they do, they also lower the equilibrium probability that a thief actually engages in theft. These technologies do not change the equilibrium probability that owners protect their property.

Technologies of type b entail an increase of the equilibrium theft probability p_t^* as sole result. As a consequence, technologies that for example increase the probability of a stolen phone being returned to the owner seem to be futile: not only does the expected utility of owners remain constant, whence their willingness to pay for such technologies is nil, but it also increases the theft rate, which may be seen as a damage to the rule of law.

Technologies of type c, to which technology enforced registration of property clearly belongs, fail to affect owners' expected utility in equilibrium. As they lower the value λ of a stolen smartphone or increase the costs σ of engaging in theft in vain, they do not change the expected value of either individual. The entire effect rests in a reduction of owners' activity to reduce their susceptibility to theft. As soon as registration by producers is costly and therefore raises prices for smartphones, this simplifying model suggests that voluntary registration is not viable on a market for smartphones.

We note that these surprising results are not an artefact of or assumption that anti-theft activities of owners are perfectly effective. If we allow for some ineffectiveness of this action, i.e. assume that the activity excludes theft only with a probability of $\beta \in (0,1)$ then the only change in the payoff matrix is in the lower left cell, were the entries become $(\beta v - a, -\beta\sigma + (1 - \beta)\lambda)$ which alters the equilibrium probabilities to $(p_a^*, p_t^*) = \left(\frac{\lambda}{\beta(\lambda+\sigma)}, \frac{a}{\beta v - s} \right)$ and the corresponding expected utilities become $E(V) = v - a\frac{v-s}{\beta v - s}$ and $E(N) = 0$. The effects of technologies of type a remain unchanged, with respect to owners' expected utility at least qualitatively. Type b technologies continue to increase the probability of theft, but now this has a strictly negative effect on owners' expected utility in equilibrium (due to $\frac{\partial E(V)}{\partial s} = -a\frac{v(1-\beta)}{(\beta v - s)^2}$). Finally, technologies of type c, that only make theft less attractive for thieves, still have no effect on owners' utility, but only reduce their probability of actively fighting against theft.

However, the results to some degree are an artefact of the homogeneity assumptions with respect to owners' and thieves' valuations of phones (owned or stolen) and anti-theft and theft-preparing activities. The standard enforcement game, which is based on these homogeneity assumptions, also suffers from the drawback that the Nash equilibrium is not stable by any reasonable definition of stability. Neither is it evolutionarily stable nor is it asymptotically stable for reasonable assumptions on dynamic adaptation (see Tsebelis, 1993, Holler, 1993 and Wangenheim, 2004 for details and further references). This undesirable property vanishes as soon as one allows for heterogeneity of owners or thieves.

To introduce heterogeneity into our model, we assume that all variables occurring in Table 1 are uniformly distributed on some given interval. Taking h_x as half of the width of this interval, we can thus write:

$$x \sim U(\bar{x} - h_x, \bar{x} + h_x) \forall x \in \{v, a, \lambda, \sigma\}$$

where $U(\cdot)$ is the uniform distribution with the lower and the upper bound of the support as arguments of $U(\cdot)$. Obviously, $\bar{x}$ is the expected value of $x \in \{v, a, \lambda, \sigma\}$.

We then get the following best-reply functions:

$$p_t^*(p_a) = \begin{cases} 1 & \text{if } p_a < p_a^1 \\ 1 - \frac{p_a - p_a^1}{p_a^0 - p_a^1} & \text{if } p_a \in [p_a^1, p_a^0] \\ 0 & \text{if } p_a > p_a^0 \end{cases}$$

and

$$p_a^*(p_t) = \begin{cases} 0 & \text{if } p_t < p_t^0 \\ \frac{p_t - p_t^0}{p_t^1 - p_t^0} & \text{if } p_t \in [p_t^0, p_t^1] \\ 1 & \text{if } p_a > p_t^1 \end{cases}$$

where $p_a^0 = \frac{\bar{\lambda} + h_\lambda}{\bar{\lambda} + h_\lambda + \bar{\sigma} - h_\sigma}$, $p_a^1 = \frac{\bar{\lambda} - h_\lambda}{\bar{\lambda} - h_\lambda + \bar{\sigma} + h_\sigma}$, $p_t^0 = \frac{\bar{a} - h_a}{\bar{v} + h_v - s}$, $p_t^1 = \frac{\bar{a} + h_a}{\bar{v} - h_v - s}$. Graphically, these reaction functions change the above figure as follows (Fig. 2):

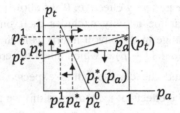

Fig. 2. Dynamic adaption with heterogeneous agents

If the equilibrium is interior, it is stable and given by $p_t^{**} = p_t^*(p_a^{**})$ and $p_a^{**} = p_a^*(p_t^{**})$, which results in:

$$p_t^{**} = \frac{(1 - p_a^0)p_t^0 + p_a^0 p_t^1}{1 + (p_a^0 - p_a^1)(p_t^1 - p_t^0)} \quad \text{and} \quad p_a^{**} = \frac{(1 - p_t^0)p_a^0 + p_t^0 p_a^1}{1 + (p_a^0 - p_a^1)(p_t^1 - p_t^0)}$$

where the numerators may be interpreted as weighted averages of the critical values of the respective probabilities and the denominator corrects for the inaccuracy of the weights. Note that lack of heterogeneity of, for example, the thieves, results in $p_t^0 = p_t^1 = p_t^*$ and thus $p_t^{**} = p_t^*$ and $p_a^{**} = (1 - p_t^*)p_a^0 + p_t^* p_a^1$. Inserting the payoffs into the equilibrium values results in complex expressions which we spare the reader as they are hard to interpret. However, the effects of the exogenous variables on p_t^{**} and p_a^{**} are easily determined from our second figure.

An increase in v or a decrease in a (equivalent to technology a) shift p_t^0 and p_t^1 downward and thus $p_t^*(p_t)$ shifts to the lower right while $p_a^*(p_a)$ remains unaffected. Hence p_t^{**} declines and p_a^{**} increases. As owners are now assumed to be heterogeneous, their average welfare is no more given by the expected utility of the average owner. However, we know that the expected utility of all individual owners who are and remain active is given by $E(V)_a = (1 - p_t^{**}(1 - \beta))v - p - a$ and thus strictly increases with these technologies. Similarly, the expected utility of all individual owners who are and remain active is given by $E(V)_{na} = sp_t^{**} + v(1 - p_t^{**}) - p$, on which the effect of such technologies is also strictly positive (v has a positive direct effect on $E(V)_{na}$ and due to $v > s$ also a positive indirect effect via the decline of p_t^{**}). Those owners who switch from inactivity to actively fight theft do so due to further gains. Hence, whether owners remain inactive or remain active or switch from inactivity to activity, they always get higher expected utilities.

Increasing the expected value that stolen phones still have for their owners has the opposite effect of increasing v on p_t^0 and p_t^1 and thus increases p_t^{**} and lowers p_a^{**}. As a consequence, expected payoffs of active owners will decline if anti-theft activity is partly ineffective ($\beta < 1$) and remain constant otherwise. However, the effect on the equilibrium expected utility of inactive owners is ambiguous: the positive direct effect of the increase in s may be offset by its negative indirect effect via the increase of p_t^{**} which is particularly strong if heterogeneity is more prevalent among owners than among thieves, which however seems implausible. If the positive direct effect prevails, owners switching from activity to inactivity may receive a higher utility and thus the total effect of the technology is ambiguous. Still, it is not necessarily positive as the negative effect which we described for the simplifying version of the model may only be partly offset.

Finally, a reduction of λ or an increase of σ (equivalent to technology b) shift p_a^0 and p_a^1 downward and thus $p_t^*(p_a)$ shifts to the lower left while $p_a^*(p_t)$ remains unaffected. In consequence, both p_t^{**} and p_a^{**} decline. This has clearly positive effects on the utility of owners: as p_t^{**} declines, both active and inactive owners gain or remain unaffected. Owners switching from activity to inactivity change their behavior because they further gain. Hence, in equilibrium the average expected utility of owners grows as a consequence of the introduction of a technology which lowers λ or increases σ. One should note, however, that the reduction of p_t^{**} which underlies the positive effect on owners' expected utility is severely mitigated by the feedback on p_a^{**} and the more so, the less heterogeneous owners are. This mitigation reduces the cost effectiveness of such technologies.

We summarize the effects of the different technologies in the following table:

Technology	p_t^{**}	p_a^{**}	Average $E(V)$	$E(V)$ in simplified model with $\beta < 1$
(a) Making self-protection easier	Declines	Grows	Grows	Grows
(b) Making recovery of stolen phones easier	Grows	Declines	Ambiguous	Declines
(c) Making theft less attractive	Declines	Declines	Grows	Constant

Eventually, registration is unlikely to reduce the value of stolen smartphones to zero. If therefore a positive risk of theft remains, registration may substitute other means of protecting one's property like keeping a close eye on it or keeping it concealed. If the substitution of anti-theft effort is strong, the main effect of registration may be a reduction of other precautions against theft and no substantial change in theft rates.[2]

3.2 Including the Producer-Owner Interaction

We so far assumed that the new technologies to reduce theft are introduced and applied by all owners. However, owners decide individually, whether they will spend costs on these technologies, either directly or by buying more expensive phones from producers that apply the technologies. But this decision is not affected by changes in the thieves' probability to prepare theft, because this probability is not owner-specific but is the same for all owners, at least as long as thieves cannot separate phones with respect to their black-market value before theft. Hence, the benefits from registration go to all potential victims of theft, while the costs remain with the registering individual. This argument is particularly relevant for technologies of type c where the positive effect on owners' expected utility hinges exclusively on the indirect effect transmitted via the change of p_t^{**}. It does not only explain why owners of smartphones are reluctant to register, but also provides reasons for why producers do not register. The latter would incur the costs of registration only if they could sell their products at a correspondingly higher price.

Thus, registration is a public good, but the additional feature of pledging may solve the public-goods problem as it is a private good jointly produced with the public good.[3]

For making recovery of stolen phones easier, the effect is reversed: while it is privately worthwhile to buy such technologies, it may be socially detrimental, depending on whether the effect on average expected utility of owners is positive or negative. If heterogeneity is small and the simplifying version of the model is thus rather close to reality or if thieves are particularly homogeneous, the effect of such technology on all owners is negative although the individual owner prefers buying it.

4 Conclusions

In this paper we have shown that registering smartphones on the blockchain may solve the problems that are impeding successful technically enforced registration in other registers so far. Our argument is that blockchain registration solves a public goods problem by joining its production with a private good.

The result is not unambiguous, though. It may be that for smartphones, the private goods jointly produced with the public good of registration to protect from theft is not valuable enough to completely solve the problem and induce voluntary registration.

---

[2] The problem has been intensively discussed in general terms for the inspection game, where reduction of the value of the illegal activity fails to reduce the frequency of the latter but rather entails a reduction of the activity which is called 'inspection' in the game and that corresponds to anti-theft activity in the case of theft of smartphones.

[3] See Vicary 1996 for the general idea of solving public-good problems by joint production and provision of the public with a private good.

Our proposal to connect the public-good aspects of registration with private-good properties may also overcome Arruñada's (2017: 22) pessimistic claim, that the main problem behind nonexistent registers is collecting and recording the data, not inappropriate storing technologies.

The possibility of registering offline movables, for which no register at all exists and thus where the blockchain opens up entirely new opportunities, has to be explored in following research.

We claim however, that the general ideas leading to our results can be transferred from smartphone registration to many other technical items connecting regularly to the internet and thus possibly to the blockchain. We thereby provide a general concept of using the blockchain to solve strategic and economic problems that other databanks cannot solve.

References

Arruñada, B.: Blockchain's struggle to deliver impersonal exchange. Minn. J. Law Sci. Technol. **19**(1), 55–105 (2018)

Armour, J.: The law and economics debate about secured lending: lessons for European lawmaking? In: The Future of Secured Credit in Europe, pp. 3–29. De Gruyter, Berlin (2008)

BITKOM (2014). http://smart-school.de/bitkom/org/noindex/Publikationen/2015/Positionspapiere/Bund-Laender-Projektgruppe-Smartphonesperre-Fragenkatalog-vom-19-Dezember-2014/2015-01-21-Stellungnahme-2-Fragenkatalog-BLPG-final.pdf. Accessed 28 June 2018

Chiu, J., Koeppl, T.: The Economics of Cryptocurrencies – Bitcoin and Beyond. In: Queen's Economics Department Working Paper No. 1389, Kingston (2017)

Collindres, J., Regan, M., Panting, G.: Using blockchain to secure Honduras land titles (2016). https://s3.amazonaws.com/ipri2016/casestudy_collindres.pdf. Accessed 26 June 2018

Deutscher Bundestag (2014). http://dip21.bundestag.de/dip21/btd/18/022/1802236.pdf. Accessed 28 June 2018

Flessner, A.: Security interests in receivables – a European perspective. In: The Future of Secured Credit in Europe, pp. 336–349. De Gruyter, Berlin (2008)

Government Office for Science: Distributed Ledger Technology: beyond block chain (2016). https://assets.publishing.service.gov.uk/government/uploads/system/uploads/attachment_data/file/492972/gs-16-1-distributed-ledger-technology.pdf. Accessed 28 June 2018

GSMA homepage (2016). https://www.gsma.com/publicpolicy/wp-content/uploads/2017/06/IMEI_Security_Technical_Design_Principles_v4.0.pdf. Accessed 28 June 2018

Holler, M.: Fighting pollution when decisions are strategic. Public Choice **76**(4), 347–356 (1993)

IBM Government Industry Blog (2016). https://www.ibm.com/blogs/insights-on-business/government/blockchain-asset-registration/. Accessed 28 June 2018

Kairos Future (2017). https://chromaway.com/papers/Blockchain_Landregistry_Report_2017.pdf. Accessed 28 June 2018

Kroll, J., Davey, I., Felten, E.: The economics of bitcoin minung or, bitcoin in the presence of adversaries. In: The Twelfth Workshop on the Economics of Information Security (WEIS 2013) Washington, DC (2013)

Livingston, M.: A rose by any other name would smell as sweet (or would it?): filing and searching in Article 9's public records. BYU Law Rev. **111**(1), 111–165 (2007)

Ministry of Communications Department of Telecommunications (2017). http://www.dot.gov.in/sites/default/files/ceir.pdf?download=1. Accessed 28 June 2018

Nakamoto, S.: Bitcoin: A peer-to-peer electronic cash system (2008). https://bitcoin.org/bitcoin.pdf. Accessed 27 June 2018

Nield, D.: You locked yourself out of your phone, now what? – Other than remembering your PIN a little better next time (2017). https://www.popularmechanics.com/technology/gadgets/how-to/a25092/locked-out-of-phone-guide/. Accessed 28 June 2018

Shin, L.: Republic of Georgia to pilot land titling on blockchain with economist Hernando De Soto, BitFury (2016). https://www.forbes.com/sites/laurashin/2016/04/21/republic-of-georgia-to-pilot-land-titling-on-blockchain-with-economist-hernando-de-soto-bitfury/#45546a9344da. Accessed 28 June 2018

Sigman, H.: Perfection and priority of security rights. In: The future of secured credit in Europe, pp. 143–165. De Gruyter, Berlin (2008)

Swan, M.: Blockchain-Blueprint for a New Economy. O'Reilly, Sebastopol (2015)

Swanson, T.: Smart Property, Colored Coins and Mastercoin (2014). https://www.coindesk.com/smart-property-colored-coins-mastercoin/. Accessed 28 June 2018

Tapscott, D., Tapscott, A.: Blockchain Revolution: How Technology Behind Bitcoin is Changing Money, Business and the World. Portfolio, New York (2016)

Tsebelis, G.: Penalty and crime: further theoretical considerations and empirical evidence. J. Theor. Polit. 5(3), 349–374 (1993)

Vicary, S.: Joint production and the private provision of public goods. J. Public Econ. 63(3), 429–445 (1996)

Wangenheim, G.: Games and Public Administration – The Law and Economics of Regulation and Licensing. Edward Elgar, Cheltenham (2004)

Wigmore, J.: The plege-idea: A study in comparative legal ideas. Harvard Law Rev. 10(6), 321–350 (1897)

Wortmann, F., Flüchter, K.: Internet of things – technology and value added. Bus. Inf. Syst. Eng. 57(3), 221–224 (2015)

On the Future of Markets Driven by Blockchain

Mario Cichonczyk[(✉)]

Bielefeld University of Applied Sciences, Campus Minden, 32427 Minden, Germany
mario.cichonczyk@fh-bielefeld.de

Abstract. When an effort is made to understand how the blockchain may influence the evolution of economies, a distinction between marketing promises and neutral assessments is required. This work aims to review the prospective development of three key economic principles under the assumed constitution of a blockchain future. It is analyzed how the concepts of intermediation, economic transparency and economic automation show characteristics under possibly disruptive impact. Their present situation is laid out and extrapolated to gain a reasoned insight into economic development driven by blockchain technology as currently promised. An argument is made that the consumers view of innovative services will be coined by nescience towards the actual data structure in use.

Keywords: Blockchain · Economy · Disruption · Future

1 Introduction

The disruptive potential of blockchain technologies seems to be one of their more emphasized characteristics. The discussion on how market areas can be transformed by the blockchain appears to be closely bound to specific use cases. The goal of this work is to examine how the blockchain can represent a progressive influence on three more abstract economic principles. The explicit aim is to not focus on tangible cases of application but rather the underlying market concepts. This approach was chosen to aid the reader in conceiving new and progressive application scenarios while also providing a glimpse into the longterm future of the cyber-physical economic system.

When categorized, three leading motifs can be observed: the influence on intermediation, the introduction of perfect economic transparency and the automation of economic processes. Each of these themes is presented and analyzed in the following sections. Finally, the concluding section shall merge the interim observations into one future vision.

2 Intermediation

The concept of economic intermediation describes the facilitation of supply and demand by independent, profit-maximizing market agents [26]. The removal of

© Springer Nature Switzerland AG 2019
W. Abramowicz and A. Paschke (Eds.): BIS 2018 Workshops, LNBIP 339, pp. 325–334, 2019.
https://doi.org/10.1007/978-3-030-04849-5_29

trading opacities by charging a commission generates revenue in the interme-diaries cashflow. Therefore, the goal is the allocation of supply->demand or demand->supply, depending on the specific use case.

Whenever market participants join the market, they see themselves con-fronted with an uncertain time delay before finding their contracting party. The outcome are search costs, which are difficult to estimate in advance. An interme-diary offers the fixation of costs and/or time that need to be invested between initiation and formation of contract. Therefore, intermediaries have a permanent presence in the market since they do not leave the place of commerce after a business transaction was concluded. Every time an asset comes into their pos-session, they forward it to buyers who value the assets worth on a higher tier. Similarly, these buyers try to procure the asset from a source which values it on a lower tier [22]. Recapitulating, intermediaries benefit whenever an asset flow is linked to a lack of knowledge about the overall market. This nescience is a consequence of the imperfect nature of real world economies in which perfect information about all producers and consumers is not available [5].

Obviously, a complex chain of sales stages can emerge [20] but the addition of such stages seems to follow a reverse trend in the age of electronic commerce [15]. Successful internet companies like Amazon consolidate complex trade chains in simple to use platforms. The business model of intermediating real world contacts seems to not be sustainable in the fast-paced internet age. Nevertheless, it is important to note that intermediaries do still exist. The heterogeneous flow of assets is merely centralizing itself in monopolistically themed intermediaries. This development can be partly attributed to an inherent characteristic of the internet as a distributed system: distrust [15]. Producers and consumers tend to gravitate to the intermediary representing the greatest amount of trust in the suspicious medium of exchange. This observation shall be understood as the fundamental basis for intermediary disruption by blockchain technologies, potentially leading to disintermediation.

Disintermediation as the principle of eliminating stages in a trade chain is not a new concept caused by the blockchain. As Gellman [9] summarizes, the first major wave of disintermediation could be observed in the 19070s. Regulatory amendments to the investment banking system caused a gap between interest payments by major banks and other forms of more direct capital investment. Consumers wandered off from established banking institutions to follow an inde-pendently managed portfolio with lower transaction costs and higher profits. Banks where no longer considered to play the sole role of monopolistic interme-diaries. Disintermediation was thereafter considered more thoroughly and found its way into economic literature and conscious reflection. Special regard was given to the rising pre-millenial significance of the internet. This phase is particularly interesting due to its correlation to the current emergence of the blockchain. Back in the 1990s, real world intermediaries saw themselves confronted with the sur-misable disintermediation through electronic commerce. Those companies which successfully transferred to the internet age as digital pioneers now face the same paradigm shift as the business they once superseded. What the internet meant for real world intermediaries in the 1990s, the blockchain now represents for trade profiteers who entered the modern era with the dotcom bubble and its aftermath.

To give a hypothetical outlook on the future of asset flows under assumed realization of blockchain markets, it seems viable to assess and interpret the economic accounting for the millennium change as a key indicator. Giaglis, Klein and O'Keefe [10] summarize that markets generally tend to push intermediaries out. Their profits lead to a direct increase in price for the consumer. Additionally, producers are thereby hindered to make exhaustive use of their products market potential. The emergence of a technology which brings producer and consumer closer together can be expected to get received well by the market participants, given the majority and austerity of this interest group. This effect now initiates three possible outcomes for intermediaries in predicament: Disintermediation, reintermediation or cybermediation [10]. The obvious, first scenario is the increasing pressure by decreasing transaction costs on facilitators who cling to their traditional role and are thereby washed out of the market. When 'disruptive potential' is mentioned, this form of complete dissolution of trade stages seems to be what is referred to. But the concept of reintermediation presents a more natural response in the realm of a capitalistic system. In this scenario, intermediaries move into niches in which they can still exert their traditional role or provide new services. Their renewed position allows them to persist next to the transformed market. Finally, there are those who fully embrace the transformative technology and indwell in its domain. This category encompasses all actors whose business models bring in the profits of the digital age. And it is exactly these cybermediaries who now seem to face the same choice of a future scenario as their predecessors once did at the end of the last century. Different market areas are subject to such metamorphosing processes by varying extent. Nevertheless, disintermediation is observed to be the most improbable scenario [10] - in direct contradiction to the blockchain claim. Intermediaries as profit-maximizing agents have the economic stimulus to prevail even through paradigm shifts.

Without doubt, the blockchain represents a technology which can transform markets and forces all actors on all stages of commerce to pick one of the given scenarios as their future. Disintermediation is obviously not a conscious choice to be made but the result of an intermediaries inability to reposition themselves in relation to their market potential. May this be in a niche or in the transformative medium. Given that our markets are capitalistic in nature, it can be assumed that all currently present actors will strive to ensure their continuity. The greatest threat is faced by monopolistic, centralized businesses [10]. Inherently, these are at the same time the most significant participants of the current system and thereby pose the most market sway as well as have the greatest incentive to prevail through change. The underlying observations of the economic digitization at the millennium shift give the impression that the decentralized, transparent market introduced by the blockchain again appears hostile to intermediaries. An argument can be made that it is more reasonable to expect changed and/or new facilitators given that intermediaries do have a capitalistic will to survive. Disintermediation is not an outcome as probable as blockchain enthusiasts try to stipulate. It is more likely that we will see a landscape of highly specialized, innovative services.

3 Economic Transparency

The preceding section gave an outline on how an asset flows through the market while progressing over intermediate stages of trade. Therefore, the primary analytic aspect resided in the influence of blockchains on facilitating the conveyance of possessive rights. On an abstract level, this insight may be interpreted as the observance of a commodities movement. The following section will in contrast focus on its alteration.

It seems natural that a commodity is being altered to cover a demand in a market segment and thereby creating added value. If multiple steps of such alterations follow one another, the concept of a supply chain becomes apparent. Every product not directly procured from its original in-house creator is the result of a sequence of such augmentations of value. With this understanding comes the insight that supply chains allow for production, provision and distribution of commodities and associated services and therefore constitute the backbone of the global economic system [16]. Control and optimization of such chains is understood as Supply Chain Management. Cooper, Lambert and Pagh [6] describe the purpose of SCM as reducing the total expenditure of resources necessary to achieve a set market goal. This is accomplished by synchronization of customer requirements with the flow of materials, reduction of inventory investments and improvement of services. All these measures introduce a competitive advantage. It was promptly observed that the actual economic competition lies not between single business but rather optimized supply chains [6]. Therefore, product owners have an economic incentive to control the manufacturing process of their commodities in a centralized fashion spanning across multiple production stages.

The identical principle of consolidated control is utilized to accommodate regulatory needs [25]. In this case, the aim is not assuring optimal profitability but rather adherence to statutory terms linked to the production of a product. Both applications profit the most if a supply chain is maximally integrated [3]. Here, integration describes the interlinkage of chain participants through information technology. Thereby, the process of a products creation projects itself onto a distributed system. The fundamental disadvantage becomes apparent: Tian [25] views modern Supply Chain Management as monopolistic, asymmetric information systems exposed to the risk of manipulation through beneficiaries who are involved either by a direct monetary investment or by economically/regulatorily imposed participation. Customers and regulators cannot track the origin of raw materials or adherence to ethical aspects in the production of a commodity without having questionable confidence in the provided information, as is typical for distributed systems with members of unknown intent [15]. For this reason, sustainability standards and certificates must be considered worthless due to a lack of verifiability since neither the information owners agenda nor their sources of data are confidently transparent [1]. Improvement of supply chain visibility is being sought after but inhibited by the historically established principles of Supply Chain Management. The blockchain acts as an ostensible solution.

Abeyratne and Monfared [1] describe how crypto-SCM is structured: products are tagged with an identifier that can be stored in the blockchain (for example an RFID chip or QR code). The identifier becomes part of the digital product profile and can be augmented by its current possessor. Given that this profile is stored in the blockchain, every party of interest can have access to the perfect information about a product and its history at all times. The data record can then be trusted in accordance with the blockchain pledge. Public-private key pairs can be unambiguously linked to supply chain participants to not only improve commodity tracking but also instill a sense of liability.

The blockchain as a transformative technology has advantages in Supply Chain Management for all stakeholders: businesses, regulators and consumers. Crypto-SCM offers regulatory control and a valid basis for sustainability standards. At the same time, it is in the customers option to track a products development history in detail before or after purchase if so desired. From a business point of view, the blockchain offers efficient SCM without the introduction of centralized distrust. Additionally, it is assumed that the blockchain solves one of the major logistic problems of SCM: the so called Bullwhip Effect [21]. It occurs through the serial propagation of demand forecasts along the chain of manufacturers. If demand changes, the first link in the chain will estimate the fluctuation a bit more generously than necessary to reduce risk. Therefore, downstream chain links see a more prominent change in demand and react with an even more accentuated forecast due to the same motive. This effect increases exponentially along the supply chain. Little oscillations at one end of the chain lead to high oscillations at the other end, introducing inefficient planning distortions. The perfectly shared information in a blockchain parallelizes inventory planning for all participants and leads to a more stable overall system.

At first sight, the blockchain entails no apparent disadvantages regarding its usage in SCM. But Apte [2] observes a fundamental problem. The given benefits can only operate under the assumption that the information within the blockchain is congruent with reality. The current state of technology gives no guarantee that the digital identifier, the attached product profile and its real world counterpart are actually symmetrical. Without this assurance, crypto-SCM brings no added value. The virtual product is subject to the blockchains transparency claim but the connection to its physical counterpart still lies within the scope of third parties of unknown intent. The question of trust is only shifted, not solved. Malign system participants continue to have a lever to effectuate their selfish interest. The alternative would be regular audits [2].

This problem makes the outlook on the future of Supply Chain Management obscure. It should be evident that crypto-SCM is desirable by all honest stakeholders. Beforehand, the unquestionable connection between virtual space and reality must become a goal for research and development. The transformative potential of the blockchain is otherwise only influencing the problem, not the solution as the necessity for audit processes already is the status quo. Francisco and Swanson [8] emphasize the increasing competitive pressure by evermore informed consumers. They no longer solely demand attractive prices but additionally adequate product transparency. It is to be expected that not the existence of the blockchain itself will transform SCM, however that it much rather poses an answer to a consumer market evolving to seek an undeceived choice.

4   Economic Automation

Up until now, it was assumed that purchase decisions are usually made by human consumers. Automated order placements are common in highly integrated supply chains but are rarely encountered in business2consumer and business2business transactions without conjoint information systems. For lack of trust and identifiability, machines were as yet hampered to independently participate in the market economy. With the uprising blockchain and the trend of the Internet-of-Things, this condition is changing dramatically: machines begin to acquire the ability to follow economic stimuli in an autarkic fashion aided by artificial intelligence [12]. Implicitly, the second section alluded to the importance of the blockchain for the banking system but let this point stress that the automation of transactions through artificial intelligence may create an entire new market volume without the need for any involvement of intermediaries [12].

The Internet-of-Things connects physical objects with the cyberspace, in which they can now become a party in economic processes. Following the inherent concept of IoT, the participation of these intelligent objects can be expected to primarily take place on an ad-hoc basis outside of established, rigid structures [27]. M2M transactions in heterogeneous environments have already been conceived and evaluated before the emergence of IoT. Back then, a lack of ubiquitous security concepts and global usability were stated as obstacles to overcome [11]. Now the blockchain is claimed as the ideal solution to these problems [14]. Smart devices which independently participate in financial transactions become part of an "Economy-of-Things" to provide an added commercial value to their users and owners [4].

The combination of IoT and blockchain allows for a monetarization of private property and thereby lays ground for the democratic, decentralized "Sharing Economy" [13]. "Smart Contracts" and "Dapps" are the tools which bring smart devices and economic incentive into a common place. Sharing as the basis of an economy describes collaborative consumption by relinquishment, rental or reciprocal exchange of resources without proprietorship [18]. The aim is to provide assets not used at full capacity to the market interest. As yet, such a rental was coupled to an active initiation and conclusion of a business transaction by the resources owner. It seems reasonable that the mercantile additional expenditure and lack of confidence in unsupervised lending acted inhibitory towards a widespread rise of the Sharing Economy. M2M transactions with support from unambiguous, evident smart contracts may ease this restraint as they lower the transaction overhead to a level that may provide acceptance and transparency to end users [23].

Redlich and Moritz [19] summarize how the future of an established Sharing Economy might look if citizens connect and work together to create value. Their presented principle of commons-based peer production introduces concepts of openness which are collaborative and decentralized in nature, contrary to traditional approaches to economy. Consumers understand themselves more as producers and thereby weaken the dependence on companies while blurring the border between the professional and non-professional sphere [19]. Companies are then obliged to subordinate themselves to the Sharing Economy, providing collaboration infrastructures or producing collaboratively created artifacts in an efficient manner [19].

This facultative future vision should be considered with care since major obstacles are to be overcome before the Sharing Economy can advance [19,24]. Even if society develops towards less distrust in autonomous smart devices and peers, the current jurisdiction was built alongside an industry that is fundamentally different from the envisioned future. Economic constructs had a top-down approach that is being challenged by the bottom-up idea and new judiciary discussions need to follow [19]. It is unlikely that progressive citizens with the intent to introduce their smart devices into the market can be modeled by taxation laws as-is. They are neither entrepreneurs nor freelancers or other forms of taxable entities. Are shared living spaces to be regulated like hotels? Are shared vehicles to be regulated like taxis? These exemplary questions are part of the current discourse and should be understood as a prelude to an upcoming in-depth discussion as problems like these are likely to be encountered in the near future.

5   Conclusion

"Disruption" is the expected notion if trust is given to the promises of blockchain start ups. This work aimed to identify the fundamental economic processes under threat of transformation by the blockchain as postulated and evaluated their respective future. In doing so, marketing promises were questioned and reviewed from a neutral perspective. Three economic principles where analyzed: intermediation, economic transparency and economic automation. It is unlikely that the blockchain will cause widespread disintermediation. It stands to reason that current market participants will have an incentive to last through the possible changes and develop new facilitation services. These will emerge as more transparent and integrated while providing advantages for all stakeholders: businesses, consumers and regulators. Especially the consumer will likely develop towards the role of a more involved user of an intelligent economy.

It is a complex question by which severity these aspects will shape the future. The separate sections outlined problems hindering the promised transformations. The blockchain as a disruptive technology in combination with the augur of its advocates allows for parallels to be drawn with the disruptive prophecies bestowed by the cypherpunk movement of the late 1980s. Innovative algorithms in asymmetrical cryptography were promised as a guaranteed means for the destabilization of established institutions and governments. Ubiquitously enforceable privacy was pledged to significantly change the social and political landscape [17]. Nowadays, these cryptographic technologies found their way into everyday life and are used self-evidently without apparent knowledge of their existence by the common user. At the same time, the aftermath of the global surveillance disclosures by Edward Snowden is still being discussed. It seems improbable that this is the future envisioned by the cypherpunk movement.

These parallels emphasize that the blockchain future should be thought of reservedly. It will surely bring transformations, but with a perspective comprised of more subtle changes than currently promised. Consumers will likely use the services of the intelligent economy with a self-evidence that is detached from knowledge about the existence of the underlying blockchains. Therefore, transitions are likely more pronounced on a macroscopic scale. Unrelated to the blockchain, Felber [7] outlines how an economy can develop from an egotistic to an altruistic motivation. Decentralization, economic transparency and mutual cooperation are given as key steps to take. Additionally, the migration away from possessive maximization tendencies towards democratized companies and banks are mentioned. Inadvertently, the blockchain may hence subtly lead to an economy of the common good if the presented obstacles are dealt with.

References

1. Abeyratne, S., Monfared, R.: Blockchain ready manufacturing supply chain using distributed ledger **5** (2016)
2. Apte, S.: Will blockchain technology revolutionise excipient supply chain management? J. Excipients Food Chem. **7**(3), 76–78 (2016). https://ojs.abo.fi/ojs/index.php/jefc/article/view/1465
3. Bagchi, P.K., Ha, B.C., Skjoett-Larsen, T., Soerensen, L.B.: Supply chain integration: a European survey. Int. J. Logistics Manage. **16**(2), 275–294 (2005). https://doi.org/10.1108/09574090510634557
4. Beck, R., Czepluch, J.S., Lollike, N., Malone, S.: Blockchain-the gateway to trust-free cryptographic transactions. In: Research Papers, p. 153 (2016)
5. BusinessDictionary.com: What is intermediation? Definition and meaning (2018). http://www.businessdictionary.com/definition/intermediation.html. Accessed 29 Apr 2018
6. Cooper, M.C., Lambert, D.M., Pagh, J.D.: Supply chain management: more than a new name for logistics. Int. J. Logistics Manage. **8**(1), 1–14 (1997). https://doi.org/10.1108/09574099710805556
7. Felber, C.: Die Gemeinwohl-Ökonomie das Wirtschaftsmodell der Zukunft. Deuticke, Wien (2010)
8. Francisco, K., Swanson, D.: The supply chain has no clothes: technology adoption of blockchain for supply chain transparency. Logistics **2**(1), 2 (2018). https://doi.org/10.3390/logistics2010002
9. Gellman, R.: Disintermediation and the internet. Gov. Inf. Q. **13**(1), 1–8 (1996). https://doi.org/10.1016/S0740-624X(96)90002-7

10. Giaglis, G.M., Klein, S., O'Keefe, R.M.: Disintermediation, reintermediation, or cybermediation? The future of intermediaries in electronic marketplaces. In: Proceedings 12th Electronic Commerce Conference on Global Networked Organizations, pp. 7–9. Moderna Organizacija (1999)
11. Gonçalves, V., Dobbelaere, P.: Business scenarios for machine-to-machine mobile applications. In: 2010 Ninth International Conference on Mobile Business and 2010 Ninth Global Mobility Roundtable (ICMB-GMR), pp. 394–401, June 2010. https://doi.org/10.1109/ICMB-GMR.2010.61
12. Hegadekatti, K.: Automation processes and blockchain systems. SSRN Electron. J. (2016). https://doi.org/10.2139/ssrn.2890435
13. Huckle, S., Bhattacharya, R., White, M., Beloff, N.: Internet of things, blockchain and shared economy applications. Procedia Comput. Sci. **98**, 461–466 (2016). https://doi.org/10.1016/j.procs.2016.09.074. The 7th International Conference on Emerging Ubiquitous Systems and Pervasive Networks (EUSPN 2016)/The 6th International Conference on Current and Future Trends of Information and Communication Technologies in Healthcare (ICTH-2016)/Affiliated Workshops
14. Kravitz, D.W., Cooper, J.: Securing user identity and transactions symbiotically: Iot meets blockchain. In: 2017 Global Internet of Things Summit (GIoTS), pp. 1–6, June 2017. https://doi.org/10.1109/GIOTS.2017.8016280
15. Mattila, J.: The blockchain phenomenon: the disruptive potential of distributed consensu architectures. In: ETLA Working Papers: Elinkeinoelämän Tutkimuslaitos, Research Institute of the Finnish Economy (2016)
16. Nagurney, A., Liu, Z., Woolley, T.: Sustainable supply chain and transportation networks. Int. J. Sustain. Transp. **1**(1), 29–51 (2007). https://doi.org/10.1080/15568310601060077
17. Narayanan, A.: What happened to the crypto dream? part 1. IEEE Secur. Priv. **11**(2), 75–76 (2013). https://doi.org/10.1109/MSP.2013.45
18. Puschmann, T., Alt, R.: Sharing economy. Bus. Inf. Syst. Eng. Int. J. Wirtschaftsinformatik **58**(1), 93–99 (2016). https://EconPapers.repec.org/RePEc:spr:binfse:v:58:y:2016:i:1:p:93–99
19. Redlich, T., Moritz, M.: Die Zukunft der Wertschöpfung - dezentral, vernetzt und kollaborativ, pp. 1–6. Springer Fachmedien Wiesbaden, Wiesbaden (2018)
20. Schmidt, R.H., Hackethal, A., Tyrell, M.: Disintermediation and the role of banks in Europe: an international comparison. J. Financ. Intermediation **8**(1), 36–67 (1999). https://doi.org/10.1006/jfin.1998.0256. http://www.sciencedirect.com/science/article/pii/S104295739890256X
21. Seebacher, S., Schüritz, R.: Blockchain technology as an enabler of service systems: a structured literature review. In: Za, S., Drăgoicea, M., Cavallari, M. (eds.) IESS 2017. LNBIP, vol. 279, pp. 12–23. Springer, Cham (2017). https://doi.org/10.1007/978-3-319-56925-3_2
22. Shen, J., Wei, B., Yan, H.: Financial intermediation chains in an OTC market. SSRN Electron. J. (2018). https://doi.org/10.2139/ssrn.2577497
23. Sun, J., Yan, J., Zhang, K.Z.K.: Blockchain-based sharing services: what blockchain technology can contribute to smart cities. Financial Innov. **2**(1), 26 (2016). https://doi.org/10.1186/s40854-016-0040-y
24. Sundararajan, A.: The Sharing Economy: The End of Employment and the Rise of Crowd-Based Capitalism. MIT Press, Cambridge (2016). http://www.jstor.org/stable/j.ctt1c2cqh3
25. Tian, F.: An agri-food supply chain traceability system for china based on RFID blockchain technology. In: 2016 13th International Conference on Service Systems and Service Management (ICSSSM), pp. 1–6, June 2016

26. Walter, B., Hess, T., Picot, A.: Intermediation und Digitalisierung: Ein Ökonomisches Konzept Am Beispiel Der Konvergenten Medienbranche. Gabler Edition Wissenschaft: Markt- und Unternehmensentwicklung, Deutscher Universitätsverlag (2007)
27. Wilusz, D., Rykowski, J.: The architecture of coupon-based, semi-off-line, anonymous micropayment system for internet of things. In: Camarinha-Matos, L.M., Tomic, S., Graça, P. (eds.) DoCEIS 2013. IAICT, vol. 394, pp. 125–132. Springer, Heidelberg (2013). https://doi.org/10.1007/978-3-642-37291-9_14

Smart Contract-Based Role Management
on the Blockchain

Cornelius Ihle[(✉)] [iD] and Omar Sanchez [iD]

Daimler AG, Breitwiesenstrasse 5A, 70565 Stuttgart, Germany
cornelius.ihle@daimler.com
https://www.daimler.com/

Abstract. Role-based access management is essential in today's business applications. The need for such access control is indisputable, implementation in a centralized way, on the other hand, is not ideal. An improvement could be a decentralized, Smart-Contract-based approach. This paper examines whether corporate applications can use distributed ledger based authorization systems to benefit from the positive properties of blockchain technology, without losing the possibilities and strengths of existing central authorization techniques. The benefit of a prototype with a decentralized approach is to serve as a basis for future decentralized company developments. This paper deals with the implementation and validation of a blockchain-based access control solution for decentralized applications. The feasibility of this on-chain solution for role-based access control (RBAC) is verified through a proof-of-concept using a suitable distributed ledger platform.

The implementation of the authorization system aims to fulfill the evaluation requirements and does not claim to be used as a corporate service.

Keywords: Blockchain · Distributed ledger technology
Identity and access management

1 Introduction

Distributed ledger applications are successors of blockchain technology and are forming the new standard for applications inside the distributed business application domain. The goal of distributed ledger technology (DLT) is to create more resilient network applications.

One factor that limits decentralization in private and permissioned ledgers is identity and access management (IAM). Current identity and access management solutions in distributed ledger applications offer only binary access control and rely on centralized services, e.g., a Certificate Authority to handle the membership service.

Supported by organization Daimler AG.

W. Abramowicz and A. Paschke (Eds.): BIS 2018 Workshops, LNBIP 339, pp. 335–343, 2019.
https://doi.org/10.1007/978-3-030-04849-5_30

Part of this thesis is the analysis of current DLT-platforms and their capability to meet the stakeholder requirements. After a basic induction into the three most promising business DLT-platforms, an in-depth analysis of the preferred platform (Hyperledger Fabric) follows.

To access authentication certificates via smart contracts, experimental libraries where used, which were not part of the release version of Hyperledger Fabric at the time of development. Further, the PoC makes use of NodeJS, Docker, and Go to implement the system. After proofing the accessibility of identity certificates via smart contracts, the contracts are extended to allow for the RBAC functionality for user authorization.

To improve the decentralization level of role-based access control a distributed ledger-based proof-of-concept is developed. The PoC differentiates itself from state of the art RBAC-Systems, as there is no single point of failure. The outcome of this thesis offers a higher level of decentralization for the access management of business applications and additionally gives a recommendation for the further development of decentralized access management, considering future DLT-empowered identity management solutions.

Our Contribution. In this thesis, we developed a proof-of-concept of a decentralized access control system. We chose a role-based access control concept that uses an access management smart contract to reliable manage access to decentralized applications. The role-based approach gives the advantage of a reduced user management effort, while the decentralized concept allows for a higher resilience against cyber-attacks.

The PoC was developed with a focus on business applications inside the Daimler AG, but many other permitted applications are a possible operational area for such a decentralized access management solution.

The result of this thesis is a stepping-stone towards the decentralization of business applications. Within the thesis, weaknesses of current distributed ledger technology platforms are shown, and a suggestion for the architecture of future development of decentralized access control systems is given. A need for self-sovereign-identity was discovered, which presumably will be provided in the near future through projects like Civic [4], Hyperledger Indy [7], or Selfkey [5].

Classic centralized access control systems represent a honeypot inside today's business application's access management. This honeypot undergoes constant penetration and exploitation attempts. The centralized access control system we designed addresses the risks of an access controlled application.

Instead of mitigating the risks of a honeypot, this thesis has shown a new architectural solution to eliminate the honeypot entirely. The target platform of the PoC, Hyperledger Fabric, is a distributed ledger technology, and is capable of providing the necessary level of decentralization to annihilate the honeypot (single-point-of-attack).

2   Background

Blockchain. A common misconception is the usage of the word "blockchain." It is frequently confused with cryptocurrency or with distributed applications. The strict definition of blockchain only specifies a subset of distributed ledgers, where transactions are ordered in sequential batches. The correct classification is as follows:

Each blockchain is a distributed ledger, but not every distributed ledger is a blockchain. In this thesis, the intention is to use distributed ledger over the term blockchain. However, some cited sources describe a wide variety of distributed ledgers with the term "blockchain," as the wording evolved to a well-known label for any kind of distributed ledger, and is used as an umbrella term, despite its more specific origin. Descendants of the blockchain technology are often of higher performance and offer additional benefits. These ledgers provide distributed ledger technology but not necessarily inside a block-chain-structure, instead of in more complex interconnecting structures, which allow for parallelization of transactions. A promising descendant of the blockchain structure is the Directed Acyclic Graph (DAG) [1].

Bitcoin. Satoshi Nakamoto invented the blockchain in 2008. Satoshi Nakamoto is an alias, used by the unknown inventor(s). The inventor(s) of bitcoin used this alias to publish a scientific paper [2]. Satoshi Nakamoto has become the most famous name inside the blockchain community. Satoshi's work is the basis on which all future blockchains were built on.

The real identity of Bitcoins inventor stays a secret, whereby false claims and fraud are a recurring problem, as of today.

Smart Contracts. Nick Szabo is widely credited for first defining Smart Contracts [3]. Cryptography and other security mechanisms allowed Szabo to define the first Smart Contract in 1997. This definition had the goal to be used for credit contracts, content rights management, payment systems, and contracts with bearers.

Identity. On the topic of decentralized identity, several projects have made significant accomplishments. In this paper we use findings of the Hyperledger Identity Working Group [6] but also considers solutions of identity focused solutions such as Civic [4], and Selfkey [5].

A promising variant of identity is the so-called Self-Sovereign Identity [5]. This identity is strongly bound to one entity and does stay valid until the end of the entities lifetime. Such an identity can be claimed in a decentralized manner. Additionally, it cannot be taken away and therefore provides a high level of immutability. An entity might be any person, organization, object or legal entity. Today, biometrics are often used to confirm a persons Self-Sovereign Identity.

Data Immutability. Data Immutability is one of the blockchain features, that ensures the persistence of the data, by storing data immutable from censorship and unwanted manipulation. Before the era of distributed ledger technology, data immutability was primarily ensured through closed systems and trustworthy actors. Another technique to ensure data immutability was the usage of Write Once Read Many (WORM) drives [9]. WORM-Drives are a hardware solution to this problem that prevents the deletion or alteration of written data, similarly to the blockchain, but without the decentralization aspect and without offering trustless transactions.

3   Our Proposal

We propose to introduce an alternative for access management inside companies. An alternative that has a decentralized architecture, contains no single-point-of-attack, and is capable of being integrated into applications via an API.

We propose that such a solution relies on a current standard (ANSI CORE RBAC [8]) to provide a state of the art level of quality.

3.1   Platform Decision

First, we broke down the possible options of a distributed ledger platform, by focusing only on business-oriented solutions. A business-oriented solution has to offer a permitted and private network variant to match Daimler AGs requirements. We used the following decision-matrix (Table 1) to identify the most suitable distributed ledger platform for this specific project.

Table 1. Platform value analysis

Criteria	Weight	Platform value on criteria		
		Ethereum	Hyperledger fabric	R3 Corda
Accessibility of the technology	2	4	5	4
Reliability of the platform	2	4	2	3
Capability of running smart contracts	3	4	5	4
Governance of development	1	5	5	4
Modes of operation (public, private, permissioned, permissionless)	3	4	4	4
Consensus algorithm	1	2	4	1
Capability of handling a cryptocurrency	1	5	3	3
Stakeholder involvement	3	3	5	1
Licensing	3	5	5	4
Platform Value:		**76**	**83**	**61**

All constraints are stakeholder constraints which need to be considered for this project, but might differ for future blockchain projects, as the technology is improving rapidly.

The platform value analysis (Table 1) shows that Hyperledger Fabric is the favorable project with a score of 83 points. Further, qualitative aspects of Hyperledger Fabric, such as its modularity and flexibility strengthen this decision.

3.2   System Design

The PoC was developed in two iterations. At first, we developed the Fabric Development Network (Fig. 1) to allow for a rapid smart contract development process, second, we created a Fabric Sample Network (Fig. 2) to validate the concept's feasibility as a business solution.

Traditional RBAC systems make use of sessions, to control the user access over a defined time of interaction. A user would log on to the system and provide proof of his identity by providing a user password. In blockchain applications, a user signs all his messages with his unique private key to prove his identity. A user interaction results in a smart contract call. This smart contract call by default undergoes a profound checking and authentication process. These interaction wise checks make sessions-based control of user access obsolete. For this proof of concept, session management is therefore completely ignored.

Identity is a necessity in this PoC, due to the fact that the requirements of the stakeholders demand a private blockchain solution. An ideal solution seeks to utilize DID (Decentralized Identifier) to handle identities on the blockchain in a decentralized manner. The platform of choice for this prototype does not yet support DID. It is foreseeable that implementation of DIDs into Hyperleder Fabric will take place after a successful release of Hyperleder Indy. For the PoC of this thesis, the default solution of Hyperleder Fabric is used, a Membership Service Provider (MSP) based on a Certificate Authority. This MSP is interchangeable and agonistic to its implementation. As soon as decentralized identity services are available, a transition to these should be considered, to improve decentralization. It is possible to use multiple Certificate Authorities within one network, to make the network more resilient and decentralized. For the PoC, a minimal setup is used to keep the complexity manageable. For a production network, the usage of multiple CA is strongly recommended, as it is mandatory for the decentralization requirement.

3.3   RBAC Smart Contract

First, we created a development network, to develop and deploy smart contracts on.

The development environment does not contain a back-end server and therefore does not run the Fabric-SDK. There is also no graphical interface for the user interaction. Testing and development of the chaincode are done using the CLI only. The CLI compiles and deploys the chaincode. The CLI is run out of a Docker container with the same name (CLI). Go code on the machine of the smart contract developer is shared with the Docker container, to allow compilation inside the CLI-peer. In the docker-compose file, the linked folders between the docker-container and the host-system are specified to allow for shared access to the folder. Figure 1 shows the apparent simplified network structure, only containing the bare minimum entities for running, developing and testing smart contracts.

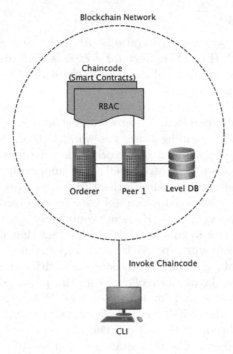

Fig. 1. Fabric Development Network structure

Table 2. Data model

TYPE	KEY	VALUE
user	userName	userID
role	roleName	{permissions}
assignment	userID	roleName

This simplified network setup allowed us to develop our RBAC-Smart Contract more quickly. The smart contract is written in "Go", a statically typed programming language in the tradition of C.

The smart contract manipulates the ledger to store the needed data in a key-value data model, containing user rights and privileges as values and using the user-id as a key. The resulting data model is viewed in Table 2.

3.4 RBAC API

We created a RESTful API To open up the on-chain RBAC implementation for applications to interact with. In order to provide the RESTful API and to move to a realistic network design, we created a "Sample Network".

The sample network is utilized to evaluate the feasibility of a business network running the on-chain RBAC chaincode. The network contains all relevant network entities for a production blockchain application.

All network entities are implemented using Docker containers, to keep the hardware demand on a minimum level and to allow for a simple debugging and management process.

A Membership Service Provider is put in place to manage user identities and to provide the public- and private-key-infrastructure for authentication.

A node back-end server creates the blockchain interface for the front-end application. This back-end interacts with the Fabric-SDK provided through the official Hyperledger Fabric repository.

Each peer inside the blockchain network has improved capabilities, through the usage of Couch DB. The database is used as a state database for the better organization of the blockchain's datasets. By default, Hyperleder Fabric uses Level DB for simple key-value states. For this PoC we use Couch DB as it is capable of handling JSON queries.

The overall sample system design is displayed in Fig. 2 and shows the network entities.

4   Use Case

As distributed ledger technology finds its way into experimental and productive business applications, the technology inevitably faces similar challenges as its centralized counterpart. Distributed ledger applications usually handle sensitive data. One of the reasons to use distributed ledgers instead of traditional solutions is the need for additional data security. Moving sensitive data onto a private, distributed ledger does effectively cancel out the single point of failure problem and provides additional resilience against many attack vectors.

Today, access to private distributed ledger applications is still handled using centralized authorization servers. Developers want to create truly decentralized applications, using truly decentralized access control. Therefore the access control data itself has to be stored and managed in a decentralized manner, e.g., on a blockchain. Interactions with this access control systems shall be enabled in a decentralized manner as well. This behavior is achieved using smart contracts (chaincode).

5   Validation

Security and resilience of applications are of great importance in the corporate world. One option to increase security and resilience is decentralization. This is why future business applications will make use of distributed ledger technology. As a consequence, standard features such as access control for business applications might migrate to decentralized solutions. The PoC implements role-based access control to meet this requirement as well as providing similar features as a state of the art access control technique such as ANSI RBAC [8].

The RPAC-API inside the PoC can be used over two interfaces. (1) The API gets called over the front-end application. (2) The API-functions can be accessed over direct API-calls using API-URLs in the browser or with the use of Postman. The interaction with the API is proven by calling Core-RBAC-Functions as supposed to and checking the responses against the expected outcome. The access control events are logged inside the hosting machine, as well as over the front-end

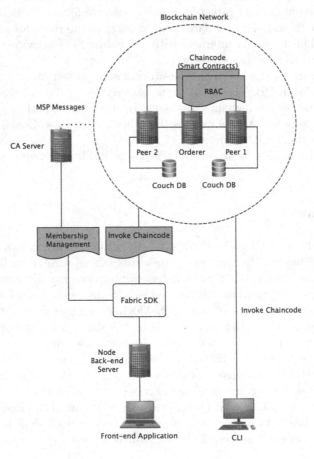

Fig. 2. Fabric Sample Network structure

application output. The API is accessible for identities with the required privileges. API calls form unknown identities, as well as API-calls from identities which do not hold the required permission or user role get declined. API calls with false parameters are also declined as intended. The development front-end is a sample for the integration into decentralized applications. It proves that arbitrary web applications can be configured or created to easily utilize the RBAC-API.

6   Conclusion

Instead of mitigating the risks of a single point of attack, this thesis has shown an architectural solution to eliminate the honeypot entirely. With the PoC running Hyperledger Fabric, as a distributed ledger, the network is capable of providing the necessary level of decentralization to annihilate the honeypot (single point of attack).

The willingness inside the hosting company Daimler AG to migrate their centralized applications to a new decentralized system is not very serious. The company has a strong trust in the immutability of its systems, as the risk of exploitation of Daimler AG's access control systems is considered marginal.

Daimler AG used the developed PoC to show an alternative to the current systems (Siteminder, OpenID Connect, SecurePIN), and to promote the relevance of decentralization.

References

1. Colomb, R.: Deductive Databases and Their Application. Taylor & Francis, Bristol (2003)
2. Nakamoto, S.: Bitcoin: a peer-to-peer electronic cash system (2008). http://www.bitcoin.org/bitcoin.pdf
3. Szabo, N.: Formalizing and securing relationships on public networks. J. First Monday (1997)
4. Civic Whitepaper. https://tokensale.civic.com/CivicTokenSaleWhitePaper.pdf. Accessed 4 Apr 2018
5. SelfKey Whitepaper. https://selfkey.org/wp-content/uploads/2017/11/selfkey-whitepaper-en.pdf. Accessed 4 Apr 2018
6. Hyperledger Indy Working Group Homepage. https://wiki.hyperledger.org/projects/indy. Accessed 4 Apr 2018
7. Hyperledger Indy Homepage. https://www.hyperledger.org/projects/hyperledger-indy. Accessed 4 Apr 2018
8. Incits: American National Standard for Information Technology - Role-Based Access Control Models. ANSI INCITS 359-2004 (2004)
9. Haustein, N.: Solving the long term archiving challenges with IBM Spectrum Protect for Data Retention Solutions (formerly SSAM) (2016)

Industrial Socio-Cyberphysical System's Consumables Tokenization for Smart Contracts in Blockchain

Nikolay Teslya(✉) 🆔

SPIIRAS, 14th line 39, 199178 St. Petersburg, Russia
teslya@iias.spb.su

Abstract. As a result of the development of the Industry 4.0 concept, the physical characteristics of production and the production process were transferred to the digital form. This process is also known as production digitalization. Digitalization allows creating so-called digital twins of production components, among which are smart objects, including machines (production robots), people, software services, processed materials and manufactured products. Digital twins allow to display not only the current state of the component, but also predict its actions according the current situation by creating behavior patterns. The interaction of digital twins is carried out through the cloud platform of the Internet of Things using an ontological representation to ensure interoperability. Interaction via cloud IoT platform causes problems associated with providing trust in the distribution of consumables between components of the industrial IoT system. One of the recent solutions to such problems is using of blockchain technology. In this paper, an example of the integration of industrial IoT and blockchain technology is presented. Each component of the system is represented by a corresponding digital twin, capable of interacting on-the-fly with ontologies in the IoT and blockchain network. To solve the problem of control and exchange of consumable resources in IIoT, this paper proposes classification and principles of resource tokenization depending on their class. The tokenization has been checked by creating smart contracts for consumables allocation on Hyperledger Fabric platform.

Keywords: Industrial IoT · Socio-cyberphysical system · Blockchain
Digitalization · Tokenization · Smart contract

1 Introduction

One of the main trends in the development of modern industries is the creation of a socio-cyberphysical systems in scope of the Industry 4.0 conception that allows to expand the globalization of production and increase its flexibility [1, 2]. The main components of the industrial socio-cyberphysical systems are smart objects, which include machines (production robots), people, software services, processed materials and products. The term "smart" in this case means that in the production process, machines, software services and people are able to analyze the current situation and make decisions based on available information about the state of production and

© Springer Nature Switzerland AG 2019
W. Abramowicz and A. Paschke (Eds.): BIS 2018 Workshops, LNBIP 339, pp. 344–355, 2019.
https://doi.org/10.1007/978-3-030-04849-5_31

production facilities [3–6], as well as processed materials and manufactured products are able to accumulate the history of interaction and analyze their own state either independently or using external services. The interaction of individual objects in the socio-cyberphysical systems is reached due to the development of software services (agents), which are digital twins of real objects that dynamically display their properties in a virtual (cyber) space and provide information exchange between them through a common information space, forming a smart factory. Unlike an automated factory, a smart factory is characterized by complete interaction of all production elements, which allows creating a flexible system that can independently optimize productivity, self-adapt to new conditions and be trained in real time as well as autonomously execute the production [7]. The problems that arise in this case are linked with ensuring the interaction between the heterogeneous components of the factories, both local (in one factory) and distributed (distributed production); consolidation of information from heterogeneous sources to obtain a new value; and the adaptation of production to rapidly changing customer requirements and production capabilities.

To ensure interoperability between components connected to the IoT, ontologies and ontology mapping mechanisms are used [8–10]. These mechanisms are developed and used in numerous projects related to socio-cyberphysical systems, the IoT and the industrial IoT, with the goal of creating a semantic description of information accessible to all components of socio-cyberphysical systems [11, 12]. The use of ontologies is helping to solve these problems with a semantic description of information that expands the knowledge of all participants about the concepts of a subject domain, which makes it possible to work not only on specific values, but also on the meaning inherent in the information [13].

Ensuring trust and monitoring the production process is relevant, mainly for the case of uniting several smart factories into a single production system. In this case, interaction between them requires the transparency of operations related to the production, supply, receipt, and processing of the product. Currently, a promising way to meet these requirements is the distributed decentralized technology of transaction ledger, also known as blockchain. With this technology, it is possible to organize a decentralized distributed immutable storage where each record, called a transaction in block, will be linked with neighboring ones, by computing the hash with a predefined complexity. Arguments of the hash function are transactions in the blockchain network and neighboring blocks [14]. Expanding the possibilities of the ledger through the use of smart contracts makes it possible to make the blockchain an active participant in the socio-cyberphysical system, which is entrusted with the role of monitoring compliance with the rules of interaction of other participants.

This paper describes the possible architecture for the interaction of socio-cyberphysical systems components based on the integration of the cloud-based IoT platform and blockchain technology. Each component is represented by a digital twin, reflecting the characteristics of a real object in the form of an ontology, as well as containing the basic behavior patterns, which allow predicting the response of a component to the current situation changes. Consumables consumption is proposed to be tracked through blockchain with smart contracts. For this purpose, the paper provides basic classification of consumables, and a possible way of their representation with blockchain tokens, taking into account the specific characteristics of each of their classes.

2 Related Work

Currently, several cloud platforms for the Internet of things are already implemented, including those adapted for the tasks of the industry. Such platforms are provided by Amazon (AWS IoT Cloud), Microsoft (Azure IoT Platform), Siemens (MindSphere), Google (Google IoT Core). In general, all of them provide the ability to connect devices of the Internet of things (sensors, robots, and computing devices) to the cloud storage of information, as well as set of built-in software services for data analysis. It should be noted that only AWS IoT Cloud provides possibility to create a digital twin of a device, called in the terms of the platform as "the device shadow", which emulates the presence of the device in case of communication or other failure. Access to all cloud platforms is provided by a paid subscription, with the source code of platforms closed, which does not allow expanding their functionality to meet new requirements to the platforms of the industrial Internet of things.

To provide interoperability between heterogeneous components in IoT that are connected to the common information space, ontologies and ontology mapping mechanisms are used [8–10]. These mechanisms are developed and successfully used in a large number of projects related to socio-cyberphysical systems, the Internet of Things and the industrial Internet of Things, with the goal of creating a semantic description of information accessible to all components of socio-cyberphysical systems and creating the ontological description of IoT components that can be viewed as digital twins [11, 15, 16].

In [17] scenarios of Industrial Internet of Things with digital twins are described:

(1) Production on demand. It is possible to create marketplaces of production services that will accept and automatically serve orders from buyers to produce highly customizable goods (for example 3D printing or computer numerical control). Production components would be smart devises tracking orders transmitted through a blockchain network.

(2) Tracing of goods through supply chains. The creation of digital twins of goods which would store information about goods life cycle—from what details they were produced, who and when owned them, information about repairs etc. Thanks to this information it is possible to track the position of the product in the supply chain, identify the products that were produced from the batch of defective parts, confirm the product license (that it is not fake or stolen) etc. The creation of digital twins with similar goals is also described in papers [2, 18, 19]. The example of a supply chain schema is described in paper [18].

(3) The organization of automatic interaction between production machines—the exchange of messages about the readiness of the product to the next stage of production. Herewith production can be decentralized—different stages of processing can be carried out by different responsible enterprises.

3 IIoT Components Interaction Through the Blockchain and IoT

Blockchain was originally considered as a distributed transaction ledger for keeping records of various operations [20]. To date, the blockchain is mainly used as a basis for cryptocurrencies, for example, in platforms like Blockchain, Ethereum, etc. However, during recent years there have been published works, describing the blockchain utilization in other areas, such as supply chain [18], medicine [21], and IoT [19].

3.1 IIoT Over Blockchain

The existing approach to ensuring the interoperability of components through the cloud-based IoT platform with using ontologies was expanded by adding a distributed digital transaction ledger based on blockchain technology to meet security requirements, long-eternity and unchangeable information [22]. As noted in the introduction, the main components of the industrial socio-cyberphysical systems are machines (production robots), people, software services, processed materials and products. Each component of the system is represented using a digital twin (Fig. 1), which interacts with other components through the use of an ontology. In addition, the digital twin provides access to the log, which allows to track the current state of the process in which it participates and update the information about the part of the process for which the relevant component is responsible. In platforms that implement blockchain technology, the capabilities of the journal can be expanded through the use of smart contracts. To ensure ontology-oriented interaction of the components of industrial socio-cyberphysical systems in a smart contract, the logic of processing the ontologies of the components and the interaction between them was determined by means of a blockchain. The idea of smart contract was first proposed in 1994 by Nick Szabo, before the appearing of blockchain technology. N. Szabo has defined a smart contract in the following way: "A smart contract is a set of promises, specified in digital form, including protocols within which the parties perform on these promises" [23].

Smart contract within blokchain technology can be viewed as a decentralized application available to all users of the blokchain. As it was mentioned in previous section, for implementation of additional protocols over an ordered list of published statements, for example, ownership and transfer of consumables, it is necessary to keep a certain state and track its change according to generally accepted rules in accordance with published statements. A possible way to implement this mechanism is to use smart contracts. This mechanism allows distribution and applying protocol rules without going beyond the blockchain. Smart contracts created with this purpose will implement methods in which appropriate checks and state updates will be made. State changes will be reflected in the smart space by means of adding/deleting relevant information.

For this purpose, a basic smart contract was developed in the detachment, which provides support for the following functions [22]:

1. Obtaining information from components presented using an ontology and determining the specific business process to which the published information relates.

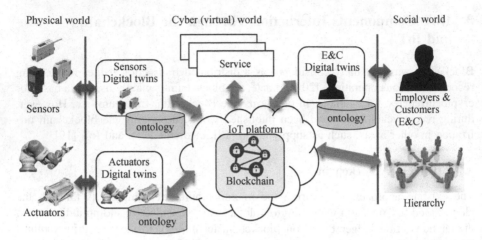

Fig. 1. Scheme of interaction for socio-cyberphysical system with blockchain integration

2. Checking the consistency of information published by the components, to an ontology defined in the industrial socio-cyberphysical system to describe these components, and, if necessary, converting information to the one of the developed ontologies. This function is relevant in the case of interaction of heterogeneous components in cloud IoT platform when using different ontologies to describe components of one category (for example, software agents of different manufacturers can use different ontologies).
3. Keeping the state of IoT platform and update it by the request of participants. Accepted rules for achieving consensus between the components should be met.

To implement the listed functions of the basic smart contract, a basic method was defined in its interface that takes two input parameters:

1. Description of changes in information classified as addition or deletion (by marking information as obsolete);
2. Description of the state of the IoT platform storage, which should be active to make changes.

The first parameter specifies the changes themselves. The seconds parameter is necessary for making changes provided that the IoT has a certain state (contains certain information). As it was noted before, the participants can form distributed business processes, using the IoT platform to take into account and conduct these processes—to publish information that initializes certain transitions between states. The state of the business process can be determined by examining the sequence of statements of its participants. When forming a new state, the participants' requests can be executed in a different order or even be discarded. Such situation can disrupt the business process and undesirable transition may occur.

Both parameters can be empty. In this case the method will return true if the changes have been made and false—otherwise. Changes will be made if the conditions, described as the second parameter are satisfied, and the changes, described as the first parameter are correct. Changes are considered as correct if they satisfy the accepted syntax and do not break the rules of consistency.

In the ontology of components, the identifier of the author of the published document, the unique identifier of the document and the mark of the relevance of the document in the form of metainformation were also added. This metainformation is available through a standard query mechanism with the ability to filter information by it. Thus, it is possible to filter information in documents by authors, publication time and relevance. The serial number is composite having the block number in which this information was published in the upper digits and the number of the information unit in the block in the lower digits. Thus, it is possible to determine the full order of records, and if the blockchain uses the block creation policy with a certain periodicity (for example, according to the documentation, in Ethereum platform parameters the frequency of forming new blocks is 17 s), then it is possible to determine approximate time of statements publication.

3.2 Smart Contract Invocation for IIoT

During the interaction between components through the IoT platform with the blockchain support, the method of basic smart contact can be called either directly through the provided transaction initiation interface in the blockchain or using other smart contacts methods. To simplify the use of custom protocols, the method of any contract should be called using the basic smart contract. To call other methods of smart contacts, participants will need to publish specially structured information in the smart space that must contain:

1. The identifier of the smart contract whose method have to be invoked;
2. The identifier of the smart contract method called by the component of the industrial socio-cyberphysical system;
3. A list of parameters passed to the called method;
4. Other service parameters specific to a particular implementation of the blockchain (for example, the amount of consumable to be transferred).

In addition to support of consumables control in industrial socio-cyberphysical system, smart contracts can be used for other purposes. For example, they can act as a representative of a certain component. The component can create a smart contract that will publish information in the IoT platform on his behalf. An example may be an enterprise that distributes certain physical resources that can be purchased and used in accordance with the terms provided. For example, an energy company can sell energy through a blockchain [17]. Purchased resources are represented by virtual tokens, through which they are controlled (in the simplest case – can be just consumed). For the distribution of tokens, a smart contract can be created, which on behalf of the enterprise can automatically create and transfer tokens (by publishing certain information to the IoT platform) at the direct request of the buyer. They can buy tokens for the currency build-in in the blockchain or for other resources (for example, bank bonds), which can also be objects of the IoT platform. The exchange of resources must be atomically, so it is necessary that a smart contract can publish information also on behalf of the component who invoked it.

So, to support the described use cases, the smart contract that reflects state of IoT platform should support:

1. The invocation of other smart contracts from the blockchain through the publication of the specially structured information.
2. The publication of information by other smart contract on behalf of itself, his creator and the transaction initiator.

In addition, to solve the presented task of developing a platform for the IIoT, another application of the smart contract should be noted. It can be used to combine heterogeneous states of several independent smart contracts in one IoT platform. That allows, for example, to perform a joint information search and conditions checks on it.

4   Digital Twins of the IIoT Components

As a result of the analysis of scenarios for the industrial socio-cyberphysical systems application, ontological models of components were developed that describe their main characteristics for the creation of digital twins. The specific ontologies that can be used as a basis for developing digital twins of components are presented below. They can be broken down to the following groups:

- Ontology of products and materials. Contains an ontological description of the types of products and raw materials. Allows to specify the type of material, its quantitative characteristics (dimensions, weight, quantity), life time, as well as the current position in the supply chain;
- Ontology of indicators of products state and functioning. This ontology is designed to track the current state of the product. Includes the time from the first use, repair marks (which component, when it was replaced), the consumables used and their value, the date of the last replenishment of consumables;
- Ontology of production machines and their capabilities. Ontology of machines, parameters of functioning and other elements necessary for the development of multi-agent systems of smart factories;
- Ontology of software services (type of service, operations performed: production of goods, delivery of materials, transportation, storage, time of operation, cost of the operation), with a description of program interfaces for the formation of orders.
- Ontology of human resources. It is used to describe workers profile (name, age, education, social id, etc.) as well as their competences (competence name and description, rating of competence for worker) and preferences (type of work, work duration, salary, etc.).

In addition, auxiliary ontologies were developed that provide a description of the relationships of the components:

- Ontology of structural relations between products and materials (components, materials used). It describes from which materials or structural components a particular product was created;

- Ontology of supply chain operations. The ontology of the operations that were performed with the products during the supply chain (materials it was produced, how, machines used in production, how it was transferred and transported, in what environmental conditions it was stored (temperature, humidity, lighting)).

The ontology of products and materials is central and is included in all other ontologies (Fig. 2). In particular, the ontology of indicators of state and functioning, as well as the ontology of structural relations, uses it as a basic one, since it requires the description of material and structural components. The ontology of software services includes the ontology of products and materials for describing input and output data. The ontology of production machines uses the ontology of products and materials to describe production processes. In the ontology of supply chain operations, it is used to describe the objects of operations. In addition, the ontology of operations in the supply chain uses the ontology of production machines and their capabilities and the ontology of software services to describe objects and specify the ontology of structural relations (it describes the operations by which relationships were formed). When creating ontologies, it is proposed to use existing ontologies to improve compatibility with existing software agents built on their basis, in particular, the following ontologies can be used: GoodRelations [24], OWL-S [25], eCl@ss [26], eClassOWL [27], and the IEC 62264 standard [28].

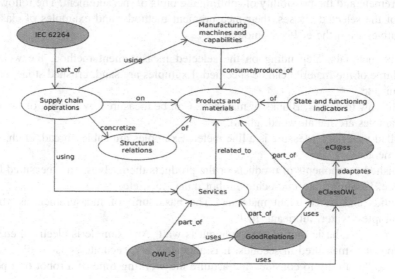

Fig. 2. Digital twins' ontologies interrelations

GoodRelations is an ontology for describing commercial offers, for example, on the sale or lease of assets, or on the provision of services. The ontology allows to describe the information about the supplier, the terms of the offer (cost, quantity, available methods of delivery, payment, etc.), as well as the proposed assets or services. To describe specific assets or services, the ontology is based on third-party standards, for example eCl@ss.

OWL-S is an ontology for describing services in the semantic web. The purpose of this ontology is to provide the ability to automatically search, call, and composition of Web services. In addition to the standard ontologies, there are several works on automation of production that describe their own ontologies that can also be used to develop machine ontologies and production capabilities, supply chain operations and ontologies of structural relationships, for example [1, 29, 30].

5   Consumables Tokenization

For the smart contracts creation associated with the control of the distribution of consumables, it is necessary to provide a description of the units of resources and materials of production in the form suitable for machine processing. This form should take into account the features of resources and materials associated with the features of their measurement and the possibility of quantization.

To compile the categories of consumables, the eCl@ss ontology was analyzed in the part related to products and materials. The classification of the presented products was carried out in such a way as to combine the materials by the method of their measurement and the possibility of splitting the units of measurement. The following is a list of the selected classes, their measurement methods, and examples of class representatives from the eCl@ss ontology.

- Bulk materials. Depending on the selected measurement method, the weight or volume of the material can be specified. Examples are sand, crushed stone, cereals, flour, etc.
- Solid raw materials. Blanks of materials. Can be measured by weight, of by pieces. Examples are metal, wood, glass).
- Rolled materials. Measure is a line meter. Examples are cable, thread, cloth, sheets of metal.
- Finished components of products or the products themselves. Are measured by the piece. Examples are microchips, robot units, cars, etc.
- Liquids and other fluent materials. The basic unit of measurement is volume. Examples: water, lubricant, fuel.
- Energy. The basic unit of measurement is watt. An example is electrical energy.
- Time. It is measured in seconds. It is allocated as a separate consumable resource due to the ability to consider and acquire the working time of a robot or a person.

Description of the consumables in a smart contract is based on the use of the ontology of products and materials. For this purpose, the following properties are defined in the classes of the ontology: the name of the material, the method of its measurement, the quantization step, the minimum and maximum amount of the resource in the system, the current amount of the resource. As an example of using the developed ontology representation of consumables, a smart contract on the Hyperledger Fabric platform has been developed [31].

```
var res Resource     //Resource to be allocated
var component Component //Component that request resource
var type []Type         //Resource type
var amount Integer      //Amount of resource

func allocateResource(stub shim.ChaincodeStubInterface,
args []string) (string, error) {
  type = [time, blank]
  component, res, amount = args[0], args[1], args[2]
  if res.type == type[1]{
    res.amount = intToTime(amount)// convert to time
  } else res.amount = amount // set blank
  if getState(res.value) > res.amount {
    stub.PutState(component.id, res.amount)
    stub.PutState(resource, res.value res.amount)
  } else askSupply(resorce, res.maxAmount - res.value))
}
```

In the example presented above, a certain number of resources is allocated to the component of the socio-cyberphysical system. In this case, it is checked whether the request from the component does not exceed the number of available resources. If the resource is sufficient, it can be allocated. Otherwise, a request is sent for the resource supplying from the remote warehouse to refill it.

6 Conclusion

The main purpose of this work was to develop a model for representing consumables in an industrial socio-cyberphysical system for the creation of smart contracts that allow for control over the allocation of resources. Resource allocation and control as well as smart contracts are implemented using the blockchain platform.

To reach this goal, a scheme was presented for the interaction of components of industrial socio-cyberphysical systems, as well as the description of components using appropriate digital twins. The development of digital twins was carried out using their ontological description, which allowed ensuring interoperability of heterogeneous components. For each type of component, the ontology of the digital twin description was developed. Individual ontologies are combined using an upper-level ontology, which provides a link between all components.

Consumables in the system are represented using an appropriate ontology. In this case, seven types of consumables were distinguished, differing in the way they specified their number. Through the allocation of classes, standard contracts were developed to allocate each of the resources. As an example, the paper presents a general view of the contract created for the Hyperledger Fabric platform.

Acknowledgements. The presented research was partially supported by the projects funded through grants # 17-29-07073, 17-07-00327 and 17-07-00328 of the Russian Foundation for Basic Research.

References

1. Cheng, H., Zeng, P., Xue, L., Shi, Z., Wang, P., Yu, H.: Manufacturing ontology development based on industry 4.0 demonstration production line. In: Proceedings of 2016 3rd International Conference on Trust System Their Application TSA 2016, pp. 42–47 (2016). https://doi.org/10.1109/tsa.2016.17
2. El Kadiri, S., et al.: Current trends on ICT technologies for enterprise information systems. Comput. Ind. **79**, 14–33 (2016). https://doi.org/10.1016/j.compind.2015.06.008
3. Bedenbender, H., Bentkus, A., Epple, U., Hadlich, T.: Industrie 4.0 Plug-and-Produce for Adaptable Factories: Example Use Case Definition, Models, and Implementation, pp. 56–62 (2017)
4. Silva, J.R., Nof, S.Y.: Manufacturing service: from e-Work and service-oriented approach towards a product-service architecture. IFAC-PapersOnLine **48**, 1628–1633 (2015). https://doi.org/10.1016/J.IFACOL.2015.06.319
5. Pisching, M.A., Junqueira, F., Filho, D.J.S., Miyagi, P.E.: Service composition in the cloud-based manufacturing focused on the industry 4.0. In: IFIP Advances in Information and Communication Technology, pp. 65–72 (2015)
6. Zhang, D., Wan, J., Hsu, C.H., Rayes, A.: Industrial technologies and applications for the internet of things. Comput. Netw. **101**, 1–4 (2016). https://doi.org/10.1016/j.comnet.2016.02.019
7. Burke, R., Mussomeli, A., Laaper, S., Hartigan, M., Sniderman, B.: The smart Factory (2017)
8. Gierej, S.: The framework of business model in the context of industrial internet of things. Procedia Eng. **182**, 206–212 (2017). https://doi.org/10.1016/j.proeng.2017.03.166
9. Zhu, T., Dhelim, S., Zhou, Z., Yang, S., Ning, H.: An architecture for aggregating information from distributed data nodes for industrial internet of things. Comput. Electr. Eng. **58**, 337–349 (2017). https://doi.org/10.1016/j.compeleceng.2016.08.018
10. Tang, H., Li, D., Wang, S., Dong, Z.: CASOA: an architecture for agent-based manufacturing system in the context of industry 4.0. IEEE Access **6**, 12746–12754 (2017). https://doi.org/10.1109/access.2017.2758160. 3536
11. Euzenat, J., Shvaiko, P.: Ontology Matching. Springer, Heidelberg (2013). https://doi.org/10.1007/978-3-642-38721-0
12. Smirnov, A., Kashevnik, A., Ponomarev, A., Teslya, N., Shchekotov, M., Balandin, S.I.: Smart space-based tourist recommendation system. In: Balandin, S., Andreev, S., Koucheryavy, Y. (eds.) NEW2AN 2014. LNCS, vol. 8638, pp. 40–51. Springer, Cham (2014). https://doi.org/10.1007/978-3-319-10353-2_4
13. Lemaignan, S., Siadat, A., Dantan, J.Y., Semenenko, A.: MASON: a proposal for an ontology of manufacturing domain. In: Proceedings - DIS 2006: IEEE Workshop on Distributed Intelligent Systems - Collective Intelligence and Its Applications, pp. 195–200. IEEE (2006)
14. Huckle, S., Bhattacharya, R., White, M., Beloff, N.: Internet of things, blockchain and shared economy applications. Procedia Comput. Sci. **98**, 461–466 (2016). https://doi.org/10.1016/j.procs.2016.09.074

15. Otero-Cerdeira, L., Rodríguez-Martínez, F.J., Gómez-Rodríguez, A.: Ontology matching: a literature review. Expert Syst. Appl. **42**, 949–971 (2015). https://doi.org/10.1016/j.eswa. 2014.08.032

16. Teslya, N., Smirnov, A., Levashova, T., Shilov, N.: Ontology for resource self-organisation in cyber-physical-social systems. In: Klinov, P., Mouromtsev, D. (eds.) KESW 2014. CCIS, vol. 468, pp. 184–195. Springer, Cham (2014). https://doi.org/10.1007/978-3-319-11716-4_ 16

17. Sikorski, J.J., Haughton, J., Kraft, M., Street, P., Drive, P.F.: Blockchain technology in the chemical industry: machine-to-machine electricity market. Appl. Energy **195**, 234–246 (2016). https://doi.org/10.1016/j.apenergy.2017.03.039

18. Abeyratne, S.A., Monfared, R.P.: Blockchain ready manufacturing supply chain using distributed ledger. Int. J. Res. Eng. Technol. **05**, 1–10 (2016). https://doi.org/10.15623/ijret. 2016.0509001

19. Jia, X., Fathy, R.A., Huang, Z., Luo, S., Gong, J., Peng, J.: Framework of blockchain of things as decentralized service platform (2017)

20. Nakamoto, S.: Bitcoin: A Peer-to-Peer Electronic Cash System, p. 9 (2008). http://www. bitcoin.org, https://doi.org/10.1007/s10838-008-9062-0

21. Hoy, M.B.: An introduction to the blockchain and its implications for libraries and medicine. Med. Ref. Serv. Q. **36**, 273–279 (2017). https://doi.org/10.1080/02763869.2017.1332261

22. Teslya, N., Ryabchikov, I.: Blockchain-based platform architecture for industrial IoT. In: Proceeding of the 21st Conference of FRUCT Association, pp. 321–329 (2017)

23. Szabo, N.: Formalizing and securing relationships on public networks. First Monday **2** (1997). https://doi.org/10.5210/fm.v2i9.548

24. Hepp, M.: Goodrelations: an ontology for describing products and services offers on the web. In: Gangemi, A., Euzenat, J. (eds.) EKAW 2008. LNCS (LNAI), vol. 5268, pp. 329–346. Springer, Heidelberg (2008). https://doi.org/10.1007/978-3-540-87696-0_29

25. Martin, D., et al.: OWL-S: Semantic Markup for Web Services (2004). https://www.w3.org/ Submission/OWL-S/. Accessed 22 Feb 2018

26. Gräser, O., et al.: White paper AutomationML and eCl@ss integration (2015)

27. Hepp, M., Leenheer, P., Moor, A., Sure, Y.: Ontology Management. Springer, Boston (2008). https://doi.org/10.1007/978-3-540-88845-1_2

28. IEC: IEC 62264-1 Enterprise-control system integration – Part 1: Models and terminology (2003)

29. Usman, Z., Young, R.I., Case, K., Harding, J.: A manufacturing foundation ontology for product lifecycle interoperability. Enterprise Interoperability IV Making Internet Future Enterprises, pp. 147–155 (2010). https://doi.org/10.1007/978-1-84996-257-5_14

30. Martinez Lastra, J.L., Delamer, I.M.: Ontologies for production automation. In: Dillon, T.S., Chang, E., Meersman, R., Sycara, K. (eds.) Advances in Web Semantics I. LNCS, vol. 4891, pp. 276–289. Springer, Heidelberg (2008). https://doi.org/10.1007/978-3-540-89784-2_11

31. Androulaki, E., et al.: Hyperledger Fabric: A Distributed Operating System for Permissioned Blockchains, p. 15 (2018)

SmartExchange: Decentralised Trustless Cryptocurrency Exchange

Filip Adamik$^{(\boxtimes)}$ and Sokol Kosta

CMI, Aalborg University Copenhagen, Copenhagen, Denmark
fadami15@student.aau.dk, sok@es.aau.dk

Abstract. Trading cryptocurrency on current digital exchange platforms is a trust-based process, where the parties involved in the exchange have to fully trust the service provider. As it has been proven several times, this could lead to funds being stolen, either due to malicious service providers that simply disappear or due to hacks that these platforms might suffer. In this work, we propose and develop a decentralised exchange solution based on smart contracts running on the Ethereum network that is open, verifiable, and does not require trust. The platform enables two parties to trade different currencies, limited to Ethereum and Bitcoin in the current status of the system. A smart contract, deployed on the Ethereum blockchain, functions as an *escrow*, which holds a user's funds until a verified transaction has been made by the other party. To make the smart contract able to detect a Bitcoin transfer, we implement our solution by utilising an *oracle*. We define the system architecture and implement a working platform, which we test in a model scenario, successfully exchanging Bitcoin and Ether on the blockchain test networks. We conclude the paper identifying possible challenges and threats to such a system.

Keywords: Cryptocurrency · Distributed · Exchange · Blockchain
Smart contract · Oracle · Ethereum · Bitcoin

1 Introduction

Researchers and developers have proposed cryptocurrency as early as 1983, when anonymous digital money was first introduced [1]. Today's cryptocurrencies, such as Bitcoin, Litecoin, Ethereum, etc., are thus only the continuation of a long lasting effort on developing a currency with sufficient guarantees against misuses, such as double-spending or theft. The wide-spread adoption of these currencies indicates that the guarantees against misuse are indeed sufficient – in other words, that the users trust the cryptocurrencies. If this was not the case, they probably would not be used. There are numerous reasons why users buy cryptocurrency, ranging from value-holding purposes to short-term trading. However, the trust in the cryptocurrency is somewhat unavoidable. Regardless of the motivation, whenever people acquire a cryptocurrency, they believe that it will retain value, at least until they exchange it for other services or goods.

© Springer Nature Switzerland AG 2019
W. Abramowicz and A. Paschke (Eds.): BIS 2018 Workshops, LNBIP 339, pp. 356–367, 2019.
https://doi.org/10.1007/978-3-030-04849-5_32

Indeed, exchanging cryptocurrencies has become a regular task for an increasing number of people. There are countless different platforms that offer this service, ranging from simple wallets that embed currency exchange as additional service, to massive trading platforms with daily market cap of millions of dollars, such as *Bitfinex*[1], *Coinbase*[2], or *Bitstamp*[3], among others. All these exchanges, however, share one common feature: when making a transaction, users need to trust them with their funds. For example, whenever a user exchanges USD to Bitcoin, she transfers the USD funds to the company's account, which converts them to Bitcoin. Until the user does not withdraw the converted amount, the platform has full control over her money. If the company suddenly goes out of business, or gets attacked, the user may never get her funds back! This situation is not hypothetical, there have been various cases where deposited funds were lost or stolen, with the most famous case of the Japanese-based Bitcoin exchange Mt. Gox, where USD 380 million worth of Bitcoins were stolen in 2014 [2]. As such, the trust in the exchange platforms is quite questionable. Some experts advise not to store any funds in these systems for long periods of time and to make deposits to a secured wallet right away, since it is believed the funds are more vulnerable in an exchange platform [3].

In this work, we address this problem and propose an exchange system where the trust in the currency is used for making the exchange process of exchange safer. To accomplish this task, we use the Ethereum system, which is the second most popular cryptocurrency as of today. Ethereum gives the possibility of running *smart contracts* – small programs that are run by many computers around the world at the same time. This provides assurance that no-one will tamper with the code and that no-one can manipulate the outcome of a smart contract. We design and implement a system that deploys smart contracts to the Ethereum network, which are used to control the trading process and function. We show that having a distributed exchange platform is not only feasible, but is highly beneficial for the users, since it removes the trust from a single entity. Moreover, to facilitate the utilization of the exchange system, we implement an Android demo application that we use for testing purposes. We demonstrate the operation of this prototype in a model scenario, where we transfer Bitcoin and Ether between two trading parties.

The rest of this work is structured as follows: First, in Sect. 2 we investigate the existing systems and platforms related to our proposal; Then, in Sect. 3 we describe the system architecture and the implementation details of our platform and demo application; In Sect. 4 we present the evaluation of the distributed exchange platform, deploying it on the test blockchain networks and performing Ethereum to Bitcoin currency exchange; In Sect. 5 we present a short discussion about the limits of our proposal; and finally, in Sect. 6 we conclude the work presenting the final remarks and considerations for future improvements.

---

[1] www.bitfinex.com.
[2] www.coinbase.com.
[3] www.bitstamp.com.

2   Related Work

Blockchain is a distributed ledger that records sets of *changes* in a system [4]. A *change* could be any data – for example it could be details of the latest currency transactions [5] or newly deposited business agreements [6]. Blockchain is usually distributed among several independent parties to prevent centralisation of the system and to avoid easy manipulation with the blockchain data by a malicious party [7]. The most notable use of the blockchain is the decentralised peer-to-peer cryptocurrency Bitcoin, where the blockchain is used to keep record of all currency transactions among its users [5]. Researchers identify the transaction-recording as the most standard use of the blockchain [7,8]. However, the possible uses of the blockchain extend further than that – blockchains can be used for operating decentralised applications [9], storing documents [6], financial uses, or outside the financial world [7].

Smart contracts are small programs run in a decentralised manner by all the nodes participating in the network, which are the heart of financial utilization of blockchains. A smart contract consists of a program code, a balance, and a storage space [10,11]. The most prominent system that operates smart contracts is the Ethereum platform. Ethereum fuses the blockchain with a Turing-complete programming language run by the *Ethereum Virtual Machine (EVM)* [12]. The states of this machine are altered by transactions. Besides invoking functions of a smart contract, an Ethereum transaction can also be used to transfer Ethereum's native cryptocurrency *Ether*. For any transaction to be executed by the EVM, users need to purchase command-execution units called *gas*. Users purchase gas to pay for the operation of the EVM – every smart contract must have enough gas to cover for all of its instructions, otherwise it will not be executed [13].

Researchers identify benefits of using the blockchain beyond the finance sector by providing a decentralised and trusted storage system. There are exemplary uses by IBM and Microsoft, who provide the blockchain as a cloud-based service for storing data and assuring their existence [14], or an e-commerce platform implementation by a china-originated multinational conglomerate operating in the transport industry HNA group, which implemented a blockchain-enabled e-commerce platform with three main uses: issuing cryptocurrency, protecting sensitive business information, and lowering the boundaries between different business units [15].

Even though blockchain is considered a robust and secure technology, it still has certain vulnerabilities. The authors of [16] examine these vulnerabilities and find that the crucial risks are related to the *51% attack*, where the attacker controls the majority of the nodes in the network, the double spending attack, or the problem of insufficient private key security. Moreover, other more advances issues are due to vulnerable or under-optimised smart contracts, which result to stolen or wasted funds. The paper further considers attacks independent from the use of blockchain, such as selfish mining attack, where the attacker does not immediately broadcast a new valid block that was mined, leading to unnecessary work performed by the other nodes in the network, or the Eclipse attack, which consists of preventing a particular network node from receiving up-to-date messages from the network and therefore limiting its functionality and/or performance.

In 2014, a security weakness was exploited in a popular cryptocurrency exchange, namely Mt. Gox, which led to subsequent crash of this exchange [2]. While this case was widely covered by the mainstream media, there were numerous other cases that didn't make the news, where the exchange was attacked and users lost their funds. The authors of [17] provide a comprehensive overview over these attacks, and conclude that the probability of a security breach in a cryptocurrency exchange is positively correlated with the transaction volume of that exchange.

All the cryptocurrency exchanges mentioned in [17] were "traditional", in a way that they require the user to deposit funds to the exchange and withdraw the exchanged funds afterwards. To the best of our knowledge, there is no fully decentralised implementation of cryptocurrency exchange available today. There are many exchange platforms offering trading Ethereum based tokens[4], but these tokens do not exist outside Ethereum realm. The only existing proposal for a trust-less digital assets exchange is introduced by Hallgren et al. [18], but this proposed architecture does not completely remove the system centralisation issue, since funds still need to be deposited to the Hallex system. Conversely, our solution is a fully decentralised cryptocurrency exchange platform, built on blockchains and smart contract technology.

The problem of interaction of two separate blockchains is examined closely in [19], where the author introduces several ways to enable cross-chain operability. These include notaries (a trusted group of entities, which operate and exchange assets on both blockchains) and relays (where one of the blockchains carries out a task to learn the status of the other blockchain). A detailed proposal of a notary has been described in [20]. A relay has been described and implemented in the BTC Relay system[5], which allows users to pay for execution of smart contracts on the Ethereum network with Bitcoins. While the exchange of the funds on different blockchains is not the primary aim of this system, it could be extended to support this use case.

3   Design and Implementation

To avoid the necessity of trust between the two trading parties, we propose an architecture where a smart contract functions as a digital escrow holding service. An escrow is a piece of property, temporarily held by a third party until a certain condition has been met[6]. The smart contract therefore holds user's funds, until a condition agreed upon by both users is true. An example of such a condition could be: *"Ether funds can only be released to Bob, if Bob has transferred his Bitcoin to Alice"*. In this scenario, after an initial agreement between Alice and Bob, Alice proceeds to deploy the smart contract with an embedded condition

---

[4] https://angel.co/0xproject/, https://idex.market/.
[5] http://btcrelay.org/.
[6] https://www.investopedia.com/terms/e/escrow.asp.

to the network. She then transfers her Ether to this smart contract, where it will pose as an escrow. This transaction, together with the smart contract code is public and can be verified by Bob. When Bob sees that the funds are deposited in the smart contract, he can transfer his Bitcoins to Alice in an ordinary transaction. The smart contract queries the Bitcoin blockchain for Bob's transaction, and once it has been completed, the smart contract releases Alice's funds to Bob. If Bob tries to cheat Alice by not sending Bitcoins, the condition specified in the smart contract would not be met and the smart contract would not release the funds to Bob. If Alice attempts to cheat Bob by deploying a smart contract with incorrect condition, Bob would discover this by exploring the Ethereum blockchain. A trading scenario between Alice and Bob is illustrated in Fig. 2, while in Fig. 3 we provide a high-level overview of our system architecture. The logic of the smart contract is described in Fig. 1.

```
class my-smart-contract {
        receive funds;
        check transaction status;
        if (transaction happened):
                forward funds to destination;
        else
                return funds to sender;
}
```

Fig. 1. High-level notation of the logic inside a half black-box.

Pre-conditions Alice wants to sell Ether and buy Bitcoins. Bob wants to buy Ether and sell Bitcoins. They agree on the details of the transaction via a side channel.

1. Alice sends Ether to the smart contract.
2. Bob verifies this transaction.
3. Bob sends Bitcoins to Alice.
4. Smart contract verifies Bob's transaction.
5. Smart contract releases Ether to Bob.

Post-conditions: Alice has Bob's Bitcoin, Bob has Alice's Ether.

Fig. 2. Trading scenario where Alice and Bob trade Ethereum and Bitcoin with the help of the smart contract.

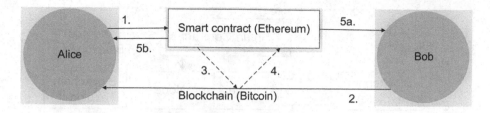

1. Initiate transaction
2. Transfer currency (BTC)
3. Query blockchain for payment
4. Return payment status
5a. Payment made: release funds to Actor B
5b. Payment not made: return funds to Actor A

Fig. 3. System architecture, reflecting the scenario in Fig. 2.

The complexity of implementing this scenario lies mainly in step number 4, where the smart contract must verify the Bitcoin transaction. The difficulty arises from the fact that Ethereum and Bitcoin blockchains are two separate entities that operate on different networks, with different protocols, and are isolated in their respective realms. Indeed, the smart contract resides on the Ethereum blockchain, and to verify Bob's transaction it would need to get data from the Bitcoin blockchain. To address this problem, we make use of *oracles*, which are specialised data sources that translate real-world, off-chain information, into data that can be processed by the smart contract. Oracles watch the blockchain for specified events and respond by publishing the results of a query back to the smart contract [21]. A simple oracle could be a server that listens for these events on the Ethereum network, fetches the real-world data from the web or other location and then delivers the results back to the contract, sending them as a part of a transaction [22,23].

Currently, there are several open source projects that provide *oracle* services – the biggest one being *Oraclize*[7], which offers simple integration with the Solidity language, which is one of the programming languages for smart contracts. Oraclize offers queries to multiple off-chain data sources, including simple HTTP queries or Wolfram Alpha. In our implementation we use Oraclize, however our platform is quite flexible, and other oracles can be integrated very easily.

3.1 Implementation of the System Components

The proposed system consists of several components that interact together, as presented in Fig. 4. The main point of user interaction for both primary and secondary users is the system front-end, which communicates with the Ethereum blockchain via an Ethereum node to deploy a custom smart contract that

---

[7] http://www.oraclize.it (https://github.com/oraclize).

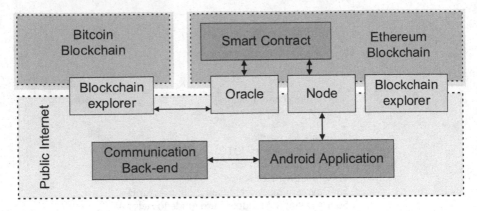

Fig. 4. Overview of the system parts: *Android application* fetches the data about existing offers from the communication back-end and sends new smart contracts to the Ethereum node. *Node* communicates with other nodes in the Ethereum network, maintains the status of the blockchain and deploys new smart contracts to the network. *Smart contract* contacts the oracle after the deployment and holds the funds until the oracle has cleared the transaction as approved. The *oracle* queries the Bitcoin block explorer to learn about the status of the transaction and communicates the result back to the smart contract. *Communication back end* communicates only with the Android application. It holds details about users' offers and supports the trading interaction between the users.

operates the logic of the transaction, and with a back-end, which acts as a communication channel between users. To operate its logic, the smart contract communicates with an oracle, which queries a blockchain explorer provider to learn about the status of a transaction and sends the updates back to the smart contract.

Smart Contract. We program the contract using the Solidity language on Remix, an in-browser IDE, which allows sandbox contract testing[8]. Smart contracts written in Solidity get compiled into BIN (binary) and ABI (Application Binary Interface) format, using the *solc* compiler. The BIN file contains the Solidity code compiled into Ethereum Virtual Machine bytecode and the ABI file contains information about how to interact with the Smart Contract. The encoding of the ABI file is part of the Ethereum protocol specification. Then, we use the Web3j command line tools[9] to transform the BIN and ABI files into Java representation of the smart contract. The Java file includes wrapper methods to invoke the custom constructor and the methods of the contract.

Node. To be able to deploy the smart contracts, we need to have a node in the Ethereum blockchain network. For this purpose, we make use of Infuria, a node-hosting service[10]. Infura endpoints accept connections from any client and

---

[8] https://remix.ethereum.org/.

[9] https://github.com/web3j/web3j.

[10] https://infura.io/.

no authentication is needed. This is not an issue, since by design, our system signs the transaction on device, before it is deployed to the network, meaning that no private information is uploaded on the node.

Oracle. We use the Oraclize service, as it is currently the most widely used in the community and includes extensive documentation and testing environment. The smart contract implements a `callback` method to register for replies from Oraclize, which is called by an Oraclize-issued smart contact together with the result. It is in this method that the smart contract handles the response.

Blockchain Explorer. This entity is needed for the oracle to understand if a transaction has been performed in the Bitcoin network. In our system, we use the *Simple Query API* provided by the Blockchain.info platform, even though any other service could be used without affecting the functionality of our platform.

Application Front-end. To demonstrate the functionality of the prototype, we implement an Android application, which provides a user interface that allows users to engage in a transaction and to deploy smart contracts on the network. It also provides guidance through the transaction process, displaying prompts to the users when their intervention is needed. Lastly, it provides a link to the smart contract, once it has been deployed, so that users can easily locate and verify it on the blockchain. To deploy the smart contract from the Android application, we use a special Java class, which holds the binary representation of the compiled Solidity code and wrapper methods that could be used to communicate with an already deployed smart contract.

Communication Back-end. The data processed by the communication back-end consists of users' Bitcoin and Ether offers. Besides storing users' offers, the back-end also serves as the coordination channel for the users. When a user performs an action in the application that advances the progress of the transaction, a particular field in the database is updated. To implement the back-end platform, we use Firebase, which is a noSQL database storing data in JSON format.

4   Evaluation

In this experiment we demonstrate a transaction between two persons: a primary user Eve, who wants to sell Ether and buy Bitcoin, and a secondary user Mike, who wants to buy Ether and sell Bitcoin. Both users run the application on their phones. Eve has her own Ethereum wallet with some Ether she wishes to sell, while Mike has his own Bitcoin wallet he will use to make the transaction. Eve's and Mike's wallets are standalone systems, independent from our system. The scenario of the transaction is as follows:

1. Mike creates a Bitcoin offer in the Android application by inputting:
    - Amount in Bitcoin he wishes to sell.
    - Amount in Ether he wishes to receive.

  - Ethereum address, where he wishes to receive the Ether.

  Mike then confirms and the offer is pushed on the Firebase database.

2. Eve's device reacts to the change in the database and fetches the latest offers. Eve can now see Mike's offer. She selects it and confirms.

3. Eve is presented with a temporary Ethereum address that will be used to deploy the smart contract. To continue, Eve must transfer her funds to the temporary address. This address is generated on the device by our system, and no other party besides Eve's Android application has access to the private key.

4. Eve then creates an empty Bitcoin address where she will receive funds from Mike. She then inputs her public key to the Android application, so that Mike knows where to send the Bitcoin funds. Eve does not reveal her private key in the process.

5. A smart contract is deployed from the temporary Ethereum address with the following properties:

   - Mike's Ethereum address.
   - Eve's Bitcoin address.
   - Amount of Bitcoin, that needs to be received by Eve, before the smart contract releases the Ether.

   Besides these properties, which are specified in the smart contract constructor as data fields, the creation of a contract also carries two other significant information:

   - Sender's Ethereum address – this is used to return the funds in case of unsuccessful transaction.
   - Value, associated with the transaction – this is funds Eve is sending to Mike.

6. After the smart contract has been deployed, the transaction hash is displayed to both Mike and Eve. Mike needs this transaction hash to find and verify that Eve deployed the smart contract with the agreed properties.

7. After Mike verifies the correctness of the information in the smart contract, he proceeds transferring funds to the Bitcoin address in the smart contract.

8. Right after the deployment, the smart contract sends a query to Oraclize. The query consists of the following data:

   - Blockchain.info API endpoint reference.
   - Eve's Bitcoin address.
   - Delay, after which the API query is executed (600 s).

   Oraclize registers this query and starts a timer. After 10 min, it contacts the specified API endpoint with the specified Bitcoin address. This endpoint returns the unspent transaction output of the queried address in Satoshi as a plain string. After Oraclize receives this reply from the Blockchain.info, it passes the result to the smart contract by calling its `callback` method.

9. The contract compares whether the result fulfils the condition (i.e. if the unspent balance of the Bitcoin address received from the Blockchain.info is equal or greater than the balance specified by Eve, when she deployed the contract). If this condition is true, the smart contract sends its Ether balance to Mike. If it is false, it returns the Ether back to Eve.

This scenario was successfully executed with two Android devices, a Parity Ethereum wallet, and a GreenAddress Bitcoin wallet. The transactions were made on the Ethereum *Kovan* test network and Bitcoin *testnet3* test networks. Eve's device was a OnePlus A5000 running Android 8.1.0 Oreo, while Mike's device was a Samsung AM-A510F, running Android 7.0.0 Nougat and both devices had a stable internet connection. The whole process took approximately 20 min, out of which 10 min is the oracle response delay. The cost of the smart contract deployment was approximately 0.05 kETH[11] and was paid by Eve. This process can be replicated on the test networks at any time. The prerequisites are a balance of kETH and testnet BTC and transaction amount greater than 0.1 kETH.

5 Discussion

In this section, we present some challenges that need to be considered, which might prove to be crucial for the adoption of the system.

Cost of a Transaction. As mentioned earlier, there is a cost associated with every smart contract. The deployment of the smart contract used in the prototype uses approximately 2 million gas (as a comparison, a simple transfer of Ether uses exactly 21,000 gas). The price payed for this amount of gas depends on the market conditions and on how fast the user wants the transaction to be processed. Limiting the amount of work preformed on the EVM by the smart contract can reduce the cost of the contract deployment and therefore the costs of the transaction. Moreover, it is also important to note that the smart contract we have used in this implementation is related to the API provided by Oraclize. It is possible that using another oracle provider might reduce the price for the smart contract deployment.

Contract Verification. The transaction process relies on the fact that the secondary user needs to verify the smart contract deployed by the primary user. While the smart contract can be found on the blockchain using the blockchain explorer, it is only the compiled bytecode that is being stored. As such, verifying that the contract is correct is not an easy task in the current version of our system, which needs to be simplified and automatised.

One Contract per Transaction. The current prototype always deploys a new contract whenever a transaction is made. This contract is then executed and discarded afterwards. Another approach would be to only deploy a single contract for the whole system. New transactions would simply call methods defined by this contract and the contract would be handling multiple transactions simultaneously. Naturally, the smart contract would need to be more complex, but the costs for its operation would be shared among all of its users.

Scalability. Trading pair Bitcoin/Ethereum can be commonly found in the portfolio of digital currency exchanges. According to Coinmarketcap platform[12], the

---

[11] *kETH* is used to indicate Kovan Ether.

[12] https://coinmarketcap.com/.

volume of the transactions between Bitcoin and Ether makes up to around 9% of the overall transaction volume across the 10 biggest digital currency exchanges. In the future, this number is likely to increase further, as cryptocurrencies further establish in the society. While this is not a problem for Ethereum and Bitcoin blockchains, it could affect our proposed system. With increasing number of queries, oracle(s) could change their pricing model which would further increase the transaction costs.

To handle larger number of users, the communication back-end would also need to be reconsidered, to allow interaction of many individuals, while not unnecessarily limiting the transaction making process.

6   Conclusions and Future Work

In this project, we proposed, designed, and implemented a system that enables a distributed and secure trade of cryptocurrencies between two parties. We built the system on the Ethereum platform and used smart contracts for the core of its operation. The smart contract holds the users' funds, until the other side of the transaction from the other party has been made. To demonstrate the process, we implemented an Android prototype, and showed that it is possible to successfully exchange Ethereum to Bitcoin, and vice-versa, without the need of a centralized service. Even though we performed the tests on the testing blockchain networks *Kovan* and *testnet3*, moving to the real ones is straightforward and is just a matter of deployment.

As plans of future development, we intend improving the system mainly on the following two aspects:

Use of Multiple Nodes. To avoid the single-node issue, since the node could refuse to perform a transaction or the provider could simply go offline, we will extend the system to use multiple nodes.

Use of Multiple Oracles and Multiple Blockchain Explorers. The current version of the system only uses one oracle and one blockchain explorer provider. Similarly as the node, they could prevent transactions from happening, if either of the two goes offline. A possible solution is to use multiple oracles, which in turn query different blockchain explorers.

References

1. Chaum, D.: Blind signatures for untraceable payments. In: Chaum, D., Rivest, R.L., Sherman, A.T. (eds.) Advances in Cryptology, pp. 199–203. Springer, Boston (1983). https://doi.org/10.1007/978-1-4757-0602-4_18
2. Popper, N., Abrams, R.: Apparent Theft at Mt. Gox Shakes Bitcoin World - The New York Times, February 2014
3. McIntosh, R.: How to Choose Crypto Exchanges, Store Money and Avoid Scams. Finance Magnates, January 2018

4. Chen, L., Xu, L., Gao, Z., Shah, N., Lu, Y., Shi, W.: Smart contract execution - the (+-)-biased ballot problem. In: Okamoto, Y., Tokuyama, T. (eds.) 28th International Symposium on Algorithms and Computation (ISAAC 2017), vol. 92, pp. 21:1–21:12, Dagstuhl, Germany, Schloss Dagstuhl - Leibniz-Zentrum fuer Informatik (2017)
5. Nakamoto, S.: Bitcoin: A Peer-to-Peer Electronic Cash System
6. Hackett, R.: J.P. Morgan Chase Is Building an Ethereum-Based Blockchain: Here's Why (2016)
7. Swan, M.: Blockchain: Blueprint for a New Economy, 1st edn. O'Reilly Media Incorporated, Sebastopol (2015)
8. Michael, N., Gomber, P., Oliver, H., Dirk, S.: Blockchain. Bus. Inf. Syst. Eng. 59(3), 183–187 (2017)
9. Buterin, V.: A next-generation smart contract and decentralized application platform (2014)
10. Delmolino, K., Arnett, M., Kosba, A., Miller, A., Shi, E.: Step by step towards creating a safe smart contract: lessons and insights from a cryptocurrency lab. In: Brenner, M., et al. (eds.) Financial Cryptography and Data Security, pp. 79–94. Springer, Heidelberg (2016). https://doi.org/10.1007/978-3-319-70278-0
11. Mik, E.: Smart contracts: terminology, technical limitations and real world complexity. Law Innov. Technol. 9(2), 269–300 (2017)
12. Patrick, M., Shahandashti, S.F., Feng, H.: A smart contract for boardroom voting with maximum voter privacy. In: Kiayias, A. (ed.) Financial Cryptography and Data Security, pp. 357–375. Springer, Cham (2017). https://doi.org/10.1007/978-3-319-70972-7_20
13. Dannen, C.: Introducing Ethereum and Solidity. Apress, Berkeley (2017)
14. Mansfield-Devine, S.: Beyond Bitcoin: using blockchain technology to provide assurance in the commercial world. Comput. Fraud Secur. 2017(5), 14–18 (2017)
15. Ying, W., Jia, S., Du, W.: Digital enablement of blockchain: evidence from HNA group. Int. J. Inf. Manage. 39, 1–4 (2018)
16. Li, X., Jiang, P., Chen, T., Luo, X., Wen, Q.: A survey on the security of blockchain systems. Future Generation Computer Systems (2017)
17. Moore, T., Christin, N.: Beware the middleman: empirical analysis of bitcoin-exchange risk. In: Sadeghi, A.R. (ed.) Financial Cryptography and Data Security, pp. 25–33. Springer, Heidelberg (2013). https://doi.org/10.1007/978-3-319-70278-0
18. Hallgren, J., Hallgren, M., Fisher, S., Larsen, N., Hautop, J., Ross, O.: Hallex: a trust-less exchange system for digital assets. SSRN Electr. J. (2017)
19. Buterin, V.: Chain interoperability (2016)
20. Poon, J., Dryja, T.: The Bitcoin lightning network: scalable off-chain instant payments. Draft version 0.5 9, 14 (2016)
21. Weldon, J.: Building an "Oracle" for an Ethereum contract (2016)
22. Oraclize documentation (2018)
23. Dourlens, J.: Oracles: bringing data to the blockchain (2017)

A Public, Blockchain-Based Distributed Smart-Contract Platform Enabling Mobile Lite Wallets Using a Proof-of-Stake Consensus Algorithm

Alex Norta[1]([✉]), Patrick Dai[2], Neil Mahi[2], and Jordan Earls[2]

[1] Department of Software Science, Tallinn University of Technology,
Akadeemia tee 15A, 12816 Tallinn, Estonia
alex.norta.phd@ieee.org
[2] Qtum Foundation, Singapore, Singapore
foundation@qtum.org

Abstract. Blockchain-enabled smart contracts that employ proof-of-stake validation for transactions, promise significant performance advantages compared to proof-of-work solutions. For broad industry adoption, other important requirements must be met in addition. For example, stable backwards-compatible smart-contract systems must automate cross-organizational information-logistics orchestration with lite mobile wallets that support the unspent transaction output (UTXO) protocol and simple payment verification (SPV) techniques. The currently leading smart-contract solution Ethereum, uses computationally expensive proof-of-work validation, is expected to hard-fork multiple times in the future and requires downloading the entire blockchain. Consequently, Ethereum smart contracts have limited utility for large industry applications. This paper fills the gap in the state of the art by presenting the Qtum smart-contract framework that allows for managing transaction headers in lite mobile wallets in addition with using a proof-of-stake (PoS) consensus algorithm.

Keywords: Smart contract · Blockchain · Mobile · Lite wallet · PoS
Abstraction layer · SVP · UTXO

1 Introduction

Orchestration and choreography protocols that facilitate, verify and enact with computing means a negotiated agreement between consenting parties, are termed smart contracts that initially find application in diverse domains such as financial-technology [5], Internet-of-Things (IoT) applications [15], and so on. An essential aspect of smart contracts is a decentralized validation of transactions, initially by means of so-called proof-of-work (PoW) [20]. The core technology that enables smart contracts is a public distributed ledger termed

© Springer Nature Switzerland AG 2019
W. Abramowicz and A. Paschke (Eds.): BIS 2018 Workshops, LNBIP 339, pp. 368–380, 2019.
https://doi.org/10.1007/978-3-030-04849-5_33

the blockchain, which records transaction events without requiring a trusted central authority. Blockchain technology spreads in popularity with the inception of Bitcoin [13], a peer-to-peer (P2P) cryptocurrency and payment system that comprises a limited set of operations on the protocol layer. Bitcoins use PoW for transaction validation that is computationally expensive and electricity intensive.

In contrast to Bitcoins, many smart-contract systems are equipped with the Turing-complete language Solidity[1] that resembles JavaScript syntax and targets for enactment, e.g., the Ethereum Virtual [21] machine. Ethereum is the de-facto leading smart-contract system despite being plagued by several deficiencies as we show in Sect. 2. PoW transaction validation diminishes scalability to the point where Ethereum is considered to not be feasible for most industry applications. One of the primary goals of Qtum is to build the first UTXO-based smart-contract system with a proof-of-stake (PoS) [18] consensus model. The latter means the creator of the next block is chosen based on the held wealth in crypto-currency. A simpler version would be "Instead of mining blocks they are minted or forged. Each new block grants an additional reward to the forger. This means additionally to the transaction fees; the forger receives an "interest" of the total amount of funds at stake. Qtum is compatible with the Bitcoin- and Ethereum ecosystems and aims at producing a variation of Bitcoin with Ethereum Virtual Machine (EVM) compatibility. Note that differently to Ethereum, the Qtum EVM is constantly backwards compatible. Pursuing a pragmatic design approach, Qtum employs industry use cases with a strategy comprising mobile devices. The latter allows Qtum promoting blockchain technology to a wide array of Internet users and thereby, decentralizing PoS transaction validation.

While smart-contract systems such as Ethereum attract attention, a widespread industry adoption does not exist for the above discussed reasons. This paper addresses the gap by specifying the Qtum[2] framework for smart-contract systems that answers the question of how to develop a smart-contract platform to satisfy critical customer requirements for scalable smart-contract systems? To establish a separation of concerns, we pose the following sub-questions. What are the key differentiating functions of Qtum to enhance scalability? What virtual-machine adaptations support the enhanced scalability? What token model matched the adapted virtual machine? Note that this paper is based on the Qtum technical whitepaper [9] that comprises the extended background information.

The remainder of this paper is structured as follows. First, Sect. 2 gives preliminaries for the rest of the paper. Section 3 focuses on concrete advantages of the Qtum framework for achieving technologically performance increases in comparison to related solutions. Section 4 discusses the extensions of the Ethereum virtual machine in Qtum for achieving scalability. Section 5 presents the Qtum abstraction layer that allows for lite smart-contract wallets on mobile devices.

---

[1] http://solidity.readthedocs.io/en/develop/.
[2] https://qtum.org/en.

Section 6 briefly evaluates the resulting Qtum smart-contract platform by reporting about the existing ecosystem of distributed applications (Dapps) Finally, Sect. 7 concludes this whitepaper together with discussing limitations, open issues and future development work.

2 Preliminaries

While Qtum uses the Ethereum Virtual Machine (EVM) for a current lack of more suitable alternatives, according to [12], the EVM has deficiencies such as earlier experienced attacks against mishandled exceptions and against dependencies such as for transaction-ordering, timestamps, and so on. It is also desirable for a smart-contract system to achieve industry-scalability with employing sidechains [8] and unspent transaction outputs (UTXO) [8], achieving compatibility to other blockchain systems such as Bitcoins [13], or Colored coins [17]. Furthermore, an adoption of features from the Bitcoin Lightning Network [16] yields scalability via bidirectional micropayment channels.

More reasons limit widespread Ethereum industry adoption [7]. For example, secure and stable virtual machines for blockchains with better performing proof-of-stake [2] transaction validation, lite wallets that do not require downloading the entire blockchain, and mobile-device solutions for smart contracts with simple payment verification (SPV) [10]. The latter means that clients merely download block headers when they connect to an arbitrary full node [13].

3 Qtum Performance Advantage

As Ethereum uses an account model for wallets, it is necessary to download the entire blockchain, which does not allow for wallets to operate on mobile devices with limited storage capacity. Furthermore, PoS is a performance bottleneck for large-scale industrial applications of smart contracts in blockchains. Thus, we explain the Qtum approach for overcoming these shortcomings of Ethereum. The remainder is structured as follows. Section 3.1 compares the advantages of Bitcoin UTXO versus the Ethereum account model. Next, Sect. 3.2 discusses the consensus platform for the Qtum blockchain.

3.1 UTXO Versus Account Model

In the UTXO model, transactions use as input unspent Bitcoins that are destroyed and as transaction outputs, new UTXOs are created. Unspent transaction outputs are created as change and returned to the spender [1]. In this way, a certain volume of Bitcoins are transferred among different private-key owners, and new UTXOs are spent and created in the transaction chain. The UTXO of a Bitcoin transaction is unlocked by the private key that is used to sign a modified version of a transaction. In the Bitcoin network, miners generate Bitcoins with a process called a coinbase transaction, which does not contain any inputs. Bitcoin uses a scripting language for transactions with a limited set of operations[3]. In the Bitcoin network, the scripting system processes data by stacks (Main Stack and Alt Stack), which is an abstract data type following the LIFO principle of Last-In, First-Out.

In the Bitcoin client, the developers use `isStandard()` function [1] to summarize the scripting types. Bitcoin clients support: P2PKH (Pay to Public Key Hash), P2PK (Pay to Public Key), MultiSignature (less than 15 private-key signatures), P2SH (Pay to Script Hash), and `OP_RETURN`. With these five standard scripting types, Bitcoin clients can process complex payment logics. Besides that, a non-standard script can be created and executed if miners agree to encapsulate such a non-standard transaction.

For example, using P2PKH for the process of script creation and execution, we assume paying 0.01BTC for bread in a bakery with the imaginary Bitcoin address "Bread Address". The output of this transaction is:
`OP_DUP OP_HASH160 <Bread Public Key Hash> OP_EQUAL OP_CHECKSIG`
The operation `OP_DUP` duplicates the top item in the stack. `OP_HASH160` returns a Bitcoin address as top item. To establishes ownership of a bitcoin, a Bitcoin address is required in addition with a digital key and a digital signature. `OP_EQUAL` yields `TRUE` (`1`) if the top two items are exactly equal and otherwise `FALSE` (`0`). Finally, `OP_CHECKSIG` produces a public key and signature together with a validation for the signature pertaining to hashed data of a transaction, returning `TRUE` if a match occurs.

The unlock script according to the lock script is:
`<Bread Signature> <Bread Public Key>`
The combined script with the above two:
`<Bread Signature> <Bread Public Key> OP_DUP OP_HASH160`
`<Bread Public Key Hash> OP_EQUAL OP_CHECKSIG`
Only when the unlock script and the lock script have a matching predefined condition, is the execution of the script combination true. It means, the Bread Signature must be signed by matching the private key of a valid Bread Address signature and then the result is true.

Unfortunately, the scripting language of Bitcoin is not Turing-complete, e.g., there is no loop function. The Bitcoin scripting language is not a commonly used programming language. The limitations mitigate the security risks by preventing the occurrence of complex payment conditions, e.g., generating infinite loops, or other complicated logic loopholes.

In the UTXO model, it is possible to transparently trace back the history of each transaction through the public ledger. The UTXO model has parallel processing capability to initialize transactions among multiple addresses indicating the extensibility. Additionally, the UTXO model supports privacy in that users can use Change Address as the output of a UTXO. The target of Qtum is to implement smart contracts based on the innovative design of the UTXO model.

---

[3] https://en.bitcoin.it/wiki/Script.

Versus the UTXO model, Ethereum is an account based system[4]. More precisely, each account experiences direct value- and information transfers with state transitions. An Ethereum account address of 20 bytes comprises a nounce as a counter for assuring one-time processing for a transaction, the balance of the main internal crypto fuel for paying transaction fees called Ether, an optional contract code and default-empty account storage.

The two types of Ether accounts are on the one hand, private-key controlled external and on the other hand, contract-code controlled. The former code-void account type creates and signs transactions for message transfer. The latter activates code after receiving a message for reading and writing internal storage, creating contracts, or sending other messages.

In Ethereum, balance management resembles a bank account in the real world. Every newly generated block potentially influences the global status of other accounts. Every account has its own balance, storage and code-space base for calling other accounts or addresses, and stores respective execution results. In the existing Ethereum account system, users perform P2P transactions via client remote procedure calls. Although sending messages to more accounts via smart contracts is possible, these internal transactions are only visible in the balance of each account and tracking them on the public ledger of Ethereum is a challenge.

Based on the discussion above, we consider the Ethereum account model to be a scalability bottleneck and see clear advantages of the Bitcoin-network UTXO model. Since the latter enhances the network effect we wish to offer, an essential design decision for the pending Qtum release is the adoption of the UTXO model.

3.2 Consensus Management

There are ongoing discussions about consensus and which platform meets the needs of respective project requirements. The consensus topics most widely discussed are: PoW [20], PoS [2], Dynamic PoS[5], and Byzantine Fault Tolerance [6] as discussed by HyperLedger. The nature of consensus is about achieving data consistency with distributed algorithms. Available options are, e.g., the Fischer Lynch and Paterson theorem [4] that states consensus cannot be reached without 100% agreement amongst nodes.

In the Bitcoin network, miners participate in the verification process by hash collision through PoW. When the hash value of a miner is able to calculate and meet a certain condition, the miner may claim to the network that a new block is mined:

$$Hash(BlockHeader) \leq \frac{M}{D}$$

For the amount of miners M and the mining difficulty D, the Hash() represents the SHA256 power with value range [0, M], and D. The SHA256 algorithm used

---

[4] https://github.com/ethereum/wiki/wiki/White-Paper.
[5] http://tinyurl.com/zxgayfr.

by Bitcoin enables every node to verify each block quickly, if the number of miners is high versus the mining difficulty.

The 80 byte BlockHeader varies with each different Nonce. The overall difficulty level of mining adjusts dynamically according to the total hash power of the blockchain network. When two or more miners solve a block at the same time, a small fork happens in the network. This is the point where the blockchain needs to make a decision as to which block it should accept, or reject. In the Bitcoin network, the chain is legitimate that has the most proven work attached.

Most PoS blockchains can source their heritage back to PeerCoin[6] that is based on an earlier version of Bitcoin Core. There are different PoW algorithms such as Scrypt[7], X11[8], Groestl[9], Equihash [3], etc. The purpose of launching a new algorithm is to prevent the accumulation of computing power by one entity and ensure that Application Specific Integrated Circuits (ASIC) can not be introduced into the economy. Qtum Core chooses PoS based on the latest Bitcoin source code for basic consensus formation.

In a traditional PoS transaction, the generation of a new block must meet the following condition:

$$ProofHash < coins \times age \times target$$

In ProofHash, the stake modifier [19] computes together with unspent outputs and the current time. With this method, one malicious attacker can start a double-spending attack by accumulating large amounts of coin age. Another problem caused by coin age is that nodes are online intermittently after rewarding instead of being continuously online. Therefore, in the improved version of PoS agreement, coin-age removal encourages more nodes to be online simultaneously.

The original PoS implementation suffers from several security issues due to possible coin age attacks, and other types of attacks [11]. Qtum agrees with the security analysis of the Blackcoin team [19] and adopts PoS 3.0[10] into the latest Qtum Core. PoS 3.0 theoretically rewards investors that *stake* their coins longer, while giving no incentive to coin holders who leave their wallets offline.

4   Scalability-Extension of the Virtual Machine

The EVM is stack-based with a 256-bit machine word. Smart contracts that run on Ethereum use this virtual machine for their execution. The EVM is designed for the blockchain of Ethereum and thus, assumes that all value transfer use an account-based method. Qtum is based on the blockchain design of Bitcoin and uses the UTXO-based model. Thus, Qtum has an account-abstraction layer that

---

[6] https://peercoin.net/.
[7] https://litecoin.info/Scrypt.
[8] http://cryptorials.io/glossary/x11/.
[9] http://www.groestlcoin.org/about-groestlcoin/.
[10] http://blackcoin.co/.

translates the UTXO-based model to an account-based interface for the EVM. Note that an abstraction layer in computing is instrumental for hiding the implementation details of particular functionality to establish a separation of concerns for facilitating interoperability and platform independence. All transactions in Qtum use the Bitcoin Scripting Language, just like Bitcoin. In Qtum however, there exist three new opcodes.

- OP_EXEC: This opcode triggers special processing of a transaction (explained below) and executes specific input EVM bytecode.
- OP_EXEC_ASSIGN: This opcode also triggers special processing such as OP_EXEC. This opcode has as input a contract address and data for the contract. Next follows the execution of contract bytecode while passing in the given data (given as CALLERDATA in EVM). This opcode optionally transfers money to a smart contract.
- OP_TXHASH: This opcode is used to reconcile an odd part of the accounting abstraction layer and pushes the transaction ID hash of a currently executed transaction.

Traditionally, scripts are only executed when attempting to spend an output. For example, while the script is on the blockchain, with a standard public key hash transaction, no validation or execution takes place. Execution and validation does not happen until a transaction input references the output. At this point, the transaction is only valid if the input script (ScriptSig) does provide valid data to the output script that causes the latter to return non-zero.

Qtum however, must accommodate smart contracts that execute immediately when merged into the blockchain. As depicted in Fig. 1, Qtum achieves this by the special processing of transaction output scripts (ScriptPubKey) that contain either OP_EXEC, or OP_EXEC_ASSIGN. When one of these opcodes is detected in a script, it is executed by all nodes of the network after the transaction is placed into a block. In this mode, the actual Bitcoin Script Language serves less as a scripting language and instead carries data to the EVM. The latter changes state within its own state database, upon execution by either of the opcodes, similar to a Ethereum contract.

For easy use of Qtum smart contracts, we have to authenticate the data sent to a smart contract as well as its creator stemming from a particular pubkeyhash address. In order to prevent the UTXO set of the Qtum blockchain from becoming too large, OP_EXEC and OP_EXEC_ASSIGN transaction outputs are also spendable. OP_EXEC_ASSIGN outputs are spent by contracts when their code sends money to another contract, or to a pubkeyhash address. OP_EXEC outputs are spent whenever the contract uses the suicide operation to remove itself from the blockchain.

5   Qtum Account Abstraction Layer

The EVM is designed to function on an account-based blockchain. Qtum however, being based on bitcoin, uses a UTXO-based blockchain and contains an

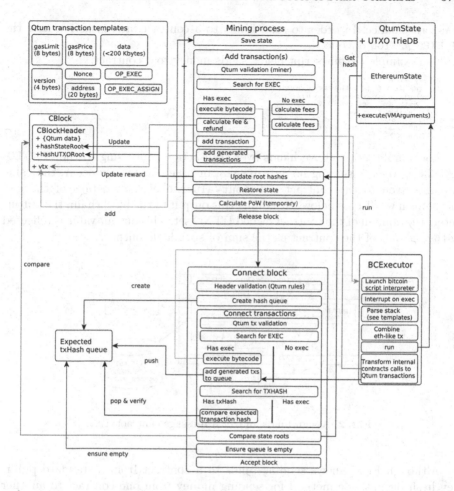

Fig. 1. Qtum transaction processing.

Account Abstraction Layer (AAL) that allows the EVM to function on the Qtum blockchain without significant modifications to the virtual machine and existing Ethereum contracts.

The EVM account model is simple to use for smart-contract programmers. Operations exist that check the balance of the current contract and other contracts on the blockchain, and there are operations for sending money (attached to data) to other contracts. Although these actions seem fairly basic and minimalistic, they are not trivial to apply within the UTXO-based Qtum blockchain. Thus, the AAL implementation of these operations may be more complex than expected.

A Qtum-blockchain deployed smart contract is assigned and callable by its address and comprises a newly deployed contract balance set to zero. There is currently no protocol in Qtum that allows a contract to be deployed with a non-zero balance. In order to send funds to a contract, a transaction uses the OP_EXEC_ASSIGN opcode.

The example output script below sends money to a contract:

```
1; the version of the VM
10000; gas limit for the transaction
100; gas price in Qtum satoshis
0xF012; data to send the contract
(usually using the Solidity ABI)
0x1452b22265803b201ac1f8bb25840cb70afe3303;
ripemd−160 hash of contract txid
OP_EXEC_ASSIGN
```

The simple script above hands over transaction processing to the OP_EXEC_ASSIGN opcode. Assuming no out-of-gas, or other exceptions occur, the value amount given to the contract is OutputValue. The exact details of the gas mechanism we discuss below. By adding this output to the blockchain, the output enters the domain of the contract owned UTXO set. This output value is reflected in the balance of the contract as the sum of spendable outputs.

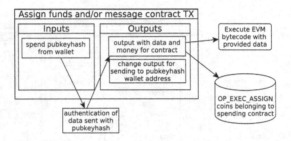

Fig. 2. Assign funds and/or a message contract TX.

Although Fig. 2 shows sending funds to a contract from a standard public key hash output, the method for sending money from one contract to another is nearly identical. When the contract sends funds to another contract or public key hash address, the former spends one of its owned outputs. The sending contract involves Expected Contract Transactions for the fund sending. These transactions are special in that they must exist in a block to be valid for the Qtum network. Expected Contract Transactions are generated by miners while verifying and executing transactions, rather than being generated by consumers. As such, they are not broadcast on the P2P network.

The primary mechanism to perform Expected Contract Transactions is the new opcode, OP_TXHASH that is part of Fig. 3. Internally, both OP_EXEC and OP_EXEC_ASSIGN have two different modes. Upon their execution as part of the output script processing, the EVM is executed. When the opcodes are executed as part of input script processing, however, the EVM is not executed to avoid double execution. Instead, the OP_EXEC and OP_EXEC_ASSIGN opcodes behave similar to no-ops and return either 1 or 0, i.e., spendable or not spendable respectively, based on a given transaction hash. This is why OP_TXHASH is so important to the functioning of this concept. Briefly, OP_TXHASH is a new opcode added

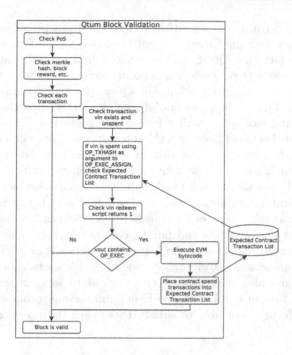

Fig. 3. Qtum block validation showing the Expected Contract Transaction List.

which pushes the current spending transaction's SHA256 hash onto the Bitcoin Script stack. The `OP_EXEC` and `OP_EXEC_ASSIGN` opcodes check the Expected Contract Transaction List during a spend attempt.

After the transaction passes (usually from `OP_TXHASH`) to the opcodes that exist in the Expected Contract Transaction List, the result is 1, or spendable. Otherwise, the return is 0, or not spendable. In this way, `OP_EXEC` and `OP_EXEC_ASSIGN` using `vouts` are only spendable when a contract and thus, the Account Abstraction Layer, requires that the `vout` is spendable, i.e., while the contract attempts sending money. This results in a secure and sound way of allowing contract funds to be spent only by a respective contract in alignment with a normal UTXO transaction.

Due to page limitations, we must unfortunately for now refer the reader to [9] for further details about the Qtum abstraction layer.

6   Evaluation and Discussion

Given the release of the Qtum project on GitHub[11] last years, a considerable set of Dapp projects[12] have been built using Qtum. The mobile lite wallet[13] of

---

[11] https://github.com/qtumproject/qtum.
[12] https://qtumeco.io/dapps.
[13] https://qtumeco.io/wallet.

Qtum where a PoS consensus algorithm yields significant performance and scalability advantages over the Ethereum platform, is a reason for Dapps choosing the former. The fact that Qtum also uses the Solidity smart-contract development language means that developers who are experienced with the Ethereum platform, find it easy to quickly adopt the Qtum platform instead.

One notable Qtum Dapp we point out is Datawallet that is a data-ownership assuring blockchain wallet for privacy-protected data exchange [14]. The available-for-download Datawallet[14] is a response to the de-facto theft and unilaterally decided upon monetization of user-generated data by well known social-media companies and a secretive data-brokerage industry. Instead, the user-controlled Datawallet with a blockchainbased smart-contract system using the Qtum platform, allows for a transparent and mutually beneficial exchange of data between consenting parties for so-called DXT tokens, i.e., between social-media users who generate data and paying commercial consumers of such data sets. The widespread adoption of the Datawallet depends on PoS efficiency for carrying out transactions. Additionally, social-media users generate data via mobile phones and also want to monetize their data sets via such fast transactions. To the best of our knowledge Ethereum, or any other smart-contract blockchain platform is not able to satisfy these essential user requirements as Qtum is able to.

7   Conclusions

This paper presents the Qtum-framework for a novel smart-contract block- chain-technology solution as a short version based in the extended whitepaper in [9]. We show the specific Qtum transaction-processing implementation that uses proof-of-stake validation. Furthermore, Qtum integrates the Ethereum virtual machine (EVM) together with the Bitcoin unspent transaction output protocol. Note that the Qtum EVM constantly remains backwards compatible.

The adoption of proof-of-stake into Qtum constitutes a considerable saving of computational effort over the not scaling Ethereum alternative that still uses proof-of-work. While Ethereum plans to also adopt proof-of-stake, it is unclear when such a new version will be released. Also the use of unspent transaction outputs is more scalable in comparison to the account management of Ethereum. In combination with simple payment verification, Qtum already develops a smart-contract mobile-device solution. While the not scaling Ethereum solution does not allow for mobile solutions, Qtum aims to achieve a democratized and highly distributed proof-of-stake transaction validation with its mobile strategy.

The Qtum framework has a clear understanding of quality criteria that future developments must satisfy. With respect to functional requirements, Qtum plans to develop an application layer for smart-contract lifecycle management. Most importantly, such lifecycle management is important for vetting collaborating parties to reduce security breaches such as those Ethereum recently experienced, resulting in multiple hardforks of the latter.

---

[14] https://datawallet.com/index.html.

References

1. Antonopoulos, A.M.: Mastering Bitcoins (2014)
2. Bentov, I., Gabizon, A., Mizrahi, A.: Cryptocurrencies without proof of work. In: Clark, J., Meiklejohn, S., Ryan, P.Y.A., Wallach, D., Brenner, M., Rohloff, K. (eds.) FC 2016. LNCS, vol. 9604, pp. 142–157. Springer, Heidelberg (2016). https://doi. org/10.1007/978-3-662-53357-4_10
3. Biryukov, A., Khovratovich, D.: Equihash: asymmetric proof-of-work based on the generalized birthday problem. In: Proceedings of NDSS 2016, San Diego, CA, USA, 21–24 February 2016 (2016). ISBN 1-891562-41-X
4. Bisping, B., et al.: Mechanical verification of a constructive proof for FLP. In: Blanchette, J.C., Merz, S. (eds.) ITP 2016. LNCS, vol. 9807, pp. 107–122. Springer, Cham (2016). https://doi.org/10.1007/978-3-319-43144-4_7
5. Bussmann, O.: The future of finance: fintech, tech disruption, and orchestrating innovation. In: Francioni, R., Schwartz, R.A. (eds.) Equity Markets in Transition, pp. 473–486. Springer, Cham (2017). https://doi.org/10.1007/978-3-319-45848-9_19
6. Cachin, C.: Architecture of the hyperledger blockchain fabric. In: Workshop on Distributed Cryptocurrencies and Consensus Ledgers (2016)
7. Christidis, K., Devetsikiotis, M.: Blockchains and smart contracts for the internet of things. IEEE Access 4, 2292–2303 (2016)
8. Croman, K., et al.: On scaling decentralized blockchains. In: Clark, J., Meiklejohn, S., Ryan, P.Y.A., Wallach, D., Brenner, M., Rohloff, K. (eds.) FC 2016. LNCS, vol. 9604, pp. 106–125. Springer, Heidelberg (2016). https://doi.org/10.1007/978-3-662-53357-4_8
9. Dai, P., Mahi, N., Earls, J., Norta, A.: Smart-Contract Value-Transfer Protocols on a Distributed Mobile Application Platform (2017). https://qtum.org/user/pages/03.tech/01.white-papers/Qtum%20Whitepaper.pdf
10. Frey, D., Makkes, M.X., Roman, P.L., Taïani, F., Voulgaris, S.: Bringing secure Bitcoin transactions to your smartphone. In: Proceedings of the 15th International Workshop on Adaptive and Reflective Middleware, ARM 2016, pp. 3:1–3:6. ACM, New York (2016)
11. Kiayias, A., Konstantinou, I., Russell, A., David, B., Oliynykov, R.: A provably secure proof-of-stake blockchain protocol (2016)
12. Luu, L., Chu, D.H., Olickel, H., Saxena, P., Hobor, A.: Making smart contracts smarter. In: Proceedings of the 2016 ACM SIGSAC Conference on Computer and Communications Security, CCS 2016, pp. 254–269 (2016)
13. Nakamoto, S.: Bitcoin: a peer-to-peer electronic cash system. Consulted 1(2012):28 (2008)
14. Norta, A., Hawthorne, D., Engel, S.L.: A privacy-protecting data-exchange wallet with ownership-and monetization capabilities. In: 2018 International Joint Conference on Neural Networks (IJCNN), pp. 1–8. IEEE (2018)
15. Ouaddah, A., Elkalam, A.A., Ouahman, A.A.: Towards a novel privacy-preserving access control model based on blockchain technology in IoT. In: Rocha, Á., Serrhini, M., Felgueiras, C. (eds.) Europe and MENA Cooperation Advances in Information and Communication Technologies. AISC, vol. 520, pp. 523–533. Springer, Cham (2017). https://doi.org/10.1007/978-3-319-46568-5_53
16. Poon, J., Dryja, T.: The Bitcoin lightning network: scalable off-chain instant payments (2015)
17. Rosenfeld, M.: Overview of colored coins. White paper, bitcoil.co.il (2012)

18. Serguei, P.: A probabilistic analysis of the Nxt forging algorithm. Ledger **1**, 69–83 (2016)
19. Vasin, P.: Blackcoin's proof-of-stake protocol v2 (2014)
20. Vukolić, M.: The quest for scalable blockchain fabric: proof-of-work vs. BFT replication. In: Camenisch, J., Kesdoğan, D. (eds.) iNetSec 2015. LNCS, vol. 9591, pp. 112–125. Springer, Cham (2016). https://doi.org/10.1007/978-3-319-39028-4_9
21. Wood, G.: Ethereum: a secure decentralised generalised transaction ledger. Ethereum Project Yellow Paper (2014)

Risk Engineering and Blockchain: Anticipating and Mitigating Risks

Michael Huth[1]([⊠]), Claire Vishik[2], and Riccardo Masucci[2]

[1] Imperial College London, London, UK
m.huth@imperial.ac.uk
[2] Intel Corporation, Santa Clara, USA
{claire.vishik,riccardo.masucci}@intel.com

Abstract. Complex systems require an integrated approach to risks. In this paper, we describe risk engineering, a methodology to incorporate risks at the planning and design stage for complex systems, and introduce some of its components. We examine, at a high level, how risk engineering can help improve the risk picture for blockchain technologies and their applications and outline challenges and benefits of this approach.

Keywords: Risk engineering · Blockchain · Ontology · Reasoning
Integrated risk analysis

1 Intrinsic Complexity of Environments and Risk Analysis

Modern ICT environment is highly integrated and operates as a system of systems sharing the same infrastructure and processes. The ecosystem is dynamic and diverse, and this diversity increases with the incorporation of every new generation of connected technologies. The evolution of the technology, including its usage models, is very rapid, resulting in co-existence of legacy and cutting-edge technologies and situations where new devices, technologies, and frameworks are added to existing systems. All emerging technology contexts, from smart grid and connected automotive systems to blockchain technology, exhibit considerable complexity and diversity of operational requirements.

The operational contexts are organizationally, technologically, and geographically diverse today, the impact of failure is enormous due to very large user populations of connected systems and processes. Around 40% of the world population used the Internet in 2014, up from 1% of the population in 1995 [1].

This dynamic and complex environment requires new strategies to evaluate and manage risks. Single-domain approaches are no longer sufficient for this task, especially in distributed environments such as blockchain. Not only integrated risk models and viable approaches to risk composition are needed, but also a modification of system design and development processes to include integrated risk considerations at the earliest stages of the design process (see Fig. 1 below). Nevertheless, several obstacles make integrated risk analysis challenging.

W. Abramowicz and A. Paschke (Eds.): BIS 2018 Workshops, LNBIP 339, pp. 381–392, 2019.
https://doi.org/10.1007/978-3-030-04849-5_34

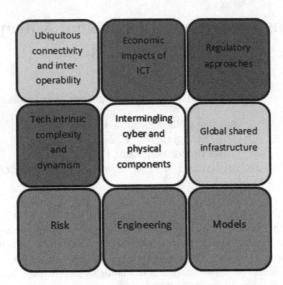

Fig. 1. Integration of different domains of modern computing environments in risk engineering models.

No Standard Way to Evaluate Security of Complex Systems. The modern computing environment is a combination of multiple frameworks, each using its own security and threat models. A framework is an abstraction providing generic functionality and a reusable environment, with specific use cases implemented via additional development. Without objective approaches to estimate risks of complex systems under operational conditions, and with neither standards or metrics to apply to diverse environments in which these systems operate, it is difficult to anticipate the consequences of system level or environmental changes for safety, security, dependability, privacy or other salient risk domains. This complexity and ambiguity of environmental context also apply to data and data protection, requiring a re-think of fundamental concepts in computer and information science such as anonymity and data interoperability.

No Viable Approach to Risk Composition. The increased complexity of the computing environment is the result of the aggregation of various frameworks and the often implicitly assumed composability of their underlying security, privacy, safety, and other aspects of risk. There are architectural patterns for composing systems that are often expressed in so-called architectural description languages [2], and could be a means of mitigating risk at an early design stage. However, such risk-mitigation techniques do not anticipate interaction within open and integrated systems.

Regulations Add to the Complexity of the Analysis. It is not only the technology design that defines its success. Deployment of innovative technologies depends on the success of technology commercialization, and this, in turn, is connected to the regulatory environments. Risk aversion of governments and regulators could translate in an increase in liability for manufacturers unless companies put proactive accountability measures in place. Regulatory requirements directly impact technology solutions and their adoption and therefore they should be considered as another metrics necessary to model and evaluate risks in complex systems.

2   What Is Risk Engineering?

Traditionally, risk models for security include three dimensions: people, processes, and technology. Risk-management approaches for more complex fields integrate additional risk domains, such as assurance and resilience [3].

The trend towards the integration of risk domains for modern systems is a premise for the concept of risk engineering denoting the need to incorporate risk into engineering processes at the design stage. An example of an integrated risk framework combining risk domains of security, privacy, safety, reliability, and resilience is illustrated in Fig. 2 and can be found in the draft deliverable of the Public Working Group on Cyber-Physical Systems [4]. However, the CPS Framework provides an excellent model to decompose integrated risks, not a framework supporting their composition or reasoning about them.

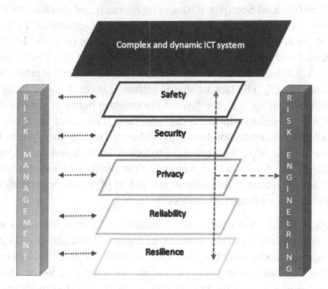

Fig. 2. Analysis of a complex and dynamic ICT system through risk management or risk engineering models (management vs. composition of risks).

We define risk engineering as **"incorporation of integrated risk analysis into system design and engineering processes"**.

Typically, risk assessments are done for specific aspects of operations: e.g., for the reputational risk that a new make of car and its marketing campaign may pose to the manufacturer or the security risk that software may behave in unexpected, malicious or fraudulent ways. These assessments are conducted in isolation from other categories of risks. In reality, various categories of risks are connected. For example, security flaws in connected home appliances can result in privacy breaches, physical damage to the house, or operational safety attacks against the appliance management systems.

3 Existing Approaches

The management of complex risks can be greatly improved if ICT systems themselves could be engineered with consideration of risks of their future use in their operational contexts. Risk engineering therefore requires a process that enables the developers to articulate, define, and sometimes quantify risks in different risk domains. The communities of research and practice for safety, security, privacy, reliability, and resilience have developed methodologies for expressing such risk specifications for their domain, with the ability to analyze consequences that such risks may bring. However, there is relatively little work on making such specifications composable to scale, as well as on specifying risks that stem from the combination or interaction of different system aspects. And adjacent areas, such as Secure Development Lifecycle (SDL) are helpful in enumerating risk areas and remedies, but do not extend to the composition.

Integration of Safety and Security Risks. The research and practitioner communities develop informal ontologies, methodologies, and best practices to address their domains, but there is limited integration of different points of view. Even the vocabulary is different. For example, "incident" refers to an event that has no safety-critical consequences in safety, whereas it usually denotes a serious breach in computer security – as noted in [5]. The lack of shared semantic context is one of the challenges to integrated risk modelling. Yet, the flow of information between various risk domains already exists, e.g., in defense-in-depth [6]. Similarly, fault trees in safety inspired the design of attack trees to understand security vulnerabilities at the system level.

Frameworks such as the "Technology Dialectics" developed in [7] or theoretical models that have predictive power, for example the number of security vulnerabilities in a code base as a function of its lifetime, studied in [8] could be extended to explore such issues during the engineering process

Quantification of Risks. We may think of security risks in at least two ways. In one approach, we are interested in the sequence of events that leads to a security breach. Techniques such as model checking [9] can be used for that. Another approach is inspired by fault tree analysis in safety, where we are interested in the capabilities that are required to realize a security breach, not in their actual operationalization as a sequence of attack, camouflage or obfuscation events. Attack-countermeasure trees (ACT) are a good example of this approach [10].

Domain Specific Languages. The design and use of domain-specific languages should also help with creating and deploying more reliable blockchain technology. For example, decentralized access control that uses blockchain for credential management and cybersecurity protocols for decentralized authentication could become a paradigm for controlling machine-to-machine and human-to-machine interactions, including the delegation of access from resource owners. This would require a Distributed Applications Store model in which apps would be written for the creation of new services.

Domain-specific languages would then be able to abstract cybersecurity and blockchain mechanisms so that developers can focus on service creation and access control, while code generators would see to the proper instantiation of such protection mechanisms.

Risk Metrics. Attack-Countermeasure Trees (ACT) [10] and similar models allow us to compute useful metrics, such as the probability of an attacker's to success in the security breach (e.g. an escalation of access privileges specified in an aforementioned domain-specific language) or the overall cost of an attack to the attacker. The tools for fault tree analysis developed in reliability theory use different computational engines to establish the probability of attack success or the cost of an attack. They can inform security metrics such as one that multiplies the attacker's success probability p with a term that trades off system impact with the attacker's cost – an established arithmetic pattern in risk metrics, including those used in the insurance business. It is also important that tools that compute such metrics provide evidence that users can interpret to gain confidence into such results.

4 Ontologies and Risk Engineering

To summarize our discussion, the main obstacles for effective risk engineering include:

- Lack of common vocabulary and semantic context;
- Absence of consistent metrics;
- Lack of techniques for risk composition.

In order to overcome these challenges, it is helpful to develop ontologies that span multiple system aspects and risk domains, to create methodologies to cope with numerical information spanning several orders of magnitude, and to conduct more empirical research to gain reliable quantitative information for aspects that traditionally are expressed in qualitative terms only. Finally, we need approaches to the integration and composition of diverse risk domains and their respective expertise and practice.

One of the main goals of the field of Knowledge Representation (KR) is the development of methodologies and tools that enable us to accurately capture knowledge. Knowledge specifications can be formulated in a purely *declarative form* without any consideration for the algorithmic nature of such statements and their validation [11]. The semantics of such a representation language defines the meaning of these specifications in a precise and unambiguous fashion. For computation, algorithms forming an inference engine can be separately defined to establish that a fact is true based on a given knowledge base.

Work on ontologies and inference engines relies largely on logical languages and qualitative reasoning. Although this makes it possible to identify system flaws, it does not automatically support the management of quantitative risk or the interaction of risk considerations across system aspects such as safety, security, and privacy. Nonetheless, the use of ontologies to manage quantitative or logistical interactions, e.g., movements of robots, indicates that the development of qualitative inference engines is possible.

The development of quantitative inference engines would first require a thorough understanding of how to specify such interactions so that quantitative results are relevant to decision makers such as system designers (e.g., the level of risk of a planned design change) as well as to end users (e.g., the perceived privacy risk). This is a daunting task, when a domain is complex and upper and lower ontologies are needed (Fig. 3). However, the challenges in creating ontologies capable of supporting models and modeling languages used for integrated risk engineering do not appear to be insurmountable. In addition, the benefits for designers, operators, and end users will be significant.

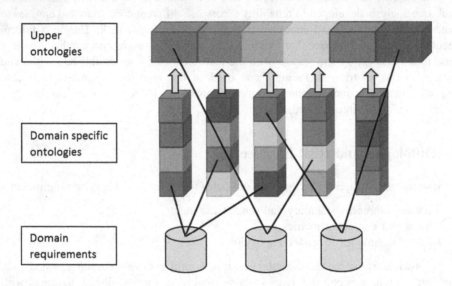

Fig. 3. Risk engineering describes multidisciplinary knowledge: domain requirements can be described by specific domain ontologies and upper ontologies.

Ontologies have been used as a methodology to improve information-based models for security threats and mitigations. An early example of this work is [12]. As security and privacy became increasingly prominent, ontologies dedicated to this area have been defined, including a multi-domain technology-focused example created in [13] or a broader ontology put together in [14] that extends to non-technology components. Ontologies to be used in modeling have been created, such as [15] or [16].

This knowledge representation and reasoning framework becomes especially useful in situations in which knowledge from multiple fields must be taken into account at the same time, as is the case for blockchain environments.

5   Case Study: Blockchain Technology

We now demonstrate how proposed risk-engineering approaches can be used in connection with an emerging technology space, blockchains and crypto-currencies. We demonstrate how these techniques could be applied at a high level, with a detailed analysis of some areas expected to form one of the subjects for future work.

In 2009, Bitcoin [17] emerged as the first digital currency in which there is no need to trust a central third party. Instead, a distributed and decentralized public ledger of transactions records the authentic history of approved transactions, and does so in a pseudo-anonymous manner. Cryptocurrencies based on blockchain technology constitute a remarkable piece of innovation, solving a well-known coordination problem in Distributed Systems [18].

Bitcoin and blockchain technology solve it through a concept called *Proof of Work (PoW)*. But there are now other consensus proposals such as Intel's Sawtooth Proof of Elapsed Time (PoET), Hedera's Hashgraph, Proof of Authority, and many more, still awaiting serious practical tests. At the same time, tokens – crypto assets maintained on a blockchain – may be utilities, securities, or some other financial instrument. There is regulatory uncertainty/regional variability on how a blockchain, token, and investment mechanism (e.g. Initial Coin Offerings) need to be treated by regulators. This poses risks to start-ups in that space, but also to established enterprises that mean to invest into or explore blockchain technology. Risk engineering can clarify such issue by supporting more sophisticated risk models.

5.1   Risks in Blockchain Design Space

Lack of Broadly Applicable Shared Semantics. Risk engineering for blockchain can be supported by an ontology that identifies dimensions of the blockchain design space, so that dependencies and trade-offs in technological and other decisions are better understood and modeled. Such an ontology may reflect complex constructs such as business cases, governance, lifecycle requirements, and particular choices of technology. Not surprisingly, the ISO Technical Committee for Distributed Ledgers (ISO TC 307)[1] started one of its workstreams by focusing on semantics and definitions.

With an ontology in place, it is possible to reason about financial requirements, revenue models, competition, and use cases for a blockchain instance. We would be able to see relationships of various concepts that form governance, including access, ownership, and regulation. Lifecycle would consider aspects such as inter-blockchain interfaces, major protocol requirements, production, retirement, and related concepts. In the technology aspect, we could examine consensus mechanisms, network protocols, payload logic, and other requirements (Fig. 4).

A broadly applicable blockchain ontology could permit us to examine properties (i.e. relationships) in its concepts such as consensus, as well as related simple axioms, e.g., an axiom stating that choosing PoW as consensus mechanism implies that the blockchain system does not possess finality of consensus. An axiom for finance can stipulate that an Initial Coin Offering that does a flawed technical implementation in regards to Anti Money Laundering (AML) or Know Your Customer (KYC) requirements is likely to pose a legal risk to leads of the ICO company even if the token of that blockchain is deemed to be a utility and not a security. Ideally, such reasoning could also help with proposing technology choices. For example, if a high level of resiliency

---

[1] Blockchain and distributed ledger technologies, https://www.iso.org/committee/6266604.html.

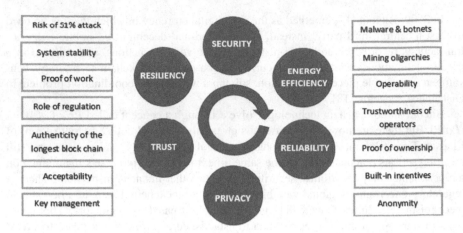

Fig. 4. Risk engineering in Bitcoin: interplay of relevant challenges.

is sought, but the energy cost of PoW should be contained, an axiom could state that Proof of Kernel Work (PoKW) [19] is an energy-efficient version of PoW.

We believe the development and use of such ontologies for the blockchain/cryptocurrency design space would have value, not only for technology development, but also to decision makers in Finance, Enterprises, and Regulatory Authorities.

5.2   Risk Engineering of Crypto-Currencies

For crypto-currencies such as Bitcoin, it is vital to consider human factors in analyzing risks for the privacy, availability, security, and correctness of systems that rely on blockchain technology. We need to develop appropriate abstractions of blockchain technologies and their deployment and adoption models. Such abstractions can help in engineering new methods for risk prevention, detection, and mitigation that inform risk management over the entire lifecycle of such complex artefacts and increase trust in the uses of such systems. In Bitcoin, e.g., low-cost transactions are not confirmed by one or more blocks within the blockchain at the time of transaction, limiting its trustworthiness. In addition to modeling and analysis capabilities, risk engineering could help deal with the tensions that could undermine the level of trust in cryptocurrency systems.

The economic aspect of crypto-currencies would benefit from the use of conventional and new models analyzing asymmetric information in crypto-currency markets, the evolved role of monetary economic models, and the impact of aggregation and intermediation. Multi-domain ontologies coupled with appropriate reasoning methodologies and risk models as described above may help overcome these limitations.

A very long lifecycle for crypto-currencies could also represent a limitation, but these issues have been addressed in emerging risk frameworks for cyber-physical and industrial control systems, that also have great variability of lifespans, ranging from one time use to several decades. A risk language proposed as an element of risk engineering foundational tools could be used to codify and quantify additional domain specific risks as they appear at the initial stages of design and amend them with empirical metrics obtained during the operations of the framework.

5.3 Modelling Languages and Solvers for Blockchain Design and Validation

Computer Science and Mathematics communities have a lot to offer in terms of expertise, methods, and tools that can de-risk the design, implementation, and deployment of blockchain-based systems. **Non-linear optimization tools**, e.g., can be used to compute initial configurations of system parameters to gain desired trade-offs between security, cost, and availability of a consensus mechanism – as used in [19] for configuring Proof of Kernel Work. Such tools can also be used to probe the composability of different blockchain systems or methods, as, e.g., is illustrated in [19] where a combination of PoET and PoKW may make the energy-efficient PoKW more fair and democratic.

Formal methods – including established tools from programming language design, verification, and compiler construction – hold great potential to shape designs of blockchain systems. This is particularly true for the distributed virtual machines and the smart-contract generated machine code they operate on: we need domain-specific languages for programming smart contracts so that the idioms in such a language are expressive enough to be useful, yet restrictive enough to allow for certifiable verification and compilation of such code into executable code. **A DSL for re-insurers**, e.g., will use different programming idioms than **a DSL for a smart contract to do crowdfunding**. Existing modelling languages as well as ontologies are useful to understand the gaps between legal code and technical code embodied in smart contracts. Such a deeper understanding can influence the blockchain architecture when the governance model becomes more sensitive to 'legal interrupts' present in the legal code that cannot be operationalized in the smart contracts and their execution environment alone.

Another potential application of verification tools for blockchain is the analysis of access-control mechanisms managed by a blockchain system. For example, in a system in which access to resources is controlled by credentials or cryptographic tokens that are made resilient through a blockchain fabric, it is important to be able to verify that the policies for such access, including the administrative policies (ability to install, modify or remove policies), do not lead to the escalation of privilege.

5.4 Richer Risk Models for Blockchain Systems: Challenges

We have established that the use of semantic tools, such as an ontology, could be instrumental in this area. The use of an ontology suggests a preference for models in the form of graphs, in the form of declarations in some logical formalism or in a combination of graph-based models and declarative constraints. One challenge is to devise support for multi-modal annotations of such graphs that express constraints, expectations, assumptions or guarantees about risk, security, privacy, reliability, regulatory constraints, or resilience. Such annotations need to be devised in a form that is understandable to end users and system developers. These annotations need to define formal semantics necessary for the analysis of their interaction. Can one devise a modeling framework with such capabilities that can be instantiated to specific application domains such as crypto currencies or blockchain-protected identities? In order to address this question, it is necessary to capture common characteristics across application domains in appropriate form, e.g., reference models or architectures.

The need for annotated models for communication and analysis is not confined to the design and implementation of a system or integrating systems into complex environments. The risk engineering paradigm needs to apply to the entire system lifecycle, including its requirements capture, development, operational and change management, and retirement. It is unlikely that the same modelling formalism would apply to each of these stages or for expressing risk pertaining to the lifecycle of the system itself.

Another challenge in creating tools and methodologies for risk engineering is the need to combine information and metrics from different risk domains, such as privacy, security, regulatory constraints, and sometimes safety, and ensuring the result is meaningful for analysis.

Although calculi can play an important role in validating, monitoring, and controlling the risk in future ICT systems, a set of principles that can express risk and its management through policy will complement this. For cybersecurity policies, Schneider and Mulligan have proposed the use of doctrines [20] as a "lens" to examine policy proposals or suggest new ones. Their Doctrine for Risk Management says there is insufficient data about threats and vulnerabilities to reliably inform the values of confidentiality, integrity, the cost of an attack and other metrics.

Although tools and approaches for risk engineering already exists, the transition from these mechanisms to integrated and quantifiable risk engineering is challenging. However, we believe that environments like blockchain will lead to the emergence of viable risk-engineering approaches, similarly to the emergence of designed-in-security paradigm after the introduction of complex multi-tenanted environments in Cloud and IoT.

6   Conclusions and Future Work

The complexity of the compute environment makes it impossible to assess risks in operational context only; it is imperative today to *inform the system development processes of the integrated acceptable risk requirements*. Thus, risk engineering is an area that should become a focus of research and practical evaluation, in order to usher in a new generation of systems that are *risk conscious by design*. Blockchain technologies provide a fertile domain to explore and validate risk-engineering techniques.

We think that key approaches needed to build these systems already exist, but need to be adjusted for risk engineering. The major components of this risk engineering are:

- Multi-domain ontology for blockchain to capture risk semantics in this space and comprising interlinked upper and multiple domain-specific ontologies.
- Modeling approaches that could be combined with such an ontology, including graph-based models and declarative constraints-based approaches.

- Risk languages that can be used to both annotate and analyze risks and are capable of supporting specific use cases.

Creating a risk engineering framework for blockchain and its applications faces several issues. They include limitation of the existing approaches; need for broadly applicable metrics; differences in terminology and metrics used in different risk domains; limited inventory of approaches to risk composition; and difficulties in developing a comprehensive multi-domain ontology. These challenges are significant, but probably not insurmountable. More research should focus on these issues to improve our understanding of risks in blockchain and risk engineering in general. Adjacent issues, such as vulnerability and threat analysis should also be taken into consideration.

References

1. InternetLiveStats.com. http://www.internetlivestats.com/internet-users/
2. Software Engineering Institute (SEI): Carnegie Mellon University, Architecture Tradeoff Analysis Method (2015). http://www.sei.cmu.edu/architecture/tools/evaluate/atam.cfm
3. Katsumata, P., Hemenway, J., Gavins, W.: Cybersecurity risk management. In: Military Communications Conference, 2010-MILCOM 2010. IEEE (2010)
4. Cyber-Physical Systems Public Working Group: Framework for Cyber-Physical Systems. Release 0.8. DRAFT, September 2015
5. Piètre-Cambacédès, L., Bouissou, M.: Cross-fertilization between safety and security engineering. Rel. Eng. Sys. Safety **110**, 110–126 (2013)
6. International Atomic Energy Agency (IAEA): International nuclear safety group (INSAG), Defence in depth in nuclear safety, INSAG-10, STI/PUB/1013 (1996)
7. Sweeney, L.: Technology Dialectics: Constructing Provably Appropriate Technology. Data Privacy Lab, Fall (2006). http://dataprivacylab.org/dataprivacy/projects/dialectics/index.html. Accessed 26 Aug 2015
8. Ozment, A.: Software security growth modeling: examining vulnerabilities with reliability growth models. In: Gollmann, D., Massacci, F., Yautsiukhin, A. (eds.) Quality of Protection. Advances in Information Security, vol. 23, pp. 25–36. Springer, Boston (2006). https://doi.org/10.1007/978-0-387-36584-8_3
9. Sheyner, O., Haines, J.W., Jha, S., Lippmann, R., Wing, J.M.: Automated generation and analysis of attack graphs. In: IEEE Symposium on Security and Privacy, pp. 273–284 (2002)
10. Roy, A., Kim, D.S., Trivedi, K.S.: Attack countermeasure trees (ACT): towards unifying the constructs of attack and defense trees. In: Security and Communication Networks, vol. 5(8), pp. 929–943, John Riley & Sons (2012)
11. Vishik, C., Balduccini, M.: Making sense of future cybersecurity technologies: using ontologies for multidisciplinary domain analysis. ISSE 2015, pp. 135–145. Springer, Wiesbaden (2015). https://doi.org/10.1007/978-3-658-10934-9_12
12. Mylopoulos, J., Jarke, M., Koubarakis, M.: Telos – a language for representing knowledge about information systems. ACM Trans. Inf. Syst. **8**(4), 327–362 (1990)
13. Herzog, A., Shahmehri, N., Duma, C.: An ontology of information security. Int. J. Inf. Secur. **1**(4), 1–23 (2007)
14. Fenz, S., Ekelhart, A.: Formalizing information security knowledge. In: ASIACCS 2009, pp. 183–194 (2009)

15. Mouratidis, H., Giorgini, P., Manson, G.: An ontology for modelling security: the tropos approach. In: Palade, V., Howlett, Robert J., Jain, L. (eds.) KES 2003. LNCS (LNAI), vol. 2773, pp. 1387–1394. Springer, Heidelberg (2003). https://doi.org/10.1007/978-3-540-45224-9_187

16. Massacci, F., Mylopoulos, J., Paci, F., Tun, T.T., Yu, Y.: An extended ontology for security requirements. In: Salinesi, C., Pastor, O. (eds.) CAiSE 2011. LNBIP, vol. 83, pp. 622–636. Springer, Heidelberg (2011). https://doi.org/10.1007/978-3-642-22056-2_64

17. Nakamoto, S.: A Peer-to-Peer Electronic Cash System. https://bitcoin.org/bitcoin.pdf

18. Lamport, L., Shostak, R., Pease, M.: The Byzantine generals problem. ACM Trans. Program. Lang. Syst. **4**(3), 382–401 (1982)

19. Lundbaek, L., Beutel, D., Huth, M., Kirk, L., Jackson, S.: Proof of kernel work: a resilient & scalable blockchain consensus algorithm for dynamic low-energy networks. xain.io/assets/downloads/XAIN_Yellowpaper_PoKW_Version_1.3.pdf

20. Schneider, F.B., Mulligan, D.: Doctrine for cybersecurity. Daedalus **140**, 70–92 (2011). Fall

IDEA Workshop

IDEA 2018 Workshop Chairs' Message

Digitization is the use of digital technologies for creating innovative digital business models and transforming existing business models and processes. Information is captured and processed without human intervention using digital means. Digitization creates profound changes in the economy and society. Digitization has both business and technological perspectives. Digital business models and processes are essential for many companies to achieve their strategic goals.

Digitization impacts the product, the customer and the value-creation perspective. Digitized products are dynamic; their functionalities can be extended on the fly by using external services. They are capable of reflecting on their own status and thus morph the selling of physical assets to services. Digitization changes the relationships with the customer significantly. Personal interaction is replaced by self-service and proactive action. The customer interacts with the enterprise using a multitude of implicit touch points provided by the Internet of Things. Digitization fosters new models of value creation such as Service-Dominant Logic. Value is also created by plat-form and network effects.

The goal of the workshop was to identify challenges from digitization for enterprises and organizations and to advance Digital Enterprise Engineering and Architecture to cope with these challenges. The workshop allowed identifying and developing concepts and methods that assist the engineering and the management of digital enterprise architectures and the software systems supporting them.

To achieve the goals of the workshop the following themes of research have been pursued:

- Methods for the Design and Management of Digital Enterprises
- Alignment of the enterprise goals and strategies with the digital enterprise architecture
- Digital Strategy and Governance
- Architectural patterns for value-co-creation, dynamic and servitized products
- Service in digital enterprises
- Business process management in Digital Enterprises
- Advanced Analytics for the Support of Digital Enterprises
- Self-service and automation in Digital Enterprises
- Customer journeys and relationship management in digital enterprises
- Internet of Things and Digital Enterprises
- Impact of digitization on society and economy
- Security in Digital Architectures

We wish to thank all the people who submitted papers to IDEA 2018 for having shared their work with us, as well as the members of the IDEA 2018 Program Committee, who made a remarkable effort in reviewing the submissions. We also thank the organizers of BIS 2018 for their help with the organization of the event.

Rainer Schmidt
Alfred Zimmermann
Selmin Nurcan

Organization

Chairs

Rainer Schmidt	Munich University of Applied Sciences, Germany
Alfred Zimmermann	Reutlingen University, Germany
Selmin Nurcan	University Paris 1 Panthéon-Sorbonne, France

Program Committee

Said Assar	Institut Mines-Telecom, France
Lars Brehm	Munich University of Applied Science, Germany
Robert Hirschfeld	Hasso-Plattner-Institut, Germany
Michael Möhring	Munich University of Applied Science, Germany
Selmin Nurcan	Université de Paris 1 Panthéon – Sorbonne
Kurt Sandkuhl	University of Rostock
Rainer Schmidt	Munich University of Applied Sciences
Alfred Zimmermann	Reutlingen University

IT Infrastructure Capability and Health Information Exchange: The Moderating Role of Electronic Medical Records' Reach

Rogier van de Wetering(⊠)

Faculty of Management, Science and Technology,
Open University of the Netherlands, Valkenburgerweg 177,
6419 AT Heerlen, The Netherlands
rogier.vandewetering@ou.nl

Abstract. This research investigates the hypothesized relationship between a hospital's IT infrastructure capability and the degree to which hospital can exchange health information. Enhanced information exchange within and between hospitals is currently considered to be critical for modern hospital operations in the big data era. In this research, we build on the resource-based view of the firm to position the deployment and usage of IT capabilities as a unique, valuable, appropriable and difficult-to-imitate resource of value for hospitals. Following the resource-based view of the firm, this study argues IT is a strategic source of value for hospitals. Guided by our research model we test two related hypotheses using Partial least squares (PLS)-based Structural Equation Modeling (SEM) on a large-scale cross-sectional dataset of 1155 European hospitals. Results show that IT infrastructure capability is a crucial antecedent of health information exchange. Finally, we found that the degree to which hospitals deploy hospital-wide systems that electronically maintain and share health data and information, i.e., Electronic Medical Records, influences the strength of this particular relationship. These particular findings suggest that although IT investments in hospitals continue to grow, IT plans and strategies to enable health information exchange will require ongoing attention. Hence, our research provides valuable insights into how IT can be targetted and exploited to support capabilities in clinical practice. Specifically, we demonstrate the conditions under which hospitals can leverage their IT resources to enhance levels of patient and health information exchange within the hospital and beyond its boundaries.

Keywords: IT infrastructure capability · Health information exchange
PLS-MGA · IT capability · The resource-based view of the firm (RBV)
Hospitals

1 Introduction

Modern hospitals currently deal with many interrelated and multi-faceted challenges, e.g., intense pressures to enhance clinical quality, take into account the dynamics of the changing environment, continuously need to innovate, change and collaborate and deal with quickly changing stakeholders wishes and demands. It seems only self-evident

© Springer Nature Switzerland AG 2019
W. Abramowicz and A. Paschke (Eds.): BIS 2018 Workshops, LNBIP 339, pp. 397–407, 2019.
https://doi.org/10.1007/978-3-030-04849-5_35

that hospital enterprises that want to be more competitive need to align their business operations and IS/IT resources. From extant literature has emerged the widely accepted conclusion that information technology (IT) can be beneficial for hospital enterprises to positively influence the health of individuals and the performance of providers [1, 2]. Therefore, hospitals are making substantial IT investments and look for appropriate digital strategies to cultivate the enterprise-wide adoption and usage of the systems that electronically maintain information concerning patients' individual's health status and care. Moreover, we now see that hospitals and other medical institutions are currently leveraging health IT to improve the quality of care, expand access, reduce operational costs, and enhance patient engagements [1, 3, 4]. In doing so, the management and decision-makers want to make sure that their resources and investments in IS/IT are harnessed successfully [5].

We currently see a trend toward rapid digitization of patient data and information and particular investment guided to engage in health information exchange (HIE) [6–8]. This development is partly also driven by regulatory pressures (e.g., the General Data Protection Regulation (GDPR). HIE allows hospitals to go beyond traditional silos within the organization and share clinical information, e.g., radiology reports, medical images, clinical documentation, and medication lists across the organizations' boundaries [9]. Therefore, this technology is getting center-stage in modern hospitals. Numerous studies highlight the value of HIE in clinical and administrative contexts. However, currently, we have a limited understanding of how hospitals can successfully leverage their IT investments, facilitate and enable HIE in a safe and privacy-minded context to create value.

Furthermore, the literature is not explicit about how hospitals can leverage and deploy HIE as a foundation to enhance quality and services benefits. The effective development and deployment of HIE in clinical practice require deliberate and targeted IT resource investments. However, few empirical studies examine the relationship between measures of IT resources and HIE. In addressing this particular issue, an IT infrastructure capability is widely recognized as a critical element to firm competitiveness and innovativeness [10–14]. Synthesizing from both Information System (IS) and health informatics studies over the past years [15–17], we see that having a flexible IT infrastructure capability is essential for organizations to enhance business processes, innovativeness and even competitiveness [10–14]. This capability underpins the formation of IT-enabled capabilities [18] and can be regarded as a key priority for organizations as they generate significant and sustainable performance enhancements.

Within this study, we draw upon the foundations of the resource-based view of the firm (RBV) [19, 20], to position the deployment and usage of IT as a unique and difficult-to-imitate resource of value for hospitals [17]. However, this source of value cannot operate on its own. For this paper, we follow Bharadwaj [21] and develop the concept of IT as a 'capability,' and empirically examine the degree to which an IT infrastructure capability drives HIE within hospitals. In line with this discussion, we also claim that this particular relationship is strengthened by the presence of an Electronic Medical record (EMR) that has enterprise-wide reach [22–26]. EMRs, in general, can be considered repositories of patient data in digital form, that store, and exchange data securely. Therefore, we guide our research through the following two research questions: '*To what extent does an IT infrastructure capability influence the formation of HIE within hospitals?'* moreover, *'Does the reach of an EMR influence the strength of this particular relationship?'*

We structured the remainder of this study as follows. Frist, we first review the literature on the RBV and IT infrastructure capabilities. These two aspects form the theoretical foundation of this work and strengthen our contribution to the IS community. Next, we propose the research model and the six hypotheses. In the coming section, we present the methods in and present the most important results. Finally, this work concludes with a discussion of the implications of the outcomes. We also identify inherent limitations and present various avenues for future research.

2 Theoretical Background

2.1 IT Infrastructure Capability

The RBV is a contemporary strategy and management information systems (IS) theory that explains how organizations can obtain a competitive advantage as a result of the resources they own or have under their control [19, 20]. This theory gained a considerable research interest in research over the past years in IS studies and healthcare [5, 17, 27] and seemed to be a fitting lens for hospitals to leverage their IT resources. IS and RBV scholars acknowledge that it is imperative for organizations to identify those organizational capabilities that IT should target to address rapidly changing business environments [12, 13, 28]. Therefore, we build on the RBV and synthesize from the extant literature that an organization's IT infrastructure capability is a significant resource for process enhancement and competitive advantage. We can define an organization's IT infrastructure capability as an integrated set of reliable IT assets, resources, and services available to support both existing applications and new initiatives [29]. Extant literature asserted that such a capability could be refined into various quality attributes. These critical qualities include shareability and reusable across the organization [30], the degree to which standards and policies have been established and how applications connect and interoperate with each [31], and the level of integration of applications [10, 32]. Also, and business connectivity can be considered a quality through which an IT infrastructure capability can be assessed [10, 32]. Prior literature defined business connectivity through the infrastructure's particular (i) reach and (ii) range [10]. While reach primarily refers to interconnected locations, the range typically refers to the degree of encapsulated functionality (i.e., information and transaction processing) or services that share automatically.

2.2 Information Sharing and Health Information Exchange

During the late 80s and the beginning of the 90s scholars recognized that information sharing between organizations is essential in partnerships and collaborations between companies [33] and pivotal in achieving a competitive advantage. Scholars now elaborate on the benefits of sharing information in various markets and domains [34, 35]. Studies showcase that most of the benefits for the participants in information sharing relate to an enhancement of information provisioning to achieve business strategies, goals, enhanced efficiency of business processes and better network capabilities. Let us now turn to HIE, which in fact, is all about sharing and exchanging information in networked settings. HIE, thus, allows hospital enterprises to share securely and real-time use of health data and information [8] and enables providers to share and process health data and information among doctors, patients, and other stakeholders within the networked ecosystem. There is substantial evidence that HIE can improve hospital efficiency, reduce health care costs, and improve outcomes for patients [8, 36]. HIE, in that regard, can make a significant contribution to the process of generating a complete patient image.

3   Research Model

3.1   IT Infrastructure Capability and HIE

Extant literature shows that an IT infrastructure capability can be a substantial resource for process enhancements and advantages in a competitive industry [10, 26, 37]. As such, this capability can be considered an integrated set of reliable IT assets, resources and services available to support both existing applications and new initiatives [29]. Studies highlighted the role and contribution of IT infrastructure capability on day-to-day business operations. For example, Duncan [30] demonstrated how infrastructure services could be directed toward the re-engineering of business processes using this capability. Therefore, this capability has great potential to improve operations within the hospital. HIE is considered to be critical for modern hospital operations as it enables hospitals to share and exchange clinical information. This particular aspects makes HIE a promising approach to improve resource utilization, and hence, improve the quality of healthcare delivery [9]. Typically, HIE exchanges vast amounts of patient information and data. It is, therefore, paramount that HIE is enabled by IT that supports both connectivity (i.e., hospital infrastructures reach and range, and level of standardization) [10, 11] and high levels of shareability and integration within the hospital [38]. In summary, if hospitals are equipped with a state-of-the-art IT infrastructure capability[1] and are efficient in targeting and deploying IT resources and assets, we foresee that they will display enhanced levels of HIE. Thus, we expect that IT infrastructure capability will positively influence IC and HIE. Hence, we suggest the following hypothesis:

Hypothesis 1. *IT infrastructure capability has a positive impact on HIE.*

3.2   The Moderating Role of EPDs' Reach in Health Information Exchange

Previous studies contend that EMRs are essential to essential to high-performing healthcare systems around the world [39–41]. EMRs can enhance doctors' standardized work practices, the availability of information, and the safety and quality of care, and

---

[1] And thus also the associated IT-related investments.

enhances operational efficiency within and between hospitals, among many other benefits [39, 42, 43]. Although the use of EMR, in practice, seems promising, the outcomes and contribute to the quality of care have been challenged [44]. These systems are accessible by multiple authorized users within the hospital and beyond the boundaries of a hospital enterprise including other care institutions [45]. It is necessary to have clinical IS/IT capabilities and competencies in providers' setting to have EMRs efficaciously exchange (patient) information between providers [39, 43]. Thus, EMRs are a crucial ingredient of hospitals IT portfolio. Motivated by prior literature on enterprise-wide EMR deployments and health IS maturity studies [22–25], we now contend that the presence of an enterprise-wide EMR will strengthen the impact of hospitals' IT infrastructure capability on HIE. This is not to say that hospitals that have multiple local, or departmental EMRs are not capable of sharing data. Notwithstanding, we argue that for hospitals to fully enable health data and information exchange, and leverage infrastructural investments, they need an enterprise-wide reach, so all the clinical service departments share its key functionality. This argument is also consistent with a claim made by Sambamurthy et al. [26] that high reach of IT is tightly associated with both the design and implementation of business operations that tie activities and information flows across the organization and beyond its boundaries. Therefore, we define:

Hypothesis 2. *The positive effect of IT infrastructure capability on HIE is moderated by EMRs' reach such that this positive effect is further strengthened when EMR's reach becomes high.*

4   Methods

4.1   Cross-Sectional Data Collection

In this work, we follow a deductive approach. Therefore, we ground our work in theory, focus on facts, and craft persuasive arguments to substantiate our claims. To do so, we need a substantial amount of cross-sectional data from hospitals to test the two hypotheses. For this, we found a unique and large-scale dataset: European Hospital Survey: Benchmarking deployment of e-Health services (2012–2013)[2]. This survey covers a wide range of aspects from IT applications, technical infrastructure, information, and data exchange, security/privacy issues, IT functionalities. It benchmarks the level of eHealth adoption and uses in acute hospitals across 30 countries in Europe. In total 1,753 hospitals completed an interview. Interviews lasted on average 45 min, and the data collection team used Computer-Aided Telephone Interviewing (CATI) with native-speaking interviewers. The Benchmark was carried out by PwC EU Services, in cooperation with Global Data Collection Company (GDCC).

Given our primary aim and to make a justified assessment, this study focusses on those hospitals in our dataset that use EMRs for information sharing. Specifically, we want to know, whether or not, hospitals that have EMRs with enterprise-wide reach, are

---

[2] The survey is accessible through: https://ec.europa.eu/digital-single-market/en/news/european-hospital-survey-benchmarking-deployment-ehealth-services-2012-2013.

better equipped to drive HIE than hospitals that have local or departmental systems (see also Sect. 3.2). Therefore, we removed cases that did not include EMRs that share information or do not use an EMR at all. Hence, we removed 598 cases in total. The final dataset included a total of 1155 hospitals, representing most of the European countries.

Finally, we applied Harman's single factor test (using SPSS v24) to control for common method bias (CMB). Hence, we could not identify a single factor that attributes to the majority of the variance. So, we can conclude that our sample is not affected by CMB [46].

4.2 Measurement Items and Construct Development

Following established work, we now measure hospital's IT infrastructure capability (represented by a second-order construct) through (1) business connectivity and (2) IT assets, both modeled as first-order constructs. We measure the first latent construct through the level of (I) standardization [31] (standards and policies establish how applications connect and interoperate with each other) and (II) hospitals' infrastructures range and reach. We now follow the comprehensive operationalization by Broadbent et al. [10, 11]. Hence, we define this measure as the product of hospitals' reach of a computer system (from computers that are not part of a hospital-wide system toward systems are part of regional or national networks) and a broad range of services the hospital is managing. Our second latent construct, IT assets, is reflected by two indicators, i.e., (I) the variety of critical applications (i.e., critical care information system (e.g., emergency, operating room), business intelligence, tele-homecare/telemonitoring services, medical/nursing document management system, appointment booking system, service order placing, transmission of clinical results and health events reporting system) and (II) the degree to which applications within the hospital are integrated.

For HIE (our dependent first-order construct) we devised a set of four survey items from the European Hospital Survey. These questions are: does your hospital exchange electronically: (1) clinical care information about patients (for instance, clinical history or results from medical tests)? (2) laboratory results about patients? (3) medication lists information about patients? And (4) radiology images and reports about patients. Respondents could select multiple of the following answers: (a) with a hospital or hospitals outside your hospital system, (b) external general practitioners, (c) external specialists, (d) health care providers in other EU countries, (e) health care providers outside the EU countries, (f) other. All the above items were rescaled to a Likert scale from 1 to 5.

We measured the moderating variable, i.e., the presence of a hospital-wide EMR, using a binary scale. In our model all latent (first- and second-order) constructs are modeled reflectively, so manifest variables are affected by the latent variables [47, 48]. Hence, measurement items reflect and depict the construct.

5   Model Estimation and Results

We use a second generation Structural Equation Modeling (SEM), Partial least squares (PLS)-based technique, to evaluate the appropriateness of our research model [49]. PLS (or component-based SEM) algorithms estimate model parameters to maximize the variance explained for all endogenous constructs in the model through a series of ordinary least squares (OLS) regressions, depending on the model specification [48, 50, 51]. The usage of PLS fits an integrative mode of thinking about theory construction, measurement problems, and data analysis. We use SmartPLS version 3.2.7. [52] for model estimations. Also, we used a non-parametric bootstrapping procedure [51] (with 500 replications) to compute the significance levels of the regression coefficients. Our sample of 1155 responses exceeds all minimum requirements concerning the measurement and structural model.

5.1 Analyses of the Measurement Model

We subjected our first-order constructs to internal consistency reliability, convergent validity, and discriminant validity tests through SmartPLS [52] to assess the psychometric model properties. Hence, we computed the composite reliability (CR)[3] values for each construct and established that their values were above the threshold of 0.70. Table 1 shows that all our CR values are above the threshold. We also assessed the obtained construct-to-item loadings. Our model did not contain any indicators with a loading of less than 0.6. Next, we assessed convergent validity by examining if the average variance extracted (AVE) is above the generally accepted lower limit of 0.50. All our calculated AVE values exceed the minimum threshold value. In a subsequent step, we assessed discriminant validity. First, we assessed if the cross-loadings on other constructs are less than the outer loading on the associated construct. Second, we assessed the Fornell-Larcker criterion. In doing so, we investigated if the square root of the AVEs was substantially larger than the inter-construct correlations [47] (see entries in bold in Table 1 along the matrix diagonal). All square root values are higher than the shared variances of the constructs with other constructs in the model. We found further evidence of discriminant validity by using the relatively new heterotrait-monotrait (HTMT) ratio of correlations approach by Henseler, Ringle, and Sarstedt [53].

PLS calculates this ratio based on the mean of the correlations of indicators across constructs measuring different constructs, relative to the average correlations of indicators within the same construct. All values are well below the upper bound (HTMT ratio value $\leq$ 0.90).

5.2 Analyses of the Structural Model

To test our two hypotheses, we estimated the structural model using the PLS algorithm and an additional non-parametric multi-group analysis (PLS-MGA) [54]. In these analyses, we mainly investigated the significance and association of each hypothesized path and the coefficient of determination (R^2); a measure of the model's predictive power.

Results show that hospital's IT infrastructure significantly influences HIE ($\beta = 0.428$; $t = 15.815$; $p < 0.0001$), thereby confirming our first hypothesis. The

---

[3] Composite reliability is similar to Cronbach's alpha without the assumption of the equal weighting of variables.

Table 1. Assessment of reliability, convergent and discriminant validity of reflective constructs

	1	2	3
1. Business connectivity	**0.759**		
2. IT assets	0.353	**0.848**	
3. Health information exchange	0.263	0.413	**0.806**
AVE	0.577	0.720	0.649
Composite reliability	0.731	0.837	0.880

model shows a substantial coefficient of determination, $R^2 = 0.181$. During the structural analyses we controlled our model for 'size' (amount of beds), 'hospital type' (private or public) and 'IT budget' all showing non-significant effects. For our second hypothesis, we employ a regression-based approach to test the effects of categorical moderating variables [55]. Therefore, we divided our dataset into two separate groups following [49], i.e., (1) $N = 843$ (hospital-wide EMR shared by all clinical service departments) and (2) $N = 312$ (multiple local/departmental EMRs) and statistically assessed the difference between the same parameter estimates but for the two distinct groups [54]. We employed the PLS-MGA algorithm in SmartPLS to execute this particular analysis. Outcomes show a statistically significant difference ($p = 0.028$)[4] between the assessed groups. The results for the separate path model analyses are as follows. Group 1 ($\beta = 0.459$, $t = 8.460$, $p < 0.001$) shows a significantly higher path coefficient than this particular estimate in group 2 ($\beta = 0.333$, $t = 8.460$, $p < 0.001$). As we expected, the model run for group 1 explains 21.5% of the variance for HIE. More so, the model's inner model for group two has an $R^2 = 0.118$. These outcomes, thereby confirm our second hypothesis.

6 Discussion, Conclusions, and Limitations

Drawing on the RBV, this study empirically examined the degree to which an IT infrastructure capability drives HIE within hospitals. For this, we used data from a large-scale cross-sectional survey, distributed by the European Commission. We argued that hospitals that are equipped with a state-of-the-art IT infrastructure capability would display enhanced levels of HIE. Moreover, we corroborated that this effect would be even stronger for a hospital that uses an EMR with enterprise-wide reach. We found support for our hypotheses and thus our essential claims through the use of various PLS model estimations and analyses. Therefore, hospitals' IT infrastructure capability has great potential to improve HIE operations within the hospital. It, now, also goes without saying that hospitals can leverage their HIE potential by providing an enterprise-wide reach for EMRs.

Like all research, our research is constrained by some limitations. Hence, the outcomes need to be interpreted with caution. First, we only included IT infrastructure capability as an antecedent in our research model. Driven by other IS studies [13, 14,

---

[4] At the 5% probability of error level.

21, 56], it likely the case that other capabilities, organizational aspects, and condition factors influence HIE in practice. Second, we did not compare groups (and types) of hospitals across countries. Such an analysis would contribute to the generalizability of our findings. Finally, we did not investigate the specific subgroups in detail.

To conclude, our study contributes to the literature by unfolding specific conditions under which hospitals can leverage their IT resources and capabilities to enhance levels of patient and health information exchange within the hospital and beyond its boundaries. Outcomes of this research are likewise relevant for practitioners as these outcomes can help decision-makers in the process of efficiently allocating IT resources, mature their IT infrastructure, and make purposeful IT investments.

References

1. Buntin, M.B., et al.: The benefits of health information technology: a review of the recent literature shows predominantly positive results. Health Aff. **30**(3), 464–471 (2011)
2. Kohli, R., Tan, S.S.-L.: Electronic health records: how can IS researchers contribute to transforming healthcare? MIS Q. **40**(3), 553–573 (2016)
3. Sheikh, A., Sood, H.S., Bates, D.W.: Leveraging health information technology to achieve the "triple aim" of healthcare reform. J. Am. Med. Inform. Assoc. **22**(4), 849–856 (2015)
4. Hendrikx, H., et al.: Expectations and attitudes in eHealth: a survey among patients of Dutch private healthcare organizations. Int. J. Healthc. Manage. **6**(4), 263–268 (2013)
5. Van de Wetering, R., Versendaal, J., Walraven, P.: Examining the relationship between a hospital's IT infrastructure capability and digital capabilities: a resource-based perspective. In: The Proceedings of the Twenty-Fourth Americas Conference on Information Systems (AMCIS). AIS, New Orleans (2018)
6. Van de Wetering, R., Versendaal, J.: How a flexible collaboration infrastructure impacts healthcare information exchange. In: The Proceedings of the 31st Bled eConference Digital Transformation – Meeting the Challenges, Bled, Slovenia (2018)
7. Walker, J., et al.: The value of health care information exchange and interoperability. Health Aff. **24**, W5 (2005)
8. Hersh, W.R., et al.: Outcomes from health information exchange: systematic review and future research needs. JMIR Med. Inform. **3**(4), e39 (2015)
9. Vest, J.R., et al.: Challenges, alternatives, and paths to sustainability for health information exchange efforts. J. Med. Syst. **37**(6), 9987 (2013)
10. Broadbent, M., Weill, P., Neo, B.-S.: Strategic context and patterns of IT infrastructure capability. J. Strateg. Inf. Syst. **8**(2), 157–187 (1999)
11. Weill, P., Subramani, M., Broadbent, M.: Building IT infrastructure for strategic agility. MIT Sloan Manage. Rev. **44**(1), 57 (2002)
12. Mikalef, P., Pateli, A., van de Wetering, R.: IT flexibility and competitive performance: the mediating role of IT-enabled dynamic capabilities. In: The Proceedings of the 24th European Conference on Information Systems (ECIS) (2016)
13. Van de Wetering, R., Mikalef, P., Pateli, A.: A strategic alignment model for IT flexibility and dynamic capabilities: toward an assessment tool. In: The Proceedings of the Twenty-Fifth European Conference on Information Systems (ECIS), Guimarães, Portugal (2017)
14. Van de Wetering, R., Mikalef, P., Helms, R.: Driving organizational sustainability-oriented innovation capabilities: a complex adaptive systems perspective. Curr. Opin. Environ. Sustainability **28**, 71–79 (2017)

15. Henderson, J.C., Venkatraman, N.: Strategic alignment: leveraging information technology for transforming organisations. IBM Syst. J. **32**(1), 4–16 (1993)
16. Melville, N., Kraemer, K., Gurbaxani, V.: Review: information technology and organizational performance: an integrative model of IT business value. MIS Q. **28**(2), 283–322 (2004)
17. Wade, M., Hulland, J.: Review: the resource-based view and information systems research: review, extension, and suggestions for future research. MIS Q. **28**(1), 107–142 (2004)
18. El Sawy, O.A., Pavlou, P.A.: IT-enabled business capabilities for turbulent environments. MIS Q. Exec. **7**(3), 139–150 (2008)
19. Barney, J.: Firm resources and sustained competitive advantage. J. Manag. **17**(1), 99–120 (1991)
20. Wernerfelt, B.: A resource-based view of the firm. Strateg. Manag. J. **5**(2), 171–180 (1984)
21. Bharadwaj, A.S.: A resource-based perspective on information technology capability and firm performance: an empirical investigation. MIS Q. **24**, 169–196 (2000)
22. Siegel, E.L., Reiner, B.: Filmless radiology at the Baltimore VA Medical Center: a 9 year retrospective. Comput. Med. Imaging Graph. **27**, 101–109 (2003)
23. Van de Wetering, R., Batenburg, R.S.: A PACS maturity model: a systematic meta-analytic review on maturation and evolvability of PACS in the hospital enterprise. Int. J. Med. Inform. **78**(2), 127–140 (2009)
24. Evans, D.C., Nichol, W.P., Perlin, J.B.: Effect of the implementation of an enterprise-wide electronic health record on productivity in the veterans health administration. Health Econ. Policy Law **1**(2), 163–169 (2006)
25. Carvalho, J.V., et al.: A maturity model for hospital information systems. J. Bus. Res. **94**, 388–399 (2017)
26. Sambamurthy, V., Bharadwaj, A., Grover, V.: Shaping agility through digital options: reconceptualizing the role of information technology in contemporary firms. MIS Q. **27**, 237–263 (2003)
27. Gordon, S.R., Tarafdar, M.: How do a company's information technology competences influence its ability to innovate? J. Enterp. Inf. Manage. **20**(3), 271–290 (2007)
28. Kohli, R., Grover, V.: Business value of IT: an essay on expanding research directions to keep up with the times. J. Assoc. Inf. Syst. **9**(1), 23 (2008)
29. Weill, P., Vitale, M.: What IT infrastructure capabilities are needed to implement e-business models? MIS Q. **1**(1), 17 (2002)
30. Duncan, N.B.: Capturing flexibility of information technology infrastructure: a study of resource characteristics and their measure. J. Manage. Inf. Syst. **12**, 37–57 (1995)
31. Weill, P., Ross, J.: A matrixed approach to designing IT governance. MIT Sloan Manage. Rev. **46**(2), 26 (2005)
32. Broadbent, M., Weill, P.: Management by maxim: how business and IT managers can create IT infrastructures. MIT Sloan Manage. Rev. **38**(3), 77 (1997)
33. Konsynski, B.R., McFarlan, F.W.: Information partnerships–shared data, shared scale. Harvard Bus. Rev. **68**(5), 114–120 (1990)
34. Lotfi, Z., et al.: Information sharing in supply chain management. Procedia Technol. **11**, 298–304 (2013)
35. Bagheri, S., et al.: Classification framework of knowledge transfer issues across value networks. In: Procedia CIRP, vol. 47, pp. 382–387 (2016)
36. Patel, V., et al.: Physicians' potential use and preferences related to health information exchange. Int. J. Med. Inform. **80**(3), 171–180 (2011)
37. Overby, E., Bharadwaj, A., Sambamurthy, V.: Enterprise agility and the enabling role of information technology. Eur. J. Inf. Syst. **15**(2), 120–131 (2006)

38. Ross, J.W., Beath, C.M., Goodhue, D.L.: Develop long-term competitiveness through IT assets. Sloan Manag. Rev. **38**(1), 31 (1996)
39. Jaana, M., Ward, M.M., Bahensky, J.A.: EMRs and clinical IS implementation in hospitals: a statewide survey. J. Rural Health **28**(1), 34–43 (2012)
40. Sittig, D.F., Gonzalez, D., Singh, H.: Contingency planning for electronic health record-based care continuity: a survey of recommended practices. Int. J. Med. Inform. **83**(11), 797–804 (2014)
41. DesRoches, C.M., et al.: Adoption of electronic health records grows rapidly, but fewer than half of US hospitals had at least a basic system in 2012. Health Affairs (2013). https://doi.org/10.1377/hlthaff.2013.0308
42. Park, S.Y., Lee, S.Y., Chen, Y.: The effects of EMR deployment on doctors' work practices: a qualitative study in the emergency department of a teaching hospital. Int. J. Med. Inform. **81**(3), 204–217 (2012)
43. Boonstra, A., Broekhuis, M.: Barriers to the acceptance of electronic medical records by physicians from systematic review to taxonomy and interventions. BMC Health Serv. Res. **10**(1), 231 (2010)
44. Zhou, L., et al.: The relationship between electronic health record use and quality of care over time. J. Am. Med. Inform. Assoc. **16**(4), 457–464 (2009)
45. Häyrinen, K., Saranto, K., Nykänen, P.: Definition, structure, content, use and impacts of electronic health records: a review of the research literature. Int. J. Med. Inform. **77**(5), 291–304 (2008)
46. Podsakoff, P.M., et al.: Common method biases in behavioral research: a critical review of the literature and recommended remedies. J. Appl. Psychol. **88**(5), 879 (2003)
47. Chin, W.: Issues and opinion on structural equation modeling. Manage. Inf. Syst. Q. **22**(1), 7–16 (1998)
48. Wetzels, M., Odekerken-Schröder, G., Van Oppen, C.: Using PLS path modeling for assessing hierarchical construct models: guidelines and empirical illustration. MIS Q. **33**(1), 177–195 (2009)
49. Hair Jr, J.F., et al.: A Primer on Partial Least Squares Structural Equation Modeling (PLS-SEM). Sage Publications, Thousand Oaks (2016)
50. Reinartz, W., Haenlein, M., Henseler, J.: An empirical comparison of the efficacy of covariance-based and variance-based SEM. Int. J. Res. Mark. **26**(4), 332–344 (2009)
51. Tenenhaus, M., et al.: PLS path modeling. Comput. Stat. Data Anal. **48**(1), 159–205 (2005)
52. Ringle, C.M., Wende, S., Becker, J.-M.: SmartPLS 3. SmartPLS GmbH, Boenningstedt (2015). http://www.smartpls.com
53. Henseler, J., Ringle, C.M., Sarstedt, M.: A new criterion for assessing discriminant validity in variance-based structural equation modeling. J. Acad. Mark. Sci. **43**(1), 115–135 (2015)
54. Henseler, J., Ringle, C., Sinkovics, R.: The use of partial least squares path modeling in international marketing. In: Advances in International Marketing, vol. 20, pp. 277–319 (2009)
55. Baron, R.M., Kenny, D.A.: The moderator–mediator variable distinction in social psychological research: conceptual, strategic, and statistical considerations. J. Pers. Soc. Psychol. **51**(6), 1173 (1986)
56. Chen, Y., et al.: IT capability and organizational performance: the roles of business process agility and environmental factors. Eur. J. Inf. Syst. **23**(3), 326–342 (2014)

The IT Department as a Service Broker: A Qualitative Research

Linda Rodriguez and Oscar Avila[(⊠)]

Department of Systems and Computing Engineering, School of Engineering,
Universidad de los Andes, Bogotá, Colombia
{ls.rodriguezc, oj.avila}@uniandes.edu.co

Abstract. The accelerated increase of new IT suppliers and services is allowing organizations to easily access to specialized outsourced services. Consequently, IT departments are increasingly developing fewer IT services and relying more on external providers to satisfy the needs of their customers. This new context requires a change in the IT function, which should move from its traditional role of service builder and operator to a new role of service integrator and broker. However, IT managers do not know in most of the cases which are the capabilities and IT expert roles and skills required in the IT area to implement this new role. To cope with this lack, we propose a management model built in two steps: (i) a review of the literature that help us to identify and analyze the current contributions in the IT service brokering area, and (ii) a qualitative research that includes a focus group and a survey to IT professionals in order to validate the findings made in the literature review. The presented model aims at establishing the basis for a complete approach to help IT organizations to adopt the IT service broker role.

Keywords: IT unit · Focus group · Survey · Outsourcing · Intermediator
Integrator · Aggregator

1 Introduction

The development of the digital market and the accelerated increase of Information Technology (IT) suppliers in the last few years has produced a growing offer of increasingly specialized and robust IT services. In this context, business areas of the organizations are self-supplying IT services because they can find easy access and rapid response to their needs in the external market [1]. In many cases, they contract and access to external services without making requests, seeking approvals or consulting the IT department [2]. According to [3], 83% of employees in business areas of U.S. companies uses IT services and applications that are not authorized by the IT department to carry out their daily work. If this is the case, this could mean that the business areas would be meeting a part of their needs and taking advantage of the benefits offered by external services without the intervention of the IT area. However, this scenario could bring security threats since users would be overlooking the information security policies and requirements of their organizations [4]. Considering the potential benefits and risks associated to such scenario it could be said that the IT

© Springer Nature Switzerland AG 2019
W. Abramowicz and A. Paschke (Eds.): BIS 2018 Workshops, LNBIP 339, pp. 408–419, 2019.
https://doi.org/10.1007/978-3-030-04849-5_36

department should, on the one hand, facilitate the use of external IT services in order to allow business areas to reap the benefits they offer, and, on the other hand, govern the procurement and access to such services in order to reduce potential risks.

To succeed in, IT departments need to assume a new management model allowing them to intermediate between the external suppliers and the business customer in order to ease and control the supply of IT services. This model has been defined by [5, 6] as IT service brokering. According to these works, in this model IT exercises the role of intermediary between external suppliers and internal customers in the provision of IT services, with the aim of focusing its own efforts on the delivery of solutions that leverage the business strategy. In this new role, the IT department acts as a strategic partner and as the sole responsible for the provision of IT services to the business. But the reality is that in most of cases IT departments do not know how to take on this new model because there is a lack of knowledge about the organizational capabilities, roles, skills and resources that need to be changed or implemented in the IT function in order to offer a unique and flexible catalog from the aggregation and integration of external services.

Considering the need above mentioned, the main objective of this research work is to contribute a conceptual model to broker IT services offered by external IT suppliers and consumed by internal business customers. This conceptual model was built through two steps: (i) to review the existing literature in the IT service brokering area in order to identify the capabilities, roles, skills and resources that the IT function needs to broker IT services; (ii) to validate and complete the literature review findings through a qualitative research that includes both a focus group and a survey. The focus group is intended to help us set up the questionnaire that will be used during the survey. The survey aims to gather the opinions and reactions of professionals and managers working in IT areas about the elements identified in the literature review in order to propose the conceptual model.

This paper presents our work as follows: Sect. 2 presents the literature review by following a systematic method. Section 3 presents the qualitative research method and the findings of the focus group activity and the survey. Section 4 introduces the resulting management model. Finally, Sect. 5 concludes the paper.

2 Literature Review

The following steps were used to conduct the review process: (i) Planning: This stage focuses on planning the search to identify the most relevant contributions. We define thus in this step the review objective and questions in order to conduct the search as well as select and validate the most pertinent works. (ii) Realization: It consists in making an exhaustive search for works by defining the search criteria and assessing the found approaches in order to select those that answer the research questions. (iii) Analysis: This stage is related to the extraction of the relevant information of the selected works and to synthesized it in order to answer the review questions.

2.1 Planning

The objective of this review is to identify and analyze the main organizational elements of the IT Service Brokering model stated in the literature. To perform this analysis, we propose the following review questions:

- What are the capabilities required by the IT area in the Service Brokering model?
- What are the IT expert roles required by the IT department in the Service Brokering model?
- What are the skills needed by IT experts in the Service Brokering model?
- What are the resources required by IT experts in the Service Brokering model?

2.2 Realization

With the purpose of finding potential research works answering the research questions previously announced, the Scopus database was used by introducing the following criteria:

- Search area: Computer Science, Business, Management and Accounting and Engineering.
- Document type: book, book chapter, article, conference paper and journal paper.
- Search field type: Abstract, title and keywords.
- Language: English.

The query introduced in the database was:

TITLE-ABS-KEY (("brokering" OR "broker" OR "mediator" OR "inter-agency" OR "interagency" OR "inter agency" OR "builder" OR "integrator" OR "integration" OR "composition" OR "composer" OR "decomposition" OR "decomposer" OR "break down" OR "breakdown" OR "unbundled" OR "unbundling" OR "brokerage") AND ("IT service" OR "ITC service" OR "cloud service" OR "saas" OR "paas" OR "iaas" OR "cloud computing" OR "cloud management" OR "outsourcing" OR "Information technology" OR "enterprise mashup") AND ("IT department" OR "CIO" OR "IT function" OR "IT area" OR "IT unit" OR "IT functional unit" OR "IT business unit" OR "IT functional area" OR "enterprise IT" OR "emerging trends" OR "academic research"))

With these criteria, the Scopus search engine returned 98 candidate articles. To evaluate the pertinence of these works, firstly, a review of the articles titles was carried out. This filter reduced the number to 35. Secondly, a reading of articles abstracts was undertaken to filter those works that do not present evidence of answering any of the analysis questions. This filter limited the number of articles to 12. Lastly, a complete reading of the articles was performed to select the final set of research works made up of 7 articles which were identified and included in the analysis.

Considering the low number of academic works that were found, we decided to carry out a Google search to find articles, books or white papers concerning our research objective. As a result, 5 white papers from technology companies that talk about the model were found. In addition, to include to our analysis the contributions made by practitioners in existing standards, best practices and reference frameworks in the area of IT service management, we include the following works to our review:

IT4IT (Information Technology for Information Technology) [7], ITIL (Information Technology Infrastructure Library) [8], FitSM [9] and COBIT (Control Objectives for Information Systems and related Technology) [10].

2.3 Analysis

A synthesis of the literature review with reference to the review questions is presented in Table 1. A discussion of the found values is described below.

Table 1. Summary of the literature review results.

Question	Found values
What are the capabilities required by the IT area in the Service Brokering model?	Supplier management Service catalog management Requirement management Request fulfillment Service level management Offer management Demand management Information security management Customer relationship management Service portfolio management
What are the IT expert roles required by the IT department in the Service Brokering model?	Supplier and contract manager Service manager Service portfolio manager IT integration specialist Enterprise architect Financial manager/controller Strategic Advisor Business relationship manager Business analyst Service level manager Catalog manager Knowledge manager
What are the skills needed by IT experts in the Service Brokering model?	Soft skills and customer orientation Software integration skills Relationship with suppliers and negotiation Financial skills Strategic thinking Service improvement
What are the resources required by IT experts in the Service Brokering model?	IT strategic plans Business cases Service performance reports Business requirements Contracts and SLAs Business objectives achievement report Service portfolio and catalog

Concerning capabilities, the reviewed literature shows that today IT departments require organizational-type capabilities such as supplier management, service level management and offer management, in order to supply the organization with external services. Regarding roles of IT experts, we identified roles in the following areas: (i) Management, IT experts who coordinate and manages IT suppliers, contracts, services and customers and their requirements; (ii) Consultancy, experts who advise to make sound decisions; (iii) Technology: IT experts that integrate external IT services to offer a unique service to the internal customers. In addition, such experts require new skills in strategic thinking, financial aspects, negotiation and customer orientation in order to prioritize business needs and offer a service portfolio with an adequate cost-benefit balance. Regarding resources, they follow the same way that capabilities in the sense that IT departments are moving towards management resources (such as contracts and SLAs) allowing them to manage suppliers and customers.

Although this set of common organizational elements constitutes a first step to help IT departments to move towards a IT service brokering role, we did not find neither a study that validates the extent to which these are pertinent in the industry nor a conceptual model that links such elements and states their relationship. To fulfill this lack, we decided to carry out the qualitative analysis presented in the next section.

3 Qualitative Research

3.1 Focus Group Activity

A focus group is a popular qualitative research technique, which consists in small groups of people guided by a moderator through an unstructured and spontaneous discussion with the aim of obtaining relevant information about a research problem [11]. For this research work, the focus group activity lasted approximatively 90 min and included 8 IT professionals working in different positions in large international companies. It was intended to help us design the questions and validate the response options for the survey questionnaire. To this end, we used the literature review results in order to ask questions and guide the activity. The main results are described as follows:

- General conclusions: All the participants affirmed that there is a strong inclination towards the intermediation of services in their departments since more than 50% of the services offered by them are contracted to external suppliers. However, 75% of the participants (6 out of 8) argued that the transition to this role has been slow because of the lack of best practices and guidelines.
- Capabilities: Most of the capabilities identified in the literature review have been implemented or are in implementation processes in at least one participant's IT department. As request fulfillment was the only capability no referred by any participant, we decide to do not include this capability in the questionnaire. Because of the unstructured and spontaneous nature of the activity, there was room for participants to talk about other IT capabilities that are not necessarily involved in the service brokering model such as availability and incident management. They argued that although those more "technical" capabilities are becoming less

common, these still exist in their departments. Taking in consideration such affir-
mation, we decided to add two "technical" response options to the question related
to capabilities: (i) Service desk, problem and incident management and (ii) availability and continuity management.

- Roles: All the roles identified in the literature review have been implemented in the
  IT departments of participants. However, there was consensus that integration
  specialists are normally contracted as an external resource for one-time projects so
  that we decided to do not include this role in the questionnaire. As development and
  operation roles such as software developer, as well as server, DB and network
  administrators, were also referred, we decided to include them into the
  questionnaire.
- Skills: In addition to the skills identified in the literature review, the participants
  stated that contract handling and SLA monitoring and follow-up are very important
  skills to deal with external providers when brokering services. As a result, these
  were added to the questionnaire. Furthermore, they expressed spontaneously that
  traditional technical skills in software, hardware, operating systems and DB are still
  required in their departments, and new technical skills in cloud computing and
  DevOps are becoming increasingly required. As a result, we included such skills in
  the questionnaire.
- Resources: The participants agreed on the importance today of the resources
  identified in the literature review. However they emphasized that their IT departments still have infrastructure resources such as development tools, applications,
  servers, networks, etc., so that we decided to include a response option for such type
  of resources in the questionnaire.
- Relationships: The relaxed atmosphere of the activity allowed participants to talk
  about the relationships between the elements mentioned above. The conclusions of
  this discussion helped us to describe the management model presented in the next
  section.

3.2 Survey to IT Professionals

Based on the results of the focus group, a questionnaire was designed to gather IT
professional's opinions and validate the findings of the literature review. The questionnaire included 23 questions, each one with several predetermined choices and an
open-ended choice to gather different responses or opinions to the proposed in the
predefined choices. Initially we thought to include as predetermined choices all the
values found for each question in the literature review. However, as seen in the previous subsection, the focus group helped us eliminate options that were not relevant
and add others that definitely made sense in the industry context. Besides, listening to
the recordings made in the focus group, we also realized that for the question related to
the capabilities some of the options could be grouped, such as catalog management and
portfolio management. This allowed us to reduce the number of options per question in
order to make the questionnaire easier to fill out. The questionnaire was sent to about
650 students and 600 graduates of our postgraduate school in computer science and
information systems that work mainly in large and medium size companies in a South-
American country. We obtained a response percentage of approximately 10,8%. From

the responses, we selected for the analysis those of 74 professionals working in large and medium size companies on which the service brokering model could been implemented. Considering that in this country there are about 4000 large and medium size companies, a sample size of 74 companies provides us a confidence level of 92% and an uncertainty of 10% on the results obtained. A favorable factor for the analysis is that 80% of the respondents have management positions (CxO and medium level management), which indicates that they have a holistic view of the IT processes in the organization. We describe as follows the responses to 3 out of the 23 questions, that included in addition, questions like *What percentage of the IT services you provide are acquired through external suppliers? What is the main reason for contracting IT services with external suppliers? Which of the following resources and assets do you use to provide IT services to your customers?*

Capabilities. To the question *what of the following capabilities have been implemented within your IT department?* the most implemented capabilities for IT service brokering in the respondents' IT departments were requirement management (80%), and supplier management (70%), and the least adopted was offer management (10%) (see Fig. 1). The "technical" capabilities added to the questionnaire have been highly implemented even by the respondents that claimed to be transitioning their IT areas to the brokering model (security management 85%, service desk, problem and incident management 95%, and availability and continuity management 75%). As a conclusion, we can say that such technical capabilities are independent of whether the department acts as a broker or not, that is, they are cross-cutting capabilities of the traditional IT developer and operator role as well as the broker role of the IT area. Additionally, when analyzing the answers to the open-ended choice associated to this question, demand and knowledge management were described by the participants as important so that those are included to the model.

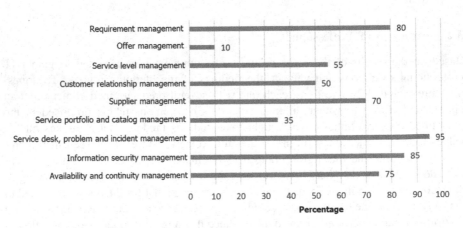

Fig. 1. Frequency of capabilities used in IT departments

Roles. When analyzing the frequency percentage of responses to the question *what of the following roles exist within your IT department?* there is a considerable percentage of organizational roles for business linking and intermediation, such as business analysts (50%), financial manager/controller (45%), supplier manager (40%), IT service and portfolio manager (40%), and strategic advisor (35%). Further, the frequency percentage of the "technical" roles shows that companies still have technological infrastructure and internal services, since 95% have infrastructure support professionals such as server and DB administrators and 65% have network technicians and administrators. In addition, thorough the open question *"which changes in the roles of your IT organization have you carried out to implement the service broker role"* proposed to the respondents, we found that the following changes were the most common: (i) the number of business analysts increased, (ii) the first and second support lines of service desk professionals were subcontracted, (iii) new management positions were created such as supplier and contract managers; and (v) business and strategic advisors increased (Fig. 2).

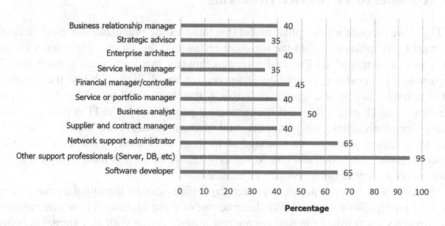

Fig. 2. Frequency of roles used in IT departments

Skills. When analyzing the results to the question *which of the following skills do you consider are important in your IT department?* We can see, on the one hand, that soft skills for dealing with customers and external providers are becoming important, e.g., relationship with suppliers and negotiation (65%), soft skills and customer orientation (65%) and contract handling and SLA monitoring, and on the other hand, it is evident that technical skills in software, hardware, DB, etc., are indispensable in the IT department since 100% of the respondents selected this option. In addition, new technical skills in cloud computing and DevOps are becoming more common (Fig. 3).

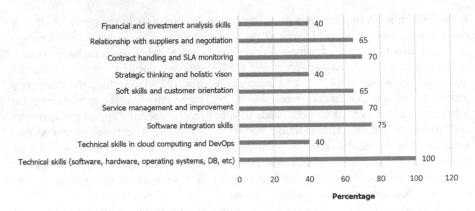

Fig. 3. Frequency of skills required in IT departments

4 A Model to IT Service Brokering

In Fig. 4 we propose a conceptual model that includes the organizational elements and their relationship found within the literature review and the survey. This model shows six types of elements: (i) External role: stakeholders that participate outside the IT department, i.e., customers, suppliers and executive board. (ii) Capability: it concerns a set of activities to obtain a specific objective. Capabilities are described in bold font in the figure. (iii) IT expert role: it relates groups of people within the IT department with related responsibilities, e.g., supplier and partner manager or business analyst. (iv) Management resource: an essential element or asset used by the IT function to broker services, e.g., contracts and SLAs. (vi) Relationship: it is used to represent the connections or interactions between capabilities.

Several integration sequences between capabilities can be identified by navigating the relationships between them. We describe one of these sequences in which business requirements are fulfilled through contracting a new service with an external supplier (see Fig. 4): The customer raises requirements that can be gathered by the requirement management (in the case of functional requirements), business relationship management (in the case of strategic requirements) or service level management (in the case of service level requirements) capabilities. Such requirements are correlated by the demand management capability in order to identify similar existing demand or create new demand. Demand is then prioritized and converted in requests for new or modified services according to the strategic business plan. These requests are then addressed by the portfolio management capability through the identification of several service options and sourcing models that could fulfill them. For each service request, a business case including financial, risk and functional aspects is thus built in order to evaluate different options that includes insourcing, outsourcing and co-sourcing alternatives. The business case is then presented to the company's Executive Board that decides for the best option. If the selected option is to contract an external service, the supplier management capability will contact the respective supplier and jointly with the service level management capability will negotiate and agree SLAs and contracts. Once

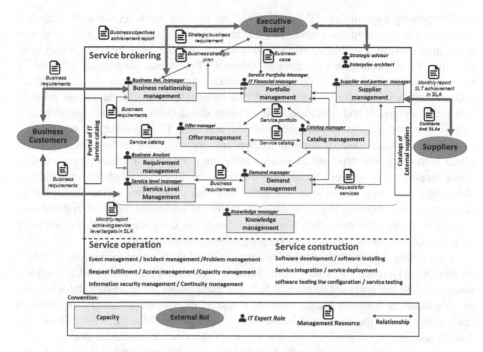

Fig. 4. Conceptual model to IT service brokering

the contract has been signed, the service catalog and portfolio are updated by the catalog and portfolio management capabilities respectively. In addition, an entry with the new service will be added into the service portal by the offer capability in order to make it accessible by the customer. In the portal customers can consult detailed information about the service and when a customer is interested in it, she makes a request that is managed by the offer management. Transversely to all the aforementioned interaction, the knowledge management capability gathers and registers knowledge generated by suppliers and the IT department in order to make it available to other capabilities and customers.

Even though the focus group and the survey allow us to identify that capabilities, roles, skills and resources involved in the "traditional" developer and operator role of the IT area are still required, we only include the capabilities in the model without describing the interaction between such elements and the ones involved in the role of the IT function as a service broker. In fact, it is outside of the scope of our main objective and additional research work would be necessary to this end.

5 Conclusions

This article proposes a conceptual model which synthesizes the main organizational elements that need to be implemented by the IT area when working as a service broker. The main conclusions of the work made are described as follows.

Concerning capabilities, IT departments are moving from focusing on technical capabilities to organizational ones. For instance, today IT departments require a supplier management capability, similar to the one of the procurement department, allowing the organization to access to external IT services. Regarding roles of IT experts, we identified an increase in new organizational roles in areas like management and consultancy. In addition, we found that although technical traditional roles in service development and operation such software developer and DB administrator, are still very important, the respondents affirmed that their IT organizations are increasingly shifting them towards supplier companies. Instead, new technology experts in cloud computing, DevOps and IT service integration and customization are each time more important, however, those are being normally contracted in outsourcing. Regarding resources, they follow the same way that capabilities in the sense that IT departments are moving from focusing on technical resources (such as applications, servers or routers) to management resources (such as contracts and SLAs) allowing them to manage intermediation between suppliers and customers.

Concerning future work, further research is needed in order to improve the conceptual model presented in this work. First, it is necessary to carry out a complete analysis of all the potential sequences between capabilities by analyzing the whole set of relationships between them. Second, research efforts are necessary in order to understand how is the interaction between the capabilities of the IT Service Brokering model and the capabilities of the traditional IT service development and operation models. Third, to validate the model, it is necessary to use additional methodology tools such as case studies or surveys. This could add more information from more companies and different sources.

Concerning the IT service brokering as a subject of study, one of the main findings is the lack of academic and industrial research works and best practices in this domain, which has had repercussion in the ability of companies to migrate to this model. [12] shows that most IT executives see the IT Service Brokering model as a priority but only 25% have made a progress in its adoption. Furthermore, according to [13], there is a clear gap in academic research in the area. From the literature review presented in this work, we can observe that the reviewed works are too focused on presenting the urgency of a change in the IT function, however, these works fail in proposing a set of good practices or formal frameworks to carry out such change. Only IT4IT [7] has specifically proposed the Request to Fulfill (R2F) workflow that helps IT organizations to move towards a service intermediary model. As a consequence, we consider that there is a need for academics and practitioners to get involved in studies regarding organizational change and transformation such as in [14]. Last but not least, the link of this research domain with the decision-making domain is necessary in order to provide a holistic approach to practitioners allowing them to cover from service and provider choice to service performance follow-up [15].

References

1. Zimmermann, S., Rentrop, C.: On the emergence of shadow IT - a transaction cost-based approach. In: 22nd European Conference on Information Systems, CIS (2014)
2. Hoyer, V., Stanoevska-Slabeva, K.: The changing role of IT departments in enterprise mashup environments. In: Feuerlicht, G., Lamersdorf, W. (eds.) ICSOC 2008. LNCS, vol. 5472, pp. 148–154. Springer, Heidelberg (2009). https://doi.org/10.1007/978-3-642-01247-1_14
3. Stratecast: Thinking of adopting an IT service broker model? These four reasons will convince you the time is right. Stratecast (2016)
4. Gefen, D., Ragowsky, A., Stern, M.: The changing role of the CIO in the world of outsourcing: lessons learned from a CIO roundtable. Commun. Assoc. Inf. Syst. **28**, 233–242 (2011)
5. Erbes, J., Nezhad, H., Graupner, S.: From IT providers to IT service brokers: the future of enterprise it in the cloud world. Computer **99**(2), 66–72 (2012). HP Laboratories, 123
6. Rackspace: 7 tips on becoming an IT service broker, pp. 1–11. Rackspace (2014)
7. The Open Group.: the open group IT4IT reference architecture (2017)
8. AXELOS ITIL publication reviews. https://www.axelos.com/best-practice-solutions/itil/itil-publications. Last Accessed 13 Nov 2017
9. The FitSM standard. http://fitsm.itemo.org. Last Accessed 12 Nov 2017
10. ISACA.: COBIT 5 (2012)
11. Greenbaum, T.: The Practical Handbook and Guide in Focus Group Research. D. C. Heath, Lexington (1988)
12. Rackspace: Managing the transition to IT as a service broker, pp. 1–10. Rackspace (2014)
13. Wadhwa, B., Jaitly, A., Suri, B.: Making sense of academia-industry gap in the evolving cloud service brokerage. In: 1st International Workshop on Software Engineering Research and Industrial Practices, pp. 6–9 (2014)
14. Avila, O., Garcés, K.: Change management support to preserve business-information technology alignment. J. Comput. Inf. Syst. **57**(3), 218–228 (2016)
15. Ruiz, J., Avila, O.: Identifying criteria for evaluating Cloud Services in the Colombian public sector. In: Americas Conference on Information systems, Boston, MA, USA (2017)

Foster Strategic Orientation in the Digital Age

A Methodic Approach for Guiding SME to a Digital Transformation

Manuela Graf(✉) [iD], Marco Peter [iD], and Stella Gatziu-Grivas [iD]

University of Applied Sciences and Arts Northwestern Switzerland,
Riggenbachstrasse 16, 4600 Olten, Switzerland
{manuela.graf,marco.peter,
stella.gatziugrivas}@fhnw.ch

Abstract. The goal of this paper is to demonstrate the need for a structured framework and instrument to support SME in adjusting their organizational strategy to environmental changes in the digital age. Since SME in particular face many challenges transforming their business, a structured and easy to use approach that takes into account the challenges and opportunities of an SME such as limited resources or high flexibility offer a high potential for success. A framework-based method named Transformation Compass extends previous instruments in including all relevant business aspects of an enterprise such as marketing, processes, change management or innovation and allowing a "thinking outside the box" approach while the impacts of the digital age are seen as digital enabler. Combing the different aspects of an enterprise based on basic principles of business management, the instrument is divided into four main building blocks that are Customer Centricity, Business Models, Operational Excellence and Organizational Excellence. Hence, the Transformation Compass serves as a starting point for strategic discussion and possible reorientation of the company.

Keywords: Strategic orientation · Digital Transformation
Customer Centricity · Operational Excellence · Business Model
Organizational Excellence

1 Introduction

Digital transformation refers to "the changes associated with the application of digital technology in all aspects of human society" [1]. Hence, digital technologies are changing the way we work, consume, live, and interact with each other [2]. This ongoing change poses not only a major challenge for companies but also great opportunities [3]. An unclearly defined strategy seems to be a key challenge for many enterprises [1]. On the other hand, Companies can benefit in digitalizing their business by gaining a competitive advantage, higher efficiency, cost reduction, higher performance and faster decisions [1]. In fact, handling Digital Transformation and its changes on the company requires reshaping and aligning the traditional strategies to the possibilities of the digital age in formulating adapted or new strategies for a successful

© Springer Nature Switzerland AG 2019
W. Abramowicz and A. Paschke (Eds.): BIS 2018 Workshops, LNBIP 339, pp. 420–432, 2019.
https://doi.org/10.1007/978-3-030-04849-5_37

transformation [4–6]. A Digital Transformation strategy can be seen as the overall strategy of a company that takes into account all strategies of an organization and aligns these based on the digital opportunities to move the company towards the digital age [7].

Nowadays, small and medium-sized enterprises (SME) are facing more and more the challenge and importance to transform their business into the digital age [8]. Compared to big companies, most SME do not have a dedicated department or team that is in charge of the Digital Transformation [9]. However, many SME are aware of the importance of digitalization in different areas of their business such as in relation to processes, employees or culture [10]. Different studies have shown that SME are already making efforts in the direction of Digital Transformation [8, 10, 11].

Nevertheless, one of the main challenges is that SME only have limited resources at their disposal and lack required capabilities for the Digital Transformation [12]. Not only the budget for investments and projects is low, SME do not have the technical equipment and expert knowledge needed for successfully transforming their business [8, 13, 14]. According to a study from a Swiss university regarding the digitalization of Switzerland, SME with more than 100 employees have difficulties regarding ,change management and unclear responsibilities [13].

In general, the studies have demonstrated that most companies are not satisfied with their current activities regarding Digital Transformation, despite a high demand from the industries for Digital Transformation approaches. Thus, SME need external support to improve their transformation projects and efficiently and successfully transform their business. Many of these projects are implemented bottom-up and miss a strategic positioning of the top management. Hence, a top-down implementation is the key to success in Digital Transformation projects [5]. In order to support SME in the Digital Transformation, a methodic and time-efficient approach taking into account all relevant areas of a business is essential [2]. An approach to achieve strategic orientation in the digital age can be carried out by a Digital Transformation Consultancy (DTC). DTC is a way to support stakeholders such as CEOs or other business leaders to benefit from the "efforts to leverage Digital technologies that enable the innovation of their entire business or elements of their business and operating models" [15]. Out of this, SME can use the potential and benefits from increased sales through new digital products and services, improved customer experience that leads to a higher customer loyalty, cost reduction, and an increased efficiency in operation [11, 13].

The aim of this paper is to introduce the Transformation Compass, a structured framework, and method to support and lead SME into the digital age. Furthermore, it serves as a starting point for strategic discussions within the organization and allows possible alignment or reorientation of the company. Transformation Compass is an instrument for consultancies or enterprises itself that assists SME in the transformation of their organization.

The paper is organized as follows: in Sect. 3, the related work is shortly explained followed by Sect. 4, where an overview of existing frameworks and models that describe relevant elements of Digital Transformation is given. Based on the literature research, the structure of a specific framework and approach for SME towards Digital Transformation is elaborated in Sect. 5. Section 6 focuses on the evaluation of the developed framework and method. The last section evinces the conclusion of this research paper.

2 Research Methodology

The research for this paper was done by applying a design research approach, which is a design-oriented research strategy with the aim to develop an artifact [16]. Based on the five phases of the design research model that are awareness of problem, suggestion of a solution, development, evaluation and the conclusion, the Transformation Compass as artifact was developed.

In a first step, Digital transformation and its specific aspects were analyzed to get a basis understanding of the topic. In several interviews, with mainly SME, data was gathered and then reviewed for defining requirements of a specific framework for SME to handle Digital Transformation. Moreover, in order to receive inputs for the development of the framework, a literature research regarding frameworks and models in the context of Digital Transformation has been performed. The findings of the first phase were analyzed to suggest a first draft of the framework for evaluation. However, based on several expert interviews and workshops with companies, an evaluation of the framework took place to finalize the artefact with the inputs from the evaluation phase.

The research is embedded within the topic of Digital Transformation and not on the digitization of a business, thus, the technical assessment tools are not being compared as part of this research. Instead, the Digital Transformation methods for a holistic approach to be used by companies are being investigated. In addition, the research is limited to publications about the role SME play in the digital age and not focused on how big companies deal with the Digital Transformation.

3 Related Work on Frameworks and Models in the Digital Age

Six major frameworks and models for Digital Transformation were found suitable to match the requirements and have been analyzed in detail for this research. The selection of frameworks is rather diverse such as frameworks form universities or consulting companies for a holistic analysis of different approaches how to define a framework. However, due to the limitation of scope of this paper several other approaches are not included.

Two of these frameworks have been developed by universities, one has been developed during the creation of a scientific book and three have been developed by well-established consulting companies. Table 1 shows the six different frameworks which have been analyzed for this research based on their purpose and whether they are SME specific or not:

Each of the mentioned frameworks in Table 1 is based on different building blocks that include various different aspects of a business for navigating through the Digital Transformation. SME specific in the context of these frameworks means whether they have specific SME oriented aspects included that are applicable for SME or not.

In order to further compare the six frameworks, a cluster of building blocks has been determined based on the majority of common or very similar aspects of each framework. The comparison reveals that there are seven main building blocks a Digital

Table 1. Overview of existing frameworks

Framework	Publisher	Purpose	SME specific
Digital innovation and transformation framework	Gerhard Oswald & Michael Kleinemeier	create a comprehensive digital strategy with the customer [17]	no
Digital Transformation Framework	Capgemini & MIT Center for Digital Business	help organizations navigate through their Digital Transformation [18]	no
Digital Portfolio	Ernst & Young	deliver integrated business solutions that empower enterprises [19]	no
McKinsey Model	McKinsey	the impact of technology on various areas in a business [20]	no
Digital Transformation Framework	Cognizant	develop a Digital Transformation blueprint [21]	no
Digital Maturity Model	University of St. Gallen	typical transformation stages and the prioritization made by the organization [22]	no

Transformation consists of. However, these "success dimensions" include various criteria of Digital Transformation from the literature research. The following Table 4 shows an overview of the frameworks and the building blocks that are covered in the frameworks:

Table 2. Overview of relevant building blocks based on existing frameworks

Framework	Offering	Processes & Systems	Organization	Customer (experience)	Business Modell	Digital Capacities	Employees
Digital innovation and transformation framework [17]	✓	✓	✓	✓	✓	✓	✓
Digital Transformation Framework by Capgemini & MIT [18]	✓	✓	✓	✓	✓	✓	
Digital Portfolio [19]	✓	✓		✓	✓		✓
McKinsey Model [20]	✓	✓		✓	✓		✓
Digital Transformation Framework by Cognizant [21]	✓	✓	✓	✓			
Digital Maturity Model [22]	✓	✓	✓	✓			✓

As the comparison reveals, only the first framework takes all the identified aspects of a Digital Transformation into account. The second analyzed framework has been identified as another framework for covering most of the common building blocks. However, it is difficult to justify whether the frameworks covering all the aspects are better than the others as covering a great breadth might not imply a great depth. Comparing the frameworks, three main findings have been identified. First, there is no instrument specifically tailored to the needs of SME on the market available. A second finding is that many of these models use a technical starting point by asking questions such as about the integration of tools in the organization or the automation degree of processes. However, Digital Transformation is much more than just a shift from analog to digital as it has high impacts on the existing business models [1, 17]. As a third finding, the application of the frameworks are unclear and seem to be hard to apply for SME.

Summarizing, the literature research shows that the presented frameworks are so generic that they may be tailored to virtually any type of organization. Yet, they might be transferred to SME as well but most do not consider the specific challenges and opportunities of SME. In addition, consulting companies develop most of the frameworks.

To conclude, almost every model ends with giving an evaluation of the current or target strategic focus but does not include specific recommendations on how to improve the current situation. Furthermore, the research proofs that the digital age changes the recommendation of previous research on organizational alignment and dynamic capabilities specifically for SME. Hence, SME need a framework that allows them a simple approach to define focus areas in the context of digital transformation with an output in form of specific recommendations on how to optimize or change the current situation.

4   Development of the Transformation Compass

The Transformation Compass allows SME to define the current and targeted strategic focus of a company and to align it with existing digital technologies and other activities to foster Digital Transformation in the organization. This takes place in showing SME different possibilities on how the company can either optimize or change its current business. Since most SME will need to adapt their current business conditions, the method has also the term Transformation in it, as the SME will most likely have to change or scrutinize their current strategy to match their business to the conditions of the digital age.

4.1   The Four Building Blocks of the Transformation Compass

The four main building blocks are defined by the common building blocks of the related work and frameworks extended by aspects identified in the general literature research towards Digital Transformation.

Customer experience is one key motivation towards Digital Transformation [18]. Customer centricity is the journey of a customer, which includes customer experience

[8]. A customer journey is split into phases of attracting the customer, interacting with the customer, the experience of a customer and how a company empowers its customers [17, 23]. Thus, a first building block of the Transformation Compass is the Customer Centricity.

Another key area for SME is to improve operational processes [24]. Not only processes but also the strategy and corporate management, such as the importance of data within the organization, are important aspects of Digital Transformation [18, 25]. All these aspects are combined in a second building block of the Transformation Compass named Operational Excellence.

A third building block is the Business Model. This building block represents innovation in form of for example new products and services or Cooperation with other companies as an enabler for a market growth [17, 24, 26]. Acquisition might be a further aspect but due to the usually very low number of acquisitions with SME, this category is not included in the Transformation Compass [27].

As a fourth building block, Organizational Excellence addresses the organization with its culture, the way people are managed and lead, as well as how employees are interacting with each other [17, 25]. Another important aspect is how companies deal with changes and implement them into the organization [17].

Table 3. Mapping of the four Transformation Compass buildings blocks

Building blocks of Transformation Compass	Offering	Processes & systems	Organization	Customer (experience)	Business modell	Digital capacities	Employees
Customer Centricity	✓			✓		✓	
Operational Excellence		✓				✓	
Business Model	✓				✓	✓	
Organizational Excellence			✓			✓	✓

Yet, the following question remains: How do these four building blocks for the Transformation Compass compare to the seven building blocks shown in Table 2 that are restricted to the elements observed during comparison of existing frameworks. After the literature review was completed and the classification scheme of the seven building blocks was defined and united, the goal was to include all the identified seven building blocks for the to-be-developed method. Table 3 shows how the four defined building blocks have been mapped with the existing seven aspects from the literature review.

The two aspects Offering and Digital Capacities might be the two building blocks from the literature, which at first glance are not fully understandable of how their mapping has been done to new building blocks. The aspect Offering is included within Customer Centricity and Business Model because the services and products a company offers, need to be defined as part of the Business Model with the customer in focus. The aspect Digital Capacities is part of each of the four new building blocks because these capacities are regarded to be relevant for each subcategory of the Transformation Compass as enabling drivers for the Digital Transformation of the SME. The literature reveals that "specific capabilities include consulting services for digital strategy and transformation, digital operations, and digital customer experience" [15].

In order to visualize, the four building blocks can be organized in a matrix, as shown in Fig. 1, where one axis represents the external or internal perspective and the other axis the focus on a human-oriented or business-oriented strategic orientation. All of the building blocks are linked with each other to illustrate that a change or optimization on one category might have an impact on another category as well.

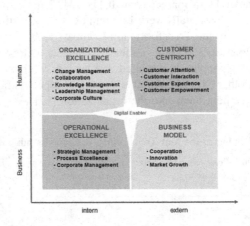

Fig. 1. Overview of the Transformation Compass building blocks

Nevertheless, all of the above-mentioned building blocks are applicable for big companies as well. The differentiation results from defining the aspects of every single building block as explained earlier in this section at the example of acquisitions and in how the Transformation Compass is applied.

4.2   The Structure of the Transformation Compass

Each of the four building blocks, discussed in the previous chapter, consist of several main categories, 15 in total. In order to achieve an optimal structure for a methodical procedure, the 15 main categories are further divided into a total of 50 subcategories.

To determine the 15 main categories and its corresponding subcategories, a deep literature search was conducted. Thus, the Transformation Compass has a structure that takes into account the most important aspects of Digital Transformation found in the literature in general and aligned to the needs of an SME. The structure of the Transformation Compass is visualized in Fig. 2:

Hence, all areas, processes, and stakeholders of a company such as marketing, strategy or culture are included in the framework. The structure of the Transformation Compass is organized as follows: the horizontal line based on level 1 shows the broad

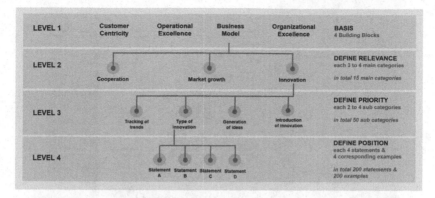

Fig. 2. Structure and application process at the example of Business Model

scope of the aspects regarding the Digital transformation. Hence, the other three levels, vertically structured, represent the various different aspects within a building block.

4.3 Working with the Transformation Compass

The main idea is to apply the Transformation Compass in workshops where a coach, who is trained on this method, guides the companies in defining the relevance, priority, and position of their current and targeted strategic alignment.

We start with the following scenario. Customers are interested to analyze how their company can develop a new Business Model. Therefore, at Level 1 the building block Business Model is the relevant one. In a next step, the workshop coach defines together with the customer whether the main categories, represented in Level 2, such as Cooperation or Innovation are relevant or not in the organization's context. Following, if the discussion reveals that Innovation is relevant for their business, the priority is defined for every single subcategory of Innovation, such as 'Type of innovation', represented on Level 3. The priority options rank from low, middle, or high. In the last step, based on the subcategories, the current and targeted position of the strategic orientation for the subcategory is selected. This finally represents Level 4.

To support the coach during the workshop, there are several instruments available such as posters to every building block and fact sheets with relevant information based on level 3 and 4 from Fig. 2. In addition, a web-based tool allows the coach to enter all the data such as the relevance, priority, current and target position to receive an automatically generated output that is further elaborated in Chap. 4.4.

As a support for the coaches to facilitate their workshop moderation, fact sheets for each of the 50 subcategories have been developed. These fact sheets help to visualize the content on a single page and combine all necessary information to answer the relevance, priority, and positioning of the customer's business. Figure 3 shows a fact sheet for the subcategory 'Type of innovation' with the corresponding statements.

Each of the 50 fact sheets is structured in the exact same way. The visualization and organization of the four statements are done in form of a matrix. By combining both axes, a general statement of where the company sees its strategy, currently and in the

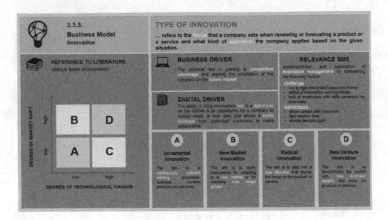

Fig. 3. Fact sheet based on the example of the subcategory 'Type of Innovation'

future, is made possible. In addition, for every single statement, an example is available in order to support the explanation of the statement so that the customer can map the own business in a facilitated way.

The content of the fact sheets has been developed by the use of sentence pattern. A clear structure fosters an easier understanding of the content even for people without a background in the given topic. In addition, it allows adapting and implementing new categories or statements efficiently. The sentence pattern follows for every type of definition, statement, or example a specific syntax in giving a clear structure how to define the texts and what kind of information to enter or add. As an example, keywords such as Incremental Innovation are used to complete systematically the sentence pattern for defining the statements. Key benefits of using a sentence pattern are standardized results and a reduced risk of multiple interpretations [28].

4.4   Outcome of Transformation Compass

As a result, from performing the Transformation Compass the gap between the current and target position, as well as the priority lead to one or several focus areas and specific recommendations are given to the SME. The recommendations are a combined set in form of a strategy map including the relevant processes to either adapt or implement, necessary skills as well as rolls an organization should define, and the technical support in form of systems or tools that are applicable for the SME. In addition, the software tool evaluates automatically the focus areas and gives out an overview in form of a spider diagram and a table, a benchmark as well as the specific recommendations according to the focus area.

5 Evaluation of the Transformation Compass

In order to evaluate the Transformation Compass, the tool has been applied in several workshops with various SME of different industries, such as retail or hospitality, and of different sizes. Each of the workshops held was identically organized and led by an experienced coach with a profound knowledge of Digital Transformation and the Transformation Compass. This coach guided the participants of the workshop through the Transformation Compass. The following table shows an overview of the in total 12 different real case studies:

Table 4. Overview of real case studies

Industry	Size of company	Focus	Number of workshops
Building industry	300 employees (SME)	Company	1
Insurance industry	9 employees (SME)	Company	1
Retail industry	86,000 employees	Department	1
IT industry	59 employees (SME)	Company	1
Food industry	5,800 employees	Department	1
Engineering industry	50 employees (SME)	Company	1
Consulting industry	23 employees (SME)	Company	1
Hospitality industry	25–50 employees (SME)	Company	5
Accounting industry	8 employees (SME)	Company	1

In addition, the framework and its application method have been applied as a case study in a class about Digital Transformation of a further education program at the University of Applied Sciences and Arts Northwestern Switzerland (FHNW). The 24 participants of this class were from different industries, SME as well as big companies and with different backgrounds. Furthermore, several interviews with experts from academic and business were conducted to evaluate the content of the artefact.

Although the workshops were quite successful, some feedback raised up that it is important to define in advance the workshop attendees from the customer's side. Depending on the topics discussed during the workshop, it is recommendable to invite the key stakeholders of that topic, such as the head of marketing if the topic is regarding Customer Centricity. This contributes by adding value to the discussion and includes the specific people that have a deeper knowledge of the corresponding building block or category. In addition, the workshop-based evaluation of the framework has shown that in most cases a pre-selection of the 15 main categories by the workshop coach together with the company is necessary for workshops where managers cannot afford spending too much time in applying the Transformation Compass with all its categories. A pre-selection allows a more concrete workshop on the topics identified as relevant and assists in defining the participants of the workshop. Hence, as the Transformation Compass is a generic instrument for all industries, for some specific industries such as hospitality generic terms such as "customer" needs to be changed into specific terms like for example "hotel guest".

Another outcome of the evaluation is, that the material provided for the workshops as well as the structured approach has been proven successful through the evaluation of the workshop participants. As a supportive instrument for the coaches, the fact sheets help the participants to understand what kind of strategy they currently apply. In addition, it fosters participants to broaden their horizon in exploring what other options exist in this specific area. To sum up, the fact sheets provide a good overview of the current discussion and the structured approach allows that results can be reused in a further workshop.

6   Conclusion

As the Digital Transformation is omnipresent and poses a high potential, SME are facing the challenge of taking steps into the digital age by performing a Digital Transformation on their business. However, due to the limited resources that SME have at their disposal, there is a high need for an approach that guides SME efficiently and systematically towards Digital Transformation. Whenever an SME is faced with moving from the well-known into something new or even disruptive, it is essential to get on the path and start the journey towards the digital age. The Transformation Compass offers a way to incrementally optimize or change the organization by taking small steps and if needed to reflect from time to time if the way is still applicable due to the current and future situation.

The structured method with its scientific background convinces through a standardized approach and user-friendly design. It allows the user to understand the concept of its procedure easily and apply it to the own company. As the keywords of the statements are based on generally well-known economic concepts or terms and come with examples, the interaction with the top management is facilitated. The focus areas and recommendations that are defined together with the participants, serve as a basis to define a concrete Digital Agenda in a further workshop. Different elements such as the technological and economic environment, organization, operations, competences, and resources based on the output of the Transformation Compass offer opportunities for some further research in the researched field of Digital Transformation for SME.

As Digital Transformation is beyond transforming the whole company into a fully digitalized environment, the Transformation Compass ensures a unique transfer of knowledge and supports a company in "thinking outside the box". Hence, the instrument offers SME to find new ways to do business by using the potentials the digital age has to offer and to set their individual strategic focus. To conclude, the Transformation Compass allows the participants of the workshop to develop a deeper understanding of the key areas and aspects of a Digital Transformation with specific regards to SME.

References

1. Parviainen, P., Tihinen, M., Kääriäinen, J., Teppola, S.: Tackling the digitalization challenge: how to benefit from digitalization in practice. Int. J. Inf. Syst. Proj. Manag. **5**, 63–77 (2017)
2. El Sawy, O.A., Pereira, F.: Digital business models: review and synthesis. Business Modelling in the Dynamic Digital Space. Springer Briefs in Digital, pp. 13–20 (2013)
3. Peter, M., Gatziu Grivas, S.: An approach to model industry ecosystems - enabling an ecosystem for service platforms. In: ICServ17 – The 5th International Conference on Serviceology, pp. 83–90 (2017)
4. Yeow, A., Soh, C., Hansen, R.: Aligning with new digital strategy: a dynamic capabilities approach. J. Strat. Inf. Syst. **27**, 43–58 (2018)
5. Peter, M., Grivas, S.G.: The need of a framework for the digital transformation of industry ecosystems – handling intercompany collaborative workflows. In: COLLA 2016, The Sixth International Conference on Advanced Collaborative Networks, Systems and Applications, pp. 66–69 (2016)
6. Street, C., Gallupe, B., Baker, J.: Strategic alignment in SMEs: strengthening theoretical foundations. In: Communications of the Association for Information Systems, pp. 420–442 (2017)
7. Matt, C., Hess, T., Benlian, A.: Digital transformation strategies. In: Business & Information Systems Engineering, pp. 339–343 (2015)
8. Peter, M.K.: KMU-Transformation: Als KMU die Digitale Tranformation erfolgreich umsetzen. Forschungsresultate und Praxisleitfaden. 1st edn. Marc K. Peter, Olten (2017)
9. Vieru, D., Bourdeau, S., Bernier, A., Yapo, S.: Digital competence: a multi-dimensional conceptualization and a typology in an SME context. In: Proceedings of the Annual Hawaii International Conference on System Sciences, pp. 4681–4690 (2015)
10. PwC Homepage. http://www.pwc.ch/de/publications/2016/pwc_digitalisierung_wo_stehen_schweizer_kmu.pdf. Accessed 27 Jan 2018
11. KMU Tag Homepage. http://www.kmu-tag.ch/. Accessed 27 May 2018
12. Cragg, P., Caldeira, M., Ward, J.: Organizational information systems competences in small and medium-sized enterprises. Inform. Manag. **48**, 353–363 (2011)
13. HWZ Homepage. https://fh-hwz.ch/news/digital-switzerland-2017/. Accessed 29 Jan 2018
14. Ashurst, C., Cragg, P., Herring, P.: The role of IT competences in gaining value from e-business: an SME case study. Int. Small Bus. J. **30**, 640–658 (2012)
15. Gartner Homepage. https://www.gartner.com/it-glossary/digital-transformation-consulting-dtc. Accessed 29 Jan 2018
16. Hevner, A.R., et al.: Design science in information systems research. MIS Q. **28**(1), 75–105 (2004)
17. Oswald, G., Kleinemeier, M.: Shaping the Digital Enterprise. Springer International Publishing, Cham (2017)
18. Westerman, G., et al.: Digital transformation: a road-map for billion-dollar organizations. MIT Center for Digital Business and Capgemini Consulting, pp. 1–68 (2011)
19. EY Homepage. http://www.ey.com/Publication/vwLUAssets/EY-digital-transformation/$FILE/EY-digital-transformation.pdf. Accessed 20 Jan 2018
20. McKinsey Homepage. https://www.mckinsey.com/business-functions/digital-mckinsey/our-insights/finding-your-digital-sweet-spot. Accessed 20 Jan 2018
21. Cognizant Homepage. https://www.cognizant.com/InsightsWhitepapers/a-framework-for-digital-business-transformation-codex-1048.pdf. Accessed 20 Jan 2018

22. University of St. Gallen. https://aback.iwi.unisg.ch/fileadmin/projects/aback/web/pdf/digitalmaturitymodel_download_v2.0.pdf. Accessed 20 Jan 2018
23. Sathananthan, S., et al.: Realizing digital transformation through a digital business model design process. In: 2017 Internet of Things Business Models, Users, and Networks, pp. 1–8 (2017)
24. MIT Sloan Management Review Homepage. https://sloanreview.mit.edu/article/the-nine-elements-of-digital-transformation. Accessed 22 Jan 2018
25. Gimpel, H., Roglinger, M.: Digital transformation: changes and chances—insights based on an empirical study. Project Group Business and Information Systems Engineering (BISE) of the Fraunhofer Institute for Applied Information Technology FIT (2015)
26. Achtenhagen, L., Melin, L., Naldi, L.: Dynamics of business models– strategizing, critical capabilities and activities for sustained value creation. Long Range Plan. **46**(6), 427–442 (2013)
27. Schweizerische Eidgenossenschaft Homepage. https://www.kmu.admin.ch/kmu/de/home/aktuell/news/2017/fusionen-und-uebernahmen-der-schweizer-kmu-stabil.html. Accessed 22 Jan 2018
28. Eckhardt, J., Femmer, H., Vogelsang, A.: An approach for creating sentence patterns for quality requirements. In: 2016 IEEE 24th International Requirements Engineering Conference Workshops, pp. 308–315 (2016)

TEA - A Technology Evaluation and Adoption Influence Framework for Small and Medium Sized Enterprises

Dominic Spalinger[1], Stella Gatziu Grivas[1(✉)], and Andre de la Harpe[2]

[1] University of Applied Science Northwest Switzerland, Windisch, Switzerland
stella.gatziugrivas@fhnw.ch
[2] Cape Peninsula University of Technology, Cape Town, South Africa

Abstract. Emerging technologies compel small and medium sized enterprises (SMEs) to advance their digital transformation. However, a conclusive and applicable overview on influencing factors for the evaluation and adoption of new technologies, on a sensitizing level, is nonexistent. Previous work has focused on adoption frameworks on an implementation level, disregarding the interconnectedness with evaluation and an appropriate application for SMEs. To empower SMEs to develop a transformation strategy considering these influencing factors, the Technology Evaluation and Adoption Influence (TEA) Framework has been designed. It covers nine influence factors operating from the external and internal company environment. To determine the factors, 56 insurance brokers distributed in Switzerland, South Africa and Turkey were interviewed and existing frameworks were analyzed. The design process went through three iterations involving experts for verification and testing. Within a field test with an expert user, the framework proved its conclusiveness, applicability, and significance for SMEs.

Keywords: Technology · Evaluation and adoption · Transformation
Digitalization · SME

1 Introduction

Digitalization plays an important role in all industries [4, 7]. Existing business models are being disrupted and IT takes the role of an enabler (if aligned with business) to push digital transformation in all areas of the economy. This transformation is changing the value chain in almost all businesses. Traditional industry boundaries are fading away. The evaluation and adoption of new technologies has thus become critical for business success [4, 7].

While large enterprises have specialized units to manage the challenge of digitalization, small and medium enterprises (SMEs) who are similarly affected by the transformation do not have these specialized functions [3, 6] and often lack adequate knowledge and resources. This is alarming, given their important and dominant role in the economy of many countries worldwide. Empirical evidence supports the importance of SMEs for their contribution towards job creation, productivity, and economic growth in developing and developed countries [37]. All market economy enterprises,

© Springer Nature Switzerland AG 2019
W. Abramowicz and A. Paschke (Eds.): BIS 2018 Workshops, LNBIP 339, pp. 433–444, 2019.
https://doi.org/10.1007/978-3-030-04849-5_38

irrespective of their legal form and activity, are classified as SMEs if they employ fewer than 250 persons, i.e. have between 1 and 249 employees [24].

It is therefore important that SMEs understand what influences them on their journey of digital transformation. There are several best practices how to evaluate and implement technology [8]. However, most of them are not suitable for SMEs due to their unique characteristics, for example a general shortage on resources. Existing publications do not cover the specific factors influencing SME's evaluation and adoption of technology on a sensitizing level to support strategy development. They rather focus on the adoption of technology on an implementation level. Most existing work disregards the interconnectedness of evaluation and adoption, and as a result does not enable an SME-appropriate application.

For SMEs, the evaluation and adoption process has to be simplified compared to bigger organizations. An approach can consist of three main phases: initial adoption stage, implementation stage, and post adoption stage [8]. According to Lin, Huang and Burn IT investment evaluation methodologies have a direct positive relation to the technology adoption readiness of a company [16]. The aim of this study is to develop a framework for SMEs to foster the awareness of digital transformation. Therefore, we present a framework that merges the two aspects of evaluation and adoption and analyzes influence factors for both aspects interconnectedly. The framework is on the sensitizing level, corresponding to the Animate-phase of the ABILI-method [23]. The ABILI-method helps SMEs in all industries with a pragmatic and company size appropriate approach to tackle the digital transformation. The development of the framework was led by three design science research iterations: a prototyping iteration, a refinement iteration, and in the end a finalizing iteration.

The paper is organized as follows: In Sect. 2 the research method is presented. In Sect. 3 the design artefact requirements are formulated. The literature review representing an analysis on existing relevant frameworks is presented in Sect. 4. In Sect. 5 the designed artefact with its nine influencing factors is described. The application integration of the artefact is described in Sect. 6. The paper concludes with a brief summary and an outlook on future research in Sect. 7.

2   Research Methodology

The research relies on a design science approach. Figure 1 displays an overview of the development phases, which reflect the authors' interpretation of design science research based on a model by Kuechler and Vaishnavi [15], and the DSR cycle of Hevner [13]. The research strategy of this paper consists of three iterations. Each iteration added new insights to the framework and was evaluated with an unstructured expert interview. In the first iteration, interview data from South Africa (15 interviews) and Turkey (25 interviews) built the base for a first framework draft. In the second iteration a review of existing frameworks, selected with a key word search strategy using google scholar, as well as 16 interviews from Switzerland were used. In the third iteration the application was designed. All 56 interviews were semi-structured and had an average duration of 40 min. Interviewees were non-randomly, purposively selected convenience sampling and conducted between 2014 and 2017. The collected frameworks and interviews were analyzed by a process of summarizing, categorizing, and structuring. Themes represented the analysis output which were used within the iterations to define the influence factors.

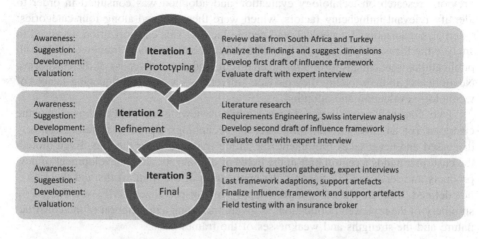

Fig. 1. Adapted design science research cycles; own interpretation based on [13, 15]

3 Requirements to the TEA Influence Framework

The requirements summarized in Table 1 were guiding the development of the framework. It is important to define the requirements of an artefact considering user and stakeholder involvement to ensure the expected quality on an artefact, especially if the artifact is developed iteratively [27]. The requirements were engineered within the iterations drawing back on interview data and a literature review.

Table 1. List of the requirements

Requirement	Description
Resource-friendly	If applied, all information needed shall be accessible through SME appropriate methods with a reasonable time effort, as SME resources are in general scarce [8]
Adaptability	All SMEs are having their singularities, thus the designed artefact must be flexible to meet customer needs [24]
Applicability	If applied, it must be easy to use, as this rises the chances of application according to an interviewed industry expert. The user must be led through the process of application with a clear structure and guidelines [23]
Conclusive	All relevant influencing factors across a company's environment shall be included to enable a profound strategy development [23]
Sensitizing	The designed artefact must sensitize the user on the aspects influencing them on their transformation due to the complexity [24]
Simplifying	The designed artefact must simplify the complex environment of influencing factors to enable the user to gain a better understanding of the impacts to the business [8]

4 Related Work on Influence Frameworks

Previous research on technology evaluation and adoption was consulted in order to identify relevant influencing factors, which were then grouped along four categories: external, organizational, technical, and people factors. This categorization was used to analyze the focus, and strength and weaknesses of the theories and frameworks. Not all publications were equally strong in the enclosure and conclusiveness of the categories. Nevertheless, in their totality they provide a diverse view on the influencing factors of technology evaluation and adoption.

Two conspicuousness were detected while reviewing the publications. First, the customer (of an SME) as an influencer on technology adoption is rather scarcely discussed and never takes prominent role in the frameworks or theories. Even though the customer builds a central part in the fields of digitalization and development of new products and services [23]. Second, the application of the frameworks and theories is not defined; they are therefore hard to apply for unspecialized SMEs. In Table 2, a summary of the reviewed publications is given, including a description of the construct nature and the strengths and weaknesses of the frameworks.

Table 2. Summary of frameworks and theories

Authors	Construct nature	Strength and weaknesses
Rogers [26]	DOI is a theory about how, why, and at what pace new technology or innovations get adopted in a company	W: does not include the environment context but professional networks S: widespread and recognized model, has been applied and adapted in various ways [21]
Tornatzky and Fleischer [33]	Focusing on technological innovation decision making, including technology-organization and environment aspects	W: for more complex and newer technology adoption, additional models are needed to achieve better understanding S: has a solid theoretical basis and is considered as more complete than DOI [21]
Ghobakhloo et al. [8]	Conceptual model of effective IT adoption process within SMEs, focusing on implementation	W: guidelines laid-out for the implementation phase, ignoring the animate phase S: based on profound theory including a conclusive set of influencing dimensions
Al-Mamary et al. [2]	Theoretical framework specifically for MIS (Management Information System) adoption	W: no environmental context S: summarizes all influencing factors in two internal dimensions where everything runs together
Padilla-Vega et al. [22]	Theoretical framework specifically for mobile technology adoption based on technology organization and environment aspects	W: scarce description of the influencer and how they affect the adoption S: includes an international perspective on the adoption challenges

The comparison of the existing frameworks with the pre-defined requirements revealed two major desiderata: First, a focus on guidance for applying the frameworks is missing. Therefore, the adaptability of the frameworks is either not evaluable or not approved. Second, the existing frameworks lack a sensitizing aspect. Most frameworks do not sensitize the user on aspects of both, evaluation and adoption, but rather focus on the implementation act of the technology.

5   The TEA Influence Framework

The Framework has two dimensions, the external and internal environment, containing influencing factors, which are described using influence categories. Figure 2 illustrates the TEA Influence Framework (Technology Evaluation and Adoption Influence Framework). The green fields represent the external environment of an organization with its four influencing factors: Government, competitive field, partner and customer, and consultant and vendor. The yellow fields on the other hand, represent the internal environment of a company such as the IT landscape, resources, IT knowledge, used practices, and culture. The distinction between the two dimensions has its origin in the data collection, as they were derived from the 56 interviews as well as from the framework analysis. In this chapter we elaborate the several fields of our framework giving examples form the insurance broker industry.

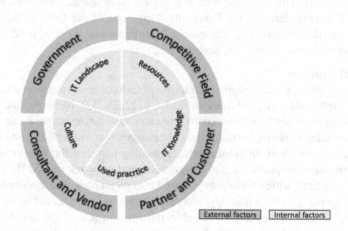

Fig. 2. TEA influence framework (Color figure online)

5.1   The External Environment

Government
There is a significant positive relationship between government support and IT adoption [8]. SMEs generally depend more on external resources and support than bigger companies, due to their limiting size [24]. Government regulations, according to the

interviews, should not only focus data security regulations but especially on official **industry standards** for interfaces between the several parties, enabling developing new solutions and interconnecting their systems. The awareness of **subsidy** programs for ICT adoptions reduces the perceived cost barrier within SMEs and therefore fosters their digitalization [28]. Even if the government offers subsidy programs, SMEs are not always aware of their existence. Swiss brokers see tax savings from IT investments as a driver (and form of subsidy) for technology evaluation and adoption. Government policies also affect the **infrastructure** companies are using. Examples are electricity and access to efficient broadband as well as projects such as the development of 5G networks in Switzerland.

Competitive Field

According to [24], competitive pressure is rather a small driver for SMEs to foster digital transformation. Nevertheless, the competitive field has its impact on the choice and usage of new technologies and therefore on the innovation strategy of a firm [36]. Direct **competitors** are for many firms a pressure point to keep up with the technological change and providing a means to survival, growth, and competitive advantage [8]. This was also clearly identified in the interviews; industry standards in the broker industry such as IG B2B from Switzerland influence the technology adoption. The competitive field does not only consist of market competitors such as other insurance brokers, but also of **technology startups**. The **technology market trends** as an environmental influencer of technology adoption are clearly recognized by the TOE framework [21, 33]. These trends, with a focus on economical, industrial, and social factors, are also considered in the Panoramic Lens, one of the tools in the Animate-phase of the ABILI-method [10]. The output from Panoramic Lens is used as an input for this framework (for details see Sect. 6).

Partner and Customer

The influencer "partner and customer" in terms of technology evaluation and adoption is not considered in the analyzed frameworks [2, 8, 22, 26, 33]. Nevertheless, the Swiss insurance brokers as well as the experts consider this factor as vital, as insurance brokers act as intermediaries between insurance company (partner) and end consumer (customer) and must cover different needs. Regarding partners, the framework mainly refers to **insurance companies** and to the **professional network** of a SME. Partners in many cases "dictate" which technology must be implemented. Professional networks have a positive impact on technology adoption as they provide access to key contacts and support, as well as novel and valuable information also regarding the possible success of innovation projects [26]. Furthermore, **customer** needs are central in the choice of technology and a customer base analysis on the readiness of new technologies is useful and meaningful.

Consultants and Vendor

The technology characteristics of **IT products** available in the market are significant determinants in the evaluation and adoption process of SMEs [9]. The interviews have clearly shown that SMEs outsource the technology evaluation. The professional abilities of **consultants** as well as **vendors** have a positive impact on the technology evaluation and adoption, as SMEs lack on internal IT expertise [2, 5]. Therefore, access to quality IT-expertise is crucial for the innovativeness of SMEs [30]. The information quality (availability, understandability, and accuracy) and complexity (features, usability, reliability, and flexibility) of a new IT product determine the technology acceptance as well as future readiness of a company [2, 20, 22, 31, 33]. Additionally, the technology acceptance is influenced by the **licensing structure** since this structure is often not accurate enough for smaller companies.

5.2   The Internal Environment

IT Landscape

Several studies over several decades have indicated that the **business and IT alignment** is a universal problem in companies [17]. The business needs and goals must be met by the new technology to improve business processes and the overall business value of the firm. Therefore, if considering a new system, it must be insured that the **technology-fit** is perceived consistent and matches with the current IT landscape, business goals and processes [22]. Most technology-fit models are based on the four elements from Henderson and Venkatraman [11] (business strategy, IT strategy, organizational infrastructure, and IT infrastructure) that need to be aligned [17]. The current IT landscape is determined by what **hardware** and **software** tools are already implemented in an organization. According to some of the Swiss interview participants, the current infrastructure tends to be a limiting influence factor on the choice of technologies, as industry standards for matching interfaces are missing. A major challenge for companies is therefore to understand the effects of new technology on the existing IT landscape with its implemented hardware and software [1].

Resources

SMEs in general suffer from a limited access to particular resources, such as money, time, staff, and company size, which distinguishes them from lager companies [8, 26, 33]. **Financial** resources are the key performance requirements and are critical success factors for SMEs based on the resource based theory [25]. According to Madrid-Guijarro et al., financially constraint companies are less likely to invest in new technology [18]. Most of the interview participants judge the financial slack. The perceived cost-benefit ratio of a new technology becomes a major influencing factor. The evaluation process itself is highly influenced by the shortcoming on **time** within the interview participants' companies. IT product variety is perceived as huge and participants do not have time for a profound screening, as the **staff** evaluating, and consulting customers can be the same due to the **company size**. In addition to a shortcoming on staff there is a lack in specialization (especially in IT), as mostly generalists are employed and wanted in SMEs.

IT Knowledge

Resistance to change has a direct link to IT knowledge within SMEs and the prerequisites for making optimum use of new technologies are the introduction and **training** of employees to the new technologies and the development of **IT skills** [2, 8, 24]. A company and its employees must adapt to the new technologies so that they can be integrated into the products, services, corporate culture, and strategy in order to achieve positive benefits. IT skills as well as experience and training do affect the attitude of staff towards new technologies and therefore influence technology acceptance or its evaluation and adoption process. There is often a lack on IT knowledge in SMEs [8]. A better understanding and higher expertise on technology encourages organizational members in participation, however it may make it more difficult to achieve consensus [26]. Sufficient training on a new system and on IT skills in general increases the **computer self-efficacy** of the firm's employees. Self-efficacy refers to the belief of the employees that they have the skills to manage a certain task successfully [2, 35]. Summarizing, the more IT-knowledge in a company, the lower the risks of IT adoption [32].

Used Practices
The interviews and the literature research show that there is a lack on **structured approaches** to evaluate new technologies. Structured tools and guidelines are rarely used and a standardized process for evaluation and adoption is usually not implemented. **User involvement** or participation is a major influencer on the technology acceptance and therefore on the success of such a project [8]. The **communication** process within a SME including the interconnectedness of the employees (means how well they are linked among each other) is crucial for a successful IT acquisition [26, 33]. In an environment of constant change, internal communication processes play an important role in improving the work environment and hinder instability and uncertainty among the companies employees [19].

Culture
The corporate culture affects the evaluation, adoption, and usage of ICTs; thus, SMEs should start investigating their cultures, analyzing how they are expressed, and describe the culture [34]. The interviews have shown that the **decision** culture of a SME is influenced by top **management** [8]. This centralization of technology acquisition decisions negatively affect the innovativeness of a company [26]. Top management and its courteous support and openness on a new technology or system also effects the perceived usefulness and user satisfaction of the employees [2]. However, IT-related projects usually enjoy insufficient attention by management, which is considered as one of the main problems in the computing area of small firms [5]. The culture of **failure** (trial and error on technology experiments) was mentioned by some of the interview participants as an influencer on technology evaluation and adoption. Especially the evaluation and selection phase can involve a long trial and error period [14]. However, only the minority of the SMEs do have a trial and error culture for technology experiments as these projects are expensive and SMEs usually suffer a scarcity of resources [8]. Sosna et al. emphasizes the importance of trial-and-error learning for businesses aiming towards digital transformation [29].

Change management is a big challenge for a technology implementation and is helpful to respect actions that foster technology acceptance among employees, such as user involvement in the evaluation and adoption process. Some of the interview participants mentioned a **generation issue** within the insurance broker industry, meaning that young people (millennials) do not see this business as attractive anymore. As older generations have a less familiar relationship to technology compared to the millennials, this becomes an influencing problem [12].

6 Application

The application of the TEA Influence Framework is based on the Question Catalogue and the Workshop Templates. The Question Catalogue consists of a range of questions structured along the influence factors and the corresponding influencing categories. The workshop templates offer application advice and structure the documentation of the workshop on a clear and pragmatic one-pager (see for example Fig. 3).

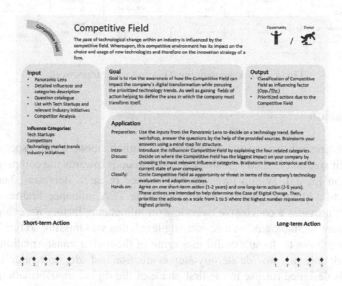

Fig. 3. Competitive field guideline template

The TEA Influence Framework supports the Animate-phase of the ABILI Methodology developed at the FHNW. The ABILI-method merges several digital transformation methods into a sequence of five phases [23]. In the first phase, the Animate Phase SMEs are being sensitized and prepared. The Panoramic Lens is the main tool for the prioritization of the trends in the environment of SMEs. The output of the Animate Phase is a case of digital change that helps the management to define the digital transformation strategy [23]. The TEA Influence Framework takes the trends from the Panoramic Lens and delivers input for the case of digital change [23]. Through the framework, SMEs become aware of the influencers affecting them while pursuing the prioritized technology trend. Furthermore, they gain fields of action helping to define the area in which the company must transform. As an exemplified insight one can take an SME that prioritized the technology trend of artificial intelligence. The TEA Influence Framework can therefore be used to determine the challenges for evaluating and adopting related technologies. As depicted in Fig. 4, the preparation involves the output of the Panoramic Lens. The highest prioritized technology trend is recommended for the workshop preparations based on the TEA Influence Framework question catalogue. The last stage is the workshop according a guideline template. The next two steps are group discussions involving IT as well as business management. The expert who applied and evaluated the application of the framework in the third iteration confirmed the conclusiveness, applicability, and importance of the artefact.

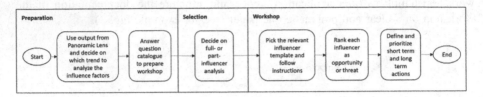

Fig. 4. Working with the TEA influence framework

7   Conclusion

This paper addressed the various challenges of digitalization, which especially affect SMEs as their size and limited resources are obstructions towards the company's digital transformation [3, 23]. Within three design science research iterations, based on 56 interviews and a literature review, an artefact – the TEA Influence Framework – was developed. It provides a conclusive overview on influencing factors for evaluation and adoption of new technologies on a sensitizing level, that was missing so far. This paper therefore contributes to the successful mastering of the digital transformation of SMEs.

This work does not provide step-by-step evaluation and adoption guidelines, as the framework is designed for use in the first phase of the digital transformation, which is dedicated to the preparation and animation of the transformation [23]. The framework is applicable within the Animate-phase of the ABILI-method in correspondence with the Panoramic Lens [10]. Future research may build on this research for further developments and a seamless interplay of the tools within the Animate-phase of the ABILI-method.

Furthermore, the TEA Influence Framework is designed to be applied as a tool in a workshop to create a case of digital change. However, the framework application in its current state is paper-based and not digitalized nor automated. In further research, the framework might be used to develop a digital tool (Surface-hub application) that supports the case of a digital change workshop in real time. Based on the proposed influencing factors of this paper, the future tool might be able to capture upcoming opportunities or threats of a potential technology in real time. The data gathered while applying the TEA Influence Framework can be used to develop a benchmark tool. According to an industry expert, who evaluated the TEA Influence Framework in iteration two, the user of such a tool is especially interested in comparing the own influencers with other companies in the market to assess the own maturity.

References

1. Adomavicius, G., Bockstedt, J.C., Gupta, A., Kauffman, R.J.: Making sense of technology trends in the information technology landscape: a design science approach. MIS Q. **32**, 779–809 (2008). https://doi.org/10.2307/25148872
2. Al-Mamary, Y.H., Shamsuddin, A., Aziati, N.: Factors affecting successful adoption of management information systems in organizations towards enhancing organizational performance. Am. J. Syst. Softw. **2**, 121–126 (2014). https://doi.org/10.12691/ajss-2-5-2
3. Cappiello, A.: Technology and the Insurance Industry: Re-configuring the Competitive Landscape. Springer, Cham (2018). https://doi.org/10.1007/978-3-319-74712-5
4. Châlons, C., Dufft, N.: Die Rolle der IT als Enabler für Digitalisierung. In: Abolhassan, F. (ed.) Was treibt die Digitalisierung?, pp. 27–37. Springer, Wiesbaden (2016). https://doi.org/10.1007/978-3-658-10640-9_2
5. Cragg, P.B., Zinatelli, N.: The evolution of information systems in small firms. Inf. Manag. **29**, 1–8 (1995)
6. Dufft, N., von Bassewitz, B.: Digitalisierung in der Versicherungsbranche (2017)
7. Gatziu Grivas, S., Peter, M., Giovanoli, C., Hubli, K.: FHNW maturity models for cloud and enterprise IT. School of Business, University of Applied Sciences and Arts Northwestern Switzerland (2017)
8. Ghobakhloo, M., Hong, T.S., Sabouri, M.S., Zulkifli, N.: Strategies for successful information technology adoption in small and medium-sized enterprises. Information **3**, 36–67 (2012). https://doi.org/10.3390/info3010036
9. Grandon, E.E., Pearson, J.M.: Electronic commerce adoption: an empirical study of small and medium US businesses. Inf. Manag. **42**, 197–216 (2004)
10. Heeb, D., Lanaia, A., Zimmermann, P., Gatziu Grivas, S., Peter, M.: The panoramic lens model, assessment of economic, industrial, and social factors to support enterprises in realizing the urgency of a digital transformation. University of Applied Science Northwest Switzerland (2018)
11. Henderson, J.C., Venkatraman, H.: Strategic alignment: leveraging information technology for transforming organizations. IBM Syst. J. **32**, 472–484 (1993). https://doi.org/10.1147/sj.382.0472
12. Hershatter, A., Epstein, M.: Millennials and the world of work: an organization and management perspective. J. Bus. Psychol. **25**, 211–223 (2010). https://doi.org/10.1007/s10869-010-9160-y
13. Hevner, A.R.: A three cycle view of design science research. Scand. J. Inf. Syst. **19**, 4 (2007)
14. Kintsch, A., DePaula, R.: A framework for the adoption of assistive technology. In: SWAAAC 2002 Supporting Learning Assistive Through Technology, pp. 1–10 (2002)
15. Kuechler, W., Vaishnavi, V.: Design Science Research Methods and Patterns: Innovating Information and Communication Technology. CRC Press, Boca Raton (2015)
16. Lin, C., Huang, Y.-A., Burn, J.: Realising B2B e-commerce benefits: the link with IT maturity, evaluation practices, and B2BEC adoption readiness. Eur. J. Inf. Syst. **16**, 806–819 (2007). https://doi.org/10.1057/palgrave.ejis.3000724
17. Luftman, J., Lyytinen, K., ben Zvi, T.: Enhancing the measurement of information technology (IT) business alignment and its influence on company performance. J. Inf. Technol. **32**, 26–46 (2017). https://doi.org/10.1057/jit.2015.23
18. Madrid-Guijarro, A., García-Pérez-de-Lema, D., Van Auken, H.: Financing constraints and SME innovation during economic crises. Acad. Rev. Latinoam. Adm. **29**, 84–106 (2016)
19. Martinez, L.A.M., Hurtado, S.R.F.: Internal communication issues in the firms: does it affect the productivity? Rev. Eur. Stud. **10**, 1 (2018). https://doi.org/10.5539/res.v10n2p1

20. Martinsons, M., Davison, R., Tse, D.: The balanced scorecard: a foundation for the strategic management of information systems. Decis. Support Syst. **25**, 71–88 (1999). https://doi.org/10.1016/S0167-9236(98)00086-4

21. Oliveira, T., Martins, M.F.: Literature review of information technology adoption models at firm level. Electron. J. Inf. Syst. Eval. **14**, 110–121 (2011)

22. Padilla-Vega, R., Sénquiz-Díaz, C., Ojeda, A.: Toward a conceptual framework of technology adoption: factors impacting the acceptance of the mobile technology in the international business growth. Int. J. Sci. Technol. Res. **4**, 81–86 (2015)

23. Peter, M., Graf, M., Gatziu Grivas, S., Giovanoli, C.: Die ABILI-Methodik: inspiration und Navigation bei der Digitalen transformation mit Fokus auf KMU. Institut für Wirtschaftsinformatik IW (2018)

24. Peter, M.K.: KMU-transformation: Als KMU die Digitale transformation erfolgreich umsetzen: Forschungsresultate und Praxisleitfaden. BoD–Books on Demand (2017)

25. Rangone, A.: A resource-based approach to strategy analysis in small-medium sized enterprises. Small Bus. Econ. **12**, 233–248 (1999)

26. Rogers, E.M.: Diffusion of Innovations, p. 12. The Free Press, New York (1995)

27. Schön, E.-M., Thomaschewski, J., Escalona, M.J.: Agile requirements engineering: a systematic literature review. Comput. Stand. Interfaces **49**, 79–91 (2017). https://doi.org/10.1016/j.csi.2016.08.011

28. Sin Tan, K., Choy Chong, S., Lin, B., Cyril Eze, U.: Internet-based ICT adoption: evidence from Malaysian SMEs. Ind. Manag. Data Syst. **109**, 224–244 (2009)

29. Sosna, M., Trevinyo-Rodríguez, R.N., Velamuri, S.R.: Business model innovation through trial-and-error learning: the Naturhouse case. Long Range Plann. **43**, 383–407 (2010). https://doi.org/10.1016/j.lrp.2010.02.003

30. Soto-Acosta, P., Popa, S., Martinez-Conesa, I.: Information technology, knowledge management and environmental dynamism as drivers of innovation ambidexterity: a study in SMEs. J. Knowl. Manag. (2018). https://doi.org/10.1108/jkm-10-2017-0448

31. Stair, R., Reynolds, G.: Fundamentals of Information Systems. Cengage Learning, Boston (2017)

32. Thong, J.Y.: An integrated model of information systems adoption in small businesses. J. Manag. Inf. Syst. **15**, 187–214 (1999)

33. Tornatzky, L., Fleischer, M.: The Process of Technology Innovation. Lexingt Books, Lexington (1990). Trott, P.: The role of market research development of discontinuous new products. Eur. J. Innov. Manag. **4**, 117–125 (2001)

34. Westrup, C., Jaghoub, S.A., Sayed, H.E., Liu, W.: Taking culture seriously: ICTs, cultures and development. In: Proceedings of IFIP WG9. 4 Working Conference on ICTs and Development: New Opportunities, Perspectives and Challenges (2018)

35. Zhao, L.: Study on online banking adoption and its predictors. In: 2010 Second International Conference on Multimedia and Information Technology (MMIT), pp 155–158. IEEE (2010)

36. Zouaghi, F., Sánchez, M., Martínez, M.G.: Did the global financial crisis impact firms' innovation performance? The role of internal and external knowledge capabilities in high and low tech industries. Technol. Forecast. Soc. Change (2018). https://doi.org/10.1016/j.techfore.2018.01.011

37. Small and medium-sized enterprises and decent and productive employment creation. In: International Labour Conference (2015)

iDEATE Workshop

iDEATE 2018 Workshop Chairs' Message

With big data and business analytics now becoming increasingly more prevalent in contemporary enterprises, there is a growing interest on how such technologies can be leveraged to provide a competitive edge. Recent commentaries, reports, and empirical studies highlight that many attempts to deploy big data analytics in the organizational fabric fail for reasons other than the technology itself or the data used to generate insight. It is now becoming increasingly more apparent that big data analytics is an organizational effort and requires changes in multiple levels in order to result in any measurable business value. Another critical issue is how exactly can the value of big data analytics be measured, and through what means are such targets realized. We often hear about big data analytics contributing towards innovation, increased business efficiency, reducing time and cost of processing data, and even in aiding or replacing human decision-making. Yet, despite such claims we still know very little about how big data analytics projects need to be planned, what aspects need to be taken into consideration when piloting projects, how such projects can be matured and scaled up, as well as how they can be benchmarked with regard to performance outcomes.

While we now know more about the key organizational aspects that influence outcomes of big data projects, such as, the level of human skills in technical and business roles, the culture surrounding big data analytics, governance practices, data-driven decision-making structures and processes, as well as key hindrances. Nevertheless, the quest on how to differentiate from competition in leveraging big data analytics still remains open. There is considerable work to be done on how big data analytics should be employed to drive strategy, and how a difficult to imitate digital strategy building on should be developed and deployed. In addition, we have seen in the last few years the emergence of some companies that put forth innovative business models which build on the power of big data analytics, yet there is still limited research on the viability and emergence of such new forms of conducting business. Our belief is that the opportunities enabled though big data analytics and other emerging technologies will have a significant impact on how digital strategies and developed and how companies and public organizations think of developing digital capabilities for sustained performance.

The aim of this workshop was to bring together people who have an interest in how big data analytics changes the way business is conducted and seek to explore mechanisms in which this can be achieved. We have had an open call for papers and invited researchers and practitioners from both industry and academia to submit original results of their completed or ongoing projects. The scope of our call has been broad in order to include all relevant aspects relating to big data analytics, organizational transformation and business value. We have encouraged the submission of empirical work and innovative studies.

The workshop received 6 submissions, of which the program committee selected 3 for presentation at the workshop. We would like to thank all members of the program committee, authors and local organizers for their efforts and support.

Patrick Mikalef
Ilias O. Pappas
Michail N. Giannakos
John Krogstie
George Lekakos

Organization

Chairs

Patrick Mikalef	Norwegian University of Science and Technology (NTNU), Norway
Ilias O. Pappas	Norwegian University of Science and Technology (NTNU), Norway
Michail N. Giannakos	Norwegian University of Science and Technology (NTNU), Norway
John Krogstie	Norwegian University of Science and Technology (NTNU), Norway
George Lekakos	Athens University of Economic and Business, Greece

Program Committee

Anastasia Griva	Athens University of Economics and Business, Greece
Konstantina Spanaki	Loughborough University, UK
Milena Stróżyna	Poznań University of Economics and Business, Poland
Mikael Berndtsson	University of Skövde, Sweden
Björn Johansson	Lund University, Sweden
Jeffrey Saltz	Syracuse University, USA
Rogier Van de Wetering	Open Universitet, UK
Maria Boura	Athens University of Economics and Business, Greece
Dirk Ahlers	Norwegian University of Science and Technology, Norway
Johan Versendaal	Hogeschool Utrecht, the Netherlands
Demetrios Sampson	Curtin University, Australia

Prescriptive Analytics: A Survey of Approaches and Methods

Katerina Lepenioti[1](✉), Alexandros Bousdekis[1],
Dimitris Apostolou[1,2], and Gregoris Mentzas[1]

[1] Information Management Unit (IMU), Institute of Communication and
Computer Systems (ICCS), National Technical University of Athens (NTUA),
9 Iroon Polytechniou Street, 157 80 Zografou, Athens, Greece
{klepenioti,albous,gmentzas}@mail.ntua.gr
[2] Department of Informatics, University of Piraeus,
80 Karaoli & Dimitriou Street, 185 34 Piraeus, Greece
dapost@unipi.gr

Abstract. Data analytics has gathered a lot of attention during the last years. Although descriptive and predictive analytics have become well-established areas, prescriptive analytics has just started to emerge in an increasing rate. In this paper, we present a literature review on prescriptive analytics, we frame the prescriptive analytics lifecycle and we identify the existing research challenges on this topic. To the best of our knowledge, this is the first literature review on prescriptive analytics. Until now, prescriptive analytics applications are usually developed in an ad-hoc way with limited capabilities of adaptation to the dynamic and complex nature of today's enterprises. Moreover, there is a loose integration with predictive analytics, something which does not enable the exploitation of the full potential of big data.

Keywords: Prescriptive analytics · Business analytics · Data analytics
Big data · Literature review

1 Introduction

Big data technologies and algorithms along with their applications have attracted significant attention over the past few years. An increasing number of enterprises invest on big data analytics and try to exploit their potential in order to obtain useful insights about their performance and gain a competitive advantage [1]. To this end, the scientific field of data analytics has emerged, going beyond a simple raw data analysis on large datasets [1]. Analytics, as a multidisciplinary concept, is defined as the means to acquire data from diverse sources, process them to elicit meaningful patterns and insights, and distribute the results to proper stakeholders [2].

Data analytics is categorized to three main stages characterized by different levels of difficulty, value, and intelligence [3]: (i) descriptive analytics, answering the questions "What has happened?", "Why did it happen?" and "What is happening now?". (ii) predictive analytics, answering the questions "What will happen?" and "Why will it happen?" in the future. (iii) prescriptive analytics, answering the questions "What

W. Abramowicz and A. Paschke (Eds.): BIS 2018 Workshops, LNBIP 339, pp. 449–460, 2019.
https://doi.org/10.1007/978-3-030-04849-5_39

should I do?" and "Why should I do it?". The maturity of the first two stages has been substantiated by the large amount of research works, associated platforms and business solutions. The current paper investigates the literature on prescriptive analytics and identifies the existing research challenges on this topic. To the best of our knowledge this is the first literature review on prescriptive analytics.

The rest of the paper is organized as follows. Section 2 presents an overview of prescriptive analytics along with three use cases in order to explicitly show the differences between the three stages of analytics. Section 3 describes our methodology for the literature review, while Sect. 4 presents the results of the literature review. Section 5 provides a discussion of the results and identifies the research challenges, while Sect. 6 concludes the paper.

2   Towards Prescriptive Analytics

Prescriptive analytics is able to suggest (prescribe) the best decision options in order to take advantage of the predicted future and illustrates the implications of each decision option [3]. It incorporates the predictive analytics output and utilizes artificial intelligence, optimization algorithms and expert systems in a probabilistic context in order to provide adaptive, automated, constrained, time-dependent and optimal decisions [4–6]. Prescriptive analytics has two levels of human intervention: decision support, e.g. providing recommendations; decision automation, e.g. implementing the prescribed action [6]. It is the most sophisticated type of business analytics and can bring the greatest intelligence and value to businesses [3]. The effectiveness of the prescriptions depends on how well these models incorporate a combination of structured and unstructured data, represent the domain under study and capture impacts of decisions being analysed [3, 5]. In order to show the potential of prescriptive analytics, we illustrate the following motivating scenarios from three different application domains.

Industry 4.0
Industry 4.0 indicates the current trend of automation and data exchange in manufacturing technologies in order to facilitate manufacturing. For example, consider the case of predictive maintenance in which sensors generate a multitude of data dealing with indicators of equipment's degradation. *Descriptive analytics* algorithms monitor the current condition of the manufacturing system and provide alerts in cases of abnormal behaviours. This is achieved by comparing the actual measurements of several parameters that constitute indicators of degradation. When they vary from the normal values, an alert triggers the *predictive analytics* algorithms. The alert is evaluated and, if it indicates a potentially hazardous state of the manufacturing equipment, the predictive analytics algorithms generate predictions about the future health state of the manufacturing system, e.g. a prediction about the time-to-failure. On the basis of this prediction, ***prescriptive analytics*** algorithms are able to provide recommendations about the optimal mitigating actions and the optimal time for their implementation in a way that the expected loss and the risk are minimized. The Industry 4.0 scenario is based upon the research works of [7] and [8].

Transportation

The traffic congestion control concerns more and more modern, crowded cities. To this end, there are attempts to release the city centers from the traffic jams. Currently, sensors can detect vehicles that pass corresponding areas. This data along with historical data from traffic monitoring networks can be utilized for further analysis by *descriptive analytics* algorithms. These algorithms can derive outcomes such as induction loop information and vehicle location information in an aggregated form. These results feed into the *predictive analytics* algorithms which provide predictions about the traffic flow (congestion level) of the system. To do this, they also exploit predictive models that have been developed based on historical data and that take into account contextual information (e.g. peak times). The predictions trigger the ***prescriptive analytics*** algorithms which execute actions with the aim to reduce the congestion level proactively (e.g. traffic lights control). The actions will change the current states of the system and affect the future states in order to maximize the total reward (reduction of congestion). The transportation scenario is based upon the research work of [9].

Healthcare

Healthcare is a key domain that can benefit from data analytics due to the regulatory requirements and the large amounts of data that have the potential to improve the quality of healthcare delivery. In several cases, reliable analytics can mean the difference between life and death (e.g. trauma monitoring for blood pressure, operating room monitors for anesthesia). For example, capturing real-time large volumes of data from in-hospital and in-home devices can feed into *descriptive analytics* algorithms for safety monitoring. When hazardous correlations of streams of physiological data related to patients with brain injuries are detected, an alert is received by *predictive analytics* algorithms, which provides a prediction about a bleeding stroke from a ruptured brain aneurysm. On this basis, ***prescriptive analytics*** algorithms provide medical professionals with critical and timely prescriptions in order to aggressively treat complications. The healthcare scenario is based upon the research work of [10].

3 Literature Review Methodology

In this Section, we outline the methodology of the literature review which is based upon the methodology proposed by [11]. We searched the following scientific databases: ACM, ArXiv, Elsevier, Emerald, IEEE and Springer. Since prescriptive analytics is a new and emerging research field, we used only the query term "prescriptive AND analytics". For the first phase, we queried the scientific databases to find papers that contain the query in their full record, including the full text of the publication. As shown in Fig. 1, there is almost an exponential growth of the use of the term "prescriptive analytics" in publications throughout the last years. This trend outlines an increase of interest for this domain and constitutes a motivation for our literature review.

The first phase of our search resulted in 2,971 papers. Since the first phase of the search includes works that do not necessarily contribute to the field of prescriptive analytics, we conducted a second phase in order to look for research works with the

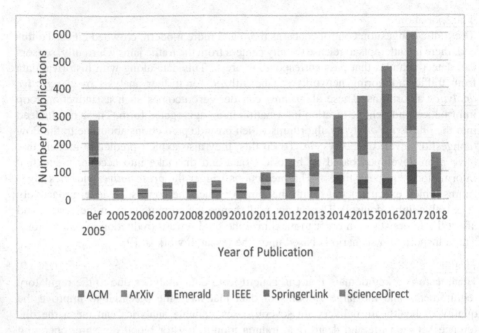

Fig. 1. The trend for the "Prescriptive Analytics" term

query term in their metadata, i.e. title, abstract, keywords or other metadata of their record. The second phase resulted in 107 papers. The third phase of our search was conducted according to the following inclusion criteria: (i) The papers contribute to the field of prescriptive analytics; (ii) the publication date is between January 2010 and February 2018; (iii) the publication type is journal, book or conference. The third phase resulted in 44 papers, consisting of 13 journal articles and 31 conference papers. The results of the three phases are shown in Table 1.

Table 1. The three phases of search

Source	First phase	Second phase	Third phase
ACM	26	3	3
ArXiv	529	3	3
Emerald	288	11	0
IEEE	511	42	17
ScienceDirect	552	27	4
SpringerLink	1065	21	17
TOTAL	2,971	107	44

4 Analysis

4.1 Classification of Reviewed Papers

We classified the reviewed papers in four categories according to their contribution: (i) conceptual models, frameworks and architectures; (ii) algorithms and methods; (iii) information systems; (iv) algorithms and methods along with information systems. This classification along with the number of papers in each category and the specific references is shown in Table 2. The fact that most of the reviewed papers propose prescriptive algorithms or/and platforms indicates that the potential of prescriptive analytics is already recognized from the research community. Therefore, the researchers focus on exploring the aspects of its applicability and utilization.

Table 2. Classification of papers

Type of contribution	#	References
Conceptual model/framework/architecture	6	[2, 8, 12–15]
Algorithm/method	18	[16–33]
Information system	13	[34–46]
Algorithm/method and information system	7	[47–53]

The most prominent application domains of prescriptive analytics in the reviewed literature are shown in Table 3, while individual approaches for other domains, e.g. aerospace, travelling and computer industry, are also proposed. Moreover, we found that nineteen (19) out of the forty four (44) papers deal with generic approaches for prescriptive analytics, while twenty five (25) papers deal with domain-specific approaches. This classification points out that the research interest to address specific topics with a prescriptive solution is almost equal with the quest for widely applicable prescriptive solutions.

Table 3. Application Domains

Application domain	References
Manufacturing	[8, 13, 14, 17, 20, 22, 24, 46, 49, 50]
Sales	[16, 17, 38, 44, 47]
Education/research	[2, 39–41, 48, 52]
Retail	[23, 27]

4.2 Methods and Techniques for Prescriptive Analytics

A broad coverage of the reviewed literature proposes optimization methods and techniques. Optimization has been considered to be the most appropriate approach for addressing prescriptive analytics [14, 17]. Indicative methods and approaches include: linear optimization, including mixed-integer, binary integer and fractional programming

[16, 19, 26–28, 37, 44, 47], non-linear optimization methods like binary quadratic and mixed integer non-linear programming [23, 24], stochastic optimization for handling uncertainty in the decision making process [38], distributionally robust optimization and statistical bootstrap of Efron [33]. In addition, simulation methods and approaches have been developed as an enabler of prescriptive analytics [2, 13, 14, 17, 20, 50, 51, 54].

Since the business data may be non-numeric, their business solutions may rely on qualitative analysis, logic, reasoning, collaboration and negotiation [55]. This encourages the utilization of decision rules and decision trees in the decision-making process. Relevant research works include: decision rules for continuously improving business processes using real-time predictions and recommendations [22]; business rules in combination with a simulation and optimization prescription mechanism [2]; an information system for prescriptive maintenance in which the decision is derived according to rules in combination with mathematical functions [50]; an architecture with the use of proactive event processing rules by combining complex event processing (CEP) engines with predictive analytics [31].

Although, the role of machine learning in predictive analytics is well-established, the research works dealing with machine learning in prescriptive analytics is rare. Four (4) of the reviewed papers deploy machine learning techniques: decision trees and real-time Random Forests (RF) to support production maximization and cost minimization of natural gas and hydrocarbon liquids [49]; k-Nearest Neighbors (k-NN), kernel methods, trees and ensembles in order to construct the weights of a prescription problem [38]; Random Forest, Bayesian Belief Network (BBN) and Auto-Regressive Integrated Moving Average (ARIMA) in combination with stochastic simulation in order to identify significant KPIs and estimate the earnings per share in computer industry [18]. Finally, twelve (12) papers propose more sophisticated solutions that consist of combinations of optimization, simulation, custom ratings and measures, search policies and other heuristic techniques [8, 20, 25, 27, 32, 34, 39–41, 48, 52, 53].

4.3   Prescriptive Model Lifecycle

Based on a synthesis of the literature review, a prescriptive model lifecycle consists of three conceptual steps: model building, model solving and model adapting. These steps are further described below.

Model Building. Model building may rely on expert knowledge, on data or on a combination of both. The literature review reveals a clear interest on modelling the problem in the best possible way. The first approach refers to the manual building of the model from an expert based on domain knowledge. The second approach is based on the statement that the optimization problem can be inferred or learned from previously observed decisions taken by an expert [56]. In this sense, the model can be built based on the collected data involved in past cases in a data-driven way without any user interference. The third approach has to do with learning and mining the model parameters/weights from data and provide them as input into a static model predefined by the domain expert. In the last two approaches, machine learning and rule-based techniques have been used.

Model Solving. Model solving takes place after model building and provides the expected prescription. This step is a well-studied area. The majority of model solving approaches deal with optimization algorithms. Examples include: a modification of the Goemans-Williamson's MAX-CUT approximation algorithm for solving a binary quadratic programming problem related to price optimization [23] and the gradient-projection algorithm for solving a mixed-integer non-linear optimization problem related to industrial maintenance [24]. Other approaches have been developed during the last years, such as the evaluation and filtering of rules for recommendation-based business processes [22].

Model Adapting. Model adapting is conducted in two different ways according to the approach followed for model building: rebuilding and training the model based on the observed data from prescriptions; updating the parameter values of a static model after mining and analyzing the gathered data. Model adapting usually includes model validation with the aim to assure reliability of the model. For example, feedback and adaptation mechanisms can be utilized in order to validate the accordance of the prescriptions with the system objectives [2].

Table 4 classifies the reviewed papers according to whether model building is conducted solely by the domain expert, solely in a data-driven way or in combination of both as well as according to whether it incorporates the step of model adapting. It should be noted that thirty (30) papers recognize and attempt to exploit the era of big data. In thirteen (13) out of the forty four (44) reviewed papers model building is conducted based on the knowledge of the domain expert, while in twenty four (24) papers, the domain knowledge is combined with the collected data. There are six (6) papers that provide a fully data-driven solution for model building. Moreover, six (6) papers consider the development of a mechanism for model adapting. One (1) of them deals with adapting a model that is fully built in a data-driven way, while five (5) of them deal with adapting models that have been built based on both domain knowledge and data.

Table 4. Model building and model adapting in the reviewed papers

References	Model building		Model adapting
	Domain expert	*Data-driven*	
[21, 25, 27, 28, 36, 37, 39–41, 44, 45, 47, 52]	X	N/A	N/A
[22, 31, 32, 42, 48]	N/A	X	N/A
[8, 13–16, 18–20, 23, 24, 26, 29, 30, 34, 35, 38, 46, 50, 53]	X	X	N/A
[33]	N/A	X	X
[2, 12, 17, 49, 51]	X	X	X

5 Discussion and Research Challenges

Due to the emergence of big data technologies, there is the need for methodologies and algorithms capable of analyzing all these data and deriving useful insights. To this end, during the last years, there is an increasing amount of research works dealing with prescriptive analytics. However, the power of data is not yet fully incorporated in the prescriptive analytics solutions proposed in the literature. Currently, the field of prescriptive analytics is still immature due to several challenges.

Prescriptive analytics applications are usually developed in an ad-hoc way with domain-specific prescriptive models, while many generic approaches have been described only at a conceptual level. In some works, the prescriptive model is built by the domain expert but the values of its parameters are obtained through historical data. Since data-driven modelling has just started to emerge, there is the possibility to go a step beyond, with prescriptive models that are built by analyzing data in a batch mode for automated data-driven model building. Future research can focus on developing widely applicable approaches, more independent on domain knowledge.

The dynamic and complex nature of today's enterprises causes a continuous change of a problem formulation, e.g., new types of constraints have to be added or there is a change in problem environment. To this end, approaches and algorithms for model adapting are required. Such approaches become even more important in a real-time/streaming computational environment. Currently, the research works using feedback mechanisms for tracking the suggested recommendations and for continuously improving the prescriptive models are limited, while the relevant research works deals mainly with conceptual frameworks.

Although it is clear by the definition of prescriptive analytics that it is applied on the basis of predictive analytics output, the related works existing in literature have a loose integration with predictive analytics, e.g. in [12, 19, 21, 25, 34, 39–41, 45, 48, 52]. This research direction would require methods, algorithms and systems enabling the flow of the prediction output to prescriptive analytics and its utilization for uncertain decision making ahead of time. To do this, several interoperability issues between predictive and prescriptive analytics should be researched.

Finally, the vast majority of the existing research works in prescriptive analytics deal with "decision support" in the sense that they provide recommendations and the human should implement the prescriptions. The research works dealing with "decision automation", i.e. automated implementation of actions, is rather limited. This direction is expected to evolve throughout the next years due to the emergence of Internet of Things leading to a higher level of data analytics maturity.

6 Conclusion

Prescriptive analytics is an emerging and promising field of data analytics that aims to prescribe decisions on the basis of the predictive analytics outcomes. There is an increasing interest in literature on this topic due to its potential for advancing data analytics and enabling enterprises to gain a competitive advantage. In this paper, we conducted a literature review on prescriptive analytics, we formulated the prescriptive model lifecycle and we identified the existing research challenges. Moreover, we discussed potential future directions of research. Due to the emergence of big data technologies, there is the need for methodologies and algorithms deriving useful insights. Currently, prescriptive analytics applications are usually developed in an ad-hoc manner. Moreover, they are not usually able to adapt through feedback mechanism to the modern dynamic and complex business environment. To this end, data-driven model building and adapting has started to emerge in an attempt to build and update the prescriptive model by analyzing the existing data. Finally, there is a loose integration between predictive and prescriptive analytics, while decision automation has not been sufficiently investigated yet.

Acknowledgements. This work is partly funded by the European Commission project H2020 UPTIME "Unified Predictive Maintenance System" (768634).

References

1. Mikalef, P., Pappas, I., Krogstie, J., Giannakos, M.: Big data analytics capabilities: a systematic literature review and research agenda. Inf. Syst. e-Bus. Manag. **16**, 547–578 (2017)
2. Soltanpoor, R., Sellis, T.: Prescriptive analytics for big data. In: Cheema, M.A., Zhang, W., Chang, L. (eds.) ADC 2016. LNCS, vol. 9877, pp. 245–256. Springer, Cham (2016). https://doi.org/10.1007/978-3-319-46922-5_19
3. Šikšnys, L., Pedersen, T.B.: Prescriptive analytics. In: Liu, L., Özsu, M. (eds.) Encyclopedia of Database Systems. Springer, New York (2016). https://doi.org/10.1007/978-1-4899-7993-3
4. Engel, Y., Etzion, O., Feldman, Z.: A basic model for proactive event-driven computing. In: Proceedings of the 6th ACM International Conference on Distributed Event-Based Systems - DEBS 2012 (2012)
5. Basu, A.T.A.N.U.: Five pillars of prescriptive analytics success. Anal. Mag. **8**, 8–12 (2013)
6. Gartner: Planning Guide for Data and Analytics (2017). https://www.gartner.com/binaries/content/assets/events/keywords/catalyst/catus8/2017_planning_guide_for_data_analytics.pdf. Accessed 03 Apr 2018
7. Bousdekis, A., Magoutas, B., Apostolou, D., Mentzas, G.: A proactive decision making framework for condition-based maintenance. Ind. Manag. Data Syst. **115**, 1225–1250 (2015)
8. Krumeich, J., Werth, D., Loos, P.: Prescriptive control of business processes. Bus. Inf. Syst. Eng. **58**, 261–280 (2015)
9. Wang, Y., Geng, S., Gao, H.: A proactive decision support method based on deep reinforcement learning and state partition. Knowl.-Based Syst. **143**, 248–258 (2018)
10. Raghupathi, W., Raghupathi, V.: Big data analytics in healthcare: promise and potential. Health Inf. Sci. Syst. **2**(1), 3 (2014)
11. Fink, A.: Conducting Research Literature Reviews. Sage Publications, Thousand Oaks (1998)
12. Nechifor, S., Puiu, D., Tarnauca, B., Moldoveanu, F.: Prescriptive analytics based autonomic networking for urban streams services provisioning. In: 81st Vehicular Technology Conference (VTC Spring), pp. 1–5. IEEE (2015)
13. Ringsquandl, M., Lamparter, S., Lepratti, R.: Graph-based predictions and recommendations in flexible manufacturing systems. In: 42nd Annual Conference of the IEEE Industrial Electronics Society, pp. 6937–6942. IEEE (2016)

14. Brodsky, A., Shao, G., Krishnamoorthy, M., Narayanan, A., Menascé, D., Ak, R.: Analysis and optimization based on reusable knowledge base of process performance models. Int. J. Adv. Manuf. Technol. **88**, 337–357 (2016)

15. Tan, J.S., Ang, A.K., Lu, L., Gan, S.W., Corral, M.G.: Quality analytics in a big data supply chain: commodity data analytics for quality engineering. In: Region 10 Conference (TENCON), pp. 3455–3463. IEEE (2016)

16. Kawas, B., Squillante, M.S., Subramanian, D., Varshney, K.R.: Prescriptive analytics for allocating sales teams to opportunities. In: 13th International Conference on Data Mining Workshops. IEEE (2013)

17. Shroff, G., Agarwal, P., Singh, K., Kazmi, A.H., Shah, S., Sardeshmukh, A.: Prescriptive information fusion. In: 17th International Conference on Information Fusion (FUSION), pp. 1–8. IEEE (2014)

18. Wang, C., Cheng, H., Deng, Y.: Using Bayesian belief network and time-series model to conduct prescriptive and predictive analytics for computer industries. Comput. Ind. Eng. **115**, 486–494 (2018)

19. Wu, P.J., Yang, C.K.: The green fleet optimization model for a low-carbon economy: a prescriptive analytics. In: International Conference on Applied System Innovation, pp. 107–110. IEEE (2017)

20. Stein, N., Meller, J., Flath, C.: Big data on the shop-floor: sensor-based decision-support for manual processes. J. Bus. Econ. **88**, 593–616 (2018)

21. Ghoniem, A., Ali, A., Al-Salem, M., Khallouli, W.: Prescriptive analytics for FIFA World Cup lodging capacity planning. J. Oper. Res. Soc. **68**, 1183–1194 (2017)

22. Gröger, C., Schwarz, H., Mitschang, B.: Prescriptive analytics for recommendation-based business process optimization. In: Abramowicz, W., Kokkinaki, A. (eds.) BIS 2014. LNBIP, vol. 176, pp. 25–37. Springer, Cham (2014). https://doi.org/10.1007/978-3-319-06695-0_3

23. Ito, S., Fujimaki, R.: Optimization beyond prediction: prescriptive price optimization. In: Proceedings of the 23rd ACM SIGKDD International Conference on Knowledge Discovery and Data Mining, pp. 1833–1841. ACM (2017)

24. Goyal, A., et al.: Asset health management using predictive and prescriptive analytics for the electric power grid. IBM J. Res. Dev. **60**, 4:1–4:14 (2016)

25. Chalamalla, A., Ilyas, I.F., Ouzzani, M., Papotti, P.: Descriptive and prescriptive data cleaning. In: Proceedings of the 2014 ACM SIGMOD International Conference on Management of Data, pp. 445–456. ACM (2014)

26. Varshney, K.R., Varshney, L.R.: Food steganography with olfactory white. In: Workshop on Statistical Signal Processing (SSP), pp. 21–24. IEEE (2014)

27. Lo, V., Pachamanova, D.: From predictive uplift modeling to prescriptive uplift analytics: a practical approach to treatment optimization while accounting for estimation risk. J. Mark. Anal. **3**, 79–95 (2015)

28. Baur, A., Klein, R., Steinhardt, C.: Model-based decision support for optimal brochure pricing: applying advanced analytics in the tour operating industry. OR Spectr. **36**, 557–584 (2013)

29. Schwartz, I., York, P., Nowakowski-Sims, E., Ramos-Hernandez, A.: Predictive and prescriptive analytics, machine learning and child welfare risk assessment: the Broward County experience. Child Youth Serv. Rev. **81**, 309–320 (2017)

30. Lentzakis, A., Ware, S., Su, R., Wen, C.: Region-based prescriptive route guidance for travelers of multiple classes. Transp. Res. Part C: Emerg. Technol. **87**, 138–158 (2018)

31. Christ, M., Krumeich, J., Kempa-Liehr, A.W.: Integrating predictive analytics into complex event processing by using conditional density estimations. In: Enterprise Distributed Object Computing Workshop (EDOCW), pp. 1–8. IEEE (2016)

32. Loh, C.S., Li, I.H.: Using Players' gameplay action-decision profiles to prescribe training: reducing training costs with serious games analytics. In: International Conference on Data Science and Advanced Analytics (DSAA), pp. 652–661. IEEE (2016)

33. Bertsimas, D., Van Parys, B.: Bootstrap robust prescriptive analytics. arXiv preprint arXiv: 1711.09974 (2017)

34. Ghosh, R., Gupta, A., Chattopadhyay, S., Banerjee, A., Dasgupta, K.: CoCOA: a framework for comparing aggregate client operations in BPO services. In: International Conference on Services Computing (SCC), pp. 539–546. IEEE (2016)

35. Hong, S., Shin, S., Kim, Y., Seon, C.N., Um, J., Song, S.: Design of marketing scenario planning based on business big data analysis. In: Nah, F.F.-H., Tan, C.-H. (eds.) HCIB 2015. LNCS, vol. 9191, pp. 585–592. Springer, Cham (2015). https://doi.org/10.1007/978-3-319-20895-4_54

36. Hupfeld, D., Maccioni, R., Sesemann, R., Ravazzolo, D.: Fleet asset capacity analysis and revenue management optimization using advanced prescriptive analytics. J. Revenue Pricing Manag. **15**, 516–522 (2016)

37. Jiang, C., Jensen, D.L., Cao, H., Kumar, T.: Building business intelligence applications having prescriptive and predictive capabilities. In: Chen, L., Tang, C., Yang, J., Gao, Y. (eds.) WAIM 2010. LNCS, vol. 6184, pp. 376–385. Springer, Heidelberg (2010). https://doi.org/10.1007/978-3-642-14246-8_37

38. Bertsimas, D., Kallus, N.: From predictive to prescriptive analytics. arXiv preprint arXiv: 1402.5481 (2014)

39. Song, S., Jeong, D.H., Kim, J., Hwang, M., Gim, J., Jung, H.: Research advising system based on prescriptive analytics. In: Park, J., Pan, Y., Kim, C.S., Yang, Y. (eds.) Future Information Technology. LNEE, vol. 309, pp. 569–574. Springer, Heidelberg (2014). https://doi.org/10.1007/978-3-642-55038-6_89

40. Lee, M., Cho, M., Gim, J., Jeong, D.H., Jung, H.: Prescriptive analytics system for scholar research performance enhancement. In: Stephanidis, C. (ed.) HCI 2014. CCIS, vol. 434, pp. 186–190. Springer, Cham (2014). https://doi.org/10.1007/978-3-319-07857-1_33

41. Song, S.-K., et al.: Prescriptive analytics system for improving research power. In: 16th International Conference on Computational Science and Engineering (CSE), pp. 1144–1145. IEEE (2013)

42. de Aguiar, M., Greve, F., Costa, G.: PrescStream: a framework for streaming soft real-time predictive and prescriptive analytics. In: Gervasi, O., et al. (eds.) ICCSA 2017. LNCS, vol. 10404, pp. 325–341. Springer, Cham (2017). https://doi.org/10.1007/978-3-319-62392-4_24

43. Ramannavar, M., Sidnal, N.S.: A proposed contextual model for big data analysis using advanced analytics. In: Aggarwal, V.B., Bhatnagar, V., Mishra, D.K. (eds.) Big Data Analytics. AISC, vol. 654, pp. 329–339. Springer, Singapore (2018). https://doi.org/10.1007/978-981-10-6620-7_32

44. Aref, M., et al.: Design and implementation of the LogicBlox system. In: Proceedings of the 2015 ACM SIGMOD International Conference on Management of Data, pp. 1371–1382. ACM (2015)

45. Osmani, V., Forti, S., Mayora, O., Conforti, D.: Enabling prescription-based health apps. arXiv preprint arXiv:1706.09407 (2017)

46. Ceravolo, P., Zavatarelli, F.: Knowledge acquisition in process intelligence. In: International Conference on Information and Communication Technology Research (ICTRC), pp. 218–221. IEEE (2015)

47. von Bischhoffshausen, J.K., Paatsch, M., Reuter, M., Satzger, G., Fromm, H.: An information system for sales team assignments utilizing predictive and prescriptive analytics. In: 17th Conference on Business Informatics (CBI), pp. 68–76. IEEE (2015)

48. Du, F., Plaisant, C., Spring, N., Shneiderman, B.: EventAction: visual analytics for temporal event sequence recommendation. In: Conference on Visual Analytics Science and Technology (VAST), pp. 61–70. IEEE (2016)
49. Anderson, R.N.: 'Petroleum analytics learning machine' for optimizing the internet of things of today's digital oil field-to-refinery petroleum system. In: International Conference on Big Data (Big Data), pp. 4542–4545. IEEE (2017)
50. Matyas, K., Nemeth, T., Kovacs, K., Glawar, R.: A procedural approach for realizing prescriptive maintenance planning in manufacturing industries. CIRP Ann. **66**, 461–464 (2017)
51. Giurgiu, I., et al.: On the adoption and impact of predictive analytics for server incident reduction. IBM J. Res. Dev. **61**, 9:98–9:109 (2017)
52. Cho, M., Song, S.K., Weber, J., Jung, H., Lee, M.: Prescriptive analytics for planning research-performance strategy. In: Park, J., Stojmenovic, I., Jeong, H., Yi, G. (eds.) Computer Science and Its Applications. LNEE, vol. 330, pp. 1123–1129. Springer, Berlin (2015). https://doi.org/10.1007/978-3-662-45402-2_159
53. Mendes, P.N., et al.: Sonora: a prescriptive model for message authoring on Twitter. In: Benatallah, B., Bestavros, A., Manolopoulos, Y., Vakali, A., Zhang, Y. (eds.) WISE 2014. LNCS, vol. 8787, pp. 17–31. Springer, Cham (2014). https://doi.org/10.1007/978-3-319-11746-1_2
54. Delen, D., Demirkan, H.: Data, information and analytics as services. Decis. Support Syst. **55**, 359–363 (2013)
55. Sun, Z., Strang, K., Firmin, S.: Business analytics-based enterprise information systems. J. Comput. Inf. Syst. **57**, 169–178 (2016)
56. Bärmann, A., Pokutta, S., Schneider, O.: Emulating the expert: inverse optimization through online learning. In: International Conference on Machine Learning, pp. 400–410 (2017)

Challenges from Data-Driven Predictive Maintenance in Brownfield Industrial Settings

Georgios Koutroulis[1]($\boxtimes$) and Stefan Thalmann[1,2]($\boxtimes$)

[1] Pro2Future GmbH, Inffeldgasse 25F, 8010 Graz, Austria
georgios.koutroulis@pro2future.at
[2] Institute of Interactive Systems and Data Science,
Technical University of Graz, Inffeldgasse 13, 8010 Graz, Austria
stefan.thalmann@tugraz.at

Abstract. In the last years many companies made substantial investments in digitization of production and started collecting a lot of data. However, the big question arises how to make sense of all these data and to create competitive advantage? In this regard maintenance is an ever-urged topic and seems to be a low hanging fruit to realize benefits from analyzing large amounts of sensor data now available. This is however, very challenging in typical industrial environments where we can find a mixture of old and new production infrastructure, called brownfield environment. In this work in progress paper we want to investigate this context and identify challenges for the introduction of Big Data approaches for predictive maintenance. For this purpose, we conducted a case study with a world reputed electronic components company. We found that making sense out of sensor data and finding the right level of detail for the analysis is very challenging. We developed a feedback app to incorporate the employees' domain knowledge in the sense making process.

Keywords: Predictive maintenance · Big data · Brownfield environment
Industrial analytics · Manufacturing

1 Motivation

In our data-driven world, we collect more and more data from machines, processes, products, plants, and infrastructure resulting in an explosion of collected data [1]. According to a report from International Data Corporation (IDC), in 2017, the data volume worldwide in 2025 will be increased by nearly ten times to a huge amount of approx. 163 zettabytes [2].

These big amounts of data from the production bring about new opportunities and are considered to be the next big productivity driver for manufacturing enterprises [4]. However, this pile of raw data is considered useless without any further processing, analyzing and integrating to enhance the knowledge and information discovery asset [3]. Big Data Analytics promises enormous opportunities, but also brings new challenges [5].

Predictive maintenance offers improved decision support to reduce maintenance costs and to avoid unexpected downtimes and thus to increase the reliability of the

W. Abramowicz and A. Paschke (Eds.): BIS 2018 Workshops, LNBIP 339, pp. 461–467, 2019.
https://doi.org/10.1007/978-3-030-04849-5_40

production system [6]. Due to a heterogeneous mixture of machinery at most modern production settings, making use of the data is a serious challenge [3]. Hence, machines that can be based on quite "old fashioned" technologies are operated in a discrete mode without any interoperability with the new ones, in which proprietary or even custom-made protocols are used [8].

This paper focuses on the challenges of introducing predictive maintenance in a brownfield environment. In a case study with an electronics components company, we investigate this challenge and address the following research questions:

RQ1: What are the challenges of introducing predictive maintenance in an industrial brownfield environment?
RQ2: What are suitable approaches to address the identified challenges?

2 Background

Nowadays, manufacturing industry needs to operate in a dynamic changing complex environment with different performance objectives [7]. This demands a continuous monitoring of the entire manufacturing process. Research showed that advanced maintenance activities can significantly increase company's productivity and profitability as the right maintenance policy can be a profit generating function [9].

Maintenance strategies can be classified as corrective and preventive ones. Corrective maintenance also well known as run-to-failure is deployed once breakdown of a component or equipment occurs, then immediate prescribed actions need to be taken [10]. In this regard current Big Data research promises to make the detection of faults much easier and more precise and ultimately predictive approaches more attractive.

Predictive maintenance incorporates a more probabilistic approach from real-time data collection. Main goal of this strategy is to evaluate a priori the equipment's failure horizon and ultimately determine the optimal time for maintenance action before early downtime occurs [11].

As brownfield sites in manufacturing, we define plants operating with legacy automation equipment, that may even be decades old and in many cases designed and installed by the personnel within the company [8]. Brownfields have a unique fingerprint for every production setting and the infrastructure is sensitive to changes. Thus, new technologies such as Big Data need to be introduced with care. Our case study emphasizes the importance for an enterprise to clearly define the weaknesses of the system as well as the goals of a seamless maintenance strategy.

3 Case Study

In the following section a case study is presented to point out the challenges of introducing predictive maintenance in an industrial brownfield environment. Case studies, are an accepted research strategy in information system research to explore relevant phenomena [13]. We conducted the case study with an electronic components company, focusing on a production line for sensors for automotive applications.

Therefore, we conducted five workshops with four to six professionals from the company. The professionals head of production, lead engineers, research and development professionals and IT specialists. Within the first workshop we also visited the manufacturing line and talked to shop floor workers. In the workshops we discussed how predictive maintenance can be introduced and which challenges need to be solved. The workshops were conducted within a period of six months to jointly reflect on the progress and solution approaches conducted in the meantime. We made notes during the workshops and discussed the key findings with the lead engineer. We discussed with the lead engineers and the R&D experts about the interpretation of data and with the experts from the IT department about the existing maintenance information system.

The production line is specifically designed for the manufacturer and can be classified as a brownfield environment. The production line evolved over the last ten years and new and old sensors are in place to monitor the entire production process. Sensors collect data about all relevant technical components and produce messages about derivations or other critical defined states of the machine.

A significant amount of unfiltered messages from all sensors are stored in a database to be further processed. Data were populated with timestamps and other critical attributes such as the error code and other cryptic (and depending on the manufacturer of the subcomponent, also in different languages) descriptions. Most of the error messages were designed by the manufacturer of the machines and our company tries to use these data and to make sense out of them. The messages coming in continuously or batch-wise, are stored in a database.

More specifically a machine malfunctioned for an unknown reason could trigger dispersed events or even harmless warnings to various spots at different workstations. In this case error sequences on the sensors' level across the entire production line can mislead the maintenance personnel regarding the detection of the real error and increase significantly downtime costs. To illustrate the significance of this issue, occasionally a worker can simply forget to close the protective door of the machine and a minor warning such as the "safety door opened" could cause false alarms and even unnecessary stoppages in the production. For this purpose, a filtering of error messages was implemented to reduce the "level of noise". However, for a data analytics project this filtering approach needs to be challenged.

3.1 Challenges

Level of Detail for Sense Making. The most important challenge in this case, was to find a suitable level of detail for analyzing and processing the sensor data. The machines of the production line continuously generated error messages based on the sensor data. However, the error messages are designed by the electronic components company and they are not designed to support predictive maintenance. As a consequence, these errors have mostly no observable effect, e.g. in cases of tolerance deviations, are messages of the human-machine interaction or they cause only minimal failures which can be solved within seconds.

To make sense out of such messages, the company introduced a feedback system in which workers could label serious failures by using an open text box. However, an analysis of these data revealed that the feedback from the end users was no suitable basis for the analysis and the sense making process. The data from the text box were inconsistent and also domain experts could not make sense out of it. Due to the sudden stoppage in the production line the workers were urged hastily to find a solution and thus not give attention to their input where sometimes could be a two-word sentence such as "computer reset". Another reason was the *usability* and especially the interface. Further, the time between failure and giving feedback was very long as users had to use a desktop computer dislocated from the machine for giving feedback. Finally, the users reported, that they get no feedback on how their input was used or they could benefit from it.

The second reason were *missing guidance* and incentives, as just a text box was offered for giving feedback and no incentive was given. Stakeholders were thus not able to incorporate in the maintenance system their valuable domain experience as well as knowledge. The last and most important reason was the *delay* for giving feedback, as the messages appeared in the desktop computer on average 29 min after the failure was solved. The main reason for this delay was the old and heterogeneous infrastructure, which was not designed for ad-hoc analysis.

Heterogeneous Infrastructure not Designed for Data Analytics. Due to the increased needs and demands for the production line which emerged over the years, new technology and especially a new middleware was added step by step. As a result, data incompatibilities and high latency issues become visible. An important reason for the long delays was the data transfer in batches from many old components causing unpredictable situations in case of concurrent triggered events. However, the buffering and batch processing was necessary as the network infrastructure was not able to transfer all the data at the same time. In extreme situations, the production line stopped due to the increased data traffic caused by sensor data.

As a result, data availability and data quality, e.g. as timestamps were difficult to relate, was poor and not suitable for introducing a predictive maintenance system. To cope with these challenges, the company used several filters and rules to preprocess the data (using MS Excel) and to discuss statistics on a weekly basis. This however reached its limits and only the "peak of the iceberg" was analyzed.

3.2 Solution Approach

In our project, we addressed the identified challenges by developing a feedback app for maintenance workers. The app targeted the challenge of finding the right level of detail and making sense out of the data. During the first phase of the project, the developed app guides the worker with drop-down menus of spatial information for an optimal fault documentation. This lead later to a "cleaner" most importantly to a labeled dataset and the app also provided guideline to the workers by presenting suitable instructions. Thereby, the new app deployed in tablets, addressed the usability challenge as new messages popped up and the employees received push messages. Further, employees could document their solution approaches via pictures and videos. These videos are accessible for other employees helping them to cope with failures. In this way an error-cause-solution classification scheme can be developed for recommending of the right maintenance action to optimize equipment health conditions and reduce costly downtime events. The participants reported, that the help function really motivated employees to contribute.

Regarding the guidance, a first structure of the real-time data sequence from the existing maintenance system was created. Therefore, we analyzed the large collection of past events. At first, data were clustered according to error codes and spatial information of the error source (machine type, components and subcomponents). Numerical attributes were aggregated to get the error counts as well as the mean value of the downtime as recorded. Furthermore, the free text messages imputed by the workers on site for every corresponded case were also aggregated with text tokenization to verify them with the actual error caused from the maintenance database system. Grouped error codes showed that quite different combinations of them could trigger similar errors. Based on this initial analysis, experts proposed classification concept for the most frequent failures using a pareto analysis. Drop-down fields providing guidance for employees were implemented in the app.

4 Discussion

We identified two major challenges in our research. First, the challenge to aggregate and prepare the data in such a way that the desired information can be extracted. For this purpose, it is not enough to collect data from the right sensor at the right time, but also to have sufficient knowledge about the meaning of the sensor data. This is particularly true in brownfield settings where sensors are mostly not intended to deliver suitable data for predictive maintenance. Based on our case, it seems crucial to incorporate the knowledge of the employees at the shop floor into the data analytics component [14]. For this purpose, we developed an app providing a structured and easy to use interface for collecting feedback. The involvement of shop floor workers in the data analytics part of the predictive maintenance project also increased their commitment to the project. Furthermore, deploying a human-in-the-loop approach helped to build an informative and labeled dataset that will be later utilized for training classification algorithms.

The second major challenge was that the heterogeneous infrastructure was not designed for data analytics application. Data quality in brownfields plays a significant role and can leverage the interoperability between different data sources coming from the production [12]. Our recommendation is to focus on the core predictive maintenance goals and improve the infrastructure for the required data targeted for these goals. In our case, integrated near real-time data are now seamlessly passed to the updated ICT infrastructure so that the worker can be guided through a novel classification scheme for predictive maintenance purposes.

5   Conclusion and Future Work

We presented the preliminary findings of a case study in which a data driven predictive maintenance system was introduced in a brownfield industrial setting. In such settings the heterogeneous infrastructure is challenging for the data processing. However, the major challenge was to make sense out of the collected sensor data and to link these data to the employees' knowledge. We plan to continue our work by evaluating the developed app and by verifying if the app can address the identified challenges. Finally, we want to show how predictive maintenance systems can be introduced in brownfield settings.

In future research it seems very promising to investigate the economic analysis for updating the brownfield infrastructure in more detail. Other way to extend the capabilities of our research is to incorporate data from other sources. Enterprise resource planning could provide additional insights regarding product specifications and spare part inventory. Further, we will integrate the predictive maintenance application into the production line. Data will be collected, and we will evaluate the impact on the production processes and eventually on the overall maintenance workflow.

Having the updated and cleaner datasets from the new application, future work will focus to validate and integrate it to other workstations in the production line. Real-time data collection could help further to explore novel advanced techniques from the field of artificial intelligence (Machine Learning, Time Series Analysis, Prognostics) and hence to boost the decision making on the maintenance process.

Acknowledgement. Pro^{2}Future is funded within the Austrian COMET Program—Competence Centers for Excellent Technologies—under the auspices of the Austrian Federal Ministry of Transport, Innovation and Technology, the Austrian Federal Ministry for Digital and Economic Affairs and of the Provinces of Upper Austria and Styria. COMET is managed by the Austrian Research Promotion Agency FFG.

References

1. Wee, D., Kelly, R., Cattel, J., Breunig, M.: Industry 4.0—How to Navigate Digitization of the Manufacturing Sector. McKinsey & Company, p. 58 (2015)
2. Reinsel, D., Gantz, J., Rydning, J.: Data Age 2025: The Evolution of Data to Life-Critical. Don't Focus on Big Data; Focus on the Data That's Big. IDC White Paper (2017). http://www.seagate.com/www-content/our-story/trends/files/Seagate-WP-DataAge2025-March-2017.pdf
3. Yan, J., Meng, Y., Lu, L., Li, L.: Industrial big data in an industry 4.0 environment: challenges, schemes, and applications for predictive maintenance. IEEE Access 5, 23484–23491 (2017)
4. Lasi, H., Fettke, P., Kemper, H.G., Feld, T., Hoffmann, M.: Industry 4.0. Bus. Inf. Syst. Eng. 6(4), 239–242 (2014)
5. Khan, M., Wu, X., Xu, X., Dou, W.: Big data challenges and opportunities in the hype of Industry 4.0. In: 2017 IEEE International Conference on Communications (ICC), pp. 1–6. IEEE, May 2017

6. Yam, R.C.M., Tse, P.W., Li, L., Tu, P.: Intelligent predictive decision support system for condition-based maintenance. Int. J. Adv. Manuf. Technol. **17**(5), 383–391 (2001)
7. Davis, J., Edgar, T., Porter, J., Bernaden, J., Sarli, M.: Smart manufacturing, manufacturing intelligence and demand-dynamic performance. Comput. Chem. Eng. **47**, 145–156 (2012)
8. O'Donovan, P., Leahy, K., Bruton, K., O'Sullivan, D.T.J.: An industrial big data pipeline for data-driven analytics maintenance applications in large-scale smart manufacturing facilities. J. Big Data **2**(1), 25 (2015)
9. Alsyouf, I.: The role of maintenance in improving companies' productivity and profitability. Int. J. Prod. Econ. **105**(1), 70–78 (2007)
10. Prajapati, A., Bechtel, J., Ganesan, S.: Condition based maintenance: a survey. J. Qual. Maint. Eng. **18**(4), 384–400 (2012)
11. Park, C., Moon, D., Do, N., Bae, S.M.: A predictive maintenance approach based on real-time internal parameter monitoring. Int. J. Adv. Manuf. Technol. **85**(1–4), 623–632 (2016)
12. Aljumaili, M., Wandt, K., Karim, R., Tretten, P.: eMaintenance ontologies for data quality support. J. Qual. Maint. Eng. **21**(3), 358–374 (2015)
13. Klein, H.K., Myers, M.D: A set of principles for conducting and evaluating interpretive field studies in information systems. MIS Q. **23**, 67–93 (1999)
14. Vathoopan, M., Brandenbourger, B., Zoitl, A.: A human in the loop corrective maintenance methodology using cross domain engineering data of mechatronic systems. In: 2016 IEEE 21st International Conference on Emerging Technologies and Factory Automation (ETFA), pp. 1–4. IEEE, September 2016

Big Data is Power: Business Value
from a Process Oriented Analytics Capability

Rogier van de Wetering[1(✉)], Patrick Mikalef[2], and John Krogstie[2]

[1] Faculty of Management, Science and Technology,
Open University of the Netherlands, Valkenburgerweg 177,
6419 AT Heerlen, The Netherlands
rogier.vandewetering@ou.nl
[2] Department of Computer Science, Norwegian University of Science
and Technology, Sem Saelandsvei 9, 7491 Trondheim, Norway
{patrick.mikalef,john.krogstie}@ntnu.no

Abstract. Big data analytics (BDA) has the potential to provide firms with competitive benefits. Despite its massive potential, the conditions and required complementary resources and capabilities through which firms can gain business value, are by no means clear. Firms cannot ignore the influx of data, mostly unstructured, and will need to invest in BDA increasingly. By doing so, they will have to, e.g., necessitate new specialist competencies, privacy, and regulatory issues as well as other structural and cost considerations. Past research contributions argued for the development of idiosyncratic and difficult to imitate firm capabilities. This study builds upon resources synchronization theories and examines the process to obtain business value from BDA. In this study, we use data from 27 cases studies from different types of industries. Through the coding analyses of interview transcripts, we identify the contingent resources that drive, moderate and condition the value of a BDA capability throughout different phases of adoption. Our results contribute to a better understanding of the importance of BDA resources and the process and working mechanisms through which to leverage them toward business value. We conclude that our synthesized configurational model for BDA capabilities is a useful basis for future research.

Keywords: Big data · Big data analytics capabilities · Qualitative coding Resource-based view (RBV) · Process stages

1 Introduction

The current political, economic, social, technological and environmental climate in which firms currently operate, is becoming more and more dynamic and complex. As today's firms are feeling pressure to improve their decision-making capabilities, big data provides a path to higher value and can potentially provide them with a competitive edge [1]. Therefore, currently, firms are exploring the role and use of big data as a means to address the ever-increasing complexities and as a strategic information technology (IT) investment. Since there are many definitions of terms like 'business intelligence,' 'data analytics,' 'business analytics' and 'analytics'—a term that has

W. Abramowicz and A. Paschke (Eds.): BIS 2018 Workshops, LNBIP 339, pp. 468–480, 2019.
https://doi.org/10.1007/978-3-030-04849-5_41

emerged as a catch-all term—we define big data as the massive amounts of various observational data which support different types of decisions [2]. In practice, big data enables business and IT managers and executives with a strategic tool, if leveraged effectively, can provide real-time information that can guide future moves. Although big data provides firms with many valuable opportunities, there are, however, many challenges that need to be addressed and overcome. Think, for instance, about identifying the best possible hardware and software and determining the best suitable infrastructure solution. Also, think about the cost of maintaining relevant data quality dimensions (e.g., completeness, the validity of data, consistency, accuracy), and also privacy issues related to the direct and indirect use of big data sources. In light of the above, big data analytics capabilities (BDACs) have become increasingly important in both the academic and the business environment. For now, we regard these particular capabilities as an overall competence that has multiple complementary dimensions that collectively enable firms to be competitive. BDACs are widely considered to enable enterprises to transform their current business models and value-added processes [3, 4]. If we have to believe the white papers, industry reports, and consulting studies, e.g., from Gartner, Forrester, McKinsey, Deloitte, big data analytics (BDA) will be among the most actively investigated and piloted technologies by enterprises over the next couple of years. However, talent shortages, privacy, cost concerns, and nascent offerings may impede effective firm adoption.

Despite valuable contributions in this particular domain, there is still limited understanding on how firms need to change to embrace, adopt and deploy these data-driven innovations, and the business shifts they entail [5]. Over the last years, the scope and approach of most scholarly efforts concerning BDA primarily focus on infrastructure, intelligence, and analytics tools. In turn, these contributions substantially disregard other related resources, as well as how these socio-technological developments should be incorporated into strategy and operations thinking. Dealing with these particular and aligning all organizational and IT capabilities is thus considered to be one of the grand challenges ahead to get sustainable results from technological innovations, including BDA [6, 7]. However, synthesizing from extant literature, we contend that the previously mentioned predicaments remain largely unexplored [5], severely hampering the business and strategic potential of big data. This apparent lack of foundational empirical work significantly hinders research concerning the value of BDA. Furthermore, it leaves practitioners in unchartered territories when faced with implementing such initiatives in their firms while addressing the challenges and opportunities associated with BDA.

In summary, big data is not a magical panacea; it is still data that daily processes and enterprise-wide capabilities need to incorporate. Against this background, this current paper tries to explore the process through which BDA value is obtained and explores the resources that are important when investigating BDA and how they relate to successful adoption. Achieving business value from BDA is crucial because ultimately, this value is what gives firms a competitive advantage [8]. IS research may address this particular challenge by exploring the process to generate value from BDA and which contingent resources play a crucial role in this complex, multifaceted process. While limiting our current scope, we follow the core notion of BDA value by

Grover et al. [8] and regard BDA value as 'the novel and valuable insights to exploit new business opportunities or defend competition threats.'

Thus, our research questions are *'Through which process stages do firms have to go for big data analytics initiatives to add business value?'* Moreover, *'What configurations of big data analytics capability resources—for each of the distinct, but related process stages—should firms then pay attention to during the implementation of big data analytics initiatives?'*

We structure the rest of the paper as follows. The next section concerns the theoretical background of this study. Then, we proceed to outline the research methodology, present the data collection methods and our sample, as well as how we uncover patterns, relationships through the use of qualitative coding. We end this paper with main findings, followed by a discussion and suggestions for future research.

2 Theoretical Background

The vast majority of current scholarship in the area of IT-business value research have grounded their arguments on the RBV of the firm [9]. The RBV is a widely acknowledged theory that explains how firms achieve and sustain a competitive advantage as a result of the resources they own or have under their control. The RBV is grounded in foundational economic scholarship concerned with firm heterogeneity and imperfect competition [10]. A 'resource' in modern research was subsequently split to encompass the processes of resource-picking and capability-building, two distinct facets central to the RBV [11]. Scholars also defined resources as tradable and non-specific firm assets, and capabilities as non-tradable firm-specific abilities to integrate, deploy, and utilize other resources within the firm Amit and Schoemaker [12]. In general, information systems (IS) studies that embrace this particular theoretical view, postulate that IT resources that are valuable, rare, inimitable and non-substitutable (VRIN) will be more likely to outperform competitors. The scholarship recognizes that competence in leveraging IT-based resources in combination with other organizational resources is a source of competitive and advantage across various industries [13–15]. These studies also suggested that firms that fail to invest in particular types of resources under specific conditions may cause the collapse of the value of the rest. Although the RBV perspective may provide some critical insights on the necessary types of IT resources that a firm must own or have under its control, it does not define how they collectively should be leveraged to derive value from them. As can be gleaned from the above, there is a need to reframe the theoretical standpoint from which IT-business value and also the value of BDA can be examined. We now focus on what BDA is.

2.1 Big Data Analytics

IDC [16] expects that from 2005 to 2020 the digital universe will grow by a factor of 300, from 130 exabytes to 40,000 exabytes. This data growth, coupled with technology advances such as open source technologies, mobile and app innovations, cloud computing, will fuel enterprises' demand for integrated BDA solutions. In the context of big data, it is important to identify the different types of resources, since the level of their infusion in various business functions can be a source of competitive differenti-ation [17]. When these resources and their related activity systems have complemen-tarities, they are more prone to lead to competitive advantage [18]. To date there have been studies that attempt to define the buildings blocks of firms' big data analytics capability, that is the resources that are necessary to build upon [4, 5, 19, 20]. In essence, these scholarly contributions adopt their conceptualizations from previous IT (capability) literature, with little regard towards the particularities and conditions of the big data context. Scholars argue that it is essential to comprehend the full spectrum of factors that are relevant to obtain business value form BDA [5]. Most research is somewhat fragmented which makes it difficult to evaluate the business value.

3   Research Methods

3.1   Critical Literature Review

The purpose of this research is to explore the process through which firms create business value from BDA and which contingent resources play a crucial role in this complicated, multifaceted process. To achieve this, we contend that it is necessary to explore the underlying phenomena and processes of BDA and explore the core body of literature to develop a clear overview and taxonomy of the phenomena of interest. Henceforth, we started a critical literature review with the primary focus on the building blocks of a BDA capability and on the possible catalysts and hindrances in attaining business value. We employed a relatively comprehensive review of BDA with the primary aim to identify the central concepts that underlie the dimensions of the theories used within the context of big data. As a final step, we tried to understand the importance of these concepts through firms that have initiated big data projects and initiatives. Table 1 shows the result of our literature review and hence the identified BDA resources and capabilities.

3.2   Case Studies and Data Collection Procedure

As our primary aim is to explore how BDA value is obtained and identify those BDA resources that are important throughout different phases of adoption, we followed a multiple-case study approach. This approach is suitable for our research, mainly because we want in-depth information about BDA phenome in practice; it allows us to present rich evidence and a clear statement of theoretical arguments [21]. This methodology is well-suited to study organizational issues [22] and allows us to gain a better understanding of how BDA resources and capabilities add value. Moreover, this approach allows us to apply a replication logic through which we treat all cases as a series of experiments that confirm or negate emerging conceptual insights [23]. We collected data through a series of in-depth, semi-structured interviews—to avoid biased responses—with field expert and senior managers from different (international) orga-nizations, i.e., public, private, industry and consulting. Interviews are a highly efficient way to gather rich and empirical data.

Table 1. Thematic support for critical big data analytics resources and capabilities

Big data analytics resources and capabilities	References
Tangible	
- *Technology:* New technologies are essential to handle the large volume, diversity, and speed of data accumulated by firms. Further, firms employ novel approaches for extraction, transformation, and analysis of data	[19, 20]
- *Data:* Firms tend to capture data from multiple sources, independently of structures and on a continuous basis. Aspects concerning data such as quality, sources, methods for curating are important in deriving business value	[24, 25]
- *Financial:* Financial resources can be considered as direct investments in support of these technologies or working hours allocated to experimentation with utilizing the potential of big data	[20, 4]
Human skills	
- *Technical Skills:* Technical skills refer to the know-how that is necessary to leverage the new forms of technology and to analyze the varied types of data to extract intelligence from big data	[19, 20]
- *Managerial Skills:* Managerial skills pertain to competencies of employees to understand and interpret results extracted from big data analytics and utilize them in meaningful ways	[20, 26]
Intangible	
- *Organizational Learning:* Organizational learning concerns the degree to which employees are open to extending their knowledge in the face of new emerging technologies	[27]
- *Data-driven Culture:* A data-driven culture describes the degree to which top management is committed to big data analytics, and the extent to which it makes decisions derived from intelligence	[19, 20]

Also, the interviews allowed us to carefully identify both the technical aspects related to implementation, as well as the interaction with the business side of the company. Interviewees were carefully selected using a systematic, convenient, non-probabilistic technique to gain maximal insights from different respondents who cover each relevant BDA aspect. We identified experts that have the knowledge and experience of working in a competitive and highly dynamic market which necessitated the adoption of big data as a means to remain competitive. See Table 2 for an overview of all respondents. All interviews were performed face-to-face, except two interviews that were taken using Skype, in a conversational style, opening with a discussion on the nature of the business and then proceeding on to the themes of the interview guideline. When necessary, questions were clarified to encourage more accurate responses. Overall a semi-structured study protocol was followed during the investigation and during the process of collecting data [28]. In total 27 interviews were held with key and senior informants from different firms, departments—through which we obtained additional secondary company-related documents—including big data and analytics strategists, CIOs, and senior business managers. We recorded all interviews with upfront (signed) consent and subsequently transcribed them.

Table 2. Profiles of the interviewees

Firm	Industry	Employees	BDA objective	Key respondent* (Years in the firm)
1	Consulting services	15.000	Risk management	Big Data and Analytics Strategist (4)
2	Oil & Gas	16.000	Operational efficiency, Decision-making	CIO (6)
3	Media	7.700	Market intelligence	CIO (3)
4	Media	380	Market intelligence	IT Manager (5)
5	Media	170	Market intelligence	Head of Big Data (4)
6	Consulting services	5.500	New service development	CIO (7)
7	Oil & Gas	9.600	Process optimization	Head of Big Data (9)
8	Oil & Gas	130	Exploration	IT Manager (6)
9	Basic materials	450	Decision-making	CIO (12)
10	Telecommunications	1.650	Market and service intelligence	CDO (5)
11	Financials	470	Auditing	IT Manager (7)
12	Retail	220	Marketing, Customer intelligence	CIO (15)
13	Industrials	35	Operational efficiency	IT Manager (5)
14	Telecommunications	2.500	Operational efficiency	IT Manager (9)
15	Retail	80	Supply chain management	CIO (11)
16	Oil & Gas	3.100	Maintenance, Safety	IT Manager (4)
17	Technology	40	Quality assurance	Head of IT (3)
18	Technology	180	Customer relationship management	IT Manager (7)
19	Oil & Gas	750	Decision making	CIO (14)
20	Technology	8	Business intelligence	CIO (3)
21	Basic materials	35	Supply chain management	CIO (6)
22	Technology	3.500	New business model development	CDO (8)
23	Technology	380	Personalized marketing	IT Manager (2)
24	Basic materials	120	Production optimization	IT Manager (4)

(*continued*)

Table 2. (continued)

25	Technology	12.000	Customer satisfaction	CIO (15)
26	Technology	9	Product function/machine learning	CIO (2)
27	Telecommunications	1.550	Fault detection, Energy preservation	CIO (9)

* Note: CIO = Chief Information Officer, CDO = Chief Digital Officer

3.3 Coding, Classifying and Mapping Procedure

We used qualitative coding techniques to systematically analyze, organize and visualize the data [29]. We reviewed, analyzed, organized and documented all obtained data on different occasions using open coding schemes [28]. Together with the outcomes of the critical literature study as well as all transcripts from the interviews, we clustered data into a tabular structure. This approach allowed us to identify those resources and capabilities, across three phases of development, which applied to each respective case in our research. We used the applied technique iteratively to gain as much insight as possible. Two of the co-authors completed the independent coding of the transcripts by the defined themes. Each coder read the transcripts independently to find specific factors related to the required resources of a BDAC, as well as on business value derived from such investments. We repeated this process until the inter-rater reliability of the two coders (matched in pairs) was greater than 90% [30].

4   Findings

4.1   Phases in the Development of Big Data Analytics Capabilities

Organizations need to focus on the full range of (IT) resources which are needed to build a difficult to replicate BDAC and understand through what mechanisms and under what conditions it can deliver business value [20]. We, therefore, tried to synthesize and integrate the above theoretical perspectives and working mechanisms, and combined with extant literature and outcomes from the interviews on BDA and explore their importance in driving business value. The outcome is the Configurational Big Data Analytics Capability Model (CBDACM), see Table 3. The CBDACM consists of two complementary aspects, i.e., (1) the three different phases and (2) different configurations of BDA resources and capabilities tailored per phase and type of organization (i.e., SMEs and large firms). The phases—a firm has to go through in obtaining value from BDA—consist of (I) Strategic initiation, (II) Use-cases and data-driven pilots, and finally (III) Adoption and maintenance. Our model accentuates the process-oriented view on how firms can use, align and efficaciously adopt BDA to create business value. As this model is grounded in complementary resources, capabilities, and working mechanisms, it is consistent with the RBV of the firm [9], and recent literature on BDA [3, 4, 20, 31, 32]. We address each of these distinct phases in the next sections.

Phase I: Strategic Initiation. The first phase according to the interviewees is about the initiation of BDA within the firms. Firms usually have to identify strategic priorities and ask 'crunchy questions.' This first step in the initiating phase is independent of the underlying data (4Vs) and therefore applicable to both traditional and BDA. Therefore, this phase requires senior management involvement and a project champion that support this significant development. Example crunchy questions might be "what are customers currently saying about our organization?", or "how loyal are our customers," "which indicators measure and represent our enterprise-wide performance?" Part of this first phase (and this might even be considered a sub-phase) is also the assessment of the current BDA capabilities. This particular assessment, by the judgment of the experts, is crucial for the identification of both the scope and requirements for BDA initiatives as well as the capabilities. The standard assessment could include (but is not limited to) data and systems, general BI and analytics maturity and capabilities and related skills sets[1], potentially other relevant aspects like formulated IT strategies, priorities, policies, associated budgets, and investments. These capability assessments are crucial for identification of the scope and requirements of data-driven and big data initiatives.

"...Data, infrastructure, system and application assessments allow us to provide valuable information about the data assets that can be leveraged."

Phase II: Use-Cases and Data-Driven Pilots. Based on our analyses, we identified a second phase, i.e., Use-cases and data-driven pilots. Interviews show that the first step in this second phase is the identification and definition of various 'Use Cases.' In this step, challenges within strategic focus areas are identified based on specific and explicit business need, ambitions, requirement and also possible suitability for BDA, i.e., 'the problem.' Various experts pointed out that these use cases (or stories for that matter) should define 'the problem' relative to the foreseen analytical data lifecycle (consisting of the following cycle steps: collecting, processing, analyzing, reporting and archiving/maintenance). After this, firms should, in essence, define a technical approach by identifying a suitable approach based on the data lifecycle, volume, variety, and velocity (or even 4V). Moreover, in this process, a clear distinction should be made between analytical techniques that scale up existing (analytic/data) assets and the once that provide the firm with new relevant data perspectives. Our coding process suggested that this part of the Use Case is followed by the refining of a particular business decision based on analytic results. Outcomes suggest that a second sub-phase of the Use-cases and data-driven pilots phase, thus, concerns the roll-out of pilots and possible prototypes. This phase is an essential part of this phase as it could save valuable time and money for firms as firm target value providing initiatives. A key attribute for data-driven pilots is the involvement of the leadership. The following excerpt from a senior manager clarifies this view:

"Ensure direct connection to the business decisions and stakeholders involved to generate and evaluate results quickly."

---

[1] As no single person has all the required skills for BDA success, typical assessments should cover skill sets across teams, departments in order to identify possible skill gaps and development needs.

Table 3. Configurational big data analytics capability model (CBDACM)

	Phase I			Phase II		Phase III		
	I	II	III	IV	V	VI	VII	VIII
Context								
Large	●	●		●		●	●	
SME			●		●			●
Resources								
Tangible								
Technology		○		●	●		●	
Data		○		●		●	●	●
Financial	●	●	●		●	●		
Human skills								
Technical Skills	○			●	●	●		
Managerial Skills	●	●				●	●	
Intangible								
Organizational Learning				●	●	●		●
Data-driven Culture	●	●		●		●	●	

In this process firms should also seek for low-risk, high-value pilot projects as these might be able to contribute to the foundation for BDA capabilities while simultaneously cultivating early, and sustaining sponsorship.

Phase III: Adoption and Maintenance. The final phase is about the adoption and maintenance of BDA initiatives. Conceptualization of our coding procedures suggests that adoption situationally requires both organizational change and a robust technical environment should be maintained. Interviews suggest that within this phase firms need to exploit talent, user skills, innovative technologies, and best-practices to continuous iterative exploration and investigation of past business performance to gain insight and drive business strategy. This step also links this final phase to the first one. So, our outcomes suggest that for every type of big data solution firms need to embrace agility, while at the same time (technical) data governance needs to be in place to deliver business insights cost-effectively. What we understand from all the interviewees is that BDA capability transformations require both hard and soft skills and firm resources. Moreover, as most firms have been heavily investing in enterprise systems to streamline their processes and recently started cultivating a mindset that focusses on analyzing data and information to improve performance.

"We see a clear shift from what modern firms and business and IT executives need to do, an innovative process of automating, to what they need to know on a daily basis."

4.2 Configurations Among the Big Data Analytics Capabilities

Through our analyses, we identified a coherent set of concepts and notions. Collectively, these resources, i.e., 'Tangible,' 'Human Skills,' and 'Intangible,' comprise what is referred to in the literature as a big data analytics capability. In this research, we apply a practical mapping approach following a configurational approach [33] using our rich qualitative data from the interviews. Configuration theory views a multitude of variables simultaneously through a 'holistic' lens. Thus, different configurations of these (BDA) capabilities can yield superior performance (or 'business value'). Hence, we visualize each possible combination of resources and capabilities of these solutions (of grouped firms) in the form of a matrix. In our research, we use black circles (●) to denote that the particular resource was important. Blank circles (○), on the other hand, indicate the absence of it in the investigated cases. In doing so, we try to elucidate patterns of elements that collectively lead to our focal outcome of interest.

We currently do not distinguish between the main elements of a particular configuration with larger circles and minor elements (less critical) with smaller ones. Blank spaces can be considered an indication that the specific condition is insignificant or a don't care situation in which the condition may be either present or absent. Also, for each phase, we distinguish patterns of elements for two types of firms, i.e., (A) SMEs and (B) large firms. Table 3 shows the importance of each resource across the three phases.

Solutions I and II correspond to large firms. In both solutions, financial and managerial skills are essential for the initiation of BDA within the firms. Solution III, however, applies to SMEs where analyses showed explicit support for financial resources as a direct investment in the support for BDA. Within Phase II we can distinguish two solutions (IV and V). Firms of solution IV (corresponding to large firms), showed a strong presence of tangible and intangible resources, and human skills. The focus for these firms in this phase is now on the know-how that is necessary to leverage BDA technology and to analyze data. On the other hand, firms of solution V, which were in the SME size-class, continued to show the presence of technological and financial resources as well as slight focus to extend employee knowledge in the face of emerging technologies. Finally, within the final phase, we identified three solutions of grouped firms. Solutions VI and VII focus on strong tangible resources, while the final solution (SME size-class) shows agility in tangible resources and human skills, while the focus is on accentuating and strengthening the already present data-driven culture and knowledge extension capability. These configurational forms in which firms create business value from BDA capabilities demonstrate an asymmetrical relation as their composition differs across three different phases differ. These fine-grained outcomes shed light on necessary capability conditions that co-exist and drive business value. Our outcomes align well with recent studies that argue that specific combinations of firm resources, competence, and capabilities enable firms to survive, thrive, and support evolutionary fitness with the external environment [34, 35].

5   Discussion, Concluding Remarks and Future Work

This study tried to unfold and get a better understanding—through 27 interviews with field experts—of the process through which BDA value is obtained and explores the importance of complementary resource and capabilities, as well as factors that enabled or hindered the potential value of big data investments, throughout the different phases.

This research, therefore, makes several contributions to the current BDA research base. First, our study contributes to the emerging literature of capturing the business value of BDA investments [4, 19, 20]. Second, we examined the different configurational forms in which firms generate business value from BDA. Finally, this study synthesized the CBDACM from the literature and subsequently extended and validated this model through interviews with big data field experts and consultants. Moreover, our configurational model highlights the importance of different configurations of resources tailored per phase. These configurations—that views a multitude of variables simultaneously through a 'holistic' configurational lens—differ per phase, as each phase focusses on different BDA aspects to create business value. These outcomes are essential because we demonstrate and contend that several important factors need to consider when implementing big data projects and initiatives. In terms of practical implications, our study unveils to managers the potential process and core-resources they should focus on when planning to delve into a big data analytics projects. Our model suggests it is imperative to turn data into actionable intelligence by developing the BDA capability to look forward, inform and optimize decision making. What is important, is that firms keep aligning their BDA initiatives with business needs. Practitioners should, therefore, understand the firms' ambitions, the business strategy, and key performance indicators, and then work backward to determine what information and analysis are needed to support those priorities. Big data must cut across the entire firm, and executives and decision-makers have a crucial role in creating awareness. Typically SMEs can achieve this easier than larger firms. When most important stakeholders know why big data is essential and how they are expected to contribute, firms can avoid significant missteps. Training and education, in that respect, are key tools for making sure everyone is on board. Also, BDA quite often requires widespread changes to processes, data standards, governance, organizational structures, governance, and IS/IT. Firms should therefore effectively focus attention on building broad-based support and helping the organization overcome resistance to change. As a first step, firms should be deploying an honest assessment—in understanding the current BDA capabilities—and the emerging gaps they will need to close to get more value from BDA investments.

There are limitations regarding our study. First, we currently only did interviews with the goal of obtaining a deep and rich understanding of BDA. Although our study is a decent starting point, we cannot generalize the outcomes based on the current scope of analyses. Future research could build on these outcomes and further validate the constructs through, e.g., survey research. A large-scale quantitative analysis could provide more granularity towards the conditions and limits to which big data analytics add value, and shed some light on contextual factors that are of importance, mainly using a complexity science approach [35]. Also, we currently did not explicitly compare across industries, companies of different size and countries. These are also avenues for future research. Future research could then also explore how firms can synthesize and define improvement activities that best meet firms' current and future innovation needs. Finally, future research could investigate the conditions that coerce firms to start investing in big data, such as competitive pressures, as well as lag effects which may delay the realization of business value.

To conclude, our contribution to the big data theory and practice accentuates the process-oriented view on how firms can use, align and efficaciously adopt BDA to create a sustained business advantage. We argue that the CBDACM is a useful contribution to the literature on how firms gain value from BDA efforts.

Acknowledgments

 This project has received funding from the European Union's Horizon 2020 research and innovation programme, under the Marie Sklodowska-Curie grant agreement No. 704110.

References

1. Constantiou, I.D., Kallinikos, J.: New games, new rules: big data and the changing context of strategy. J. Inf. Technol. **30**(1), 44–57 (2015)
2. Goes, P.B.: Editor's comments: big data and IS research. MIS Q. **38**(3), p. iii-viii (2014)
3. Akter, S., et al.: How to improve firm performance using big data analytics capability and business strategy alignment? Int. J. Prod. Econ. **182**, 113–131 (2016)
4. Wamba, S.F., et al.: Big data analytics and firm performance: effects of dynamic capabilities. J. Bus. Res. **70**, 356–365 (2017)
5. McAfee, A., Brynjolfsson, E., Davenport, T.H.: Big data: the management revolution. Harvard Bus. Rev. **90**(10), 60–68 (2012)
6. Van de Wetering, R., Mikalef, P., Pateli, A.: A strategic alignment model for IT flexibility and dynamic capabilities: toward an assessment tool. In: The Proceedings of the Twenty-Fifth European Conference on Information Systems (ECIS), Guimarães, Portugal (2017)
7. Mikalef, P., et al.: Big data analytics capabilities: a systematic literature review and research agenda. Inf. Syst. e-Bus. Manag. **16**, 1–32 (2017)
8. Grover, V., et al.: Creating strategic business value from big data analytics: a research framework. J. Manag. Inf. Syst. **35**(2), 388–423 (2018)
9. Barney, J.: Firm resources and sustained competitive advantage. J. Manag. **17**(1), 99–120 (1991)
10. Chamberlin, E.H.: Monopolistic or imperfect competition? Q. J. Econ. **51**(4), 557–580 (1937)
11. Makadok, R.: Toward a synthesis of the resource-based and dynamic-capability views of rent creation. Strateg. Manag. J. **22**(5), 387–401 (2001)
12. Amit, R., Schoemaker, P.J.: Strategic assets and organizational rent. Strateg. Manag. J. **14**(1), 33–46 (1993)
13. Pavlou, P.A., El Sawy, O.A.: From IT leveraging competence to competitive advantage in turbulent environments: the case of new product development. Inf. Syst. Res. **17**(3), 198–227 (2006)
14. Ravichandran, T., Lertwongsatien, C.: Effect of information systems resources and capabilities on firm performance: a resource-based perspective. J. Manag. Inf. Syst. **21**(4), 237–276 (2005)
15. Van de Wetering, R., Versendaal, J., Walraven, P.: Examining the relationship between a hospital's IT infrastructure capability and digital capabilities: a resource-based perspective. In: The Proceedings of the Twenty-Fourth Americas Conference on Information Systems (AMCIS). AIS, New Orleans (2018)

16. Gantz, J., Reinsel, D.: The digital universe in 2020: big data, bigger digital shadows, and biggest growth in the far east. IDC iView: IDC Anal. Futur. **2012**(2007), 1–16 (2012)
17. Davenport, T.H.: Competing on analytics. Harv. Bus. Rev. **84**(1), 98 (2006)
18. Eisenhardt, K.M., Martin, J.A.: Dynamic capabilities: what are they? Strateg. Manag. J. **21** (10–11), 1105–1121 (2000)
19. Kamioka, T., Tapanainen, T.: Organizational use of big data and competitive advantage-exploration of antecedents. In: PACIS (2014)
20. Gupta, M., George, J.F.: Toward the development of a big data analytics capability. Inf. Manag. **53**(8), 1049–1064 (2016)
21. Eisenhardt, K.M., Graebner, M.E.: Theory building from cases: opportunities and challenges. Acad. Manag. J. **50**(1), 25–32 (2007)
22. Benbasat, I., Goldstein, D.K., Mead, M.: The case research strategy in studies of information systems. MIS Q. **11**(3), 369–386 (1987)
23. Battistella, C., et al.: Cultivating business model agility through focused capabilities: a multiple case study. J. Bus. Res. **73**, 65–82 (2017)
24. Erevelles, S., Fukawa, N., Swayne, L.: Big data consumer analytics and the transformation of marketing. J. Bus. Res. **69**(2), 897–904 (2016)
25. Janssen, M., van der Voort, H., Wahyudi, A.: Factors influencing big data decision-making quality. J. Bus. Res. **70**, 338–345 (2017)
26. Braganza, A., et al.: Resource management in big data initiatives: processes and dynamic capabilities. J. Bus. Res. **70**, 328–337 (2017)
27. Espinosa, J.A., Armour, F.: The big data analytics gold rush: a research framework for coordination and governance. In: 2016 49th Hawaii International Conference on System Sciences (HICSS). IEEE (2016)
28. Yin, R.K.: Case Study Research: Design and Methods. SAGE publications, Thousand Oaks (2013)
29. Miles, M.B., Huberman, A.M.: Qualitative Data Analysis: An Expanded Sourcebook, 2nd edn. SAGE Publications, Thousand Oaks (1994)
30. Boudreau, M.-C., Gefen, D., Straub, D.W.: Validation in information systems research: a state-of-the-art assessment. MIS Q. **25**, 1–16 (2001)
31. Mikalef, P., van de Wetering, R., Krogstie, J.: Big data enabled organizational transformation: the effect of inertia in adoption and diffusion. In: Abramowicz, W., Paschke, A. (eds.) BIS 2018. LNBIP, vol. 320, pp. 135–147. Springer, Cham (2018). https://doi.org/10.1007/978-3-319-93931-5_10
32. Mikalef, P., et al.: Information governance in the big data era: aligning organizational capabilities. In: Proceedings of the 51st Hawaii International Conference on System Sciences (2018)
33. Fiss, P.C.: A set-theoretic approach to organizational configurations. Acad. Manag. Rev. **32** (4), 1180–1198 (2007)
34. Aral, S., Weill, P.: IT assets, organizational capabilities, and firm performance: how resource allocations and organizational differences explain performance variation. Organ. Sci. **18**(5), 763–780 (2007)
35. Van de Wetering, R., Mikalef, P., Helms, R.: Driving organizational sustainability-oriented innovation capabilities: a complex adaptive systems perspective. Curr. Opin. Environ. Sustain. **28**, 71–79 (2017)

SciBOWater Workshop

SciBOWater 2018 Workshop Chairs' Message

The SciBOWater workshop focused on the topics related to water managements. Currently, the processes in water resources management are undergoing major transformations during its transition from the sectoral approaches of the past (e.g., water use for only irrigation, hydro-power, or navigation) to contemporary ones that are integrative and comprehensive approaching watersheds as complex system with interrelated processes surrounding the water cycle. This transformation comes at a time when acute problems are rising in water resources by direct (land use change) or indirect (climate change) human interventions in the natural systems within which we live. Among the most obvious example of extreme events related to water are floods, droughts, excessive pollutant in streams, and an increasing demand of fresh water to sustain economic and social needs.

The new management approaches require processing of a huge amount of information with different levels of accessibility and availability and in various formats (from digital to hard-copy formats). Given the relevance of the data for practice, often the data acquisition needs to be acquired, transmitted and accessed in real time. Not all the required data neither is critical nor of equal quality, therefore screening and conditioning has also to be conducted in real time. Equally important is to have access to historical data (raw, statistics and post-processed) for calibration and validation of the models. With regard to the accessibility of stakeholders to information, there are as well different situations. There are situations when information is to be accessed only by designated stakeholders, but there is a huge amount of information that is, and should be handled, as public information.

Thus, the workshop addressed relevant aspects of business information systems putting accent on the conference theme "Digital Transformation – an imperative for today's business markets", with focus on water related problems. The authors coming from 9 countries (Denmark, Germany, Greece, Italy, Netherlands, Portugal, Romania and Sweden) submitted 12 papers and 16 reviewers evaluated 10 of them as "clear accept", one as "probably accept" and one was rejected. Each paper was evaluated by 2 to 4 evaluators. The workshop organizers decided to select 6 of the best evaluated papers for oral presentation and publication in the Proceedings volume. Further four papers were accepted for poster presentation. Thus, the acceptance rate for publication in the Workshops Proceedings lies to 50.

Mariana Mocanu
Antonio Candelieri

Organization

Chairs

Mariana Mocanu   University Politehnica of Bucharest, Romania
Antonio Candelieri   University of Milano-Bicocca, Italy

Program Committee

Antonio Candelieri   University Bicocca of Milan, Italy
Petru Cascaval   Technical University "Gh. Asachi" of Iaşi, Romania
Valentin Cristea   University Politehnica of Bucharest, Romania
Ciprian Dobre   University Politehnica of Bucharest, Romania
Elisabetta Fersini   University Bicocca of Milan, Italy
Anca Hangan   Technical University of Cluj-Napoca, Romania
Anca Daniela   IONITA University Politehnica of Bucharest, Romania
Andreja Jonoski   IHE Delft Institute for Water Education, The Netherlands
Ciprian Lupu   University Politehnica of Bucharest, Romania
Mariana Mocanu   University Politehnica of Bucharest, Romania
Florin Pop   University Politehnica of Bucharest, Romania
Dan Popescu   University Politehnica of Bucharest, Romania
Florina Ungureanu   Technical University "Gh. Asachi" of Iaşi, Romania
Lucia Vacariu   Technical University of Cluj-Napoca, Romania
Ito Wasito   University Epoka from Tirana, Albania

A Multiple-Layer Clustering Method for Real-Time Decision Support in a Water Distribution System

Alexandru Predescu[1], Cătălin Negru[1], Mariana Mocanu[1(✉)], Ciprian Lupu[1], and Antonio Candelieri[2]

[1] Department of Computer Science, University POLITEHNICA of Bucharest, Bucharest, Romania
mariana.mocanu@cs.pub.ro
[2] Department of Computer Science, University of Milano Bicocca, Milan, Italy

Abstract. Machine learning provides a foundation for a new paradigm where the facilities of computing extend to the level of cognitive abilities in the form of decision support systems. In the area of water distribution systems, there is an increased demand in data processing capabilities as smart meters are being installed providing large amounts of data. In this paper, a method for multiple-layer data processing is defined for prioritizing pipe replacements in a water distribution system. The identified patterns provide relevant information for calculating the associated priorities as part of a real-time decision support system. A modular architecture provides insights at different levels and can be extended to form a network of networks. The proposed clustering method is compared to a single clustering of aggregated data in terms of the overall accuracy.

Keywords: Decision support system · Machine learning
Multiple-layer clustering

1 Introduction

Nowadays, smart cities use Information and Communications Technology (ICT) systems for management of water resources. There are some challenges that need to be overcome, such as efficient water exploitation, elimination of water loss because of broken pipes or ensuring good water quality. Also, these ICT systems gather data about water production, distribution and consumption aiming to optimize different stages of water cycle and to inform all the actors implies (e.g. operators, city services providers and citizens) [7].

In the ever expanding large scale water distribution systems, the task of the operator has become increasingly difficult and most commonly there is little insight on the system as a whole. Therefore, a decision support system is useful for increasing the efficiency and handling events based on priorities and cost effectiveness. A typical situation where Machine Learning algorithms are used is the classification of consumers based on their behavior.

© Springer Nature Switzerland AG 2019
W. Abramowicz and A. Paschke (Eds.): BIS 2018 Workshops, LNBIP 339, pp. 485–497, 2019.
https://doi.org/10.1007/978-3-030-04849-5_42

Water resource management for complex networks is a subject of ongoing research. This includes the estimation of water demand from smart meter data, which allows for efficient planning and detection of anomalies as described in [1]. There are also described solutions which allow for handling the vast amount of data in such systems. The k-means algorithm is used for data clustering in the context of unsupervised learning. The demand patterns of different consumer types can be extracted from AMR (Automatic Meter Reading) meters which provide 24-h time series as described in [2].

The paper is organized as follows: In Sect. 2 we present the context of research in the area of Machine Learning and defined strategies for increasing the efficiency of resource spending in water distribution systems. In Sect. 3 we propose a method for integrating modern technologies and results from the field of Machine Learning into a decision support system for prioritizing maintenance works and repairs, defining a method for data clustering, priority evaluation and implementation. In Sect. 4 we use the proposed method on a data set provided by measurements and we present the results in terms of accuracy and the level of detail that is obtained by a multiple-layer data clustering architecture, in comparison with a single layer architecture. The effect of an additional consumer on the existing clusters is also evaluated.

2   Related Work

Machine Learning (ML) is the state-of-the-art for Artificial Intelligence (AI), based around the idea that the machines should have access to and learn from available data. It is currently being used in a broad range of applications to extract relevant information in fields such as Internet of things (IoT) where wireless sensor networks (WSN) provide increasingly large amounts of data. The algorithms and strategies for addressing functional and non-functional requirements for this domain are described in [3]. Data clustering and aggregation is one of the main functional requirements for data processing in a WSN. Outlier detection is defined as a performance enhancement, though it can be the main focus in some applications.

Clustering methods have been applied in domains such as energetics for finding the energy consumption patterns [8], finance for evaluating the financial trends [10], medicine for detecting brain activity [11], robotics for improving autonomous capabilities [12] and psychology for analyzing user behavior in the context of social networks [13].

For water distribution systems, a proactive strategy allows for increasing the efficiency of resource spending for pipe renewal by addressing the most important assets first as stated in [6]. A proactive strategy is recommended for low probability and high consequence situations while a reactive strategy implies analyzing the breakdown history and scheduling the repair accordingly and is often used for high probability and low consequence situations.

In [4], by using the k-means algorithm and the results of multiple clusterings it is possible to accumulate evidence in the context of unsupervised learning. In this paper we study a multiple clustering strategy by defining multiple layers, each providing additional information about the entire data set in a proactive approach to water network management.

3   Proposed Solution

We propose the integration of a multiple-layer clustering algorithm into a decision support system for prioritizing pipe replacements in a water distribution system.

The priorities are defined as a function of the calculated daily demand patterns and the consumer types. There are different types of consumers such as residential, commercial and industrial, each having different requirements for water and service quality [2].

In our proposed algorithm, each consumer node is assigned a priority. With pipes being the scope of most repair works, the associated priorities have to be calculated. Considering a tree structure and using a bottom-up approach, each parent node is assigned the average priority of its child nodes. The pipe priority is defined as the average priority of its end nodes.

We propose two questions related to the integration of this method into a real-time decision support system that we further address in Sect. 4:

(i) **Network reconfiguration**
   The first question is related to the effect of adding a new consumer to the network on the associated priorities (e.g. by installing an additional smart meter providing data for the particular node).
   When comparing this scenario to the ideal case where all the data is known in advance, the discrepancy between the two scenarios is a measure of the overall accuracy of the method in real-life operating conditions.
(ii) **Comparison and parameter optimization**
   The second question is related to the advantages and disadvantages of using a multiple-layer clustering method over a single clustering method and the effect on the overall accuracy correlated with the number of clusters.

3.1   Data Clustering Method

For identifying the consumer patterns from measured data, unsupervised learning algorithms are used. We considered a two-layer clustering method which finds patterns for each consumer and then for the entire network as shown in Fig. 1. This method allows for distributed processing of consumer patterns for the first layer while reducing the bandwidth required for the second. An extension to n-layer clustering, where the system can be divided into subsystems is a subject of a future paper.

The following steps outline the proposed clustering method:

(i) **Individual consumer clustering**
   The clustering algorithm is run for each individual consumer node to obtain

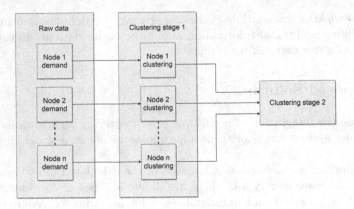

Fig. 1. Dual-layer clustering method

the daily consumption pattern over the entire time frame. This allows for an accurate visual representation of the consumer behavior for the particular node.

The optimal number of clusters for each consumer node is determined using a silhouette analysis on k-means clustering as having a silhouette coefficient that indicate a lower degree of overlapping with the other clusters [9].

(ii) **Consumer group clustering**

The cluster centroids from the individual consumer clustering are used as the input to the second clustering algorithm. The result of this second-layer represents the consumer demand patterns for the network/network section. The method is the same as for individual consumer clustering, with the additional specification of the number of clusters that should emphasize the patterns for the consumer group. The requirement is that the number of clusters for the higher layer is not higher than the number of aggregated clusters from a particular layer.

The effect is that the main characteristic of the current layer is used for data processing for the higher layers. Therefore, the data can be processed in a more organized way that is similar to the Hierarchical Clustering method.

(iii) **Priority evaluation**

Each time series corresponding to the particular node is assigned to one of the identified patterns for the entire network. The assignment of individual consumers to a cluster is evaluated by finding the most frequent assignment of the associated time series. Therefore, the consumer priority is selected based on the most relevant assignment that results from the measured data.

As a result, the main consumer categories can be defined as residential consumers with peaks in the morning and in the evening, commercial consumers with higher demand during the business hours and industrial consumers which can have either a uniform demand during the day or an irregular pattern in the case of irrigation systems.

In a supervised learning strategy, these characteristics can be defined and compared to the identified clusters using a similarity measure such as the euclidean distance [8].

For multiple layers, the clustering method is similar. Each layer would provide patterns for the lower layers. The consumer layer is considered as the first layer, showing the individual consumer patterns.

3.2 Priority Assignment Method

The network is represented as a directed graph. For the sake of simplicity, we considered a single source (i.e. pumping station) as the root node, consumers as leaf nodes and intermediary nodes.

After the individual consumers are clustered using the method described in Sect. 3.1, the associated priorities can be calculated as a function of the consumer type and demand profile.

The final objective is to assign priorities to the pipes in the network in order to provide decision support for the maintenance operations. For this, we define an indirect method using the previously calculated priorities for consumer nodes where the pipe priority is calculated as the average priority of the connected nodes. This assumes that the priority of the intermediary nodes has to be calculated, in this case as the average priority of the adjacent consumer nodes.

At the algorithm level, a breadth-first graph traversal is used and the priorities are calculated in reverse order, from the leaf nodes up to the root node.

For the n-layer clustering, the node priorities are calculated at each layer using the data from the lower layers. Each layer should be able to operate either as an autonomous entity or as part of a higher layer decision system. The priority associated to a layer can be defined according to the specific requirements (e.g. location, average priorities from lower layers). The edge priority is then calculated in a similar way as described for the two-layer scenario.

3.3 Python Implementation

The Python language is used as there is a vast ecosystem of open-source libraries which can be used for scientific purpose. The first step is loading the data from CSV files into a numpy array that is used in many libraries requiring data processing capabilities such as numpy, scipy and matplotlib. The server functionality is implemented using the Flask framework providing a REST (Representational State Transfer) architecture. The core functionality is represented by the data processing methods that implement the clustering algorithms and the priority evaluation. This requires the integration of Machine Learning algorithms with the network representation and with the API that is exposed to the AngularJS application.

The *scikit-learn* package provides tools for Machine Learning applications and implements some of the most common algorithms in this field [5]. For unsupervised learning the *KMeans* class from the *sklearn.cluster* package implements the general clustering algorithm that can be used for a broad range of applications:

```
kmeans=KMeans(n_clusters=3)
```
The algorithm clusters data with the specified parameters (number of clusters, maximum number of iterations) and allows the initialization of centroids with previous values. The method *fit* is actually used for k-means clustering of the input data (array-like or sparse matrix):
```
res=kmeans.fit(data)
```
The algorithm is initialized with a sample from the data set or with the specified centroids and then iteratively recalculates the centroids after assigning new samples until the new centroids do not change significantly. The results (e.g. centroids, assignments) can be extracted from the returned object, for example the centroids:
```
centroids=res.cluster_centers_
```
The method *predict* returns the assignment of the data samples to the closest corresponding cluster without modifying the centroids. This is useful for assignment of additional data to a cluster as it allows using the training data set as well as additional data:
```
assignments=res.predict(data)
```
In the case of new samples that have to be added to a cluster, an additional parameter is used that initializes the algorithm with the previous centroids and ensures the same order when updating the clusters:
```
KMeans(n_clusters=3,init=centroids)
```

For graph representation and related algorithms, the *networkx* package is used. First, the network is defined in JSON format, suitable for data exchange with a GIS (Geographic Information System) server. The measurements are assigned to the corresponding network node and the priorities for the other nodes and pipes are calculated from the consumer layer to the upper layers.

The application is built with a client-server architecture. The Python API handles the data and algorithms, and the SPA (Single Page Application) shows the user interface for the proposed decision support system. The data exchange is implemented using HTTP requests and the MVC architecture allows for separation of concerns.

4   Results

The data that we used in this paper is obtained from smart meters that were installed in a water distribution system from Italy. The data is stored in CSV files corresponding to each node. Each file contains daily 24-h time series for individual consumers having a sampling time of 1 h over a time-frame of several months. The structure of the network is not required for the experiments presented in this paper and an experimental model is used instead.

First, we obtain the consumer patterns from the data set for individual consumers. This initial clustering reveals some typical consumer patterns. For example, in Fig. 2, the characteristic shows two peaks corresponding to the average residential consumer pattern and in Fig. 3, the pattern is that of an industrial consumer with a single peak during the working hours.

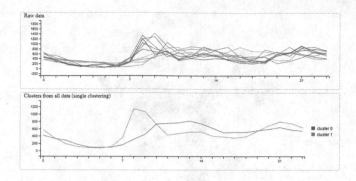

Fig. 2. Residential consumer pattern

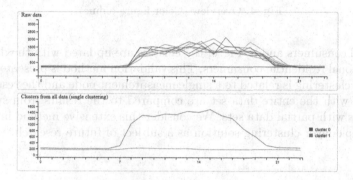

Fig. 3. Industrial consumer pattern

Then, using the second-layer clustering, the general consumer patterns are obtained and the individual consumers are assigned to one of the identified patterns to calculate the associated priority. For an effective visual overview, the network nodes and pipes and the two-layer clustering results are shown as a graph having a colormap representation of the associated priorities. The higher priorities are shown in red and the lower priorities are shown in blue. The size of the element is also proportional to the priority. In Fig. 4, a simple network is shown with the results obtained from the available data set. When a node is selected, the time series and cluster centroids are shown to the operator.

Therefore, we defined a method for priority evaluation using clustering algorithms as part of a visual decision support system. There are some aspects that have to be clarified regarding the accuracy and reliability of the proposed method in real-life scenarios.

4.1   Network Reconfiguration

For answering the first question that we proposed in Sect. 3, we analyze the partial recalculation (update) of the clusters when a consumer node is added to the network configuration. In Fig. 5, the clusters are calculated from two

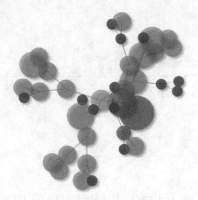

Fig. 4. Overview (Color figure online)

residential consumers and in Fig. 6, the clusters are updated with the data from two additional residential consumers. This validation method is presented in [14], where the clustering is related to a single measurement node and the results from clustering with the entire data set are compared to the results from successive clusterings with partial data sets. We consider this extensive method in the case of a multiple-layer clustering solution as a subject of future research.

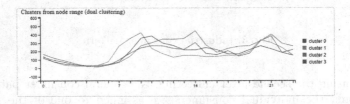

Fig. 5. Network reconfiguration (before)

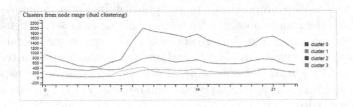

Fig. 6. Network reconfiguration (after)

In the analyzed scenario, the cluster assignments and main characteristics are maintained between the two cases. The third cluster is changed in terms of consumer demand, while having a similar profile with two peaks. The other clusters present a slight change from the initial clustering. This shows the possibility of using the clustering algorithm with initialization from previous iteration under dynamic conditions.

In the case of new time series which are being created on the same network configuration, the assignment to one of the clusters can be done without prior recalculation of centroids as described in [14].

4.2 Comparison and Parameter Optimization

For evaluating the accuracy of the two-layer clustering method, the resulting centroids are compared to a control method. The control method implements a single-layer clustering using the data from each node as input. We consider the silhouette analysis to find the optimal number of clusters for the first-layer as we are not interested in a specific number of individual consumer patterns. The second-layer clustering has a predefined number of clusters that represent the general patterns for the entire data set (e.g. residential consumers, industrial consumers).

The resulting centroids obtained using the optimal number of clusters for each node and 3 final clusters are shown in Fig. 7. The control method (green) provides a reference for testing the accuracy of the proposed method (blue).

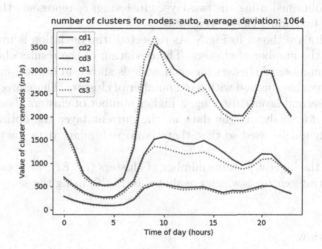

Fig. 7. Dual-layer with optimal number of individual clusters (Color figure online)

For answering the second question that we proposed in Sect. 3, we define an extensive evaluation of the overall deviation from the control method for the entire range of parameters. Instead of using the optimal number of clusters for the first-layer clustering, we evaluate the deviation over the entire range of possibilities, in this case between 2 and 82 clusters. The upper limit is given by the number of available time series for each node.

The deviation is calculated as the euclidean norm of the individual cluster deviation.

$$x_i \in \mathbb{R}^N, \ i = 1 \ldots NC \tag{1}$$

$$y_i \in \mathbb{R}^N, \ i = 1 \ldots NC \tag{2}$$

$$\delta_i = \sqrt{\sum_{j=1}^{N} (x_{i,j} - y_{i,j})^2} \in \mathbb{R}, \ i = 1 \ldots NC \tag{3}$$

$$\|\delta\| = \sqrt{\sum_{i=1}^{NC} \delta_i^2} \in \mathbb{R} \tag{4}$$

The formulas describe the method for calculating the overall deviation between the two methods, where $N = 24$ is the dimension of each cluster centroid and $NC = 3$ is the number of clusters used for the second layer, x_i represents a cluster centroid obtained using the control method and y_i represents a cluster centroid obtained using the two-layer clustering, δ_i represents the deviation between two individual cluster centroids.

The results are shown in Fig. 8. As expected, the deviation is inversely proportional to the number of clusters. The deviation of the results obtained with the optimal number of clusters for each node is shown in orange, and is generally higher than the method with fixed number of clusters. Therefore, we propose that for the second-layer clustering, a higher number of clusters should be used. Nonetheless, for analyzing the data at the current layer the optimal number of clusters should be used so that there is no redundant data for the decision system.

By using the highest possible number of clusters (i.e. 82), we obtain the most similar resulting centroids which are shown in Fig. 9, using the same convention as in Fig. 7.

4.3   Overview

The final result of the clustering algorithm consists in the identified consumer patterns that allow for an accurate classification of the consumers and calculating the associated priorities. In the case of a multiple-layer clustering, the identified patterns characterize a particular sub-network that can have an associated priority as well. The resulting decision support system is characterized by a similar organized architecture that allows for coordinating a large-scale water distribution system. With additional results presented in [14], the real-time requirements can range from a daily evaluation of priorities to a much more frequent evaluation with the actual sampling time of the data.

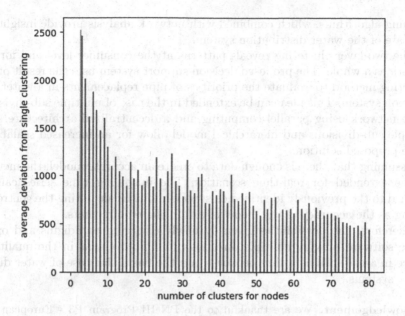

Fig. 8. Overall deviation (Color figure online)

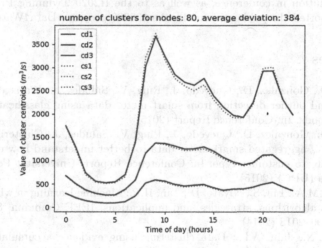

Fig. 9. Dual-layer with highest number of individual clusters

5 Conclusion

In this paper, Machine Learning algorithms are used as the basis of a decision support system for water distribution systems. Data clustering is used for consumer type identification and further data from consumers is then assigned to the identified clusters. This makes use of both unsupervised and supervised Machine

Learning algorithms, which combined with network analysis provide insights to the state of the water distribution system.

The two-layer clustering reveals patterns at the consumer level and for the network as a whole. The proposed decision support system uses the result of the clustering method to evaluate the priorities of pipe replacements in a water distribution system. This idea can be extended in the case of multiple sub-divisions of the network using parallel computing and a decentralized architecture. The multiple sub-divisions and hierarchical model allow for an increased scalability of the proposed solution.

Assuming that there is enough data to create an accurate model, the method can be extended for real-time scenarios. The upcoming time series can be assigned to the previously identified clusters without recalculating the centroids, as long as the accuracy of the model is within the requirements.

Therefore, the possibilities given by newly emerging paradigms and open-source software provide multiple directions for improvement in the quality of service in areas such as utility networks and the particular case of water distribution systems.

Acknowledgement. We are thankful to the PN III Program P3 - European and International Cooperation, UEFISCDI, that supported the research activity and part of the presentation in conference, as well as to the H2020 Twinning Program, that partially supported the publication under the 690900 project - Data4Water

References

1. Garcia, D., Gonzalez, D., Quevedo, J., Puig, V., Saludes, J.: Water demand estimation and outlier detection from smart meter data using classification and big data methods. In: Conference Report (2015)
2. García, D., Gonzalez, D., Quevedo, J., Puig, V., Saludes, J.: Clustering and classification of aggregated smart meter data to better understand how demand patterns relate to customer type. In: Conference Report, Universitat Politécnica de Catalunya (UPC) (2015)
3. Alsheikh, M.A., Lin, S., Niyato, D., Tan, H.P.: Machine learning in wireless sensor networks: algorithms, strategies, and applications. IEEE Commun. Surv. Tutor. **16**(4), 1996–2018 (2014)
4. Fred, A.L.N., Jain, A.K.: Data clustering using evidence accumulation. Object recognition supported by user interaction for service robots, vol. 4, pp. 276–280 (2002)
5. scikit-learn developers (BSD License) (2007). http://scikit-learn.org/stable/auto_examples/cluster/plot_kmeans_silhouette_analysis.html
6. Moglia, M., Burn, S., Meddings, S.: Decision support system for water pipeline renewal prioritisation. ITcon **11**, 237–256 (2006)
7. Umar, M., Uhl, W.: Integrative Review of Decentralized and Local Water Management Concepts as Part of Smart Cities (LoWaSmart). Norsk institutt for vannforskning (2016)
8. Iglesias, F., Kastner, W.: Analysis of similarity measures in times series clustering for the discovery of building energy patterns. Energies **6**(2), 579–597 (2013)

9. scikit-learn. http://scikit-learn.org/stable/
10. Kumar, M., Patel, N.R., Woo, J.: Clustering seasonality patterns in the presence of errors. In: Proceedings of Eighth ACM SIGKDD, pp. 557–563 (2002)
11. Wismüller, A., et al.: Cluster analysis of biomedical image time-series. Int. J. Comput. Vis. **46**(2), 103–128 (2002)
12. Ramoni, M., Sebastiani, P., Cohen, P.: Multivariate clustering by dynamics. In: Proceedings of the National Conference on Artificial Intelligence, pp. 633–638 (2000)
13. Zhu, J., Wang, B., Wu, B.: Social network users clustering based on multivariate time series of emotional behavior. J. Chin. Univ. Posts Telecommun. **21**(2), 21–31 (2014)
14. Predescu, A., Negru, C., Mocanu, M., Lupu, C.: Real-time clustering for priority evaluation in a water distribution system. In: AQTR 2018, Cluj, Romania (2018, accepted)

Automated Updating of Land Cover Maps Used in Hydrological Modelling

Muhammad Haris Ali[(✉)], Thaine H. Assumpção, Ioana Popescu,
and Andreja Jonoski

Integrated Water Systems and Governance,
IHE Delft Institute for Water Education, Delft, The Netherlands
haris_irfan@hotmail.com

Abstract. Urbanization and rapid growth in population are common development in many catchments and flood plains, often leading to increased flood
risks. In hydrological models of regions with urban spread out, the parameters
representing changes in land cover need to be frequently updated for obtaining
better estimations of the discharge (runoff). This article presents an automated
method for incorporating updated model parameters (SCS curve numbers) as per
new land cover maps, and using them in a hydrological model. The presented
work is developed for one part of Kifisios catchment in Greece, which is a pilot
area of the Horizon 2020 SCENT research project (https://scent-project.eu/),
focused on producing updated land use/land cover maps using crowdsourcing
data provided by citizens, combined with data from remote sensing and drone
images.

The method uses a newly available land cover map, which, together with
other data, is automatically geo-processed in ArcGIS to provide updated SCS
curve numbers. This is achieved using Python programing language and the
ArcPy libraries of ArcGIS. The updating of the pre-developed HEC-HMS
hydrological model with new SCS curve numbers is implemented in MATLAB,
through a specialized API for changing inputs to the HEC-HMS model. The
whole process is executed via a GUI developed in MATLAB, which also allows
to run the HEC-HMS automatically, and present updated results - discharge
hydrographs.

Keywords: ArcGIS · HEC-HMS · Automatic geo-processing
Flood modelling

1 Introduction

Quantifying the consequences of land cover changes on the runoff dynamics in a
catchment has always been an area of interest for hydrologists and water researchers.
The cities are growing worldwide and a large amount of urbanization has already been
witnessed [1]. Currently, 54% of the population of the world lives in cities and this
percentage is projected to increase to 66% by 2050 [2]. Urbanization poses a serious
threat to flooding and water quality [3]. Catchment urbanization seals the natural
surfaces, which leads to increase in imperviousness, resulting in reduced rainfall
infiltration into sub-soils and smaller surface storage capacity [4]. Combined effects on

© Springer Nature Switzerland AG 2019
W. Abramowicz and A. Paschke (Eds.): BIS 2018 Workshops, LNBIP 339, pp. 498–506, 2019.
https://doi.org/10.1007/978-3-030-04849-5_43

discharge runoff are: overall increase of volume [5, 6], base flows reduction [7], and decrease of response times of catchments [8]. Consequently, more flashy response of the catchment to the rainfall events occurs, which may result in faster floods with higher peak discharges [9]. Urbanization and land cover changes thus provide a challenging task to urban planners, as the development in formerly rural/natural catchments changes the hydrologic response of the area. Careful planning is required that can accommodate these altering responses in such catchments [10].

Urban planners and managers seek help from modelling results for assessing the increased flood risks and to formulate preventive and response strategies [11]. Models use different input data to simulate the runoff generated as a response to a rainfall event, including spatially varying land cover parameters, which also represent urban extent and imperviousness of the catchment. Hydrological models developed for regions of urban spread out need to frequently update the input parameters representing changes in land cover for better estimations of the discharges (runoffs).

SCENT, an ongoing research project funded under the Horizon 2020 program, has the goal of engaging citizens in environmental monitoring of land cover/use changes and to quantify the impact of such changes on flood risks and spatio-temporal inundation patterns, assessed with appropriate hydrodynamic and hydrological models. The crowdsourced data by citizens is combined with information from remote sensing and drone images within a platform that will provide regularly updated land cover maps. However, further processing is required to use such data in the hydrological models upon each update. The required data processing is generally done manually, using multiple software packages, which are often laborious and time consuming activities.

In this study a convenient method has been developed that can support the modelers in pre-processing of the land cover maps and integrating them as relevant parameters in a hydrological model, therefore keeping the developed models updated. For this purpose MATLAB was used as main software package to interact with ArcGIS and HEC-HMS through batch files and Python scripts. The methodology is implemented on a specific case study in the Kifissos catchment, in Greece, as discussed in Sect. 2.

2 Study Area

The study area is located in Greece and is a sub-basin of Kifissos catchment (Fig. 1). The natural streams in surrounding mountainous area flow down forming Kifissos River, which passes thought the city of Athens and discharges into the Saronic Gulf. The area of whole Kifissos catchment is 374.6 km² while the study area covers 136.5 km² in the upstream part of the catchment. The area has mostly retained its natural form, but rapid changes in land cover are observable. The lower portion of the catchment is already fully urbabanised. The climate is Mediterranean. August is hottest month while January is coldest, with mean temperatures of 27.7 °C and 10.4 °C respectively [12]. Average mean annual rainfall is 332.2 mm but maximum daily rainfall has enough potential to generate flash floods in the area [13]. Topography varies from moderate to steep [14].

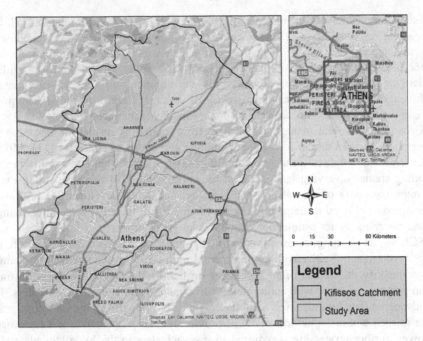

Fig. 1. Location of study area

The catchment is highly urbanized as 40% of the national population of Greece lives in the metropolitan city Athens and 31 surrounding municipalities. The area used to be drained by natural streams in the past but due to extensive urbanization, the natural streams were ignored in the urban management and most of them were concealed under streets and/or built upon, consequentially making the area flood prone [15, 16].

3 Methodology

The automated method developed to update the land cover information in the hydro-logical model includes calculation of new parameters based on the updated land cover map. An event-based hydrological model was developed for the study area using the HEC-HMS modeling system. The pre-processing of the available Digital Elevation Model (DEM) was done in ArcGIS using HEC-GEO-HMS toolbox and the catchment was delineated into 21 sub-basins based on their physical characteristic and flow regime (see Fig. 2 left). Data of two rainfall events (19–20 November 2000 and 14–15 January 2001) with corresponding discharge at the outlet were available. The model parameters were calibrated for the first one rainfall event and validated for the second event.

SCS curve number method was used for the calculation of runoff in each sub-basin. The method uses empirical formulae for determining runoff from a given catchment, which include different parameters (curve numbers) for different land covers. These

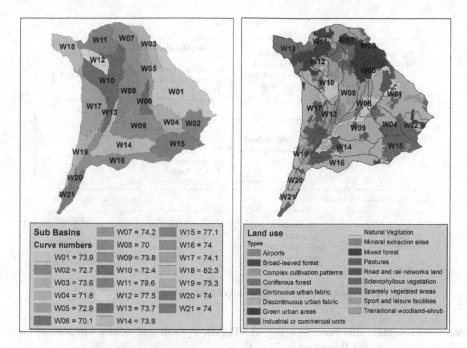

Fig. 2. Delineated sub-basins (left) and land use map (right, [17])

were calculated by pre-processing in ArcGIS of three maps: land cover map, hydrological soil group map and imperviousness map. The required steps are shown in Fig. 3.

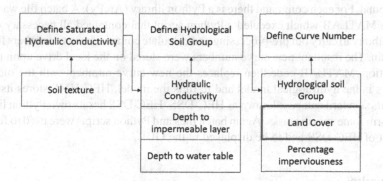

Fig. 3. Flowchart for determination of curve numbers (Color figure online)

The red box in Fig. 3 is showing the main input (land cover map) in the whole process while other data remain same, as long as the area under consideration remains same. Each time land cover changes, curve numbers will change and so does the runoff generation capacity of catchment. So curve numbers need to be updated in the model and the laborious task of pre-processing needs to be repeated. The solution proposed

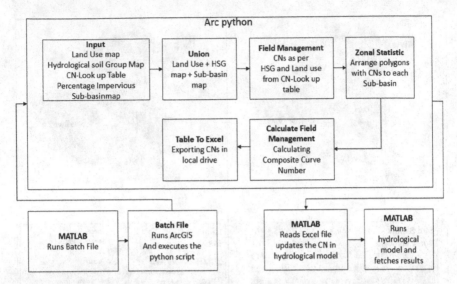

Fig. 4. Flowchart to update land cover map in the hydrological model

hereis to automate this process using MATLAB, Python and ArcPy libraries of Arc-GIS, as shown in the flowchart in Fig. 4.

The Curve Number (CN) lookup table was generated, which contains the list of curve numbers corresponding to general land cover taxonomy and hydrological soil group classification. CN look up table, Hydrological soil group map, percentage imperviousness map and sub-basins shape file were exported to the default data base of ArcGIS as these remain same. A GUI was developed in MATLAB for controlling and executing all steps in the application. ArcGIS tasks were executed using Python scripts running in background. For each command there is a Python library (ArcPy). A batch file was called through MATLAB which executed a Python script that contained all necessary calls to AcrPy library to carry out pre-processing and calculate composite curve numbers for each sub-basin. The resultant new curve numbers were stored on the local drive upon process completion. MATLAB code then replaces the new curve numbers with the old curve numbers in the hydrological model and re-runs the model. HEC-HMS stores its output data in its standard database known as HEC-DSS. HEC-DSS has its own Python libraries to perform some specific tasks. Again batch files and Python scripts were used to fetch the data out of HEC-DSS and to be displayed in the GUI.

4   Results

The MATLAB GUI is shown in Fig. 5. It provides functionalities to upload new land cover map, integrate the newly extracted curve numbers into HEC-HMS hydrological model, control the HEC-HMS model run and fetch the data out of HEC-DSS for plotting.

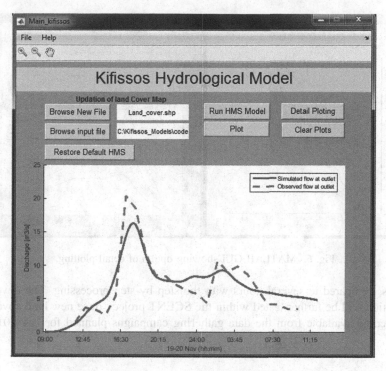

Fig. 5. MATLAB GUI for the hydrological model (Color figure online)

The graph in Fig. 5 is discharge hydrograph of catchment at the outlet for the rainfall event of November, 2000 and using the original land cover map as shown in Fig. 2 (right). Blue line in graph is representing the simulated discharge hydrograph by the model while red one is representing actual observed discharge hydrograph at the outlet. Efficiency of the hydrological model was measured in terms of Nash-Sutcliffe coefficient and RMSE which were equal to 0.85 and 1.6 m^3/s respectively.

The GUI enables fetching data out of HEC-DSS and provides the opportunity to the user to obtain results at other points of interest in the catchment, by referring to points on the image of the detailed river network in the catchment (see Fig. 6).

A number of scenarios were prepared an executed to test the working of the application. Here we present one such scenario where it was assumed that urbanization took place in the catchment and leading to increased curve numbers by 10% compared to their original values shown in Fig. 2 (left). The model was run and it was found out that peak discharge would raise to about 19 m^3/s (from 16.2 m^3/s) while the second peak has shown even higher relative increase in discharge from 8.5 m^3/s to 14 m^3/s. Cumulative volume of surface water has also increased in the catchment (see Fig. 7). Using the developed application this analysis can now be carried out in a matter of

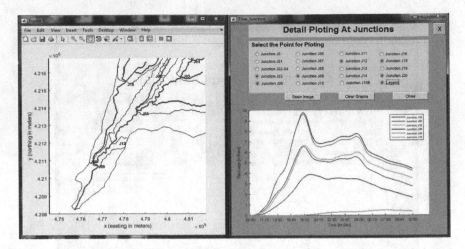

Fig. 6. MATLAB GUI showing option of detail plotting.

seconds, compared to several hours with the step by step processing. The developed application will be further tested within the SCENT project, once new land cover data will become available from the data gathering campaigns planned for late 2018 and 2019.

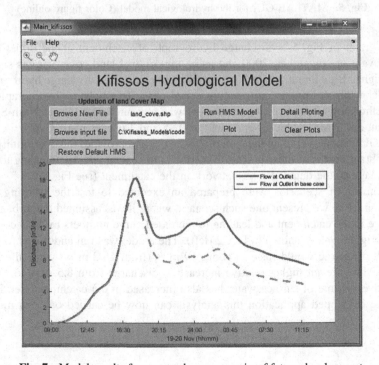

Fig. 7. Model results for assumed case scenario of future development.

5 Conclusions

This study has explored and implemented procedures for automated running of HEC-HMS, ArcGIS and extracting the output of HEC-HMS from HEC-DSS. The codes developed can provide assistance to link these software packages to other tools for different purposes. Specifically, in this study the land cover map was linked with curve numbers method used in HEC-HMS, but methods of updating spatial data inputs to HEC-HMS models can also be explored with the same or modified procedures. The application can be improved further by better visualization of results, providing additional functionalities modifying more input parameters of the model, or to change input precipitation data to the model, as main (and also rather uncertain) driver of the hydrological processes. Overall, such tool can provide the modelers with an opportunity to conduct fast analysis about land cover change in the catchment, can control different software packages using one application and can keep the developed hydrological model updated.

Acknowledgements. This study has received support from the SCENT project (grant agreement No. 688930) and Data4Water project (grant agreement No. 690900) of the European Union's Horizon 2020 research and innovation programme.

References

1. UN-Habitat, State of the world's cities 2010/2011, Earthscan, London (2010)
2. World Urbanization Prospects, United Nations, Department of Economic and Social Affairs, Population Division, World urbanization prospects: The 2014 Revision (2015)
3. Miller, J.D., Hutchins, M.: The impacts of urbanisation and climate change on urban flooding and urban water quality: a review of the evidence concerning the United Kingdom. J. Hydrol. Reg. Stud. **12**, 345–362 (2017)
4. Booth, D.B.: Urbanization and the natural drainage system – impacts, solutions, and processes. Northwest Environ. J. **7**(1), 93–118 (1991)
5. Brun, S.E., Band, L.E.: Simulating runoff behavior in an urbanizing watershed. Comput. Environ. Urban Syst. **24**(1), 5–22 (2000)
6. Kjeldsen, T.R., Miller, J.D., Packman, J.C.: Modelling design flood hydrographs in catchments with mixed urban and rural land cover. Hydrol. Res. **44**(6), 1040–1057 (2013)
7. Simmons, D.L., Reynolds, J.: Effect of urbanisation on the water balance of a catchment with shallow groundwater. J. Hydrol. **485**, 162–176 (2013)
8. Smith, J.A., Baeck, M.L., Meierdiercks, K.L., et al.: Field studies of the storm event hydrologic response in an urbanizing watershed. Water Resour. Res. **41**(10), 1–15 (2005)
9. Baker, D.B., Richards, R.P., Loftus, T.T., et al.: A new flashiness index: characteristics and applications to midwestern rivers and streams. J. Am. Water Resour. Assoc. **44883**, 503–522 (2004)
10. Miller, J.D., Hess, T.: Urbanisation impacts on storm runoff along a rural-urban gradient. J. Hydrol. **552**, 474–489 (2017)
11. Sikorska, A.E., Scheidegger, A., Banasik, K., Rieckermann, J.: Bayesian uncertainty assessment of flood predictions in ungauged urban basins for conceptual rainfall-runoff models. Hydrol. Earth Syst. Sci. **16**(4), 1221–1236 (2012)

12. Bathrellos, G.D., Karymbalis, E., Skilodimou, H.D., Gaki-Papanastassiou, K., Baltas, E.A.: Urban flood hazard assessment in the basin of Athens Metropolitan city, Greece. Environ. Earth Sci. **75**(4), 319 (2016)
13. Baltas, E.A., Mimikou, M.A.: Considerations for optimum location of a C-band weather radar in the Athens area. In: ERAD, pp. 348–351 (2002)
14. Mazi, K., Koussis, A.D.: The 8 July 2002 storm over Athens: analysis of the Kifissos River/Canal overflows. Adv. Geosci. **7**, 301–306 (2006)
15. Diakakis, M.: An inventory of flood events in Athens, Greece, during the last 130 years. Seasonality and spatial distribution. J. Flood Risk Manag. **7**(4), 332–343 (2014)
16. Mimikou, M., Baltas, E., Varanou, E.: A study of extreme storm events in the Greater Athens area, Greece. In: The Extremes of the Extremes, Extraordinary Floods. IAHS-AISH Publication, 271 (2002)
17. European Union: Copernicus Land Monitoring Service, European Environment Agency (EEA) (2012)

High-Performance Computing Applied in Project UBEST

Ricardo Martins$^{(\boxtimes)}$, João Rogeiro$^{(\boxtimes)}$, Marta Rodrigues$^{(\boxtimes)}$,
André B. Fortunato$^{(\boxtimes)}$, Anabela Oliveira$^{(\boxtimes)}$,
and Alberto Azevedo$^{(\boxtimes)}$

Hydraulics and Environment Department,
LNEC – National Laboratory for Civil Engineering, Lisbon, Portugal
{rjmartins,jrogeiro,mfrodrigues,afortunato,aoliveira,
aazevedo}@lnec.pt

Abstract. UBEST aims at improving the global understanding of present and future biogeochemical buffering capacity of estuaries through the development of Observatories, computational web-portals that integrate field observation and real-time MPI (Message Passing Interface) numerical simulations. HPC (High-Performance Computing) is applied in Observatories to serve both on-the-fly frontend user requests for multiple spatial analyses and to speed up backend's forecast hydrodynamic and ecological simulations based on unstructured grids. Backend simulations are performed using the open-source SCHISM (Semi-implicit Cross-scale Hydroscience Integrated System Model). Python programming language will be used in this project to automate the MPI simulations and the web-portal in Django.

Keywords: HPC · Estuaries · Numerical models · Parallel computing
Forecasts · SCHISM · UBEST

1 Introduction

High-Performance Computing (HPC) plays an important role in the solution of computationally-demanding problems in areas such as health, physics and mathematics. For instance, HPC is used by the coastal and estuarine modeling community to solve complex, long-term and large-scale problems using shared computational resources such as grid clusters, parallel computing or cloud computing [2]. Indeed, the complexity of coastal processes and related partial differential equations, along with the need to simultaneously resolve small spatial and temporal scales makes coastal modeling a natural candidate for HPC use.

Estuaries are one of the most productive ecosystems on Earth. They support various species and habitats and protect the adjacent coastal zone from terrestrial contaminants (e.g. increased nutrient loads). Human activities (e.g. fishing, tourism) and climate change can, however, increase the pressures on the estuarine ecosystems and change their dynamics [1].

The project UBEST seeks to understand the changes on the biogeochemical buffering capacity of the estuaries and its susceptibility to future scenarios. This is

© Springer Nature Switzerland AG 2019
W. Abramowicz and A. Paschke (Eds.): BIS 2018 Workshops, LNBIP 339, pp. 507–516, 2019.
https://doi.org/10.1007/978-3-030-04849-5_44

achieved by developing web-portals, denoted Observatories, which integrate field observations and real-time, high-resolution numerical model predictions. Two distinct observatories are being developed: for the Tagus estuary, one of the largest estuaries in Europe, and for the Ria Formosa, the most important coastal ecosystem in the southern coast of Portugal (Algarve region). From a computational viewpoint, these frameworks have two main components: (i) the frontend (web-portal), where data and model results are made available and processed through both pre-defined indicators and on-the-fly user requests, and (ii) the backend, where daily high-resolution model simulations are carried out to provide short-term predictions of the water and ecosystem dynamics of the two systems. UBEST's backend uses SCHISM (Semi-implicit Cross-scale Hydroscience Integrated System Model) [3], a parallelized model that uses the MPI (Message Passing Interface) paradigm.

In the scope of UBEST, HPC will play a double role: to support realistic, high-resolution simulations of circulation and ecosystem dynamics in the two coastal systems, and to provide computational power to process data and model results through pre-defined, automatic products or user requests at the web-portal. The main purpose of this paper is thus to describe how HPC will be an asset in the Observatories developed within UBEST and the strategies to use it efficiently to achieve faster predictions and provide better usability and user experience on the web-portal. The implementation of HPC in UBEST using the INCD - the Portuguese National Infrastructure for Distributed Computing - will also be discussed.

This paper is organized as follows. Section 2 will cover the related work; Sect. 3 will present the analysis of HPC usage in the scope of computational model forecasts in UBEST; Sect. 4 will present the UBEST web-portal and its architecture, and Sect. 5 will present a strategic analysis on how HPC can be used in UBEST's web-portal. Finally, Sect. 6 is the conclusion which anticipates the forthcoming work.

2   Related Work

Recent advances in computational infrastructures have promoted the widespread usage of HPC to support multiple applications in many areas. In the field of environmental sciences, typical usage of these resources is associated with high-resolution numerical models, often solving multiple scales and processes, from hydrodynamics to ecological dynamics.

HPC has large relevance in coastal and ocean modeling [2], and the recent computational infrastructure advances have promoted a vast knowledge improvement in many areas using numerical models, and in turn has encouraged the search for broader, further detailed modeling studies that bring these computational resources to the limit [4]. Different HPC approaches were used by applying parallel computing in cloud resources [4, 5] or in grid environments [6].

In coastal and estuarine modeling, unstructured grid numerical models have been used for several decades to simulate coastal zones [7], but achieving the adequate high resolution is still a challenge due to the associated computational costs. There is a need to apply numerical models to predict key variables, such as velocities or biogeochemical concentrations, to address complex problems such as analyzing the impacts of climate change in these regions or simulating the interaction between physical and biogeochemical processes. HPC is one of the avenues that many models have been pursuing and applying successfully. Several models are available to simulate hydro-dynamic and ecological dynamics [8], many of which can take advantage of HPC resources through MPI parallelization. In this paper, we explore the model SCHISM, which evolved from the model SELFE (semi-implicit Eulerian–Lagrangian finite-element), both parallelized using MPI.

Both models SELFE [9] and SCHISM [3] are hydrodynamic models that solve three-dimensional (3D) conservation equations for mass and momentum to calculate the free-surface elevation and the 3D water velocity, salinity and temperature. SELFE integrates modules for oil spills [10], fecal contamination [11] and ecological dynamics [12]. ECO-SELFE is a fully coupled 3D hydrodynamic and ecological model which has been used in several nutrient dynamic studies. SCHISM evolved from SELFE and is distributed with an open-source Apache v2 license, with many enhancements and upgrades including new extension to large-scale eddying regime and a seamless cross-scale capability from creek to ocean [3]. Currently, ECO-SELFE is integrated within SCHISM's modeling suite.

The need to predict estuarine and coastal zones dynamics has brought the useful-ness of HPC in coastal modeling to a bigger dimension. Forecast systems fulfill this need by providing predictions of relevant variables at short time scales, through the integration of numerical models and field data [13]. Forecast systems produce high-resolution simulations of multiple variables, to be delivered in a timely way every day. These stringent spatial and temporal requirements make the use of HPC and paral-lelized models essential [4].

LNEC has a large experience in the development of new models, integrated in community-based open source modeling suites, and in the integration of coastal model applications in new web platforms. Since 2007, LNEC has been developing a generic forecast framework, supported by several high-resolution models. The WIFF (Water Information Forecast Framework) is a forecast platform to address estuarine and coastal dynamics, from physical processes to biogeochemistry [13]. It uses computational models for hydrodynamic prediction (SELFE [2] and SCHISM [13]), wave-current circulation (SCHISM-WWM, [13]), coupled hydrodynamic and fecal contamination or ecological dynamics (ECO-SELFE [11]) and oil spills (VOILS [10]). WIFF process workflow consists in preparing input data from external services, such as NOAA, NCEP or Copernicus that feed the computational model simulations in real time and generate visualization products made available through Web interfaces. MOLINES [13] and SPRES [14] are examples of Web interfaces that give access to customized deployments of WIFF to estuarine inundation and oil spill risks prediction, respectively.

WIFF has been deployed in multiple computing environments, from workstations, grids and on the cloud [4]. The use of the cloud has been shown to be an alternative, flexible, and scalable, out-of-the-box paradigm to handle forecast stringent require-ments, given its flexibility of accessing additional resources on request and a consid-erable effort on providing service platforms to facilitate its use.

3 HPC Usage in Model Applications in UBEST

As explained in the Sect. 1, there will be two uses for HPC in UBEST: one for the frontend, where data and model results are made available and processed through both pre-defined indicators and on-the-fly user requests (Fig. 1), and the other in the backend, where daily high-resolution simulations are carried out to provide short-term predictions of the dynamics of the two systems.

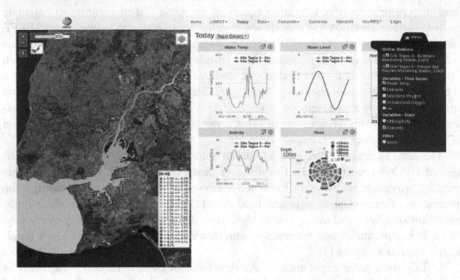

Fig. 1. UBEST web-portal 'Today' interface

UBEST numerical simulations, results analyses and multi-source data processing can benefit from HPC. This is possible by using the already integrated MPI parallelization in the modeling suite SCHISM and will be explored elsewhere. MPI is a communication protocol used in parallel computing where processes communicate with each other by message exchange to assure its synchronization. For example, model SELFE supports parallelization through MPI, improving its efficiency to more than 80% in a 2 million-node grid case on a TeraGrid cluster [6]. On the other hand, SCHISM supports parallelization by MPI protocol in all its modules, with generally excellent scalability [3]. The main parallelization strategy adopted by these two models consists in dividing the simulation grid of the domain into several sub-grids that are later allocated to each node of the computational cluster. This type of parallelization is performed by using the ParMETIS graph partitioning library to decompose the domain into smaller regions.

SCHISM forecast workflow in UBEST numerical simulations starts by processing various data inputs from regional atmospheric and ocean models, to provided boundary and over the domain conditions for the forecast. Then it applies a highly efficient and accurate semi-implicit finite-element/finite-volume method with Eulerian-Lagrangian algorithm to solve the Navier-Stokes equations in parallel mode. Executing the

SCHISM model within WIFF is achieved by a set of scripts that offload the execution to HPC resources, handling most aspects of the process automatically, including the amount of MPI processes to be run in parallel, for optimal performance according to the number of grid nodes.

SCHISM has an optimum number of CPUs dependent of the number of grid points, in the order of 1 CPU for each 1000 horizontal grid points. Studies like [4] and [2] corroborate this hypothesis through the implementation of several scalability tests in different computational environments (HPC and Cloud). The choice of the adequate HPC resources is mandatory to guarantee the fastest delivery of the model predictions.

In order to exploit the HPC resources, additional scripts will be used to combine the model outputs and convert them to formats that can readily be integrated in the Web interface, such as GIS layers and output files in standard *netcdf* formats.

The HPC usage in backend mode will be applied for the Forecasts and Scenarios pages. Both pages use the SCHISM as an information provider. The backend for the Forecasts runs on a Linux operating system, and is managed by a set of scripts, scheduled to run periodically. The workflow consists in creating a folder structure to run the forecast simulation for each day. In this folder a set of input files are stored, these files are generated based on the results of the previous run, tidal, regional circulation and atmospheric forecasts to define the boundary forcing conditions, and data from in situ sensors. Therefore, the system interacts with forcings databases to retrieve input data to force the daily simulations, including river flows, water temperature and atmospheric data. The scheduled scripts must retrieve all the information before the launch of the model SCHISM for each forecast. Afterwards, other scripts compare the results of the SCHISM model with the available in-situ data retrieved from the field sensors.

The UBEST project also makes use of HPC in the construction of the scenarios database, which will feed the Scenarios page on the web-portal. These scenarios will be set according with the expected climate changes for the Portuguese coast, in particular for both domains of UBEST project, the Tagus estuary and the Ria Formosa. The future scenarios will also take into consideration possible changes in anthropogenic sources of biogeochemical contaminants that will affect the characterization of both estuaries. The scenarios are created running the SCHISM model for a predefined set of initial conditions and specific forcings instead of the daily inputs used by the forecast system. These scenarios will be used to study the biogeochemical buffer capacity and resilience of each estuary to future environmental conditions.

4   UBEST Web-Portal and Parallelization Strategies

4.1   UBEST Web-Portal

The UBEST web-portal is developed using Django, a Python web framework that has a frontend and a backend. The frontend is the presentation layer of the web application, the web framework loads the pages to the user to interact and request data from them. The backend is the engine running on the back of the portal that processes user requests and returns requested information. The UBEST frontend is composed by 'Home/Today', 'Data Access', 'Forecasts', 'Scenarios' and 'Indicators' pages.

The 'Today' page (Fig. 1) is an operational dashboard for the daily tasks of the end-users, highly configurable for their particular needs and embeds all estuary data and model predictions from the current day, providing interaction mechanisms to show or hide data users wish to see. The 'Home' page is just a simplified 'Today' page but with less information and more restricted interactivity.

The 'Data Access' page (Fig. 2) gives the user the ability to view the available data by selected station name and by variables, and to search available data using filters, allowing the user to view or download the data required for their job.

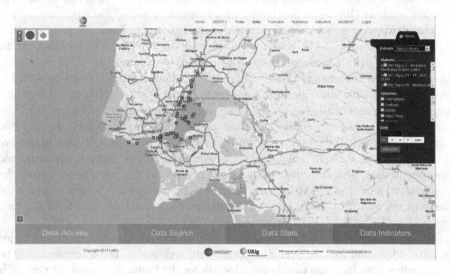

Fig. 2. UBEST 'Data Access' page

The 'Forecasts' page shows a 48-h forecast from the models, and adds the possibility to interact with these results by building derivative products such as transects and model probing.

The 'Scenarios' page presents the estuary susceptibility in future scenarios, and the 'Indicators' page alerts the user for possible behavior changes in the estuary dynamics and biogeochemistry.

4.2   UBEST Architecture and Possible Problems

The actual UBEST architecture flow diagram is presented in Fig. 3. The frontend is able to fetch WFS/WMS model results from a Map Server, by sending AJAX requests. The backend processes user requests and calls the repository hosted in another server to fetch data from Observatories as JSON.

This architecture can have some performance issues due to the size and complexity of the requests. For instance, the 'Forecast' page allows users to build derivative

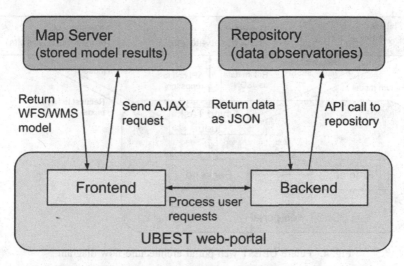

Fig. 3. Current UBEST web-portal architecture flow diagram

products and requires calling asynchronously multiple times the Map Server to fetch data from WFS/WMS models. The 'Today' and 'Data Access' pages give the user the ability to view the available data and that requires doing multiple API calls to the repository to load data by multiple variables, multiple estuary stations and by several start/end dates.

This issue has an impact on the server performance, degrading the user's experience. Some parallelization strategies are being studied for application in the UBEST web portal to overcome this issue, and will be described in the next section.

5 Applying Parallelization

5.1 Parallelization Strategies

Parallelization can be applied on web-portals to speedup processing user requests. There are some solutions that can be used on web-portals, such as using multithreaded servers (Apache) or using HPC RESTful web-services [15]. In the scope of the UBEST web-portal, the existing Django's default web-server will be replaced by a more suitable, flexible and robust web-server that will be explained in the final subsection.

An asynchronous task queue service will be implemented to queue requests from the users and process them asynchronously. UBEST's web-portal backend will use this service to queue and process frontend user requests with defined parameters, and to return model results on-the-fly. As described in Fig. 4, this new architecture will allow flexibility and scalability on the requests.

For the 'Forecasts' page, in addition of loading stored models results from the Map Server, a new approach to load models on-the-fly will be applied, by using SCHISM and with the benefit of using the included MPI parallelization to speedup model

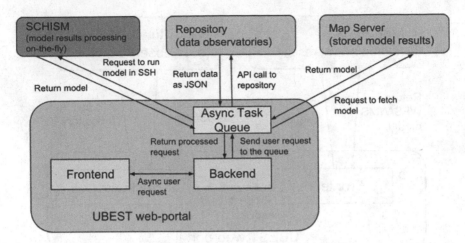

Fig. 4. Future UBEST web-portal architecture flow diagram

processing. The requests to run the SCHISM model processing will be done remotely by SSH on the backend side.

For the 'Data', 'Today' and other pages, other HPC strategies in Python will be applied inside of the backend to load data from repository. We believe that will improve the performance on processing user requests and fetching (and calculating) them, by using *Threading* or *Multiprocessing* packages. *Threading* spawns threads inside of a process, while *Multiprocessing* spawns processes.

There's a difference between threads and processes, threads are lightweight and use shared memory, while processes are heavy and use their own process memory. Threads have problems with shared memory, when an object is stored on shared memory and multiple threads access it at once, leading to memory corruption errors. To overcome that, Python implements the Global Interpreter Lock (GIL) that protects access to a Python object from other threads when it's already held by a thread, but its complexity and overhead brought performance issues that are impossible to get rid. Because of that, we decided to use processes instead of threads. Many Python applications already use multiprocessing, processes are memory safe and do not have the GIL associated overhead. Other alternatives are being studied to be used, such as MPI for Python (mpi4py).

5.2   UBEST Production Deployment

UBEST web-portal and forecast system will follow the architecture defined in Fig. 4, and will be integrated on the INCD initiative, the Portuguese National Infrastructure for Distributed Computing, to take advantage of their resources for the model processing, and to deploy the web-portal.

For this case, some changes will be made to assure scalability, security and performance of the server when handling many concurrent user requests at same time, by changing Django's internal development server to Gunicorn web-server, and the SQLite database to a more production suitable one, the PostgreSQL database. An asynchronous task queue will be used to run on the web-portal's backend side for processing queued user requests asynchronously (Celery+RabbitMQ broker). As a side note, Gunicorn and Celery do use multiprocessing.

As explained previously, the interaction between UBEST web-portal and the model processing will be similarly implemented as in [4] that describe a possible way to run the ECO-SELFE model remotely.

6   Conclusions

This paper addresses the use of HPC within coastal Observatories processing needs, for backend model calculations and frontend data/model automatic processing and on-the-fly user requests. The analysis is based on the experience gained on UBEST's developments and former projects, on the use of parallel computing to support high-resolution daily model forecasts and multiple scenarios analysis. The analysis is complemented with a strategic assessment for the use of HPC in frontend web applications as well, namely to support the processing of large information datasets as part of a web-portal automatic product operations and user requests products.

The analysis suggests that the good performance obtained in the backend, using model SCHISM in HPC environments, can also be obtained in the frontend. The strategies highlighted anticipate that it is possible to make UBEST a coupled web-portal and forecast system with full HPC support. The future work will focus on adding support to the ecological model of SCHISM in the forecast framework WIFF and analyzing its performance in an HPC environment. The increase in computational power needed to achieve timely forecasts, on a daily basis, of high resolution ecological variables is a major challenge. Processing these and other results, as well as data for the web-portal constitutes the second challenge. Again, HPC is the adequate way to address this challenge, in particular in the scope of managing multiple observatories in the Portuguese coast.

Acknowledgements. The authors would like to thank Dr. Y. Zhang for making the models SCHISM and SELFE openly available. This work was developed in the scope of project UBEST (PTDC/AAG-MAA/6899/2014), funded by the Fundação para a Ciência e a Tecnologia (FCT). The third author was also funded by FCT through grant (SFRH/BPD/87512/2012).

References

1. Rodrigues, M., Fortunato, A.B., Freire, P.: Salinity evolution in the Tagus estuary relative to climate change. In: 4as Jornadas de Engenharia Hidrográfica, Lisbon, June 2016
2. Costa, M., Oliveira, A., Rodrigues, M., Azevedo, A.: Application of parallel, high-performance computing in coastal environmental modeling: circulation and ecological dynamics in the Portuguese coast. In: Proceedings da 3rd Iberian Grid Infrastructure, pp. 375–386 (2009)
3. Zhang, Y., Ye, F., Stanev, E.V., Grashorn, S.: Seamless cross-scale modeling with SCHISM. Ocean Model. **102**, 64–81 (2016)

4. Rogeiro, J., et al.: Running high resolution coastal models in forecast systems: moving from workstations and HPC cluster to cloud resources. Adv. Eng. Softw. **117**, 70–79 (2017). ISSN 0965–9978
5. Glenis, V., McGough, A.S., Kutija, V., Kilsby, C., Woodman, S.: Flood modelling for cities using cloud computing. J. Cloud Comput. **2**(7), 1–14 (2013)
6. Zhang, Y., Witter, R.W., Priest, G.P.: Tsunami-tide interaction in 1964 Prince William Sound Tsunami. Ocean Model. **40**, 246–259 (2011)
7. Dietrich, J.C., et al.: Modeling hurricane waves and storm surge using integrally-coupled, scalable computations. Coast. Eng. **58**(1), 45–65 (2011). https://doi.org/10.1016/j.coastaleng.2010.08.001
8. Hashioka, T., Yamanaka, Y.: Ecosystem change in the western North Pacific associated with global warming using 3D-NEMURO. Ecol. Model. **202**, 95–104 (2007)
9. Zhang, Y., Baptista, A.M.: SELFE: a semi-implicit Eulerian-Lagrangian finite-element model for cross-scale ocean circulation. Ocean Model. **21**(3–4), 71–96 (2008)
10. Azevedo, A., et al.: An oil risk management system based on high-resolution hazard and vulnerability calculations. Ocean Coast. Manag. **136**(1), 1–18 (2017). https://doi.org/10.1016/j.ocecoaman.2016.11.014
11. Rodrigues, M., Guerreiro, M., David, L.M., Oliveira, A., Menaia, J., Jacob, J.: Role of environmental forcings on fecal contamination behavior in a small, intermittent coastal stream: an integrated modelling approach. J. Environ. Eng. **142**(5), 05016001 (2016)
12. Rodrigues, M., Oliveira, A., Queiroga, H., Fortunato, A.B., Zhang, Y.J.: Three-dimensional modeling of the lower trophic levels in the Ria de Aveiro (Portugal). Ecol. Model. **220**(9–10), 1274–1290 (2009). ISSN 0304-3800
13. Fortunato, A.B., et al.: Operational forecast framework applied to extreme sea levels at regional and local scales. J. Oper. Oceanogr. **10**(1), 1–15 (2017)
14. Freire, P., et al.: A local-scale approach to estuarine flood risk management. Nat. Hazards **84**(3), 1705–1739 (2016)
15. Cholia, S., Skinner, D., Boverhof, J.: NEWT: a RESTful service for building high performance computing web applications. In: 2010 Gateway Computing Environments Workshop (GCE), New Orleans, LA, pp. 1–11 (2010). https://doi.org/10.1109/gce.2010.5676125

A Comparative Study on Decision Support Approaches Under Uncertainty

Panagiotis Christias[1,2](✉)

[1] Piraeus University of Applied Sciences, Piraeus, Greece
xristias@puas.gr
[2] University Politehnica of Bucharest, Bucharest, Romania

Abstract. This paper presents a comparative study between two approaches for decision support examined to the reference problem of energy retrofit and indoor environment quality in buildings. Two approaches will be presented. The first concerns a proposition based on multi-criteria analysis methodology and the second is based on Bayes' mathematical theory. The aim is to examine ways of constructing decision support systems which can produce credible decisions under uncertainty. For this purpose, criteria relevant to the given problem will be examined, while attempting to choose those which need less measured or audited information to perform calculations.

Keywords: Decision support · Multi-criteria analysis · Bayes approach
Probabilistic uncertainty · Energy retrofit · Thermal-optical comfort
Water resources management

1 Area of Application

The examined decision support approaches focus around the application of actions which improve the energy consumption of a building and relate to air conditioning equipment and water resource management. The decision support mechanisms will take into account information relevant to buildings in order to shape proposals for improvement. Moreover, audit and measurement data will be used in order to compare and evaluate the results of the decision processes. The energy classification methodology of buildings is based on real energy consumption records. They consist of electricity consumption on heating, water cooling or pressurization and lighting values. Total energy consumption is calculated from the cumulative sensor measurements. The result is the labeling of the building in energy categories (A > B > C > D > E) according to its state, with E being the lower energy level [2]. Buildings are divided into groups according to their use: office buildings, residences, hotels, schools and warehouses. Table 1 shows indicatively the limits of the classification categories for air conditioned office buildings.

W. Abramowicz and A. Paschke (Eds.): BIS 2018 Workshops, LNBIP 339, pp. 517–526, 2019.
https://doi.org/10.1007/978-3-030-04849-5_45

Table 1. Energy labels limits for air conditioned office buildings (kWh/m^2/year).

Label	Heat/Cool	Heat/Cool + Electricity
A	[0,67)	[0,122)
B	[67,122)	[122,172)
C	[122,199)	[172,240)
D	[199,278)	[240,348)
E	≥ 278	≥ 348

2 The Multi-criteria Decision Support Approach

The classification of a building into better energy category labels is the core goal of the decision support outcome. The process can propose a selection from a set of alternative scenarios related to the building operation or infrastructure. These scenarios concern interventions or implementations in the building, targeting the improvement of thermal and optical comfort and the optimal use of water resources.

The problem of finding and proposing the most useful alternative scenarios to improve comfort and reduce energy consumption in the building is initially approached with multi-criteria decision making. In multi-criteria problems there are multiple and conflicting criteria for assessing alternative decisions. The number of criteria and the relationship between them have an effect on the decision maker's preference hierarchy. Multi-criteria decision analysis assume a value system which represents the preferences of the decision makers over a set of alternative actions. This value system is taken into account upon creation of the utility function and the priorities relative weights. The decision maker will choose the most useful solution through a set of conditions [6]. The set of available alternatives is a finite set of options during the decision making process and is denoted:

$$A = \{a_j, j = 1, 2, \ldots, n\} \qquad (1)$$

A 'criterion' is defined as a real function g, with domain a set A of the alternative actions and with a codomain Y where the preferences of the decision maker are expressed [6]:

$$g : A \rightarrow Y \qquad (2)$$

The outcome $g(a)$ reflects the estimation of the alternative action a on criterion g. If $g(a) > g(b)$, a is considered better than b. Given a set of criteria $\{g_1, g_2, \ldots g_n\}$, an alternative action-choice a dominates over an alternative b if:

$$\forall j. g_j(a) \geq g_j(b) \qquad (3)$$

and

$$\exists j | g_j(a) > g_j(b) \tag{4}$$

In our problem, the alternative scenarios form set A. The criteria are four:

- g_1: Reduction of energy consumption
- g_2: Improvement of air quality
- g_3: Improvement of thermal comfort
- g_4: Better exploitation of water resources

Based on multi-attribute utility theory [6], a utility function U composes the criteria together in order to reflect the decision maker's preferences. The weighted sum method is chosen to represent the utility of an action and is calculated by the following formula:

$$u(a) = \sum_{j=1}^{4} w_j * g_j(a) \tag{5}$$

The coefficient w_j is a positive real number that express the weight of the corresponding criterion, i.e. the preference-priority on the given criterion. Preference weights have a sum of *1*. The weight coefficient has also a physical meaning: it indicates tradeoffs among criteria. The degree of tradeoff for criterion i against criterion j is defined as the quantity on criterion j that the decision maker wishes to give up in order to obtain a unit of criterion i [1]. The weights of the four criteria in this case are assigned by experience and they are displayed in Table 2.

Table 2. Weight coefficients in multi-criteria decision approach.

Criterion	Weight
Reduction of energy consumption	0.3
Improvement of air quality	0.25
Improvement of thermal comfort	0.2
Optimization of water resources usage	0.25

Since the actual values of the four criteria are expressed in different numerical units, they are normalized so they will map to the range *[0, 1]* following the rule:

$$v_j = \frac{(g_j - min(g_j))}{(max(g_j) - min(g_j))} \tag{6}$$

The utility function is shaped as follows:

$$u(a) = 0.3 * g_1(a) + 0.25 * g_2(a) + 0.2 * g_3(a) + 0.25 * g_4(a) \tag{7}$$

The decision support system will seek the alternative which maximizes the outcome of (7). If two alternatives produce equal outcomes, it will chose the one which causes greater improvement to the criterion with the larger weight.

The multi-criteria approach has disadvantages which led to abandoning the actual implementation. More specifically:

1. The preference weights are arbitrarily defined, orienting the utility function towards our subjective preferences rather than the system's initiative.
2. It is difficult to acquire the alternative actions evaluations on the given criteria for each and every building.
3. The criteria values are altered in the same way as the first criterion which is energy saving. That is, improving air quality will lead to the indoor environment improvement but also with positive impact on energy consumption.
4. Perfect information gathering is a mathematical tool that puts the decision system closer to the perception of reality. This would mean retrieving all the energy consumption, air quality, thermal comfort and water management data from all the buildings under consideration. While perfect information gives a clear picture of the problem, it is almost impossible to collect.

3   Probabilistic Decision Making

3.1   Decisions Under Uncertainty

Almost all decision-making procedures involve uncertainty [8]. The term 'uncertainty' implies that an initial state can be interpreted and evaluated differently among decision makers. In addition, the available alternative actions that can be adopted to alter the initial state lead to similar results, and their effect cannot be predicted accurately. The problems of decision making under uncertainty are: the amount of data we own on possible outcomes, the information value, the way circumstances change dynamically over time, the usefulness of alternatives and our own subjective preferences which are vague and controversial [5]. In this methodology the concept of Bayes' classic probabilistic approach is introduced.

3.2   Decision Making with Bayes Approach

Statistical decision making theory is based on the fact that uncertainty in the future can be characterized as a probability [8]. The future outcome of the problem under consideration is divided into a number of states. In the current case they consist of the energy consumption labels to be assigned to the building in study after the implementation of alternatives scenarios. In Bayes' theory, future states are characterized as probability events [7]. All possible future states are declared:

$$S = \{s_1, s_1, \ldots, s_n\} \tag{8}$$

And their probabilities set:

$$P = \{p(s_1), p(s_2), \ldots, p(s_n)\} \tag{9}$$

The above probabilities are the marginal probabilities. For buildings, the energy consumption states are five and the states as they were recorded for buildings in Greece [3] are shown in Table 3.

Table 3. Energy consumption labels for buildings total.

Energy consumption category	Percentage of total // Probability
A	20% // 0.2
B	15% // 0.15
C	25% // 0.25
D	25% // 0.25
E	15% // 0.15

Thus, (8) and (9) become:

$$S = \{A, B, C, D, E\} \tag{10}$$

And their probabilities set:

$$P = \{0.2, 0.15, 0.25, 0.25, 0.15\} \tag{11}$$

The energy conservation actions chosen for this case study are:

1. Constant Air Volume to Variable Air Volume air conditioning conversion
2. Water consumption, ice storage/conversion and waste water facilities upgrade
3. Window glazing retrofit
4. Indoor temperature adjustment and water flow pressure/rate variation in air conditioning pumping/circulation system
5. Motor replacement
6. Daylight Control plan

For each scenario a_j, we assign a utility value u_{ji} provided the resulting state after its implementation is s_i $(i = A,B,C,D,E)$. Utility values express cost or advantage for each pair of alternative action – future state. Information which was not strictly related to the energy consumption or the indoor environment quality participated in this decision making process. The factors defining each alternative's utility were chosen to be [4]:

- The financial benefit on the overall electricity consumption when choosing the specific alternative
- The capital payback time period after applying an alternative

The data used derived after auditing a common office building [4]. Table 4 presents those values for every alternative scenario application:

Table 4. Financial benefit and capital payback period per alternative scenario

Alternative scenario	Financial savings (%)	Capital payback period (years)
1	11.8	3.5
2	0.6	8
3	1.7	15
4	3	0.5
5	1.1	5
6	6	4

Apparently, the higher the profit and the shorter the time horizon, the better for that scenario. The challenge in this approach was to build the utility values matrix in an as objective manner as possible by using relevant information and not pure energy measurements. The steps for producing the formula are:

Initially, a utility index is attributed to each future state in a similar way to the weights attributed in the multi-criteria approach:

$$A \rightarrow 10 \quad B \rightarrow 8 \quad C \rightarrow 5 \quad D \rightarrow 2 \quad E \rightarrow 0.5 \tag{12}$$

The values for the two utility factors (Table 4) are normalized in the range $[0, 1]$ based on (6). Because the shorter the payback period the better for the decision, the normalized payback period value is subtracted from 1. The sum of the two normalized values is multiplied by the corresponding utility index and thus the utility value is determined:

$$u_{ji} = \left[v\_financial_{j\,norm} + \left(1 - v\_payback_{j\,norm} \right) \right] * utility_i \tag{13}$$

The higher the energy label, the higher the utility index will be in order to increase the utility value for that particular pair of alternative action – future state. For this reason, index values increase as we approach category A. Additionally, in (12) a non-successive numbering was chosen, because in this way scenarios with close values on financial savings and payback period can still hold the lead if they refer to higher energy labels. The utilities matrix where alternatives relate to states is shaped as follows (Tables 5 and 6):

Table 5. Utility values matrix

Altern$_j$ State$_i$	A	B	C	D	E
a_1	17.931	14.345	8.966	3.586	0.897
a_2	4.828	3.862	2.414	0.966	0.241
a_3	0.982	0.786	0.491	0.196	0.049
a_4	12.143	9.714	6.071	2.429	0.607
a_5	7.343	5.874	3.671	1.469	0.367
a_6	12.408	9.926	6.204	2.482	0.620

Table 6. Expected utility values per alternative scenario

Alternative scenario	$E(u_j)$
1	9.010
2	2.426
3	0.494
4	6.102
5	3.690
6	6.235

The expected utility referred to alternative j therefore is [8]:

$$E(u_j) = \sum_{i=1}^{5} u_{ji} * p(s_i) \tag{14}$$

The decision will point to the alternative with the highest expected utility:

$$E(u^*) = \max_j E(u_j) \tag{15}$$

Scenario 1 is proposed first and scenarios 6 and 4 follow. The same sequence was proposed, after measuring real consumption and simulating consumption behavior [4]. Simulation results were produced by the DOE-2 energy use and cost analysis software.

3.3 Using Derivative Information

We can get more information on the outcome of future states so we can approach safer the probability for those events in set S (10). Suppose the elements of the 'new' information are grouped together in set X. These objects are used in the Bayes methodology approach to upgrade the marginal probabilities. With the help of conditional probabilities we can express the probability of 'new' information given that a future state is true. These are the conditional probabilities of the type: $p(x_k|s_i)$.

Using the above, we can deduce the probability: $p(s_i|x_k)$, which express the probability of the building moving to an energy label when the specific alternative was applied. According to Bayes' law [8]:

$$p(s_i|x_k) = \frac{p(x_k|s_i)}{p(x_k)} * p(s_i) \tag{16}$$

The denominator is not known $(p(x_k))$. However, according to law of total probability [8]:

$$p(x_k) = \sum_{i=1}^{5} p(x_k|s_i) * p(s_i) \tag{17}$$

The 'new' information is called imperfect information because it expresses certainty (through conditional probabilities) by approximating that one of the future states *i* will occur. Typically, in decision making problems the type of 'new' information chosen relates to future states indirectly. The closer the new information is to the alternatives we have, the more credible the decision can be [8]. In the problem of deciding which scenario to propose for improving the buildings energy labels, we set as 'new' information the very same application of alternatives in relation to the energy state of the building. From the existing observations in buildings, it is possible to determine the conditional probability: *'What is the probability for a building with a known energy label to have a scenario already applied?'*

From Eqs. (16) and (17) we can lead to the assessment of a future state when implementing the scenario. Therefore, the definition of imperfect information can be documented on the basis of the buildings examined in the past. However, this logic has disadvantages:

1. It is very difficult to collect all this information for such a large population of buildings.
2. It is not scientifically correct to use the results of applying a particular scenario to a building in order to produce an approximate estimate of its application to a different building.

Despite that above, we examined how the usage of conditional probabilities can contribute to the decision process. Because there were no recorded data of the 'new' information, we resided to simulation results which when executed (on the basis of the parameters that model the building), provide direct estimates for the alternative applications in the building. In this case-study the estimates were produced by the DOE-2 software and are shown in Table 7. [4].

Table 7. Conditional probabilities

	a1	a2	a3	a4	a5	a6
$p(A|a_k)$	1	0	0	0	0	0
$p(B|a_k)$	0	0	0	0	0	1
$p(C|a_k)$	0	0	0	1	0	0
$p(D|a_k)$	0	1	0	0	1	0
$p(E|a_k)$	0	0	1	0	0	0

Simulation will produce results which may deviate from the real reaction of the building to the applied interventions. Therefore, the result will indicate one resulting category with high portion of reliability, while there is a small room that the building can actually result in a neighbor category. The flexibility of results should be mathematically represented in every column by showing a distribution of the probabilities values among more than one energy categories. Those probabilities (which express estimates) should therefore be less than *1* and be allocated to the nearby energy categories where the building is about to move to. The sum of each column's probabilities must equal to *1*. In the present problem, that approach was not adopted and the label provided after DOE-2 simulation is considered as the only transition possible. This means that abusively the decision process approximates perfect information. The expected utility that refers to the alternative j under the condition of 'new' information is then:

$$E(u_j|a_k) = \sum_{i=1}^{n} u_{ji} * p(s_i|a_k), n = 5 \tag{18}$$

And the maximum expected utility:

$$E(u^*|a_k) = \max_j E(u_j|a_k) \tag{19}$$

To determine the maximum unconditional expected utility for each alternative in (18) the marginal probability is used:

$$E(u_x^*) = \sum_{k=1}^{r} E(u^*|a_k) * p(a_k) \tag{20}$$

In (20) r is the cardinality of the 'new' information and equals to the number of alternative actions (six). We assume that the implementation of alternatives is equally-liked $(P = 1/6 = 0.166)$. Table 8 shows the new results:

Table 8. Utility values matrix for imperfect information

	a1	a2	a3	a4	a5	a6
$E(u_1|a_k)$	17.931	4.826	0.982	12.143	7.343	12.408
$E(u_2|a_k)$	3.586	0.966	0.196	2.429	1.469	2.482
$E(u_3|a_k)$	0.897	0.241	0.049	0.607	0.367	0.620
$E(u_4|a_k)$	8.966	2.414	0.491	6.071	3.671	6.204
$E(u_5|a_k)$	3.586	0.966	0.196	2.429	1.469	2.482
$E(u_6|a_k)$	14.345	3.862	0.786	9.714	5.874	9.926
$E(u^*|a_k)$	17.931	4.826	0.982	12.143	7.343	12.408

We notice that the first alternative would be chosen again like in the case of the unconditional elements.

4 Conclusions

A multi-criteria and a probabilistic approach based on Bayes theory were examined based on various actions on a building. Those intervention scenarios may involve altering the air-condition temperature ranges, upgrading equipment or materials and adjusting water related processes like pressurized flow for high altitude supply, high/low temperature flow for heating/cooling, etc. The target was to examine how such measures address decision support towards energy savings. The implementation of the multi-criteria approach falls short at the following:

1. The definition of preference weights is arbitrarily defined, setting the utility function in favor of our subjective preferences rather than the system's initiative.
2. The amount of data on such a large number of criteria is difficult to collect.
3. The criteria are changed in the same pattern as the decision objective. For example, adjusting the temperature or prolonging the preparation period for heating or cooling water will reduce energy consumption. This means, improving thermal comfort implies an improvement in the overall indoor environment quality, while improving energy consumption at the same time.

The implementation of the probabilistic approach based on Bayes' theory has the following advantages:

1. The system depends on one factor set, the energy consumption estimates.
2. Preferences that determine which alternatives are more useful are not defined by experience but using the utility matrix table calculated procedure.

Future work will try to improve the way of modeling the states a system can result into after applying alternative actions and further incorporate better approaches in order to produce expected utilities in a more objective manner.

References

1. Matsatsinis, N.F.: Decision Support Systems, Course Lectures. Technical University of Crete, Department of Production Engineering and Management, Crete (2004)
2. Hellenic Ministry of Environment and Energy. http://www.ypeka.gr/Default.aspx?tabid=338
3. Center for Renewable Energy Sources and Saving. http://www.cres.gr/energyhubforall/2.2. html
4. Krarti, M.: Energy Audit of Building Systems: An Engineering Approach, 2nd edn. CRC Press, Boca Raton (2011)
5. Schuster, A., Adamson, K., Bell, D.A.: Decision making on fuzzy pieces of evidence. In: Intelligent Data Analysis in Medicine and Pharmacology (IDAMAP 99), Washington DC, pp. 114–116 (1999)
6. Roy, B.: Multicriteria Methodology for Decision Aiding. Kluwer Academic Publishers, Dordrecht (1996)
7. Yuille, A.L., Bülthoff, H.H.: Bayesian decision theory and psychophysics. In: Knill, D.C., Richards, W. (eds.) Perception as Bayesian inference, pp. 123–161. Cambridge University Press, New York (1996)
8. Bertsekas, D., Tsitsiklis, J.: Introduction to Probability. Athena Scientific, Belmont (2002)

Plastic Grabber: Underwater Autonomous Vehicle Simulation for Plastic Objects Retrieval Using Genetic Programming

Gabrielė Kasparavičiūtė[1]($\boxtimes$), Stig Anton Nielsen[2]($\boxtimes$), Dhruv Boruah[3]($\boxtimes$), Peter Nordin[1]($\boxtimes$), and Alexandru Dancu[4]($\boxtimes$)

[1] Chalmers University of Technology, Gothenburg, Sweden
gabkas@student.chalmers.se, nordin@fy.chalmers.se
[2] IT University Copenhagen, Copenhagen, Denmark
sani@itu.dk
[3] thethamesproject.org, London, UK
dhruv@boruah.com
[4] MIT Media Lab, Cambridge, USA
dancu@mit.edu

Abstract. We propose a path planning solution using genetic programming for an autonomous underwater vehicle. Developed in ROS Simulator that is able to roam in an environment, identify a plastic object, such as bottles, grab it and retrieve it to the home base. This involves the use of a multi-objective fitness function as well as reinforcement learning, both required for the genetic programming to assess the model's behaviour. The fitness function includes not only the objective of grabbing the object but also the efficient use of stored energy. Sensors used by the robot include a depth image camera, claw and range sensors that are all simulated in ROS.

Keywords: Underwater autonomous vehicle · Plastic collector
Genetic programming

1 Introduction

Plastic pollution is an ever rising environmental and health issue. Global plastic production had reached 288 million tons in the year 2012 [16], out of which 10% reached the ocean [20]. There are estimated to be 5 trillion pieces of plastic that weigh over 250,000 tons afloat at sea [7].

The highest ranking categories of plastic items in the sea are: plastic bottles (11%), plastic bags (10%), food packaging (9%), beakers, plates and cutlery (5%) [8,15]. "Microplastics" are defined as pieces of plastic less than 5 mm in diameter and originate from macroplastics that have been broken down or are the waste from cosmetics abrasives and blasting media. Microplastics are ingested

W. Abramowicz and A. Paschke (Eds.): BIS 2018 Workshops, LNBIP 339, pp. 527–533, 2019.
https://doi.org/10.1007/978-3-030-04849-5_46

by aquatic organisms thus endangering their health and survival. It has been estimated that by the year 2050 the mass of plastic in the ocean will outweigh the fish [6].

When the plastic reaches the oceans it poses a health issue through ingestion by birds, fish, marine mammals, but also by humans that consume the fish [4].

We propose having an autonomous underwater vehicle (AUV) that is able to plan its path and retrieve plastic objects from the sea. Planning the path and the control of such a vehicle involves the use of a multi-objective function.

Our first step is to explore the simulation of the AUV behaviour using genetic programming.

2   Related Work

2.1   Current Solutions for Plastic Retrieval

There have been different solutions proposed to address this environmental concern. Among these are civic programs that involve the collection of plastics on shores [15] or there are more ambitious programs, such an example can be found in the work done by Ocean Cleanup. Here a 1–2 km circular pipe is deployed, in the high density debris areas of the ocean, to collect and concentrate plastics [3].

Another solution is to deploy aquadrones, robotic vehicles that would collect the plastics. Aquadrones like Blueye [2] are used for inspection in shipping and aquaculture. These aquadrones can also be used to retrieve waste and collect environmental data. Remote controlled vehicles navigating urban rivers have been crowdfunded [21], this project involves citizen participation to identify and retrieve a floating object. Another commercial product is WasteShark [19] that is able to autonomously navigate rivers, canals, ports, marinas and collect debris.

2.2   Genetic Programming for AUVs

Genetic programming is a technique that comes from the field of artificial intelligence, that is based on the biological principles of evolution, learning and developing by using mechanisms of; fitness, crossover, random mutation and such. Genetic programming (GP) is able to find an approximate solution to a problem, its capabilities had been demonstrated a few decades ago, for example, by controlling a robots land based navigation functions [12,13]. The AUV's design suggested in this paper employs a multi-objective fitness function, these objectives can be grouped into two categories: navigation and object detection.

Path planning (navigation) is a crucial part of underwater vehicles. It allows the AUVs to operate autonomously in a variety of applications, ranging from gathering ocean samples to monitoring current ocean state. It has been shown that it is difficult to employ path planning in AUVs due to a high degree of uncertainty in the AUV's movement caused by ocean currents. Zeng et al. [22] also list other problems that affect an underwater vehicles autonomy, such as drag reduction, AUVs skin friction, power consumption, battery lifetime and so on.

Fortunately, these issues have been solved to some extent and the state of path planning is being continuously improved. Path planning has been solved by using genetic programming in a simulated environment. Fogel and Fogel [9] have proven this by choosing a fitness function that is the number of visited sites in a critical time. This of course does not include the constraint of the manner in which the AUV gets to the required sites. Alvarez et al. [1] demonstrated successful AUV navigation after adding an energy optimization constraint to the AUV's path planning fitness function. A more recent example successfully conducted by Cheng et al. [5], using the same constraints as Alvarez et al., also shows promise. Even though Alvarez et al. and Cheng et al. solved this by using genetic algorithms, this just displays that it is also feasible through the use of genetic programming.

The AUV suggested in this paper does not only utilize the proven genetic programming methods for path planning, but also applies its techniques for plastic detection using neural networks. A recent article by Fulton et al., demonstrates the possibility of detecting marine litter using neural networks [10].

3   Design

3.1   Simulation

Genetic programming has been abandoned in the field of the AUVs. One speculation of this abandonment is that it requires a large number of tests to train the model. In the past decade there has been a great improvement in underwater simulations, some of these simulations have emerged completely as open source, for example, Robot Operating System (ROS). ROS is a great platform to develop software by reproducing underwater environments to a suitable extent [18]. Such an example is a package in ROS that is called UWSim that stands for UnderWater SIMulator [17], this simulator reproduces the ocean environment and allows the user to tune parameters such as; wind force, speed, ocean's depth, surface height, wave scale and so on (see Fig. 1).

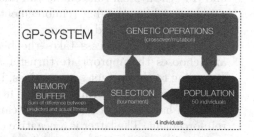

Fig. 1. An example of an underwater simulation from [17].

Fig. 2. Schematic view of the AUV's memory applied system based on [14].

UWSim grants the ability to replicate a choice of AUVs that have different sensors, varying from depth cameras, range sensors to object pickers, and IMUs.

3.2 Model

The extent of plastic contamination is not only confined to the surface, but extends to lower depths of the ocean [11]. This requires the work of an AUV that is based on the shore. When the AUV leaves the home base and dives deeper, it is able to use a range sensors to evaluate any nearby plastics and then detect them. When the plastic has been detected, the AUV moves towards it in a way that utilizes optimized and efficient path planning algorithms, then the AUV grabs the plastic using a claw or by using a similar mechanism. The latter tool then aids in placing the detected plastic object into a container. After the vehicles container has been filled or its power has reached a low threshold, the AUV returns to the surface, by using a lifting bag. The motivation behind using a lifting bag is that it does not require as much power to reach the surface. By utilizing solar power, the AUV would then be able to charge its battery required to have sufficient power to return to the home base. To manage these tasks, the initial robot's design includes 3 thrusters, one video camera, 4 sonar sensors, and a grabber in the shape of a claw.

The model in the ROS simulator combines two interfaces, a subscription and a publication. The former consists of nodes that send information about the AUV. For example, the information sent includes images from camera, grabber mechanism's joint state, position of the AUV and other sensor data that the AUV observes. The publication interface acts as an environment or world, thus it includes nodes that send data to the AUV, for example, GPS data.

The plastic object detection task is addressed by using neural networks. However, the neural networks are trained using genetic techniques. This deploys not only evolved weights in neural networks, but evolved neural network architecture and hyper-parameters required to best tune the plastic detection model.

In genetic programming terms, the goal of the AUV controlling system is to evolve obstacle avoidance and grabbing behaviors. Following example in [12] and [14], the system runs online and adapts itself to noisy sensor data within the simulator while applying reinforcement learning. The algorithm has two main processes: learning and planning.

The planning process takes the best individual from the learning process and chooses the appropriate thruster speed and grabber action for the AUV according to the current sensor values, i.e., the speed and grabber length depend on sensor values that bring the prime fitness value. The process receives feedback that can have two options: either it can give positive reinforcement or negative reinforcement. The latter is a negative contribution to the fitness function which can be also calculated from total data of the proximity sensors. This ensures that the AUV is penalized if it gets too close to an object. The positive reinforcement contribution protects the AUV from staying put by giving positive reinforcement points for moving fast and forward. An example of negative reinforcement is a scenario where the AUV gets too close to obstacles. On the contrary, an instance of a positive reinforcement is if the AUV detects a plastic bottle and moves towards it. After the AUV has received the feedback it stores the input and output values into the memory buffer, i.e., list of vectors.

The learning process looks at all the vectors of events and using the GP system finds the best individual according to the memories (see Fig. 2). The memory buffer consists of the following elements:

$$(s_1, s_2, s_3, s_4, t_1, t_2, t_3, c_1, g_1, fitness) \tag{1}$$

It takes into consideration the sonar sensors, thruster speed, grabber length, and the fitness and then finds the best program (set of instructions) that generalises all the memories according to the elements and fitness.

$$g(s_1, s_2, s_3, s_4, t_1, t_2, t_3, c_1, g_1) = fitness \tag{2}$$

Each individual, i.e., program or set of instructions, is completely independent of the others. The GP-system follows a steady-state GP algorithm that cycles through the following executions [14]:

1. Choose randomly 4 individuals from the population.
2. Calculate the fitness value for all 4 individuals.
3. The highest scoring individuals are copied for genetic operations.
4. The lowest scoring individuals are swapped with the highest scoring ones which are put through crossover and mutation.
5. Repeat steps 1 to 4.

This allows the system to run the fitness function against only 4 members at a time instead of the total population. The genetic operations include crossover and mutation. After the number of individuals reaches the number of the initial population size, it counts this as a generation. The idea behind this model is that it approximates the solution to the problem by finding the correct function. When the best individual is found, it sends it to the planning process and the cycle repeats itself where the best values for thruster's speed and grabber length are chosen for the current scenario.

When the robot has a low battery charge, the GP system turns off and a simple navigation system allows the AUV to return to the home base.

4   Discussion

This section includes the genetic programming system's strengths and limitations followed by future work.

Genetic programming allows the ability to produce computer programs that advance themselves automatically as new data from the AUV's sensors is received. This is especially helpful for the AUVs as GP also adapts to noisy sensor data that can arise from being situated below the ocean surface. By permitting GP to train in different underwater environments, it aids the robot's model (computer programs) to generalise and prepare for a large variety of problematic situations. For example, the AUV can be placed in a scenario where plastic objects are far away from the home base or where plastic objects vary in size and so on. By combining reinforcement learning with GP, the AUV is capable of accomplishing complexed tasks, while at the same time providing a high level representation of the best solution.

4.1 Limitation

This artificial intelligence technique has its drawbacks. For example, when creating the initial population, it may take a lot of generations to create a population that is not stuck at a local minima, e.g., the AUV can provide the best individual that just causes it to move forward and backward. It may also require a large number of generations to come up with a decent solution, which means it would take a lot of time to find the convergence. Lastly, choosing the correct fitness function requires a deep understanding of the problem at hand.

For realistic path planning, exclusion zones need to be implemented, safety and rollback must be considered, as well as recovery and liability.

4.2 Future Work

The next step would be the investigation into the use of a genetic programming system for a fleet of autonomous underwater vehicles. This fleet could be working from the shore, but could also be based in the middle of oceans. This would allow the underwater robots to collect plastic objects and return them to a buoyant station without any human interaction, allowing the entire plastic retrieval and disposal system to be autonomous. Furthermore, an enhanced system for plastic grabbing by the AUV could be looked into.

References

1. Alvarez, A., Caiti, A., Onken, R.: Evolutionary path planning for autonomous underwater vehicles in a variable ocean. IEEE J. Oceanic Eng. **29**(2), 418–429 (2004)
2. Autonomous Marine Operations and Systems (AMOS) at NTNU: Blueye. https://www.blueyerobotics.com/pages/professional
3. Boyan Slat: Ocean cleanup (2013). https://www.theoceancleanup.com/technology/
4. Cauwenberghe, L.V., Janssen, C.R.: Microplastics in bivalves cultured for human consumption. Environ. Pollut. **193**, 65–70 (2014). https://doi.org/10.1016/j.envpol.2014.06.010. http://www.sciencedirect.com/science/article/pii/S0269749114002425
5. Cheng, C.T., Fallahi, K., Leung, H., Chi, K.T.: A genetic algorithm-inspired uuv path planner based on dynamic programming. IEEE Trans. Syst. Man Cybern. Part C (Appl. Rev.) **42**(6), 1128–1134 (2012)
6. Ellen Macarthur Foundation: The new plastics economy rethinking the future of plastics (2013). https://goo.gl/vF2rxP

7. Eriksen, M., et al.: Plastic pollution in the world's oceans: more than 5 trillion plastic pieces weighing over 250,000 tons afloat at sea. PLOS ONE **9**(12), 1–15 (2014). https://doi.org/10.1371/journal.pone.0111913
8. Floating Horizon: Marine litter. http://www.floatinghorizon.org/marine-litter.htm
9. Fogel, D.B., Fogel, L.J.: Optimal routing of multiple autonomous underwater vehicles through evolutionary programming. In: 1990 Proceedings of the Symposium on Autonomous Underwater Vehicle Technology, AUV 1990, pp. 44–47. IEEE (1990)
10. Fulton, M., Hong, J., Islam, M.J., Sattar, J.: Robotic detection of marine litter using deep visual detection models. arXiv preprint arXiv:1804.01079 (2018)
11. Lavender Law, K., van Sebille, E.: How much plastic is there in the ocean? https://www.weforum.org/agenda/2016/01/how-much-plastic-is-there-in-the-ocean/
12. Nordin, P., Banzhaf, W.: Genetic programming controlling a miniature robot. In: Working Notes for the AAAI Symposium on Genetic Programming, AAAI 1995, vol. 61, p. 67. MIT, Cambridge (1995)
13. Nordin, P., Banzhaf, W.: An on-line method to evolve behavior and to control a miniature robot in real time with genetic programming. Adapt. Behav. **5**(2), 107–140 (1997)
14. Nordin, P., Banzhaf, W.: Real time control of a khepe. ra robot using genetic programmmg. Control Cybern. **26**(3) (1997)
15. Ocean Conservancy: Report 2017 (2017). https://goo.gl/v9R5zN
16. Plastics Europe: Plastics - the facts 2013 : an analysis of European latest plastics production, demand and waste data (2013). https://goo.gl/hf6FT6
17. Prats, M., Pérez, J., Fernández, J.J., Sanz, P.J.: An open source tool for simulation and supervision of underwater intervention missions. In: 2012 IEEE/RSJ International Conference on Intelligent Robots and Systems (IROS), pp. 2577–2582. IEEE (2012)
18. Quigley, M., et al.: ROS: an open-source robot operating system. In: ICRA Workshop on Open Source Software, Kobe, Japan, vol. 3, p. 5 (2009)
19. Ranmarine: Aquadrone wasteshark. https://www.ranmarine.io/aquadrone-wasteshark
20. Thompson, R.C.: Plastic debris in the marine environment: consequences and solutions. Mar. Nat. Conserv. Europe **193**, 107–115 (2006)
21. Urban Rivers: Trash robot (2018). https://goo.gl/jNfqbq
22. Zeng, Z., Lian, L., Sammut, K., He, F., Tang, Y., Lammas, A.: A survey on path planning for persistent autonomy of autonomous underwater vehicles. Ocean Eng. **110**, 303–313 (2015)

Adaptation of Irrigation Systems to Current Climate Changes

George Suciu[✉], Teodora Uşurelu, Cristina M. Bălăceanu,
and Muneeb Anwar

Beia Consult International, 16 Peroni Road, Bucharest, Romania
{george, teodora.usurelu,
cristina.balaceanu, ma}@beia.ro

Abstract. Irrigation is a hydroameliorative measure, which involves controlled water management, in addition to natural water, to ensure and increase crop yield and harvest quality. The idea of artificially wetting agricultural crops to guarantee great produce has emerged since antiquity. Civilizations in arid areas of the globe have had to adapt to climate conditions to ensure their existence by developing irrigation systems that give them greater control over farming practices. Over time, due to the increase in greenhouse gas emissions, several climatic changes have taken place: temperatures have risen, precipitation patterns have changed, glaciers have melted, sea and ocean levels have increased. To ensure its existence, the contemporary population needs irrigation systems adapted to the current environmental conditions. In this point, Beia and the Polytechnic University of Bucharest have developed a decision support system for an irrigation system that considers parameters such as: air and soil humidity and temperature, plant evapotranspiration, precipitation intensity, wind direction and speed, and relative pressure, to ensure the efficient use of water and energy resources in agriculture. The decision support system aims to develop a startup command for irrigation pumps for a certain amount of time-based on the information received from the transducers. This order is passed to the farmer in the form of an irrigation report as a support in his decision, but the decision to use the proposed arrangement is exclusive to the farmer.

Keywords: Irrigation system · Control strategies · Telemetry

1 Introduction

Irrigation is a set of operations that artificially bring and administer water on a vegetation ground to help increase crop yields, restore vegetation to modified land through construction work to mitigate the effects of late frosts, or to create a wetter microclimate during periods of drought and excessively hot weather. Irrigation is the primary measure to combat the effects of drought on cultivated plants. It is sometimes used in combination with desalination to improve salinated soils or to avoid salinization of irrigated and/or decayed soils [1].

The idea of artificially wetting crops to guarantee great products has emerged since antiquity. Civilizations in the arid areas of the globe (e.g., in ancient Egypt) had to adapt to climate conditions to ensure their existence by developing irrigation systems

© Springer Nature Switzerland AG 2019
W. Abramowicz and A. Paschke (Eds.): BIS 2018 Workshops, LNBIP 339, pp. 534–549, 2019.
https://doi.org/10.1007/978-3-030-04849-5_47

that gave them greater control over farming practices [2]. Over time, due to the increase in greenhouse gas emissions, several climatic changes have taken place: temperatures have risen, precipitation patterns have changed, glaciers have melted, and sea and ocean levels have increased. Just as in antiquity, to ensure its existence, the population needs irrigation systems adapted to the current environmental conditions.

The automated irrigation system proposed by Beia and University Politehnica of Bucharest considers various parameters related to soil, plant evapotranspiration, precipitation, wind direction and speed, to efficiently use water and energy resources. The decision system aims to develop a startup command for irrigation pumps for a certain amount of time based on the information received from the transducers. This decision is passed to the farmer in the form of an irrigation report, but in the end the decision to use the proposed system command belongs to the farmer.

The article is structured in five sections as follows: the first section is the introduction, the second briefly presents information on climate change, the third section mentions parameters monitored in the irrigation management, the fourth section presents the proposed solution and the section five conclusions.

2 Related Work

Researchers have wholly investigated factors influencing adoption of advanced irrigation technology. Though, almost a few studies have introduced climate variables in functional analyses. Knowledge of irrigation technology adoption has often centered on small geographic areas, such as a single irrigation region. The geographic scope of such reviews can be too narrow to measure impacts of climate. Long-term climate proportions change limited over time, and localized studies may have deficient variation in climate to recognize for econometric analysis. Put, over too narrow a geographic range; potential climate variables do not vary [3].

Patricia Mejias Moreno addressed a survey of irrigation in the meaning of climate change. She set out several levels for climate change response in irrigation and focused the attention of (a) climate-proofing of investment plans for expanding large-scale irrigation systems, (b) location-specific appraisals for the credentials of response options, and (c) the attention of climatic drivers in the water cycle.

The fundamental climate change influences on the water cycle that affect irrigation are likely to shift in precipitation patterns (including increased intensity or lack of rainfall), inducing floods and droughts; raising air temperatures, causing heightened evapotranspiration, increased crop water demand; and rising sea levels, causing salinization of water supplies [4].

It is challenging to associate any single event directly to climate change; rising temperatures signify that the atmosphere can endure more water vapor, providing both for higher rates of rainfall and runoff when the air is steeped and for drier conditions unless. In other words, though overall rates of evaporation are not changing much, utmost in precipitation are becoming less familiar but more intense, and as an end, rainfall patterns are downshifting across the world. Since 2013, extreme drought has affected the Western U.S in California, 2015 was the driest year on record, supplanting 2013; and 2014 had been the third-driest. Somalia, Kenya, and other East African countries have undergone below-average rainfall since the late 1990s, providing to a 30% reduction in crop yields and starvations in 2010, 2011, and 2016 [5–9].

3 Climate Change

From 1950 to the present (see Fig. 1), the number of warm days and nights has grown globally, and cold days and nights have fallen. In most dry subtropical regions, climate change has led to significant reductions in renewable resources of surface water and groundwater. This phenomenon becomes a problem in the field of agriculture, ecosystems, and industry, affecting water, energy and food supply [10].

By the end of the 21st century, climate change may increase the occurrence of weather and agricultural droughts and may negatively influence freshwater ecosystems by changing the flow of water and its quality [11].

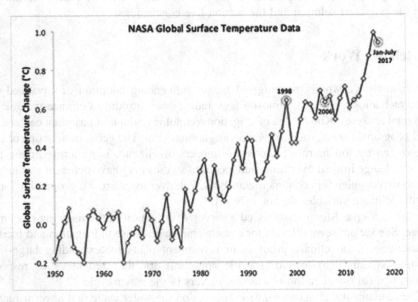

Fig. 1. Global average surface temperature data from the NASA [12] Goddard Institute for Space Studies [13]

The climate of Romania is temperate continental, with four distinct seasons, with oceanic influences from the West, South-Western Mediterranean modulations and excessive continental effects in the North East. The climatic variations are due to the geographical elements, the various relief forms, and the position of the central mountain chain, their altitude and the location of the Black Sea in the South-East part of the country (see Fig. 2) [14].

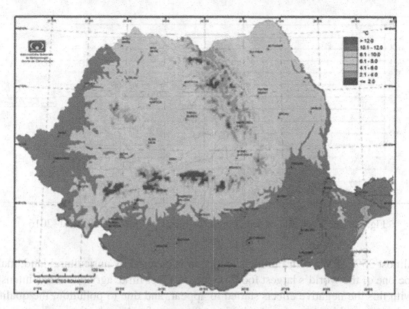

Fig. 2. Multiannual mean of air temperature (°C) for the interval 1961–2016

In Table 1 you can see the average annual Romania's temperature varies with latitude.

Table 1. Temperature variation in different areas of Romania

Region	North	South	Mountains	Plains
Temperature	8	12	2.6	11.7

The highest annual average temperature recorded in Romania was 11.6 °C in 2015, and the lowest annual average temperature in Romania was recorded in 1940 and measured 8 °C [14].

In Table 2 you can see the minimum and maximum temperatures recorded in Romania until now.

Table 2. The minimum and maximum temperatures recorded in Romania

Year	1942	2015
Minimum/maximum temperature	−38.5	44.5
Region	Bod, Brașov	Ion Sion, Bărăgan

From 1901 to the present, the average annual temperature has risen by 1 °C, with growth being observed since 1971 [14].

Also, as shown in Fig. 3, after 1981 there is a tendency to increase the intensity of the burning heat. During the summer of 2007 in Giurgiu, the maximum intensity of the burning index reached 223 units for a total of 61 days, with a maximum temperature of more than 32 °C [14].

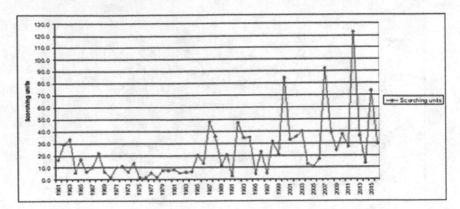

Fig. 3. The evolution of scorching heat intensive in Romania 1961–2016

Almost 35% of Western Europe's land area is covered by agricultural land, making Europe one of the world's largest food producers. Over time, agriculture has intensified and with this the negative effects started to appear, and due to pollution, the quality of water decreases, this phenomenon also has effects on food production and ecosystems, which also affects the health of humans and animals [15].

Romanian agricultural land is frequently affected by drought, leading to erosion and landslides. As can be seen in Fig. 4, areas with high risk of drought are those of plains, the most important areas for agriculture [14].

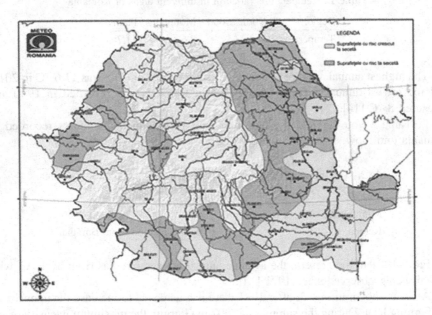

Fig. 4. Agricultural surfaces in Romania affected by drought for the interval 1961–2016

Looking on the Figs. 4 and 5 you can see that, unfortunately, the most important areas for agriculture are the warmest and record the smallest annual rainfall of 400–600 mm/sqm*year.

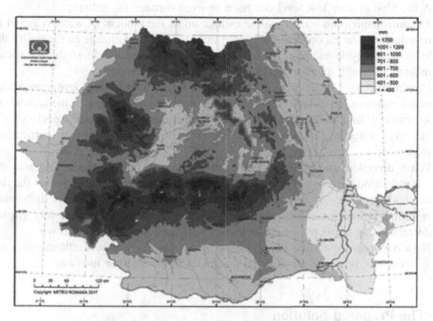

Fig. 5. Multiannual mean of precipitation amount in mm for the interval 1961–2016

4   Monitored Parameters in Irrigation Management

Proper irrigations and measurements are of particular importance for agricultural productivity. Too much or too little water can affect plant health and, implicitly, crops [16].

Also, each culture depends on a certain climatic region and is more productive on a particular type of soil. This dependence expresses the influence of the weather on the quality of agricultural crops.

There are a number of generally applicable parameters that influence crop quality [16].

- **pH value** - a pH of less than 7 indicates an acidic soil. If its value is greater than 7, then the soil is alkaline. A neutral soil has a pH value of 7. Typically, the most fertile soils are those with pH 6.5 and organic soils with pH 5.5;
- **Humidity** - most of the crops are destroyed in predominantly wet climates. At the same time, moisture can be an essential factor for plants that grow best in high humidity conditions;
- **Temperature** - Temperature is a valuable physical property of the soil and controls many chemical and biological processes in the ground. To germinate the seeds, they

need a specific temperature of the soil. If the temperature is too high or too low, the roots of the plants will be destroyed;

- **Moisture** - irrigations are completely dependent on the level of soil moisture. For good plant growth, it is necessary to maintain a certain level of moisture in the soil. A too high or very low level can harm or even damage the culture;
- **Evapotranspiration** - refers to the estimation of the amount of water required to irrigate crops, based on evaporation physics [17]. Climate change can intensify the hydrological cycle and bring about changes in evapotranspiration, so this parameter requires thorough monitoring [18];
- **Precipitations** - The limiting of water is decisive regarding plant development and maintenance of physiological and chemical processes. Regardless of the area where agricultural land is located, water has a fundamental role, and aspects of the quantity, duration, frequency, and intensity of precipitations are particularly important;
- **Wind direction and speed** - Prolonged exposure to strong winds increases the water demand for crops, due to increased evapotranspiration, and increases the risk of root cropping. At the same time, the strong wind has negative influences regarding pollination. Wheat gluten content and protein content in pasture grasses decreased due to the protection of these crops from total exposure to wind;
- **Relative pressure** - Atmospheric pressure does not have a direct influence on crop growth. It is, however, an essential parameter in the weather forecast.

5   The Proposed Solution

Following the study of existing automated irrigation systems and current climate conditions [19], Beia Consult International, in collaboration with the Polytechnic University of Bucharest, has developed such an automation and telemetry solution based on principles of reliability, robustness, and efficiency in consumption energy. The system called SA-TERRA (see Fig. 6) is divided into three levels of interest: telemetry station, command, and control level and process level.

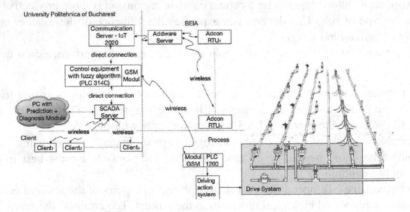

Fig. 6. Architecture of the SA-TERRA system

The telemetry station consists of the A753 remote monitoring unit, the A850 data storage unit, temperature transducers, soil and air humidity measurement. The sensors operate autonomously, powered by a solar panel and accumulators. On the addVANTAGE Pro platform, all measured data can be accessed. The measured parameters are transmitted to the SCADA system via an RTU and a communications server.

At the command and control level, there is an IoT 2020 equipment that allows the acquisition of data from the Adcon server and which further provides this data to a PLC314 programmable controller in charge of the control side. Before being sent to the programmable machine, data is converted to a standard format. The programmable device contains a Fuzzy algorithm that, based on the data provided by the telemetry station and based on a prediction method, sends commands to the process level.

At the same time, the PLC has a built-in GSM module that sends commands to the programmable pump controller. This is the S7 1200 model and contains the pump control program and is connected to an HMI interface to facilitate user interaction.

The system is under the supervision of a station responsible for diagnosing possible defects that may occur on the data acquisition side or the communications side.

The process level contains the S7-1200 PLC and receives information from the control station via a GSM module. The automatic implements the force-based command logic that is built from starter software, motors, pumps, valves, relays, and protections. The irrigation pumps are operated using three three-phase motors with a short-circuit rotor. There is also a pilot pump that can be operated directly. The three asynchronous motors are Siemens 1LA7070-4AB60 with a voltage of 400 V, a nominal power of 0.25 kW and a speed of 1350 rpm.

To start the main pumps, the Siemens 3RW3013-1BB14 starter with the 480 V nominal voltages, the start time of 0–3 s and the rated current of 3.6 A was used. The starter offers a gradual start of the motor starting from the set start voltage main tension.

The S7-1200 PLC was used to implement the AC motor control mechanism. It can work at high-temperature differences; it is resistant to vibration and immune to electrical noises. The control program is performed in the device memory via the STEP7 program.

Motor protection is provided by Siemens 3RV 1021-0JA10 tripolar switches.

In case of engine power, three-contact contactors and an auxiliary contact were included, and the Human Machine Interface (HMI) interface was implemented to facilitate interaction with the system.

Pumps and valves have low power consumption to ensure increased system efficiency.

6   Scenarios of Operation and Testing

Several scenarios have been defined for testing the system as it follows

1. Automatic control of a system of 3 irrigation pumps

There are 3 main pumps as well as a pilot pump used for irrigation, which will provide water to maintain soil moisture to an acceptable level (see Fig. 7).

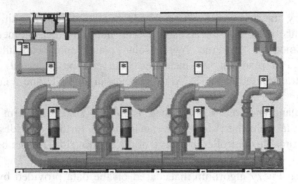

Fig. 7. Pump system

It is possible to make a choice between manual and automatic modes, switching from one mode to another is done by activating a key switch for each pump. Also, a hardware interlock mechanism has been implemented between the two modes of operation in such a way as to prevent possible simultaneous operation.

The control of the three-phase motors operating the pumps is executed according to the logic implemented on the programmable machine. Each output in the automaton is connected to the coil of an electromagnetic relay. On the input side of the programmable logic are auxiliary contacts of the protections, as well as contacts that signal the automatic mode or the manual mode.

In order to ensure the energy efficiency of the irrigation system, the three M1, M2, M3 three-phase asynchronous motors are started in turn by a starter software in a triangle connection. It is connected to the input with an automatic circuit breaker for overload protection or thermal protection. Similarly, the motors are connected to a protection switch. This equipment has ancillary contacts connected to several lamps to signal possible defects during operation.

Depending on the control logic, the programmable controller will alternately activate the M1, M2, M3 motors via the K1, K2, K3 contacts. Normally, each engine should have been connected to a starter software, but to make energy consumption more efficient, a single starter software was used to connect each engine to each motor as needed.

The command algorithm was implemented on the TIA Portal platform and then loaded on the PLC 1200 PLC. The programming language chosen for implementation is the Ladder Diagram.

The first part of the algorithm focuses on verifying the operation of the soft starter and the motors. For example, as can be seen in Fig. 8, when the auxiliary contact MQ0 associated with the protection connected to the starter input is activated, the bit associated with the variable "Starter Error" will become 1. Further, this fault will be signaled corresponding to the human machine interface (HMI) through a message. Similarly, it is also used to signal engine failure defects.

Also, on the same principle, it is checked whether the starter is used by a pump at a certain time, respecting whether the starter is already working. Specifically, when a soft starter command is sent, a timer will be triggered. If the contactor linking the soft starter

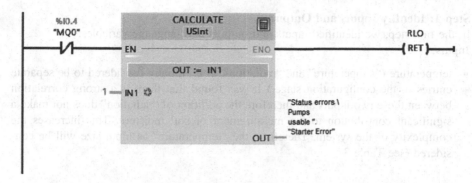

Fig. 8. Detecting errors that may occur in the starter software operation

to the pump does not engage after a predetermined time, an error message will be displayed. To start the soft starter, a hardware and software interlock mechanism was implemented. On the software side, startup of the starter is based on three variables, one associated with each main pump.

The selection of pumps is based on the monitoring of soil moisture evolution. The selection principle is based on the evolution of soil moisture at certain intervals.

Specifically, if the soil humidity is below a minimum U threshold, the main pumps alternate. They remain switched on until the humidity in the ground exceeds the minimum U threshold.

At that point, the pilot pump will start, which does not have the same strong influence on soil moisture as the main pumps, but it will remain on until the humidity exceeds a U threshold of at least h and will enter the area of a desired value.

If the permissible zone is exceeded and the maximum U threshold h, the pilot pumps and the main pumps will be stopped one after the other, if they are already started.

The pumps are also started in two stages. In the first stage, the pump to be started receives authorization from the control program. During the authorization period, an additional pump check will be performed over a time interval counted by a timer. At the end of the time, if no malfunction has occurred, the pump will start effective.

2. Fuzzy irrigation control system

There are a number of parameters that influence the amount of water used for irrigation. Some of these parameters are constant over a season and are of agricultural nature (type of crop, soil type, growth phase, etc.).

For the design of the system, a fuzzy type controller with Mamdani type inference and the centroid diffusion method were chosen. The rule consists of 44 rules such as "if A is X then B is Y", where A and B are fuzzy variables and X and Y are linguistic values.

Step 1: Identify Inputs and Outputs

In the first step, we identified inputs and outputs and language variables.

Inputs:

- temperature ("temperature" and "radiation" were initially considered to be separate entries in the configuration stage.) It was found that there is a strong correlation between these two inputs and therefore the addition of "radiation" does not make a significant contribution to the measurement of soil moisture. This increases the complexity of the system. Therefore, the "temperature" as input size will be considered (see Table 3);

Table 3. Temperature

Temperature [°C]	Language value	Range
The ambient temperature in Celsius degrees obtained from the temperature sensor	Very cold	[0 0 10 15]
	Cold	[10 15 20 25]
	Normal	[20 25 30 35]
	Warm	[30 35 40 45]
	Very warm	[40 45 50 50]

- relative humidity. (RH 100% means extremely humid, and 50% indicates very dry air conditions, see Table 4);

Table 4. Relative environmental humidity

Air humidity [%]	Language value	Range
Relative humidity (RH) of the medium expressed as a percentage [0 100]	Low	[0 0 15 30]
	Medium	[15 30 45 60]
	High	[45 60 75 90]
	Very high	[75 90 100 100]

- leaf humidity (see Table 5);

Table 5. Leaf humidity

Leaf humidity [U]	Language value	Range
Lead moisture expressed in units [0 20]	Dry	[0 0 3 6]
	Normal	[3 6 9 12]
	Wet	[9 12 15 18]
	Very wet	[15 18 20 20]

- precipitations (have a significant role in irrigation, contributing directly to soil moisture, see Table 6);

Table 6. Precipitations

Precipitations [mm/h]	Language value	Range
Precipitation in mm/h [0 20]	Low	[0 0 1 3]
	Medium	[1 3 5 7]
	High	[5 7 9 11]
	Very high	[9 11 20 20]

The output variable is water scarcity (see Table 7).

Table 7. Water shortage

Water shortage	Language value	Range
Water deficit refers to the missing water requirement to have soil moisture corresponding to the reference and is measured in units [0 3.5]	Normal	[0 0 0.5 1]
	Low	[0.5 1 1.5 2]
	Medium	[1.5 2 2.5 3]
	High	[2.5 3 3.5 3.5]

Step 2: Identification of Language and Language Variables

At this stage the linguistic variables were identified and the linguistic values for each variable were calculated (Figs. 9, 10, 11, 12, 13 and 14).

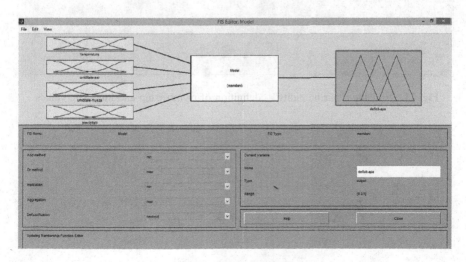

Fig. 9. Fuzzy model

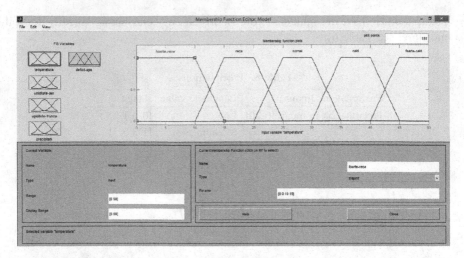

Fig. 10. Temperature variable - definition of membership and linguistic values

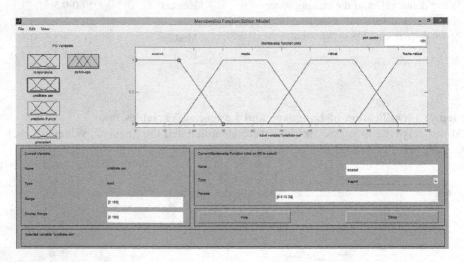

Fig. 11. Variable - "air humidity" - definition of membership and linguistic values

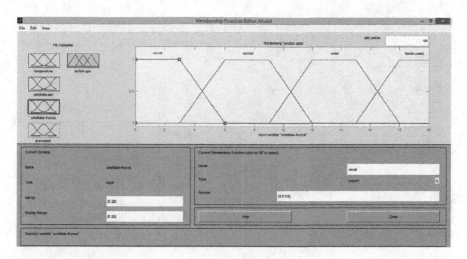

Fig. 12. Variable - "leaf humidity" - definition of membership and linguistic values

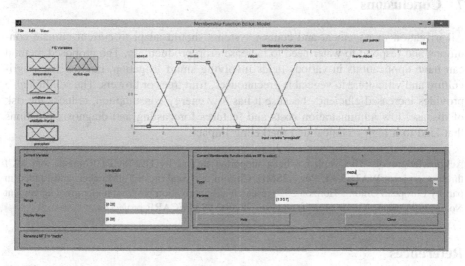

Fig. 13. Variable - "precipitations" - definition of membership functions and linguistic values

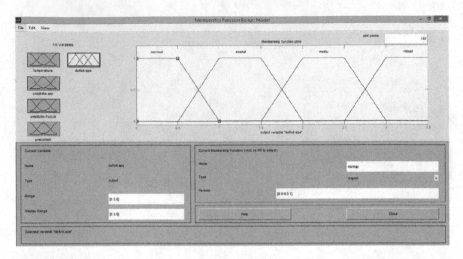

Fig. 14. Variable - "water deficit" - definition of membership functions and linguistic values

7 Conclusions

All irrigation management and control systems should adapt to current climate conditions and respond to water need to increase crop productivity. The proposed method can have applications in various fields involving smart irrigation, ranging from agriculture and viticulture to vegetable greenhouses, fruit trees or flowers. The solution also provides increased efficiency because it has low energy consumption, reduces the risk of disease, low administration costs and features forecasting and diagnosis functions that lead to a high technical and marketing impact.

Acknowledgment. This work has been supported in part by UEFISCDI Romania and MCI through projects WATER-M, Power2SME, CitiSim and SeaForest, TelMonAer, and funded in part by European Union's Horizon 2020 research and innovation program under grant agreement No. 777996 (SealedGRID project) and No. 787002 (SAFECARE project).

References

1. Pascale, S.D., Costa, L.D., Vallone, S., Barbieri, G., Maggio, A.: Increasing water use efficiency in vegetable crop production: from plant to irrigation systems efficiency. HortTechnology **21**(3), 301–308 (2011)
2. Janick, J.: Ancient Egyptian agriculture and the origins of horticulture. ISHS Acta Horticulturae **582**, 23–39 (2002)
3. Frisvold, G., Bai, T.: Irrigation technology choice as adaptation to climate change in the Western United States. J. Contemp. Water Res. Educ. **158**, 62–77 (2016)
4. Basic texts of the food and agriculture organization of the United Nations, Vol. I and II (2017). http://www.fao.org/3/a-mp046e.pdf
5. Global Warming and the Science of Extreme Weather. https://www.scientificamerican.com/article/global-warming-and-the-science-of-extreme-weather/

6. DROUGHT: 2015 water year is hottest and driest on record. https://www.pe.com/2015/09/29/drought-2015-water-year-is-hottest-and-driest-on-record/
7. Water Conditions. http://www.water.ca.gov/waterconditions/
8. Across Africa, the worst food crisis since 1985 looms for 50 million. https://www.theguardian.com/global-development/2016/may/22/africa-worst-famine-since-1985-looms-for-50-million
9. Typhoon Haiyan death toll tops 6,000 in the Philippines. https://edition.cnn.com/2013/12/13/world/asia/philippines-typhoon-haiyan/
10. Burkett, V.R., et al.: Point of departure. In: Climate Change 2014: Impacts, Adaptation, and Vulnerability. Part A: Global and Sectoral Aspects, pp. 169–194. Cambridge University Press, Cambridge (2014)
11. Cisneros, J., et al.: Freshwater resources. In: Climate Change 2014: Impacts, Adaptation, and Vulnerability. Part A: Global and Sectoral Aspects. Contribution of Working Group II to the Fifth Assessment Report of the Intergovernmental Panel on Climate Change, pp. 229–269. Cambridge University Press, Cambridge (2014)
12. NASA. https://www.nasa.gov
13. Skeptical science. https://www.skepticalscience.com/2017-2nd-hottest-year.html
14. Burnete C., et al.: Romania's 7th National Communication under the United Nations Framework Convention on climate change, UNFCCC, Bonn, Germany (2017)
15. Kovats, R.S., et al.: 2014: Europe. In: Barros, V.R., et al. (eds.) Climate Change 2014: Impacts, Adaptation, and Vulnerability. Part B: Regional Aspects. Contribution of Working Group II to the Fifth Assessment Report of the Intergovernmental Panel on Climate Change, pp. 1267–1326. Cambridge University Press, Cambridge (2014)
16. Galande, S.G., Agrawal, G.H., Bangal, S.P.: Automatic parameter monitoring and analysis of irrigation system in agriculture. Int. J. Sci. Eng. Technol. Res. 4(9), 2491–2495 (2015)
17. Jensen, M.E., Allen, R.G.: Evaporation, Evapotranspiration, and Irrigation Water Requirements, April 2016
18. Jung, M., Reichstein, M., Zhang, K.: Recent decline in the global land evapotranspiration trend due to limited moisture supply, October 2010
19. SA-TERRA. http://www.beiaro.eu/sa-terra

QOD Workshop

QOD 2018 Workshop Chairs' Message

The First Workshop on Quality of Open Data, QOD 2018, was organized during 21st Business Information Systems conference and took place in Berlin, Fraunhofer FOKUS. Its goal was to bring together different communities working on quality of information in Wikipedia, DBpedia, Wikidata and other open knowledge bases.

There were 11 papers submitted for the conference and the program committee decided to accept five papers. There were 24 members in the program committee, representing 22 institutions from 10 countries.

The first paper "ADEQUATe: A Community-Driven Approach to Improve Open Data Quality" presents a platform for improving the quality of open data. The plat-form consists of several components supporting various activities: monitoring, quality assessment, data profiling, semantic interpretation. One of the exposed features is the feedback for data maintainers. The second paper "Situation-Dependent Data Quality Analysis for Geospatial Data Using Semantic Technologies" focuses on quality evaluation of geospatial data. Un-like non-semantic approached the authors leveraged common vocabularies and reasoning. The proposed framework was validated using OpenStreetMap.

The third paper "Indicating Studies' Quality Based on Open Data in Digital Libraries" carries out an interesting analysis of digital libraries with regard to information they can provide. This was used to construct the taxonomy of available information and then investigate its suitability for quality assessment.

The fourth paper "Syntactical Heuristics for the Open Data Quality Assessment and Their Applications" is concerned with the quality of open data originally available in CSV files. It describes DataChecker, a JavaScript library for providing data type inferencing and cleaning suggestions.

The last paper "Access Control and Quality Attributes of Open Data: Applications and Techniques" contributes to the usually ignored topic of access control in open data. It introduced the notion of Data Sharing Agreements and proposes a quality language for data quality.

Amrapali Zaveri
Krzysztof Węcel
Włodzimierz Lewoniewski

Organization

Chairs

Amrapali Zaveri	Maastricht University, The Netherlands
Krzysztof Węcel	Poznań University of Economics and Business, Poland
Włodzimierz Lewoniewski	Poznań University of Economics and Business, Poland

Program Committee

Maribel Acosta	Karlsruhe Institute of Technology, Germany
Riccardo Albertoni	CNR-IMATI, Italy
Wouter Beek	Vrije Universiteit Amsterdam, the Netherlands
Vittoria Cozza	University of Padua, Italy
Quang-Vinh Dang	Inria, France
Anastasia Dimou	Ghent University, Belgium
Suzanne Embury	The University of Manchester, UK
Ralf-Christian Härting	Aalen University, Germany
Antoine Isaac	Europeana & VU University Amsterdam, The Netherlands
Tomas Kliegr	University of Economics, Prague, Czech Republic
Tomas Knap	Semantic Web Company, Austria
Magnus Knuth	Leipzig University, Germany
Elisabeth Lex	Graz University of Technology, Austria
Shuangyan Liu	The Open University, UK
Finn Årup Nielsen	Technical University of Denmark, Denmark
Matteo Palmonari	University of Milano-Bicocca, Italy
Simon Razniewski	Max Planck Institute for Informatics, Germany
Anisa Rula	University of Milano-Bicocca, Italy
Thomas Steiner	Google Germany GmbH, Hamburg, Germany
Arjen de Vries	Radboud University, The Netherlands
Morten Warncke-Wang	Wikimedia Foundation

ADEQUATe: A Community-Driven Approach to Improve Open Data Quality

Lőrinc Thurnay[1]([✉]), Thomas J. Lampoltshammer[1], Sebastian Neumaier[2],
and Tomáš Knap[3]

[1] Danube University Krems, Krems an der Donau, Austria
{loerinc.thurnay,thomas.lampoltshammer}@donau-uni.ac.at
[2] Vienna University of Economics and Business, Vienna, Austria
sebastian.neumaier@wu.ac.at
[3] Semantic Web Company, Vienna, Austria
t.knap@semantic-web.at

Abstract. This paper introduces the ADEQUATe project—a platform to improve the quality of open data in a community-driven fashion. First, the context of the project is discussed: the issue of quality of open data, its relevance in Austria and how ADEQUATe attempts to tackle these matters. Then the main components of the project are introduced, outlining how they support the goals of the project: Portal Watch managing monitoring, quality assessment and enhancement of data, the ADEQUATe Knowledge Base providing the backbone to the search and semantic enrichment components, the faceted Search functionality, Dataset profiles presenting an enriched overview of individual datasets to users, ADEQUATe's GitLab instance providing the community dimension to the portal, and Odalic, a tool for semantic interpretation of tabular data. The paper is concluded with an outlook to the benefits of the project: easier data discovery, increased insight to data evolution, community engagement leading to contribution by a wider part of the population, increased transparency and democratization as well as positive feedback loops with data maintainers, public administration and the private sector.

Keywords: Community engagement · Open data portal
Open Governmental Data · Semantic web · Linked data

1 Introduction

Open data has become an important factor in furthering social and economic development [10]. Throughout the last ten years Open Government Data (OGD) is particularly recognized for its potential of increasing transparency, citizen participation and innovation in society [6].

Open data can be defined as freely accessible data on the Internet, reusable under open licenses, provided in appropriate machine-readable formats [4]. However, the value of open data is not realized in its full potential simply by meeting

W. Abramowicz and A. Paschke (Eds.): BIS 2018 Workshops, LNBIP 339, pp. 555–565, 2019.
https://doi.org/10.1007/978-3-030-04849-5_48

the criteria of the definition above. The quality of data that is released openly is one of the important factor that determine to which extent the data can be reused to bring about added value [11,13]. Data quality can be assessed from a number of viewpoints and can concern data as well as metadata that describes the data. Poor quality of OGD is indeed a common issue that has a negative impact on the value of OGD globally [1]. It is this understanding that initiated the ADEQUATe project Austria.

Other research projects have addressed the quality issue of open data as well. For example, the textitOpenDataMonitor[1] provides a comprehensive set of quality assessment metrics for open data sources/portals such as open licenses, machine readability, availability, and metadata completeness. However, it does not provide any means of correcting identified issues. Another example is the *COMSODE* project[2]. The project introduced a concept for an open data platform to foster reuse of open data via enrichment and linking of data. While the platform includes tools for data processing, it does not provide means of 1:1 integration to portals nor does it provide capabilities for users to jointly work on the improvement of data. One more project towards increased open data quality is present via the *Project Open Data*[3], initiated by the U.S. White House. It is a collection of tools and best-practices to provide open data. However, it is not an integrated solution and the results vary heavily on the resources and the know-how of the adopting party.

The ADEQUATe project aims to increase the value of OGD by tackling quality issues of metadata and data and strengthening interoperability between data sources. It does so with a combination of data- and community-driven efforts, including (1) the continuous assessment of data quality of open data portals based on a comprehensive list of quality metrics, (2) the application of (semi)-automatic algorithms along with crowd-sourcing approaches to improve identified quality issues, and (3) the use of Semantic Web Technologies to transform legacy open data sources (mainly common text formats) into Linked Data.

To accommodate the needs of the open data community, the ADEQUATe project based its requirements elicitation on a community survey involving several focus groups representing all key stakeholders (i.e., lay-persons, open data interested individuals, platform providers, as well as scientists). User interface design, testing, and the creation of training materials were carried out considering three distinct user personae to address relevant levels of expertise of potential users: (1) *rookies*, who have experience working with tabular data, but not with OGD, (2) *intermediate users*, with working experience of processing OGD, capable of identifying quality issues, and (3) *pros*, with deeper understanding of data science, linked data, capable of improving datasets.

---

[1] https://www.opendatamonitor.eu.
[2] https://www.comsode.eu.
[3] https://project-open-data.cio.gov.

The datasets available on the ADEQUATe portal are sourced from the two national open data portals of Austria[4]—data.gv.at and Open Data Portal Austria. ADEQUATe imports the catalogues and datasets of both portals, thus unifying them under one platform.

data.gv.at is the central Austrian open data platform for Open Governmental Data and Public Sector Information of the federal, state, and municipal governments and other state organizations. With nearly 20 000 datasets hosted, data.gv.at is jointly operated by the Austrian Federal Ministry for Digital and Economic Affairs and the City of Vienna.

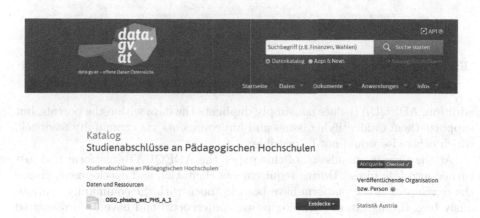

Katalog
Studienabschlüsse an Pädagogischen Hochschulen

Studienabschlüsse an Pädagogischen Hochschulen

Daten und Ressourcen

OGD_phsabs_ext_PHS_A_1

Veröffentlichende Organisation bzw. Person

Statistik Austria

Fig. 1. Integration of the ADEQUATe platform into data.gv.at

Open Data Portal Austria[5] is the sister portal of data.gv.at. This portal provides infrastructure for sharing open data from the private sector, culture, NGOs and NPOs, academia, and civil society. It currently hosts nearly 500 datasets. Open Data Portal Austria is a project of Wikimedia Österreich.

The data on both portals are disjoint on purpose. Data.gv.at hosts exclusively data from public administration (along the PSI directive [2]), while its sister portal opendataportal.at is accessible for everybody (e.g. companies, individuals, NGOs) for publishing data.

The ADEQUATe platform—in comparison with the before-described relevant research endeavours—does not only make use of the data hosted on open data portals, but is an integrated part of them. Both Austrian portals link their datasets to their ADEQUATe counterparts via the "ADEQUATe checked" button, as it can be seen in Figs. 1 and 2. Thus, users can easily navigate between the original data and its improved and modified community version. Consequently, the communication channel with the original authors is kept alive. In

---

[4] Though not in the scope of the project, ADEQUATe is easy to integrate with further Open Data Portals that provide CKAN API, having several functions adapt to new portals automatically, and some that must be adjusted manually.

[5] https://www.opendataportal.at.

Fig. 2. Integration of the ADEQUATe platform into the Open Data Portal Austria

addition, ADEQUATe does not simply duplicate the data within the portals, but supports them in identifying issues and improvements via community feedback, which otherwise would not be possible.

At the time of submission of this paper the ADEQUATe platform had just turned into *beta* phase. During requirements elicitation and development phases the developers of the platform have been in touch with the community continuously (e.g. through meet-ups, blog posts, conferences) and have been reassured of the community's interest in the project. The project members are also in close communication with governmental stakeholders regarding the current status of the project through interactive exchange during regular events such as the Open Government Platform meetings in Vienna[6] or the Cooperation OGD Austria[7] meetings. The ADEQUATe platform is available at https://adequate.at.

2   Main Components of the Platform

In this section we give an overview of the main technological components that serve as building blocks for the ADEQUATe platform. The components of are loosely coupled to allow for the usage of the most fitting languages and technologies for each component and to increase the resilience of the infrastructure to the potential service interruption of individual components. Components are hosted on one physical infrastructure, in separate Docker containers. They are for the most part integrated by RESTful APIs. As there are several components that serve content for the front-end of the portal (e.g. *Search*, *Dataset profiles*, *Odalic*), requests from the Internet are routed amongst components by an nginx server. ADEQUATe's main components are the following.:

---

[6] https://open.wien.gv.at/site/open-data/danke-ogd/.
[7] https://www.data.gv.at/infos/cooperation-ogd-austria/.

Portal Watch – The data management, monitoring, and quality assessment of the open data portals' datasets is based on the Open Data Portal Watch framework [13]. This component automatically performs the following four tasks of the ADEQUATe platform: (1) data download, (2) quality assessment, (3) versioning, and (4) enrichment and cleansing of resources. The steps performed by the Portal Watch are displayed in Fig. 3 and explained in more detail in the following.

Fig. 3. The steps performed by the Portal Watch component.

The component downloads all the datasets' metadata descriptions and resources (i.e. the actual corresponding content) once a week, using the public APIs of the data portals. To allow users to track potential changes and to retrieve prior versions of the datasets, all the metadata descriptions and resources get stored in the ADEQUATe *GitLab* instance: each dataset is versioned in a separated Git repository; new versions get pushed to these projects allowing users to look into the diffs for each individual file and/or metadata instance.

A major quality issues across open data portals is the heterogeneity of metadata and file formats [13]. To provide users a consistent and standardized access, the datasets' metadata and quality assessments (displayed on *dataset profiles*, cf. Fig. 5) are stored using W3C standard vocabularies, namely the DCAT metadata vocabulary [12], and the Data Quality Vocabulary (DQV) [3] for describing quality metrics and measures. In case of CSV files, Portal Watch enriches the existing metadata by generating *CSV on the Web* (CSVW) metadata (e.g., the CSV's delimiter, headers, and file encoding) [16]. In-depth description of these vocabularies, as well as the enrichment and re-publishing processes employed are published in [14].

The predominant file format in open data catalogues is CSV, and they appear in a variety of non-standard variants, e.g. varying in the use of the delimiting character, the use of (multiple) header rows, differing character encodings between files, etc. To ease access of open data CSVs, the pipline aligns the portals' CSVs by providing an additional, "cleaned" version of the file to the ADEQUATe Gitlab repository, compliant with the RFC 4180 standard [15]: we adjust the encoding (UTF-8) and delimiter (","), and provide a single header row (in case of missing/multiple header rows). The improved/enriched metadata and cleaned CSV files get re-published in the respective GitLab repositories.

Knowledge Base – The ADEQUATe platform is built around the ADEQUATe Knowledge Base; a knowledge base that is built on-top of a manually created and curated ontology for the Austrian data portals: it contains entities, classes, and relations appearing in the data available at Austrian open data portals. The Knowledge Base is used by the portal's search engine as a basis for its faceted search functionality, and also by *Odalic* for (semi-)automatically linking terms within the input data to Linked Data entities. The Knowledge Base is maintained via the *PoolParty Thesaurus Manager*, a component of the PoolParty Semantic Suite.[8]

Search – The platform includes an advanced search functionality (see Fig. 4), backed by the *PoolParty GraphSearch*[9] search engine. It lets users to perform full-text and faceted search in metadata of datasets, filtering results based on the classes and entities derived from *ADEQUATe Knowledge Base*. To prepare search facets, ADEQUATE employs *UnifiedViews* (a management service for RDF data processing tasks) [8] that runs *PoolParty extractor*, a tool for automatic annotation of unstructured data with entities derived from the Knowledge Base.

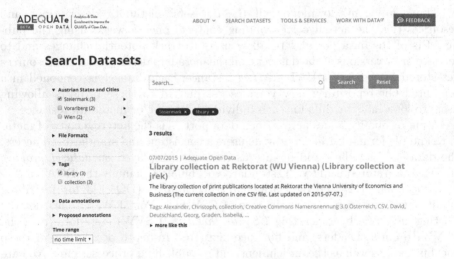

Fig. 4. Faceted search on the ADEQUATe portal

Dataset profiles serve as landing pages for datasets, providing an overview of the content, the quality, and the community engagement related to the dataset. Here users can review the dataset's basic attributes such as the publishing and maintaining organizations, dates of publishing and updating, keywords and description. The list of distributions available for the dataset shows distribution-specific details, including what data quality issues were corrected automatically by *Portal Watch*. For CSV distributions users may import the file into *Odalic* for semantic linking and enrichment by clicking a the "Import to Odalic" button.

---

[8] https://www.poolparty.biz.

[9] https://www.poolparty.biz/poolparty-semantic-graph-search-server/.

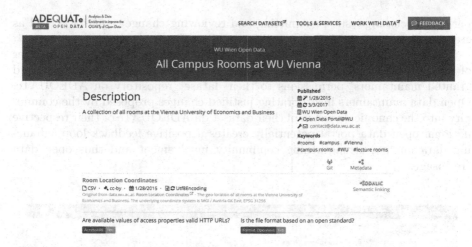

Fig. 5. The profile of a dataset on the ADEQUATe portal (http://opendataportal. pages.adequate.at/all_campus_rooms/)

Automatically generated by *Portal Watch*, a list of quality assessment attributes regarding formatting, standards, licenses, contactability, etc. are displayed, informing users and maintainers of the general quality of the data and metadata, along with suggestions for quality improvement. Under the quality assessment section is an overview of the discussions and issues related to the dataset are displayed, along with a list and a timeline illustrating the history and frequency of changes to the dataset (cropped from Fig. 5).

GitLab – The community engagement and crowd-sourcing dimension of the ADEQUATe platform is provided by a self-hosted GitLab[10] installation. GitLab is an open-source, web-based manager for the popular Git version control system[11] including features not provided by Git, such as issue tracking.

Managing data and metadata in a version control system gives users of the portal insight into the history of the dataset—visualizing how the quality and the content of the data and metadata changed over time and who initiated these changes (e.g. the data provider, the ADEQUATe community, ADEQUATe's automated quality enhancement algorithms, etc.). As per the current scope of the ADEQUATe project changes to data distributions, and dataset forks that are carried out by the community on ADEQUATe are not automatically reflected in the respective metadata file—community updates must be manually updated in metadata files. Automatizing the metadata generation for community activity will be considered for further versions of the platform.

Version controlling also allows users with varying levels of technical skills to participate in the improvement of the quality of data and metadata by report-

---

[10] https://about.gitlab.com.
[11] https://git-scm.com.

ing and discussing issues, submitting and reviewing change requests as well as
creating and maintaining forks, as illustrated on Fig. 6.

Pull requests requested by the community may be reviewed by the maintainer
of the dataset. The maintainer of a dataset is automatically notified about, and
granted maintainers' permissions to their dataset repository on ADEQUATe.
Open data maintainers incorporating justified changes proposed by the community into the canonical version of their dataset on ADEQUATe or their respective
national open data portal potentially creates a positive feedback loop enhancing data quality, strengthening community involvement and thus open data
(re-)usage.

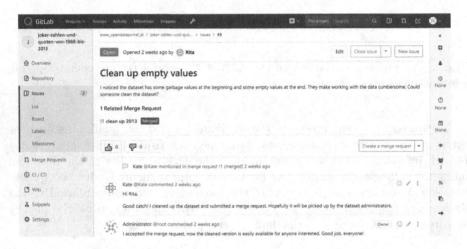

Fig. 6. ADEQUATe's GitLab interface—the community discussing and improving a
dataset's quality.

Odalic is a tool for the semantic interpretation of input tabular data (CSV files)
and their subsequent publication as Linked Data [7]. A user can run Odalic on an
input tabular data and get suggestions for table *annotations* (see Fig. 7). Odalic
distinguishes the following types of annotations: (1) classifications of columns,
(2) disambiguations of cell values, and (3) discovered relations between columns.

Odalic provides annotations based on the *ADEQUATe Knowledge Base*, its
own internal semantic table interpretation algorithm, as well as user feedback:
users may fine-tune suggested annotations, e.g., by marking certain disambigua-
tion as incorrect, manually setting column classifications, or by proposing new
relations.

Data that have been semantically interpreted by Odalic can be exported as
RDF/Linked Data, saved back to the ADEQUATe platform, and thus not only
providing the enriched version to the community but also further improving the
results of ADEQUATe's search engine.

Tasks ▾   Input files ▾   Knowledge bases ▾   ⚙ My account

Classifications and disambiguations   Subject columns   Relations

Column classifications and disambiguations of the values in cells

NUTS1		NUTS2		NUTS3		DISTRICT_CODE		DISTRICT
NUTS 1 (scheme:NUTS1)		NUTS 2 (scheme:NUTS2)		NUTS 3 (scheme:NUTS3)				Stadt (scheme)
AT2		AT22		AT221		601		Graz-Stadt
AT2 (data:44f421cd-ab78-4d4e-96cb-860ea5807acb)		AT22 (data:7d0f3723-2fa4-480e-9edd-ceb28987d886)		AT221 (data:db7166db-17f4-436f-8551-74830da56bb8)				Graz-Stadt (data:a44dd)
AT2		AT22		AT225		603		Deutschland
AT2 (data:44f421cd-ab78-4d4e-96cb-860ea5807acb)		AT22 (data:7d0f3723-2fa4-480e-9edd-ceb28987d886)		AT225 (data:c4e4e1e7-30fb-4b1e-81cb-eec44ac9e324)				Deutschland (data:e2356)
AT2		AT22		AT225		603		Deutschland
AT2 (data:44f421cd-ab78-4d4e-96cb-860ea5807acb)		AT22 (data:7d0f3723-2fa4-480e-9edd-ceb28987d886)		AT225 (data:c4e4e1e7-30fb-4b1e-81cb-eec44ac9e324)				Deutschland (data:e2356)
AT2		AT22		AT225		603		Deutschland
AT2 (data:44f421cd-ab78-4d4e-96cb-860ea5807acb)		AT22 (data:7d0f3723-2fa4-480e-9edd-ceb28987d886)		AT225 (data:c4e4e1e7-30fb-4b1e-81cb-eec44ac9e324)				Deutschland (data:e2356)

Fig. 7. Odalic—classifications and disambiguations for tabular data (https://datagv.pages.adequate.at/land-stmk_lebendgeboreneindersteiermark/)

3 Emerging Benefits

Working with data—open data in particular—holds many difficulties to be dealt with. One of the main stumble blocks that the ADEQUATe platform can support users with concerns interaction with open data. Via its integrated and semantically enhanced search capabilities, the ADEQUATe platform eases the task of locating the desired data from the open data portals. In addition, the extended metadata provides all required information to decide whether these data are suitable for the task at hand, including the assessed quality criteria. With these at hand, a better understanding of the content as well as the inherent structure of the data becomes possible. Furthermore, potential users can directly get in contact with the creator of the data, provide maintainers with critical and constructive feedback, as well as request missing information regarding the data at hand.

Another important area of contribution of ADEQUATe lays in the field of the Open Science Movement[12]. The ADEQUATe platform with its integrated *GitLab* instance allows for the interaction of interested people and the discussion of current issues of data. This enables an increased level of knowledge exchange between stakeholders in open data, and amongst them between individuals with varied degrees of skills and expertise. Furthermore, as both the discussion about datasets as well as the modifications of the data or metadata resulting from discussions are visible to the public, the evolution of data—how data was modified, who modified it, why modifications were made—becomes

---

[12] http://www.unesco.org/new/en/communication-and-information/portals-and-plat forms/goap/open-science-movement/.

increasingly transparent. As modifications are made on a fork-based approach, damaging the original data to the point of irreversibility is not possible. Without a risk of participation and with a discussion- and review-centric environment that ADEQUATe provides, the platform allows for the participation of entry-level users as well, such as students or members of coding clubs, who are interested to get into coding and application areas of open science (like citizen-driven geographic information science [9]) but would otherwise not have the means, skills or expertise to actively participate in the open data community.

Open data portal providers and the main data contributors respectively will also have the potential to benefit from ADEQUATe, as the introduced platform increases the ease with which datasets provided and managed by them can be found. In addition, companies that host their data on, e.g., Open Data Portal Austria can use ADEQUATe to initiate data challenges about certain issues with data, mobilize the open data community and monitor the overall activity around and interest in their datasets.

Finally, not only companies can benefit besides citizens; the public administration too can profit from ADEQUATe. As the public sector has a responsibility to open its data—in part due to the *Directive on the re-use of public sector information* [2]—the platform can support administrations in the identification of quality issues with their data, the areas of particular societal interest in data, as well as towards open science. The enhanced data managed by ADEQUATe may be used as basis for citizen scientists to get a better understanding of policy decisions made by the public administration and thus also allow them to participate in public matters in a democratic manner with direct feedback and suggestions towards the policy-cycle [5].

4 Outlook

The ADEQUATe projects intends to actively involve all stakeholders of open data to contribute to the creation, improvement, enrichment, review, reuse and dissemination of open data. It does so by employing semantic interpretation and enhancement technologies, an advanced data discovery function, automated data quality assessment tool providing insight to the data and recommending improvement measures, as well as automatic data quality enhancement. The GitLab component enables discussion, cooperation, the submission and management of changes, facilitating the community-driven quality improvement of data managed on ADEQUATe.

With increased usability, exposure, transparency, democratization, as well as lowered barrier of entry for participation, and the potentials for citizen science, the involvement of the larger open data community in open data quality improvement efforts using ADEQUATe directly benefits all stakeholders of open data, and indirectly the society and economy in general.

Acknowledgement. The ADEQUATe project is funded by the Austrian Federal Ministry of Transport, Innovation and Technology (BMVIT) under the program "ICT of the Future" (grant no. 849982) between October 2015 and June 2018.

References

1. Open Data Barometer: Open data barometer global report. World Wide Web Foundation (2017)
2. Council of European Union: Directive 2003/98/EC of the European Parliament and of the Council of 17 November 2003 on the re-use of public sector information. Off. J. **46**, 90–96 (2003). https://eur-lex.europa.eu/legal-content/EN/TXT/?uri=celex:32003L0098
3. Debattista, J., Dekkers, M., Guret, C., Lee, D., Mihindukulasooriya, N., Zaveri, A.: Data on the web best practices: data quality vocabulary. W3C Working Group Note (2016). https://www.w3.org/TR/2016/NOTE-vocab-dqv-20161215/
4. Dietrich, D., et al.: Open data handbook documentation, p. 11 (2012)
5. Höchtl, J., Schossböck, J., Lampoltshammer, T.J., Parycek, P.: The citizen scientist in the epolicy cycle. In: Ojo, A., Millard, J. (eds.) Government 3.0 – Next Generation Government Technology Infrastructure and Services: Roadmaps, Enabling Technologies & Challenges. Public Administration and Information Technology, vol. 32, pp. 37–61. Springer, Cham (2017). https://doi.org/10.1007/978-3-319-63743-3_3
6. Jetzek, T., Avital, M., Bjorn-Andersen, N.: Data-driven innovation through open government data. J. Theor. Appl. Electron. Commer. Res. **9**(2), 100–120 (2014)
7. Knap, T.: Towards Odalic, a semantic table interpretation tool in the ADEQUATe project. In: Proceedings of the 5th International Workshop on Linked Data for Information Extraction Co-located with the 16th International Semantic Web Conference (ISWC 2017), Vienna, Austria, 22 October 2017, pp. 26–37 (2017). http://ceur-ws.org/Vol-1946/paper-04.pdf
8. Knap, T., et al.: UnifiedViews: an ETL tool for RDF data management. Semant. Web J. (2018, to appear). http://www.semantic-web-journal.net/content/unifiedviews-etl-tool-rdf-data-management-0
9. Lampoltshammer, T.J., Scholz, J.: Citizen-driven geographic information science. In: Ceccaroni, L., Piera, J. (eds.) Analyzing the Role of Citizen Science in Modern Research, pp. 231–245. IGI Global, Hershey (2017)
10. Lampoltshammer, T.J., Scholz, J.: Open data as social capital in a digital society. In: Kapferer, E., Gstach, I., Koch, A., Sedmak, C. (eds.) Rethinking Social Capital: Global Contributions from Theory and Practice, pp. 137–150. Cambridge Scholars Publishing, Newcastle upon Tyne (2017)
11. Lóscio, B.F., et al.: Data on the web best practices. W3C Working Draft (2017). https://www.w3.org/TR/2017/REC-dwbp-20170131/#quality
12. Maali, F., Erickson, J., Archer, P.: Data catalog vocabulary (DCAT). W3C Recommendation (2014). https://www.w3.org/TR/2014/REC-vocab-dcat-20140116/
13. Neumaier, S., Umbrich, J., Polleres, A.: Automated quality assessment of metadata across open data portals. J. Data Inf. Qual. (JDIQ) **8**(1), 2 (2016)
14. Neumaier, S., Umbrich, J., Polleres, A.: Lifting data portals to the web of data. In: WWW2017 Workshop on Linked Data on the Web (LDOW2017), Perth, Australia, 3–7 April 2017 (2017)
15. Shafranovich, Y.: Common Format and MIME Type for Comma-Separated Values (CSV) Files. RFC 4180, October 2005. https://doi.org/10.17487/RFC4180, https://rfc-editor.org/rfc/rfc4180.txt
16. Tennison, J.: CSV on the Web: a primer. W3C Working Group Note (2016). https://www.w3.org/TR/2016/NOTE-tabular-data-primer-20160225/

Situation-Dependent Data Quality Analysis for Geospatial Data Using Semantic Technologies

Timo Homburg[(⊠)] and Frank Boochs

Mainz University of Applied Sciences, Lucy-Hillebrand-Straße 2,
55128 Mainz, Germany
{timo.homburg,frank.boochs}@hs-mainz.de

Abstract. In this paper we present a new way to evaluate geospatial data quality using Semantic technologies. In contrast to non-semantic approaches to evaluate data quality, Semantic technologies allow us to model situations in which geospatial data may be used and to apply costumized geospatial data quality models using reasoning algorithms on a broad scale. We explain how to model data quality using common vocabularies of ontologies in various contexts, apply data quality results using reasoning in a real-world application case using OpenStreetMap as our data source and highlight the results of our findings on the example of disaster management planning for rescue forces. We contribute to the Semantic Web community and the OpenStreetMap community by proposing a semantic framework to combine usecase dependent data quality assignments which can be used as reasoning rules and as data quality assurance tools for both communities respectively.

Keywords: Data quality · GIS · Reference data · Machine learning
OpenStreetMap

1 Introduction

In the last years, the question of data quality became more and more relevant in the geospatial community. For endusers of map data it is crucial to know if the given is suitable for the task at hand. Unfortunately, map data can be used in a variety of contexts, making a general notion of data quality assessment usually infeasible. In fact, in many open geospatial data sources, even official governmental resources, data quality enrichments are very rare or most of the time non-existent. Instead, governmental data is usually declared the de-facto or de-jure standard for geospatial data and is perceived by the respective community as such. Sometimes general measurements of positional accuracy and provenance information are added as well. Therefore, despite of the geospatial community discovering a variety of data quality metrics which could be applied using a reference source or on the geometry itself, data quality results

W. Abramowicz and A. Paschke (Eds.): BIS 2018 Workshops, LNBIP 339, pp. 566–578, 2019.
https://doi.org/10.1007/978-3-030-04849-5_49

are usually geometry-centric and non-application case specific. OpenStreetMap communities such as the wheelmap (https://wheelmap.org/map/) or OpenRailwayMap (https://www.openrailwaymap.org) benefit from a more usecase-centric data quality assessment, as other aspects of data quality than the ones commonly provided might be important for the communities. In fact, the positional accuracy of a building is less important for the wheelmap than if the annotation wheelchair=yes is given or not, giving its data quality expectations a very different perspective. In addition OpenStreetMap is used in a variety of contexts which are not obviously documented and backed by an official OpenStreetMap community. One example of such a usecase is the usage of OpenStreetMap for rapid disaster response in which OpenStreetMap was quickly remapped using satellite images to assist rescue forces [23]. The authors therefore think that the OpenStreetMap community can benefit from the creation of a general framework of OpenStreetMap activities, e.g. usecases for OpenStreetMap data and the description of necessary quality parameters. In the long run such a general framework could increase the following aspects of working with OpenStreetMap data:

1. Quality Indication: Users for a respective task can evaluate the map according to their usecase or given enough data quality templates, a similar usecase
2. Quality Formalization: Formalization and collection of data quality metrics and calculating tools
3. Usecase dependent views: Creation of situation and usecase dependent data quality layers on the fly for common usecases
4. Semantic Reasoning: Creation of a repository of map use cases in the Semantic Web for the automated evaluation of map data using reasoning algorithms

We therefore use Sect. 2 to summarize common approaches in geospatial data quality and integration, explain in Sect. 3 how we can use semantics to integrate and enrich geospatial data and discuss in Sect. 4 how we implemented this approach in our prototype. Section 5 explains how we applied our approach on a real-world usecase in disaster management and how this can benefit disaster management applications in Germany today. In Sect. 6 we summarize our results and discuss how to extend the approach to other usecases.

2 State of the Art

This section discusses work on geospatial data quality assurance, geospatial data integration and data quality assessment in OpenStreetMap in particular.

Definitions of Data Quality
In the literature GIS data quality is defined in various ways [29] and different contexts. The GIS community commonly uses the ISO8000 [18] standard definition to describe data quality as "Quality is the degree to which a set of inherent characteristics fulfils requirements". Data quality is then further distinguished in the five categories of Lineage [31], Positional Accuracy [10], Attribute Accuracy [12], Logical Consistency [19], Geometry and Attribute Completeness [14],

Temporal Accuracy [7] and Semantic Accuracy [26]. To quantify data quality in the several categories, quality metrics have been defined in either an extrinsic fashion using a reference data source or in an intrinsic way [3] using characteristics of the geometry itself such as geometry validity. Reference data sources are in this context commonly defined as data sources that people perceive to have a better data quality either because they were collected by experts and are are therefore used as a goldstandard even in cases that have not been fully quality-assured itself. In our publication we use data quality metrics of those different categories as a foundation for our situation-dependent quality assessment.

Data Quality in OpenStreetMap
Data quality in OpenStreetMap has commonly been limited to the following approaches:

- Geometrical comparisons of OpenStreetMap data to a goldstandard
- Intrinsic data quality comparisons on time revisions of the same map data source
- Quality assurance by authority i.e. de-jure data quality assurance whereas data is provided by an authority and declared the goldstandard by law
- Preliminary analysis of OpenStreetMap metadata for the purpose of detecting (non-)trustworthy contributors

[13] conducted a first quality analysis of OpenStreetMap roads in England. [21] proposed metrics to compare OpenStreetMap data to a reference dataset by applying feature tag analysis, source tag analysis, coverage analysis and a ground-truth comparison with data about Ireland. Comparative analysis to ground-truth data have been conducted by [11] in several parts of Germany. First work in the direction of metadata and user behavior has been done by [22] who created comprehensive statistics of OpenStreetMap user behavior. Intrinsic data quality analysis on OpenStreetMap have been examined by [3]. We can see that OpenStreetMap has been evaluated in various ways with various data quality metrics. What is missing is the inclusion of metrics which are usecase-dependent and an integrational concept on how usecase dependent metrics relate to established metrics. We hope to improve this fact in this publication.

Semantic Geospatial Data Integration
In the last years there has been related work on providing geospatial data as linked data in order to profit from synergies provided by a global linked data infrastucture as described in [6]. Since 2013, the GeoSPARQL standard [4] allows the execution of geospatial comparison operations in triple stores, laying the foundations of query procession for a geospatial semantic web. Since then several approaches of (semi-)automatic data integration either on a database level like R2RML [8] or on the level of class detection and the subsequent interlinking of datasets have been made [27] in a general fashion and in a more specialized fashion for geospatial data by [17, 25] in which ways to import geospatial datasets of unknown origins, datasets in known OGC dataformats and in databases have been explored. [20] shows other efforts to create geolinked data in the field of earth observation and interlinkage. Additional semantic information

such as provenance information and in [16] first data quality metric information were attached to the integrated data in order to provide ways to select data based on data quality factors while querying a semantic database. While many of the aforementioned approaches have worked on integrating and interlinking geospatial data in a semantic way and even some have integrated provenance and lineage annotations, none of the aforementioned approaches were explicitly integrating geospatial data and geospatial data quality metrics combined with an anticipated usage of the dataset.

3   Modelling

In this section we propose our model of semantic situation-dependent data quality analysis. In order to model situation dependent data quality we propose to model requirements of possible usecases in a semantic way. If requirements of possible usecases can be modelled in a standardized fashion, this would allow a reasoning system to decide if map data and also other data sources for that matter are reliable enough for the anticipated task by the user. In our usecase of map data, this requires a formalization of data quality metrics and situation dependant consistency criteria.

From Data Integration to Enriched Data Integration
We propose a combination of several established ontologies and vocabularies to model each set of data quality requirements beforehand both for reasoning and data quality assurance. In [25], following [17], a method for semi-automated geospatial data integration has been proposed for the purpose of the integration of heterogeneous geospatial data. [2] showed that it is possible to create an ontology on top of OpenStreetMap that categorizes the different elements available on the map. Integrations of further different common geospatial data formats can be predefined using costumized ontologies as shown in [30] and as results of the SemanticGIS project (https://i3mainz.hs-mainz.de/en/projekte/semanticgis) for common German standards like XPlanung and ALKIS (https://github.com/i3mainz/SemGISOntologies) Many such ontologies provide interlinked class structures to Wikidata [28] and provide geometries according to the GeoSPARQL specification [4] or a geocoordinate usable for matching and integration purposes. We extend this integration approach by defining data quality metrics and requirement profiles as described in the following section during the import process of geospatial data.

Data Quality Dimensions and Metrics
Figure 1 depicts the dimensions of data quality we think are appropriate to be considered when evaluating geospatial data. We consider intrinsic, extrinsic and usecase specific data quality metrics to evaluate the quality of the geometry. These metrics include the completeness of specific points of interest for the usecase or the uncertainty degree of geometries in a certain area. Further important aspects are metadata quality metrics such as the freshness of the

current map and provenance considerations. For OpenStreetMap provenance data, a user analysis is performed to evaluate the contribution activity of users and their edit history. User statistics were hereby provided by a webtool by Neis (https://neis-one.org/2010/12/osm-rank/) and provided indicators like for example a user contribution rank, areas in which the user has contribution experience and how often the users edits have been corrected. Another possible dimension of data quality is the quality of the service, e.g. how often the data service is accessible, if it provides necessary formats and comes in correctly licensed data for the application case. Commonly, such information is provided as appendices to web feature services hosted by governmental authorities or they can be evaluated manually using a long enough timeframe for testing the service conditions. Lastly, logical consistency criteria of the current map can be interesting for data quality assessment. In this field several tools e.g. KeepRight (https://www.keepright.at/index.php?lang=de), Osmose (http://osmose.openstreetmap.fr/de/) indicate inconsistencies in OSM data.

Fig. 1. Data Quality Dimensions with examples (excerpt)

Map Change Prediction

In addition, predictive measures can be applied to find out how data quality varies and is likely to vary in future iterations of map data, i.e. OpenStreetMap. [16] suggested, a Machine learning predictor of map behavior could be used as a metadata quality metric for specific events.

Data Quality Requirements Definition. For a usecase, data quality requirements are measurements of certain characteristics of geospatial data, which are supposed to be in a certain value range in order for the usecase to be executed properly. We define a set of requirements as a data quality requirement profile: "A data quality requirement profile is a prioritized set of data quality metrics with preferred value ranges which is used to classify the feasibility of executing a certain usecase to the satisfaction of the usecase definition." A data quality metric is hereby described as a function measuring a certain aspect of the data quality dimensions highlighted in Fig. 1. We describe an example of such a requirement profile definition in listing 1.1:

```
1  {"requirements" = [ {"FireBrigadeMission":[
   {"title":"color",10:{"color":"darkred","label":"very bad"}...100:{"color":"darkgreen",
       "label":"perfect"}},
3  {"title":"Freshness","metrictype": "RELATIVEMETRIC",
   "unit": "http://data.nasa.gov/qudt/owl/unit#Day",
5  "urival": "http://www.w3.org/2001/XMLSchema#integer",
   "category": "IndividualMetric","ranges":[{"from": "0.0","to":"365.0"}],
7  "optimalValue": "0.0", "priority":2,dealbreaker:false,
   "comment":"The freshness of the respective geometry in passed days since the last
       edit.","uri": "http://semgis.de/stat#freshness"} ....]}
```

Listing 1.1. Requirement Profile Excerpt (Freshness <1 year)

Here, the metadata quality metric of the freshness of a dataset is described as one example of data quality metrics for the usecase of the planning of a fire brigade mission. Each metric consists of:

1. A metric type describing the result of the metric as relative (percentage), absolute or within a range
2. The unit of the metric value given by the QUDT ontology [15]
3. An xsd datatype in which the value is to be interpreted
4. A metric category equivalent to the metrics dimension
5. Acceptable value ranges
6. An optional optimal value if it exists
7. The value calculated by the metric function
8. The priority of the metric function within the usecase
9. A title and comment for clarification
10. The uri of the metric for unique identification purposes

In addition a metric can affect a usecase in such a way, that this usecase is not executable if the metric returns a certain value. A metric can indicate this with the dealbreaker attribute. If no such attribute is set, the data quality results can be calculated among certain usecase dependent statistical aggregation methods. In the development of the data quality assurance method with our cooperation partners we found that endusers usually prefer a weighted priority average method of aggregation, as usually some metric results will impact the outcome of a usecase more likely than other metric results. For example: The freshness metric is considered less important for the execution of a fire brigade mission than the completeness of the points of interest on the map which may represent possible rescue targets for the fire brigade mission.

Data Quality Requirements as Reasoning Rules

Requirement Profiles can easily be converted into reasoning rules which classify map data in certain categories of feasibility of execution according to the available usecases. The freshness rule defined in listing 1.1 could be translated to a SWRL rule (listing 1.2):

```
1   FireBrigadeMission(?mission) & hasQualityMeasurement(?mission,?measurement) &
    Freshness(?measurement) & hasValue(?measurement,?measurementvalue) &
    smallerThan(?measurementvalue, "365.0"^^xsd:float) −> Feasible(?mission)
```

Listing 1.2. Requirement Profile Reasoning Rule

As reasoning rules and data quality metrics are applied per geometry, they can be queried by a GeoSPARQL query using a triple store implementation and an appropriate webservice as shown in listing 1.3.

```
1   ASK  { ?x geo:hasGeomety ?geom . ?geom geo:asWKT ?geomWKT .
    ?x rdf:type semgis:FireBrigadeMission . ?x rdf:type semgis:Feasible .
3   Filter(bif:st_intersects (?geomWKT, st_geomFromText("POLYGON((...))"),0.1)) }
```

Listing 1.3. Sample GeoSPARQL Query to find out the Feasibility of a Rescue Mission for a set of geometries defined by a Bounding Box

```
1   SELECT ?geomWKT ?metric ?value ?interpretation WHERE  {
2   ?x geo:hasGeomety ?geom . ?geom geo:asWKT ?geomWKT .
    ?x daq:hasQualityMeasurement ?metric . ?measurement daq:hasMetric ?metric .
4   ?metric daq:hasValue ?value . ?measurement rdf:type ?interresult .
    ?interpretation rdfs:subClassOf semgis:Interpretation . ?interpretation semgis:
      isPositive ?interresult .
6   Filter(bif:st_intersects(?geomWKT, st_geomFromText("POLYGON((...))"),0.1))}
```

Listing 1.4. Sample GeoSPARQL Query to select quality parameters and their individual interpretation

The statistical view in listing 1.4 allows for other programs to conduct further interpretations that have not yet been added to the ontology, to incorporate further definitions of quality not immediately available in the triple store reasoning rules or just an opportunity of interpretation for the enduser to find out about the reason why the reasoner found the approach to be feasible/not feasible in the current area of operation. A sample query output is shown in listing 1.5.

```
1   POLYGON(...) | Freshness | 40.0^^xsd:double | true^^xsd:boolean
```

Listing 1.5. Sample Query Result

Ontological Representation. Our ontological representation of quality-assured geodata is depicted in Fig. 2. In our application cases we include geodata which we represent according to the GeoSPARQL standard [4], possibly links between different representations of geodata (e.g. LinkedGeodata) represented with owl:sameAs relations, interlinks to relevant ontologies like Wikidata and DBPedia to represent geodata attributes, as well as concepts of the W3C provenance ontology [5]. To model data quality metrics we rely on the daQ ontology [9] which allows to categorize data quality dimensions and data quality metrics. Lastly, we model usecase requirements using the requirement profile descriptions we introduced in Sect. 2.

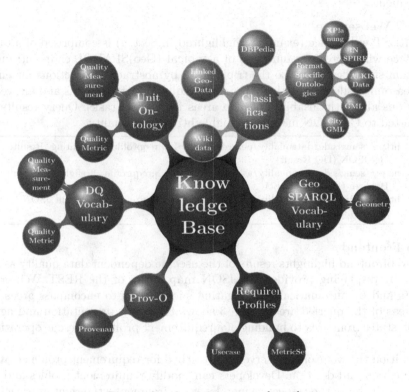

Fig. 2. Ontological structure [1,2,9]

4   Implementation

The implementation of our approach can be divided in a frontend web application allowing to display data usecase dependent data quality on a Leaflet map view and allowing the editing of requirement profiles, a datastore backend represented by a triplestore, a Java implementation of about 60 data quality metric function and a REST webservice masking SPARQL [24] queries discussed in Sect. 3.

Data Quality Assessment Tool and Data Storage
To provide quality-assured geospatial data, we rely on the data import process described in [25], which converts data sources such as SHP, GeoJSON etc. to RDF and provides mappings of attributes as well as owl:sameAs relationships to geometries in OpenStreetMap using geometry matching algorithms. In addition a statistical module enriches the imported dataset using data quality metric functions as discussed in Sect. 2 and saves them in a unified ontology representation described in Fig. 2 in the parliament triple store implementation. Using a webservice we can subsequently include reasoning rules into the triple store, so that an integrated reaasoner can produce reasoning results for data quality assessment.

REST Webservice
The REST webservice (examples highlighted in Sect. 4) is comprised of a query interface which provides functions of a typical (Geo)SPARQL endpoint and in addition simplifies access to the triple store by abstracting functions for entering reasoning rules, extracting reasoning results for certain areas and answering questions about the usability of map areas for certain tasks. Query results are converted to GeoJSON map layers highlighting data quality.

```
1   http://semgis.de/dataquality/perarea?bbox=[...],reqprofile=firefighting  Result:
      GeoJSON (DQ Result)
    http://semgis.de/dataquality/askquery?bbox=[...],reqprofile=firefighting  Result:
      Boolean (Feasible or not)
3   http://semgis.de/dataquality/reqprofile?reqprofile=firefighting  Result:JSON (
      Reqprofile definition)
```

Web Frontend
The webfrontend highlights results of the usecase dependent data quality assessment, by displaying provided GeoJSON map layers of the REST Webservice results and by automatically aggregating such results to encompass areas and subareas of the queried area. Figure 3 shows the result presentation and aggregation states from area to building of a requirement profile for rescue operations.

In addition the webfrontend serves as a testbed for requirement profile creation, modification and deletion. Developers can modify requirement profiles and test them on the fly in the respective map layer environment - the right approach for an empirically driven data quality assessment.

5   Applications

We applied our concept on one example in disaster management to show its potential for a firebrigade planning a rescue mission in a disaster management case. In disaster management, a common usecase is the planning of a firebrigade rescue mission using map data for navigational purposes. We can create a requirement profile for a firebrigade rescue mission map as follows: Higher prioritized data quality metrics are in this usecase the completeness of the road network,

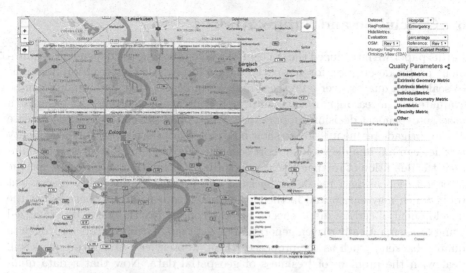

Fig. 3. Requirement Profiles visualized using Leaflet

the completeness of points of interests, i.e. buildings in the map that need to be rescued including important information such as firebrigade:number of cars, hospital:number of beds as well as possibly the building type of the buildings to be rescued (Table 1). The similarity of the building and/or road geometries in comparison to a reference source (Hausdorffdistance) is less important, as the firebrigades primary target is to find the buildings to be rescued and then commonly needs to decide how to proceed with the rescue operation on arrival at the respective building. A data quality result of this kind can have implications for the firebrigade to use or not use the map data or to get an indication in which areas map data is not entirely suitable for the tasks they need to pursue. This may imply that the firebrigade exercises more caution in such areas and is warned about map inconsistencies.

Table 1. Requirement profile description for a firebrigade rescue mission

Metric	Category	Value	Unit	Priority (1–5)
Freshness	Metadata	<365	Days	2
Completeness of POI	Usecase Spec	>90	Percent	1
Completeness of addresses	Usecase Spec	>90	Percent	3
Completeness of roads	Extrinsic	>90	Percent	2
HausdorffSimilarity	Extrinsic	>95	Percent	4
POI Information	Intrinsic	>80	Percent	2

6   Conclusion and Future Work

In this paper we introduced the concept of a semantic usecase dependent requirement profile description for geospatial data and proposed aggregation functions
to scale data quality over a greater area. We indicated that data quality can be
evaluated by a reasoner in a semantic web context and become the basis for a
usecase-dependent decision support tool. We applied the concept on the usecase
of a firebrigade rescue mission to show how a correct prioritization of data quality
metrics can aid in a decision support scenario. For the OpenStreetMap community, the definition of further usecases including its situation and usecase-specific
interpretation using a reasoning backend can produce data quality assessment
tools which may enrich and in the case of machine learning further predict the
development of certain map aspects. For the community those can be visualized
using the semantically driven generation of data quality map layers and/or data
quality backends such as the proposed REST webservices. Our future work will
deal with the problem of freshness of geospatial data. Now that a data quality evaluation in is place, we want to predict if and how the data quality of
the given map changes by using map changes of the past as a training set for
future map change classifications. We think of this as a first step into classifying which quality characteristics of a map are expected to be stable over time
and which characteristics have a tendency to vary in quality. Incorporating this
notion of changing map data quality could be useful for a variety of usecases to
be automatically interpreted by reasoning algorithms.

Acknowledgements. This work was funded by the German Federal Ministry of Education and Research under project reference number 03FH032IX4.

References

1. Auer, S., Bizer, C., Kobilarov, G., Lehmann, J., Cyganiak, R., Ives, Z.: DBpedia:
a nucleus for a web of open data. In: Aberer, K., et al. (eds.) ASWC/ISWC -2007.
LNCS, vol. 4825, pp. 722–735. Springer, Heidelberg (2007). https://doi.org/10.
1007/978-3-540-76298-0_52
2. Auer, S., Lehmann, J., Hellmann, S.: LinkedGeoData: adding a spatial dimension
to the web of data. In: Bernstein, A., et al. (eds.) ISWC 2009. LNCS, vol. 5823, pp.
731–746. Springer, Heidelberg (2009). https://doi.org/10.1007/978-3-642-04930-
9_46
3. Barron, C., Neis, P., Zipf, A.: A comprehensive framework for intrinsic openstreetmap quality analysis. Trans. GIS **18**(6), 877–895 (2014)
4. Battle, R., Kolas, D.: Enabling the geospatial semantic web with parliament and
geosparql. Semant. Web **3**(4), 355–370 (2012)
5. Belhajjame, K., et al.: PROV-O: the PROV ontology. W3C Working Draft (2012)
6. Berners-Lee, T., Hendler, J., Lassila, O., et al.: The semantic web. Sci. Am. **284**(5),
28–37 (2001)
7. Chaudhuri, G., Clarke, K.C.: Temporal accuracy in urban growth forecasting: a
study using the SLEUTH model. Trans. GIS **18**(2), 302–320 (2014)

8. Das, S., Sundara, S., Cyganiak, R.: R2RML: RDB tO RDF mapping language. w3c recommendation, 27 September 2012. World Wide Web Consortium (W3C), Cambridge (2012). www.w3.org/TR/r2rml
9. Debattista, J., Lange, C., Auer, S.: daQ, an ontology for dataset quality information. In: LDOW (2014)
10. Drummond, J.: Positional accuracy. In: Elements of Spatial Data Quality, pp. 31–58. Elsevier, Amsterdam (1995)
11. Fan, H., Zipf, A., Fu, Q., Neis, P.: Quality assessment for building footprints data on openstreetmap. Int. J. Geogr. Inf. Sci. **28**(4), 700–719 (2014)
12. Goodchild, M.F.: Attribute accuracy. In: Elements of Spatial Data Quality, pp. 59–79. Elsevier, Amsterdam (1995)
13. Haklay, M., Weber, P.: Openstreetmap: user-generated street maps. IEEE Pervasive Comput. **7**(4), 12–18 (2008)
14. Hecht, R., Kunze, C., Hahmann, S.: Measuring completeness of building footprints in openstreetmap over space and time. ISPRS Int. J. Geo-Inf. **2**(4), 1066–1091 (2013)
15. Hodgson, R., Keller, P.J.: QUDT-quantities, units, dimensions and data types in OWL and XML (2011). http://www.qudt.org
16. Homburg, T., Boochs, F., Roxin, A., Cruz, C.: Map change prediction for quality assurance. In: The 14th Conference on Location Based Services. ETH Zurich (2018)
17. Homburg, T., et al.: Interpreting heterogeneous geospatial data using semantic web technologies. In: Gervasi, O., et al. (eds.) ICCSA 2016. LNCS, vol. 9788, pp. 240–255. Springer, Cham (2016). https://doi.org/10.1007/978-3-319-42111-7_19
18. Data quality - Part 8: Information and data quality: Concepts and measuring. Standard, International Organization for Standardization, Geneva, CH, November 2015
19. Kainz, W.: Logical consistency. In: Elements of Spatial Data Quality, pp. 109–137, 202. Elseiver, Amsterdam (1995)
20. Koubarakis, M., Bereta, K., Papadakis, G., Savva, D., Stamoulis, G.: Big, linked geospatial data and its applications in earth observation. IEEE Internet Comput. **4**, 87–91 (2017)
21. Mooney, P., Corcoran, P., Winstanley, A.C.: Towards quality metrics for openstreetmap. In: Proceedings of the 18th SIGSPATIAL International Conference on Advances in Geographic Information Systems, pp. 514–517. ACM (2010)
22. Neis, P., Zipf, A.: Analyzing the contributor activity of a volunteered geographic information project–the case of openstreetmap. ISPRS Int. J. Geo-Inf. **1**(2), 146–165 (2012)
23. Palen, L., Soden, R., Anderson, T.J., Barrenechea, M.: Success & scale in a data-producing organization: the socio-technical evolution of openstreetmap in response to humanitarian events. In: Proceedings of the 33rd Annual ACM Conference on Human Factors in Computing Systems, pp. 4113–4122. ACM (2015)
24. Prud, E., Seaborne, A., et al.: SPARQL query language for RDF (2006)
25. Prudhomme, C., Homburg, T., Jean-Jacques, P., Boochs, F., Roxin, A., Cruz, C.: Automatic integration of spatial data into the semantic web. In: WebIST 2017 (2017)
26. Salgé, F.: Semantic accuracy. In: Elements of Spatial Data Quality, pp. 139–151. Elsevier, Amsterdam (1995)
27. Volz, J., Bizer, C., Gaedke, M., Kobilarov, G.: Silk-a link discovery framework for the web of data. In: LDOW, vol. 538 (2009)
28. Vrandečić, D., Krötzsch, M.: Wikidata: a free collaborative knowledgebase. Commun. ACM **57**(10), 78–85 (2014)

29. Wang, R.Y., Strong, D.M.: Beyond accuracy: what data quality means to data consumers. J. Manag. Inf. Syst. **12**(4), 5–33 (1996)
30. Würriehausen, F., Homburg, T., Müller, H.: Using an inspire ontology to support spatial data interoperability. In: INSPIRE 2016, Barcelona, Spain, September 2016
31. Yue, P., He, L.: Geospatial data provenance in cyberinfrastructure. In: 2009 17th International Conference on Geoinformatics, pp. 1–4. IEEE (2009)

Indicating Studies' Quality Based on Open Data in Digital Libraries

Yusra Shakeel[1,2(✉)], Jacob Krüger[1], Gunter Saake[1], and Thomas Leich[2,3]

[1] Otto-von-Guericke University, Magdeburg, Germany
{shakeel,jkrueger,saake}@ovgu.de
[2] METOP GmbH, Magdeburg, Germany
[3] Harz University of Applied Sciences, Wernigerode, Germany
tleich@hs-harz.de

Abstract. Researchers publish papers to report their research results and, thus, contribute to a steadily growing corpus of knowledge. To not unintentionally repeat research and studies, researchers need to be aware of the existing corpus. For this purpose, they crawl digital libraries and conduct systematic literature reviews to summarize existing knowledge. However, there are several issues concerned with such approaches: Not all documents are available to every researcher, results may not be found due to ranking algorithms, and it requires time and effort to manually assess the quality of a document. In this paper, we provide an overview of the publicly available information of different digital libraries in computer science. Based on these results, we derive a taxonomy to describe the connections between this information and discuss their suitability for quality assessments. Overall, we observe that bibliographic data and simple citation counts are available in almost all libraries, with some of them providing rather unique information. Some of this information may be used to improve automated quality assessment, but with limitations.

Keywords: Citation counts · Quality assessment
Literature analysis · Digital libraries

1 Introduction

Scientific publications are the most important means for the research community to communicate findings. To advance, researchers build on such findings and, to this end, cite them [4]. Consequently, especially citation counts, average citations, and the number of published papers are often considered as indicators for importance, visibility, and impact of researchers. Thus, such metrics are used not only to evaluate research [6,11], but also to rank publications, for example in Google Scholar [1]. However, there are discrepancies in how these metrics are determined [13,21]. Moreover, due to the increasing number of publications [24] and technical limitations of digital libraries [27], such rankings can bias which publications are found. For example, researchers often rely on these

© Springer Nature Switzerland AG 2019
W. Abramowicz and A. Paschke (Eds.): BIS 2018 Workshops, LNBIP 339, pp. 579–590, 2019.
https://doi.org/10.1007/978-3-030-04849-5_50

metrics, especially citation counts [9], when they retrieve existing publications—threatening the completeness of their search and potentially missing important research. Still, some information that could indicate quality are publicly available, in contrast to the actual publications, allowing to compute metrics and, thus, facilitating the daily work of researchers. To this end, it is necessary to understand the publicly available information, how they are connected, and if they can indicate quality.

Utilizing such information can be particularly interesting in assessing the quality of retrieved primary studies for a literature analysis, especially systematic literature reviews [14]. While in some domains the citation count is used during this phase [9], there are ongoing discussions and criticisms on how well it represents the quality of research [4,18,22]. In particular, the context in which the research has been published, for example, the year, availability, and publication venue can have an impact. With an increasing number of publicly available information, quality assessments may be improved considerably. While a detailed quality assessment arguably includes reading the selected publications, such metrics can provide initial insights.

Using such metrics is especially interesting, because many digital libraries do not block the necessary information sources with pay-walls—in contrast to the full papers that usually are not open-access. In this paper, we investigate several of these libraries, namely the ACM Digital Library, CiteSeerX, DBLP, Google Scholar, IEEE Xplore, ScienceDirect, Scopus, Springer Link, and Web of Science. We derive an overview of the available information in each library that can be utilized to assess quality. Furthermore, we derive a taxonomy that displays the relationships between the information and discuss how they can indicate quality. Having such insights can help researchers to improve the automation of literature analyses and facilitate the identification of relevant, qualitative publications.

The remainder of this paper is structured as follows: In Sect. 2, we describe our research approach and results, providing an overview of the information available in digital libraries and of our taxonomy. Within Sect. 3, we discuss the implications concerning the quality of information in digital libraries as well as their suitability for quality assessments of publications. Afterwards, we discuss the major threats to validity in Sect. 4, describe related work in Sect. 5, and conclude in Sect. 6.

2   An Overview of Digital Libraries

We base our analysis on nine digital libraries that are regularly used for reviews in computer science [16,30]. Note that we also include Scopus and Web of Science as a comparison, despite the fact that they do not provide free access to most of their information. For each of these libraries, we search for a set of publications on the web interface and investigate the information that are available. Moreover, we analyze author and publication venue pages to understand which additional information on these are provided. This procedure has been performed separately by the first two authors. Afterwards, we merged the results, checked them again, and analyzed the identified information as well as their relationships.

Table 1. Overview of the information provided (●) by digital libraries that may be useful for assessing quality of publications.

Information	ACM DL	CiteSeerX	DBLP	Google Scholar	IEEE Xplore	Science Direct	Scopus	Springer Link	Web of Science
on Publication									
Citations (by)	●	●	○	●	●	●	●	●	●
(Avg.) Citations/Year (by)	○	○	○	●	○	○	●	○	●
Self-Citations	○	●	○	○	○	○	●	○	●
FWC-Impact	○	○	○	○	○	○	●	○	○
Downloads	●	○	○	○	●	●	○	●	○
(Avg.) Downloads/Year	○	○	○	○	●	○	○	○	○
References (by)	●	●	○	○	●	○	●	●	●
Index Terms	●	○	○	●	○	●	○	○	○
on Author									
Affiliation (History)	●	○	○	●	●	●	●	●	●
Publication Years	●	○	●	●	●	○	●	○	●
Publication Count	●	○	○	○	●	○	●	○	●
Citations	●	○	○	●	○	○	●	○	○
(Avg.) Citations/Article	●	○	○	●	○	○	○	○	○
(Avg.) Downloads/Article	●	○	○	○	○	○	○	○	○
(Avg.) Citations/Year	○	○	○	●	○	○	●	○	○
h-Index	○	○	○	●	○	○	●	○	○
i10-Index	○	○	○	●	○	○	○	○	○
Co-Authors	●	○	●	●	●	○	●	○	●
Publication Venues	○	○	●	○	●	○	●	○	●
on Venue									
Acceptance Rate	●	○	○	○	○	○	○	○	○
Citation Count	○	○	○	○	○	○	●	○	○
CiteScore	○	○	○	○	○	○	●	○	○
SJR	○	○	○	○	○	○	●	○	○
SNIP	○	○	○	○	○	○	●	○	○
Impact Factor	○	○	○	○	○	○	○	●	●

(by): May also refer to concrete publications; (Avg.): May only provide an average instead of precise value; (History): May provide a history rather than only the current value

2.1 Research Objective

In the remainder of this section, we present the results of our analysis concerning the information provided in different digital libraries that may be useful for quality assessments. We remark that we do exclude standard bibliographic data, such as a publication's authors, year of publication, and page numbers. These information are provided by all the digital libraries and are already used as parameters to determine a publication's quality. Our focus remains on more specific information that are supported and made available exclusively by some libraries, such as, citation information and metrics on publications, authors, and venues. Thus, we can summarize our **research objective**:

RO We aim to compare the publicly available information of different digital libraries to investigate their usability for quality assessments.

We remark, that some of the considered libraries are limited in the number of results they retrieve for a search query [27]. Furthermore, additional restrictions can apply that are also due to technical reasons. For instance, Web of Science can only report citations for up to 10,000 search results. If a query returns more publications, the citation count feature becomes inactive. Furthermore, there can be differences when using APIs [27] and it is important to consider that digital libraries evolve. Consequently, we provide an overview on the currently available information, but this may change over time.

2.2   Results

In Table 1, we summarize all information we identified in the investigated digital libraries. We can see that there are several discrepancies among these libraries. For instance, most of them (except DBLP) count the number of citations for a publication, while only few of them have other metrics, such as self-citations or Field-Weighted Citation Impact (FWC-Impact). This is depending on the purpose of each digital library: Does it only help identify literature (e.g., DBLP), aim to summarize existing research and provide an overview on publications and authors (e.g., Scopus, Google Scholar), or is it a publisher's library (e.g., ACM Digital Library, IEEE Xplore)? For example, the h-index [3] is an author-level metric intended to measure the productivity and citation impact of a researcher that is only supported by Google Scholar and Scopus. Interestingly, none of the libraries seems to be "complete" in the sense that it supports all or at least most information that is available in other libraries. Closest to this may be Scopus, but it does not provide all its information for free.

The only information that is rather consistently provided is the citation count, partly with references to the citing publications. Only DBLP is an exception in this regard, due to its intended purpose and limitations [17]. In contrast, DBLP is one of the few libraries that allows users to link the search results either to an author's or venue's profile page and list corresponding publications.

We find several additional information that are interesting and can improve automated quality assessments, but are supported only by few libraries. Consider, as an example, self-citations, which refer to the number of citations that belong to one of the publication's authors: They are reported separately in Cite-SeerX, Scopus, and Web of Science. While such citations are important to refer to own, previous work, it is unclear to which extend they represent quality as the count could be biased if authors misuse self-citations [28].

Overall, the results seem to verify that the citation count is considered to be an important information and it is made publicly available in most libraries. As this number reflects on the impact of a publication, it may be possible to use this measure for an assessment of quality. However, there are several other information that are tangled with the number of citations, for example, publication year, self-citations, and index terms that are often neglected. In order to improve this situation, we need to refine our understanding of the relationships between the different information. To this end, we put the identified information from Table 1 into a taxonomy that helps us to structure them.

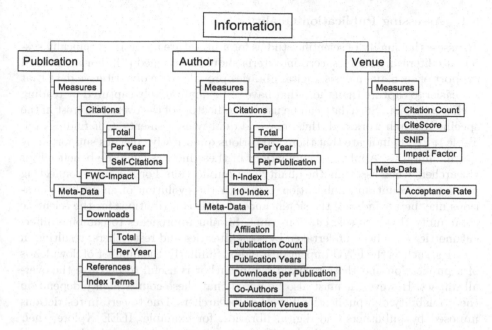

Fig. 1. Taxonomy of information provided by digital libraries.

2.3 A Taxonomy of Available Information

We display our taxonomy in Fig. 1. The top-level represents the categories of information we already used in Table 1: Publication, author, and venue. However, we introduce two additional layers within the taxonomy: Measures refer to concrete metrics and numbers that are computed by the digital libraries and can potentially reflect on the impact of research. Meta-data are not metrics, but a collection of information that can indicate different quality aspects. For example, the list of references may indicate well-founded background, a library's index terms can more precisely cluster publications, and the list of co-authors may show established, reliable cooperators. Again, we can see that across all information, the citation metric and its sub-metrics seem to be established. Still, there are some relationships (and fuzzy distinctions into our layers) between the information, for example, the number of downloads of a publication will somehow impact the number of its citations. In the remaining paper, we discuss the information shown in our taxonomy.

3 Discussion

In this section we discuss dependencies of the identified information and their potential to indicate quality. We further discuss some shortcomings of digital libraries, mainly highlighting the issues of incomplete information. Moreover, we find that inconsistencies of information across libraries makes comparative analysis between them challenging or even impossible.

3.1   Assessing Publication Quality

To assess the quality of scientific studies for a literature analysis, specifically systematic literature reviews, certain criteria should be defined [14]. For automated support of such an analysis, digital libraries provide some quantitative data that are easier to capture than those that have to be qualitatively captured by reading each publication. Such data can be used as indicators of the overall interest in the specific research work and, thus, may aid quality assessments. Our findings (cf. Table 1, Fig. 1) indicate that there are various quantitative metrics supported by specific libraries. Applying combinations of these metrics could be beneficial for researchers when assessing the quality of a publication. For instance, connecting publication count and publication year with the evolution of an author's citations may better indicate the significance of their contributions for the scientific community than the sole citation count. Similar approaches to combine different metrics have been undertaken by some libraries and researchers, resulting in metrics, such as the FWC-Impact or h-index. Similarly, the number of downloads of a publication and those received by an author is useful to perceive the overall impact. However, it must also be noted that these counts highly depend on the availability of a publication for other researchers. Due to certain restrictions imposed by publishers and digital libraries, for example, IEEE Xplore, their content is not publicly available [27]. Consequently, it is possible that a good quality publication has a lower number of (measured) downloads and citations, as researchers are not able to access it.

During a literature review, researchers usually use some common factors for the quality assessment, including the impact of a publisher, citation counts, popularity of authors, and number of pages [26]. Citation analysis is one of the most important technique that could facilitate researchers for evaluating research [4]. However, there are other factors that influence the citation count, such as, the year of publication. Consequently, researchers can define different metrics to evaluate the quality of a publication that may include the citation count received by an author, the impact factor of the publishing venue, and the number of times a publication has been downloaded. Such information can communicate the overall interest of the scientific community and the role of such factors may be considered for the assessment.

The findings that we display in Table 1 show that digital libraries provide several information, especially about the citation count of the publications. However, there is inadequate support for the self-citations count, which may be an important factor that must be considered. Self-citations, if unbiased, fairly presented by authors and accurately citing the previous works performed by the co-authors and collaborators, could be a suitable quality indicator [12]. However, there is still extensive evidence on how poor the citation of previous work can be in the scientific literature [7, 23]. This may mislead researchers aiming to evaluate a research work and propagate invalid analyses. In this regard, researchers must aim to determine relevant references to minimize bias and improve reliability of the citation counts.

Certain factors can also influence the data for evaluating quality of a publication. The publication count of authors over the years is an indicator of their contributions, however, it is also possible that these may not necessarily reflect their impact [18]. In some situations, it is possible that authors keenly contribute towards a research topic through valid and reliable publications. However, they may become less active later on—which can negatively influence such quantitative data. Thus, the metrics depending on such factors must be examined and their effects on the information must be minimized for valid quality assessment.

3.2 Dependencies of Information

The open data supported by various digital libraries may provide an indication of the significance of a research work. However, we must also analyze the usability of available information for the quality assessment. As we mentioned earlier, the most consistent information that libraries support are the citation counts for a publication. Still, advanced citation metrics for authors and publishing venues are only provided by few libraries. The quality assessment criteria that researchers usually define to perform the evaluation are based on the cumulative effect of the authors, publishing venues, and publications.

Citation metrics that measure the influence of individual researchers and authors, such as h-index and i10-index, are also important information useful to assess a publication. It is evident in Table 1 that ACM DL, Google Scholar, IEEE Xplore, Scopus, and Web of Science support several useful items of information regarding the authors. In contrast, while being popular digital libraries in the field of computer science, CiteSeerX, ScienceDirect, and Springer Link lack the support of such features. These factors are a good indicator of the author's credibility and the reliability of the performed research. Furthermore, meta-data of authors, such as their affiliation history, number of downloads and citations received per publication, can also reflect quality. These significant aspects represent the expertise of an author regarding the topic and how well their work is able to capture the attention of the audience.

Moreover, digital libraries may support features that allow users to obtain an understanding regarding the impact of publishing venues. Through our analysis, we conclude that there is inadequate, or no support at all, for information regarding publication venues across digital libraries (except Scopus). Although, it is partially possible to assess articles based on the publication type, for instance, journal papers are often considered to have a greater impact compared to conference and workshop proceedings or parts of a book. However, to improve the evaluation, additional information, such as, impact factor, SNIP, and acceptance rate, are useful. These information represent the importance and standard of a publishing venue, thus, supporting the quality assessment of publications.

3.3 Incomplete Data

The digital libraries we investigated are commonly used by scientific researchers to retrieve promising publications. However, during our investigation, we realized that information of the unique parameters are not always provided for all publications. The probability of incomplete data hamper the analysis even if only a single digital library is being examined [27]. For example, if the acceptance rate is under consideration for determining the quality and is missing for any publication, it would become unreasonable to investigate this parameter completely. Thus, developers of digital libraries must ensure completeness of the data provided to the users, allowing them to perform valid quality evaluations.

Similarly, it is also possible that the information about the author in some libraries, such as, Google Scholar, is missing. Due to such limitations, an evaluation based on data that is missing for some results makes it challenging to perform automated analyses. Similarly, only few libraries collect information on venues or connect them. In particular, there are often incomplete information, for instance, on acceptance rates or the proceedings series. The latter prevents time series assessments of conferences, as the publications are not linked to each other. We also realized that the computed metrics and meta-data provided by digital libraries are solely based on the content present in this database. Due to variations in the coverage of publications across digital libraries, for example, Google Scholar has a larger coverage compared to Scopus, using them in isolation does threaten consistency and completeness.

3.4   Uncertain Parameters

Generally, the citation statistics provided by libraries are based on the scholarly content available in the specific library's database itself. Thus, overview libraries, such as Google Scholar, may be better sources for citation counts as they provide an overall count of a publication. While using most of the other libraries, the analysis of this parameter may lead to an incomplete result, as the counts are confined within a certain database only.

Furthermore, the author statistics are often only consistent in libraries if the authors maintain their profiles in each library. Thus, such information may be insufficient or not available for other authors without a profile. To obtain certain interpretation of the information metrics provided by digital libraries, it must be clearly stated which parameters are under observation.

3.5   Inconsistent Data

Based on our findings in Table 1, we notice the inconsistency of parameters supported by different digital libraries. Assessing the quality of publications obtained from a number of libraries for any literature analysis becomes quite challenging, or even impossible, due to inconsistent information provided. For example, analyzing the publishing venue is only possible by using Scopus, as the rest of the digital libraries have limited or even no support for such features.

The inconsistency in the features supported by different digital libraries is a limitation for automated quality assessments. For instance, the same search query may not be reused in different libraries, due to missing search fields [27].

Thus, to overcome this problem, the support for significant parameters that reflect quality must be enabled across libraries.

3.6 Indicating a Publication's Quality

The research metrics can be used inappropriately: Using one metric in isolation may lead to undesirable outcomes. Thus, using multiple evaluation metrics based on the different types of measurements, such as, document, authors, and venues, is helpful. For example, the author's measures and meta-data along with the document metrics could be used to indicate the credibility of a publication. Thus, the identified information metrics can be useful to answer important questions, despite their limitations:

- How credible are the findings of a study regarding a research topic?
- What is the impact of a study on the overall research being performed?
- How relevant is a certain publication in a specific research domain?

Overall, we argue that using multiple metrics to assess the quality of literature is beneficial—at least improving over the citation count as a metric. A combination of such information provides a clearer understanding of the significance of research.

3.7 Limitation of Using Meta-information

On a final note of our discussion, we want to emphasize that a sole automated quality assessment based on meta-information is usually not feasible. It can help to indicate important and reliable research, helping to reduce the set of publications. However, only by carefully reading a publication, researchers can assess its relevance, importance, and quality. The purpose of automating such analyses is to facilitate the time-consuming and effort-full process of literature analysis, especially in the context of systematic literature reviews.

4   Threats to Validity

We see the following three major issues that may threaten the validity of our results: First, we focused on a subset of all available digital libraries. However, we relied on the arguably most important ones for software engineering, reducing this threat. Moreover, our research goal is to assess the available unique information (other than the standard bibliographic meta-data, such as, year of publication) and their suitability for quality assessments. Thus, we may have missed some information, but we arguably captured the most regular ones and our discussions on their suitability are not threatened.

Second, we derived all information and discussed them by ourselves. Consequently, other researchers may face more access restrictions (e.g., for Scopus and Web of Science), which limits the availability of these information. While our focus is on the openly available data (e.g., ACM Digital Library, DBLP, IEEE

Xplore, and Google Scholar), we used such libraries as references. Thus, other researchers may come to different conclusions, depending on their access restrictions, the considered subject systems, and implications they derive. However, we carefully described our procedure and derived our results with caution, meaning that they can be reproduced by others.

Third, digital libraries evolve over time, with a prominent example being CiteSeer's update to CiteSeerX [8,20,25]. Consequently, the available information may change over time, making our results obsolete. Of particular interest may be the extension with further metrics or the consolidation of digital libraries into single repositories—similar to Scopus, DBLP, and Google Scholar— to solve technical issues [27]. While we cannot overcome this threat, capturing the state-of-the-art is important to investigate the evolution of information in digital libraries. Additionally, several pieces of information are likely to be always relevant, for example, the citation count.

5   Related Work

Concerning related work, we are aware of several works that are discussing the suitability of different publication metrics [2,3,29]. Mostly discussed may be the citation count and its meaning [1,15,21], with particular attention being paid to self-citations [12,28]. Other works focus on the evolution [8,20,25], overlap [5,19], and technical issues [10,27] of digital libraries. Still, none of these papers is based on an analytical comparison of established digital libraries, except for Neuhaus and Daniel [21]. Thus, this work may be the closest to ours, but does only focus on the search functionalities of the considered libraries. In contrast to existing works, we are focusing on—especially publicly available—information that can be used to assess the quality of publications. We are not aware of a similar overview and taxonomy as the one we derived.

6   Conclusion and Future Work

In this paper, we provide an overview of the available information in various digital libraries that can support the quality assessment of scientific publications. We present a first insight through our analysis and aim to continue further research in this regard. Our investigation shows that there are some useful features, such as, self-citation count and unified indexing, that are still not supported by all libraries. As indicated in previous works, the citation count and its subsumed metrics (e.g., self-citations, citations per year) represents an established metric and can be useful—if considered with care. Some other information can also be useful and assist quality assessments, in particular aiming to provide automation based on open data. We believe that further analysis and tooling to assess quality using publicly available information can have several benefits, for example:

- Reduce the necessary time to analyze a large set of publications, as is necessary for literature analyses.

- Improve the ranking of publications to not only rely on citations and, thus, identify potentially more relevant works.
- Help researchers to find publications that are most suitable for their needs, for example, if they aim to explore a new research area.
- Potentially extend the search capabilities of digital libraries to allow for more fine-grained searches.

To this end, we aim to extend our research to improve our understanding regarding the connection between the different information and quality of publications.

In the future, we plan to evaluate different metrics to interpret the quality of scientific research works. For the current paper, we mainly focused on highlighting the support for certain features of various commonly used digital libraries. The results will provide the basis for our research, allowing us to scope automated quality assessments. Furthermore, we aim to explore how well these information can support and guide systematic literature reviews, for which some approaches on automated quality assessment have been proposed [26].

Acknowledgments. This research is supported by the DAAD STIBET Matching Funds grant.

References

1. Beel, J., Gipp, B.: Google Scholar's ranking algorithm: the impact of citation counts (an empirical study). In: International Conference on Research Challenges in Information Systems (RCIS), pp. 439–446 (2009)
2. Bergstrom, C.T., West, J.D., Wiseman, M.A.: The eigenfactor^{TM} metrics. J. Neurosci. **28**(45), 11433–11434 (2008)
3. Bornmann, L., Daniel, H.D.: What do we know about the h index? J. Assoc. Inf. Sci. Technol. **58**(9), 1381–1385 (2007)
4. Bornmann, L., Schier, H., Marx, W., Daniel, H.D.: What factors determine citation counts of publications in chemistry besides their quality? J. Inf. **6**(1), 11–18 (2012)
5. Brophy, J., Bawden, D.: Is Google enough? Comparison of an Internet search engine with academic library resources. In: Aslib Proceedings, vol. 57, no. 6, pp. 498–512 (2005)
6. Daniel, H.D.: Publications as a measure of scientific advancement and of scientists' productivity. Learn. Publ. **18**(2), 143–148 (2005)
7. Giannakakis, I.A., Haidich, A.B., Contopoulos-Ioannidis, D.G., Papanikolaou, G.N., Baltogianni, M.S., Ioannidis, J.P.A.: Citation of randomized evidence in support of guidelines of therapeutic and preventive interventions. J. Clin. Epidemiol. **55**(6), 545–555 (2002)
8. Giles, C.L.: The future of citeseer: citeseer^x. In: Fürnkranz, J., Scheffer, T., Spiliopoulou, M. (eds.) ECML 2006. LNCS (LNAI), vol. 4212, p. 2. Springer, Heidelberg (2006). https://doi.org/10.1007/11871842_2
9. Harnad, S.: Open access scientometrics and the UK research assessment exercise. In: Conference of the International Society for Scientometrics and Informetrics, pp. 27–33 (2007)
10. Harter, S.P.: Scholarly communication and the digital library: problems and issues. J. Digital Inf. **1**(1), 147–156 (2006)

11. Hemlin, S.: Research on research evaluation. Soc. Epistemology **10**(2), 209–250 (1996)
12. Ioannidis, J.P.A.: A generalized view of self-citation: direct, co-author, collaborative, and coercive induced self-citation. J. Psychosom. Res. **78**(1), 7–11 (2015)
13. Jacso, P.: As we may search - comparison of major features of the web of science, scopus, and google scholar citation-based and citation-enhanced databases. Curr. Sci. **89**(9), 1537–1547 (2005)
14. Kitchenham, B.A., Charters, S.: Guidelines for performing systematic literature reviews in software engineering. Technical report, Keele University and University of Durham (2007)
15. Kulkarni, A.V., Aziz, B., Shams, I., Busse, J.W.: CoLus: Comparisons of citations in web of science, scopus, and Google Scholar for articles published in general medical journals. JAMA: J. Am. Med. Assoc. **302**(10), 1092–1096 (2009)
16. Lausberger, C.: Konzeption von Suchprozessen und Suchstrategien für systematische Literatur Reviews. Master's thesis, University of Magdeburg, German (2017)
17. Ley, M.: DBLP—some lessons learned. Proc. VLDB Endowment **2**(2), 1493–1500 (2009)
18. Lindsey, D.: Using citation counts as a measure of quality in science measuring what's measurable rather than what's valid. Scientometrics **15**(3–4), 189–203 (1989)
19. Meier, J.J., Conkling, T.W.: Google Scholar's coverage of the engineering literature: an empirical study. J. Acad. Libr. **34**(3), 196–201 (2008)
20. Meyyappan, N., Chowdhury, G.G., Foo, S.: A review of the status of 20 digital libraries. J. Inf. Sci. **26**(5), 337–355 (2000)
21. Neuhaus, C., Daniel, H.D.: Data sources for performing citation analysis: an overview. J. Doc. **64**(2), 193–210 (2008)
22. Phelan, T.J.: A compendium of issues for citation analysis. Scientometrics **45**(1), 117–136 (1999)
23. Robinson, K.A., Goodman, S.: A systematic examination of the citation of prior research in reports of randomized controlled trials. Ann. Intern. Med. **154**(1), 50–55 (2011)
24. Schröter, I., Krüger, J., Ludwig, P., Thiel, M., Nürnberger,A., Leich, T.: Identifying innovative documents: quo vadis? In: International Conference on Enterprise Information Systems (ICEIS), pp.653–658. ScitePress (2017)
25. Schwartz, C.: Digital libraries: an overview. J. Acad. Libr. **26**(6), 385–393 (2000)
26. Shakeel, Y.: Supporting quality assessment in systematic literature reviews. Master's thesis, University of Magdeburg (2017)
27. Shakeel, Y., et al.: (Automated) literature analysis - threats and experiences. In: International Workshop on Software Engineering for Science (SE4Science), pp. 20–27. ACM (2018)
28. Thijs, B., Glänzel, W.: The influence of author self-citations on bibliometric meso-indicators. The case of European Universities. Scientometrics **66**(1), 71–80 (2006)
29. Walter, G., Bloch, S., Hunt, G., Fisher, K.: Counting on citations: a flawed way to measure quality. Med. J. Australia **178**(6), 280–281 (2003)
30. Zhang, H., Ali Babar, M.: On searching relevant studies in software engineering. In: International Conference on Evaluation and Assessment in Software Engineering (EASE), pp. 111–120. BCS Learning & Development Ltd. (2010)

Syntactical Heuristics for the Open Data Quality Assessment and Their Applications

Donato Pirozzi[✉] and Vittorio Scarano

Dipartimento di Informatica, Universtà degli Studi di Salerno,
Fisciano, Salerno, Italy
dpirozzi@unisa.it, vitsca@dia.unisa.it

Abstract. Open Government Data are valuable initiatives in favour of transparency, accountability, and openness. The expectation is to increase participation by engaging citizens, non-profit organisations, and companies in reusing Open Data (OD). A potential barrier in the exploitation of OD and engagement of the target audience is the low quality of available datasets [3,14,16]. Non-technical consumers are often unaware that data could have potential quality issues, taking for grant that datasets can be used immediately without any further manipulation. In reality, in order to reuse data, for instance to create visualisations, they need to perform a data clean, which requires time, resources, and proper skills. This leads to a reduced chance to involve citizens.

This paper tackles the quality barrier of raw tabular datasets (i.e. CSV), a popular format (Tim-Berners Lee tree-stars) for Governmental Open Data. The objective is to increase awareness and provide support in data cleaning operations to both PAs to produce better quality Open Data and non-technical data consumers to reuse datasets. DataChecker is an open source and modular JavaScript library shared with community and available on GitHub that takes in input a tabular dataset and generate a machine-readable report based on the data type inferencing (a data profiling technique). Based on it the Social Platform for Open Data (SPOD) provides quality cleaning suggestions to both PAs and end-users.

Keywords: Open data · Quality assessment · Type inferencing

1 Introduction

During the G8 summit in 2013, member countries signed the G8 Open Data Charter [21], an agreement that officially recognises the importance of OD in order to increase transparency, accountability [5], and participation by civil society. The agreement evolved around the commitment on five core principles. A principle of "releasing open data by default", in which the key term *open* means that "anyone can freely access, use, modify, and share data for any purpose" [22].

© Springer Nature Switzerland AG 2019
W. Abramowicz and A. Paschke (Eds.): BIS 2018 Workshops, LNBIP 339, pp. 591–602, 2019.
https://doi.org/10.1007/978-3-030-04849-5_51

It means that governments implement OD policies, releasing all data under an open license (legally open [14]) unless there are security or privacy concerns, in non-proprietary and machine-readable formats (technically open [14]), following principles of *"ensuring high quality"* and *"making data usable by all"*.

As consequence, public agencies (PAs) started to release a large amount of data with open license on their portals. Barriers in accessing OD exists, which limit the success of these initiatives. Among the barriers reported in literature, there is the concern about the Open Data quality. The Open Data Goldbook [14] by the European Data Portal (EDP) reports two important barriers: data is not sufficiently accurate and it will cost too much to transform the data to a standard format. The Open Data Barometer found that *"government data is typically incomplete and low quality"* [16]. The motivation is due to the fact that *"data catalogues are manually fed"* [16] due to the informal data management. These barriers about the quality make hard and costly to use datasets. For example, in order to visualise a low quality dataset, it must be cleaned (e.g., remove characters from numerical values), which requires data skills and time. It is an important message for PAs to publish datasets with a better quality in order to reduce the re-use costs [8] and engage citizens.

The research question of this paper is *"how does the open data quality assessment can support data producers in improving the quality of three-stars data they publish as well as data consumers in exploiting three-stars open data?"*.

The paper approaches the quality assessment along two ways: PAs that need to produce open data with a higher quality to reduce the cost of their use, and the data consumers (e.g., citizens, non-profit organisations, and so on) that need to use the data and be aware of their quality. It is worthwhile to mention a typical situation of the second scenario. A citizen, finds an interesting dataset of hundreds of records, for instance, about the spending in road maintenance in her/his city, and she/he desires to create a chart to understand on which category there is the greatest spending. In order to create such a chart the dataset must have no quality issues, meaning that the numerical column about the maintenance cost should have no null values, strange characters, symbols, and so on. Users need to be aware of possible quality issues and know exactly where they are.

Tabular datasets are plain textual files. They are stored on the open data portals as CSV or TSV files. Hence, they do not have any semantics attached as well as they do not have any additional information on the schema, for instance, they do not contain the domains of columns, something that is typical for instance in the context of relational databases.

Since the term quality is broad, it is worth to specify its meaning in this paper. The objective is to have datasets in which each column has a data type and all values in the column are coherent with its data type. This is straightforward clear when datasets are extracted from databases, but it does not in the OD world, where often CSV files are exported from spreadsheet software that leave a high degree of freedom to the user. Indeed, it happens that a column that should contain only numerical values, contains numbers with spaces, symbols, and so on, making costly to re-use it (e.g., to create visualisations) because it requires a cleaning activity. Furthermore, users are not aware of this quality issues, especially when datasets are large with many rows.

The idea is to infer the data type for each column of the tabular dataset and use it for data quality assessment. DataChecker is an open source javascript library available on GitHub. It has a variety of applications within the OD field and beyond. In particular, this paper identifies specific points named *data quality assessment checkpoints* in the process of opening data performed by PAs as well as in the process of using Open Data by the public (e.g., citizens, non-profit organisations, companies). It is exploited in SPOD (Social Platform for Open Data) both to support the production and the exploitation of Open Data. These features can be tried at spod.routetopa.eu.

2   Related Work

The objective of data quality assessment "is to identity erroneous data items and estimate their impact on data-driven processes" [19]. The first part can be assisted by data profiling techniques in order to collect statistics and information about data [20]. Data profiling can consider a single column or involve multiple columns. Single column approach include the number of null values and distinct values of a column, the data type and additional patterns [20]. This paper exploits the traditional data type inferencing on a single column over OD in tabular format in order to discovering syntactic heterogeneity [20]. The inferred data type is not limited only to the quality assessment. Pirozzi et. al [23] exploited the data type inferencing in order to automatically propose a bunch of compatible visualisations based on chosen dataset fields.

The *five stars rating system* [4], introduced by Tim Berners-Lee in 2006, classifies datasets based on their property, which include license, proprietary or not, machine-readable or not, and the usage of Semantic Web technologies. The aforementioned rating does not give indication on the quality of dataset content. Indeed, OD in three-stars could have quality issues. Dawes et al. [10] interviewed users who explored the use of land records and parcel data. Interviewed persons requested better quality data. Authors observed that in order to get fit-for-use data, users spent considerable resources trying to improve the data.

The European Data Portal [7] (EDP) developed and maintained by European Commission harvests metadata of open datasets made available across Europe. The analysis of datasets on the EDP portal is useful to have a broad overview about the actual quality of data published by governments across Europe. The Open Data Maturity Report [6] annually gives indication on the maturity of open data in Europe, reporting also statistics about the content available on the portal. In the 2017, a moderate 66% of datasets are available in machine-readable format, the remaining datasets are still published in non machine-readable or proprietary formats (e.g., PDF, XLS, DOC). Machine-readable format means that data can be read and processed by a software [18], for example CSV (comma separated values), JSON and XML are machine-readable formats. The EDP is based on CKAN, which provides an overview of available formats along with the number of datasets for each one, making very easy and quick to check these statistics. In particular, in order to give an idea, at time of writing accessing to the EDP, 34.33% of datasets are one-stars or two-stars, 29.26% are three-stars, and only 1.17% are four-stars datasets, the remaining are compressed (i.e., ZIP, RAR), geographical data, other formats, or with wrong indication of format. Hence, a large quantity of datasets on OD portals are three-stars (e.g., CSV, TSV), this means that there is a demand to make simpler their usage, tackling the data quality issues, considering that they are plain textual data with no attached semantics amd without a schema.

Metadata are additional information to describe the dataset content. Metadata are essential to find desired datasets within open data catalogues. Furthermore, they are essential to understand the dataset content, the context in which it has been created, the version, the last update and so on. Issues in the quality of metadata exists as widely pointed out in literature; quality issues in metadata is out of scope of this paper, other works already faced this issue.

A common approach to infer types is to use the cast operator provided by programming languages or any equivalent function. An example of such approach is adopted in the project Messytables[1]. Since the aim is to provide feedback to the user about the dataset content, there are values for which the casting fails but using regular expressions is more powerful. For instance, a numerical string with the currency symbol, very common in open data CSV, it can not be casted, but it can be recognized by a proper regular expression. An example of using regular expressions to recognize data types is presented in Döhmen et al. [13], which provides also a wide introduction to all the kind of CSV issues categorized in syntax, file-level, table level, and column/cell issues. Of course, in this paper we focus on the quality assessment at column level. This paper also uses regular expressions but with a different approach. Döhmen et al. [13] approach "tries to parse iteratively column content until all values were successfully parsed. If not all cells can be successfully, the column is per default a string column". Our approach aims to increase awareness of issues and help citizens in fixing issues so we use a different approach based on thresholds.

3   Heuristics for Data Quality Assessment

The objective is to automatically infer additional information on the dataset content and perform a data quality assessment. Technically, the idea is to run a set of heuristics over the content of plain textual dataset to infer the data type of each column based on the values that it contains. The content of this paper has been implemented in `DataChecker` library, an open source (LGPL), modular, and reusable library implemented in JavaScript. It is available on GitHub[2].

---

[1] Messytables documentation https://messytables.readthedocs.io/en/latest.
[2] DataChecker open source library available on GitHub at https://github.com/donpir/ JSDataChecker.

3.1   Dataset Notation

The tabular dataset is denoted with R, it has n rows and m columns. Columns are denoted with $C = \{C_1, ..., C_m\}$. The dataset is a matrix, so we use the standard notation $R[i][j]$ to get the textual value in the row i and column j, $\forall 1 \leq i \leq n, 1 \leq j \leq m$. Usually when working for instance with rational databases, there is also the relational schema S, its attributes $attr(S) = \{A_1, ..., A_m\}$, and for each attribute $A_i \in S$, the domain $dom(A_i)$. In the open data context, tabular data are in CSV formats, hence, the schema and domains are not provided.

3.2   Data Types Hierarchy

A data type defines what kind of values a column can contain. Usually in DBMS the relational schema defines the type for columns. In plain tabular datasets (i.e., CSV, TSV), there is not the declaration of the data type, so it must be inferred. As in programming languages, data types form a hierarchy. Figure 1 depicts the data type hierarchy adopted and embedded in the DataChecker library.

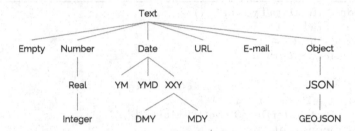

Fig. 1. A tree data structure (DTS) that represents the hierarchy among data types within the DataChecker data quality assessment library.

The hierarchy is a tree data structure $DTS = (T, E)$, where T is the sets of data types. The root is text since the dataset is textual. E is the set of interconnections between data types. Data types have parent-child relationship. For instance, the data type real denotes the range of mathematical real numbers which includes the mathematical integer numbers.

The function inferDataTypeOfValue in DataChecker takes in input the textual value $R[i][j]$ and returns the inferred data type $dt \in T$ (Fig. 1). The inferring of a type is implemented by running a sequence of regular expressions, that we omit here, since they are classical and can be found in the source code. A human supplies the Hierarchy and the set of regular expressions, one for each data type.

A value can match multiple data types (e.g. a number is also a text); there is an ordering of regular expressions so that the type with the narrowest range is chosen and the hierarchy implicitly keeps track of the possible conversions though parent-child relationships. A value can have a variety of formats, for instance, a date can have the DMY or MDY format (e.g. 1/1/2018); in this case the XXY type is placed in the hierarchy as intermediate common data type.

3.3 Infer the Column Data Type

Given the dataset R, the objective is to infer the $type(C_j), \forall 1 \le j \le m$ for each column of the dataset. Considering all the values in the column C_j, they could have different data types due to quality issues (i.e., typos in numerical values) or just because values are effectively of different types. An example of the first case is when the column contains mostly numbers that are inferred as number data type, but there are typos in some values (e.g., spaces, strange symbols) that are recognized as text. Figure 3 shows a dataset with a typos in the cell $R[7][3] = 2a$ that is evaluated as a text, instead all the other values are integer.

In order to consider this situation, we introduce a weighted function of the data types in T named $occurs : T-> \mathbb{N}$ that assigns to each data type dt the number of values that have the type $dt \in T$ in the column C_j.

The approach is to loop through all the values in the column j, calling n times the function inferDataTypeOfValue, one for each value of the column and annotate the number of data types occurrences on the tree. Practically, it checks every value in the column against the sequence of regular expressions to infer the data type.

```
function inferDataType(T, j) {
    //Initialization
    for each dt ∈ T
        occurs(dt) = 0;

    //for each value of the column Cj
    for (i=1; i ≤ n; i++) {
        dt = inferDataTypeOfValue(R[i][j])
        occurs(dt)++;
    }

    return occurs;
}
```

The algorithm creates the DTS for each column, annotating each node $dt \in T$ (data type) with the number of occurrences $occurs(dt)$ as well as adding references to cells recognised as dt type. The inferred data type of the column is the one that has the most occurrences, hence the one with the highest occurs value. There is a special case, in which a column contains two data types mixed together in equal amounts, in this case the DTS is used to choose a common data type by navigating the tree up towards the root. Furthermore, the annotated DTS can be used to inform user where exactly issues are placed, that are cells that do not match the inferred data type.

4   Open Data Process and Data Quality Assessment

This section describes specific *data quality assessment* functionalities within the process of opening data by PAs as well as when public audience (e.g., citizens) uses open data. Hence, it proposes a variant of the conceptual representation of the open data process described in Helbig et al. [17], annotated with the data quality assessment functionalities which are based on the heuristics described in Sect. 3. Technically speaking these functionalities use features provided by `QualityChecker` but presenting, using and interacting with the quality assessment results in a different ways and with different degree of control.

This paper considers the following functionalities distinguished between two main stages, the production of open data made by PAs and the usage of open data usually made by citizens:

- QA1 *Support data cleaning* (production): quality assessment to support and guide users and making them aware of the potential quality issues in the data they are collecting, creating and cleaning;
- QA2 *Check quality before publication* (production): quality assessment of datasets before the official publication on the OD portal (i.e. CKAN);
- QA3 *Raise quality awareness* (exploitation) raise awareness of possible quality issues in the dataset;
- QA4 *Prevent mistakes while creating visualisations* (exploitation): prevent user impossible action while users are creating visualisations, for instance, prevent the creation of charts when the dataset has no numerical columns.

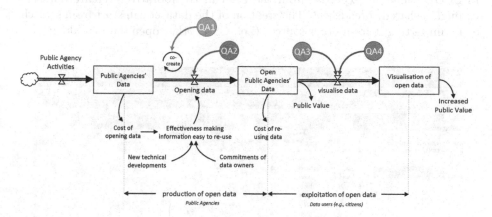

Fig. 2. Process of opening data (adapted form [17]), integrated with the exploitation of OD and enhanced with quality assessment features.

Figure 2 depicts the process of opening data (see [11] for more details) annotated with the quality assessments steps. *Public Agency datas* is the set of data [14] that a Public Agency collects by performing its activities. PAs follow a process and make the effort to turn a subset of these data in *open government data*, according to privacy, legal, and technical requirements. Helbig et al. [17] depicted the abstract process by using stock-and-flow diagrams. The process has seen as a hydraulic valve that based on the effort and allocated resources changes the rate at which the quantity of the data made publicly available.

Obviously, many other quality assessment functionalities can be envisioned and exploited both in the open data context that outside. SPOD [9] is a Social Platform for Open Data (http://spod.routetopa.eu) that supports both the collaborative creation and the exploitation of Open Data. SPOD includes the quality assessment functionalities previously listed. Functional requirements have been collected by closely working with five public administrations, including the Council of Campania Region and Prato municipality, in Italy as well as a pilot project in the Cultural Heritage field named Hetor which involved non-profit organisations, group of citizens and students in producing and using open data for the protection, preservation and promotion of Campania Cultural Heritage [1]. As previously specified, the paper focuses on three stars Tim Berners-Lee datasets in tabular format, hence, all functionalities work only on this type of datasets. This section describes in detail the four functionalities which run the quality assessment library DataChecker, described in the previous Sect. 3.

4.1 QA1 Support Data Cleaning

Usually the opening of data is not a one-shot activity, but involves many iterations where multiple roles within the PA collaboratively create the dataset. In SPOD, different expertise from the PA can collaboratively create datasets through a shared spreadsheet. The creation of the dataset can start from scratch or by importing it from other sources (i.e., CSV, other open data catalogues).

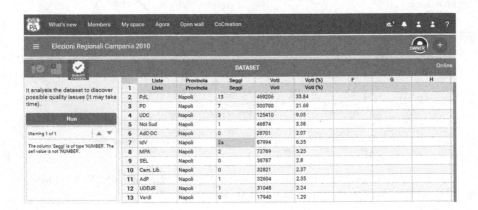

Fig. 3. SPOD data Co-creation, a shared spreadsheet enhanced with quality assessment functionalities to run a set of heuristics to check the quality of the dataset while is being created. The snapshot shows a numerical column with a cell that contains a typos as identified by the tool.

The shared spreadsheet has specific functionalities to support the quality assessment that is always under the user full control. It is the user that decides when to run quality checks by clicking on the dedicated function. The functionality suggests potential quality issues by listing them, but leaves the user the full control on the dataset content, indeed, she/he decides whether to change the signalled value or not. This feature is especially useful when the datasets have hundreds of rows because often issues are difficult to identify over large datasets.

4.2 QA2 Check Quality Before Publication

When the dataset is considered ready, there is a formal decision to make it public, publishing it on the official PA open data catalogue (e.g., CKAN), making it visible to the general audience over Internet and available to be harvested by other open data portals at various levels (i.e., national, European level).

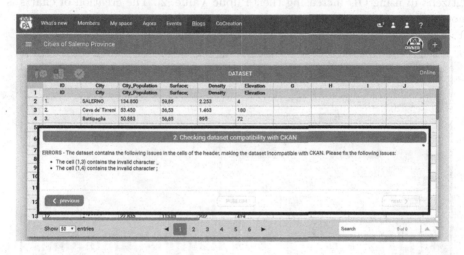

Fig. 4. Checking whether the dataset is compliant with the target open data catalogue.

SPOD has a wizard that guides the authorized user in publishing the dataset directly on the OD catalogue. The wizard has multiple steps, one of them (Fig. 4) is the quality assessment before the publication. It reports the same issues already signalled within the shared spreadsheet, plus additional checks (with specific regular expressions) based on the target OD catalogue. Since there are several catalogues, each one with its specific conventions and accepted content to be sure that the data is compliant with catalogue. For instance, the CKAN platform does not accepts underscore and semicolon characters in the header. The DataChecker performs these checks in the publication step finding these issues and blocking the publication on the portal. Technically, the dataset is sent to the `QualityChecker`, that is initialised with these additional checks.

4.3 QA3: Usage of Open Data

Target audience for Open Data are citizens, non-profit organisations, and companies. Often this audience does not have the needed data skills to identify, understand and fix potential quality issues within datasets. The idea is to raise the quality awareness by visualising a table that lists the potential quality issues. In this way, citizens can request better quality dataset to their public administrations. In De Donato et al. [12] there is a full description of the use case with relevant screenshots (see Fig. 5 in [12]).

4.4 QA4: Visualising Open Data

SPOD exploits visualisations (e.g., charts, maps) named Datalets [12] to engage citizens in using OD increasing their Public Value [2]. The creation of charts is not easy for untrained citizens and without a tool that guides the process.

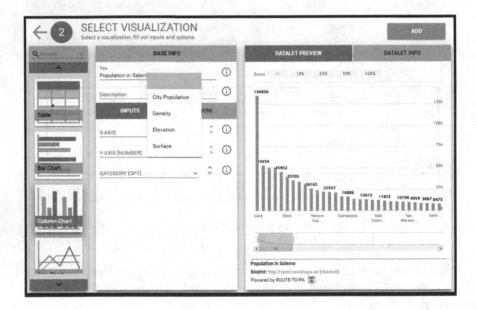

Fig. 5. By automatically inferring data types of the dataset, the system can guide the user in making the right choice. The chart accepts a number on the y-axis, hence, based on the types inferred by the DataChecker, the system shows only the numerical values, excluding the city that is textual (see the table header of Fig. 3.)

The quality of datasets can impact on the possibility to create charts. For instance, line charts can not be created when numbers have typos or other strange characters inside. The identification of potential issues can help citizens in filtering unusable rows. Moreover, the identification of data types from the dataset can be used to guide the user and prevent the wrong selection of fields to visualize. For instance, Fig. 5 shows how selecting a column for the y-axis of a bar chart, the system reports only the numerical columns, hiding other types, the city name in the list is omitted because is textual.

5 Conclusions

The idea, approach and open source software presented in the paper have wide applicability also outside the Open Data world, for instance in the engineering field, where engineers create charts from a variety of data sources [15]. The extraction of data types from tabular datasets can be exploited to assist users in transforming tabular data in linked data, moving from three-stars to four-stars datasets. There is the possibility to provide the open data quality assessment as service. In this way it can be used by any other third part software. Of course, assessment messages provided to users need to be adapted according to the application. Furthermore, there is the need to include domain-specific and language-specific heuristics (e.g., recognizing city names, addresses, and others). Part of the future work will be the user evaluation to understand and measure the improvements of the approach as well as evaluate the usability of tools.

Acknowledgements. The research leading to results presented in this paper has been conducted in the project ROUTE-TO-PA (www.routetopa.eu) that received funding from the European Union's Horizon 2020 research and innovation programme under grant agreement No. 645860. We gratefully acknowledge discussions with the project participants, who stimulated our work. Authors would like to thanks the anonymous reviewers for the interesting and valuable feedback.

References

1. Ambrosino, M.A., et al.: Protection and preservation of campania cultural heritage engaging local communities via the use of open data. In: Proceedings of the 19th International Conference on Digital Government Research. ACM (2018). https://doi.org/10.1145/3209281.3209347
2. Andriessen, J., et al.: Increasing public value through co-creation of open knowledge. In: 2017 Fourth International Conference on eDemocracy & eGovernment (ICEDEG), pp. 47–54. IEEE (2017)
3. Beno, M., Figl, K., Umbrich, J., Polleres, A.: Open data hopes and fears: determining the barriers of open data. In: 2017 Conference for E-Democracy and Open Government (CeDEM), pp. 69–81. IEEE (2017)
4. Berners-Lee, T.: Linked data - design issues. http://www.w3.org/DesignIssues/LinkedData.html. Accessed 03 May 2018
5. Castro, D., Korte, T.: Open data in the G8: a review of progress on the open data charter (2015). Accessed 23 May 2018
6. Commission, E.: Open data maturity in Europe 2017 (2017). https://www.europeandataportal.eu/sites/default/files/edp_landscaping_insight_report_n3_2017.pdf
7. Commission, E.: Open data portal (2017). https://www.europeandataportal.eu/data/it/dataset

8. Commission, E.: Re-using open data (2017). https://www.europeandataportal.eu/sites/default/files/re-using_open_data.pdf
9. Cordasco, G., et al.: Engaging citizens with a social platform for open data. In: Proceedings of the 18th Annual International Conference on Digital Government Research, pp. 242–249. ACM (2017)
10. Dawes, S.S., Helbig, N.: Information strategies for open government: challenges and prospects for deriving public value from government transparency. In: Wimmer, M.A., Chappelet, J.-L., Janssen, M., Scholl, H.J. (eds.) EGOV 2010. LNCS, vol. 6228, pp. 50–60. Springer, Heidelberg (2010). https://doi.org/10.1007/978-3-642-14799-9_5
11. De Donato, R., et al.: Agile production of high quality open data. In: Proceedings of the 19th Annual International Conference on Digital Government Research: Governance in the Data Age, p. 84. ACM (2018)
12. De Donato, R., et al.: Datalet-ecosystem provider (deep): scalable architecture for reusable, portable and user-friendly visualizations of open data. In: 2017 Conference for E-Democracy and Open Government (CeDEM), pp. 92–101. IEEE (2017)
13. Döhmen, T., Mühleisen, H., Boncz, P.: Multi-hypothesis CSV parsing. In: Proceedings of the 29th International Conference on Scientific and Statistical Database Management, p. 16. ACM (2017)
14. European Data Portal: Open data goldbook for data manager and data holders. https://www.europeandataportal.eu/sites/default/files/goldbook.pdf. Accessed 23 May 2018
15. Fish, A., Gargiulo, C., Malandrino, D., Pirozzi, D., Scarano, V.: Visual exploration system in an industrial context. IEEE Trans. Industr. Inf. 12(2), 567–575 (2016)
16. Foundation TWWW: Open data barometer 4th (edn.) Global Report, May 2017. http://opendatabarometer.org/doc/4thEdition/ODB-4thEdition-GlobalReport.pdf
17. Helbig, N., Cresswell, A.M., Burke, G.B., Luna-Reyes, L.: The dynamics of opening government data. Center for Technology in Government (2012). http://www.ctg.albany.edu/publications/reports/opendata. Accessed 23 May 2018
18. International OK: Open data handbook. http://opendatahandbook.org/glossary/. Accessed 05 May 05 2018
19. Maydanchik, A.: Data Quality Assessment. Technics Publications, Denville (2007)
20. Naumann, F.: Data profiling revisited. ACM SIGMOD Rec. 42(4), 40–49 (2014)
21. Open Data Charter: Open data charter web site. https://opendatacharter.net. Accessed 23 May 2018
22. Open Knowledge International: Open definition (2018). https://opendefinition.org/od/2.1/en/. Accessed 05 May 2018
23. Pirozzi, D., Scarano, V.: Support citizens in visualising open data. In: 20th International Conference on Information Visualisation (IV), pp. 271–276. IEEE (2016)

Access Control and Quality Attributes of Open Data: Applications and Techniques

Erisa Karafili[1]([✉])(iD), Konstantina Spanaki[2], and Emil C. Lupu[1]

[1] Department of Computing, Imperial College London, London, UK
{e.karafili,e.c.lupu}@imperial.ac.uk
[2] School of Business and Economics, Loughborough University, Loughborough, UK
k.spanaki@lboro.ac.uk

Abstract. Open Datasets provide one of the most popular ways to acquire insight and information about individuals, organizations and multiple streams of knowledge. Exploring Open Datasets by applying comprehensive and rigorous techniques for data processing can provide the ground for innovation and value for everyone if the data are handled in a legal and controlled way. In our study, we propose an argumentation and abductive reasoning approach for data processing which is based on the data quality background. Explicitly, we draw on the literature of data management and quality for the attributes of the data, and we extend this background through the development of our techniques. Our aim is to provide herein a brief overview of the data quality aspects, as well as indicative applications and examples of our approach. Our overall objective is to bring serious intent and propose a structured way for access control and processing of open data with a focus on the data quality aspects.

Keywords: Data quality · Argumentation reasoning · Open data
Data access

1 Introduction

Open Data as a term is often questioned in literature and public debates; however the definition of open data addresses two core concepts: the openness and the features of the data (quality aspects) required to be characterized as 'open data'. Open Data are more than public data, they include also private sector data, and therefore their use can be controversial in regards to the ownership of the data. In our paper we accept the definition of Lindman et al. ([24], p. 740) for the open data as *"data, which is legally accessible through the Internet in a machine-readable format"*. The roots of open data stem from the context of open source [10] in combination with the background of open innovation [6,23] and open access [38]. The main difference of open source and open data as it is highlighted by Lindman et al. [24,25] is the fact that *"data is used for storage and, the application is used for different operations based on data"* ([25], p. 1240) where the application is the open source.

© Springer Nature Switzerland AG 2019
W. Abramowicz and A. Paschke (Eds.): BIS 2018 Workshops, LNBIP 339, pp. 603–614, 2019.
https://doi.org/10.1007/978-3-030-04849-5_52

We also include here similar assumptions for our examples as in our previous work [21] that the data are open for use/reuse/redistribution and in a form that can be accessible to everyone who has the rights to access them. Data should be accessible, assessable, and reliable and in a state that judgments and sense-making can be made so as value is created [14,15]. Data should give the opportunity for the audience to make intelligent judgments or assessments once they are scrutinized. Another important aspect of the open data is around their format, so as the data can be used or reused for different purposes, including information and meta-data or linked data. Opportunities and innovation around the concept of open data can bridge the social divide and equality issues by their use from all the social levels [14]. In organizational level large numbers of enterprises have tried to open their data and they have generated new services and applications for individuals. The entrepreneurial movement towards open data shared the view for transparency and accountability of organizational practices and also the collaborative potential around the data with other organizations and individuals for innovative purposes [24,25].

However, some major challenges for the supporters of open data come mostly in the form of privacy issues related to personal data (identities, privacy and regulatory landscape). The privacy issues are more prevalent lately in line with the new GDPR regulations. Some other challenges can be considered as the costs of collecting, producing and releasing the datasets, as well as the diversity of interests and behaviour in opening the data for the public use or even the actual use of the data.

The proposed approach extends the concept of open data with a focus on the quality aspects and processing techniques and the associated data sharing agreements (DSAs). The study proposes an expressive policy analysis language for representing the DSAs enriched with data quality attributes to capture specified aspects of the data. The introduced analysis, based on argumentation and abductive approach, permits the construction of correct and efficient DSAs that can be applied in different contexts during the processing of data.

We introduce briefly the related work for data quality and data access and usage control in Sect. 2. In Sect. 3 we present the used techniques for representing the data quality properties and permitting the correct access of open data. We show an application of our methodology in Sect. 4, where we work with immigration movement open data. Finally, we conclude in Sect. 5 and discuss some future research directions.

2   Related Work

2.1   Data Quality

Data quality as a concept was initially presented through the data manufacturing analogy. Data as a "raw material" was initially introduced by Brodie [5] through the analogy between product manufacturing and data manufacturing process when data quality was a major concern in transforming data to valid information and knowledge [1,11,29]. Studies as those of Fox et al. [11] and Wang and colleagues [32,36,37] focused on the analysis of 'data quality', in terms of dimensions, attributes, as well as the upcoming issues and research areas. The so called 'dimensions' for data quality representation as they were presented by Fox et al. [11]: accuracy, freshness, completeness, and consistency. In our study, we will base our proposed approach on the dimensions and quality aspects as they were described in the literature of data quality.

Some of the most indicative studies around the quality aspects have developed the concept of data manufacturing analogy in order to find out the path for better data quality [13,26,28,35] and they designed frameworks that describe and track data manufacturing processes [2,30,35,36]. A simple framework of input-process-output describing the similarities between the two manufacturing processes is proposed by Wang et al. [36] and calls for continuously defining, measuring, analysing, and improving data quality. Mostly, the data manufacturing analogy was focusing on data quality and the ways to ensure that we can trust the data we use in manufacturing processes. Recent studies in data quality research, apply the data manufacturing analogy, in order to explain the tailoring techniques and the potential of data marketplaces within the context of supply chain [12,31].

2.2   Data Access and Usage Control

Due to the increasing connectivity between users, there is a parallel increase of the associated security breaches and attacks. Protecting and securing the environment where the data is transferred/stored/used or even re-used [20] remains a major challenge for all interested parties. Data-centric security solutions have dominant position in the literature [3,27,34] and specifically the protection of the data transfers and transactions. Data-centric security solutions present two main challenges associated with the access and the usage control of the data. Both of them, have been widely studied and the research has developed multiple solutions for solving such problems [9,22].

Before creating, sharing and using the data, the data subject, controller and processor should agree regarding the different rules that describe how the data should be treated, called the *data sharing agreements*, denoted by DSAs [33]. The DSAs describe not only the agreements between the data subject, controller, and processor, but also the compliance of the different business and regulatory contexts for data sharing. Thus, the DSAs require an expressive language to represent the agreements. Given the heterogeneous nature of the agreements, various conflicts can be generated, especially between legal and business rules, or legal rules and user requirements. The authors in previous studies [17,18,21] propose a policy language that represents complex agreements, and an analysis process for capturing the conflicts and solving them. The approach is based on abductive [16] and argumentation based reasoning [4,8], as this technique can facilitate decision making mechanisms under conflicting knowledge.

3   Methodology

The methodology presented in this study assumes that data are processed by different entities. Data Sharing Agreements (DSAs) are established between the entities for data processing and are composed of various constraints and rules. As in previous work [21], an expressive policy analysis language is used for representing the DSAs. Data quality is the main focus of the data processing mechanism; therefore the policy language is enriched to capture various data quality properties like accessibility, timeliness and accuracy. The used policy language permits the analysis of the various policies and the detection of the rising conflicts, redundancies or the missing cases. We follow argumentation and abductive reasoning to build our proposed methodology to capture and solve conflicts between context dependent rules. The introduced analysis permits the construction of precise DSAs that can be applied in various contexts during data processing phase.

3.1   A Policy Language for DSAs and Data Quality

To represent the various data sharing agreements that incorporate extensive types of information, we use a policy analysis language [18]. The used policy language is an extension of the one introduced by Craven et al. [7], where the used extension supports efficiently the data access of open data and the data quality properties. Let us introduce briefly the policy language, which represents the requirements of accessing, using and sharing the data.

The policy language is composed of rules that are predicates and domain descriptions, and represent the authorization and obligation rules. The first three predicates are authorization rules and have in their structure a specific subject, as well as specified targets, and actions, while the last one is a domain description predicate.

$$permitted(Sub, Tar, Act, T)$$
$$denied(Sub, Tar, Act, T)$$
$$obl(Sub, Tar, Act, T_s, T_e, T)$$
$$holdsAt(Predicate, T)$$

The above predicate represents correspondingly: the permission $permit$ for a given subject Sub to perform an action Act to a target object Tar at the instant of time T; the prohibition $denied$ for a given subject Sub to perform an action Act to a target object Tar at the instant of time T; the obligation obl for a given subject Sub to perform an action Act during the period of time from T_s to T_e; the domain description predicate $holdsAt$ means that a given property/predicate $Predicate$ is true in a given instance of time T.

The used policy language can represent the permission, denial and obligation concepts for the DSAs, e.g., the owner of the data can access to her/his own data.

$$permitted(Sub, Data, access, T) \leftarrow holdsAt(owner(Sub, Data), T).$$

In the above formula, the preconditions are on the right side while the conclusion is on the left side of the arrow. Thus, if it is true (represented by using the *holdsAt* predicate) that subject *Sub* is the owner of the data, described as *owner*(*Sub, Data*), at the instant of time *T*, then the subject is permitted to access the *Data* at the instant of time *T*.

Following the above example, let us introduce how a prohibition predicate can be constructed, e.g., if the subject is not the data owner then s/he cannot access the data,

$$denied(Sub, Data, access, T) \leftarrow \mathbf{not}\ holdsAt(owner(Sub, Data), T).$$

An obligation force the data user to perform certain actions to the data. The enforcement is made possible by using the sticky policy mechanism, where the rules are attached to the data and enforce to them various constraints, e.g., temporal, geographical etc. Continuing with the example, an obligation can use temporal constraints where it asks for a particular data to be deleted after a certain amount of time from when the data was accessed.

$$obl(Sub, Data, delete, T, T', T) \leftarrow holdsAt(access(Sub, Data), T),$$
$$T' = T + 6.$$

In the above case the subject has the obligation to delete the data from the moment s/he accessed them *T*, until after 6 years from that instant of time, and the obligation is enforced from the moment s/he accessed the data *T*.

Representation of the Quality and Sharing Aspects

The sharing and usage of data raises issues around the description of other properties related to the quality of the collected data. The data quality is an important factor when we are working with data consumers[1], where data quality is defined as data that fit the data consumers' requirements. The used policy language permits to represent various *data quality* properties.

An important data quality property is *accessibility*. Our methodology ensures that data accessibility respects the imposed constraints e.g., security, legal and business constraints. The *permitted, denied* and *obl* regulation rules enforce a correct data accessibility, by permitting the allowed users to access the data, prohibiting the users that do not satisfy the needed requirements for accessing the data and putting obligations on the users about the use/access and sharing of the rules.

When collecting data with the purpose on releasing them as open data, not all part of the data can become public. Our methodology permits to classify the data depending on their level of privacy. An example would be the data collected from individuals for statistical purpose. When the data are being public, their private information are not released to the public.

$$denied(Sub, Data, access, T) \leftarrow holdsAt(private(Data), T),$$
$$holdsAt(member(Sub, public), T).$$

$$permitted(Sub, Data, access, T) \leftarrow holdsAt(private(Data), T),$$
$$holdsAt(member(Sub, staff), T).$$

---

[1] The data consumers are called the entities that use/share/access the data.

The above predicates state that if the subject is a member of the public, then s/he cannot access the private data, while if the subject is a member of the staff, thus working with the data, then s/he is permitted to access the data.

Accuracy is another data quality attribute that our methodology is able to represent. When data are collected, e.g., by an human actor or IoT devices, an obligation for satisfying a particular accuracy level when collecting and storing the data is enforced.

$$accuracy(Data, T, level) \leftarrow holdsAt(collect(Device, Data), T),$$
$$holdsAt(capacity(Device, level), T).$$

In the above predicate, a certain level of accuracy is ensured, when the device that collects the data, use the capacity of that level of accuracy. The accuracy can also be restricted/manipulated in order to give different level of accuracy to different data consumers, or depending on the type of data. An example would be the visual data collected by drones in certain area. The image quality (the accuracy of the images) can be restricted when is released publicly, in case of sensitive data.

The notion of data *freshness* is part of the timeliness as a data quality aspect. Data freshness is the degree data represent reality in the required point in time. In our methodology it is represented as a predicate that expresses that the data represented by Tar are fresh at the instant of time T: $freshness(Tar, T)$.

An example of freshness is that data is collected in the last 10 min.

$$freshness(Data, T) \leftarrow holdsAt(collect(Device, Data), T'),$$
$$T \leq T' + 10.$$

3.2   Analysis and Conflict Resolution

Given the heterogeneity of the rules that compose the DSAs is natural to have conflicts between rules. There exists a conflict between the DSAs rules when an action is both permitted or denied on the same instant of time.

$$permitted(Sub, Tar, Act, T) \qquad denied(Sub, Tar, Act, T)$$

Another type of conflict is when an action is denied and obliged to occur at the same instant of time.

$$obl(Sub, Tar, Act, T_s, T_e, T) \qquad denied(Sub, Tar, Act, T) \qquad T_s < T$$

The conflicts exists not only between exactly matching entities, but also when a certain entity is subset of another one. Going back to the previous example of public data, suppose *Bob* is a member of the public $member(Bob, public)$ and **not** $member(Bob, staff)$ therefor, he should not access the private data, because of the following rule.

$$r_1 : denied(Sub, Data, access, T) \leftarrow holdsAt(private(Data), T),$$
$$holdsAt(member(Sub, public), T).$$

As *Bob* is the owner of the data *owner*(*Bob, Data*), he should have access to his own data, even the private ones, because of the following rule

$$r_2 : permitted(Sub, Data, access, T) \leftarrow holdsAt(owner(Sub, Data), T).$$

The two above rules are in conflict between each other.

To capture the above conflicts and conflicts similar to the ones shown previously, we introduce an analysis process to the DSAs [18], based on the abductive reasoning, that identifies conflictual policy regulation rules. The analysis is able to identify gaps between rules as well as redundancies. Once the conflicts are identified, we use a conflict resolution based on the argumentation reasoning, that solve the conflicts by introducing priorities between them. In specific, for the previous example of *Bob* permitted and denied to access the private data, rule r_1 and r_2 are in conflict, then we decide that r_2 is stronger than r_1, denoted by $r_2 > r_1$ for the case when the data subject is the owner of the data.

4 Use Case: Immigration Movement Open Data

In this section we show our proposed methodology applied in a realistic case scenario taken from the *immigration movement open data*. The open immigration data are gathered from governmental and humanitarian organisations from refugees camps, as well as the immigrants while trying to proceed with their travel document applications. The collected data enclose various and multiple properties, e.g., age, country of origin, type of immigration (e.g., political, economic), education level, legal/illegal immigration. The properties of the data, as well as their accuracy and timeliness, compose aspects around the quality of the data. Revealing immigration data to the general public by humanitarian, statistical, and governmental entities can be important. On the other hand, it is crucial to anonymized the data, before they are made public. Exposing to the public all these types of data (anonymized) can sometimes be dangerous or beyond the human rights, e.g., revealing sensitive information about the refugees camps in unstable or conflicting geopolitical areas. Hence for publicizing immigration movement data, we can divide the data in three categories, that represent also their quality: *basic, medium*, and *detailed* data.

The *basic* data are open data of the immigration movement. Such data are published every year, and support the categorization of immigrants in three age groupings (i.e., children, adults, and elder people), the sum of these groupings give the total number of immigrants per country.

The *medium* data can be accessed only by national statistics agencies. Such data can be updated monthly, and have the exact age of the immigrants, the type of immigration (e.g., political, economic), the country of origin, education level, legal/illegal immigration.

The *detailed* data can be accessed only by governmental and UN entities. Such data have the same properties as the medium one but are updated weekly, instead of monthly.

We are able to deal with this division of data quality, by using the argumentation reasoning approach. Before introducing the rules that describe how the access to data is made by agents with different roles, we define the *freshness* of data for this use case as below.

$$
\begin{aligned}
Fresh(Data, T) \leftarrow\ & holdsAt(update(Data), T_i), \\
& holdsAt(update(Data), T_j), \\
& \mathbf{not}\ holdsAt(update(Data), T_k), \\
& T_j < T_k < T_i,\ T_i - T_j \leq 7, \\
& T \geq T_i,\ T - T_i \leq 7.
\end{aligned}
$$

The above predicate, states that *Data* is *Fresh* at the instant of time T, if it was updated at the instant of time T_i, (where T is bigger than T_i of maximum 7 days), the previous time when the data was updated is T_j (where T_j is at most 7 days before T_i) and there was no update made between T_i and T_j.

The data quality is divided into three categories, depending on the three types of public where these categories are released. Given an *Agent* that wants to access the data, it can be a general entity/individual denoted by *Public(Agent)* (in this case the data is open access), a statistical entity *Statistic(Agent)*, or an individual/entity part of the UN or Governmental Entities, denoted by *UN/Gov(Agent)*. Depending on the role of the agent a freshness restriction is made *Cast_Fresh*, as described below.

$$
\begin{aligned}
Cast\_Fresh(Agent, Data\_In, Data\_Out) \leftarrow\ & Public(Agent), \\
& Fresh(Data\_In, T), \\
& holdsAt(update(Data\_Out), T'), \\
& T - T' \leq 365, T' = X.
\end{aligned}
$$

$$
\begin{aligned}
Cast\_Fresh(Agent, Data\_In, Data\_Out) \leftarrow\ & Statistic(Agent), \\
& Fresh(Data\_In, T), \\
& holdsAt(update(Data\_Out), T'), \\
& T - T' \leq 30, T' = Y.
\end{aligned}
$$

The predicate *Cast_Fresh* depends on the type of *Agent*. Thus, given the fresh data *Data_In*, it gives to the *Public* the data collected at most 1 year ago *Data_Out*, and to the *Statistic* institute the data collected at most 1 month ago, where X and Y are fixed time range correspondingly representing when the data are released every year, e.g., X = [01/01 − 07/01], while Y when the data are released every month, e.g., $Y = [01 − 07]$ of every month.

We make use of another predicate, *Cast*, that removes some of the immigration data properties. Thus given *Cast(Data_In, Data_Out)* where *Data_In* is the fresh data that has different properties, the result of this restriction/alteration is *Data_Out* that does not have any more the following properties: immigration type, education level, country of origin, legal/illegal immigration, and the age property is aggregated into three categories, i.e., children, adult, elder. For constructing the *Cast* predicate, we use a similar mechanism as the one introduced in [19].

We can now represent the rules that describe who can access the data. In case the original data, $Data'$, are not anonymized ($Anonym(Data', Data)$), then nobody can access the data, as described in rule (1). Rule (2) describes that agents that are from the UN or/and governments can access the data unaltered and the data should be fresh and anonymized. In case the agent is not part of UN/Gov then it cannot access the data, even though the data is anonymized, as described in rule (3).

$$denied(Agent, Data, access, T) \leftarrow \textbf{not } Anonym(Data', Data) \qquad (1)$$

$$permitted(Agent, Data, access, T) \leftarrow UN/Gov(Agent), \; Fresh(Data', T), \\ Anonym(Data', Data)$$
$$(2)$$

$$denied(Agent, Data, access, T) \leftarrow \textbf{not } UN/Gov(Agent), \\ Anonym(Data', Data) \qquad (3)$$

$$permitted(Agent, Data, access, T) \leftarrow Statistic(Agent), \; Fresh(Data', T), \\ Cast\_Fresh(Agent, Data', Data''), \\ Anonym(Data'', Data)$$
$$(4)$$

$$permitted(Agent, Data, access, T) \leftarrow Public(Agent), \; Fresh(Data', T), \\ Cast\_Fresh(Agent, Data', Data''), \\ Cast(Agent, Data'', Data'''), \\ Anonym(Data''', Data)$$
$$(5)$$

Rule (4) represents that $Statistic$ institutes can access the data with a minor freshness restriction, maximum 30 days. Rule (5) represents that the generic $Public$ can access the data with a freshness restriction of maximum 1 year, and the data quality is restricted. In both rules the data is anonymized.

While constructing the rules using our argumentation framework the various conflicts are detected. Rule (3) is in conflict with rules (4) and (5). In this case, as they are special cases of rule (3), we give priority to rules (4) and (5) over rule (3), denoted by (4) > (3) and (5) > (3).

5   Conclusion and Future Work

In our paper, we explained in brief our proposed approach for data processing and access control. Theoretically the approach is structured using the data quality background applied for the context of open data and open knowledge databases. Through our case scenario we present our method and example applications. However, through our presentation we identified additional issues pertinent to data quality which were not discussed in this study and should be further investigated. In this study we did not focus or discuss a specific conceptualization for data quality in open data context, although it is of great importance and one of our future goals. Another important topic that should be discussed in future research is the measurement of data quality and also a particular focus on multi-source and multi-format data and the supply chains around them. Further directions also could include topics as how the open data could create value for individuals, governments and organizations, in terms of financial growth, well-being, innovation, ethics and also sustainability.

Acknowledgments. Erisa Karafili was supported by the European Union's H2020 research and innovation programme under the Marie Skłodowska-Curie grant agreement No. 746667.

References

1. Arnold, S.E.: Information manufacturing: the road to database quality. Database **15**(5), 32–39 (1992)
2. Ballou, D., Wang, R., Pazer, H., Tayi, G.K.: Modeling information manufacturing systems to determine information product quality. Manag. Sci. **44**(4), 462–484 (1998)
3. Bayuk, J.: Data-centric security. Comput. Fraud Secur. **2009**(3), 7–11 (2009)
4. Bondarenko, A., Dung, P.M., Kowalski, R.A., Toni, F.: An abstract, argumentation-theoretic approach to default reasoning. Artif. Intell. **93**, 63–101 (1997)
5. Brodie, M.L.: Data quality in information systems. Inf. Manag. **3**(6), 245–258 (1980)
6. Chesbrough, H.: The era of open innovation. MIT Sloan Manag. Rev. **44**(3), 35–41 (2003)
7. Craven, R., Lobo, J., Ma, J., Russo, A., Lupu, E.C., Bandara, A.K.: Expressive policy analysis with enhanced system dynamicity. In: Proceedings of the 2009 ACM Symposium on Information, Computer and Communications Security, ASIACCS, pp. 239–250 (2009)
8. Dung, P.M.: On the acceptability of arguments and its fundamental role in non-monotonic reasoning, logic programming and n-person games. Artif. Intell. **77**(2), 321–358 (1995)
9. Ferraiolo, D.F., Kuhn, D.R.: Role-based access controls. In: 15th National Computer Security Conference (1992)
10. Fitzgerald, B.: The transformation of open source software. MIS Q. Manag. Inf. Syst. **30**, 587–598 (2006)
11. Fox, C., Levitin, A., Redman, T.: The notion of data and its quality dimensions. Inf. Process. Manag. **30**(1), 9–19 (1994)
12. Hazen, B.T., Boone, C.A., Ezell, J.D., Jones-Farmer, L.A.: Data quality for data science, predictive analytics, and big data in supply chain management: an introduction to the problem and suggestions for research and applications. Int. J. Prod. Econ. **154**, 72–80 (2014)
13. Huh, Y., Keller, F., Redman, T., Watkins, A.: Data quality. Inf. Softw. Technol. **32**(8), 559–565 (1990)

14. Janssen, M., Charalabidis, Y., Zuiderwijk, A.: Benefits, adoption barriers and myths of open data and open government. Inf. Syst. Manag. **29**, 258–268 (2012)
15. Janssen, M., van den Hoven, J.: Big and Open Linked Data (BOLD) in government: a challenge to transparency and privacy? Gov. Inf. Q. **32**, 363–368 (2015)
16. Kakas, A.C., Kowalski, R.A., Toni, F.: Abductive logic programming. J. Log. Comput. **2**(6), 719–770 (1992)
17. Karafili, E., Kakas, A.C., Spanoudakis, N.I., Lupu, E.C.: Argumentation-based security for social good. In: AAAI Fall Symposium Series (2017)
18. Karafili, E., Lupu, E.C.: Enabling data sharing in contextual environments: policy representation and analysis. In: Proceedings of the 22nd ACM on Symposium on Access Control Models and Technologies, SACMAT 2017, Indianapolis, IN, USA, 21–23 June 2017, pp. 231–238 (2017)
19. Karafili, E., Lupu, E.C., Cullen, A., Williams, B., Arunkumar, S., Calo, S.B.: Improving data sharing in data rich environments. In: 2017 IEEE International Conference on Big Data, BigData 2017, Boston, MA, USA, 11–14 December 2017, pp. 2998–3005 (2017)
20. Karafili, E., Nielson, H.R., Nielson, F.: How to trust the re-use of data. In: Foresti, S. (ed.) STM 2015. LNCS, vol. 9331, pp. 72–88. Springer, Cham (2015). https://doi.org/10.1007/978-3-319-24858-5_5
21. Karafili, E., Spanaki, K., Lupu, E.C.: An argumentation reasoning approach for data processing. Comput. Ind. **94**, 52–61 (2018)
22. Lazouski, A., Martinelli, F., Mori, P.: A prototype for enforcing usage control policies based on XACML. In: Fischer-Hübner, S., Katsikas, S., Quirchmayr, G. (eds.) TrustBus 2012. LNCS, vol. 7449, pp. 79–92. Springer, Heidelberg (2012). https://doi.org/10.1007/978-3-642-32287-7_7
23. Lichtenthaler, U.: Open innovation: past research, current debates, and future directions. Acad. Manag. Perspect. **25**, 75–93 (2011)
24. Lindman, J., Kinnari, T., Rossi, M.: Industrial open data: case studies of early open data entrepreneurs. In: 47th Hawaii International Conference on System Sciences, pp. 739–748 (2014)
25. Lindman, J., Rossi, M., Tuunainen,V.: Open data services: research agenda. In: 46th Hawaii International Conference on System Sciences, pp. 1239–1246 (2013)
26. March, S.T., Hevner, A.R.: Integrated decision support systems: a data warehousing perspective. Decis. Support Syst. **43**(3), 1031–1043 (2007)
27. Mont, M.C., Pearson, S.: Sticky policies: an approach for managing privacy across multiple parties. Computer **44**, 60–68 (2011)
28. Redman, T.C.: The impact of poor data quality on the typical enterprise. Commun. ACM **41**(2), 79–82 (1998)
29. Redman, T.C., Blanton, A.: Data Quality for the Information Age. Artech House Inc., Norwood (1997)
30. Ronen, B., Spiegler, I.: Information as inventory: a new conceptual view. Inf. Manag. **21**(4), 239–247 (1991)
31. Spanaki, K., Gürgüç, Z., Adams, R., Mulligan, C.: Data supply chain (DSC): research synthesis and future directions. Int. J. Prod. Res. **56**(13), 4447–4466 (2018)
32. Strong, D.M., Lee, Y.W., Wang, R.Y.: Data quality in context. Commun. ACM **40**(5), 103–110 (1997)
33. Swarup, V., Seligman, L., Rosenthal, A.: Specifying data sharing agreements. In: 7th IEEE International Workshop on Policies for Distributed Systems and Networks, POLICY, pp. 157–162 (2006)

34. Wang, C., Wang, Q., Ren, K., Lou, W.: Privacy-preserving public auditing for data storage security in cloud computing. In: 2010 Proceedings of INFOCOM, pp. 1–9. IEEE (2010)
35. Wang, R.Y.: A product perspective on total data quality management. Commun. ACM **41**(2), 58–65 (1998)
36. Wang, R.Y., Reddy, M.P., Kon, H.B.: Toward quality data: an attribute-based approach. Decis. Support Syst. **13**(3), 349–372 (1995)
37. Wang, R.Y., Strong, D.M.: Beyond accuracy: what data quality means to data consumers. J. Manag. Inf. Syst. **12**(4), 5–33 (1996)
38. Willinsky, J.: The Access Principle: The Case for Open Access to Research and Scholarship. The MIT Press, Cambridge (2006)

Doctoral Consortium

Doctoral Consortium 2018 Chair's Message

The Doctoral Consortium was held in conjunction with BIS 2018 conference, a well-respected event joining international researchers to discuss the wide range of the development, implementation, application and improvement of business applications and systems. The Consortium provided doctoral students with the chance to present and obtain comment on their research, to hear about the work of their peers at other universities, and to interact today's leading researchers from different universities and countries. It was also an opportunity to meet interesting people and make new friendships. We invited students at different career stages: advanced students who have a clear topic and research approach as well as less experiences students, on the beginning of their PhD track.

The Consortium was divided into two parts: plenary sessions and mentoring session. During the plenary session each student presented his or her work (research ideas, the current progress, future plans) and then received constructive criticism and insights that relate to his or her paper. There were organized 3 sessions and 11 PhD Students from 3 countries were invited to attend the conference. The mentoring session took place after the plenary sessions. Consortium Mentors were assigned to each student to provide individual feedback, advice on the paper, the focus of the work and further developments.

After reviewing process, 7 papers were accepted for publication in the proceedings at hand. Although every proposal is related to the Big Data topic, the scope of all proposals is wide-ranging. We hope it will be an interesting reading and a great inspiration for further analysis and research.

Florin Pop

Organization

Chair

Florin Pop   University Politehnica of Bucharest, Romania

Program Committee

Man Ho Allen Au   The Hong Kong Polytechnic University, China
Lidia Bajenaru   National Institute for R&D in Informatics – ICI,
                                                    Bucharest, Romania
Aniello Castiglione   University of Salerno, Italy
Marta Chinnici   ENEA, Italy
Kim-Kwang Raymond Choo   The University of Texas at San Antonio, USA
Valentin Cristea   University Politehnica of Bucharest, Romania
Ciprian Dobre   University Politehnica of Bucharest, Romania
Daniel Grosu   Wayne State University, USA
Nina Khairova   National Technical University, Kharkiv
                                                    Polytechnic Institute, Ukraine
Christian Leyh   Technische Universität Dresden, Chair of
                                                    Information Systems, Germany
Kuan-Ching Li   Providence University, Taiwan
Constandinos Mavromoustakis   University of Nicosia, Cyprus
Mariana Mocanu   University Politehnica of Bucharest, Romania
Gabriel Neagu   National Institute for R&D in Informatics – ICI,
                                                    Bucharest, Romania
Cătălin Negru   University Politehnica of Bucharest, Romania
Bogdan Nicolae   Argonne National Laboratory, USA
Francesco Palmieri   University of Salerno, Italy
Adrian Paschke   Fraunhofer FOKUS Berlin, Germany
Florin Pop   University Politehnica of Bucharest, Romania
Nirvana Popescu   University Politehnica of Bucharest, Romania
Ioan Salomie   Technical University of Cluj-Napoca, Romania
Maarten van Steen   University of Twente, the Netherlands
Laurence T. Yang   St. Francis Xavier University, Canada

Mentors

Christian Leyh	Technische Universität Dresden, Chair of Information Systems, Germany
Mariana Mocanu	University Politehnica of Bucharest, Romania
Cătălin Negru	University Politehnica of Bucharest, Romania
Gary Klein	University of Colorado Boulder, USA
Florin Pop	University Politehnica of Bucharest, Romania

Measures for Quality Assessment of Articles and Infoboxes in Multilingual Wikipedia

Włodzimierz Lewoniewski$^{(\boxtimes)}$ (iD)

Department of Information Systems, Poznań University of Economics and Business,
al. Niepodległości 10, 61-875 Poznań, Poland
{wlodzimierz.lewoniewski}@ue.poznan.pl
http://kie.ue.poznan.pl

Abstract. One of the most popular collaborative knowledge bases on the Internet is Wikipedia. Articles of this free encyclopaedia are created and edited by users from different countries in about 300 languages. Depending on topic and language version, quality of information there may vary. This study presents and classifies measures that can be extracted from Wikipedia articles for the purpose of automatic quality assessment in different languages. Based on a state of the art analysis and own experiments, specific measures for various aspects of quality have been defined. Additional, in this work they were also defined measures for quality assessment of data contained in the structural parts of Wikipedia articles - infoboxes. This study describes also an extraction methods for various sources of measures, that can be used in quality assessment.

Keywords: Wikipedia · Data quality · Quality measures · DBpedia
Wikidata · Quality dimensions · Web 2.0 · Encyclopedia

1 Introduction

Nowadays, often decision making in different areas depends on information that is found in the various open sources. On the one hand, peoples care about having access to as wide range of related data as possible. On the other hand, the quality of the data is also important. Therefore, searching for relevant information, Internet users need to understand how choose data and information with high quality from the Web.

Technologies Web 2.0 for more than 10 years allow everyone to contribute to common human knowledge on the Internet. One of the best examples of such online repositories is Wikipedia with over 48 million articles [76]. Information in this free encyclopaedia can be edited even by anonymous users independently in about 300 various language versions. The most developed is English version with over 5.7 million articles. However, this does not mean that this language

© Springer Nature Switzerland AG 2019
W. Abramowicz and A. Paschke (Eds.): BIS 2018 Workshops, LNBIP 339, pp. 619–633, 2019.
https://doi.org/10.1007/978-3-030-04849-5_53

version contains data and information of the best quality. Despite its popularity (the 5th most visited website in the world [2]) Wikipedia often criticized for the poor quality of content [21]. That quality depends on topic and language version of the articles [48].

Community of Wikipedia users separately in each language version defined rules and criteria to be followed by contributor when creating and editing the content of the articles. When all (or almost all) criteria are met, the article can get special award for quality. For example, in English Wikipedia the best articles have name "Featured" [23] (when all criteria are met) and "Good" [24] (when almost all criteria are met). In other language versions can be found equivalents for these awards with different spelling. However, very small number of articles in each language version of Wikipedia can boast such high quality content - they have a share of less than 1% [48].

In some language versions of Wikipedia articles can get other (lower) grades for quality. Articles assessment requires initiative and time from users, which should check whether the content meets the accepted quality criteria. Additionally, the content of the previously evaluated article can be corrected and updated at any time several times, which does not mean that the quality grade will also be corrected. Therefore, a large number of articles in different language versions do not have an assessment or have an irrelevant grade.

Quality in Wikipedia is broad topic in scientific works [77] and there are different researches in the field of automatic predicting of quality grade of the Wikipedia articles. Each study usually used own set of measures and specific algorithm to build a model to solve this task. This work presents known and new measures which can be related for different quality dimensions of the Wikipedia articles.

Articles in Wikipedia often includes dedicated table with main facts about the subject infobox. Depending on topic, the presence of an infobox can affect the quality of whole article. Infobox usually placed on a visible part of the page. That one of the most important elements. In wiki markup infobox contains list of items "parameter = value". However, sometimes it data can be inserted automatically from other sources: from Tabular Data [26] or WikiData [74]. Example of such infobox with its data sources is shown in Fig. 1.

These infoboxes are also used to enrich other others public knowledge bases such as DBpedia [18]. Data from such bases have been successfully applied in a number of domains: Life Sciences, Web Search, Digital Libraries, Maritime Domain, Art Market and others [1, 29, 66]. So this article presents also dimensions and measures for quality assessment of the infoboxes.

2 Quality Dimensions of the Wikipedia Articles

Quality can be defined as a degree to which information has content, form, and time characteristics, which give it value to specific end users [57]. If we take into the account user needs, quality will be the degree to which information is meeting this needs according to external, subjective user perceptions. [69]. In other words, quality of information is fitness for use [36].

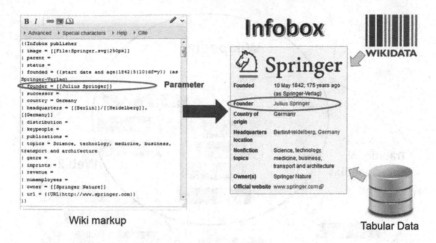

Fig. 1. Infobox with its data sources in English Wikipedia about publisher in article "Springer Science+Business Media"

According to ISO 8402, quality is "the totality of features and characteristics of a product or service that bear on its ability to satisfy stated or implied needs" [58]. For the needs of this work, the concept of quality from ISO 8402 will be used.

There are different approaches that defined measures and dimensions of information quality in the literature. For example, Eppler proposed 70 characteristics (or dimensions) of information that narrows down to 16 most important [27]. Depending on a source of information, complementary definitions of quality, outlining the various important dimensions of quality (e.g. accuracy, timeliness, etc.) can be defined.

Due the fact that on the one hand Wikipedia is an encyclopedia, and on the other hand - a representative of Web 2.0 services, based on the literature below are presented the most important quality dimensions for three sources of information:

- **Traditional encyclopedias:** Authority, Completeness, Format, Objectivity, Style, Timeliness, Uniqueness
- **Web 2.0 services:** Accessibility, Completeness, Credibility, Involvement, Objectivity, Readability, Relevance, Reputation, Style, Timeliness, Uniqueness, Usefulness
- **Wikipedia:** Completeness, Credibility, Objectivity, Readability, Relevance, Style, Timeliness

Figure 2 shows coverage of the quality dimensions of three mention sources of information.

Short description of each quality dimension are presented below:

- **Credibility:** whether the information provided can be checked with reliable sources

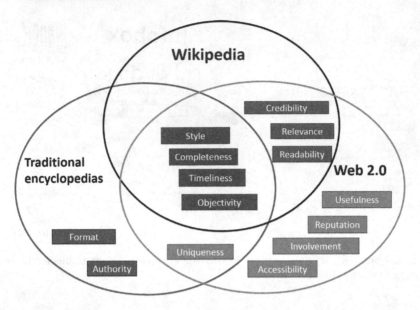

Fig. 2. Coverage of the quality dimensions of three sources of information: traditional encyclopedias, Wikipedia, Web 2.0 services. Source: own study.

- **Completeness:** how comprehensive the description of the topic is in article
- **Objectivity:** to what extent the content of the article meets the criterion of a neutral point of view, does it contain pictures and other multimedia materials related to this article
- **Readability:** to what extent the text is understandable and free from unnecessary complexity
- **Relevance:** to what extent the article is relevant (important) for readers/users
- **Style:** How the content of the article is organized.
- **Timeliness:** to what extent the article describes the current state of a certain reality (degree to which information is up-to-date).

3   Quality Measures of the Wikipedia Articles

Each of 7 quality dimension of the Wikipedia cave has own set of measures. Each measure can be represented as statistical value. In section describes the most popular quality measures of the Wikipedia Articles related to particular quality dimension.

3.1   Credibility

Using reliable sources in Wikipedia is one of the important criteria for writing articles with high quality [22]. Readers of the encyclopedia must be able to check where the information come from [25]. Therefore, one of the most commonly used measure related to credibility is number of the references in Wikipedia articles [6,13,15,17,28,43,46–48,61,64,65,72,81,84] or external link count [6,13,15,28, 30,47,65,68,72,82]. On of the related research has shown that depending on the references users can assess the trustworthiness of Wikipedia articles [52].

Here it can be also taken info the account not only quantity, but also quality of the sources. On of the possibilities is to estimate popularity of the reference and its domain based on visiting count or number of incoming links from other websites. For this, data from search engines can be useful. For this we can use data from search engines such as Google, Baidu, Yahoo, Bing, Yandex and also specific tools such as Alexa. Another possibility is to evaluate scientific references using Altmetric [3] and other tools.

3.2 Completeness

Wikipedia articles with high quality must neglects no major facts or details and places the subject in context. One of the most popular measure for this dimension is content volume measured by articles length [5,13,16,17,30,41,43, 46–48,59,64,67,68,71,72,81,82,84]. Length can be measured in different ways: bytes, characters, words and others.

3.3 Objectivity

Wikipedia article must presents views fairly and without bias. Objectivity can expected from article, which was jointly created by a large number of different users. So, the most popular measure is the number of unique authors [13,28,30,37,39,47,50,51,61,67,68,72,79–82]. Here it can be also used image count measure [6,13,15,37,43,46–48,51,63,67,68,72,81,82,84]

3.4 Readability

Measures related to this quality dimension must show to what extent the text is understandable and free from unnecessary complexity. Therefore, first of all, here it is necessary to take into account special readability formulas such as Automated Readability Index [5,16,17,30,51,59,60,62,64], Bormuth Index [4, 7], Coleman-Liau Index [5,12,16,17,30,59,64], FORCAST Readability [5,10], Flesch Reading Score [5,13,16,17,30,31,61,64,67,68,81], Flesch-Kincaid grade level [5,13,16,17,30,38,61,64,67,68,70,81], Gunning Fog Index [5,16,17,30,33, 64], LIX [16,30], Miyazaki EFL Readability Index [4,32], Dale-Chall [14,17,64], SMOG Grading [5,17,30,53,64], Linsear write formula [11,17,64] and others. These formulas often based on pre-calculated words of different types. So, this dimension can also consist various linguistic features. Depending on language version, it is possible to defined up to over 100–150 such measures [45,49]

3.5 Relevance

This dimension shows how popular or important for readers is selected Wikipedia Article. For this reason, it can be used such measures as articles age [13, 15, 28, 30, 37, 39, 41, 43, 47, 51, 59–61, 67, 68, 70, 81], number of page watchers [47, 72], number of page visits [47, 48], incoming internal link count (number of times that the article is cited by other Wikipedia articles) [15, 28, 30, 47, 65, 72] and others, including more complex (e.q. PageRank [8]). Also it can be taken into the account measures that shows number of the links from external sources, such as Reddit [56], Facebook, Youtube, Twitter, Linkedin, VKontakte and other social services [44].

3.6 Style

Wikipedia articles with high quality must follows the style guidelines, including appropriate structure. So, one of the most simplest and popular measure for this dimension is number of the sections in the article [6, 13, 15, 28, 41, 47, 70, 72, 81, 84]. Here also can be used such measures, as number of tables [4, 6], number of templates [4, 41, 43, 70].

3.7 Timeliness

Information on certain topics may change with time (living people, populated places etc.), therefore it is important that the article has actual data. Some measures can help to assess this dimension: number of unique editors and number of contributions for the last selected time. Measures of this quality dimension can be related to currency and volatility of the information [34].

3.8 Extraction Methods for Articles Measures

There are different possibilities and techniques to get measures values of the Wikipedia articles. The vast majority of the measures can be extracted from Wikipedia database dumps. Below is a list of some files for the latest dump of English Wikipedia [75] and a brief description of what can be extracted:

- **enwiki-latest-pages-meta-current.xml.bz2:** recombine all pages (including articles), current versions only. This file is used for obtaining a majority of the articles measures.
- **enwiki-latest-pages-articles.xml.bz2:** consist articles, templates, media/ file descriptions, and primary meta-pages. Can be used also for obtaining a majority of the articles measures (excluding statistics from discussion pages).
- **enwiki-latest-pagelinks.sql.gz:** wiki page-to-page link records. Used for network measures - for example incoming links from other articles.
- **enwiki-latest-categorylinks.sql.gz:** wiki category membership link records. Can be used for category count measure.
- **enwiki-latest-externallinks.sql.gz:** wiki external URL link records. can be used for external link count measure.

- **enwiki-latest-stub-meta-history.xml.gz:** contain only historical revision metadata. Can be used to extract number of the editors from different groups (bots, anonymous users, administartors etc.) and alsa number of the edits of various types (e.g. minor edits, edits comments).
- **enwiki-latest-iwlinks.sql.gz:** Interwiki link tracking records. Can be used to extract number of the unique internal links (links to other Wikipedia articles).
- **enwiki-latest-templatelinks.sql.gz:** Wiki template inclusion link records. Used for templates count measure, also it is possible to check if article has infobox
- **enwiki-latest-page.sql.gz:** base per-page data (id, title, old restrictions, etc.). Can be used to extract last edit time, page length in bytes.
- **enwiki-latest-imagelinks.sql.gz:** wiki media/files usage records. Can be used to image count measure.

Mention files can give different opportunities for extracting values of measures. For example, some of the studies count number of images by taken into the account tag [[image:...]] in the wiki markup (source code of the article) [6, 13, 15, 67, 68, 81, 82, 84]. However, other images that are inserted (for example using special templates) will not be considered. Therefore, it can be used other approach, which extracted number of the images from wiki media usage records file [43, 46–48, 63, 72].

Another example - number of internal links and number of incoming internal link (from other articles). It is possible to study the code of each article to find links, but links which was inserted by special templates will be not considered. Therefore, it can be used file with wiki page-to-page link records.

Some of the measures can not be extracted from dumps files. For example, to obtain number of page watcher for each article it is necessary to send request to Wikipedia API [20]. Measures from external resources (such as Facebook, Twitter, Reddit etc.) are also must be obtained from other sources.

3.9 Derivative Measures

Most of the related works took into the account combination of two or more measures. For instance, one of the most popular derivative measure is number of the references per article length [9, 15, 28, 43, 46–48, 59, 70, 72]. Here length can be defined as volume in bytes [9, 43, 46–48, 70, 72], number of the words [4, 15], number of the characters [28, 59]

Some approaches based on normalised measures. For example, to build synthetic measure for Wikipedia articles quality online service WikiRank [78] use normalised values of 5 measures based on the threshold from Featured articles [46, 72]. It is also possible to measure relative popularity using normalised value of some measures related to relevance quality dimension [48]. Some studies used log-transformed measures [9, 41, 47, 71, 72]

3.10   Multidimensional Quality Measures

Some measures can be related to two or more quality dimension. For example, editors count can show objectivity of the article (different point of view), but additionally can help to measure relevance of the content (more users are interested in this topic).

Another example - images count. On the one hand, pictures can help assess objectivity of the presented in the article material, but on the other hand we can measure completeness (because articles on a particular topic should contain pictures) and style (for example, to avoid writing a lot of text, the authors of the article decided to add more images).

Number of the citation templates [17,64,71,84] can help to measure quantity of the references (credibility) as well as in what degree information about the source is available for the reader (completeness).

4   Quality Measures of the Infoboxes

Interpretation of the quality of data depends on who will use this information [54]. Based on the literature [40,42,54,83]and own observations four important dimensions was selected to assess quality of the infoboxes: completeness, credibility, relevance, timeliness. Subsections below briefly describes quality measures of the infoboxes related to these dimensions.

4.1   Completeness

Completeness of the infobox can be measured as the ratio of the number of parameter values to the number of all defined parameters in the infobox of a given type. Other related to this quality dimension measure can also consider weights for each filled parameter, where weight is based on the frequency of filling this parameter [42]. Here we can also take into the account length of the infobox, number of templates and other elements that the infobox contains.

In some topics, infoboxes can consist similar parameters, which can be omitted when calculating completeness. For example, to describe cities of Poland in some language versions of Wikipedia there is a special infobox, so the parameter about country is absent. At the same time other languages to describe the same city can use common infobox for different cities in the world, so parameter about country is important there.

4.2   Credibility

As in the case of Wikipedia articles credibility is related to analysis of the references. Depending on the topic and the language version, within each infobox you can find parameters with similar references. To assess credibility it can be used such measures as number of references, number of unique references, references to filled parameters ratio.

4.3   Relevance

Data in infoboxes can be provided by different users. Relevance can be measured as number of unique authors of the infoboxes. Authors can be divided to different categories: bots, anonymous users, administrators etc.

4.4   Timeliness

For this dimension we must take into the account measure related to number of recent changes of whole infobox and its individual parameters. As in the case of Wikipedia articles, timeliness measures can be related to currency and volatility of the infoboxes.

5   Quality of the Infobox Parameter

Quality of each parameter of the infoboxes can also be evaluated. One of the important dimensions of quality is timeliness. It can be measured based on the values of specific parameters.

For example, often in infoboxes that describe cities, there is a parameter that indicates the date (year) when the population size was evaluated. However, most of the parameters do not have this additional information.

For example, in the same infoboxes about cities, there is no explicit information when the value of the parameter about the city mayor has been entered. This may be particularly important in the periods of local government elections, when the election results were announced, but officially the new mayor has still can not perform this function.

The Fig. 3 shows the history of changes in the "leader name" parameter of the Poznań infobox in the Wikipedia language versions in question from the moment of announcing the results of the exit pool on WTK television until the oath made by the new mayor of Poznań. On the basis of this figure, we can see that in Polish version changed parameter about mayor quickly after posting news on media portals. In addition, it can be seen that in the Polish Wikipedia there was no consensus on the value of the "leader name" parameter of the infobox in the article about Poznań in the presented period, because the new city mayor was formally elected, but can gain authority after taking the oath. However, in English Wikipedia there was no controversy on the subject, and the name of the new mayor was entered after the election results were announced, but a bit later than the Polish language version did. The Russian Wikipedia has twice changed the value of the parameter about the city mayor in the audited period. The first arose from the announcement of the results of the vote, and the second change arose from a minor correction of the name, according to the rules of transliteration to the Cyrillic alphabet. As for the Belarusian and Ukrainian Wikipedia - there were no changes there and the new value appeared much later. This is related to the fact that entering the value of this parameter in the Belarusian and Ukrainian version of the infobox is not mandatory, because the value can be automatically inserted from the Wikidata, where the value was updated almost 3 years after the announcement of the election and the oath.

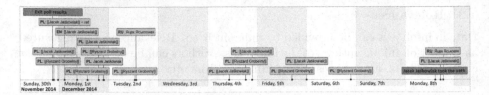

Fig. 3. History of changes of the "leader name" parameter of the infobox about Poznań in selected language versions of Wikipedia since the publication of the exit pool results on WTK television until the taking the oath by the new mayor of Poznań. Source: own study based on historical Wikipedia data.

6   Discussion and Future Work

In this paper quality measures and dimensions for quality assessment of Wikipedia articles and infoboxes were described.

Most of the previous studies works with the most developed language version of Wikipedia - English. Therefore, it is necessary to filter some of the measures (especially related to readability dimension) to be able to assess quality of articles between different languages.

Using machine learning and artificial intelligence algorithms proposed measures can help to build more accurate models for quality assessment of articles and infoboxes in different language versions of Wikipedia. To build such models it is planned to use also cloud computing platforms such as Microsoft Azure [55]. Comparing the quality of information between different language versions of Wikipedia can also be done without taking into account other external sources of the related data (that can be closer to real-world description), by analogy with the theory of relativity [19].

Additional to improve the quality models, it is planned to use data from projects, which collect data from Internet users that compare quality of the multilingual information in Wikipedia. For example, project WikiBest [73] allows to choose best language version of infoboxes of particular topic in four nominations: the best quality, the best completeness, the best credibility, the best timeliness. User ratings can help to improve projects related to infoboxes evaluation [35].

Future works will be concentrated in defining new measures and in researches that will help to find dimensions and the most important measures for quality assessment of articles and infoboxes in multilingual Wikipedia.

References

1. Abramowicz, W., Auer, S., Heath, T.: Linked data in business. Bus. Inf. Syst. Eng. **58**(5), 323–326 (2016). https://doi.org/10.1007/s12599-016-0446-0
2. Alexa: Wikipedia.org traffic, demographics and competitors. https://www.alexa.com/siteinfo/wikipedia.org
3. Altmetric: free tools. https://www.altmetric.com/products/free-tools/

4. Anderka, M.: Analyzing and predicting quality flaws in user-generated content: the case of Wikipedia. Ph.D. Bauhaus-Universitaet Weimar Germany (2013)
5. Blumenstock, J.E.: Automatically assessing the quality of Wikipedia articles. Technical report (2008). https://doi.org/10.1080/17439880802324251
6. Blumenstock, J.E.: Size matters: word count as a measure of quality on Wikipedia. In: WWW, pp. 1095–1096 (2008). https://doi.org/10.1145/1367497.1367673
7. Bormuth, J.R.: Readability: a new approach. Read. Res. Q. **1**, 79–132 (1966)
8. Brin, S., Page, L.: The anatomy of a large-scale hypertextual web search engine. Comput. Netw. ISDN Syst. **30**(1–7), 107–117 (1998)
9. De la Calzada, G., Dekhtyar, A.: On measuring the quality of Wikipedia articles. In: Proceedings of the 4th Workshop on Information Credibility, pp. 11–18. ACM (2010)
10. Caylor, J.S., Sticht, T.G.: Development of a simple readability index for job reading material (1973)
11. Chen, H.H.: How to use readability formulas to access and select English reading materials. J. Educ. Media Libr. Sci. **50**(2), 229–254 (2012)
12. Coleman, M., Liau, T.L.: A computer readability formula designed for machine scoring. J. Appl. Psychol. **60**(2), 283 (1975)
13. Conti, R., Marzini, E., Spognardi, A., Matteucci, I., Mori, P., Petrocchi, M.: Maturity assessment of Wikipedia medical articles. In: 2014 IEEE 27th International Symposium on Computer-Based Medical Systems (CBMS), pp. 281–286. IEEE (2014)
14. Dale, E., Chall, J.S.: A formula for predicting readability: instructions. Educ. Res. Bull. **18**, 37–54 (1948)
15. Dalip, D.H., Gonçalves, M.A., Cristo, M., Calado, P.: Automatic quality assessment of content created collaboratively by web communities: a case study of Wikipedia. In: Proceedings of the 9th ACM/IEEE-CS Joint Conference on Digital Libraries, pp. 295–304 (2009). https://doi.org/10.1145/1555400.1555449
16. Dalip, D.H., Gonçalves, M.A., Cristo, M., Calado, P.: Automatic assessment of document quality in web collaborative digital libraries. J. Data Inf. Quality **2**(3), 1–30 (2011). https://doi.org/10.1145/2063504.2063507
17. Dang, Q.V., Ignat, C.L.: Measuring quality of collaboratively edited documents: the case of Wikipedia. In: 2016 IEEE 2nd International Conference on Collaboration and Internet Computing (CIC), pp. 266–275. IEEE (2016)
18. DBpedia: Main Page. https://wiki.dbpedia.org
19. Einstein, A.: The Meaning of Relativity. Routledge, Abingdon (2003)
20. English Wikipedia: API sandbox. https://en.wikipedia.org/wiki/Special:ApiSandbox
21. English Wikipedia: Criticism of Wikipedia. https://en.wikipedia.org/wiki/Criticism_of_Wikipedia
22. English Wikipedia: Featured article criteria. https://en.wikipedia.org/wiki/Wikipedia:Featured_article_criteria
23. English Wikipedia: Featured articles. https://en.wikipedia.org/wiki/Wikipedia:Featured_articles
24. English Wikipedia: Good articles. https://en.wikipedia.org/wiki/Wikipedia:Good_articles
25. English Wikipedia: Verifiability. https://en.wikipedia.org/wiki/Wikipedia:Verifiability
26. English Wikipedia: Wikiproject tabular data. https://en.wikipedia.org/wiki/Wikipedia:WikiProject_Tabular_Data

27. Eppler, M.J.: Managing Information Quality: Increasing the Value of Information in Knowledge-Intensive Products and Processes. Springer, Heidelberg (2003). https://doi.org/10.1007/3-540-32225-6

28. Ferschke, O., Gurevych, I., Rittberger, M.: FlawFinder: a modular system for predicting quality flaws in Wikipedia. In: CLEF (Online Working Notes/Labs/Workshop), pp. 1–10 (2012)

29. Filipiak, D., Filipowska, A.: Improving the quality of art market data using linked open data and machine learning. In: Abramowicz, W., Alt, R., Franczyk, B. (eds.) BIS 2016. LNBIP, vol. 263, pp. 418–428. Springer, Cham (2017). https://doi.org/10.1007/978-3-319-52464-1_39

30. Flekova, L., Ferschke, O., Gurevych, I.: What makes a good biography? Multidimensional quality analysis based on Wikipedia article feedback data. In: Proceedings of the 23rd International Conference on World Wide Web, pp. 855–866. ACM (2014)

31. Flesch, R.: A new readability yardstick. J. Appl. Psychol. **32**(3), 221 (1948)

32. Greenfield, G.R.: Classic readability formulas in an EFL context: are they valid for Japanese speakers? Ph.D. thesis. Temple University (1999)

33. Gunning, R.: The Technique of Clear Writing. McGraw-Hill, New York (1952)

34. Hazen, B.T., Boone, C.A., Ezell, J.D., Jones-Farmer, L.A.: Data quality for data science, predictive analytics, and big data in supply chain management: an introduction to the problem and suggestions for research and applications. Int. J. Prod. Econ. **154**, 72–80 (2014). https://doi.org/10.1016/j.ijpe.2014.04.018

35. Infoboxes.net: quality comparison of infoboxes in Miltilingual Wikipedia. http://infoboxes.net

36. Juran, J., Godfrey, A.B.: Quality Handbook, pp. 173–178. McGraw-Hill, New York (1999)

37. Kane, G.C.: A multimethod study of information quality in Wiki collaboration. ACM Trans. Manag. Inf. Syst. (TMIS) **2**(1), 4 (2011)

38. Kincaid, J.P., Fishburne Jr, R.P., Rogers, R.L., Chissom, B.S.: Derivation of new readability formulas (automated readability index, fog count and Flesch reading ease formula) for navy enlisted personnel. Technical report. Naval Technical Training Command Millington TN Research Branch (1975)

39. Kittur, A., Kraut, R.E.: Harnessing the wisdom of crowds in Wikipedia: quality through coordination. In: Proceedings of the ACM 2008 Conference on Computer Supported Cooperative Work - CSCW 2008, p. 37 (2008). https://doi.org/10.1145/1460563.1460572

40. Kontokostas, D., et al.: Test-driven evaluation of linked data quality. In: Proceedings of the 23rd International Conference on World Wide Web, pp. 747–758. ACM (2014)

41. Lerner, J., Lomi, A.: Knowledge categorization affects popularity and quality of Wikipedia articles. PloS One **13**(1), e0190674 (2018)

42. Lewoniewski, W.: Completeness and reliability of Wikipedia infoboxes in various languages. In: Abramowicz, W. (ed.) BIS 2017. LNBIP, vol. 303, pp. 295–305. Springer, Cham (2017). https://doi.org/10.1007/978-3-319-69023-0_25

43. Lewoniewski, W.: Enrichment of information in multilingual Wikipedia based on quality analysis. In: Abramowicz, W. (ed.) BIS 2017. LNBIP, vol. 303, pp. 216–227. Springer, Cham (2017). https://doi.org/10.1007/978-3-319-69023-0_19

44. Lewoniewski, W., Härting, R.-C., Wecel, K., Reichstein, C., Abramowicz, W.: Application of SEO metrics to determine the quality of Wikipedia articles and their sources. In: Damaševičius, R., Vasiljevienė, G. (eds.) ICIST 2018. CCIS,

vol. 920, pp. 139–152. Springer, Cham (2018). https://doi.org/10.1007/978-3-319-99972-2_11

45. Lewoniewski, W., Khairova, N., Węcel, K., Stratiienko, N., Abramowicz, W.: Using morphological and semantic features for the quality assessment of Russian Wikipedia. In: Damaševičius, R., Mikašytė, V. (eds.) ICIST 2017. CCIS, vol. 756, pp. 550–560. Springer, Cham (2017). https://doi.org/10.1007/978-3-319-67642-5_46

46. Lewoniewski, W., Węcel, K.: Relative quality assessment of Wikipedia articles in different languages using synthetic measure. In: Abramowicz, W. (ed.) BIS 2017. LNBIP, vol. 303, pp. 282–292. Springer, Cham (2017). https://doi.org/10.1007/978-3-319-69023-0_24

47. Lewoniewski, W., Węcel, K., Abramowicz, W.: Quality and importance of Wikipedia articles in different languages. In: Dregvaite, G., Damasevicius, R. (eds.) ICIST 2016. CCIS, vol. 639, pp. 613–624. Springer, Cham (2016). https://doi.org/10.1007/978-3-319-46254-7_50

48. Lewoniewski, W., Węcel, K., Abramowicz, W.: Relative quality and popularity evaluation of multilingual Wikipedia articles. Informatics 4 (2017). https://doi.org/10.3390/informatics4040043

49. Lewoniewski, W., Węcel, K., Abramowicz, W.: Determining quality of articles in polish Wikipedia based on linguistic features. In: Damaševičius, R., Vasiljevienė, G. (eds.) ICIST 2018. CCIS, vol. 920, pp. 546–558. Springer, Cham (2018). https://doi.org/10.1007/978-3-319-99972-2_45

50. Lih, A.: Wikipedia as participatory journalism: reliable sources? Metrics for evaluating collaborative media as a news resource. In: 5th International Symposium on Online Journalism, p. 31 (2004)

51. Liu, J., Ram, S.: Using big data and network analysis to understand Wikipedia article quality. Data Knowl. Eng. 115, 80–93 (2018)

52. Lucassen, T., Schraagen, J.M.: Trust in Wikipedia: how users trust information from an unknown source. In: Proceedings of the 4th Workshop on Information Credibility, pp. 19–26. ACM (2010)

53. Mc Laughlin, G.H.: SMOG grading-a new readability formula. J. Read. 12(8), 639–646 (1969)

54. Mendes, P.N., Mühleisen, H., Bizer, C.: Sieve: linked data quality assessment and fusion. In: Proceedings of the 2012 Joint EDBT/ICDT Workshops, pp. 116–123. ACM (2012)

55. Microsoft Azure: Cloud computing platform & services. https://azure.microsoft.com/en-us/

56. Moyer, D., Carson, S.L., Dye, T.K., Carson, R.T., Goldbaum, D.: Determining the influence of reddit posts on Wikipedia pageviews. In: Ninth International AAAI Conference on Web and Social Media, pp. 75–82. AAAI Press Oxford, UK (2015)

57. O'Brien, J.A., Marakas, G.M.: Introduction to Information Systems, vol. 13. McGraw-Hill/Irwin, New York City (2005)

58. OECD Glossary of Statistical Terms: ISO 8402 - quality. http://stats.oecd.org/glossary/detail.asp?ID=5150

59. Ransbotham, S., Kane, G.: Membership turnover and collaboration success in online communities: explaining rises and falls from grace in Wikipedia. MIS Q. 35(3), 613–627 (2011)

60. Ransbotham, S., Kane, G.C., Lurie, N.H.: Network characteristics and the value of collaborative user-generated content. Mark. Sci. 31(3), 387–405 (2012)

61. di Sciascio, C., Strohmaier, D., Errecalde, M., Veas, E.: WikiLyzer: interactive information quality assessment in Wikipedia. In: Proceedings of the 22nd International Conference on Intelligent User Interfaces, pp. 377–388. ACM (2017)
62. Senter, R., Smith, E.A.: Automated readability index. Technical report, University of Cincinnati, Ohio (1967)
63. Shang, W.: A comparison of the historical entries in Wikipedia and Baidu Baike. In: Chowdhury, G., McLeod, J., Gillet, V., Willett, P. (eds.) iConference 2018. LNCS, vol. 10766, pp. 74–80. Springer, Cham (2018). https://doi.org/10.1007/978-3-319-78105-1_9
64. Shen, A., Qi, J., Baldwin, T.: A hybrid model for quality assessment of Wikipedia articles. In: Proceedings of the Australasian Language Technology Association Workshop, pp. 43–52 (2017)
65. Soonthornphisaj, N., Paengporn, P.: Thai Wikipedia article quality filtering algorithm. In: Proceedings of the International Multi Conference of Engineers and Computer Scientists, vol. 1 (2017)
66. Stróżyna, M., Eiden, G., Abramowicz, W., Filipiak, D., Małyszko, J., Węcel, K.: A framework for the quality-based selection and retrieval of open data - a use case from the maritime domain. Electron. Mark. 28(2), 219–233 (2018). https://doi.org/10.1007/s12525-017-0277-y
67. Stvilia, B., Twidale, M.B., Gasser, L., Smith, L.C.: Information quality discussions in Wikipedia. In: Proceedings of the 2005 International Conference on Knowledge Management, pp. 101–113. Citeseer (2005)
68. Stvilia, B., Twidale, M.B., Smith, L.C., Gasser, L.: Assessing information quality of a community-based encyclopedia. In: Proceedings of ICIQ, pp. 442–454 (2005)
69. Wang, R.Y., Strong, D.M.: Beyond accuracy: what data quality means to data consumers. J. Manag. Inf. Syst. 12(4), 5–33 (1996)
70. Warncke-wang, M., Cosley, D., Riedl, J.: Tell me more : an actionable quality model for Wikipedia. In: In: WikiSym 2013, pp. 1–10 (2013). https://doi.org/10.1145/2491055.2491063
71. Warncke-Wang, M., Ranjan, V., Terveen, L.G., Hecht, B.J.: Misalignment between supply and demand of quality content in peer production communities. In: ICWSM, pp. 493–502 (2015)
72. Węcel, K., Lewoniewski, W.: Modelling the quality of attributes in Wikipedia infoboxes. In: Abramowicz, W. (ed.) BIS 2015. LNBIP, vol. 228, pp. 308–320. Springer, Cham (2015). https://doi.org/10.1007/978-3-319-26762-3_27
73. WikiBest: Online game about comparing data quality between various languages of the wikipedia. https://wikibest.net
74. Wikidata: Main page. https://www.wikidata.org/wiki/Wikidata:Main_Page
75. Wikimedia Downloads: English Wikipedia latest database backup dumps. https://dumps.wikimedia.org/enwiki/latest/
76. Wikipedia Meta-Wiki: List of Wikipedias. https://meta.wikimedia.org/wiki/List_of_Wikipedias
77. Wikipedia Quality: Scientific works. https://wikipediaquality.com/wiki/Category:Scientific_works
78. WikiRank: Quality and popularity assessment of Wikipedia. https://wikirank.net
79. Wilkinson, D.M., Huberman, B.A.: Assessing the value of cooperation in Wikipedia. arXiv preprint arXiv: cs/0702140 (2007)
80. Wilkinson, D.M., Huberman, B.A.: Cooperation and quality in Wikipedia. In: Proceedings of the 2007 International Symposium on Wikis WikiSym 2007, pp. 157–164 (2007). https://doi.org/10.1145/1296951.1296968

81. Wu, K., Zhu, Q., Zhao, Y., Zheng, H.: Mining the factors affecting the quality of Wikipedia articles. In: 2010 International Conference of Information Science and Management Engineering (ISME), vol. 1, pp. 343–346. IEEE (2010)
82. Yaari, E., Baruchson-Arbib, S., Bar-Ilan, J.: Information quality assessment of community generated content: a user study of wikipedia. J. Inf. Sci. **37**(5), 487–498 (2011)
83. Zaveri, A., Rula, A., Maurino, A., Pietrobon, R., Lehmann, J., Auer, S.: Quality assessment for linked data: a survey. Semant. Web **7**(1), 63–93 (2016)
84. Zhang, S., Hu, Z., Zhang, C., Yu, K.: History-based article quality assessment on Wikipedia. In: 2018 IEEE International Conference on Big Data and Smart Computing (BigComp), pp. 1–8. IEEE (2018)

Supply Chain Modelling Using Data Science

Szczepan Górtowski[1,2(✉)]

[1] Department of Information Systems,
Faculty of Informatics and Electronic Economy, Poznań University of Economics,
al. Niepodległości 10, 61-875 Poznań, Poland
`szczepan.gortowski@ue.poznan.pl`
[2] Żabka Polska, Plac Andersa 7, 61-894 Poznań, Poland

Abstract. The paper describes a research results in the field of supply chain modelling. The supply chain topology model, which will be the base for further analysis, is modelled as a network where nodes represent entities and business processes between them are presented as edges. A convenience stores network with a franchising business model was chosen for the model evaluation. The analysis uncovers conflicting goals between the franchisees and the franchise holder that must be taken into account. To conduct the research the Data Mining techniques, especially Process Mining (process design, process improvement, process analysis) will be used. First insight into Information needs is described.

Keywords: Process mining · Data-driven decision making
Supply chain · Logistics · Supply chain modelling · Supply chain design

1 Introduction

The increasing complexity of business processes leads to the generation of a huge amount of data. Increasing volume of heterogeneous data as well as novel Data Science technologies and tools allow to use non-trivial calculation methods and algorithms. Building knowledge from data is an important step for achieving competitive advantage (Witten et al. 2017). The role of information in value creation is emphasised in the literature (Kubina et al. 2015; Lim et al. 2018).

Common market model is the presence of large entities that organise the supply chain and affect smaller entities. A special case of such a structure is the franchise network. Considering the market organisation, it is reasonable to build a supply chain that takes into account the interests of both the franchisee and franchise holder (Reynolds 2015; Rosado-Serrano et al. 2018). Moreover, it is reasonable to investigate possible sources of conflict in achieving the goals of individual units and decide what is more important for the network success. The model that neglects this aspect might be inaccurate and not sufficient for real-world business scenarios. Thus, there is a need for solutions that will maximise profit across the entire franchise network. The author was unable to identify

© Springer Nature Switzerland AG 2019
W. Abramowicz and A. Paschke (Eds.): BIS 2018 Workshops, LNBIP 339, pp. 634–645, 2019.
https://doi.org/10.1007/978-3-030-04849-5_54

methods for supply chain analysis taking the relationships between franchisees and franchise holder into account.

Use case chosen for the method evaluation are convenience stores from FMCG[1] sector. Successes of networks like Żabka Polska[2], Circle K[3] or 7-Eleven Inc.[4] confirm that this concept is profitable. The networks above are suitable for conducting research in the described area due to their vastness and the resulting technological flow.

The paper is composed as follows. Section 2 presents the approaches used for modelling supply networks as well as usage of Data Science for modelling or measuring the effectiveness of individual processes. Section 3 presents the thesis and research goals. Subsequently, Sect. 4 presents the supply chain topology model on which the work is based. Contradictory aspirations and potentially conflicts between links in the network that have been presented will be taken into account when building the model. This part also contains a brief description of the sample process. The final section will present conclusions from previous research as well as the future research steps.

2   Related Work

The subject of modelling and improving the supply chain is constantly discussed by many researchers, who use new IT solutions to build more effective supply chain (Gjerdrum et al. 2001; Crespo Márquez 2010; Campuzano and Mula 2011). The changes in transport, globalisation, Semantic Web and other improvements change business models. Supply chain modelling approaches could be categorised in many ways. Among several works that touch the problems, the ones worth highlighting are: (Min and Zhou 2002; Kim and Rogers 2005; Kleijnen 2005). Cited papers focus on the methodologies and highlight major approaches of modelling supply chains. There are mostly distinguish analytical and simulation models. Last one also survey a simulation tools and techniques. The following approaches are the most common in the literature:

- Analytical
    - Deterministic – It is possible to fully specify variables, that do not change within the model (Bidhandi et al. 2009; Sadghiani et al. 2015).
    - Stochastic – There are variables, which may not be fully modelled and the model will work on uncertain conditions. (Malikia et al. 2017)
    - Hybrid – (Chiadamrong and Piyathanavong 2017)
- Simulation models
    - Spreadsheet simulation – Simple analysis between restricted changing factors, relatively easy to use (Liu et al. 2013, Buchmeister et al. 2013).

---

[1] Fast Moving Consumer Goods.
[2] http://www.zabka.pl.
[3] https://www.circlek.com/.
[4] https://www.7-eleven.com/.

- System dynamics (SD) – The task of system dynamics is to understand causes and system behaviour in the case of applying changes (Pierreval et al. 2007; Crespo Márquez 2010; Ivanov 2017).
- Business games – Used in cases, where it is impossible to model some behaviour such as ones coming from human part, allowing for a dialogue between the user and programme (van Houten 2007; Panchal et al. 2015).
- Discrete event dynamic systems simulation – In contrast to system dynamics – this simulation allows for uncertainty in the model variables and occurencies (Morgan et al. 2017).

Measuring the supply chain effectiveness have been discussed in many studies such as:

- (Beamon 1998) – In this papers the author distinguished cost, customer, responsiveness, cost and customer responsiveness, cost and activity time, flexibility as a basis for measurement. Depending on basis performance could be measure as minimized cost, achieved service level, stockout probability etc.
- (Campuzano and Mula 2011) – The area of measures was divided into qualitative (e.g. described flexibility or suppliers performance) and quantitative (based on profit and based on the customer's response).

The assessment of supply chain effectiveness is very important and could be company-specific. It depends on company needs. Some methods, metrics and indicators may be used by companies from various sectors (Taylor and Fawcett 2001; Jacyna-Gołda et al. 2018) as well as more complex ones such as the case based on performance measurement system by (Tonchia et al. 2010) and the ones that are based on operational controlling (Śliwczyński 2011). According to (Tonchia et al. 2010) one can divide a performance measurement depending on dimensions (mainly cost, non-cost), type (time, quantity etc.) or the level of analysis. In the case of organisational level it could be operational, tactical or strategic measures, but it can be also divided into corporate, entity, plant, customer, product etc. level. The evaluation methods of supply chain management systems was described e.g. in (Tomczak and Rzepecki 2017). This paper described multi-criteria decision making method in supply chain.

Data Mining techniques, especially for Process Mining (process design, process improvement, process analysis) were discussed by (Witten et al. 2017, van der Aalst 2016). Both papers describe the main concept of data mining e.g. heuristic, genetic, region-based and inductive. There are also mentioned limitations and current research areas with this technologies. This techniques could be used for help the decision and build the decision making system e.g. Data-Driven Decision Making – approaches to making business decisions through extensive use of data as a kind of Decision Support System (Yu et al. 2017; Long 2018). DSS may be build independently or may evolve from previously built model such as for example simulation (Crespo Márquez 2010).

Author was not able to identify any example of modelling the entire supply chain using Data Science. There are attempts to model only fragments of supply chains (Ho et al. 2010; Gumus et al. 2010; Beutel and Minner 2011; Apte et al.

2011; Pishvaee et al. 2011; Long 2018). Summary of using analytic methods in building and improving the supply chain has been presented in e.g. (Wang et al. 2016). In the paper there are two main basis of analysis which are splitted into application groups. First one is strategy level appicated into strategy sourcing, supply chain network design, product design and development. Second level is supply chain operations e.g. demand planning, inventory. Supply chain analytics could be divided into descriptive, predictive and prescriptive methods.

3   Thesis and Research Goals

The previous section presents studies related to subject of supply chain modelling in terms of particular processes. The effectiveness of their usage on a particular part of supply chain would suggest that their use will positively affect the efficiency of the entire supply chain. Hence the thesis was formulated as follows:

> It is possible to use Data Science techniques for supply chain modelling in order to improve its efficiency.

The main research goal is to model supply chain using Data Science techniques, which improve the efficiency of the entire supply chain. In order to achieve the main research goal, several specific subgoals have been formulated:

- Presentation of the mechanisms of the supply chain used in the proposed solution. Justification of importance of modelling the supply chain, improving its efficiency with usage of Data Science.
- Selection of tools and techniques described in the literature in the field of supply chain model building, Data Mining in particular Process Mining and Data-Driven Systems.
- Collection of necessary data. The implementation of this subgoal is associated with the preparation of solutions for the analysis of individual processes in variants on the model.
- Choosing effectiveness measures, which will be used to assess the model. In particular, measures must relate to common efficiency measures for the franchisee and franchise holder on the example of convenience networks. Determining how measures interact with each other and how they translate into achieving the goals of a given entity.
- Justification which data is available in good quality and then analysed in terms of quality the possibility of using it in modelling. Due to the verification environment, a determination which is verifiable and which is not.
- Building the supply chain model using Data Science.
- Model verification based on the real-world data. Describing the curves of dependencies between indicators.
- Results evaluation. Comparison of results obtained by the model to the results of the analysed network. Analysis of deviations from expected values.
- Description of observations and conclusions obtained during the z research.

4   Research Results

The research is in the early stages. Currently one subgoal has been realised. The mechanisms of the supply chain has been described. The results will be presented in 5 subsections, that relate to efficiency measures, conflicts analysing between franchise holder and franchisee in the model of the supply chain. Moreover, an overview of data sources for analysis is presented as well as sample process.

4.1   Efficiency Measures

The supply chain model should take into account francisee and franchise holder success. Examples of detailed measures, which are valid for franchisee stores network were described in the Table 1. The measures are examplary was developed during interviews with experts in a supply chain field.

Table 1. Examplary process effectiveness measures for supply chain

	Measures and indicators	
	Strategic	Operational
Forecasting	Profit loss caused by underforecasting	Promotion coverage, products unavailability, value percentage of reproducing goods
Procurement	Order automation proposals confirmation ratio	Order balancing indicator, numbers of order per day
Transportation	Total cost of transport, average time of delivery	Truck fulfilment
Supply chain integration	Percentage of companies which the data is transferred, service level from Vendors	Automated order confirmation level
Franchisee cooperation	service level, Lost sales caused by lack of products	stock level on shelves, punctuality of deliveries, stock availability on shop
Reverse logistics	Total cost of returns process	Percentage of damage goods
Warehousing	Stock Coverage Ratio	Warehouse fulfilment, products availability

The success of the network is often determinated by selling goods to final customers. Thus, the most important measures are related to total sales. From logistics point of view the measure which might be used is profit loss from logistics issues as a total value and percentage of total sales. It aggregates many different costs originated in different areas. Second measure is product availability on shelves. For this one both the franchisee and franchise holder are responsible. Franchisee is responsible for ordering the goods on time and keep the stock. On the other hand, the franchise holder must organise the supply chain for local buying or availability in distribution centres.

4.2 Data Sources and Data Availability

Franchise networks are in privileged situation in terms of data acquisition, compared to the way, that traditional supply chain works. It is due to the kind of agreement integrate data flow and collection from the moment of supply purchase, through the elements in the middle and finishing on the actual customer. The geographical expansion on the national scale, as well as the expansion on the urban scale allows to measure sales in different environments. Looking for patterns in different data sets may take place both within and outside the enterprise. For data mining, there is need for transactional data, that consists of different sets of information of basic products, localization and external data. In the case of research within the company in the area of modelling the supply chain, the main areas are the warehouse processes (ability to apply process mining) as well as processes of external deliveries, both in and outcoming. Any actions that aim to reinforce the cooperation between providers and receivers are not always equal to full information exchange. Sample data sources grouped by type are showed below:

- Transaction data – the sources for that data can be systems like ERP or WMS as well as other transactional systems[5]. That type of data may be presented in form of event log or database records.
- Master data – the primary source of that data is the central information system – especially, when the systems are using the same information.
- External data – data from an open source, bought from other companies, that have gathered and structured it or the data shared by business partners. This data can also include secondary research conducted on the Internet.

Another issue is the way to collect and use the data. Data management while having many different sources may be difficult therefore it is important to collect and organise it in data warehouse.

4.3 Logistics Topology Model

There are many participants in the logistics network. In the Fig. 1 they are represented as nodes, connected by edges that represents business processes. The node in the picture represents object class with similar features and role in logistics chain. In the real chain it could be one or more participant instances. The arrows present the direction of the business process. Each process is illustrated using different colours.

Participants presented in Fig. 1 can be divided into several groups: warehouses, intermediary elements, shops, suppliers and customers. Warehouses, distribution centres in particular, fulfill the role of distributors in a supply chain, i.e. they accumulate deliveries and distribute them to individual points of sales. Depending on the owner and their role, these are divided into distribution centres, external warehouses and local warehouses. Intermediary elements could be

---

[5] Warehouse Management System.

for example cross-dock truck terminals. Their task is to consolidate or decon-solidate deliveries. Stores are usually the most numerous in whole supply chain. These are most diversified in terms of size and location. Suppliers due to the scope of cooperation and type of offered products, divide into local, e-service suppliers, producers, importers and wholesalers. Customers are usually individual clients, but they could also be wholesalers or public benefits organisations.

Between these nodes there are several primary business processes: product delivery, sales, materials transfer between the same kind of nodes, returns and returns of returnable packages. Product delivery is a process responsible for providing product availability in set of entities. Support for the sales process from the logistics side is to ensure an adequate stock level for sale. It is also important to ensure the availability of support products such as disposable bags, displays, thermal rolls for printing receipts, promotional materials. They are not a source of sales, but are necessary for the proper course of the process. Materials transfer between the same kind of nodes aims to balance level of stock in the network. Separate process, but very expensive is returns service, which stands as a part of the reclamation process. From logistical point of view, this process can be connected with returns of returnable packages.

The main task for processes optimisation is cost and material management for participants. Each node type could have different features and set of connections. The goal is to assure network flexibility – if the delivery by standard path is not possible, the stores should be able to use another supplier or distribution path. Depending on the product characteristics, some distribution channels are more suitable than others. Business needs, especially high profitability, indicate which channel should be used. Presented supply chain topology model might apply to any convenience stores network, but participants characteristics may vary depending on the particular company. One of the challenges in supply chain management is to calculate the optimal (i.e. the most profitable) number of nodes of each type in the network, and its characteristics like capability and location (Chiadamrong and Piyathanavong 2017). One of the biggest strategy decisions is the facility location, which will determine the costs in a long period. The cost calculation approach is described in the literature (Daskin 2005). The layout optimisation problem is described e.g. in (Marcoux 2005). The proper network construction, possible visualisation of nodes and processes along with cost prescription will support the decision-making processes.

4.4 Sample Process — Delivery

The most expanded logistics process in the convenience network is product delivery. There is a wide range of possible sources of supply (shown in Fig. 1). Some supply chains are very short, e.g. delivery from local suppliers to shops, others are long and connect many different nodes. Although the product delivery processes have different flow, the end node is always the final customer. That process has been highlighted with blue colour in Fig. 1.

Among the many costs in this process, the most significant one is transport cost. This cost is reduced by delivery consolidation. Similarly, the handling

Logistics topology model

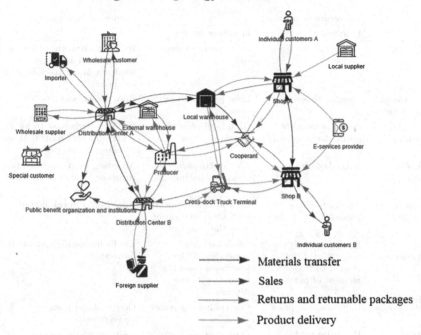

Fig. 1. Supply chain model (Icons from: https://icons8.com)

manipulation and packaging costs is going down. A higher stock level on distribution centres usually means higher level of service. When the transport and handling costs are reduced, the stock level and the capital cost increase. There might be also a problem with warehouse capacity and workload.

The franchisee in the chain may fulfill the role of coordinator through supporting the actions. The supply chain could be very short for some products, especially without any intermediary elements between suppliers and shops. In that case franchise holder only organising the process without physical workload. In the other hand there are more nodes in the process e.g. buffer warehouses, distribution centres. Sample flows of the product delivery process are as follows:

- Local suppliers/E-service providers -> Shops -> Customers
- Suppliers -> Wholesaler -> Shops -> Customers
- Producer -> Distribution Centre/Cooperant -> Cross-Dock Truck Terminal -> Shops -> Customers
- Foreign suppliers/ Importers -> Shops -> Customers
- Producer -> External Warehouse -> Distribution Centre -> Cross-Dock Truck Terminal -> Shops -> Customers

In each of presented scenarios there is a different schedule and source of cost. The interviews with data analyst experts lead to conclusion, that using

Table 2. Sample compromises between entities in franchise network

	Expectations of entity		Propose compromise
	Franchisee	Franchise holder	
Safe stock	Very small, own decision	Stock on the shops shelves	Information in the order form, in-outs[a] and strategic products msafe stock building on shops
Assortment management	Flexible choosing	Most products are the same	Core assortment
Managing standards	Selective usage of particular standards	HIgh level of network standardisation	Set Standards have to be achievable and contribute to realising the strategy
Delivery cycles	Everyday, any amount	Cost restriction, transport balancing	Adapting limits to store sales turnover, deliveries on set days
Promotions management	Ability to choose promoted products	Central management with little integration from the store	Allowing for local discounts
Stock ownership	Stock becoming ownership of the franchisee from the moment of purchase	Stock becoming ownership of the franchisee from the moment of store delivery	Credit limits, division of stock ownership
Setting price	Influence over price shifts	Central pricing policy	Geographical price diversification
Returns management	Franchise holder responsible	Franchisee responsible	Unit, which decides on allocation is responsible for returns

[a]Short shelf time products

traditional analytical methods is not sufficient to find answers to questions that assess the best practise for business scenarios. On top of that, the constant change of environment further enhances the need for proper, tailored solutions for Decision Support System for companies.

4.5   Franchising Compromises in Modelling Supply Chain

Current industry practise shows, that the franchising is strong and important element of the industry itself. However, it does not mean, that it has no flaws. The particular problem for that model is the potential tendency to take actions, that restrict sovereignty of the franchisee, on the other side, there is excessive desire to decide on their own. Avoiding that problem may lead to lack of trust between the units and potential imbalance of the idea that is behind franchise model. It is important to look for compromise from both points of view. Examples of such problems described in the literature (Rosado-Serrano et al. 2018) and the ones that are concluded out of interviews, that apply specifically to processes, that take place in the supply chain are presented in the Table 2.

5   Conclusions

The conducted research suggests that modelling supply chain topology based on Data Science for the franchise's network might result with better and more efficient supply chain processes. The described supply chain consists of several types of entities, e.g. distribution centres, warehouses, shops, suppliers.

Data sources and their potential use in the future analysis and modelling of the supply chain was pre-listed. Data from several areas is needed for supply chain analysis. The main data sources are usually internal systems, e.g. ERP, promotions, warehouse, replenishment systems. Moreover, many valuable information might be collected from external sources, e.g. received from business partners, scrapped from the Internet.

Future works include a selection of technologies which could be used for supply chain network design analysis. The supply chain measures method will be developed.

References

Apte, A.U., Rendon, R.G., Salmeron, J.: An optimization approach to strategic sourcing: a case study of the united states air force. J. Purch. Supply Manag. **17**(4), 222–230 (2011)

Beamon, B.M.: Supply chain design and analysis: models and methods. Int. J. Prod. Econ. **55**(3), 281–294 (1998)

Beutel, A.-L., Minner, S.: Safety stock planning under causal demand forecasting. Int. J. Prod. Econ. **140**(2), 637–645 (2011)

Bidhandi, H., Yusuff, R., Ahmad, M., Abu Bakar, M.: Development of a new approach for deterministic supply chain network design. Eur. J. Oper. Res. **198**(1), 121–128 (2009)

Buchmeister, B., Friscic, D., Palcic, I.: Impact of demand changes and supply chain's level constraints on bullwhip effect. Adv. Prod. Eng. Manag. **8**(4), 199–208 (2013)

Campuzano, F., Mula, J.: Supply Chain Simulation: A System Dynamics Approach for Improving Performance. Springer, London (2011). https://doi.org/10.1007/978-0-85729-719-8

Chiadamrong, N., Piyathanavong, V.: Optimal design of supply chain network under uncertainty environment using hybrid analytical and simulation modeling approach. J. Ind. Eng. Int. **13**(4), 465–478 (2017)

Crespo Márquez, A.: Dynamic Modelling for Supply Chain Management. Springer, London (2010). https://doi.org/10.1007/978-1-84882-681-6

Daskin, M.S.: Facility location in supply chain design. In: Langevin, A., Riopel, D. (eds.) Logistics Systems: Design and Optimization, pp. 39–65. Springer, Boston (2005). https://doi.org/10.1007/0-387-24977-X_2

Gjerdrum, J., Shah, N., Papageorgiou, L.G.: A combined optimization and agent-based approach to supply chain modelling and performance assessment. Prod. Plan. Control. **12**(1), 81–88 (2001)

Gumus, A.T., Guneri, A.F., Ulengin, F.: A new methodology for multi-echelon inventory management in stochastic and neuro-fuzzy environments. Int. J. Prod. Econ. **128**(1), 248–260 (2010)

Ho, W., Xu, X., Dey, P.K.: Multi-criteria decision making approaches for supplier evaluation and selection: a literature review. Eur. J. Oper. Res. **202**(1), 16–24 (2010)

Ivanov, D.: Simulation-based ripple effect modelling in the supply chain. Int. J. Prod. Res. **55**(7), 2083–2101 (2017)

Jacyna-Gołda, I., Izdebski, M., Szczepański, E., Gołda, P.: The assessment of supply chain effectiveness. Arch. Transp. **45**(1), 43–52 (2018)

Kim, J., Rogers, K.: An object-oriented approach for building a flexible supply chain model. Int. J. Phys. Distrib. Logist. Manag. **35**(7), 481–502 (2005)

Kleijnen, J.: Supply chain simulation tools and techniques: a survey. Int. J. Simul. Process. Model. **1**(1–2), 82–89 (2005)

Kubina, M., Varmus, M., Kubinova, I.: Use of big data for competitive advantage of company. Procedia Econ. Financ. **26**, 561–565 (2015)

Lim, C., Kim, K.-H., Kim, M.-J., Heo, J.-Y., Kim, K.-J., Maglio, P.P.: From data to value: a nine-factor framework for data-based value creation in information-intensive services. Int. J. Inf. Manag. **39**, 121–135 (2018)

Liu, Q., Zhang, X., Liu, Y., Lin, L.: Spreadsheet inventory simulation and optimization models and their application in a national pharmacy chain. INFORMS Trans. Educ. **14**(1), 13–25 (2013)

Śliwczyński, B.: Controlling operacyjny łańcucha dostaw w zarządzaniu wartością produktu. Wydawnictwo Uniwersytetu Ekonomicznego (2011)

Long, Q.: Data-driven decision making for supply chain networks with agent-based computational experiment. Knowl.-Based Syst. **141**, 55–66 (2018)

Malikia, F., Souierb, M., Dahanec, M., Sarib, Z.: The use of metaheuristics as the resolution for stochastic supply chain design problem: A comparison study. Int. J. Supply Oper. Manag. **4**(3), 193–201 (2017)

Marcoux, N.: Models and methods for facilities layout design from an applicability to real-world perspective. In: GERAD 25th anniversary series, pp. 123–170 (2005)

Min, H., Zhou, G.: Supply chain modeling: past, present and future. Comput. Ind. Eng. **43**(1), 231–249 (2002)

Morgan, J.S., Howick, S., Belton, V.: A toolkit of designs for mixing discrete event simulation and system dynamics. Eur. J. Oper. Res. **257**(3), 907–918 (2017)

Panchal, G.B., Jain, V., Kumar, S.: Multidimensional utility analysis in a two-tier supply chain. J. Manuf. Syst. **37**(P1), 437–447 (2015)

Pierreval, H., Bruniaux, R., Caux, C.: A continuous simulation approach for supply chains in the automotive industry. Simul. Model. Pract. Theory **15**(2), 185–198 (2007)

Pishvaee, M.S., Rabbani, M., Torabi, S.A.: A robust optimization approach to closed-loop supply chain network design under uncertainty. Appl. Math. Model. **35**(2), 637–649 (2011)

Reynolds, J.: Franchise businesses to again grow faster than rest of economy in 2015: federal regulations could significantly slow growth. Fr. World **47**(2), 42–44 (2015). (research)

Rosado-Serrano, A., Paul, J., Dikova, D.: International franchising: a literature review and research agenda. J. Bus. Res. **85**, 238–257 (2018)

Sadghiani, N., Torabi, S., Sahebjamnia, N.: Retail supply chain network design under operational and disruption risks. Transp. Res. Part E, Logist. Transp. Rev. **75**, 95–114 (2015)

Taylor, J., Fawcett, S.: Retail on-shelf performance of advertised items: an assessment of supply chain effectiveness at the point of purchase. J. Bus. Logist. **22**(1), 73–90 (2001)

Tomczak, M., Rzepecki, L.: Evaluation of supply chain management systems used in civil engineering, vol. 245. Institute of Physics Publishing (2017)

Tonchia, S., Quagini, L., Dresner, H.: Performance Measurement : Linking Balanced Scorecard to Business Intelligence. Springer, Berlin (2010). https://doi.org/10.1007/978-3-642-24761-3

van der Aalst, W.M.P.: Process Mining - Data Science in Action, 2nd edn. Springer, Heidelberg (2016). https://doi.org/10.1007/978-3-662-49851-4

van Houten, S.: A suite for developing and using business games: supporting supply chain business games in a distributed context (2007)

Wang, G., Gunasekaran, A., Ngai, E., Papadopoulos, T.: Big data analytics in logistics and supply chain management: certain investigations for research and applications. Int. J. Prod. Econ. **176**, 98–110 (2016)

Witten, I.H., Frank, E., Hall, M.A., Pal, C.J.: Data Mining: Practical Machine Learning Tools and Techniques, 4th edn. Morgan Kaufmann, Amsterdam (2017)

Yu, W., Chavez, R., Jacobs, M.A., Feng, M.: Data-driven supply chain capabilities and performance: a resource-based view. Transp. Res. Part E: Logist. Transp. Rev. **114**, 371–385 (2017)

Behavioral Biometrics in Mobile Banking and Payment Applications

Piotr Kałużny[✉]

Poznań University of Economics and Business,
Al. Niepodległości 10, 61-875 Poznań, Poland
piotr.kaluzny@ue.poznan.pl

Abstract. This paper presents an overview on the possible use of behavioral biometrics methods in mobile banking and payment applications. As mobile applications became more common, more and more users conduct payments using their smartphones. While requiring secure services, the customers often do not lock their devices and expose them to potential misuse and theft. Banks and financial institutions apply multiple anti-fraud and authentication systems - but to ensure the required usability, they must develop new ways to authenticate their users and authorize transactions. Answer to this problem comes with a family of behavioral biometric methods which can be utilized to secure those applications without hindering the usability. The goal of this paper is to describe potential areas in which behavioral biometrics can be used to ensure more secure mobile payments, increase usability and prevent frauds.

Keywords: Behavioral biometrics · Authentication
Behavioral profiling · Banking · Mobile applications · Security

1 Motivation

Modern mobile phones have became a truly ubiquitous device. According to the recent GSMA report [1] about 5 billion people all over the world use mobile phones. Nearly 60% of those devices fall into smartphone category, and 66% of those people accesses the Internet with their mobiles. This ubiquity makes those devices a basic tool for a variety of everyday tasks, including mobile payment and banking services. Banks and financial institutions need to adapt to the needs of their customers, and those include mobile banking applications. With users conducting everyday payments by mobile banking applications the new mobile–centric banking model becomes a goal to which all modern financial institutions try to adapt [2].

As 77% of European clients utilize mobile devices to keep track of their finances [3], most of them also pay for everyday services using mobile banking and e-wallet applications especially the younger generation of clients, which consider themselves "mobile money users". This dynamic is even more prevalent in

© Springer Nature Switzerland AG 2019
W. Abramowicz and A. Paschke (Eds.): BIS 2018 Workshops, LNBIP 339, pp. 646–658, 2019.
https://doi.org/10.1007/978-3-030-04849-5_55

Poland, where BLIK[1] payment service allows the customers to pay by providing short one-time codes and transfer money utilizing phone numbers. Polish customers also use mobile payments regardless of the transaction value [4]. While convenience is the main reason why users choose mobile wallets, 37% believes that safety and security are also an important benefit of e-wallet services.

In this new environment financial institutions must provide services which are not only convenient, but also secure [4] to meet their customers requirements, stabilize their position on the market and integrate with new FinTech solutions. Those traits can be ensured by the use of biometric authentication services which are already available in some of the banking applications e.g. utilizing fingerprint scanners. Unfortunately not all devices are equipped with the required sensor and about 40% of users does not secure their device in any way - be it PIN or biometrics [5]. To prevent frauds and ensure sufficient security banks and FinTech companies can use a family of recently developed behavioral biometrics methods which are especially suited for mobile environment due to the variety of sensors available on today's smartphones. This new group of methods can be used in a variety of scenarios, from enriching existing authorization processes with behavioral signature, to fraud detection or working as self sufficient layer in the authentication process.

2   Goal and Methodology

The goal of this research is to find a range of methods that can improve the security and usability of current mobile banking and payment applications through behavioral biometrics. Compared to the literature, this paper focuses on characterizing the possible features which may be used in behavioral authentication and their application in various authentication approaches. While most of the authors focus on accuracy and error rates of specific methods, this paper tries to describe the general state of the field and brings up the discussion about the evaluation methodologies and use cases in which behavioral biometrics may be utilized in different scenarios, along with possible benefits that may be achieved. The methodology behind the research follows the principles of the Design Science and the special guidelines for Information Systems [6] apply as well. The effects of the study may create multiple artifacts: methods, algorithms, techniques, frameworks, models, processes. All of those artifact should be set in a context such as design, development, use of software or maintenance. The applied methodology consist of five phases: *Awareness of Problem, Suggestion, Development, Evaluation,* and *Conclusion*. The artifacts developed during the process can cover:

- new or adopted and improved methods for behavioral biometrics authentication,
- development and evaluation of processes for potential enrichment of existing solutions with behavioral biometrics elements.

---

[1] https://blikmobile.pl/en/.

The business problem was stated and explained in the motivation section of this paper and more broad definition of the problem from scientific perspective was stated above. More broad formulation of the problem is defined by the following proposed research question:

Can behavioral biometrics methods be integrated into mobile banking and payment applications and provide satisfactory results in terms of accuracy, security of the solution and sufficient usability.

In addition, auxiliary questions were formulated:

1. *What are the possible sensors and methods which can be utilized for behavioral authentication on mobile devices?*
2. *How to choose the methods suitable for mobile devices/applications and banking/payment scenario? Can the complementary methods be chosen based on various characteristics and combined to provide satisfactory accuracy of the solution without hindering the usability?*
3. *How to benchmark and evaluate the methods results in scenarios which may present the advantages and drawbacks of proposed methods in real application scenarios?*
4. *Is it possible to use behavioral biometrics in existing solutions to enrich the current authentication models and existing processes present in the mobile application environment and fraud detection systems?*

As the state of the current research is at the beginning, those questions are up for discussion and are subject to change. To answer those questions a broad analysis of literature is required which will describe the characteristics of behavioral biometrics. Main goal of this research is to provide preliminary evaluation of the behavioral biometric methods to tackle the business problem defined. Based on the outcome of the analysis new artifacts such as new methods, frameworks or processes can be proposed. The frameworks, benchmarks and experiments evaluating the proposed assumptions can be designed. The effects in turn may be used to provide use cases validating the artifacts provided during the research.

3   Behavioral Biometrics Characteristics

Biometrics incorporates unique or at least sufficiently distinguishable traits which can be quantified and assigned to an individual for identification and confirmation of identity (authentication) [7]. Besides the "traditional" traits (already used to some extent in banking) such as: fingerprint or palm print, iris and retina and face characteristics - new family of methods consisting of behavioral traits emerged recently. While behavioral biometrics are mentioned in the literature, the dynamics of new methods development has increased recently due to the possibility of applying those methods on mobile phones utilizing different sensors available on those devices.

Those methods cover the factors that can be considered unique, non transferable, hard to forget or lose, difficult to reproduce and hide but derive from user behavior rather than physical features. While they may be worse at identification of an individual based on a biometric pattern from a large population [8], most of the today's commercial biometric use cases rely on authentication cases where the user identity is assumed based on e.g. device or account name. A definition of behavioral feature (also name factor can be used), which was utilized in previous work [9] is as follows:

Any readable and processable representation of user behavior which exhibits identifiable and repeatable patterns that can be used for identification and authentication.

Methods utilizing behavioral biometrics can have a variety of applications that can potentially enhance banking and payment applications, including:

- **Continous/implicit/transparent authentication** [10–14] - contrary to the knowledge based authentication systems (utilizing PIN numbers or passwords) and standard biometrics which work as a *point-of-entry*, their behavioral counterpart is able to authenticate users continuously based on analyzing various sensors installed in the device.
- **Non-binary authentication** [13] - as some of the methods can produce quantifiable similarity measures between the saved behavioral pattern and the current state it is possible to define various levels of authorization based on the confidence about user identity [8] or enrich fraud-detection systems with this knowledge.
- **Multi-layer and multi-modal authentication integration** [15,16] - Characteristics of the methods allow applying an ensemble of different methods [11] without additional costs in terms of user interaction or additional sensors installed on the device which translates to added security without hindering the usability [17].
- **High usability** of methods [17–19] - as also mentioned above some of the methods can work continuously without user interaction or could potentially enrich existing access methods e.g. by adding behavioral signature to a typed PIN, password or provided fingerprint scan.
- **Minimizing the danger of pattern theft** - due to the complicated and multi-modal nature of the behavioral models a "behavioral signature" utilizing a single or multiple methods can built which depends on the internal factors used in the process of its' creation. The behavior pattern captured can be subject to change over time [20] or be device dependent in case of some methods. Stealing an aggregated pattern is not useful for the attacker as the company utilizing the methods can just change factors utilized in the process of pattern creation.
- **Possibility of user identification** [11,21] - allowing to identify multiple users utilizing the same shared device (and identification of a user over multiple devices he or she uses [22]).

Applying behavioral biometrics in a working authentication system is still an unexplored field. While many methods are provided in the literature, there are also multiple topics which are not widely studied, including: the trade-off between the time required to learn the profile and accuracy, usefulness of methods in different scenarios and scenarios for enriching existing authentication systems (including standard biometrics) or fraud detection systems with those methods. Findings of the recent research questionnaire carried out by Tele-Sign [17] among 600 security, risk, and fraud professionals responsible for user authentication in large companies also confirm the potential value of behavioral biometrics. The results (which can be partially seen in Fig. 1) also point to the benefit of increasing security without usability hindering effects.

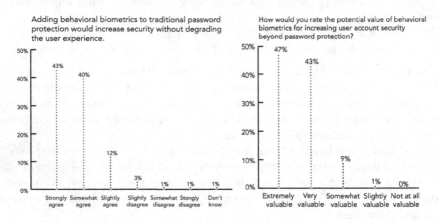

Fig. 1. Findings of the report considering behavioral biometrics. Source: [17]

The potential drawbacks connected with this family of methods may include: low accuracy (FAR/FRR) compared to the existing solutions, potential danger to the user privacy and data, problems with storing the profile and problems in methods evaluation. Also the device-specific aspects of user "behavioral signature" created may limit the use cases for the methods, as the device change may require recalculation of the model.

4 Behavioral Biometrics Methods

While the existence of behavioral biometrics is broadly acknowledged in the literature [7], the listing of possible factor proves difficult. Human behavior is complex and different aspects may differentiate users - the task of research in behavioral biometrics is to find patterns which are unique enough to successfully distinguish people based on their representation achieved by the use of specific methods. Results may vary in terms of: provided accuracy, complexity of learning process, time required for pattern extraction and also the convenience of the solution and possibility of integration with existing systems.

Listing possible factors that can be extracted proves difficult due to the constantly changing research outcomes and the overlap between the methods.

For example accelerometer can be used for profiling gait[2] pattern, recognizing user activities, as a part of behavioral profiling method or a variable enhancing user writing signature or password/pattern. It can also act as a supportive sensor in geographical profiling to improve the sampling process to lower the battery usage of GPS.

The behavior observed can be based on multiple sensors and data streams available, looking from the technical standpoint a multitude of possible behaviors can be observed based on the types of data sources available in the device. Those sensors can be used to extract a variety of factors which, based partially on [23], can be listed as:

- **gestures** - most similar to the traditional authentication factors as they require the user to provide a pattern (similar to e.g. password) which is then captured by the device. This gesture can be based on device movement [24] extracted by the accelerometer.
- **keystroke** - based on the dynamics of user typing, a family of methods can be utilized (including additional sensors like an accelerometer) to capture the unique user pattern.
- **touchscreen interaction profile** - based on the process of user interaction with the device [25] and actions performed (double clicks, scrolling, phone unlocking) [26].
- **gait and activity recognition** - which authenticate user based on the unique pattern of movement.
- **behavioral profile** - which incorporates a wide family of sensors to extract patterns of interaction with the device specific for the user, often including the context of place and time.
- **signature** (or similar written pattern) - based on recognition of user specific pattern, most of the time a standard signature, the methods capture unique pattern of user signature which can be enriched by external sensors [27].
- **voice** - the extracted characteristics of human voice can also be used for identification and authentication, where a predefined phrase may also be present to enable multi-factor authentication and increase the accuracy.

The characteristics of the above factors in already researched examples is provided in Table 1. Those factors do not exhaust all of the possibilities, as new methods are constantly developed. For example, social behavioral biometrics [28] based on user behavior and interactions with other people. Also behavioral profiling part of behavioral biometrics is quite ambiguous and currently captures all of the methods (or combinations) which do not fall into other defined factors. But there are multiple methods which may potentially extend this are into profiling of: geographical aspects expressed by a mobility pattern [9], linguistic features [29] or social interactions [28].

Analyzing and commenting the outcome visible in Table 1, those behavioral factors can be examined in depth considering multiple viewpoints.

---

[2] Profile of movement, based on unique traits that identify walk pattern specific for a user.

Table 1. Characteristics of chosen behavioral biometrics factors performance.

Factor	Sensor	Possible use	Privacy risk	Accuracy achieved
Behavioral profiling	Call and SMS logs Application usage Battery level GPS Closest BTS WiFi, Bluetooth, NFC	Constant authentication	High (depends on the sensors used and method)	EER 5% after 1 min, and 1% after 3 min [5] About 4.5% EER based only on sparse geographical trace derived from call logs [9]
Gait and activity recognition	Accelerometer	Constant authentication	Minimal	5.6% EER [30]
Keystroke analysis	Virtual keyboard	Enriching standard biometrics	Medium	2% EER [31]
Touch profile dynamics analysis	Touchscreen	Enriching standard biometrics or providing a new method	Minimal	5% [26], 2% given about 11 actions [25]
Gestures	Accelerometer, Camera	New method of authentication	Minimal	2% EER [24], 0.5% EER [32] with 25 training samples
Voice	Microphone	New method of authentication	High (depends much on user perception)	2% EER [33]
Signature	Touchscreen	Enriching standard biometrics or providing a new method	Low	0.8% EER [27]

With regards to the **security** provided by a given method a potential pattern theft scenario and other attacks should be considered. This trait can be achieved by providing high accuracy and low error rates, mostly expressed with Equal Error Rate value. This widely used indicator showcases the level at which the rate of False Positives (which in our case mean the situations where user is denied access) - expressed by FRR, is equal to the rate of False Negatives (where an impostor is allowed access into the device) - where the metric used is called FAR. While comparing EER rates between methods can help in comparison of their performance - the potential effects of impostor gaining access to the device is more important for the security of the solution. The ideal standard, specified by the EN-50133-1 European standard for access-control systems is to reach a FRR less than 1%, with a FAR of no more than 0.001%, which confirms the previous assumption towards the expected ratio of those two values. The fact is that both face recognition (with EER about 3% [34]) and voice authentication, with did not match up to this standard, are accepted and already used as a stand-alone authentication method. Behavioral biometrics on the other hand could potentially provide better EER and also work in conjunction with existing methods in the multi-factor authentication process.

The resulting accuracy of the methods varies highly [35] even for the same factor: utilizing similar methods researchers obtained anywhere from 2% to even 12% reported EER. This characteristic points to the possible issues in methodology of methods evaluation and the scale of research may be important - most of the approaches were tested on a sample of about 10–25 users. Based on the examples in the literature, the **length of the learning process**, **time required for classification** and **methodology of evaluation** are important and often not discussed widely. Those characteristics along with reluctancy in sharing the datasets may provide real EER to be larger in scenarios more close to real life applications. Also the approach of uninformed and informed attacker test classes is not utilized often, which is a common practice in security systems and has been tested in few behavioral biometrics papers [9, 20].

As for the applications of those methods in any scenario, a few characteristics need to be addressed. With regards to the **privacy** - the factors which focus on the content of user communication and activity are a possible threat to user privacy. Due to this fact - methods based on linguistic profiling and those that require access to user private data (SMS or e-mail content, conversation recordings) should not be used as a base of standard authentication system. Potentially the same can be said about voice, but this type of authentication is already used in some banks in Poland. Studies have proven that it possible to achieve about 2% EER on mobile phones for voice recognition [33] - which points to the question of performance comparison with recent behavioral biometrics methods. Even the behavioral profiling methods require sharing user sensitive data with regards to the authentication process and would require user agreement. Nonetheless the base for gathering this data is a well defined purpose: to prevent fraud and provide more convenient authentication process.

Focusing on **convenience**, some of the methods may not be used based on the context dependent nature connected with both privacy and convenience [36]. For example, user would not want to use voice when he or she is traveling in public transport - both because somebody could eavesdrop on the potential secret phrase and due to the overall usability. Similar problems could occur with face recognition methods which require additional gestures and processes. Finding a suitable combination of authentication factors that are context-independent and have high usability is required. This comes up to utilizing an **adaptive** authentication approach, which can be defined as using different authentication methods and protection methods depending on the user's context (e.g. location, networks nearby or operation importance) [37].

The methods used in banking scenario should be safe - in terms of accuracy and stopping the potential attacker trying to impersonate the original account owner. They should also be privacy respecting from user perspective and not have access to the sensitive personal data[3] and be convenient in the terms of their potential use in as many contexts as possible. Based on those assumptions, classifiers based on content (linguistic or voice profiling) will be omitted from the perspective of this work, as other classifiers can potentially provide satisfactory accuracy of the solution.

Behavioral biometrics methods can provide accuracy metrics in line (or better) with face or voice biometrics already utilized in smartphone authentication systems. Their characteristics may provide additional benefits, but the trade-offs in terms of privacy risk, convenience of use and security provided should be considered. The evaluation of those methods showcased varying results in terms of reported error rates which points to the thorough testing and benchmarking needed. Further tests in scenarios which may prove their usefulness in the environment of mobile banking and payment applications may also be necessary.

5   Proposed Use Cases and Model

With variety of methods described, a number of possible use cases can be identified, which may apply behavioral biometrics in scenarios connected with mobile banking and payment applications. Those include:

- Adaptation of behavioral biometrics methods as a new model of authentication: utilizing continuous authentication and standard access systems enriched with behavioral biometrics - a *behavioral signature* of a user.
- Providing a set of methods which can recognize the user context and adapt to it, or authentication methods that work in a context-independent manner.
- Use methods that provide high convenience and usability by e.g. continuous authentication and utilize the non binary output of behavioral biometrics to introduce risk-based authentication based on different actions possible in applications. Use of multiple methods should follow a general rule that the authentication process should not take more time (or be significantly more demanding) than the task to be performed [8].
- Integrate the methods with current fraud detection systems, which can help in improving the accuracy of current solutions in this field.

Some behavioral features mentioned before - such as signature, are not directly suited for a mobile phone scenario. Due to this fact, similar methods (touch dynamics) can be connected with already known methods to make them "sensor-enhanced" [38]. That way accuracy of password or pattern-lock methods can be enhanced with behavioral biometrics signature of a user, which builds up to a multi-modal authentication access system. An example processes including those cases which may be a part of the proposed system are presented in Figs. 2 and 3.

---

[3] Actually, the question of the extent of this privacy threatening behavior is always a trade-off, as banks e.g. keep customer actions which also contain potentially private information but if this information is used for fraud detection and widely accepted among users.

Non-continuous authentication

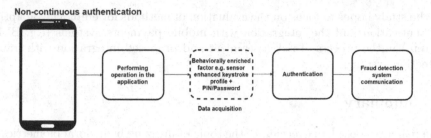

Fig. 2. Simplified process of integrated continuous non-continuous behavioral authentication and standard biometrics enrichment.

Continous Authentication

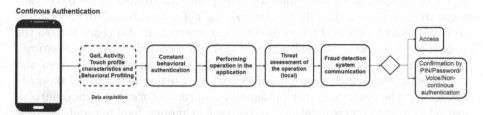

Fig. 3. Simplified process of integrated continuous authentication along with the communication with anti fraud system.

It includes a decision based authentication with an additional step of verification required utilizing already existing authentication processes, which can also be enriched with biometric elements. Additional benefit is the easy integration with local risk based assertion of actions - e.g. differentiating between presenting the account balance and making large transfers. The local system of threat assertion can be backed up by the already existing fraud detection systems. That way, based their behavioral profile, each user action can be measured in terms of similarity to the typical user behavior. This allows for decreasing the potential need for interaction in terms of low-risk transactions and ensures higher level of security for high-risk ones. The **most relevant features of the proposed model** include:

- **Multi-modal authentication** and integration with current authentication systems, increasing the security without lowering the usability of current solutions.
- Possibility of employing **continuous authentication** and lowering the number of required point-of-entry prompts for the user.
- **Adaptive authentication** based on the user context and the risk connected with the action.

The model proposed is an early draft, there are still multiple areas that need to be addressed further on. The main area of the **further work** is the choice and the evaluation possible behavioral biometrics methods performance and usability characteristics in the mentioned processes based on real data examples. Further on the study hopes to focus on the evaluation of methods for employing adaptive authentication and the integration with mobile payments systems (e.g. BLIK system) in the process of risk assessment and proposed integration with fraud-detection systems.

6 Summary

The paper proposed an overview of the topic of utilizing behavioral biometrics in mobile banking and payment applications. Compared to the current literature, the paper focuses on the characteristics of features that are available for use in the authentication processes, along with the potential improvements to the current systems which can be achieved by utilizing behavioral biometrics. Providing motivation and theoretical basics for the used methods it also characterized the approaches and methods used which may be considered behavioral features. Based on the approaches in the literature, the paper characterized them and listed the benefits which may be achieved when utilizing behavioral biometrics systems. At the end, the paper presented an outline of the behavioral authentication system use cases which may be used in mobile banking and payment scenarios. The paper tried to describe the general state of the field of behavioral biometrics and possible scenarios connected with mobile payment and banking application which may utilize those methods. The evaluation methodologies, use cases and possible benefits of applying the methods in the field were briefly discussed.

References

1. GSMA Intelligence: The mobile economy 2018 (2018). https://www.gsma.com/mobileeconomy/wp-content/uploads/2018/02/The-Mobile-Economy-Global-2018.pdf. Accessed 05 July 2018
2. Deloitte Center for Financial Services: 2018 banking outlook (2018). https://www2.deloitte.com/global/en/pages/financial-services/articles/gx-banking-industry-outlook.html. Accessed 05 July 2018
3. Visa: Annual digital payments study Europe 2017 (2017). https://www.visaeurope.com/media/pdf/45377.pdf. Accessed 05 July 2018
4. Visa: Annual digital payments study Poland 2016 (2016). https://resources.mynewsdesk.com/image/upload/thv1p2ep6thuchr66z6m.pdf. Accessed 05 July 2018
5. Fridman, L., Weber, S., Greenstadt, R., Kam, M.: Active authentication on mobile devices via stylometry, application usage, web browsing, and GPS location. IEEE Syst. J. 11(2), 513–521 (2017)
6. Hevner, A.R., March, S.T., Park, J., Ram, S.: Design science in information systems research. MIS Q. 28(1), 75–105 (2004)
7. Saeed, K.: Biometrics principles and important concerns. In: Saeed, K., Nagashima, T. (eds.) Biometrics and Kansei Engineering, pp. 3–20. Springer, New York (2012). https://doi.org/10.1007/978-1-4614-5608-7_1
8. Crawford, H., Renaud, K.: Understanding user perceptions of transparent authentication on a mobile device. J. Trust Manag. 1(1), 7 (2014)

9. Kałużny, P.: Behavioural profiling authentication based on trajectory based anomaly detection model of user's mobility. In: Abramowicz, W. (ed.) BIS 2017. LNBIP, vol. 303, pp. 242–254. Springer, Cham (2017). https://doi.org/10.1007/978-3-319-69023-0_21
10. Gascon, H., Uellenbeck, S., Wolf, C., Rieck, K.: Continuous authentication on mobile devices by analysis of typing motion behavior. In: Sicherheit, pp. 1–12. Citeseer (2014)
11. Li, F., Clarke, N., Papadaki, M., Dowland, P.: Active authentication for mobile devices utilising behaviour profiling. Int. J. Inf. Secur. **13**(3), 229–244 (2014)
12. Milton, L.C., Memon, A.: Intruder detector: a continuous authentication tool to model user behavior. In: 2016 IEEE Conference on Intelligence and Security Informatics (ISI), pp. 286–291. IEEE (2016)
13. Shi, E., Niu, Y., Jakobsson, M., Chow, R.: Implicit authentication through learning user behavior. In: Burmester, M., Tsudik, G., Magliveras, S., Ilić, I. (eds.) ISC 2010. LNCS, vol. 6531, pp. 99–113. Springer, Heidelberg (2011). https://doi.org/10.1007/978-3-642-18178-8_9
14. Gupta, S., Buriro, A., Crispo, B.: Demystifying authentication concepts in smartphones: ways and types to secure access. Mob. Inf. Syst. **2018** (2018). https://www.hindawi.com/journals/misy/2018/2649598/cta/
15. Saevanee, H., Clarke, N.L., Furnell, S.M.: Multi-modal behavioural biometric authentication for mobile devices. In: Gritzalis, D., Furnell, S., Theoharidou, M. (eds.) SEC 2012. IAICT, vol. 376, pp. 465–474. Springer, Heidelberg (2012). https://doi.org/10.1007/978-3-642-30436-1_38
16. Bailey, K.O., Okolica, J.S., Peterson, G.L.: User identification and authentication using multi-modal behavioral biometrics. Comput. Secur. **43**, 77–89 (2014)
17. Telesign: Beyond the password: the future of account security (2016). https://www.telesign.com/wp-content/uploads/2016/06/Telesign-Report-Beyond-the-Password-June-2016-1.pdf. Accessed 10 Sept 2016
18. Buriro, A., Crispo, B., Del Frari, F., Klardie, J., Wrona, K.: ITSME: multi-modal and unobtrusive behavioural user authentication for smartphones. In: Stajano, F., Mjølsnes, S.F., Jenkinson, G., Thorsheim, P. (eds.) PASSWORDS 2015. LNCS, vol. 9551, pp. 45–61. Springer, Cham (2016). https://doi.org/10.1007/978-3-319-29938-9_4
19. Xu, H., Zhou, Y., Lyu, M.R.: Towards continuous and passive authentication via touch biometrics: an experimental study on smartphones. In: Symposium on Usable Privacy and Security, SOUPS, vol. 14, pp. 187–198 (2014)
20. Kayacik, H.G., Just, M., Baillie, L., Aspinall, D., Micallef, N.: Data driven authentication: on the effectiveness of user behaviour modelling with mobile device sensors. arXiv preprint arXiv:1410.7743 (2014)
21. Ehatisham-ul Haq, M., Azam, M.A., Naeem, U., Amin, Y., Loo, J.: Continuous authentication of smartphone users based on activity pattern recognition using passive mobile sensing. J. Netw. Comput. Appl. **109**, 24–35 (2018)
22. Wang, X., Yu, T., Zeng, M., Tague, P.: XRec: behavior-based user recognition across mobile devices. Proc. ACM Interact. Mob. Wearable Ubiquit. Technol. **1**(3) (2017). Article no. 111. https://portalparts.acm.org/3140000/3139486/fm/frontmatter.pdf?
23. Alzubaidi, A., Kalita, J.: Authentication of smartphone users using behavioral biometrics. IEEE Commun. Surv. Tutor. **18**(3), 1998–2026 (2016)
24. Guerra-Casanova, J., Sánchez-Ávila, C., Bailador, G., de Santos Sierra, A.: Authentication in mobile devices through hand gesture recognition. Int. J. Inf. Secur. **11**(2), 65–83 (2012)

25. Bo, C., Zhang, L., Li, X.Y., Huang, Q., Wang, Y.: SilentSense: silent user identification via touch and movement behavioral biometrics. In: Proceedings of the 19th Annual International Conference on Mobile Computing & Networking, pp. 187–190. ACM (2013)
26. Li, L., Zhao, X., Xue, G.: Unobservable re-authentication for smartphones. In: NDSS, pp. 1–16 (2013)
27. Ngoc Diep, N., Pham, C., Minh Phuong, T.: SigVer3D: accelerometer based verification of 3-D signatures on mobile devices. In: Nguyen, V.-H., Le, A.-C., Huynh, V.-N. (eds.) Knowledge and Systems Engineering. AISC, vol. 326, pp. 353–365. Springer, Cham (2015). https://doi.org/10.1007/978-3-319-11680-8_28
28. Sultana, M., Paul, P.P., Gavrilova, M.: A concept of social behavioral biometrics: motivation, current developments, and future trends. In: 2014 International Conference on Cyberworlds (CW), pp. 271–278. IEEE (2014)
29. Saevanee, H., Clarke, N., Furnell, S., Biscione, V.: Text-based active authentication for mobile devices. In: Cuppens-Boulahia, N., Cuppens, F., Jajodia, S., Abou El Kalam, A., Sans, T. (eds.) SEC 2014. IAICT, vol. 428, pp. 99–112. Springer, Heidelberg (2014). https://doi.org/10.1007/978-3-642-55415-5_9
30. Damaševičius, R., Maskeliūnas, R., Venčkauskas, A., Woźniak, M.: Smartphone user identity verification using gait characteristics. Symmetry 8(10) (2016). https://doi.org/10.3390/sym8100100
31. Zahid, S., Shahzad, M., Khayam, S.A., Farooq, M.: Keystroke-based user identification on smart phones. In: Kirda, E., Jha, S., Balzarotti, D. (eds.) RAID 2009. LNCS, vol. 5758, pp. 224–243. Springer, Heidelberg (2009). https://doi.org/10.1007/978-3-642-04342-0_12
32. Shahzad, M., Liu, A.X., Samuel, A.: Secure unlocking of mobile touch screen devices by simple gestures: you can see it but you can not do it. In: Proceedings of the 19th Annual International Conference on Mobile Computing & Networking, pp. 39–50. ACM (2013)
33. Zou, L., He, Q., Feng, X.: Cell phone verification from speech recordings using sparse representation. In: 2015 IEEE International Conference on Acoustics, Speech and Signal Processing (ICASSP), pp. 1787–1791. IEEE (2015)
34. Bayometric: Top five biometrics: face, fingerprint, iris, palm and voice. https://www.bayometric.com/biometrics-face-finger-iris-palm-voice/. Accessed 27 Aug 2012
35. Alotaibi, S., Furnell, S., Clarke, N.: Transparent authentication systems for mobile device security: a review. In: 2015 10th International Conference for Internet Technology and Secured Transactions (ICITST), pp. 406–413. IEEE (2015)
36. Wójtowicz, A., Joachimiak, K.: Model for adaptable context-based biometric authentication for mobile devices. Pers. Ubiquit. Comput. 20(2), 195–207 (2016)
37. Ayed, M.B.: Method for adaptive authentication using a mobile device. US Patent 8,646,060, 4 Feb 2014
38. Giuffrida, C., Majdanik, K., Conti, M., Bos, H.: I sensed it was you: authenticating mobile users with sensor-enhanced keystroke dynamics. In: Dietrich, S. (ed.) DIMVA 2014. LNCS, vol. 8550, pp. 92–111. Springer, Cham (2014). https://doi.org/10.1007/978-3-319-08509-8_6

Modelling of Risk and Reliability of Maritime Transport Services

Milena Stróżyna[✉]

Poznań University of Economics and Business, Poznań, Poland
milena.strozyna@ue.poznan.pl

Abstract. Maritime transport plays nowadays an important role in the global economy. In 2017 around 80% of trade was carried by sea, therefore there is a need for constant monitoring of transport processes from the point of view of their reliability and punctuality. In order to provide up-to-date information about reliability and punctuality, a lot of data from different maritime sources needs to be collected and analysed. The paper presents concepts of two methods that based on an analysis of big amount of maritime data provide information that might be used to support various entities from the maritime domain in decision-making. The first method concerns a short-term assessment of reliability of a maritime transport service, while the second one dynamically predicts punctuality of a ship. The presented methods are part of a PhD research. The aim of the article is to provide an overview of this research, starting from motivation, its objectives and the thesis, through presentation of the methods, up to description of the main results of methods' evaluation.

1 Motivation and Justification of the Research Topic

In the current global economy, maritime transport plays a key role in transporting goods, being the backbone of international trade and the leader in terms of transport economics. Nowadays, around 80% of global trade by volume and 70% by value is carried by sea [1]. In this context, the maintenance of high reliability of maritime transport is of prime importance. The reliability means successful performance of shipment under given operating conditions, at a given time and with no damage to a cargo. This, in turn, requires appropriate risk management with regard to realization of transport services.

Another important issue of maritime transport services is the fact that it needs to be planned days in advance. Therefore, access to actual information about the ship's position, estimated time of arrival and whether there is any delay on the route, is very important for the proper operation of the supply chain. In this matter, there is still a lot to be done. The statistics show that in practice only 52% of the vessels arrive on time [2]. Moreover, in the last year the punctuality dropped further by 8.4%.[1]

---

[1] http://www.gospodarkamorska.pl/Porty,Transport/punktualnosc-kontenerowcow-spadla-w-zeszlym-roku.html, accessed: 2018-03-19.

© Springer Nature Switzerland AG 2019
W. Abramowicz and A. Paschke (Eds.): BIS 2018 Workshops, LNBIP 339, pp. 659–674, 2019.
https://doi.org/10.1007/978-3-030-04849-5_56

As a result, a precise estimation of a ship's arrival time and a prediction of its punctuality is a key issue in the logistics and supply chain management. Information about a ship's punctuality, that is additionally updated when the ship is on its way, is relevant for various entities, such as harbor authorities, logistic service providers along the supply chain (terminal owners, companies responsible for further transport, etc.), and the final customer. A better information on arrival times makes operations of these entities more efficient and helps to reduce costs [3,4].

Having these challenges in mind, the research focuses on two, interrelated topics. The first topic relates to estimation of reliability and risk of maritime transport services. The second topic concerns the prediction of a ship's punctuality, which further influences the reliability of supply. Both parts requires collection and an efficient analysis of big amount of maritime data.

In the research, two methods that cover the topic of reliability and risk estimation and the punctuality prediction are presented. The novelty of these methods results from their assumptions and characteristics. They allow to: (1) assess the risk for an individual ship; (2) take into account a wide range of possible risk variables and conditions of ships' operational environments; (3) perform this assessment in a more dynamic manner (for a shorter time horizon); and (4) analyse huge amount of maritime data from different data sources.

2   Related Work

There exist various approaches, models and techniques to maritime risk and reliability assessment (see e.g. [5–7]). They can be divided into qualitative or quantitative methods. The first includes inter alia statistic analysis based on historical data [8], Fault and Event Tree Analysis [9], Bayesian Networks [10], correlation analysis and fuzzy logic [11,12]. The quantitative methods encompass for example risk matrices, risk profiles or risk indexes/rankings [6]. The key issue in the risk assessment is to choose the right method or combination of methods, which best matches the analysed situation and available data.

The existing methods for the maritime risk assessment have some common characteristics that, in the opinion of the author, are their shortcomings. First, they focus on estimating risk of one of the three (separate) types of situations: (1) either a specified type of hazard (e.g. collision, oil spill); or (2) an undesired event in relation to a ship's technical attributes (e.g. an engine problem); or (3) a human error. As a result, they take into account only selected factors, strictly connected with a given type of hazard. Besides, the estimated risk concerns a particular group of ships (e.g. tankers) instead of a particular ship. Therefore, their results can be used only in a given context (in a selected risk scenario).

Second, the analyzed methods use a limited set of factors or only factors of a given category, like technical characteristics of a ship, experience of the crew, history of accidents. Many of them do not include such important aspects as: factors that may change in time (e.g. flag, owner, congestion on the route), current and historical anomalies in a ship's behavior, past routes, characteristics of the current route, and further risks that are related to the ship's localization (e.g. geopolitical risk, congestion, weather).

Final, the existing methods provide above all information about the long- or mid-term risk level (especially when it comes to risk of supply performed by merchant ships) [13]. Very few methods, e.g. [11,14,15], focus on the short-term risk, which concerns a given voyage, a given ship, and which additionally may change during this voyage. Taking into account that the situation at sea may change quickly, the continuous monitoring of ships' behavior and of the environment in which they operate is crucial.

The main barrier, which has also been confirmed by other researchers [16], is still a lack of comprehensive and efficient IT tools with implemented functionalities for maritime reliability and risk assessment. Despite the added value of using multiple sources of information and implementation of some analytic methods, there still exist deficits and gaps in the available maritime systems when it comes to conducting risk analysis.

3   Objective of the Research and the Thesis

The problem of assessing reliability of deliveries and transport services is an important topic in the maritime economy and is crucial for various entities working in the maritime domain. The reliability depends on punctuality and travel time of a ship. If a ship is delayed and its travel time deviates from what was planned, the reliability suffers. Thus, a relationship between the risk of a delay (low punctuality) and the reliability of a delivery can be observed - the higher the risk, the lower the reliability. In other words, lower punctuality leads to lower reliability.

Main Objective
The main objective of the research is to propose an effective, accurate and useful method for the short-term assessment of reliability of a maritime transport service, being carried out by a given ship, taking into account both static (voyage-independent) and dynamic (voyage-dependent) characteristics of a ship and attributes of its operational environment that can be retrieved from the available maritime data.

The detailed research objectives are:

- To identify and classify a ship's characteristic and attributes of its operational environment that may influence the reliability and risk of a maritime transport service (**Artifact 1**).
- To develop a method for the assessment of reliability and risk of a maritime transport service, realized by an individual ship, which takes into account the available static (voyage-independent) and dynamic (voyage-dependent) characteristics of a ship and attributes of its operational environment (**Artifact 2**).
- To develop a method for a dynamic prediction of a ship's punctuality on a given voyage (**Artifact 3**).

– To evaluate the proposed methods through experiments based on real data on ships, their movements and attributes of their operational environment.

Thesis

The short-term assessment of maritime risk that is based on individual characteristics of ships and the attributes of their operational environments allows for an estimation of the reliability and punctuality of deliveries by sea with higher accuracy

4   Research Methodology

The overall methodology applied within the research follows principles devised by design science [17]. Design science research is a paradigm in which a researcher answers relevant research questions by creating innovative artifacts, and thereby contributes new knowledge to the existing body of knowledge and scientific evidence [18]. The design science is a problem-solving paradigm. Its end goal is to build and evaluate artifact(s). Moreover, it has been proved to be a rigorous research process via its application in various domains, starting from information systems, through healthcare, e-commerce, biology, transportation, through to the fine arts.

According to the design science paradigm, the presented research has been structured into four steps: (1) Problem identification and motivation; (2) Definition of objectives for the solution (artifacts); (3) Design and development of artifacts; (4) Demonstration and evaluation. Moreover, the research has been conducted in three Design Science Research Cycles. It started with the Relevance Cycle that combines the application domain (in this case the maritime domain) with the design science research, followed by the Rigor and the Design Cycles.

With respect to the knowledge contribution, the research can be classified as *Research Opportunity* [18]. It means that the problem context is mature but there is a great need for more effective artifacts, and thus the research provides new solutions for known problems.

The important step of the design science is demonstration and evaluation. A designed artifact must be evaluated via methods that will rigorously demonstrate its utility, quality and efficacy [18]. In the research, the proposed methods have been evaluated using the FEDS framework, proposed by [19]. To this end, an artificial summative evaluation was conducted, according to the Technical Risk & Efficacy strategy [19]. It means that the evaluation was performed at the end of the development process without real users or a system in real organizational situations but included laboratory experiments using real data and a criteria-based analysis.

5   Data Sources

In order to develop and evaluate the artifacts, a set of relevant maritime data from different sources was collected. It was assumed that real data from different maritime systems and sources should be used to present and evaluate the proposed concepts on real world examples of ships and voyages. In the research, the main data source was Automatic Identification System (AIS) that makes it possible to track in real-time the movements of over 150 thousands ships worldwide. Therefore, the system generates huge amount of data every day.

On the one hand, access to AIS data creates a great potential for analytics and reasoning, stemming from (near) real time information where ships are located, where they are heading, or where they were sailing in the past. On the other hand, the analysis of such big amount of data is a complex task that requires application of appropriate technologies and tools for processing and storing them. To deal with it cloud solutions were used, which is considered as a relevant field of research in science and industry and will still play a major role in future [20].

Another sources of data used encompass additional data acquired from various maritime services and sources, such as data about ships and their characteristics, data about detentions and inspections of ships, data about classification of ships and their belonging to classification societies, data about risk indexes, ship's accidents, reported piracy and terrorist attacks as well as GIS data (e.g. national borders and Exclusive Economic Zones).

6   Research Contribution

The contribution of the research to the existing body of knowledge consists of the three Artifacts that were proposed and developed.

6.1   Artifact 1: The Typology of Maritime Risk Variables

The first artifact is the typology of a ship's characteristics and attributes of its operational environment that may influence the reliability and risk of a maritime transport service. The typology was prepared based on the conducted literature review. To this end, various approaches, methods, and systems used in the maritime domain were reviewed, followed by an analysis of risk factors that were used by different researchers. As a results, the identified maritime risk variables were assigned to eight categories, proposed by the author. Moreover, each variable was additionally classified as dependent or independent from other risk variables. The developed typology is presented in the Appendix.

This analysis allowed to answer the posted research question, which characteristics of a ship and attributes of its operational environment may be taken into account in the assessment of reliability and risk of maritime transport services. Besides, based on the developed typology, it was able to identify variables that so far have not been used, or were used only in few studies, in the assessment of reliability and risk in the maritime domain. These variables have been selected to be included in the proposed methods (Artifacts 2 and 3). Moreover, based on the conducted literature review, shortcomings in the existing solutions and methods as well as the challenges that the maritime domain needs to face, were identified. These shortcomings were then taken into account by the author while designing two methods: the method for reliability and risk assessment (MRRAM) and the method for punctuality prediction (SPP).

6.2   Artifact 2: The Method for Reliability and Risk Assessment

The first method (MRRAM) aims at providing a short-term assessment of reliability and risk of a maritime transport service, realized by an individual ship. The method utilizes the concept of the Bayesian Networks and allows for an evaluation of the reliability of a maritime transport service in a short-term horizon. The short term relates here to a given ship's voyage (e.g. from port A to port B). It is assumed that reliability is estimated at the beginning of the voyage by taking into account the variables known at the moment of conducting the estimation. This short-term horizon of the estimation, as well as an individual approach, in which estimation always concerns a particular ship and takes into account variables that relate to this ship, are the main assumptions that distinguish the approach proposed in the dissertation from the methods that already exist in the literature.

In comparison to the existing solutions for maritime risk and reliability assessment, MRRAM provides some novel functionalities and assumptions, and addresses previously identified gaps and challenges. The main characteristics of MRRAM are:

- It focuses on the reliability and risk of transport services being realized by merchant ships.
- The estimation of the reliability is conducted for a short-term horizon – a given voyage, and for a given ship.
- The reliability is determined at the beginning of a ship's voyage taking into account the static (voyage-independent) and the dynamic (voyage-dependent) characteristics of a ship and its operational environment.
- It addresses two steps of the Formal Safety Assessment Methodology – hazard identification and risk assessment.

MRRAM consists of three classifiers (Fig. 1): (1) ship-related, which includes variables about a ship's characteristics; (2) voyage-related, which includes variables about a given voyage; and (3) history-related, which includes information about the history of a ship. For each classifier, a set of variables were selected from the typology (Artifact 1). The variables were selected based on the data that were available in this research. However, the list of included variables may be modified if other data sources are available.

Finally, MRRAM yields also a confidence for the results that depends on how much information was provided as input to the method. In general, the more information is available while conducting an estimation, the higher the confidence becomes. The development of MRRAM allowed for the implementation of the second detailed objective of this research.

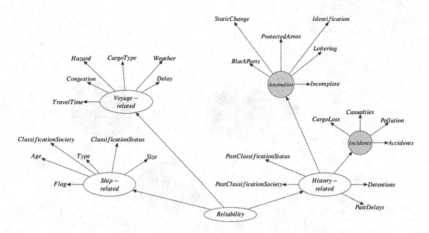

Fig. 1. Concept of the MRRAM method

6.3 Artifact 3: The Method for Punctuality Prediction

The second method developed in the dissertation provides a dynamic prediction of a ship's punctuality on a given voyage (SPP method). Its aim is to determine the estimated time of arrival of a given ship to a destination port as well as to provide dynamic updates on the predicted punctuality during the ship's voyage. Punctuality prediction is conducted in a short-term horizon – at the beginning of a ship's voyage, taking into account static and historical variables that are not going to change during the voyage (voyage-independent variables); it is the static approach. Additionally, the elaborated method makes it possible to update the predicted time of arrival at the time when the ship is already on its way, taking into account other variables that may change during the voyage (voyage-dependent variables) – the dynamic approach.

SPP consists of six components that together allow for an assessment of the ship's punctuality (Fig. 2): a route prediction to a destination, travel time estimation, the congestion factor, the hazard index, the weather factor, and the average delay. For each component, appropriate methods were developed and tested based on real data. Thanks to this, the third detailed objective of the dissertation was achieved.

7 Evaluation

7.1 Evaluation Methodology

In the research, a special focus was put on the evaluation of the developed methods. The goal of the evaluation was to demonstrate the quality, efficacy, and utility of the artifacts. This was accomplished in two phases in which SPP and then MRRAM were evaluated separately.

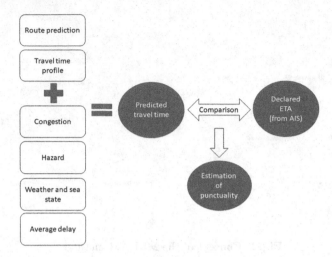

Fig. 2. Concept of the SPP method.

The evaluation started with a collection and preparation of real maritime data. The data were acquired from different maritime sources and concern inter alia features of ships, their movements, and characteristics of different maritime areas. The scope of the evaluation included merchant ships, their movements on a global scale, and the time period of one year.

7.2 Infrastructure

The conducted research was very data-intensive. Especially the evaluation process was a real challenge when it comes to analyzing huge amounts of available AIS data. It required utilization of appropriate infrastructure. The challenge of big data has been partially tackled thanks to the research grant *"Data Science and Azure-based analytics services for predicting risk and reliability of maritime transport"* that the author has received in the program Microsoft Azure for Research. The grant allowed for an application of big data technologies offered by the Azure cloud services. As a result, the maritime data on the global scale and covering a long time period could analyzed to develop and evaluate the proposed methods. Such a wide scope of analysis is the next characteristic that distinguishes the research from what has already been done.

First of all, the Azure Storage services were used to store the big amount of AIS data required for the analysis in a form which enables their fast and efficient analysis.

Then, to test and evaluate the methods also analytics solutions, which provide predictive analytics, machine learning, and statistical modeling for Big Data, had to be used. Both SPP and MRRAM were implemented using R, Spark and a Hadoop cluster to take the advantage of a large parallel analytics. This significantly speed up the computation time and the process of getting the results.

The processing of millions of AIS messages collected for a one-year period took just a few minutes, instead of a few hours or days, like it was observed in the case of other studies [21–23]. Probably, along with an extension of the cluster and providing better processing capabilities, it would be possible to decrease the processing time even more.

7.3   Results

In the first step, SPP method was evaluated. The evaluation was conducted in several steps, in which the SPP method as a whole as well as its components, were verified using real maritime data and a set of real world examples. To this end, a set of experiments were performed in which for the selected voyages and ships the routes and travel profiles were generated. Exemplary results of the route prediction are presented in Figs. 3 and 4. Then, for each analysed voyage the predicted travel time was calculated taking into the generated travel profile, congestion, potential hazards and past delays.

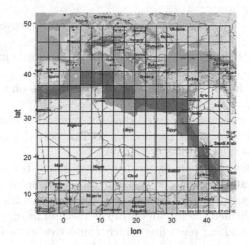

Fig. 3. Exemplary result of the route prediction method - voyage to the port of Algeciras.

The main results and conclusions of the SPP evaluation may be summarized as follow:

- Based on the conducted experiments, it was confirmed that the SPP method is effective in 88.42% of cases. It means that in general the method provides more accurate estimated time of arrival (ETA) than the time provided by a captain. This result proves also the effectiveness of the method in determining the predicted time of arrival at a given destination port, and thus its usefulness in supplying a potential user with more accurate and up-to-date information regarding estimated time of arrival of ships to a given destination.

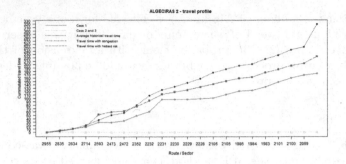

Fig. 4. Exemplary travel profile - voyage to the port of Algeciras.

– The evaluation has confirmed that it is justified to include additional information about the operational environment of the ship as well as historical information while determining the predicted travel time and the ETA. This concerns especially the information about congestion, potential hazard on the route and past delays:
  – Inclusion of the information about congestion improved the accuracy of estimations in 69% of cases.
  – Inclusion of the information about potential hazards improved the accuracy of estimations in 79.49% of cases on average.
  – Inclusion of the information about the past delays on the route improved the accuracy of estimations in 65% of cases.
– The conducted experiments proved that the method is able to appropriately indicate delayed ships. The method in 88.35% of cases correctly predicted whether a ship will or will not be delayed.
– The results of the additional experiments conducted to evaluate the *Hazard* index proved that the proposed method for determining the *Hazard* index based on three hazard factors is useful and confirms real-life observations. The experiments confirmed the usefulness of the method in supporting a potential user in decision-making regarding which route to choose for a given voyage and indicating potential hazardous areas that require special attention.
– The *Hazard* index is a factor that should be taken into account in calculating the predicted ETA, especially when there is a low propensity for risk. In the case of a high propensity for risk, the index may not influence the predicted ETA.
– All the experiments were conducted based on real, historical data, and real examples of ships' voyages. Thus, it might be said the obtained results are in compliance with what is observed in reality and the method can be used in real business processes.

The second phase of the evaluation process concerned the MRRAM method. The evaluation was conducted based on a relatively big sample of real voyages. In total, a set of 255 voyages was used to train and test models of Bayesian Networks for each MRRAM classifier. Besides, each ship and voyage was characterized by additional information that was collected from AIS data, maritime data sources available on the Internet, results of methods for maritime anomalies detection, and results provided by the SPP method (Artifact 3). Then, a set of experiments was conducted.

The main results and conclusions of the MRRAM evaluation may be summarized as follow:

- Based on the conducted experiments, it was confirmed that the MRRAM classifiers are effective tools to estimate the probability of a delay and the short-term reliability of a transport service (a supply). All classifiers are characterized by good accuracy (80.77%, 65.38%, and 84.62% accordingly, for the ship-related, the voyage-related, and the history-related classifier), and good precision (86.96%, 93.33%, and 87.50% accordingly). Thus, it might be concluded that they are able to provide accurate estimations and, as a result, might be used in the prediction of a ship's risk and reliability, taking into account the assumed risk variables (i.e. the variables that relate to the ship, its voyage, and its history).
- In the case of the voyage-related classifier, the accuracy and precision of the results is the lowest. It might result from the fact, that the weather conditions and sea state might be an important variable here. Thus, the quality of the voyage-related classifier could be improved by taking into consideration more information or more precise information about the weather conditions and sea state on the predicted route.
- The MRRAM method is able to provide accurate reliability assessment for real world examples of voyages and using real data. Depending on the propensity to take the risks (risk threshold), and the importance of different risk variables, the accuracy of the MRRAM results amounts between 73.08% (for higher risk thresholds) and 84.62% (for lower risk-thresholds).
- The MRRAM method is able to correctly predict the reliability of a ship in 73% to 84% of cases, depending on the defined risk threshold.
- MRRAM is an effective and useful tool for creating a ranking of ships from the point of view of the reliability of delivery and, as a result, could be a support in decision-making when a user needs to decide which ship is the best/ is appropriate for the realization of a punctual and reliable delivery of goods on a given route.

Based on the results of the conducted experiments, the author has confirmed that both developed methods, which relate to an individual ship and a given delivery, are able to provide more accurate estimation than a human expert (a captain of a ship). Besides, it was verified that inclusion of additional information about the operational environment of a ship and about its history in the process of punctuality prediction can improve the accuracy of estimations. Moreover, both methods were successfully validated from the point of view of effectiveness and usefulness in supplying a potential user with predictions regarding the punctuality of a ship and the reliability of a transport service. Thus, it might be concluded that the last detailed objective of the dissertation was achieved.

8   Conclusions and Future Work Directions

Summarizing, it might be concluded that in the course of the research the author successfully proved the stated thesis. Moreover, both the main and all the detailed objectives of the dissertation were successfully realized. Finally, it might be said that the developed methods are more efficient than other existing solutions when the cloud solutions are used.

The author sees the potential for the exploitation of the developed methods in business practice and their application in different business scenarios. First, the methods can facilitate an automatic monitoring of ships' reliability and a comparison of ships from the point of view of the risk they pose.

Second, the methods can be helpful in the process of planning a ship's voyage and other activities in advance. The up-to-date information about ETA and the ship's punctuality are important aspects of planning harbor operations as well as of all further logistic activities. If a ship arrives too early, it has to wait for a free dock or berth for unloading. But then, if it is too late, a time slot planned for its stop and unloading has expired and all operations have to be rescheduled. This also influences the further logistic operations, causing, for instance, the subsequent transport by trucks to be delayed. All these aspects call for extra safety stocks to be kept at companies, resulting in extra costs or lower service quality. The proposed methods may be helpful in avoiding such situations.

Final, information about potential hazards underway may be used to plan and monitor a ship's voyage from the point of view of potential maritime threats. Last but not least, thanks to SPP, ships that probably will be delayed may be quickly identified.

Thereby, both methods are potentially interesting solutions for different entities from the maritime domain in conducting a risk analysis, in determining the reliability of supplies, and thus support them in decision-making, such as logistic companies, senders and recipients of goods, port authorities. Moreover, they could be incorporated into the existing maritime and logistic systems for monitoring fleet and maritime traffic as well as in intelligent navigational systems to support users in decision making.

The methods have also potential for further development in the future. The first direction concerns taking into account new variables that can influence the reliability and punctuality of a transport service, for example historic data and forecasts about the weather and the sea state. The second direction of future work is further improvement of the developed MRRAM classifiers to increase the accuracy of the method. Finally, more in-depth analysis of relationships between different variables may be conducted (e.g., ships' characteristics, attributes of their operational environments). These relationships might be difficult to notice without an analysis of real ships' trajectories and correlating them with other information about the ship and its behavior.

Appendix

See Table 1.

Table 1. Typology of maritime risk variables

Category	Variable	Dependent/independent	Dependencies	How often used
Ship-related	Capacity/gross tonnage/size	I		11
	Dimensions (e.g. length, draft)	I		7
	Owner	I		2
	Age	I		8
	Type	I		9
	Flag	D	Owner, classification society	4
	Reputation	D	Owner, Classification society/status, crew characteristics, working conditions, management rules, delays, delivery time, past incidents, pollution events, cargo damage, number of owners, detentions, failure frequency	1
	Maintenance program	D	Owner, type, technical features, crew, flag, classification society/status	2
	Emergency system on the ship	D	Technical features, type, classification society, flag	2
	Technological features (hull, machinery, state, stability, reserve buoyancy, equipment, innovations, upgrade)	D	Owner, classification society/status, type, age	12
	Management rules	D	Owner, classification society, crew	4
	Classification society, status, advices	D	Owner, crew characteristics, working conditions, management rules, emergency system, delays, past incidents, pollution events, number of owners, detentions, failure frequency, anomaly route	2
Dynamic	Speed/heading/course	D	Technical features, type, age, owner, capacity, crew	12
	Location/position; distance evolution; ship's trajectory	D	Area, congestion, crew	3
	Time to shore	D	Speed, location	1
	Anomalous route/trajectory	D	Crew, owner	1
	Time	I		2

(continued)

Table 1. (*continued*)

Category	Variable	Dependent/independent	Dependencies	How often used
Voyage-related	Transit time	D	Technical features, type, age, owner, capacity, crew	1
	Geopolitical issues (e.g. political conflicts/unrest, piracy, hijacking, armed robbery, terrorism, crimes, corruption, civil disorders)	I		5
	Cargo type/vulnerability (e.g. dangerous)	I		5
	Congestion (at source harbor, destination harbour, sea)/traffic density	I		7
	Area (incl. characteristics of waterway, tug response time, self repair time)	I		14
History-related	Delays/downtime/timely delivery	D	Voyage-related variables, past incidents, crew/human errors, port-related variables, environmental/weather, management rules, technical features	4
	Past incidents/accidents/ship damage	D	Crew/human errors, port-related variables, environmental/weather, management rules, technical features, congestion, area, maintenance program, flag	11
	Number of casualties/fatalities	D	Crew/human errors, port-related variables, environmental/weather, management rules, technical features, area, maintenance program	2
	Pollution events	D	Crew/human error, owner, management rules, owner, maintenance program, environmental/weather	5
	Cargo loss/cargo damage/excessive loads	D	Crew/human error, owner, management rules, owner, maintenance program, environmental/weather, voyage-related variables	5
	Number of owners	D	Ship-related variables	1
	Duration of detentions	D	Ship-related variables	1
	Failure frequency (e.g. technical failure)	D	Ship-related variables, Crew/human error, environmental/weather	11

(*continued*)

Table 1. (*continued*)

Category	Variable	Dependent/independent	Dependencies	How often used
Crew	Crew characteristics (incl. knowledge, skills, experience, training, size, rotation scheme, language, culture, morale, motivation, performance, fitness for duty)	D	Owner, management rule	23
	Work conditions (complexity, workload, ergonomics, work process, stress, duty scheme)	D	Owner, management rule, type, age, technical features	5
	Human errors	D	Crew characteristics, work conditions	7
Environment	Meteorological conditions (weather) and climate	I		18
	Weather extremes (wind, fog, rain, snow, clouds) and natural hazards (earthquake, tsunami, volcano eruption)	I		4
	Sea state (sea current, waves)	I		7
	Visibility	I		5
	Time of day (Day/night, darkness)	I		5
Port-related	Port operations (e.g. berthing/unberthing procedure)	I		2
	Port capacity (water depth, shoreline length, number of berths, cranes)	I		2
	Cargo loading/unloading procedure	I		3
	Traffic management	I		2
	Personnel (competence, training)	I		1
	Geopolitical (political unrest, corruption, civil disorders, terrorism, crimes)	I		1
Other	Maritime regulations (conventions, recommendations, rules)	I		3

Source: own work

References

1. UNCTAD: Review of maritime transport 2017 (2017)
2. Vernimmen, B., Dullaert, W., Engelen, S.: Schedule unreliability in liner shipping: origins and consequences for the hinterland supply chain. Marit. Econ. Logist. **9**(3), 193–213 (2007)

3. Calkoen, C., Santbergen, P.: MetOcean services to the marine transport sector. Deliverable of Melodies Project (2016)
4. Veldhuis, H.D.: Developing an automated solution for ETA definition concerning long distance shipping. Ph.D. thesis, University of Twente (2015)
5. Goerlandt, F., Montewka, J.: Maritime transportation risk analysis: review and analysis in light of some foundational issues. Reliab. Eng. Syst. Saf. **138**, 115–134 (2015)
6. ABS: Guidance notes on risk assessement applications for the marine and offshore oil and gas industries. Technical report, American Bureau of Shipping (2000)
7. Szymanek, A.: Risk acceptation principles in transport. J. KONBiN **5**(2), 271–281 (2008)
8. Soares, C.G., Teixeira, A.P.: Risk assessment in maritime transportation. Reliab. Eng. Syst. Saf. **74**(3), 299–309 (2001)
9. Berle, Ø., Asbjørnslett, B.E., Rice, J.B.: Formal vulnerability assessment of a maritime transportation system. Reliab. Eng. Syst. Saf. **96**(6), 696–705 (2011)
10. Trucco, P., Cagno, E., Ruggeri, F., Grande, O.: A Bayesian belief network modelling of organisational factors in risk analysis: a case study in maritime transportation. Reliab. Eng. Syst. Saf. **93**(6), 823–834 (2008)
11. Balmat, J.F., Lafont, F., Maifret, R., Pessel, N.: MAritime RISk Assessment (MARISA), a fuzzy approach to define an individual ship risk factor. Ocean Eng. **36**(15–16), 1278–1286 (2009)
12. Elsayed, T.: Fuzzy inference system for the risk assessment of liquefied natural gas carriers during loading/offloading at terminals. Appl. Ocean Res. **31**(3), 179–185 (2009)
13. Kowalski, J., Kozera, J.: Mapa zagrożeń bezpieczeństwa energetycznego RP w sektorach ropy naftowej i gazu ziemnego. In: Bezpieczeństwo Narodowe, pp. 301–324. BBN, Warszawa (2009)
14. Blaich, M., Köhler, S., Reuter, J., Hahn, A.: Probabilistic collision avoidance for vessels. IFAC-PapersOnLine **48**(16), 69–74 (2015)
15. Hornauer, S., Hahn, A.: Towards marine collision avoidance based on automatic route exchange. IFAC Proc. Vol. **46**(33), 103–107 (2013)
16. Wieteska, G.: Zarządzanie ryzykiem w łacuchu dostaw na rynku B2B. Difin (2011)
17. Hevner, A., March, S., Park, J., Ram, S.: Design science in information systems research. MIS Q. **28**(1), 75–105 (2004)
18. Hevner, A., Chatterjee, S.: Design Science Research in Information Systems. Springer, Boston (2010). https://doi.org/10.1007/978-1-4419-5653-8
19. Venable, J., Pries-Heje, J., Baskerville, R.: FEDS: a framework for evaluation in design science research. Eur. J. Inf. Syst. **25**(1), 77–89 (2016)
20. Norkus, O., Sauer, J.: RABIC: a reference architecture for business intelligence in the cloud. J. Commun. Comput. **13**, 244–260 (2016)
21. MMO: Mapping UK Shipping Density and Routes from AIS. Technical report, Marine Managment Organisation, Newcastle, UK (2014). MMO Project No: 1066
22. Shelmerdine, R.L.: Teasing out the detail: how our understanding of marine AIS data can better inform industries, developments, and planning. Mar. Policy **54**, 17–25 (2015)
23. Wu, L., Xu, Y., Wang, Q., Wang, F., Xu, Z.: Mapping global shipping density from AIS data. J. Navig. **70**(1), 67–81 (2017)

Mixed Methods Approach as Requirements Analysis of a Method for Process Harmonization in Design Science Research

Irene Schönreiter[(⌧)]

Technische Universität Dresden, Dresden, Germany
irene@schoenreiter.de

Abstract. Process harmonization (PH) in the post-merger integration phase is essential for successful mergers & acquisitions (M&A). Especially in the service sector, the know-how is bundled in processes, thus PH is an essential success factor. In order to execute PH systematically under holistic consideration, a method for PH is desirable. The objective of the research project is the development of a corresponding artefact within the framework of the Design Science Research approach. To identify requirements for the artefact, the Mixed Methods (MiMe) research consisting of interviews with experts and questionnaire survey was used for the requirements analysis, whose results were already published in individual contributions. This article aims to evaluate critically the applied MiMe research and thus broaden its application in IS research. The result shows that the obtained meta-inferences hold a high validity and accordingly the requirements gained from MiMe research are an essential prerequisite for the development of an artifact for PH.

Keywords: Mixed methods research · Process harmonization
Design science · Business Process Management

1 Introduction

The number of mergers and acquisitions (M&A) activities was steadily increasing in recent years. In particular, the services sector is affected by the majority of global M&A's [1]. Post-merger integration (PMI) is the key element for a successful M&A [2, p. 105]. However, substantial value creation after M&A is quite rare [3], so the PMI must be well planned and methodically set up. Since Business Process Management plays a central role in organizational change situations [4, 5], process harmonization (PH) is essential in PMI. Stable business processes are required to maintain competitiveness throughout the change process. For a merged entity, this means harmonizing processes efficiently and implementing them in a common management system (MS). For this, a method would be desirable that systematically accompanies and performs the merged organization during the PH [6, 7]. The objective of this ongoing research is to develop and evaluate a methodology according to the Design Science Research (DSR) approach. The approach of the research follows the process model of Design Science Research Methodology (DSRM) of [8] with the following phases:

© Springer Nature Switzerland AG 2019
W. Abramowicz and A. Paschke (Eds.): BIS 2018 Workshops, LNBIP 339, pp. 675–686, 2019.
https://doi.org/10.1007/978-3-030-04849-5_57

- problem identification & motivation
- definition of the objectives of a solution
- design & development
- demonstration
- evaluation
- communication

In the research series, the "problem identification & motivation" has already been described in detail [6, 7]. The PH methodology must meet a number of requirements to ensure a beneficial and constructive support in the complex situation. In order to carry out an exhaustive and holistic requirements analysis, the know-how of already merged organizations is surveyed. These include the experience of success factors, but also wrong decisions leading to a failure or complications of a PH in the PMI. Therefore, an empirical approach based on qualitative and quantitative research and thus following the Mixed Methods (MiMe) research was chosen to identify requirements, i.e. the MiMe approach was chosen as a method for "definition of the objectives of a solution". Currently, the requirements for an artifact were already published in various individual contributions:

(a) Significance of Quality 4.0 in Post Merger Process Harmonization [9]
(b) Process Harmonization in the Post Merger Integration – Quality Criteria for the Integration Process (translated from: Prozessharmonisierung in der Post Merger Integration – Qualitätskriterien für den Integrationsprozess) [10]
(c) Process Harmonization Phase Model in Post Merger Integration [11]
(d) Successful Post Merger Process Harmonization in the Triangle of Methodologies, Capabilities and Acceptance [12]

This article focuses on the implementation of the MiMe approach for requirements analysis with the objective of a critical review. The motivation for this contribution are the following: firstly, the MiMe approach is - with less than 5 percent of the empirical studies published between 2001 and 2007 in the six major IS journals - scarcely applied in IS research [14], and secondly, the overall picture of MiMe could not be represented adequately in the individual contributions (a)–(d). As the requirements impact the design and development of an artefact significantly, the validation of the MiMe approach and requirements is mainly discussed. Thus, the goal of identifying strengths and weaknesses of the own MiMe approach in general is intended, followed by a concluding collective validation of the articles (a)–(d) with the identified requirements.

The MiMe approach is an accessible approach to inquiry for researchers and has steadily grown and developed over the years, besides others in the considerations about validity and quality [13]. The MiMe strength lies in the complementarity of qualitative and quantitative analysis. The approach is very effective in overcoming the drawbacks of a single method, and so helps to identify and understand requirements of a particular user group. The novelty presented in this paper emphasizes the combination of the scarcely applied MiMe approach in IS research to identify requirements from a helicopter perspective as an input for the design and development of an artefact.

The review is based on the approach of Venkatesh et al. [14], which focuses on: (1) appropriateness of a MiMe approach, (2) development of meta-inferences from MiMe research, (3) assessment of the quality of meta-inferences [14].

As a result, the following research questions arise:

1. *Is the MiMe research adequate in the present research project for defining the objectives of a solution according to the DSR approach?*
2. *To what extent did the requirements analysis/requirement artefacts consider the guidelines and, in particular, the validation of Venkatesh et al.* [14]*?*
3. *Which quality hold the requirements and meta-inferences?*

This article is structured as follows: Sect. 2 describes the MiMe research with its components. Section 3 illustrates the methodology used in the ongoing research project for requirements analysis, consisting of expert interviews and quantitative surveys using questionnaires, which are critically assessed in Sect. 4 by applying the guidelines of Venkatesh et al. [14]. Finally, the results are discussed and summarized.

2 MiMe Research

MiMe research is particularly used in social and behavioral sciences. However, in the research of IS (information systems) the approach is hardly applied, although the MiMe offers numerous strengths and could thus provide valuable contributions to IS research [14]. MiMe research combines quantitative and qualitative research [14, 15, p. 90], [16, p. 8], based on its data collection, analysis and inference techniques, but extends the approaches as a third paradigm choice to more informative, complete, balanced and useful research results [17]. The combination of investigative and confirmatory research allows in-depth conclusions, which would not be possible with the application of only one method, and on the other hand, the value lies in a theses review of the accompanying method leading to a repeated review of the conceptual framework for conflicting results [14].

Qualitative research is used to collect, analyze, interpret and present narrative information [16, p. 6]. In the research project, expert interviews providing deep insights into the experience of the interviewees were executed. In contrast to the quantitative methods, which are characterized by objectivity, the expert interview is rather sub-jective and interpretive [18, p. 39]. Respondents have the opportunity to explain the background and motive of decisions and actions that cannot be raised in questionnaires. Further facts and correlations can be analyzed [19, p. 7]. Qualitative research is based on individual cases - a small number of experts whose objective views are of interest and who contribute both to the hypothesis formation of a theory and to its practical application [15, pp. 86–89]. An expert is selected of a group of people with a specific experience, position and subject-specific competences. An Expert contributes signifi-cantly to the orientation in a particular situation and can influence the perspective of a specific problem [20, pp. 14–15]. The evaluation was carried out by qualitative content analysis according to [21], in which linguistic material was systematically evaluated, rigorously assessed and interpreted.

Quantitative research is used to collect, analyze, interpret, and present numerical information [16, p. 6] and deals with the presentation of empirical facts as numbers that are mathematically/statistically evaluated in means, distributions, percentages, probabilities, and relationships. The aim is to quantify issues within a large sample using a standardized approach [15, pp. 86–89]. Quantitative data are much easier to process than qualitative data and are therefore suitable for a larger number of data sets. Representativeness and generalizability of the theses is achieved with the high number. Therefore, the theses obtained in qualitative research can be validated with the quantitative approach [22, p. 8]. The questionnaire "translates" the research question into individual questions to obtain information and data for empirical investigations [23, p. 183].

3 Methodology

In this section the components of the applied research strands are explained in more detail.

3.1 Phase 1: Qualitative Analysis

The qualitative analysis was executed with expert interviews. As a variant of the expert interview, the "process knowledge" was chosen. Process knowledge includes experience of specific events and courses of action in which the respondents were involved [20, p. 18]. Furthermore, a distinction is made between different forms of the expert interview. In the present case, the "systematizing expert interview" was selected. This is characterized by the widest possible and comprehensive collection of expert knowledge and aims to gather information [20, p. 18]. For transcription, the simple transcript was chosen to focus on the content of the interviews. In the event of abnormalities or emotions the interview was followed up directly, so that no further interpretation was necessary.

The interviews were carried out semi-structured supported by an interview guideline with a mix of open and closed questions. Various aspects that were queried would not arise in a free or narrative interview [24, pp. 103–107]. Based on the experiences and insights of the interviewed persons, quantitative research results or already established theories can be validated. Concurrently, a considerable amount of background knowledge can be gained and thus allows to supplement the quantitative analysis. Best practices and lessons learned have been identified as well.

A total of 12 experts were interviewed by telephone with an average duration of 60 min. The experts are quality manager and top-level manager of various service companies with an active participation or steerage in one or more PMI's. 33% of the respondents were CEO/COO, 66% of respondents were in a quality management position in the branches computer software, supplies & services, health care, consulting, plant engineering, sheltered and home improvement industries and several industry service providers.

3.2 Phase 2: Quantitative Analysis

The quantitative analysis consists of a questionnaire survey. This was based on the results of the expert interviews and partly extended with more in-depth questions. The questionnaire holds a total of 23 questions in following sections: background information of the company, integration approach, independent variables (information on the implementation of the PH), dependent variables (measurement of the success of the PH), demographic information.

Due to the high relevance of the integration approaches absorption and symbiosis for PH, only appropriate answers were considered. A total of 61 out of the 91 answers were included in the analysis, all other cases were excluded. In order to check the representativeness of the answers, 25% of the answers were compared with the result of all answers without significant differences between the groups. Table 1 shows the composition of the participants in terms of position and industry.

Table 1. Participants of quantitative analysis

Position	In %	Branch	In %
Quality management/process management	17%	Service companies	35%
Executive board + management	52%	Production	24%
External consultant	17%	Transport, communication, energy	8%
Employees	14%	Whole sale	7%
		Others	26%

4 Results

The results are reviewed retrospectively after completion of MiMe research and assessed according to the guidelines of [14].

4.1 Appropriateness of MiMe Approach

[14] suggest several motivators for choosing the MiMe research. In the present case, the approach is chosen in particular by reason of completeness, developmental, confirmation and compensation. In order to develop a method for PH, the overall picture of the situation must be available initially to define a complete catalog of requirements for the artefact to be designed. Conclusions are drawn from the expert interviews, which are tested as hypotheses in quantitative research, so that a full confirmation of the findings is available. As described in Sect. 2, both qualitative and quantitative analysis imply weaknesses that are compensated in the MiMe approach. Insights into the experience and knowledge of versed PH professionals with obtaining a holistic understanding and its verification in that depth would not be possible with the application of one analysis only. Accordingly, the application of the MiMe approach is definitely appropriate in the present research.

4.2   Strategy for MiMe Design

The MiMe research was set up sequentially. In contrast to the simultaneous strategy, sequential research design involves qualitative and quantitative research in different phases that are integrated mutually [14]. In the present case, qualitative research was conducted to understand the overall context and theoretical framing of a PH in addition to deriving initial insights, that have been verified by quantitative research. Accordingly, the questionnaire was influenced by the results of the expert interviews.

4.3   Strategy for MiMe Data Analysis

Frequently in MiMe research, one of the two analyzes is more dominant and its data described in more detail than the other [14, 17]. In the present case, however, the qualitative and quantitative analysis receive the same attention and are specified in the same intensity. Although the sequential order started with the expert interviews, the results of the quantitative analysis are of the same importance. Though, the contributions show that qualitative and quantitative analysis have different weights when creating pre-artifacts and defining the artifact requirements. For example, only the results of expert interviews were used to define quality criteria for a successful PH (see [10]), while for testing of hypotheses in the PH triangle, consisting of methods, capabilities and acceptance, quantitative analysis was used (see [12]).

4.4   Development of Meta-inferences

Meta-inferences are theoretical conclusions drawn within the quantitative or qualitative strand of MiMe research [14]. In each of the individual contributions was answering the corresponding research questions of primary importance. As a result no common meta-inferences were formed as suggested by [14]. However, all identified requirements and "pre-artifacts" derived from MiMe research impacted the "design & development" phase as a complete package.

Quantitative Analysis

For testing the hypotheses, regression analysis was performed to examine the coherence between dependent and independent variables. Design validity, measurement validity and inference validity were tested according to [14].

The design of the questionnaire was based on the results of the qualitative analysis and tested several times with different managers involved in a post-merger PH. The answers were received from german-speaking countries (Germany, Austria, Switzerland) in order to obtain as homogeneous results as possible. For an indefinite population, the sample size cannot be specified. The hypotheses tested were structured in "methodology", "capabilities" and "acceptance". Critical to note are two aspects. Firstly, the term "conditions for acceptance" would have been more appropriate, as various items were operationalized to measure the conditions for acceptance. Secondly, the dependent variable "to what extent are you convinced that the employees of both company parts had been sufficiently informed and involved?" was used as an indicator to measure "acceptance". There may exist more indicators suitable to assess acceptance. In this case only this one variable was used, as such the point might be regarded as not sufficient enough. Otherwise the questionnaire survey is only one part of the requirements analysis– and as such the point is not negligible but will not influence the artefact in a remarkably extent.

Measurement validity was ensured by correct operationalization during the measurement with appropriate consideration of the features related in the hypothesis. Furthermore, distorting influences in the data collection were controlled in order to avoid systematic misinformation. Data processing corresponded to the underlying measurement level.

Qualitative Analysis

In qualitative analysis is - in contrast to quantitative analysis - validation often omitted because there are no generally accepted guidelines [14]. However, at least basic principles such as objectivity, reliability and validity should be considered [25]. In order to ensure the validity of the qualitative analysis, the evaluation was carried out according to the rules of [21, 25]. Qualitative content analysis is conducted by methodical handling of linguistic material and is characterized by analysis of (fixed) communication as well as systematic, rule-based, theory-led approach, with the aim to draw conclusions about certain aspects of communication [21, p. 13]. In the transcribed material, the facts from the interviews were compacted and rules derived. The tool "QCAmap", a software for qualitative content analysis, was used for qualitative content analysis. The procedure is based on the fulfillment of analytical validity [14] with regard to theoretical validity (results from the data are justifiable), reliability (the core statements repeat themselves in the course of the expert interviews and thus suggest reliable and generalizable statements), consistency (reduction of raw data to key messages through systematic compression of data and statements) and plausibility (the results derived from the compacted data reflect the statements of the experts). Thus, the results provide credible, transferable and generalizable statements in terms of design validity. The inferential validity was passively examined after evaluation of the results by providing the cumulative results to all experts. Occasional confirmations of the results and the lack of critical feedback support a confirmation of the interpretations made by the researcher. In addition, key messages were summarized by the researcher and confirmed by the interviewee during the interviews.

MiMe Validation

First of all, the corresponding nomenclature shall be used in the validation of MiMe in order to clearly distinguish it from qualitative and quantitative research [14]. Furthermore, the quality of the meta-inferences should be assessed.

Using established evaluation tools, both strands of research are considered as validated. SPSS IBM Statistics was used in quantitative research and QCAmap was used in qualitative research. In general, both analysis yield similar results. As already stated, the published contributions are related in particular to one of the two analysis, so that MiMe validation was not discussed separately in these.

There is room for improvement in the traceability of the reflection from qualitative results to the single questions in the questionnaire. A detailed mapping of questions and hypotheses to a certain result is not available. The reflection of hypotheses and questionnaires was done in a summarizing way out of the results of the expert interviews available via the software QCAmap.

The interviews were conducted under neutral conditions and evaluated anonymously. Nevertheless, attention should be drawn to possible distortions that can usually arise from the interview situation, e.g. reactivity, interview atmosphere, present third persons, selective failure, etc. [23, p. 188], [26, pp. 62–63], [27, p. 316]. These response distortions could also occur in the questionnaire. However, with the possibility of anonymous answers, the interviewer effects should be neutralized in the present case [28, p. 237]. The content analysis itself is a non-reactive method, there is no contact between interviewer and respondent. Thus, distortions cannot occur because the analysis is strictly based on a methodological evaluation through categorization and codes [28, p. 237]. Nevertheless, it cannot precluded that a speeding up of the questionnaire can lead to a falsification if the questions and possible answers are not thoroughly read [26, p. 64].

4.5   An Integrative Framework for Validation in MiMe Research in IS

Table 2 has been adopted in its structure from [14] to assess the own research contributions.

Table 2. Validation of own MiMe research

Quality aspects	Quality criteria	Assessment of own research	Contribution			
			(a)	(b)	(c)	(d)
Design quality	Design suitability/ appropriateness	The MiMe approach is appropriate to answer the research questions (see Sect. 4.1). The method was executed rigorously. Objectives and requirements for an artefact have been identified step-by-step within the MiMe research	ok	ok	ok	ok
	Design adequacy	**Quantitative:** The design components are realized by composing a questionnaire, which includes different sections, a sufficient number of data and an evaluation with established software of sound quality and appropriate rigor	ok	ok	ok	ok
		Qualitative: According to [21, 25], the basic principles of the qualitative analysis are implemented so that the results promise credibility and reliability				
	Analytic adequacy	**Quantitative:** 25% of the responses were tested by a comparison with the result of all responses to secure representativeness. No significant differences were detected. Furthermore, the values of R2, F, B, beta were reported in the regression analysis in order to ensure comprehensive transparency	ok	ok	ok	ok
		Qualitative: Validity and plausibility of the theses are achieved by the rule-based approach supported by the software QACmap				

(continued)

Table 2. (*continued*)

Quality aspects	Quality criteria	Assessment of own research	Contribution			
			(a)	(b)	(c)	(d)
Explanation quality	Quantitative inferences	Overall, the impressions from expert interviews and findings from the literature analysis have been confirmed by the results of the tested hypotheses				ok
	Qualitative inferences	The inferences resulted from the results of the qualitative content analysis, so they are credible, demonstrable and transferable	ok	ok	ok	
	Integrative inverence/meta-inference	**Integrative efficacy** means that inferences are effectively integrated into a theoretically consistent meta- inference model [14]. In this case, the key messages of qualitative and quantitative research coincide. However, in particular, the results of the qualitative analysis were coupled with other research methods (e.g. literature analysis) to gain requirements or "intermediate artifacts" as a prerequisite for the development of the final artifact. As a result, these parts of qualitative research can not be compared directly with the results of quantitative research. The same applies inversely: the questionnaire was influenced by the qualitative analysis during the preparation, but also expanded by contents that were not discussed with the experts in the first phase				
		Inference transferability assesses the extent to which meta-inferences are generalizable and transferable to other contexts and situations [14]. The gained meta-inferences are generalizable to service companies pursuing a PH after M&A. The extent to which meta-inferences could be transferred to other sectors was not examined in the research project				
		Integrative correspondence describes the extent the meta-inferences of MiMe research meet the initial purpose of using the MiMe approach [14]. The MiMe approach contributed significantly to a comprehensive picture throughout the research project. Qualitative research has been more extensively included in the requirements analysis, possibly due to the "more tangible" statements of the experts and the possibility to ask questions. In addition, the interviews with experts in the sequential series were conducted first and thus shaped the understanding of an organization in the situation of a PMI. Nonetheless, the qualitative analysis was valuable to validate key messages from the experts in a broader sense				

5   Discussion and Summary

This paper pursues the goal to review of the applied MiMe research critically. The review of the present research project according to the guidelines of [14] illustrated a detailed and convincing examination of MiMe research for requirements analysis used as an input for the development of an IS artifact. The adequacy of the MiMe approach has been clearly demonstrated. With the results and identified requirements for an artifact a successful and profitable application for the entire research project is supposed. The DSR phase "definition of the objectives of a solution" according to [8] was thus adequately conducted. Therefore, a concluding collective validation of the realized MiMe research along with the identified requirements is confirmed. It should, however, be critically noted that the formulation of the meta-inferences in the individual contributions did not explicitly take place. Thus, the very close interlocking of the qualitative and quantitative analysis in the various contributions listed in Sect. 1 was not apparent. Further, a part of hypotheses testing in the quantitative analysis was simplified in some way, but in summary adequate for the attached value within the overall project. Apart from that both qualitative and quantitative analysis have been performed with high validity, so that the generated meta-inference advocate for a qualitatively flawless result.

The meta-inferences from the overall package could be as follows:

(1) PH consists of analysis phase, conception phase, realization phase and verification phase and is divided in process level and management system level.

(2) Industry 4.0 elements are of secondary importance for PH, although service organizations could benefit enormous from the potential. However, processes should be reviewed for modernization during PH and implemented accordingly.

(3) There are quality criteria that must be considered when developing a method for PH.

(4) A method for PH does not exist. Established methods from quality and process management are not suitable for usage during PH, nor in individual phases.

(5) An early definition of the future personnel structure after M&A leads to the avoidance of power struggles and conflicts of interest. The composition of the PH project team should be aligned with the future corporate structure.

(6) A regular and systematic information policy leads to better employee acceptance and is thus an essential prerequisite for the success of a PH.

(7) The merged company requires a combination of standardized and individual processes, forced standardization leads to worse results.

(8) Mutual understanding of the merged organization with enough time for an analysis of the processes and the management system (maturity assessment) lead to better results.

(9) An optimal implementation method for the realization phase could not be identified (big-bang versus step-by-step versus pilot-operated introduction), the decision should be made on a company-specific basis.

(10) A common certification after completion of the PH project confirms the success of PH.

Negative effects associated with qualitative or quantitative research were explicitly considered and deliberately neutralized by the combination in the MiMe approach. Respective limitations were clearly formulated in the individual contributions using only one analysis type. As a limitation, it is pointed out that there may be several months between the survey and the project of PH, so corresponding gaps in the memory of respondents may occur.

The depth of application of the guidelines for MiMe research according to [14] was detailed in the previous section. The identified requirements and pre-artefacts are assessed as valid and thus hold a high quality. Meta-inferences provide valuable input for developing an artifact for PH. In addition, using the MiMe methodology in IS research has widened the knowledge base and provides further evidence of the added value of this combination. A more robust conclusion is achieved by rendering an enhanced validity through cross validation. Practitioners benefit from valid knowledge and experience of a broad set of surveys combined with expert knowledge.

References

1. Zephyr published by Bureau van Dijk: M&A Portal: M&A Review Global H1 2017 (2017)
2. Haspeslagh, P.C., Jemison, D.B.: Managing Acquisitions: Creating Value Through Corporate Renewal. The Free Press, New York (1991)
3. Toppenberg, G., Henningsson, S.: Taking stock and looking forward: a scientometric analysis of IS/IT integration challenges in mergers. In: ECIS 2014 Proceedings, pp. 0–16 (2014)
4. Rohloff, M.: Advances in business process management implementation based on a maturity assessment and best practice exchange. Inf. Syst. E-Bus. Manag. 9(3), 383–403 (2011)
5. Jochem, R., Geers, D., Heinze, P.: Maturity measurement of knowledge-intensive business processes. TQM J. 23(4), 377–387 (2011)
6. Schönreiter, I.: Bedarfe zur Prozessharmonisierung in fusionierten Dienstleistungsunternehmen im Zeitalter Quality 4.0. In: Winzer, P. (ed.) Herausforderungen der Digitalisierung, 1/2016, pp. 35–49. Shaker, Aachen (2016)
7. Schönreiter, I.: Methodologies for process harmonization in the post merger integration phase - a literature review. Bus. Process Manag. J. 24(2), 330–356 (2018)
8. Peffers, K., Tuunanen, T., Rothenberger, M.A., Chatterjee, S.: A design science research methodology for information systems research. J. Manag. Inf. Syst. 24(3), 45–77 (2008)
9. Schönreiter, I.: Significance of quality 4.0 in post merger process harmonization. In: Piazolo, F., Geist, V., Brehm, L., Schmidt, R. (eds.) ERP Future 2016. LNBIP, vol. 285, pp. 123–134. Springer, Cham (2017). https://doi.org/10.1007/978-3-319-58801-8_11
10. Schönreiter, I.: Prozessharmonisierung in der Post Merger Integration - Qualitätskriterien für den Integrationsprozess. zfo - Zeitschrift Führung + Organ. 86(04), 253–260 (2017)
11. Schönreiter, I.: Process harmonization phase model in post merger integration. In: Proceedings of the 6th International Symposium on Data-Driven Process Discovery and Analysis (SIMPDA 2016), pp. 3–22 (2016)
12. Schönreiter, I.M.: Successful post merger process harmonization in the triangle of methodologies, capabilities and acceptance. In: Teniente, E., Weidlich, M. (eds.) BPM 2017. LNBIP, vol. 308, pp. 656–668. Springer, Cham (2018). https://doi.org/10.1007/978-3-319-74030-0_53
13. Creswell, J.W., Clark, V.L.P.: Designing and Conducting Mixed Methods Research, 2nd edn. Sage Publications, Los Angeles, London, New Delhi, Singapore, Washington DC (2017)
14. Venkatesh, V., Brown, S.A., Bala, H.: Bridging the qualitative-quantitative devide: guidelines for constructing mixed methods research in information systems. MIS Q. 37(1), 21–54 (2013)
15. Hug, T., Poscheschnik, G.: Empirisch forschen die Planung und Umsetzung von Projekten im Studium, 2nd edn. UVK Verl.-Ges, Konstanz, München (2015)
16. Teddlie, C., Tashakorri, A.: Foundations of Mixed Methods Research: Integrating Quantitative and Qualitative Approaches in the Social and Behavioral Sciences. Sage, Beverley Hills (2009)
17. Johnson, R.B., Onwuegbuzie, A.J., Turner, L.A.: Toward a definition of mixed methods research. J. Mix. Methods Res. 1(2), 112–133 (2007)

18. Borchardt, A., Göthlich, S.E.: Erkenntnisgewinnung durch Fallstudien. In: Albers, S., Klapper, D., Konradt, U., Walter, A., Wolf, J. (eds.) Methodik der empirischen Forschung, 1st edn, pp. 37–54. Dt. Univ.-Verl, Wiesbaden (2006)
19. Dresing, T., Pehl, T.: Praxisbuch Interview, Transkription & Analyse. Anleitungen und Regelsysteme für qualitativ Forschende, 6th edn. Eigenverlag, Marburg (2015)
20. Bogner, A., Littig, B., Menz, W.: Interviews mit Experten: eine praxisorientierte Einführungeine praxisorientierte Einführung. Springer, Wiesbaden (2014). https://doi.org/10.1007/978-3-531-19416-5
21. Mayring, P.: Qualitative Inhaltsanalyse: Grundlagen und TechnikenGrundlagen und Techniken. Beltz, Weinheim (2015)
22. Riesenhuber, F.: Großzahlige empirische Forschung. In: Albers, S., Klapper, D., Konradt, U., Walter, A., Wolf, J. (eds.) Methodik der empirischen Forschung, 1st edn, pp. 1–18. Dt. Univ.-Verl, Wiesbaden (2006)
23. Stier, W.: Empirische Forschungsmethoden. Springer, Berlin (1996). https://doi.org/10.1007/978-3-642-58460-2
24. Gläser, J., Laudel, G.: Experteninterviews und qualitative Inhaltsanalyse: als Instrumente rekonstruierender Untersuchungenals Instrumente rekonstruierender Untersuchungen, 4th edn. VS, Verl. für Sozialwiss, Wiesbaden (2010)
25. Mayring, P.: Qualitative Content Analysis: Theoretical Foundation, Basic Procedures and Software Solution. Klagenfurt (2014). www.beltz.de
26. Raab-Steiner, E., Benesch, M.: Der Fragebogen von der Forschungsidee zur SPSS-Auswertung, 3rd edn. Facultas, WUV, Wien (2012)
27. Esser, H.: Differenzierung und Integration sozialer Systeme als Voraussetzungen der Umfrageforschung: Differentation and integration in social systems as prerequisites of survey research. Zeitschrift für Soziologie ZfS **4**(4), 316–334 (1975)
28. Friedrichs, J.: Methoden empirischer Sozialforschung, 14th edn. Westdt. Verl, Opladen (1990)

Predicting Customer Churn in Electronic Banking

Marcin Szmydt[✉]

Department of Information Systems, Poznan University of Economics and Business,
Aleja Niepodległości 10, Poznan, Poland
marcin.szmydt@ue.poznan.pl

Abstract. The following paper is an outline of the current author's research on the churn prediction in electronic banking. The research is based on real anonymised data of 4 million clients from one of the biggest Polish banks. Access to real data in such scale is a substantial strength of the study, as many researchers often do use only small data sample from a short period. Even though current research is still preliminary and ongoing, unlimited access to these data provides a great environment for further work. The study strongly connects with real business goals and trends in the banking industry as the author is also a practitioner. Described research focuses on methods for predicting customers who are likely to leave electronic banking. It contributes especially in further classification of an electronic churn and a broader definition of customer churn in general. Recommended solutions should contribute to the increase in the number of digital customers in the bank.

Keywords: Banking · Churn prediction · Electronic banking

1 Introduction

In almost every business retaining existing customers is undoubtedly cheaper than gaining new ones. In the past, banking used to be a sector with relatively low churn rate. Each customer was treated individually and offered a customised service. After years of intense competition, customers exchanged highly personalised service for a lower price, higher anonymity and reduced variety [11]. Right now, in the age of digitalisation, it is easier than ever to open a new bank account and transfer all assets without even leaving home. This situation forced banks to become more interested in the subject of customer retention. However, before taking efficient ways of retaining existing clients, it is necessary to predict those who are about to leave [1].

Furthermore, with digital transformation of the banking industry, it is also essential for banks to keep customers in electronic channels like Internet or mobile [2]. Reason for this is that digital customer is more profitable than the traditional one. There is no need for a physical branch nor a staff that is providing services to this client. The digital customer is also more willing to use

W. Abramowicz and A. Paschke (Eds.): BIS 2018 Workshops, LNBIP 339, pp. 687–696, 2019.
https://doi.org/10.1007/978-3-030-04849-5_58

additional services available in electronic or mobile banking and is susceptible to e-marketing [13]. Thanks to this trend, a new issue arose - *digital churn*. Predicting this phenomen means identifying customers who are about to leave using remote services. Leaving electronic channels may indicate that customer has opened another account in competitors bank or is just not satisfied with a banking portal or mobile application any more. An increasing number of banks do not charge customers for running accounts therefore most customers do not close bank accounts any more, they just stop using them. This is the reason why predicting churn from electronic channels might be more valuable than just predicting closing all bank accounts and products - as the churn is described in most research papers in existing literature. It is also vital to discover churn reasons of a given customer to take appropriate actions in time [7]. To the best of author's knowledge, there are no articles nor publications with the main focus on the prediction of electronic banking churn with the further classification of an electronic churn type to match adequate retention campaigns.

The above motivation gives the way to outline the main research problem analysed in this paper, which is: *How to predict customers who are leaving electronic channels and how to retain them?* To solve this problem, the following research questions need to be addressed:

Q1: Who are the customers who are leaving electronic channels and what are the reasons for their churn? (electronic churn groups)
Q2: What are the existing methods of customer churn prediction in banking?
Q3: How efficiently apply existing methods to electronic channel churn prediction and further electronic churn classification?

2   Research Methodology

Having in mind empirical and theoretical aspects of the problem, proper research methodology must be chosen. The methodology behind this research follows the principles of Design Science Research (DSR) with guidelines designed by Hevner et al. in [4]. Additionally, some recommendations provided by Webster and Watson in [14] has also been used.

DSR methodology consists of the following phases: *Awareness of Problem, Suggestion, Development, Evaluation,* and *Conclusion.* After a broad analysis of the banking sector with the main focus on electronic channels and digitalisation of the banking industry, the problem was formulated in Sect. 1. In the next stage, it was extended to a form of research questions (also Sect. 1). The literature review concerning an existing churn prediction methods in banking has been described in Sect. 3. Suggested methods to address presented issues has been provided in Sect. 4. In the same section, some evaluation tools for this methods also were proposed. Conclusions and further actions of this ongoing research are described in Sect. 5.

Following the Design Science Research Guidelines, the artifact in the form of a process has been developed. Business needs described in Sect. 1 justify research problem. In Sects. 1 and 4 environment analysis has been performed and some proposals of empirical evaluation methods were included in Sect. 4. Even though the study is still incomplete, research rigour is enforced to yield best results in current and further work (Fig. 1).

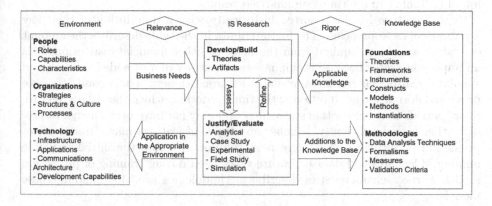

Fig. 1. Design science research with guidelines designed by Hevner et al. [4]

3   Literature Review

3.1   Searching Process

Comprehensive literature analysis has been conducted to analyse the current state of the art of research in the area of churn prediction in banking. Key recommendations provided by Webster and Watson in [14] and Hevner et al. [4] has been used as a guideline to enhance the rigour of the research process. The chosen research databases consisted of Springer, IEEExplore, ACM Digital Library, ResearchGate and ScienceDirect because they covered research papers from the fields of Information Systems, IT, Engineering and Economics. Additionally, following guidelines of Webster and Watson [14] Google Scholar and Mendeley tools were used to provide relevant articles that were not found in the databases listed above. By this means, a literature search was not limited to only top journals and databases.

The search was conducted by using the keywords and phrases: "Churn Prediction"; "Customer Attrition Prediction"; "Graph-based Churn Prevention"; "Predicting Customer Churn"; "Customer Churn Model"; "Customer Churn Analysis" and combining them with the domain keywords: "banking", "banks"; "electronic banking"; "electronic channels"; "financial sector"; "finance" and "fintech". Backwards and forward search has also been comprehensively performed to find relevant papers. The main goal of this literature review was to summarise existing knowledge in churn prediction with a primary focus on the banking domain.

Initial number of publications related to churn prediction and churn models consisted of 1427 items. After filtering papers related to the banking industry, a total number of publications decreased to 150. Not being able to describe all of them, the author tried to present the most representative cases which can be found in Table 1 in a form of summarized results.

The literature has been sorted historically with a description of their key attributes of its approaches. The first attribute in the table describes the amount of real data sample acquired from the bank or other financial institution. It is an important factor because it emphasises the utility of a provided solution and simulates real-life environment available for practitioners. The second attribute provides information on duration of the time period for which these data refer to. Short periods may not contain seasonality and may not have been enough to predict other periods efficiently. Number and types of features may strongly affect prediction performance. Therefore next columns describe the initial available number of features and dataset feature types used during training of prediction model. Further characteristics describe methodologies used for building these models.

3.2   Related Work

This section provides information about different approaches in literature related to the prediction of a customer churn with a primary focus on the banking sector.

To tackle the problem of churn prediction not only does it need to be chosen an efficient algorithm, but also it is vital to acquire proper dataset of relevant features and validate the methodology on a real customer data. [9] used logistic regression to predict customer churn on data retrieved from a Finnish bank. Their dataset included typical features of customers like socio-demographics, aggregated account transactions, banking products and services. Class imbalance problem has been addressed by using down-sizing (under-sampling) methods which reduced the number of non-churners to prevent classifying all customers into one group. Constructed models were evaluated mostly using lift curve and counting the number of correct predictions. Despite the simplicity of this approach, it predicted churners relatively well.

On the other hand, [12] worked on a data of 5000 customers aged in the range of 18 to 80 years old from Croatian bank chosen by random sampling. Class imbalance problem in this study was solved by choosing precisely half of the data that included churners and the other half with non-churners. Input data set contained similar variables to [9]. All of the variables were measured at five different points in time (t0 to t4). The fuzzy C-Means algorithm has been applied to predict customer churn. According to their research fuzzy-based methods performed better than the classical ones.

Rough set approach and flow network graph are another techniques that can be applied in predicting churners. [8] utilised these methods to a sample data of 21 000 customers from a commercial bank in Taiwan. Their data set also included demographics, psychographic and transactional features. Initially, their dataset consisted of 43 variables, but only 16 variables were selected to training phase by their experts from university marketing department and managers from the banking industry. A drawback of this study is that there is only one-month period data taken into account when training models.

Other interesting studies on churn prediction by [1] suggest that customer social network analysis can significantly improve predictive accuracy. It introduces a concept that customers do not act independently and their decisions are highly influenced by others. Therefore customer network features (i.e. a degree of centrality, betweenness centrality and density) have been added to their training data. The dataset contained real records of 244 787 customers from a European financial services company. Beside network features, it also included socio-demographic and home banking behaviour. Random forests have been applied to train model for churn prediction. Their research revealed that contextual network features are even more important than socio-demographics and account features. This approach has also been explored and applied in prior studies from the telecom industry [5].

Further research in this area [3] included Support Vector Machine (SVM) analysis and naïive Bayes tree (NBTree). A dataset of 14 814 customers used in this study was obtained from a Chilean bank that suffered from an increasing number of credit card churners. Two groups of features were available for each customer: socio-demographic and product behaviour. Accordingly to their study, by considering sensitivity alone, hybrid model of SVM + NBTree using Support vectors with corresponding predicted target values with reduced features and balanced by SMOTE (Synthetic minority over-sampling technique) yielded the best value of sensitivity.

[10] worked with data from one of the major Nigerian banks by using K-Means clustering, decision trees and JRip algorithm. The raw dataset included 1,048,576 customer records described with eleven features including socio-demographics, account information and transactional behaviour. However, only 4958 records were chosen for analysis after data cleaning and preparation. Furthermore, after sampling and variable selection only 500 customers with four attributes were included in the final data set for model training. A lot of missing values like age or customer type were a substantial problem of this research therefore only a small fraction of a whole database was used in the construction of a prediction model.

Current research seems to validate the view that simple techniques like decision trees are still widely used for churn prediction. [6] explored data using the CRISP methodology and built decision tree model for electronic banking customer churn prediction. This paper is one of few that touched the subject of electronic banking churn prediction. They randomly sampled 4383 customers of e-banking services from the bank's database with features related to customer dissatisfaction, service usage and socio-demographics. Their decision tree brings a lot of knowledge in the area of electronic churn and may be an object to draw some conclusions on reasons for customer churn.

Table 1. Summary of related literature on churn prediction in banking domain

Year	Researchers	Real data sample	Time period	Initial number of features	Dataset features	Method
2006	Teemu Mutanen, Jussi Ahola, Sami Nousiainen	151 000 customers	12 points in time (with intervals of 3 months during 34 months)	75	Socio-demographics, products, services, transactional data	logistic regression
2008	Dzulijana Popovic, Zagrebacka Banka, Bojana Dalbelo Basic	5 000 customers (choosen by random sampling from bank's database)	Does not say ("client population in 2005")	73	Socio-demographics, products, financial data, bad-behaviour	Fuzzy C-Means Clustering, Canonical Discriminant Analysis, K-means clustering
2011	Chiun Sin Lin, Gwo Hshiung Tzeng, Yang Chieh Chin	21 000 customers	1 month	43	Socio-demographics, transactional data	Rough Set Approach, Flow Network Graph
2012	Dries F. Benoit, Dirk Van Den Poel	244 787 customers	7 months	31	Socio-demographics, customer social network features, electronic banking behaviour	Random forests, Social Network Analysis (SNA)
2014	M.A.H. Farquad, Vadlamani Ravi, S. Bapi Raju	14 814 customers	Does not say ("data obtained in 2004")	22	Socio-demographic, behavioural data	Support Vector Machine (SVM), naive Bayes tree (NBTree)
2015	A.O. Oyeniyi, A.B. Adeyemo	1 048 576 customer records (model trained on only 500 records)	Does not say	11	Socio-demographics	K-Means clustering, Decision tree, JRip algorithm
2016	Abbas Keramati, Hajar Ghaneei, Seyed Mohammad Mirmoham-madi	4383 customers (choosen by random sampling from bank's database)	2 years	11	Socio-demographics, customer dissatisfaction, service usage	The CRISP Methodology, decision tree

3.3   Literature Discussion and Author's Contribution

The literature review shows that most researchers are limited to data and char-acteristics provided by the bank. Although the majority of prior research has applied a wide range of prediction tools, little attention has been paid to deter-mine what customer features lead to the churn intention. Furthermore, in most literature, churn is defined as a closure of a given product (like account or credit card) and little attention is also paid to those customers who do not formally close their products, but just stop using them. Widely applied in the telecom industry - customer social network features - has been used only in one paper referring to the financial domain. There are only few publications related to electronic banking churn. According to author's knowledge, no previous research has further classified electronic churners into different churn groups to match appropriate retention campaigns. This approach also partly addresses issues with churning without formally closing products. Few attention is also paid to actions after proper predicting of a customer who is about to leave and which retention methods yield best results. Trying to fill some of the existing gaps in the literature, below research has been conducted.

4 Research Progress and Solution Design Proposal

This section provides a brief description of analysis and gives an outline of the proposed method. Data mining on records from last three years from corporate data warehouse has been performed to get an overview of the bank's customers. After this analysis, to answer the first research question about who are the customers that are leaving electronic channels the following cases have been identified:

Group 1: Customers who are leaving electronic channels and then closing all banking products. This group of customers contains classical bank churners who are widely and frequently described in the literature. They are formally closing all banking products like accounts, credit cards and online services. Most likely, they want to end their relationship with the bank permanently.

Group 2: Customers who are leaving electronic channels and keep using banking products in offline channels. This group of customers stop using electronic channels or significantly reduce the intensity of usage of these channels. Reasons for this behaviour may vary from security concerns to switching primary bank but still using these products as a secondary option.

Group 3: Customers who are leaving electronic channels and stop using banking products (without formally closing products). These clients cease their activity in electronic as well as offline channels. In case of current accounts, as data mining of cash flows revealed, most frequently they transfer all their money to accounts in other banks in their last few months of electronic activity. However, formally they still have a bank account or other products that can be used in future. This is the biggest group but yet hard to identify during first stages. It is difficult to discover whether they decided to stop their activity permanently or just for a short period.

The proposed process of predicting and classifying electronic banking churners consists of seven stages presented in Fig. 2. First one focuses on acquiring customer data from banks databases. These sources may vary from traditional data warehouses to data retrieved from system logs and big data environment. During the second stage, data is being cleaned and prepared to use in the next stages. Later, proper methods like backward, forward feature selection or recursive feature elimination should be applied. This stage focuses on selecting best features and data sources for model training phase. After features selection, prediction models are being trained. During this stage, a variety of models created by different methodologies may be constructed. Next stage evaluates these models to choose a model with best prediction efficiency. Methods like the Area Under the ROC Curve or similar tools should be applied to evaluate the performance of the constructed models. After having a database of potential electronic churners, classification methods might be applied to further categorise these customers into three groups of electronic churners as described above. After having a database with potential churners divided into these groups, different retention methods might be applied to keep them in bank and electronic channels. This process should be carried out regularly in cycles to adapt to constantly changing environment and to keep retaining customers in electronic channels.

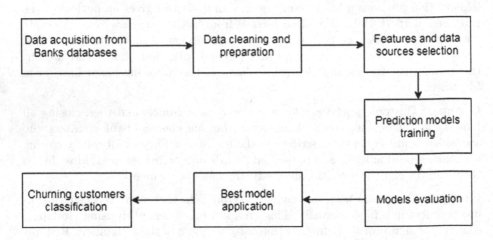

Fig. 2. Seven stages of the proposed process

5 Conclusions and Further Work

The above research reveals that electronic churn in banking industry might be an important aspect that is worth taking a closer look. The problem of electronic churn is broader then regular churn which is often described in the literature. As the customers may leave electronic channels and it may or may not mean that they churned from the bank. This approach will also reach customers that will be inactive or unsatisfied with their current electronic services. Having a proper prediction tool, banks may more successfully keep customers from churning in general and keep them in profitable electronic channels. This might be helpful to achieve bank's goals to incrase the number of a "digital customers" in the age of digital transformation of the banking industry. With the ability of further classification of electronic churners by their churn context, different retention campaigns may be used for different groups. This strategy should yield better results than just one campaign for all electronic churners.

The described analysis is only a brief indication of a problem and the research is still ongoing. The article presents a general idea for research in this field and its vision. Further work will consist of carefully application each stage of this solution in the production environment, monitoring and comparison of best prediction models, especially those with nonstandard features like social influence or behavioural characteristics. This might also lead to further data feature types prediction efficiency analysis. These actions may improve further models performance and precision. After having an ability to precisely predict churners, further retention actions must be taken. Different retention strategies may be applied for specific groups of potential churners (as described in Sect. 4) to improve their success rates. These strategies should also be part of the research with a primary goal of finding the best-performing ones. It is also interesting question how many months before actual churn these actions should be initialised. Psychological and behavioural aspects should also be taken into account during retention strategy planning. After some empirical tests, machine learning and other prediction techniques may also be applied to identify best performing retention strategies.

References

1. Benoit, D.F., Van Den Poel, D.: Improving customer retention in financial services using kinship network information. Expert Syst. Appl. **39**(13), 11435–11442 (2012). https://doi.org/10.1016/j.eswa.2012.04.016
2. Cuesta, C., Ruesta, M., Tuesta, D., Urbiola, P.: The digital transformation of the banking industry. BBVA Research (2015). https://www.bbvaresearch.com/wp-content/uploads/2015/08/EN_Observatorio_Banca_Digital_vf3.pdf
3. Farquad, M.A., Ravi, V., Raju, S.B.: Churn prediction using comprehensible support vector machine: an analytical CRM application. Appl. Soft Comput. J. **19**, 31–40 (2014). https://doi.org/10.1016/j.asoc.2014.01.031
4. Hevner, A., March, S., Park, J., Ram, S.: Design science in information systems research. MIS Q.: Manage. Inf. Syst. **28**(1), 75–105 (2004)
5. Hill, S., Provost, F., Volinsky, C.: Network-based marketing: identifying likely adopters via consumer networks. Stat. Sci. **21**(2), 256–276 (2006). https://doi.org/10.1214/088342306000000222. http://projecteuclid.org/euclid.ss/1154979826
6. Keramati, A., Ghaneei, H., Mirmohammadi, S.M.: Developing a prediction model for customer churn from electronic banking services using data mining. Financ. Innov. **2**(1), 10 (2016). https://doi.org/10.1186/s40854-016-0029-6
7. Liébana-Cabanillas, F., Nogueras, R., Herrera, L.J., Guillén, A.: Analysing user trust in electronic banking using data mining methods. Expert Syst. Appl. **40**(14), 5439–5447 (2013)
8. Lin, C.S., Tzeng, G.H., Chin, Y.C.: Combined rough set theory and ow network graph to predict customer churn in credit card accounts. Expert Syst. Appl. **38**(1), 8–15 (2011). https://doi.org/10.1016/j.eswa.2010.05.039
9. Mutanen, T., Ahola, J., Nousiainen, S.: Customer churn prediction-a case study in retail banking. In: Proceedings of the ECML/PKDD Workshop on Practical Data Mining, pp. 13–19 (2006)
10. Oyeniyi, A.O., Adeyemo, A.B.: Customer churn analysis in banking sector using data mining techniques. Afr. J. Comput. ICT **8**(3), 165–174 (2015)
11. Peppard, J.: Customer relationship management (CRM) in financial services. Eur. Manage. J. **18**(3), 312–327 (2000)

12. Popović, D., Banka, Z., Bašić, B.D.: Churn prediction model in retail banking using fuzzy C-means algorithm. Informatica **33**, 243–247 (2009). http://wen.ijs.si/ojs-2.4.3/index.php/informatica/article/viewFile/242/239
13. Sumra, S.H., Manzoor, M.K., Sumra, H.H., Abbas, M.: The impact of e-banking on the profitability of banks: a study of Pakistani banks. J. Public Adm. Gov. **1**(1), 31–38 (2011)
14. Webster, J., Watson, R.T.: Analyzing the past to prepare for the future: writing a literature review. MIS Q. **26**(2), xiii–xxiii (2002)

Assessing Process Suitability for AI-Based Automation. Research Idea and Design

Aleksandra Revina(✉) ⓘ

Technische Universität Berlin, Berlin, Germany
revina@tu-berlin.de

Abstract. Recent advancements in Big Data and Machine Learning (ML) have triggered progressive adoption of Artificial Intelligence (AI) in the enterprise domains to address growing business process complexity. What is yet largely missing in the traditional Business Process Management (BPM) approaches, are formal frameworks and guidelines for decision making support when applying AI in a company. Proposed research aims to extend existing BPM frameworks and guidelines by novel methods, this way increasing understanding of business processes in the view of recent technology developments in Big Data, AI and ML.

Keywords: Business Process Management · Business process frameworks
ITIL · Text Analytics · Text Mining · Artificial Intelligence
Process automation

1 Introduction

Business Process Management (BPM) is known as the most established way to structure, improve and control the processes, which exist in any organization. Currently, Artificial Intelligence (AI) technologies are developing faster than ever fueled by the recent advancements in Big Data, computational power, cloud computing and accessibility of Machine Learning algorithms and frameworks [28]. The conventional AI algorithms attract stronger attention in the research community, while business strategists show the renewed interest in the enterprise applications of AI.

At the time of evolvement of classical BPM discipline, AI and ML were mainly the subject of academic research. Thus, common BPM frameworks lack methods and guidance on the process domains and use case evaluation in the context of AI technologies.

In this paper, the research idea and research design will be presented. In order to reduce the knowledge domain complexity, the author suggests to focus on the ITIL (Information Technology Infrastructure Library) framework [1]. A particular motivation to revisit ITIL can be justified by two reasons: (i) nature of the framework itself, IT Service Infrastructure, which can be seen as one of the most relevant in the context of AI technologies, and (ii) its current popularity in the practitioners' community.

In order to place the research topic in a wider theoretical context correctly, it is planned to consider the guidelines by [21]. Herewith, it is differentiated among theories, best practice and pragmatic approaches. As presented later on, the author of the

W. Abramowicz and A. Paschke (Eds.): BIS 2018 Workshops, LNBIP 339, pp. 697–706, 2019.
https://doi.org/10.1007/978-3-030-04849-5_59

paper already identified some methods on the use case evaluation in the context of AI implementation for process automation. Those are widely used by vendors and business consulting companies. These approaches fall into the pragmatic group. The focus of the current research, ITIL framework, as well as many other frameworks, e.g. CMMI (Capability Maturity Model Integration), COBIT (Control Objectives for Information and Related Technologies), eTOM (Enhanced Telecom Operations Map), can be fairly classified into best practices. They are based on the cross- or industry-specific international experiences collected over many years and put together by practitioners in cooperation with scientists. These are not theories and on purpose are not directly derived from theories. Nevertheless, it is likely that one can find theories for justification of best practices [5]. Therefore, the author suggests to investigate possible theoretical baselines for ITIL, e.g. its relation to organizational, behavioral, agency, and risk theories. This formalization approach would guarantee the benefits for both theory (building, testing or expanding of theoretical baselines) and practice (increasing applicability of research findings in the enterprise context). As [20, 24] rightly mention, there is in general a lack of theoretically driven research in the area of IT Service Management (ITSM), where ITIL belongs to. This could be another valuable contribution of the suggested research.

2   Research Approach

The main research goal can be formulated as *identify, evaluate and validate a set of process meta parameters formally indicating process automation degree with AI (focus ITIL framework)*. These meta parameters or features could support the decision-making process in applying AI technologies in certain process domains. In other words, on practical level, it will allow plausible judgements regarding business value of AI technologies in a particular process use case before starting expensive proof of concepts. On theoretical level, the results will complement standard ITIL framework with the research proven approach of AI technology compliance of particular processes.

The research is divided into five phases, while the first two are executed in parallel:

1. Literature analysis on classical BPM approaches with the focus on ITIL framework and AI technology (theory, state-of-the-art research, recent practitioners' insights);
2. Practical experiment (Text Mining of ITIL framework and practitioners' documentation based on the selected process);
3. Development of a process parameter metric to measure the applicability of AI technology on a process addressing both qualitative and quantitative process features;
4. Qualitative evaluation of the metric (interviews with the process owners of IT AI-based automation projects);
5. Validation of the metric on the selected use case.

The approach does not exclude the quantitative survey in case the research findings from phases 1–4 allow.

To give a critical view on the current state-of-the-art in the topic, it is aimed to analyse relevant theoretical concepts, recent conference and journal publications, practical handbooks, and practitioners' forums. A detailed description of the literature analysis phase is provided in the section "Related Work" of the current paper. As already stated, ITIL framework is selected as the research focus.

Seamless delivery of IT Services is essential for problem-free organisational functioning. Thus, IT departments are obliged to respond quickly to changing business requirements while satisfying the needs of internal and external customers. Such process frameworks as ITIL aim to support organizations to structure and improve their IT services. Recent reports confirm ITIL certification to be among the top five to obtain [7]. This is also one of the highly discussed frameworks in relation to emerging AI-based services. The practitioners admit that ITIL provides value to organizations with its common vocabulary, consistent processes for managing IT environments and compliance with key regulations and quality standards [3, 19, 29]. At the same time, the AI and BPM-concerned communities drive multiple discussions regarding ML potential to tackle various process optimization challenges where the starting point should be IT Services. The experts also recognize one of the biggest risks related to AI implementation in the enterprise – that it could be applied to a wrong type of processes [13]. Thus, under the light of highly paced AI and ML enterprise adoption perspectives, ITIL framework needs certain reviews and updates to conform to business and IT environment [3, 19, 29].

As outlined above, the literature analysis will be enhanced with a practical experiment on Text Mining of ITIL standard framework and practitioners' documentation (e.g. resolved tickets history) based on a selected process element in the IT Change Management Ticket Processing. The goal of the experiment is to answer the following questions:

1. ITIL standard framework mining:
   a. Which process clusters can be identified in the standard framework text abstracts using state-of-the-art Text Mining techniques?
   b. Based on the identified clusters, is it possible to conclude on the AI- based automation and standardization potential of the process?
2. ITIL practitioners' documentation mining (resolved tickets):
   a. Which process clusters can be identified in the practitioners' documentation?
   b. Which process problems are most frequent ones and what are common solutions?
   c. Is it possible to automate ticket processing and resolution?

Thus, the literature analysis complemented by practical experiment serve as a basis for the design of a process parameter metric indicating the AI-based automation and standardization potential of a particular process cluster or group. In particular, using the information obtained in the literature analysis, Text Mining and the method of educated guesses or other expert techniques, AI technologies can be linked to generic problem classes they are recognized to solve. In their turn, problem classes can be mapped to relevant business processes or process groups. By an indirect transitive closure, it can be inferred that certain business processes offer an automation potential with AI technology. This might be expressed as a degree of probability that should be verified by an expert.

Such a metric can include following qualitative and quantitative parameters: process nature (e.g. strategic, operational), criticality, process dependency on other processes, process execution time, process frequency, process costs, data (e.g. its volume and quality), technology (e.g. number of systems and interfaces), people (e.g. number of process participants), performance (e.g. variance). The practitioners and BPM consultants usually apply proprietary metrics to evaluate AI-based automation project [2, 14]. However, these experiences are usually based on the common knowledge, practice and sense lacking scientific provenance and context of standard BPM frameworks and ITIL specifically.

Quality of the metric will be evaluated by means of a qualitative survey (guided interviews) with the ITIL practitioners and process owners involved in the AI-based automation projects. Finally, process parameter metric will be implemented and validated on the ITIL process use case that is undergoing evaluation for an AI automation project. Qualitative approach is selected to gain an in-depth understanding of the possibilities of intended research outcomes as this method provides insights into the setting of a problem. In the meanwhile, it can develop ideas and hypothesis for later quantitative research [27]. Therefore, quantitative approach is not excluded from the current design research framework and can be further added based on the qualitative findings.

3 Research Framework

The work is based on the Design Science Research guidelines by Hevner et al. [8] and uses common methods of Information Systems research, such as case studies, laboratory experiments, interviews, and observations [32]. Based on the model by Hevner et al., Fig. 1 explains and summarizes the application of Design Science Research in the proposed work.

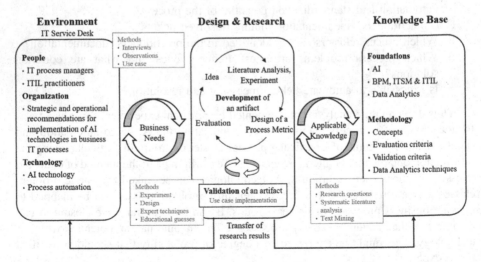

Fig. 1. Research framework based on Hevner et al. [8].

Access to the environment (enterprise context) is enabled by the author's working network and ongoing projects in the case study company. The business need for process analysis in the aspect of emerging AI technologies has been identified while observing the latest R&D achievements, growth of the market offerings, increasing enterprise process complexity and costs, as well as expanding cross-company initiatives and process optimization projects.

The knowledge base contains existing relevant sources that can be grouped into three areas: (i) AI technology in general and its diverse applications for process improvement, (ii) classical BPM approaches extended with recent intelligent technologies and (iii) the role of ITIL framework accentuated by the current discussions in the topic of ITIL, ITSM and AI-based services. One more relevant area is the research regarding the method planned for the practical experiment, i.e. Data and Text Analytics. Hereby, the knowledge sources in scope will include various external literature (theory, handbooks, research papers, publications, practitioners' forum discussions) and internal topic relevant information available to the author. The questions inferred from the main research goal serve to place the topic and guide through the literature analysis. Text Mining techniques to analyze the ITIL documentation (theory and practical process data) allow to experiment with the idea of using AI to discover the potential of AI itself for process automation.

The core of the work is development of an artefact followed by its evaluation and validation. The artefact of this research proposal (process parameter metric indicating the degree of a process AI-based automation and standardization potential) will be evaluated in the guided interviews with IT process managers responsible for automation projects. Afterwards, it will be validated on an ITIL Change Management process use case to suggest process automation candidates. The research artefact will be designed in an iterative approach.

Transfer of the research results will be possible by the research plan itself and author's engagement in the relevant projects of the use case company. Due to the author's current role and responsibilities in the company, it is supposed that developed artefact would be directly used by the research colleagues to complement running research projects as well as by business and technology partners to evaluate process pain points.

The following Table 1 explains how the seven Design Science Research guidelines by Hevner et al. will be implemented in the current work.

Table 1. Design science research guidelines and their application.

Guideline	Application
1. Design as an artefact	Development of a process parameter metric, extending ITIL and current knowledge base
2. Problem relevance	Screening of external and internal enterprise environment to analyse the problem
3. Design evaluation	Interview-based evaluation of the artefact with process experts and use case based validation

(*continued*)

Table 1. (*continued*)

Guideline	Application
4. Research contributions	Placement of the topic by means of research questions, clearly defined methodology, continuous comparison with the knowledge base
5. Research rigor	Use of common research methods of Business Informatics by Wilde and Hess [32] and research guidelines by Hevner et al. [8]
6. Design as a search process	The work addresses both theoretical and practical problems. The complexity reduction is achieved by reduction of the knowledge domain (ITIL framework) and case study approach.
7. Communication of research	By the topic nature, the work addresses both technology- and management-oriented audience

4 Related Work

As it has already been stated, the approaches to assess process fitness towards AI-based automation do exist in practice and are widely used, for example, by consulting companies. However, scientifically proven insights are missing.

Scanning the latest conferences, which aim to build the bridge between business and academic research in BPM, e.g. BPM Conference, it becomes evident that although referring to common enterprise problems (e.g. privacy enhancements of BPMN models, anomaly detection in process execution, predictive process monitoring, etc.), R&D technology roadmap is in the forefront [4].

At the same time, academic world recognizes the necessity of research on the business application aspects of current technologies in the light of the AI hype. Thus, [31] highlights that focus of the recent BPM Conferences lies on the Business Intelligence technologies per se while management aspects are not well presented.

In the current research proposal it is planned to conduct literature analysis according to the systematic literature review guidelines. A systematic literature review is an exhaustive review of research results [11, 12, 18]. The process suggested by Kitchenham et al. [11, 12] includes the following steps: (i) definition of search goals and questions, (ii) definition of the search process, (iii) exclusion/inclusion criteria, and finally (iv) data collection procedure. The main goals of this review are to identify, classify and summarize existing relevant literature and information sources according to the subject(s) of the research. Thus, starting point is to define those subject areas relevant for answering the main search question of the work and building an artefact. The author believes that these four subject areas should be studied:

1. Standalone research on AI and ML: on the whole, it has been observed that recent AI conferences have a deep technology focus. The variety and relevance of the research topics are of high value, going into the direction of potential use cases, such as Neural Networks for evaluating pricing options, Deep Learning for user intention understanding, sentiment analysis, and robotics among others [25]. The reduction of analysis complexity should be achieved by a clear focus on the extrapolation of the researched AI technology to the problems it claims to solve.

2. BPM and intelligent technologies close to practice: currently, practitioners highlight two factors driving the integration of intelligent technologies into BPM: (i) the emergence of BPM systems as general-purpose application development platforms that allow the easy integration of other technologies, and (ii) the need to automate processes and decisions for business reasons ranging from efficiency to compliance [10]. Here such technologies as Business Rules and Automated Decisioning, Predictive Analytics, Machine Learning, Process Mining, Event Processing should be considered. Very close to the context of BPM are so-called Symbolic AI approaches which aim to enrich BPM with semantic knowledge, e.g. Semantic BPM, and to automate process flows, e.g. Rule or Decision based Models [17, 23]. However, it needs to be emphasized that the goal of the intended research is not to develop a framework or tool which enables the AI-based process automation but to assess the process appropriateness for the latter. Therefore, the focus of the literature analysis at this point lies on the extrapolation of the technology to the process problem or particular process cluster/group it most successfully addresses.

3. ITIL research: observed research records either cover reasons, key success factors, outcomes and benefits of implementation [6, 9] or investigate specific topics of ITIL deployment, such as statistical methods of IT Ticket Analytics [15], mathematical algorithms for problem classification in ITIL Incident and Problem Management [26]. Based on the use case in focus, special attention should be paid to relevant publications in IT Service Desk Ticket Processing, ITIL Change Management Tickets in particular.

4. Research on the method planned for the practical experiment, i.e. Text Analytics and Mining: it is aimed to study relevant publications regarding Text Analytics in general (Text Mining of long and short texts) and in particular IT Ticket Analytics and Mining. In the context of IT Systems, relevant literature source will be Mining Software Repositories (MSR) research field which analyses the rich data available in software repositories to discover valuable information about projects and software systems. The topic has been gaining popularity since 2004 supported by a working MSR Conference, collocated with the International Conference on Software Engineering (ICSE) [16].

Keeping in mind that such concepts as Industry 4.0 and Internet of Things (IoT) are considered to be one of the strongest drivers in Big Data and Artificial Intelligence, the author believes that the intended research would highly benefit from attracting ideas of the mentioned concepts and vice versa.

Based on the methodology suggested by Kitchenham [11, 12], two main questions are defined for the literature search:

1. Addressing the subjects of the research (points 1-3 above): "What AI technology is known to solve what problem (classes of problems)?"

2. Addressing method of the research used in the practical experiment (point 4 above): "What Data and Text Analytics and Mining techniques are commonly researched and used to get valuable insights out of texts (short and long) and data in the software repositories?"

Thus, the search process will be scoped by the questions and the four subject areas. For each of the subject areas, key words and sources of recognized quality and value will be defined, i.e. leading journals, recent conferences and proceedings, practical handbooks, forums and electronic repositories in the relevant subject field.

In order to streamline the search process, following inclusion and exclusion criteria are planned to be set at the beginning:

1. Inclusion: AI (and Symbolic AI) technology and problems it is known to solve;
2. Exclusion: research on the improvement of existing technologies, models, algorithms, libraries, architectures or the development of new prototypes, technologies and tools.

Data extracted from each of the sources will be structured according to the following categories:

1. Source, full reference, authors;
2. Main topic area;
3. (Symbolic) AI technology, described method;
4. Problems it solves, application areas, use cases;
5. Summary and value for the intended research.

Methodologically, it is planned to follow the recommendation of Kitchenham et al. [12] that one researcher extracts the data, and the other verifies the extracted information and its value. In case of disagreement, the discrepancies should be discussed until agreement is met.

5   Concluding Remarks and Outlook

In this paper, the research idea regarding the analysis of AI applications for business process improvement was presented and the lack of standardized approaches was identified. In order to address this gap, it is proposed to develop an artefact, process parameter metric, which will indicate the process suitability for AI-based automation and possibly extend ITIL framework.

The value and strength of the presented approach is that it is based on the combination of the analysis of existing sources and the application of Text Mining algorithms, what could generate completely new insights. Another value is the research focus, ITIL framework, which can be considered as one of the most relevant in the context of AI technologies. Thus, the research is expected to contribute to better understanding of the core of business processes, their levels and relationships, inferring explicit indications for AI-based automation.

Further on, depending on the research proceedings and results, the author could suggest the development of a second artefact – method and set of recommendations how to apply the first artefact, process parameter metric, in an enterprise context. Additionally, author might come up with the third artefact – completely new theory on process classification under the light of AI technologies [5]. As correctly confirmed and illustrated by [30], classification approaches are as a rule clearly defined in the applied sciences domain. However, with more than 120 existing frameworks and reference models [22], the process domain lacks this clarity. The penetration of AI technologies into the business processes could allow to build a new theory around this subject.

References

1. Agutter, C.: ITIL Lifecycle Essentials. IT Governance Publishing, Ely (2013)
2. Albright, F., Banerjee, P.: ISACA Presentation - RPA & Beyond. Tata Consultancy Services (2017). https://www.isaca.org/chapters3/Charlotte/Events/Documents/Event%20Presentations/06072017/Robotic%20Process%20Automation.pdf. Accessed 30 Apr 2018
3. Andersen, A.: Who Needs ITIL in the Age of Smart Machines? LinkedIn Forum (2016). https://www.linkedin.com/pulse/who-needs-itil-age-smart-machines-allan-andersen/. Accessed 20 Apr 2018
4. Carmona, J., Engels, G., Kumar, A.: Proceedings 15th International Conference, BPM 2017. Springer, Barcelona (2017)
5. Colquitt, J.A., Zapata-Phelan, C.P.: Trends in theory building and theory testing. A five-decade study of the Academy of Management Journal. Acad. Manag. J. **50**(6), 1281–1303 (2007)
6. De Barros, M.D., Simões Gomes, C.F., da Silva, R.A., Gomes Costa, H.: Mapping of the scientific production on the ITIL application published in the national and international literature. Procedia Comput. Sci. **55**, 102–111 (2015)
7. Global Knowledge Training: IT Skills and Salary Report 2017. https://www.globalknowledge.com/us-en/content/salary-report/it-skills-and-salary-report/. Accessed 23 Apr 2018
8. Hevner, A.R., March, S.T., Park, J., Ram, S.: Design science in information systems research. MIS Q. **28**(1), 75–105 (2004)
9. Iden, J., Eikebrokk, T.R.: Implementing IT service management. a systematic literature review. Int. J. Inf. Manag. **33**, 512–523 (2013)
10. Kemsley, S.: Smarter BPM with AI. Bonitasoft (2018). https://www.bonitasoft.com/news/smarter-bpm-ai. Accessed 16 July 2018
11. Kitchenham, B.: Procedures for performing systematic reviews. Joint Technical report. Keele University, Keele (2004)
12. Kitchenham, B., Pearl Brereton, O., Budgen, D., Turner, M., Bailey, J., Linkman, S.: Systematic literature reviews in software engineering. A systematic literature review. J. Inf. Softw. Technol. **51**(1), 7–15 (2009)
13. Koplowitz, R.: Artificial Intelligence Revitalizes BPM. Forrester (2017). https://www.infosys.com/services/digital-process-automation/Documents/artificial-intelligence-revitalizes-bpm.pdf. Accessed 09 July 2018
14. Leukert, P., Vollmer, A., Reeves, M.: IT Complexity. Model, Measure and Master. Capco (2012). https://www.edmcouncil.org/downloads/MC_CAPCO.IT.complexity.Model.measure.pdf. Accessed 30 Apr 2018
15. Li, T.-H., et al.: Incident Ticket analytics for IT application management services. In: Proceedings 2014 IEEE International Conference on Services Computing, pp. 568–574 (2014)
16. Mining Software Repositories (MSR): The 15th International Conference Homepage (2018). https://conf.researchr.org/home/msr-2018. Accessed 16 July 2018
17. Object Management Group: The Decision Model and Notation Specification Version 1.1. https://www.omg.org/spec/DMN/About-DMN/. Accessed 08 July 2018

18. Okoli, C., Schabram, K.: A guide to conducting a systematic literature review of information systems research. Sprouts: Working Pap. Inf. Syst. **10**(26), 1–49 (2010)
19. Piccinno, D.: Driverless ITIL 2030. LinkedIn Forum (2017). https://www.linkedin.com/pulse/driverless-itil-2030-donato-piccinno. Accessed 28 Apr 2018
20. Proehl, T., Erek, K., Limbach, F., Zarnekow, R.: Topics and applied theories in IT service management. In: 46th Hawaii International Conference on System Sciences, pp. 1367–1375. IEEE Computer Society (2013)
21. Resch, O.: Einführung in das IT-Management. Grundlagen, Umsetzung, Best Practice. 4th edn. Erich Schmidt Verlag, Berlin (2016)
22. RMK Reference Model Catalogs. http://rmk.iwi.uni-sb.de/pub.php. Accessed 31 July 2018
23. RuleML + RR 2017 Conference Homepage. http://2017.ruleml-rr.org/. Accessed 08 July 2018
24. Shahsavarani, N., Ji, S.: Research in information technology service management (ITSM) (2000 – 2010). An overview. Int. J. Inf. Syst. Serv. Sector **6**(4), 76–94 (2014)
25. Singh, S., Markovitch, S.: Proceedings of the Thirty-First AAAI Conference on Artificial Intelligence and the Twenty-Ninth Innovative Applications of Artificial Intelligence Conference. The AAAI Press, San Francisco (2017). https://www.aaai.org/Library/AAAI/aaai17contents.php. Accessed 28 Apr 2018
26. Song, Y., Sailer, A., Shaikh, H.: Problem classification method to enhance the ITIL incident and problem. In: Proceedings 2009 IFIP/IEEE International Symposium on Integrated Network Management, pp. 295–298 (2009)
27. Taylor, G.R.: Integrating Quantitative and Qualitative Methods in Research. University Press of America, Lanham (2005)
28. Valdes, M.: Keynote. Intelligent continuous improvement. When BPM meets AI. In: Carmona, J., Engels, G., Kumar, A. (eds.) Proceedings 15th International Conference, BPM 2017, p. 14. Springer, Barcelona (2017)
29. Vekas, C.: ITIL Future. We are not Competing with Cloud Computing/AI but would be Complementing Them. LinkedIn Forum (2017). https://www.linkedin.com/pulse/itil-future-we-competing-cloud-computing-ai-would-them-chetan-vikas. Accessed 20 Apr 2018
30. von Rosing, M., Scheer, A.-W., von Scheel, H.: The Complete Business Process Handbook. Morgan Kaufmann, Amsterdam (2014)
31. Weske, M.: BPM. Reflections on a broad discipline. In: Carmona, J., Engels, G., Kumar, A. (eds.) Proceedings 15th International Conference, BPM 2017, p. 16. Springer, Barcelona (2017)
32. Wilde, T., Hess, T.: Forschungsmethoden der Wirtschaftsinformatik. Eine Empirische Untersuchung. Wirtschaftsinformatik **49**(4), 280–287 (2007). Ed. by Buhl, H.U. et al.

Author Index

Adamik, Filip 356
Albrecht, Simon 217
Ali, Muhammad Haris 498
Anwar, Muneeb 534
Apostolou, Dimitris 449
Archetti, Francesco 3
Assumpção, Thaine H. 498
Avila, Oscar 112, 408
Azevedo, Alberto 507

Bagheri, Samaneh 143
Bălăceanu, Cristina M. 534
Bieliauskas, Rytis 289
Bieser, Hemma 244
Boochs, Frank 566
Boruah, Dhruv 527
Bousdekis, Alexandros 449

Candelieri, Antonio 3, 485
Chasparis, Georgios 244
Christias, Panagiotis 517
Cichonczyk, Mario 325
Cucurull, Jordi 300
Curmi, Axel 211

da Costa Cruz, Janina 313
Dai, Patrick 368
Dancu, Alexandru 527
Danielius, Paulius 223
Davies, Philip 124
de la Harpe, Andre 433
Dormer, Alan 51

Earls, Jordan 368
Emmadi, Nitesh 229

Fakorede, Oluwatoyin 124
Filipiak, Dominik 63
Filipowska, Agata 63
Finogina, Tamara 300
Fitsilis, Panos 38
Fortunato, André B. 507
Franqueira, Virginia N. L. 197
Freund, Daniel 277

Galuzzi, Bruno G. 3
Gatziu-Grivas, Stella 420
Giordani, Ilaria 3
Goranovic, Andrija 244
Górtowski, Szczepan 634
Gourley, Scarlett 173
Graf, Manuela 420
Grefen, Paul W. P. J. 143
Gresch, Jerinas 185
Grivas, Stella Gatziu 433
Gruszczyński, Krzysztof 77

Härting, Ralf-Christian 101
Hinkelmann, Knut 136
Homburg, Timo 566
Huth, Michael 381

Ihle, Cornelius 335
Inguanez, Frankie 211

Jonoski, Andreja 498

Kabi, Oliver R. 197
Kabzińska, Katarzyna 63
Kałużny, Piotr 646
Kanchanapalli, Srujana 229
Kanhere, Salil S. 185
Karafili, Erisa 603
Kasparavičiūtė, Gabrielė 527
Knap, Tomáš 555
Kosta, Sokol 356
Koutroulis, Georgios 461
Kriksciuniene, Dalia 86
Krogstie, John 468
Krüger, Jacob 579
Kurjakovic, Sabrina 136
Kusters, Rob 143

Lampoltshammer, Thomas J. 555
Leich, Thomas 579
Leonhartsberger, Kurt 244
Lepenioti, Katerina 449
Lettner, Georg 244

Lewandowski, Roman 86
Lewoniewski, Włodzimierz 619
Lupu, Ciprian 485
Lupu, Emil C. 603

Maddali, Lakshmipadmaja 229
Mahi, Neil 368
Marksteiner, Stefan 244
Martins, Ricardo 507
Masteika, Saulius 223
Masucci, Riccardo 381
Meisel, Marcus 244
Mentzas, Gregoris 449
Mikalef, Patrick 468
Mocanu, Mariana 485
Muñoz, Leonardo 112

Narumanchi, Harika 229
Negru, Cătălin 485
Neumaier, Sebastian 555
Newell, David 124
Nielsen, Stig Anton 527
Nordin, Peter 527
Norta, Alex 368

Oliveira, Anabela 507

Perego, Riccardo 3
Perkowski, Bartosz 77
Peter, Marco 420
Pichler, Mario 244
Pirozzi, Donato 591
Popescu, Ioana 498
Predescu, Alexandru 485
Puiggalí, Jordi 300

Ragos, Omiros 38
Reichstein, Christopher 101
Revina, Aleksandra 697
Rodrigues, Bruno 185
Rodrigues, Marta 507
Rodriguez, Linda 408
Rodríguez-Pérez, Adrià 300
Rogeiro, João 507
Roman, Dumitru 258

Saake, Gunter 579
Sakalauskas, Virgilijus 86
Sanchez, Omar 335
Sandkuhl, Kurt 101, 156
Savenas, Tomas 223
Scarano, Vittorio 591
Scheid, Eder 185
Schönreiter, Irene 675
Schröder, Aenne Sophie 313
Schulz, Kai Fabian 277
Seigerroth, Ulf 156
Shakeel, Yusra 579
Shilov, Nikolay 30
Skjellum, Anthony 264
Smirnov, Alexander 30
Spalinger, Dominic 433
Spanaki, Konstantina 603
Stiller, Burkhard 185
Stróżyna, Milena 659
Strüker, Jens 217
Suciu, George 534
Szmydt, Marcin 687

Tarasov, Vladimir 156
Teslya, Nikolay 344
Tewari, Hitesh 173
Thalmann, Stefan 461
Thurnay, Lőrinc 555
Trienekens, Jos 143
Tsoutsa, Paraskevi 38

Usmani, Zeeshan-ul-hassan 289
Uşurelu, Teodora 534
Utz, Manuel 217

Vallant, Heribert 244
van de Wetering, Rogier 19, 397, 468
Vigneswaran, R. 229
Vishik, Claire 381
von Wangenheim, Georg 313
Vu, Kien 258

Waddell, Andre 289
Wieloch, Magdalena 63
Worley, Carl R. 264

Zoerner, Thorsten 217

Printed in the United States
By Bookmasters